Voices of Dissent

Critical Readings in American Politics

Sixth Edition

William F. Grover
Saint Michael's College

Joseph G. Peschek
Hamline University

PEARSON

Longman

New York San Francisco Boston
London Toronto Sydney Tokyo Singapore Madrid
Mexico City Munich Paris Cape Town Hong Kong Montreal

For our students—May you build a world more devoted to peace and justice.

Executive Editor: Eric Stano
Senior Marketing Manager: Elizabeth Fogarty
Production Manager: Denise Phillip
Project Coordination, Text Design, and Electronic Page Makeup: WestWords, Inc.
Cover Design Manager: John Callahan
Cover Designer: Maria Ilardi
Cover Photo: © Win McNamee/Reuters/Corbis
Manufacturing Manager: Mary Fischer

For permission to use copyrighted material, grateful acknowledgement is made to the copyright holders on p. 384, which are hereby made part of this copyright page.

Library of Congress Cataloging-in-Publication Data

Voices of dissent : critical readings in American politics / [edited by] William F. Grover,
    Joseph G. Peschek.—6th ed.
        p. cm.
    Includes bibliographical references.
    ISBN 0-321-32817-5 (pbk.)
        1. United States—Politics and government. I. Grover, William F., 1956– II. Peschek,
Joseph G. III. Title.

JK21.V65 2006
320.973—dc22

                                                                      2004026284

Please visit our website at http://www.ablongman.com

ISBN 0-321-32817-5

2 3 4 5 6 7 8 9 10   08 07 06

Contents

PART II: Politics and Institutions   111

PART III: Politics and Vision   293

Chapter 9: Political Challenges at Home and Abroad   294

Chapter 10: Visions of a New Democracy   330

Resources for Further Study   361

Appendix   364

Credits   384

Preface

Voices of Dissent is the only reader on the market that fundamentally challenges the political and economic status quo in America. It provides a systematic series of critical perspectives on American politics that goes beyond the range of debate between mainstream liberalism and conservatism. In developing this book we drew on some of the best examples of a diverse and energizing body of critical scholarship that is all too often overlooked in government courses. Political economy, and the tension between capitalism and democracy, is a recurrent theme in the selections. Other articles explore the ideological effects of the mass media, the ecological results of uncontrolled economic growth, and the dynamics of class, race, and gender divisions in the United States—issues central to our political life early in the twenty-first century. American governmental institutions and political processes are treated in five central chapters, but only after they are placed in the context of underlying economic and social structures, as well as the more apparent constitutional arrangements, that shape their design and impact.

Our goal is to provide students with the intellectual tools to develop a sustained and integrated critique of the workings of U.S. democracy so that as citizens they can better contribute to a broader debate about the American future. We firmly believe that students today are open to a critical analysis of their political system and are eager to participate in a discussion about fresh alternatives. We also think that many instructors are interested in exposing their students and themselves to material that makes sense of the dissatisfaction with the status quo that registers daily in America today. Our book provides a set of readings to help accomplish these goals.

Voices of Dissent is designed for introductory college-level courses in American government. It could be used as a supplement to a variety of textbooks, or in conjunction with several works that have a narrower focus. In our experience, some of the best opportunities for learning occur when alternative frameworks of analysis and explanation are matched against each other. For that reason, the pairing of our reader with a work that adopts a more conventional, or even sharply opposed, interpretation of American politics might prove quite stimulating.

The sixth edition of *Voices of Dissent* includes several new articles that will widen and deepen students' understanding of contemporary American politics. New selections by Robert Jensen and Arlie Hochschild examine in sensitive and diverse ways the impact of the "war on terrorism" on American politics and political culture. R. Claire Snyder examines the conservative political forces behind the opposition to gay and lesbian marriage. Paul Krugman explores the continued growth of economic inequality and its threat to both middle class society and democracy. A study by the public interest group Common Cause reveals the real forces that shaped the 2003 Medicare bill, one of the most significant pieces of social policy legislation in recent years. Finally, we have revised and updated our own studies of Bernie Sanders and the Congressional Progressive Caucus and the presidency of George W. Bush in light of the 2004 elections.

ORGANIZATION

We begin with a general introduction. Here we explain the intellectual and political orientation that shaped our selection of readings and contrast our outlook with what we call mainstream political science. The readings that follow are grouped into three sections. Part I looks at the broad structures that constrain and pattern American politics. The three chapters in this section look at democracy and political economy, ideology and culture, and the distinctive nature of the American state. Part II attends to the traditional subject matter of political processes and government institutions: the mass media, parties and elections, Congress, the presidency, and law and the courts. Many of the articles in this section are notable for relating familiar processes and institutions to the broader level of political analysis developed in Part I. Part III examines major political challenges facing the United States and explores visions for democratic revitalization in light of the critical analysis contained in the previous chapters.

FEATURES

Voices of Dissent contains several features that make it an attractive and original resource. Our emphasis on the contextual centrality of corporate capitalism and individualist values should deepen students' understanding of the very meaning of politics. Article introductions relate selections to key political questions and overall themes of the book. Most chapters begin with a theoretical or conceptually oriented piece that identifies underlying issues relevant to the unconventional view of American politics this book has been designed to encourage. Our 40 selections represent some of the best and most provocative writing on American politics, scholarly and journalistic, available today. Each article is followed by Discussion Questions, that are meant to facilitate class dialogue and debate. We have included a Resources for Further Study list to provide additional alternative information so students can sustain this analytic framework beyond the classroom setting where they first may have encountered it. Finally, we have an Appendix containing three classic political documents whose importance must be considered in any critical analysis.

ACKNOWLEDGMENTS

We wish to thank the following reviewers who made insightful comments and suggestions:

Larry R. Beck, New Mexico State University–Alamogordo

Andrew D. Grossman, Albion College

Daniel Kryder, Massachusetts Institute of Technology

Bradley J. Macdonald, Colorado State University

J. N. Patten, Buena Vista University

Greg Shaw, Illinois Wesleyan University

Michael Givel, University of Oklahoma

Susan Leisure, North Georgia College and State University

We also want to acknowledge the insight and encouragement of our editor at Longman Publishers, Eric Stano, and his staff. Howard D'Angelo provided valuable research assistance. Finally, we would like to thank Pat Troxell and Glenace Edwall for their continuing support and helpful suggestions.

WILLIAM F. GROVER
JOSEPH G. PESCHEK

INTRODUCTION

Why a *Critical* Reader?

> "A long habit of not thinking a thing *wrong,* gives it a superficial appearance of being *right* . . . "
>
> —Thomas Paine, *Common Sense*

In January of 1776, Thomas Paine voiced Americans' growing aspirations for freedom and independence with his radical call for an end to the monarchical rule of the British Empire. His pamphlet *Common Sense* was a phenomenal success, with upwards of 150,000 copies printed, reaching an estimated one million people, unheard of numbers for his day.[1] Paine's straightforward message found a receptive audience among ordinary people, whose often inchoate opposition to the King was impeded by entrenched deference to royal authority. With fiery reasoning in support of dissent and republican government, he cut through the haze of "what was," and crystallized a vision of "what could be."

In January of 2000, the world entered a new millennium. If a contemporary Thomas Paine were to issue a radical call for "common sense" today, would the public even be able to hear it? We wonder. As introductory students of politics, the lessons of eighteenth century America may seem like ancient history as you ponder political life in the twenty-first. The revolutions in political thinking that punctuated the end of the last century occurred elsewhere. We are now more than a decade removed from such seismic shifts as the collapse of the Berlin Wall and the break-up of Eastern Europe as a Soviet satellite, the coordination into a single market of the economies of the European Community nations, and the demise of Communism in Russia and, albeit more slowly, in China. Historic world events swept away the political, economic, military and ideological basis of the Cold War, and with it much of what we knew as foreign affairs in the post-World War II period. In the wake of these breathtakingly rapid transformations we have been treated to the predictable chorus of political pundits and "experts" in the mass media reassuring us that recent history confirms the universal appeal and unquestionable rightness of American versions of democracy and corporate capitalism. The tide of history is going our way, we are told. Why swim against it?

---

[1] For a lively discussion of the role of Paine's pamphlet *Common Sense* in galvanizing the revolutionary spirit in America, see Edward Countryman, *The American Revolution.* New York: Hill and Wang, 1985, Chapter 4.

SHIFTING TIMES/ENDURING STRUCTURE

The sentiments above have framed each edition of *Voices of Dissent*. They speak of times when changes of historic importance occurred. We continue to live in such exciting yet crisis-filled times. As authors, we certainly don't write in a vacuum. The horrendous terrorist attacks of September 11, 2001, the U.S. bombing of Afghanistan, the ongoing "war on terrorism," and war against Iraq have dominated the context of recent times. As we prepare the sixth edition of this anthology, we cannot escape the need to address issues that flow out of circumstances that have seared themselves into the consciousness of the nation. The "war on terrorism" has been the ubiquitous theme of President George W. Bush and the media. We are told on an almost daily basis that 9-11 "changed everything" in American politics. We are skeptical of that assertion. As renowned linguist and political analyst Noam Chomsky puts it in his controversial bestseller *9-11:*

> The horrifying atrocities of September 11 are something quite new in world affairs, not in their scale and character, but in the target. For the United States, this is the first time since the War of 1812 that the national territory has been under attack, or even threatened. . . . For the first time, the guns have been directed the other way. That is a dramatic change.[2]

What hasn't changed, Chomsky reminds us, are the fundamental objectives of U.S. foreign policy. Supported as they always have been by massive use of state-sponsored violence and neglect of international law, these objectives reflect the structure of corporate, military, and political power in America. Indeed, the events of 9-11 have solidified that structure and swept away potential challenges to it. Dissonant issues, which had begun to illuminate the dark side of U.S. power, seemingly disappeared overnight. Thus the remarkable rash of corporate abuses of power—from Enron and Arthur Anderson, to Global Crossing, Adelphia, ImClone, Tyco, Merrill Lynch, WorldCom, Dynergy, Qwest, and Martha Stewart Living Omnimedia—which had begun to receive media scrutiny, were shuffled off to the side after September 11. The sordid tale of corporate CEOs profiting while ordinary Americans watched their retirement savings disappear with the bursting of the 1990s dot-com bubble fell on deaf ears. All but forgotten was what columnist and political activist Barbara Ehrenreich termed the collapsing credibility of our principal institutions. Public confidence in a range of political, economic, and civic leadership positions plummeted:

> It's not only the occasional radical crank who understands that our major institutions are rapidly approaching the reliability of Amtrak.[3]

Overshadowing all of this and more—the intelligence ineptitude of the FBI and the CIA, and inquiry into the Bush administration's own complacency about warnings of terrorist attacks in the summer prior to 9-11—was the new official story line: WAR!

---

[2]Noam Chomsky, *9-11*. New York: Seven Stories Press, 2001, pp. 11–12. Chomsky explains the weakness of the Pearl Harbor analogy to 9-11, given that at the time Hawaii was a U.S. territory, a colony really, and not officially part of the country.
[3]Barbara Ehrenreich, "The Collapse of Credibility," *The Progressive,* August 2002.

That story line became the backdrop to the election of 2004. President George W. Bush campaigned as a "war president," fanning the flames of voter anxiety and challenging the war leadership credentials of Senator John Kerry, whose Vietnam War record was tarnished by unceasing Republican Party attacks. The framing of President Bush as a "war president" continued even as his shifting rationales for the war in Iraq were exposed as the product of exaggeration and deception. U.S. standing in the world sunk to new lows. While winning a very tight reelection, President Bush asserted his right to a new "mandate," announcing at his first post-reelection press conference that he intended to use his newly earned "political capital" to pursue his conservative agenda of militarism, permanent tax breaks skewed to the wealthy, privatization of social security and a rightwing social agenda laced with wedge issues. We desperately need contemporary Thomas Paines to meet the challenges posed by these times of crisis. While dissenters risk being labeled "unpatriotic," it's a risk that must be taken in a true democracy. For structures of power endure.

With this as a political and cultural backdrop, the need for a critical reader in American politics may seem less than compelling to you. As distinctions between the two political parties continue to diminish, the possibility of posing alternatives to the status quo may appear nonexistent. Indeed, the very idea of political alternatives may seem moot. Presidential politics can help bring the need for serious alternatives into sharper relief. In the immediate aftermath of President Clinton's reelection in 1996 and the Republican's retention of their congressional majorities, the two parties had so successfully dissolved into one on core issues that conservative columnist and TV commentator George Will was moved to offer the following observation of Clinton:

> The man who campaigned more conservatively than Bush now proposes to govern more conservatively than Reagan. Washington may die of boredom unless there is forced busing to achieve ideological balance.[4]

Will's wit should not be allowed to obscure the truth it seeks to illuminate: the United States increasingly has taken on the characteristics of a one-party state.

The election of 2000 only confirmed this troubling atrophy of democracy. With Democratic Vice President Al Gore and Texas Governor George W. Bush Jr. straining to spin tiny fibers of difference into dark blue suits of policy difference, only Green Party candidate and lifelong consumer advocate Ralph Nader articulated what great numbers of Americans already felt: the two-party emperor has no clothes. With corporate control of the political economy expanding, democracy in America is an endangered species, threatened by a growing "democracy gap." As Nader pointed out in a speech announcing his presidential candidacy:

> This control by the corporate government over our political government is creating a widening *democracy gap*. Active citizens are left shouting their concerns over a deep chasm between them and their government.[5]

---

[4]George Will, "Clinton and the balanced budget," *Boston Globe,* November 15, 1996.
[5]Ralph Nader, "Statement of Ralph Nader Announcing His Candidacy for the Green Party's Nomination for President," www.votenader.com, Washington, D.C., February 21, 2000. See Article 40 in Chapter 10.

Even those who seek to benefit from it, and whose political work seeks to downplay it, tacitly acknowledge this gap between citizens and government. Reflecting on the 2000 GOP national convention in Philadelphia, former Chair of the Republican National Committee Haley Barbour offered the following insight about the proceedings:

> It's all propaganda. It's all a TV show. It's not news, but it's hugely important information for the American people.[6]

Party leaders cynically offer the people made-for-TV, feel-good spectacles devoid of real decisions and real political meaning—an empty combination of pabulum and propaganda that continues into the general election and beyond. "Hugely important?" From whose perspective?

Americans clearly are not happy with the political and economic conformity that confronts them. The lingering sense that the election of 2000 was a product of a conservative Supreme Court more than a result of voter preference only heightens political disenchantment. Among the many indicators of this discontent is the stark reality of an abysmal 49 percent turnout rate in the 1996 election and an only slightly higher rate in 2000. A rise in turnout among evangelical Christians and young first-time voters led to an improved turnout rate of about 59 percent in 2004. In mid-term elections far fewer eligible voters cast ballots. Although America fancies itself as the greatest democracy on earth, in fact, the United States still remains mired at or near the bottom of all industrialized nations in terms of voter participation. Other, more hopeful signs of discontent abound. In Seattle in November of 1999, and again in April of 2000 in Washington, D.C., tens of thousands of people from around the world came together to voice growing opposition to the World Trade Organization and other global financial institutions whose decisions set the rules of economic life far removed from citizen input. This nascent social movement—uniting students, environmentalists, working people, and other activists against the elite agenda of corporate capital—has shed light on the often secretive world of international economic decision making, raising deep doubts about the presumed wisdom of globalization.[7] And in February of 2003, millions of people around the globe protested against the impending U.S. invasion of Iraq—the largest day of organized protest in the history of the world. We strongly believe that the American political system today has a superficial appearance of rightness, a veneer of public ritual and familiarity beneath which lies tremendous private (and increasingly public) discontent. Moreover, we sense students and teachers are interested in a challenging analysis of American politics that includes alternatives to conventional liberal and conservative approaches, which, we are all taught, mark the limits of "legitimate" debate. In our text we ask you to move beyond these socialized limits in an attempt to span the "democracy gap."

---

[6]R.W. Apple, Jr., "No Decisions, No Drama," *New York Times,* August 1, 2000.
[7]For an in-depth exploration of this social movement, see John C. Berg, ed., *Teamsters and Turtles? U.S. Progressive Political Movements in the 21st Century,* New York: Rowman and Littlefield, 2003.

PROBLEMS AND POSSIBLE RESPONSES

The arrival of the twenty-first century has brought stunning change, and with it has come both the dark possibilities and bright opportunities that jointly mark all periods of crisis and transition. Yet at the same time, the list of pressing problems facing the United States—indeed the world—remains long, and finding real solutions that transcend patriotic rhetoric, cynical presidential promises, nationalistic hubris, and ten-second sound bites necessarily will involve a broadening of political debate. The post 9-11 U.S. "war on terrorism" and the war in Iraq further destabilizes an already wildly unstable Middle East and weakens our ties to European allies. Other regional conflicts, particularly in South America, grow as a source of contention as the nation struggles to adjust to its changed military role in the post-Cold War world. The AIDS pandemic continues to ravish the African continent. The intensification of corporate globalization wreaks havoc on developing nations while undermining the national autonomy of all nations. Specific issues here at home also are troubling, among them: the growing gap between the rich and the poor, with the top 1 percent of households now owning more wealth than the bottom 95 percent; a stagnating standard of living for working and middle class Americans during the Reagan-Bush era that continued even amidst the much-celebrated "economic boom" of the Clinton years and has reached crisis proportions during the presidency of George W. Bush; the soaring wage differential between CEOs and average factory workers, which resulted in CEOs earning about 600 times what an average worker earned in 2001, up from 1980, when CEOs made 41 times as much; job insecurity that has accompanied the phenomenon of corporate "downsizing" and the growing power of multinational corporations in the brave new world of global "free trade"; the crisis of environmental degradation, which is reaching potentially cataclysmic proportions globally; the burgeoning financial crisis that includes, but is not limited to, both the national debt and more acutely, personal consumer debt; the well-documented inadequacies of the American educational system, which is second to many others worldwide; the health care crunch that has left upwards of 45 million Americans without any medical coverage and an equal number with woefully inadequate coverage; the persistence of poverty (especially among children), with the poverty rate rising in 2003 to 12.5 percent while median household income continued to stagnate; and lingering racism and sexism as barriers to basic equality. Perhaps more unsettling still is the underlying cancerous trend of popular nonparticipation in the political process due to widespread apathy, despair, and lack of confidence people have in their political leaders and institutions. Most Americans barely can bring themselves to go to the polls every four years to select a president, let alone play a greater role as full citizens. They have, in effect, given up on politics.

These and a host of other problems confront the student of politics. In the face of such formidable dilemmas, you are left with a few possible responses. One common response is ***resignation,*** expressed in such adages as "you can't fight city hall" and "don't rock the boat." Many students tell us they can see basic injustices but feel powerless to change anything. The continuing durability of this view is ironic, though, given the sweeping and rapid late-twentieth century changes we have seen in the Soviet Union, Eastern Europe, South Africa, and China.

Another response available to you is the ***pluralist*** interpretation of political life, which encourages piecemeal problem solving and an incremental view of change. Closely linked to an inherited cultural assumption about politics and power, the pluralist model of politics dominates contemporary Political Science. Pluralism rests on the view of society as a collection of groups, which compete over various policy areas. Through these groups, or acting as individuals through other democratic freedoms such as voting rights, representative institutions, and civil liberties, people can negotiate and compromise in an open political process. Group conflict is considered fair as long as the government serves as an unbiased umpire, maintaining a level playing field for all groups. Power is said to be diffuse so that no one group has unfair advantages. When necessary, reforms occur as groups succeed (or fail) in having their ideas triumph over competing ideas. And the end result of this pluralist interaction is understood to reasonably approximate "the public interest." On a pluralist reading of politics, the system may have its flaws, but none are so fatal that the system itself is called into question. The pluralist understanding of American politics is a relatively comfortable one, for it allows students to retain the belief that the political process is open enough, and sufficiently fluid, to adapt to virtually any contingency without changing the basic power relations of the political economy. Moreover, pluralists define "politics" narrowly—as what *government* does—so that the model overlooks other arenas of power, among them corporate capital.

We contend that neither resignation nor pluralist incrementalism will help you make sense of the American political landscape. A third, more **critical approach** is warranted, one that challenges existing power relations. As currently practiced, politics speaks largely to the concerns of the already wealthy and influential. The political system does not offer the hope of a better life for most Americans, but rather leaves unquestioned a structure of power and privilege that endures regardless of which party controls Congress and the White House. In American political history, this kind of critical questioning often has been championed though the collective action of social movements, a point emphasized by many authors in this volume.

A CRITICAL VIEW? BUT I'M NOT A "RADICAL!"

Our anthology seeks to contribute to the ongoing discussion about the need to rethink and broaden the range of political and economic options facing the country. For many of you this may be your first exposure to dissenting political orientations, which are marginalized, or rendered invisible, in the mass media and most college textbooks. Within Political Science, the field of American politics is awash in textbooks and readers that assume an orthodox pluralist perspective, or provide a small sampling of differing viewpoints (though uniformly still heavily weighted toward the mainstream) on a series of issues of the day. Against this current, we adopt a critical stance, which challenges conventional self-congratulatory accounts of the American political system. We draw articles from the rich literature of radical scholarship, along with selected mainstream pieces, which add texture to the more critical interpretation.

The book is divided into three sections. Part I examines the structure underlying political life, a structure that profoundly shapes and constrains the political choices available to us. The chapters in this section emphasize the interconnections between the political economy, ideological and cultural beliefs, and the structure of the state. Part II considers the "nuts and bolts" of political institutions and processes. Its five chapters closely parallel material found in almost all introductory textbooks and readers, albeit from a direction that contributes to a critical understanding of the political status quo by situating those institutions within the deeper structure outlined in Part I. Part III moves beyond the institutions to explore where the nation is heading, and where it *should* be heading: politics and *vision,* if you will. Selected foreign and domestic policy challenges are explored, and then we ask you to ponder the implications of the foregoing analysis for your own life, as a responsible citizen. All readings in these ten chapters are followed by Discussion Questions, a feature intended to get you thinking about the implications of the readings. We also have included a list of Resources for Further Study, a compilation of the addresses, phone numbers, and web sites of many of the leading organizations and publications that offer a critical perspective on American politics and economics. Finally, we have included in an appendix, three classic political documents whose importance must be considered in any critical analysis.

While there are many ways to use our reader in introductory courses, we believe it may be most useful as an analytic complement to any of the myriad conventional textbooks on the market. It is through the competition of ideas that you will develop your capacity to think freely and critically. Our alternative perspective—which questions the very roots of political, economic, and ideological power in the United States—grows out of a positive belief that the current distribution of power and resources seriously impedes freedom, equality, and democracy, in the fullest sense of these terms. As proponents of real political participation and social justice, we critique the system in order to improve it when possible, and change it when necessary.

With these thoughts in mind, we frankly hope our reader will make you feel uncomfortable, shake you up a bit, and ultimately stimulate you to ask deep questions about the American political and economic system. Our goal in this sense is a radical one, for we ask that in your study of American politics you "go to the root causes," the very definition of the word "radical." A nation is not a healthy democracy simply because its politicians, corporate leaders, and the mass media constantly say it is, or because other forms of more authoritarian control have tumbled down worldwide. And the democratic ideal is not close to being realized if the people continually are asked to settle for a political system that is merely "pretty good," or if at election time voters find themselves holding their noses and voting for the "lesser of two evils," or if the answers to our problems are assumed to lie in policies of a "moderate" direction. For the legacy of Thomas Paine also reminds us:

> A thing moderately good is not so good as it ought to be. Moderation in temper is always a virtue; but moderation in principle is always a vice. (1792 Letter)

A truly healthy polity can thrive only when ordinary people have meaningful control over the decisions that directly affect their lives. Nader refers to such control as "deep democracy," which facilitates peoples' best efforts to achieve social justice and self-reliance.[8] Democracy in the fullest sense should provide the societal context within which people's "instinct for freedom" can flourish, as Noam Chomsky has written in *Language and Politics:*

> I would like to believe that people have an instinct for freedom, that they really want to control their own affairs. They don't want to be pushed around, ordered, oppressed, etc., and they want a chance to do things that make sense, like constructive work in a way that they control, or maybe control together with others. I don't know any way to prove this. It's really a hope about what human beings are like—a hope that if social structures change sufficiently, those aspects of human nature will be realized.[9]

We share the hope of these two modern-day Thomas Paines, a hope that is animated by a spirit Paine would have appreciated. Its realization—and the empowerment that would accompany it—is what informed, truly democratic citizenship is supposed to be about. We welcome feedback from students and teachers so we may learn whether this reader has helped you develop the analytic skills necessary to bring this hope closer to fruition.

---

[8]Ralph Nader, "Acceptance Statement for the Green Party Nomination for President of the United States," www.votenader.com, Denver, CO, June 25, 2000. See also his book *Crashing the Party: How to Tell the Truth and Still Run for President* (New York: St. Martin's Press, 2002).
[9]Noam Chomsky, *Language and Politics* (Montreal: Black Rose Books, 1988), p. 756.

PART  I

STRUCTURE

If the foundation of your house is cracked and starting to weaken, it makes little sense to address the problem by applying a fresh coat of paint that would merely conceal the underlying reality of decay. In our view, the American political system is a lot like a house with an unstable foundation. While the possibility of collapse certainly is not imminent, the structure of the American political economy, and the ideology that sustains it, is showing signs of severe stress. Moreover, this structure belies the cherished pluralist assumption (discussed in our Introduction) that our political system is one of open, fluid competition among groups. The inherent structural advantages, and disadvantages, accorded various groups significantly bias the political and economic system toward the interests of those who wield great power.

At the outset we must acknowledge that the concept of *structure* is itself quite muddled. Mainstream political scientists often use the term "structure" in a shallow sense when discussing the institutions of government, thus equating structure with the formal machinery of politics. This reduces structure to the institutional balance of power between the executive, legislative, and judicial branches of government. While these institutional interactions obviously merit our attention, the structure-as-institutions approach ignores the deeper structure of power within which institutions operate.

In Part I we explore this deep structure of American politics, with three chapters focusing on the primary structural components of political economy, ideology, and state-constitutional arrangements. Taken as a whole they challenge you to consider whether the tensions inherent in the relationship between democracy as a political concept, and capitalism as a form of economic organization, may in fact constitute a *problem* for the nation, not the solution to our problems, as we are socialized to believe. Are capitalism and a meaningful degree of democracy really compatible, or is capitalist democracy an oxymoron? Does our political culture enable us to consider carefully a wide range of alternative policy directions in the United States? If not, are we as "free" as we like to think? Why is the power of the state so closely connected to the private power of large economic entities? Does the U.S. Constitution strengthen this connection, or provide ways to challenge it? To what extent have social movements been able to constrain and change this structure? These and many other troubling questions flow from a close reading of the selections in Part I.

Together these three structural components form the basic context—the playing field—within which political institutions operate. Understanding this structure will help you make sense of what government institutions do, and why problems so often seem to persist regardless of what policies are pursued in Washington. And it will help you come to grips with the pressures that impinge upon the foundations of American politics.

Democracy and Political Economy

Politics is much more than government. Underlying this book of readings is the conviction that politics involves all relationships of power, whether they be economic, social, or cultural, as well as the interrelationship of government institutions. In their accounts of American politics, many political scientists focus on the Constitution and the three branches of government it established more than 200 years ago. We include these traditional subjects, but place them in a broader context that, in our view, will help you to understand better their actual workings and significance. Given our approach, it should not seem strange that we begin a book on American politics with what appears to be an economic focus.

Our first set of readings emphasizes the closely interwoven connection between democracy and political economy and the importance of understanding our capitalist system if we are to understand our politics. In the late eighteenth century, political economy was a common sense way of thinking for Alexander Hamilton and other Founding Fathers, as we will see in Chapter 3. But in the twentieth century the study of economics and politics became institutionally separated in American colleges and in academic discourse more generally. In recent years this conceptual chasm has been challenged from a variety of perspectives. The selections in Chapter 1 represent a revival of a broader, integrated analysis of American politics that challenges us to think critically about the relationship of capitalism and democracy. All of the authors in this chapter should help you to see politics as much broader than what goes on in government, and as powerfully shaped and constrained by the dynamics of our economy. When this is understood it is difficult to be satisfied with a definition of democracy confined to the presence of elections and formal rights.

THIS LAND IS YOUR LAND

Jim Hightower is a best-selling author, radio commentator, public speaker, and former Texas agriculture commissioner whose populist humor sheds light on serious issues of political, economic, and social inequities. With a wit worthy of Will Rogers and an unquenchable fire in his belly, he delivers his politically subversive message to an audience increasingly fed up with a sham version of democracy in which politicians pretend to serve the interests of the people while really serving the interests of corporate America. In this selection from his book If The Gods Had Meant For Us To Vote They Would Have Given Us Candidates, *Hightower deploys his humor to celebrate the revolutionary spirit of 1776, which he reminds us was at times quite anticorporate in character. Hightower traces the evolution of the corporation, an institution initially constrained by charters that regulated their behavior and which could be revoked by state legislatures and courts if the corporation failed to live up to charter conditions. In this manner the potential dangers of vast corporate power—dangers well known to the Framers—were kept in check. But as corporations and their wealthy benefactors fought back against charters after the Civil War, what emerged was the "runaway corporate autocracy" that is an affront to meaningful democratic authority. Hightower writes of efforts today to fight back against corporate power with campaigns mounted by citizens from Wayne, Pennsylvania, to Arcata, California. Such attempts to take back democracy from the clutches of corporation boardrooms are fueled by the "fire-breathing democratic passion" reminiscent of such cultural icons as Thomas Paine, Woody Guthrie, and Martin Luther King Jr. Ultimately, then, Hightower's message is full of hope—a hope whose realization requires the time, energy, vision, and humor of political mavericks animated by the promise of democracy.*

Woody Guthrie wrote "This Land" in 1940 while living in New York City, penning all six verses in one night while staying in a no-star hotel somewhere around Times Square. The song had been forming in his fertile mind for a long time as "he roamed and rambled" all around America, "walking that ribbon of highway." He wrote it not as a sweet sing-along glorifying the American landscape but as a proudly populist anthem for the hardscrabble people he traveled among. He had

Source: Jim Hightower, *If The Gods Had Meant For Us To Vote They Would Have Given Us Candidates,* New York: HarperCollins, 2000, pp. 307–324 and 337–339.

already written hundreds of songs that chronicled the lives and struggles of these workaday folks who are the strength of our great land, performing his songs for them on picket lines, in migrant camps, and at rallies, as well as performing on radio and at their dances. His music entertained, even as it encouraged people in their battles against the Pinkertons, politicians, and other authorities who fronted for the refined men with soft hands and hard eyes who ran things from afar.

When he wrote the words *"your* land," Woody was pointedly speaking to the steelworkers in Pittsburgh and dockworkers up and down the Pacific coast, the dust-bowl people (of whom he was one) who had lost their crops to drought and their farms to bankers, the workers who risked their lives to build the Grand Coulee and the itinerant harvesters who cut the wheat and stacked the hay, "trying to make about a dollar a day." Every schoolchild has sung "This Land's" gentle verses about the "endless skyway" and "diamond deserts," but the songbooks carefully excise Woody's verses that provoke ordinary citizens to rethink the established order, to realize their democratic strength, and to rebel against the structures of privilege that lock out the majority. Verses like:

> Was a big high wall there that tried to stop me
> A sign was painted said: "Private Property."
> But on the back side it didn't say nothing
> This side was made for you and me.©[1]

Woody knew that this land is our land only if we make it so, only if we have the stomach to confront the elites and challenge the insidious forces of autocracy that are continually at work to make it exclusively their land, in the sense that they control the economic and political decisions that rule us. The essence of democracy is self-government. Anything less is a fraud. Being connected to the Internet is not democracy, having a choice between Gore and Bush is not democracy, receiv-

ing five hundred channels of digital television is not democracy, being awarded a slice of corporate-allocated prosperity is not democracy. Democracy is control. Whatever goals we strive for as a people—racial harmony, peace, economic fairness, privacy, clean water and air—all are dependent on our ability to control the decisions that affect these goals.

Pause for a moment to think of what an incredible treasure it is to have the right to govern ourselves. Precious few people in history have even had the possibility of asserting their common will over the will of the ruling powers, and the vast majority of earth's people today cannot even imagine such a right. But, in the Declaration of 1776, we have it in writing: ". . . governments are instituted among men, deriving their just powers from the *consent of the governed."* We're in charge! Not kings of feudal barons, congresses or presidents, and damned sure not corporations or World Trade Organizations.

Having it on paper, though, doesn't make it so. Indeed when it was first written, it wasn't so for very many citizens at all. In the first presidential election, 1789, only 4 percent of the American people were allowed to vote. No women voted (they were chattel), no African Americans (they were slaves), no Native Americans (they were considered heathens), and no one who was without land (they were riffraff). A broader sense of self-rule came later, and only with great effort, pain, and suffering. From abolitionists to suffragists, from populists to Wobblies, from sit-down strikes to lunch-counter sit-ins, blood has flowed as generation after generation has battled the Powers That Be for a share of "Life, Liberty, and the Pursuit of Happiness." In the 224 years since Jefferson wrote of these "inalienable rights," thousands upon thousands of Americans have died in the ongoing struggle to democratize the Declaration, to extend the possibility of self-government to more citizens. What a debt we owe to those who

---

[1]The excerpt used in this book was taken from Woody Guthrie's original manuscipt and is different from the published words.

have sacrificed so much to bring us this far, and what a gift this right to self-government is.

But will we hold on to it? Progress is never assured and democracy cannot be taken for granted, even in our country. There has been a radical backsliding of democratic control in the past few years—a majority of Americans now find themselves effectively shut out of economic and political decision making, and even greater threats of our sovereignty loom in the ominous form of the WTO, NAFTA, and other antidemocratic creations of the global corporate powers. Democratic power is never given; it always has to be taken, then aggressively defended, and retaken when it slips from our hands, for the moneyed powers relentlessly press to gain supremacy and assert their private will over the majority. Today, our gift of democracy is endangered not by military might threatening a sudden, explosive coup but by the stealth of corporate lawyers and politicians, seizing a piece of self-government from us here, then another piece from over there, quietly installing an elitist regime issue by issue, law by law, place by place, with many citizens unaware that their people's authority is slipping away.

For the past couple of decades, this has been going on, greatly accelerating in the nineties, as corporate will has been enthroned, increasingly reigning supreme over every aspect of our lives—economics, politics, culture, and nature itself. We American people find ourselves, once again, at one of those "When in the course of human events" moments, when it is our time to face the reality that a despotic force is in our midst. In the name of all American rebels who have gone before, are we going to sit by, unwilling to confront the bully in front of us, which grows more powerful the longer we wait? You and I have the lofty responsibility to follow in the footsteps of those rebels, to oppose the corporate usurpers and fight for our nation's unique and hard-won right to self-government. Progress doesn't come by merely standing on guard but, as George Bernard Shaw said about a hundred years ago, "by attacking, and getting well-hammered yourself."

WHAT THE HELL IS A CORPORATION?

This ubiquitous critter called the corporation—we're stuck with it, right? We've just got to learn to live with it, don't we, kind of like we live with cockroaches? After all, a corporation has a kind of natural right to do business, doesn't it? No, no, and no. First of all, a corporation is not a business. It's nothing but a piece of paper, a bit of legalism that does not create a business but instead creates a protective association for individuals who want to do business yet want special protections for themselves against other people, against the public at large . . . against the very workings of democracy.

You can make widgets, you can farm, you can sell hardware or groceries, you can operate a hotel, you can provide banking services, or be in any other business without being a corporation. Most of the businesses in the world are *unincorporated* enterprises—individuals, sole proprietorships, partnerships, co-ops, or other forms of operation. Taking on corporations is not antibusiness at all—we must have businesses, but that does not mean we have to have corporations.

Where did we get the corporate structure? From the jolly Brits, who devised a devilish scheme called "joint stock companies" during their colonial phase. Empire and all that, eh what? The corporate entity was (and is) a legal fiction, first invented by the crown to assist the barons, merchant traders, and bankers of the day in plundering the wealth of the Empire's colonies, including those in our fair land. It was a way to amass the large sums of capital they needed to plunder faraway places, collecting money from investors to finance the plundering, then distributing the booty back to those investors. The corporate construct is dangerous not only because it can agglomerate an absolutely domineering amount of financial power but also because it allows the owners of the corporation (the shareholders) to profit from its business activities, yet accept *no responsibility* for any harm done by their company's business activities. All gain, no pain. The corporation is a legal shield, granting its owners an extraordinary protective privilege that no other business owners are allowed. Oh, did my company spill eleven million gallons of oil into Prince William Sound (Exxon), did it kill two thousand people in a chemical explosion in Bhopal, India (Union Carbide), did it defraud thousands of senior citizens who were persuaded to put money into bad securities (Prudential), did it dump cancer-causing PCBs into the Hudson River (General Electric)? So sorry, I'm sure, but that's none of my doing—the *corporation* did it. Yet, the corporation has no ass to be kicked, no scruff of the neck to be grabbed, no body to be tossed unceremoniously into the maximum security lockup, no conscience to make it contrite, and no soul that would allow the religious among us to believe that at least this wretched enterprise will be condemned to eternal hell.

To the built-in irresponsibility of the amorphous corporate entity, add the bottom-line imperative of the CEO and board of directors. Academicians, judges, and corporation executives themselves aver that the sole role of corporate management is to make as much money as possible for the shareholders (a group that prominently includes the managers). The managers have no responsibility—none—to workers, environment, consumers, community, flag, or anything else. To the contrary, the entire incentive is for management to cut corners, to shortchange, to exploit. It is not a matter of a CEO's good intentions or bad—it is the bottom line, and it must be served. Put away all hope, ye who go in asking corporations to be "good," "responsible," "accountable." It is not in their self-interest or in their nature—you might as well expect a Rottweiler to meow.

As for corporations having natural rights, forget it. It's no longer taught in civics or history classes, and it's definitely not mentioned in today's politics or media, but corporations have no rights at all. Zero. Not even the right to exist. The state gives them the *privilege* to exist, but this existence can be narrowly defined and controlled by We the People. I realize this goes against the received wisdom, against the carefully nurtured assumption that corporations are somehow or other one of God's creatures with inherent powers that are larger and elevated above the powers of us common citizens. We can all be forgiven for assuming this, for that certainly is how it works in practice today. But it need not and should not work that way, nor was it meant to work that way when our country and most of our states were founded. Each corporation was and is the creature of the *citizenry,* allowed to exist only through receipt of a state charter. *We are the sovereign,* not them. They are supposed to serve us, not vice versa.

Back to the future: the American Revolution. Jane Anne Morris, a thinker, digger, strategist, and agitator on the issue of corporate dominance, writes: "The people who founded this nation didn't fight a war so they could have a couple of 'citizen representatives' sitting in on meetings on the British East India Company. They carried out a revolution in order to be free of oppression: corporate, governmental, or otherwise; and to replace it with democratic self-government." Adams, Jefferson, Paine, and the rest had not had a happy experience with the corporations of the crown and were unabashedly anticorporate at the founding, with Jefferson even speaking of the need "to crush in its birth the aristocracy of our moneyed corporations."

The citizens of early America knew what they were up against: raw economic power. They were rightly wary of the corporate structure itself, knowing that it allowed a few individuals in the society to stockpile a massive amount of money and power, then use this and the corporate shield to pursue their private gain to the harm of the common good. Eighteenth- and nineteenth-century Americans were prescient when it came to these entities—citizens expressed concern that corporations would use their money as bribes to pervert democratic elections and buy both legislators and judges; farmers worried that corporations would use their muscle to monopolize markets and control crop prices; and industrial and craft workers were concerned that corporations would, as historian Louis Hartz has written, turn them into "a commodity," treating them "as much an article of commerce as woolens, cotton or yarn." They knew that the unbridled corporation was antithetical to the democratic principles they espoused and a threat to the very system of self-government they had established. So they made damned sure the corporation was securely bridled.

Anyone so timid as to think that it is radical for citizens today even to consider "interfering" with the private will of corporations is not made of the same stout stuff as the citizens who created our states and our country. In America's first hundred years, applicants could get a corporate charter only by approval of their state legislature, usually requiring a two-thirds vote to win one. Few charters were awarded, and those few corporations that got them were limited in their function, in how much money they could aggregate, in how long they could exist, and in how they could function. Citizens took their hard-won sovereignty seriously, adamantly defending it against the possibility of corporate usurpation. State after state imposed strict terms on the issuance of a charter, leaving no doubt about who was in charge. This is our hidden history of proud and aggressive citizenship, and you're likely to be amazed if you look into how the people of your state have stood up to corporate power in the not-so-distant past. Jane Anne Morris dug into the records of her state of Wisconsin and found that from 1848 to as recently as 1953, the legislature had imposed such charter conditions as these:

- Corporations had to have a clearly stated reason for existing, and if they failed to fulfill that purpose or went beyond it, their charter could be revoked.
- The legislature could revoke the charter for any particular reason or, as the Wisconsin attorney general ruled in 1913, "for no reason at all."
- Corporate management and stockholders could be held liable for corporate acts.

- Directors of the corporation were required to come from among the stockholders.
- If a corporation's principal place of business was Wisconsin, it had to have its headquarters and its meetings there.
- Charters were granted for a specific period of time, like twenty years, rather than "in perpetuity."
- Corporations could not own other corporations.
- Corporations could own real estate only if it was necessary to carry out their specific purpose.
- Corporations were flatly prohibited from making any political contribution, direct or indirect, and it was a felony crime if they did so.
- All corporate records and documents were open to the legislature and to the attorney general.

From Maine to California, Wisconsin to Texas, all states had similar stipulations on their books—and they were enforced! Especially important were the revocation clauses, which allowed state legislatures or courts to yank the operating licenses of corporations that behaved badly. Imagine. The people were in charge, the general welfare was paramount over corporate profit, civic authority prevailed over CEO whim. Richard Grossman and Ward Morehouse, two thoughtful activists who codirect POCLAD (the Program on Corporations, Laws and Democracy), have published an excellent pamphlet worthy of Thomas Paine, entitled "Taking Care of Business: Citizenship and the Charter of Incorporation." It notes that the corporate charter was a sacrosanct oath: "The penalty for abuse or misuse of the charter was not a fine or a slap on the wrist, but revocation of the charter and dissolution of the corporation. Citizens believed that it was society's inalienable right to abolish an evil." Charters were routinely revoked, including those of the most powerful—in 1894, the Central Labor Union of New York City cited a pattern of abuses against John D. Rockefeller's Standard Oil Trust of New

York, asking the attorney general to request that the state supreme court revoke its charter. The AG did . . . and the court did.

After the Civil War, however, with the rise of the Robber Barons, a full-scale assault was begun by the moneyed interests against these inconvenient rules. Railroad baron Cornelius Vanderbilt issued the war cry of the antidemocratic elites when he thundered, "What do I care about the law? H'ain't I got the power?" For the next hundred years—stipulation by stipulation, state by state, bribe by bribe—the sovereign was steadily reduced to the subjugated. Corporate barons like Vanderbilt hauled sacks of money into state capitols to buy legislators and win charter changes favorable to them. The chief justice of Wisconsin's supreme court spoke as early as 1873 of "a new and dark power" that was looming, warning that "the enterprises of the country are aggregating vast corporate combinations of unexampled capital, marching, not for economical conquests only, but for political power. . . ." The Vanderbilts, Goulds, Rockefellers, and others had more money than hell has brimstone, and they used it to corrupt and dominate the same state legislatures that had been bulwarks of democratic resistance to the corporate empire builders. A Pennsylvania legislator is reported to have said, "Mr. Speaker, I move we adjourn, unless the Pennsylvania Railroad has some more business for us to transact."

Gradually, the bridle has been removed, resulting in what we have today—the runaway corporate autocracy that the founders predicted and feared. Shall we just accept it? Shall we timidly continue into another century with the status quo politics of the pathetic ClintonGore-Bradley Democrats, who demand again and again that the people must adjust to the private agenda of a handful of corporate executives and investors?

"This is an exciting time to be an American," a Californian wrote to me several months ago. "We are in a crisis. We are on the brink of failure of our old democratic processes—swamped, subverted, perverted, and filibustered by the corporate feudal system and its totalitarian dominance of our lives. We have the opportunity and the duty to overcome all that," he wrote.

Bingo! In one succinct paragraph, this citizen has nailed it, and he is but one of a growing majority who know that "consent of the governed" is a mockery today, supplanted by a crude bribery system of corporate governance that is becoming as autocratic as anything imagined by King George III and his royally chartered British East India Company, Hudson's Bay Company, and the crown charters that ruled American colonies. Just a few examples: High-handed CEOs can, by fiat, off several thousand workers from the payroll, thereby jacking up the company's stock price and enriching themselves with tens of millions in stock gains, while the workers and their families are allowed no redress for their grievances; your bank, insurance company, credit-card firm, HMO, and other corporations can secretly collect the most intimate details of your private life, then use or sell this information in any way they see fit, without even informing you; imperious biotech corporations can mess dangerously with the very DNA of our food supply for no purpose except to enhance their profits, then force families to be the guinea pigs of their Frankenfood experiments, since there is no labeling of thousands of supermarket items (including baby food) already containing these genetically altered organisms; conniving corporations routinely extract millions from townspeople as the price of building a factory or sports stadium in their town, then can renege on any pledge of job creation and, on whim, pull up stakes and abandon the town altogether; haughty HMOs can make decisions that kill you, yet Congress protects them from legal liability and punishment for your death; "speech" has been perverted to mean money, authorizing corporations and their executives to buy control of the entire political process; a chemical company can callously pollute our air, water, and food, leading to thousands of deaths, birth defects, and other horrors, yet continue doing business and continue polluting, with no punishment beyond, perhaps, a fine, which it easily absorbs and, in some cases, can deduct from its income taxes as a "cost of doing business"; a handful of media giants have attained absolute control over the content of news and the range of ideas that are broadcast on the *public's* airwaves, arbitrarily shrinking the democratic debate; the democratic decisions of a city council, state legislature, or other sovereign government can be arrogantly annulled by corporate action through antidemocratic entities established by NAFTA and the WTO.

Who the hell are these people? Who elected them to run our world? Why are we putting up with this crap? As the bumper sticker puts it: LEMMINGS OF THE WORLD UNITE! YOU HAVE NOTHING TO LOSE BUT YOUR PLACE IN LINE!

We need to crank up a political fight that has some guts to it, some fire-breathing democratic passion in it, some of the revolutionary spirit of 1776 behind it. This is not a fight about regulations or really even about corporations—it's about control, sovereignty, self-government, *democracy.* Let's force the issue and put it as starkly as it is: Are corporations going to rule, or are we? From time to time, I hear veterans of the civil rights and antiwar battles of the sixties bemoan the lack of a "Big Battle" today, one that can unite a majority across traditional political lines, one that is about justice for all, is loaded with citizen outrage, has the spark of genuine passion within it, and is worthy of bloody heads. Well, here it is: The self-evident battle of our era is to defeat corporate autocracy and establish citizen rule over our government, our economy, and our environment.

WHEN YOU FIGHT THE DEVIL, FIGHT TO WIN

Practically every progressive struggle—campaign finance reform, rain forest destruction and global warming, sweatshops, family farms, fair trade, health care for all, unionization, military spending and arms sales, tax reform, alternative energy, healthy food, media access, hazardous waste dumps, redlining, alternative medicine, you name it—is being fought against one cluster of corporations or another. But it is not that corporation over there or this one over here that is the enemy, it is not one industry's contamination of our drinking water or another's perversion of the lawmaking process that is the problem—rather it is the corporation itself that must be addressed if we are to be a free people.

In his powerful pamphlet *Common Sense,* Thomas Paine touched the heart of the American Revolution when he wrote: "Ye that dare oppose not only tyranny but the tyrant, stand forth." We can all object to consequences and seek remedial action, but will we finally face the tyrant itself? That is the questions for progressives as we step into 2000. We can continue fighting the beast as we have been, through scattershot, uncoordinated efforts—a lawsuit here, an investigation there, some legislation, more regulations, prayer, and the always useful sacrificial goat. Occasionally, these approaches succeed. But, as Grossman and Morehouse have written, "Tactically, [this approach] means limiting ourselves to resisting harms one corporate site at a time, one corporate chemical or biotechnology product at a time; to correcting imperfections of the market; to working for yet more permitting and disclosure laws; to initiating procedural lawsuits and attempts to win compensation after corporate harm has been done; to battling regulatory and administrative agencies; to begging leaders of global corporations to please cause a little less harm."

In 1998, Britain's House of Lords dealt with the weighty matter of changing the official costume worn by the Lord Chancellor, that body's top official. The outfit included a long powdered wig, breeches, tights, buckled shoes, white gloves, and black stockings. The incumbent wanted very much not to look, as one reporter described him, like "the frog footman in 'Alice in Wonderland,'" so he proposed a switch to modern business attire. Traditionalists, however, opposed any change in the seventeenth-century garb. Lord Wattington put the case for tradition forcefully, summing up by declaring, "I can see no advantage to the Queen or the public if the Lord Chancellor removes his tights."

At the national level, inside the Beltway, too many of our progressive energies and resources are spent on fights that amount to removing the Lord Chancellor's tights. The piecemeal approach to fighting corporate abuses keeps us spread thin, separated from each other, on the defensive, riveted on the minutiae, and fighting on their terms (literally over the language of *their* laws and regulations, and in *their* courts and legislatures). More often than not, regulatory agencies are shams, working to sustain the business-as-usual tactics of corporations rather than to inhibit them, and the deck is stacked against the public interest anytime we find ourselves within these legalistic meat grinders. This is nothing new—historian Howard Zinn writes about the creation of the Interstate Commerce Commission in 1887, a "reform" pushed by President Grover Cleveland, ostensibly to regulate railroads. But railroad executives were told not to worry by Richard Olney, a railroad lawyer who was soon to be Cleveland's attorney general: "The Commission . . . is or can be made, of great use to the railroads. It satisfies the popular clamor for a government supervision of railroads, at the same time that its supervision is almost entirely nominal. . . . The part of wisdom is not to destroy the Commission, but to utilize it."

Piecemeal battles must certainly continue, but there is real and immediate corporate harm to be addressed for people and communities. But it's time for our strategic emphasis to shift to the offensive, raising what I believe to be the central political issues for the new century: *Who the hell is in charge here?*

It is an open question, despite the appearance that corporations have things pretty tightly locked down. Yes, they have the money, the media, the government, the two major parties, the police and military, and the deadening power of conventional wisdom. But so did King George III. We've been here before, we've done this, and we can do it again.

We've got a couple of things going for our side in this historic struggle. For one thing, our constitutional assertion of citizen control of corporations is still there, as is much of the language

in the state codes that formally subjugates corporations to us. As Richard Grossman has found in his years of digging, "We still have the authority to *define* the corporations through their charters; we still have the authority to *amend* the charters; we still have the authority to *revoke* the charters—the language is still there. We still have the authority to *rewrite the state corporation codes* in order to *order* corporate executives to do what the sovereign people want to do." We have legal language and authority, a constitutional claim, a moral position firmly rooted in justice, and a powerful historic precedent that flows from the revolutionary patriots themselves.

We also have the common sense and revolutionary chutzpah of grassroots American agitators going for us. The commonsense side says: There are laws in our country that proclaim to human criminals "three strikes and you're out"—why not for corporations? Each year, hundreds of doctors, lawyers, accountants, and other professionals have their licenses to practice permanently revoked by the states—why not corporations? The Supreme Court has rules that the corporation is a "person" under the law; people who murder are removed from society—why not corporations?

The chutzpah side says: Let's go get 'em. And they are! The national media have been practically mum about it, but there already is an important movement among the citizenry to begin reestablishing citizen control over charters. In Wayne, Pennsylvania, the locals passed a 1998 ordinance that prohibits any corporation from doing business there if it has a history of consistently violating laws to protect workers, consumers, the environment, and so forth. In Jay, Maine, a town of paperworkers, the people were fed up with the repeated pollution of the water and air by the recalcitrant International Paper Company, so they enacted the "Jay Environmental and Improvement Ordinance," which gives the town of Jay the authority to monitor and regulate pollution by IP's Androscoggin paper mill—the townspeople have their own full-time environmental administrator with full authority to fine and shut down the mill for violations. In 1998, the people of South Dakota just said "no" to corporate hog factories in their state, voting by a sixty-to-forty margin for a constitutional amendment to prohibit corporations from owning livestock. Also in 1998, New York attorney general Dennis Vacco, a Republican, showed that the Council for Tobacco Research had acted fraudulently and illegally in pretending to do objective research when in fact it was nothing but a lobbyist and a front for the tobacco industry, leading to a settlement in which the council surrendered its corporate charter. The state's new attorney general, Democrat Elliott Spitzer, is expanding Vacco's initiative, considering all corporate charters fair game: "When a corporation is convicted of repeated felonies that harm or endanger the lives of human beings or destroy the environment, the corporation should be put to death, its corporate existence ended, and its assets taken and sold at public auction." He has hired a highly regarded public-interest attorney to oversee this effort.

Meanwhile, in the small coastal town of Arcata, California, there has been a remarkable two-year effort to put the issue of corporate usurpation of democratic authority into the public debate again. It began with Paul Cienfuegos, Gary Houser, and a few others, who organized Democracy Unlimited of Humboldt County, which in 1998 launched a citizens campaign to get on the ballot a local initiative called Measure F: Advisory Measure on Democracy and Corporations. After a few straightforward whereases about the sovereign power of people to govern themselves, the Measure resolved that "the people of Arcata support the amending of the California Constitution so as to clearly declare the authority of citizens over all corporations." The proposition then included a couple of practical steps that, very smartly, took a slow and minimalist approach toward advancing citizen sovereignty in Arcata, establishing a process for democratic discussion in town that could move people along, but not before they were ready to move. First was a simple provision that, if Measure F passed, the city council would sponsor two town hall meetings on this

topic: "Can we have democracy when large corporations wield so much power and wealth under law?" Second was for the city government to create an official committee to develop policies and programs to assert democratic control over corporations doing business in Arcata.

The citizens campaign hit the streets, and in just twenty-six days got the signatures needed to put the measure on the ballot. They gained key endorsements from Arcata mayor Jim Test and groups like the central labor council and students at Humboldt State University, and they delivered materials to the doors of nearly every household and business in this town of about seventeen thousand people. In the November 1998 election, their effort paid off: Measure F passed with nearly 60 percent of the vote. Since then, this town has been having what every town, city, neighborhood, and village green needs—a heart-to-heart airing out of the basic question of "Who's in charge?" Ralph Nader visited in 1999 in support of citizen control, likening Arcata's democracy dialogue to the ride of Paul Revere. On the other side, Kenneth Fisher, a *Forbes* magazine columnist and a financial speculator, gave a lecture entitled "Societal Ethics Are Always Unethical," bemoaning Measure F as an example of the "tyranny of democracy." Then came the town hall meetings in April and May of 1999, which produced a turnout of more than six hundred people, far surpassing expectations. The opposition had been active, too, working hard to turn out a pro-corporatist crowd, led by a couple of very vocal officials with the Yakima Corporation, which is based in the area but manufactures at a Mexican border factory. The proceedings were structured so both sides made two presentations of eight minutes each—then the floor was open to the people. The freewheeling discussions went long past the set time, putting the lie to conventional wisdom that insists people are too busy, too satisfied, too uninformed, too unconcerned, too prosperous, too conservative, too short, too stupid, too whatever to get involved with something as "boring" as their own democracy. Overwhelmingly, participants favored Measure F, and the town's people are now at work on developing the policies and programs for city hall that will put the well-being of the community above corporate whim on issues ranging from chain stores bankrupting local businesses to industry polluting the town's air and water.

Whatever the outcome at city hall, the effort already has accomplished something extraordinarily important: It has launched a citywide democratic conversation on a subject that hasn't been discussed in public for a century. Cienfuegos notes that thousands of local residents are now conversant with corporate rule and how it impacts their lives. It's a conversation that has become common in the cafés, Laundromats, in line at the post office, and elsewhere—literally taking root in the culture of the community. The groundbreaking work in Arcata continues, and it is spreading to other California towns, and to places like Olympia, Washington.

·   ·   ·

People are ready for politics that challenges the ongoing corporate grabfest. A recent series of focus-group sessions with middle-class folks (most of whom made in the range of $20,000–$60,000 a year) produced results that cannot be comforting to the Keepers of the Established Order:

- 68 percent of the people viewed corporate greed as an "equally important" or "more important" cause of working families' economic woes than big government—nearly half say corporations are the "more important" cause.
- 70 percent believe that such actions as massive downsizing, cutbacks on worker benefits, and sending U.S. jobs overseas are not motivated by the corporate need to be competitive and efficient, but by greed.
- 79 percent of Democrats in the groups, 67 percent of Republicans, and 74 percent of ticket splitters say the economic and human impacts of these corporate behaviors are seri-

ous enough to warrant purposeful government intervention.

I realize that this goes counter to the constant message from those on high who keep telling us that we Americans are a conservative people, but I find the regular folks of this country to be a gutsy bunch who, at their core, have an ingrained commitment to the ideal of democracy, a deep (and hardearned) distrust of concentrations of economic and political power, and a fighting spirit that doesn't need much kindling to flare. People are not "conservative," certainly not in the corporate sense, nor are they "liberal," in the sense of believing that more social programs and nitpicking regulations are going to clean up the messes that are being made by global corporate greed. People are antiestablishment mavericks, and they know (as any mother or kindergarten teacher can tell you) that the better plan is not to keep trying to clean up the messes but to get control over the brutes that are making the messes.

If the progressive movement is going to matter, going to make any difference at all in twenty-first-century politics, it has to understand and act on the latent radicalism (á la 1776) and maverick spirit of the true majority. The term "maverick" even has revolutionary roots—a member of the Maverick family was one of the five "liberty boys" killed at the "Boston Massacre" in 1770. But the term as we use it today actually came from another member of this same family. Samuel Maverick was his name, a pioneer Texas rancher who had fought in the 1836 revolution against the Mexican authorities. A thoroughly independent sort, Sam refused to brand his cattle. So, out on the range, any unbranded calf or steer one came across was said to be a maverick.

Go into the coffee shops and bars where middle-class workaday America hangs out, chat with the cab drivers and grocery clerks, visit working-class churches and neighborhood block parties, talk with nurses, janitors, mechanics, clerks, and restaurant workers while they're on break, shoot the breeze with the regulars at the barber shops or in the feed-and-seed stores. Here's where you'll find the maverick majority for the progressive politics I'm talking about, a constituency willing to run right at corporate power. This is where the progressive future is—not in Washington, fidgeting with policy on the fringes of power, quibbling over which of the namby-pamby corporate suck-ups running for president will do the most for "the cause."

Hey, let's gut it up, decamp from Washington, put our resources into the countryside, slug the corporate bastards right in the snout, and get it on with a grassroots politics that gives regular folks a reason to be excited and to get involved. Why not start the new century and millennium with a political crusade that is worthy of all of our energies and capabilities, a fight that is big enough, important enough, and bold enough to rally the workaday majority? It's the fight to take our government back, take our economy back, take our environment back by taking our sovereignty back—taking back our constitutional right as a people to *be in charge* of our own destinies.

"I may not get there with you," said a prophetic Martin Luther King Jr. in a sermon on the eve of his assassination, but "I've seen the promised land." The land that Reverend King saw is the same land that Woody Guthrie sang about in his cross-country rambles, and that I see today as I travel. It's *our* land, an extraordinary land where ordinary people are the strength, a place with awesome *possibility* to implement the democratic ideals of the people themselves. Through the generations, Americans have taken historic stands to hold on to and advance those ideals. Now is our time, our chance, and our duty to make real the promise of democracy—if not for ourselves, then for our grandchildren.

This *is* an exciting time to be an American.

DISCUSSION QUESTIONS

1. Hightower states that "democracy is control." In what ways does corporate power interfere with popular sovereignty or control?
2. Interpret Hightower's remark that the corporate entity was and is a "legal fiction."
3. How does the case study of citizen action in Arcata, California, relate to Hightower's view of what form progressive politics should take?

THE MARKET AS PRISON

Charles Lindblom, a political scientist, was long associated with the pluralist approach, which saw political power as broadly dispersed and balanced among an array of competing interest groups. But in his 1977 book Politics and Markets, *Lindblom argued that business occupies a "privileged position" in the political systems of market societies. Lindblom's "The Market As Prison" (1982) summarizes many themes from his book and contends that markets function to "punish" public policymakers when they attempt to make changes that are unwelcome to the business community. Lindblom's article suggests that private control of investment, which is basic to capitalism, has profound public impacts, and undermines a democratic formation of the common good by withdrawing crucial decisions from popular deliberation.*

Suppose—just to limber up our minds—that we faced the fanciful task of designing a political system or a political/economic system that would be highly resistant to change. How to do it? One way that can be imagined—but only imagined—is to design institutions of such excellence as would satisfy us without further amendment and would do so under all possible circumstances in a rapidly changing world. To identify such a possibility is to discard it as hopelessly visionary. Another possibility might be somehow to place all power in the hands of a despot or oligarch, who would thereafter deny citizens any capacity for changing the system. But doing so would of course enable the elites to change the system, and we know that some elites are more eager for change than some masses.

Another possibility is simple and fiendishly clever. It is to design institutions so that any attempt to alter them automatically triggers punishment. By "automatic" I mean that the punishment follows from the very act intended to change the system. Punishment does not wait for anyone's deliberation on whether the change is acceptable or not. Such a change-repressing system would be all the more effective if the punishments were strong; if they took the form of over-responses, like the tantrums of a spoiled child raging at even mild attempts at parental control.

How fanciful is that possibility? It is not at all clear how such a simple concept could be made effective in actual practice. Consider some of our institutions. There seems to be no way to make such a mechanism work in the case of schools. We are indeed sometimes punished in our attempts to improve them in that the attempts

Source: Charles E. Lindblom, "The Market As Prison," *Journal of Politics,* vol. 44, no. 2, May 1982, pp. 324–336.

sometimes fail and make the situation worse. But that is not a built-in feature of the school system or of our attempts to improve it. There may be no way, even if we sought one, to build in an automatic punishing recoil. The same seems to be true for labor unions. Unions possess a capacity for retaliatory punishment through strikes, but it is a weapon they must use sparingly. And it is a weapon rarely used to punish attempts of society to change the institutional role of unions but is instead largely an adjunct to bargaining over terms of employment for members. There appears to be no easily perceived possibility for automatically punishing ourselves every time we try to legislate on unions.

If we go down the line of social institutions, the possibilities for repressing change through an automatic punishing recoil appear to be either nonexistent or impossible to imagine. For the church, the family, or the various institutions of government, for example, unpunished change continues in fact from year to year even if, again, we may sometimes construe a failure in reform as a punishment. No method for guaranteeing automatic punishment is in evidence.

When we come, however, to that cluster of institutions called business, business enterprise, or the market, just such a mechanism is in fact already operating. Many kinds of market reform automatically trigger punishments in the form of unemployment or a sluggish economy. Do we want business to carry a larger share of the nation's tax burden? We must fear that such a reform will discourage business investment and curtail employment. Do we want business enterprises to reduce industrial pollution of air and water? Again we must bear the consequences of the costs to them of their doing so and the resultant declines in investment and employment. Would we like to consider even more fundamental changes in business and market—worker participation in management, for example, or public scrutiny of corporate decisions? We can hardly imagine putting such proposals as those on the legislative agenda so disturbing would they be to business morale and incentive.

In the town in which I live, a chemical plant discharges something into the atmosphere that carries both a bad odor and irritants to the eyes. Town and state governments are both reluctant to put an end to the problem for fear that the plant will find it advantageous to move to a new location in another state. Nationally, we have recently seen that a reinvigorated Federal Trade Commission has been crippled by new restrictive legislation and presidential instructions for fear that effective regulation of monopoly by the Commission will undercut business incentives to invest and provide jobs.

All this is familiar. One line of reform after another is blocked by prospective punishment. An enormous variety of reforms do in fact undercut business expectations of profitability and do therefore reduce employment. Higher business taxes reduce profitability. Bearing the costs of pollution control reduces profitability. Building safer automobiles reduces profitability. Countless reforms therefore are followed immediately—swiftly—by the punishment of unemployment.

Change is repressed, not wholly stopped. Businessmen sometimes learn to live with reforms. Sometimes also we escape the punishment because we attach to the reforms new offsetting benefits to business to keep up their incentives to provide jobs. To a growing number of environmental controls over business we attach new tax benefits or, as in the case of Chrysler, new loan guarantees. But the conflict between reform and its adverse effects on business that punish us through unemployment is a long standing and real repressant of change. As for the ubiquity of punishment, its swiftness and severity, there is nothing like it elsewhere in the social system. Nowhere else is there so effective a set of automatic punishments established as a barrier to social change.

Business people often exaggerate the conflict. Chrysler, for example, argued that its financial difficulties, for which it sought relief from government, were largely caused by environmental regulations, which is almost certainly not the case. And business people often predict dire consequences from regulations that they know they can accept if they must. Nevertheless, change in business and market institutions is drastically repressed by the frequency with which change will in actual fact produce unemployment. This is a familiar phenomenon as old as markets themselves.

Punishment is not dependent on conspiracy or intention to punish. If, anticipating new regulations, a businessman decides not to go through with a planned output expansion, he has in effect punished us without the intention of doing so. Simply minding one's own business is the formula for an extraordinary system for repressing change.

The mechanism that accounts for this extraordinary state of affairs is the same one that I referred to in *Politics and Markets* to explain the related phenomenon of the privileged position of business in the political system of all market-oriented societies. In all market-oriented societies, the great organizing and coordinating tasks are placed in the hands of two groups of responsible persons, functionaries, or leaders. One group consists of government officials at sufficiently high levels. The other group consists of business people. The tasks assigned to business people are of no less importance than those assigned to government officials. To business people is assigned the organizing of the nation's work force, and that task in itself is perhaps the largest and most basic specific problem in social organization faced by any society. Businessmen direct capital accumulation, income distribution, and resource conservation, as well as discharge more particular tasks such as organizing the production of steel, bicycles, armaments, pots and pans, and housing. Businessmen also undertake specific coordinating tasks as, for example, the bringing of farm products to urban consumers.

The defining difference between a government official and a business entrepreneur is not that one discharges important functions and the other only secondary functions, for both perform major and essential services for society. The difference is that one is directed and controlled through a system of commands while the other is directed and controlled by a system of inducements. Why societies use both systems of direction and control is a long story that we shall not undertake. But a market society is one that makes heavy use of an inducement system for directing and controlling many of its major leaders. Market systems are inducement systems. Put out of your minds the question of whether or not societies ought to use inducement systems for controlling and directing top leadership. The fact is that some do, and that is what market systems are.

Playing their roles in a command system, government officials can be commanded to perform their functions. Playing their roles in an inducement system, business people cannot be commanded but must be induced. Thus inducement becomes the nub of the automatic punishment system. Any change in their position that they do not like is a disincentive, an anti-inducement, leading them not to perform their function or to perform it with less vigor. Any change or reform they do not like brings to all of us the punishment of unemployment or a sluggish economy.

Again, the system works that way not because business people conspire or plan to punish us, but simply because many kinds of institutional changes are of a character they do not like and consequently reduce the inducements we count on to motivate them to provide jobs and perform their other functions.

The result is that across the entire array of institutional changes that businessmen themselves do not like, an automatic punishing recoil works to repress change. In that broad category, change—and often even the suggestion of change—adversely affects performance, hence adversely affects employment. Anticipations of change are enough to trigger unemployment.

Children may sulk when they do not like the way they are being treated. Professors may grumble. Workers may slow their work. But their responses differ from the responses of dissatisfied businessmen in a critical way. The dissatisfactions of these other groups do not result in disincentives and reduced performance that impose a broad, severe and obvious penalty throughout the society, which is what unemployment does. A generalized gradual slowdown of workers, if it were to occur, would ordinarily be neither measurable nor observable. Any general business slowdown is measurable and hurtful in jobs lost, and almost everyone is aware of it. A specific localized work slowdown or stoppage—say, a decision of trainmen to work by the rule-book so assiduously as to paralyze rail traffic—can be a felt injury to millions of people. But it is a tactic that can only now and then be mobilized. Instead, the penalty of unemployment is visited on us by business disincentives in any situation in which business people see themselves adversely affected, because business people are major organizers and coordinators.

Business people do not have to debate whether or not to impose the penalty. They need do no more—as I said before—than tend to their own businesses, which means that, without thought of effecting a punishment on us, they restrict investment and jobs simply in the course of being prudent managers of their enterprises.

Do I need to point out how broadly business disincentives injure a population? The unemployed suffer—that is obvious. So also do young prospective entrants into the labor force, who find that they cannot obtain jobs when business is slack. So also do businessmen themselves, large and small, as production is reduced. So also do stockholders, whose earnings decline. So also do farmers—businessmen themselves—who find markets for their outputs depressed.

What about government officials? It is critical to the efficacy of automatic punishment that it be visited on them. For it is they who immediately or proximately decide to persist in policy changes or to withdraw from such initiatives. The penalty visited on them by business disincentives caused by proposed policies is that declining business activity is a threat to the party and the officials in power. When a decline in prosperity and employment is brought about by decisions of corporate and other business executives, it is not they but government officials who consequently are retired from their offices.

That result, then, is why the market might be characterized as a prison. For a broad category of political/economic affairs, it imprisons policy making, and imprisons our attempts to improve the social world because it afflicts us with sluggish economic performance and unemployment simply because we begin to debate or undertake reform.

In his *Great Transformation,* Karl Polanyi makes the point that early English experience with policy designed to soften the harshness of the market system in eighteenth-century England demonstrated how easily regulation of the market could derange the economy. But he did not go so far as to argue that market systems imprison or cripple the policy-making process and indeed thought that more intelligent policy making could succeed where earlier attempts failed. I am arguing that the crippling of policy making in a market society may be more serious than he thought.

You may be tempted to believe that the real obstacle to social change is—as we often carelessly assert—a kind of social inertia or a tendency of societies to remain as they are. But it is not at all clear that inertia of that kind exists in the social world. Many people constantly try to change the social world. An explanation of their failure more plausible than that of inertia is to be found in the great number of other people who are vigorously trying to frustrate social change. My analysis points to a social mechanism that frustrates it. It is a highly selective mechanism, you should note, that permits change of some kinds and imposes powerful obstacles to other kinds.

Clearly, if we look at different areas of social life, ease of change varies greatly from area to area. In recent years we have seen large changes in sexual mores, for example, as well, of course, as multiple changes pressed on us by technological development. In political/economic life, society all over the world has gone through or is now going through one of the world's greatest social revolutions—the organization of almost every form of social cooperation through formal organization, especially bureaucratic organization. The bureaucratic revolution is enough to testify to the capacity of society for political and economic change. It is all the more impressive that there exists a mechanism of automatic punishing recoil that successfully retards or represses change in other aspects of political and economic life.

In just what aspects of political/economic life that mechanism operates I have not yet said, except to note that the included aspects are all those in which businessmen—or any large or critical number of them—see change as hurtful to their own prospects. You can fill in what those aspects are. They include institutions and policies that protect the decision-making authority of businessmen in their own businesses, and the customary prerogatives of management, including rights to self recruitment into corporate elites. They include policies that maintain the existing distribution of income and wealth, along with institutions and policies that hold the labor movement in check. The efficacy of the recoil mechanism is evidenced by the continuing historical failure of equalitarian aspirations to achieve a significant change in the distribution of wealth and income among social strata, and by the continuing autonomy of corporate management in a world in which increasing numbers of thoughtful people are arguing, on environmental and other grounds, that no group of leaders can be allowed to exercise so autonomous a control over our lives. A new study of corporate power by Herman opens our eyes to the extent in which business autonomy has been sustained despite decades of apparent growth in the regulation of it.

It is also the case that insofar as policy has successfully pushed into areas of which business people disapprove, it has often had to be offset by new benefits or supports to business. When that happens, policy is imprisoned not in the sense that it cannot break out of its confinement but in the sense that to release it we must pay ransom. Where there are prisons, however, there are also jailbreaks. Again, therefore, I do not argue that the market is escape-proof.

The imprisoning of institutions and policy making in market-oriented society is, I think, ordinarily brushed aside as an embarrassing feature of ostensibly democratic systems. We are not comfortable in acknowledging that popular control is crippled in these systems by an automatic punishing recoil. In the U.S. today, however, in the Reagan administration we now hear remarkably candid acknowledgments that we must learn to be happy in our prison. The new administration tells us boldly and badly that we cannot have growth, cannot have price stability, and cannot have full employment unless we stop undermining business incentives. Hence, they have told us that we cannot have an effective Federal Trade Commission, its recent energy having harmed business. Nor can we persist in recent programs of automobile safety, which must now be relaxed. Nor can we protect the landscape against strip mines. One after another of our recent reforms are being curtailed so far as the administration can achieve the result, on the grounds that our economic system—the market system—does not allow such reforms if we are to enjoy prosperity. We cannot even hold to a policy of human rights abroad. As David Rockefeller early announced and members of the Reagan administration have repeated since, our policy of protecting human rights abroad has to be subordinated to our needs for foreign markets, with which it has been an interference.

The Reagan administration is trying to make the automatic recoil mechanism even more obstructive to social change than it need be. But I credit the administration with understanding that such a mechanism exists in any market system. They are right in appreciating that policy making is imprisoned, even without their efforts to build the walls higher.

Finally, take note that my argument is that policy is imprisoned in market-oriented systems, which is a broader generalization than if I had said that it is imprisoned in private enterprise systems. The feature of market systems that is at the core of the recoil mechanism is the inducement system that we use to motivate one great category of organizers and coordinators to do their work. If we were to operate a market system composed exclusively of government owned and operated market enterprises, the recoil mechanism would still operate. The inducements necessary to get the required performance out of public managers might be fewer or less; hence the problem of automatic punishing recoil might be reduced. But it would not be eliminated unless we abandoned the inducement system in favor of a command system, thus removing the socialized enterprise from a market system of inducements.

One of the causes, I believe, of Soviet abandonment of their attempts in the 1960s to introduce more market elements into the Soviet economy is that their earliest moves were abruptly perceived as requiring top political leadership to sit on its hands, that is, not to interfere with market stimulated managerial decisions. At least dimly, they perceived that the growth of the market implied constrictions on their own ability to make policy. They, top Soviet authorities, would be imprisoned by their commitment to the market.

Some of you will hear my remarks today as constituting an argument for getting rid of the market system so that policy can escape from its prison. But that would be putting words in my mouth. I do believe that the fact that the market system imprisons policy through an automatic punishing recoil is a serious disadvantage of market systems. I would not want to deprecate, minimize, or obscure that inference. We pay a big price for the use of a market system. But whether the market ought to be maintained or abandoned calls for a weighing of its advantages and disadvantages. And that task I am not undertaking today.

In any case, the relation between democracy and market is more complex than we hear it to be from classical liberals like Hayek and Friedman. No democratic nation state has ever arisen anywhere in the world except in conjunction with a market system—surely a historical fact of enormous importance. But, according to my argument today, no market society can achieve a fully developed democracy because the market imprisons the policy-making process. We may be caught in a vise. For minimal democracy, we require a market system. For fuller democracy, we require its elimination. But its elimination might pose more obstacles to a fuller democracy than does its

continuing imprisoning of policy making. It may therefore be that a fuller democracy is never to be ours. Or, if it can be achieved, it will come only when we discover how to provide, without a market system, those minimal supports for democracy which, so far in history, only market systems have provided. Our dilemma or difficulties are extraordinary—and are not clarified for us by the current state either of market theory or democratic theory.

For Americans and many Western Europeans the market is a prison in another sense as well. Both as an institution and as an intellectual concept, it seems to have imprisoned our thinking about politics and economics.

For me, an early and memorable demonstration of imprisoned thought was many of the reviews of *Unions and Capitalism,* a book based on my doctoral dissertation and published in 1949. In it I had argued that certain incompatibilities between two major institutions of our society—collective bargaining, on one hand, and the market system, on the other—would in the future produce serious problems, including simultaneous unemployment and inflation. Not knowing what to do about the problem, I simply offered a diagnosis without a remedial prescription, naively assuming that the diagnosis implied that something had to give either on the side of collective bargaining or on the side of the market system. Almost all reviewers, however, simply took it for granted that my purpose was to make a case against collective bargaining or a case for its restriction. At least conventional academic reviewers seemed unable to contemplate the possibility that a conflict between two institutions raised questions about both of them and, *a priori,* no more about the one than the other.

Having been sensitized by that early experience, I have noted ever since that the standard formulation of one of our economic problems is that union pressure on wages causes inflation or restriction of job opportunities in the immediately affected industrial firm. *Given* a market system, that is probably true. But let me suggest the other possible formulation: given the inevitable and understandable desire of workers to increase their share of national income, a market system will produce inflation or unemployment. The second proposition is no less true than the first. The limited capacity of our thinking is revealed in our commitment in habit of mind to the first proposition to the neglect of the second. We have come to think not of human need and aspiration but of the market system as the fixed element in the light of which we think about policy. We find it difficult to think of the market as the variable.

Much of our thinking in other policy areas is similarly imprisoned, as, for example, our thinking on environmental protection. That policy made in Congress and in the White House sacrifices environmental protection to the needs of market enterprises is one thing. That those academics and other scholars, analysts, and critics who are trying to think constructively about the options open to us often themselves cannot see the market as a variable but treat it as the fixed element around which policy must be fashioned is another thing. The latter is what I mean by imprisoned thought.

A more striking example is the state of thinking about television. One of the great shapers of contemporary culture and politics is commercial broadcasting, especially television. You have all heard what once would have been thought of as astonishing figures on the number of hours adults and children spend watching and hearing what commercial advertisers and their clients decide we will see and hear. That in the United States we have permitted or chosen a broadcasting system that confers such authority on people whose motives are to sell something to us; that we accept frequent urgent interruptions in almost all programs so that we can be exhorted to buy; that we must also hear a steady diet of praise for the corporate institutions that exhort us to buy; that we grant without charge broadcasting rights to those fortunate enough to gain the enormously profitable broadcast licenses; and that we do not even ask in exchange for significant use of broadcast time for educational purposes—all these features of American broadcasting are as

plausible evidences of insanity as they are of intelligence in public policy.

For a wealthy society that can afford any of a variety of superior systems—and for a society that in any case pays all the costs of the present system—one might think that political scientists and other analysts would attend to the merits and demerits of commercial broadcasting, that so critical a shaper of politics and culture would be on the agenda for spirited debate. It is not. Our thought is imprisoned. We cannot venture intellectually—a few exceptions aside—beyond what seems normal and natural. We uncritically accept what the market provides. For American social science it is a scandal that it remains silent on so great an issue. And—to make the point precisely—it is not that commercial television is unacceptable. That is not the point. The point is that whether it is or not is a great issue on which we are incapable of thought, so imprisoned are our minds.

You will note that I am saying—and here I make it explicit—that the prison is strong enough to incarcerate not only popular thought but professional thinking in the social sciences. Further evidence lies in the controversy over pluralism in the last fifteen or so years. Dominant pluralist thought in American political science describes all policy making as a result of vectors, each vector often consisting of the influence of some group. All groups who wish to be admitted are, according to pluralist thought, admitted to the process. The attack on pluralist thought that eventually emerged argued—successfully, I think—that in some policy areas or for certain kinds of policy issues the pluralist competition of groups did not work and that class influences, traditional biases in the political culture, or processes called "mobilization of bias" made certain policy positions dominant and others impossible to advance. But on the whole these critics missed the phenomenon I am describing—the extent to which policy making has to be and is constrained by the peculiar characteristics of an inducement system in a market system. Pluralism at most operates only in an unimprisoned zone of policy making. Hence the continuing debate on pluralism, although it has greatly improved our understanding of politics, is still significantly constrained or imprisoned.

Even today, interest-group theory for the most part treats business interests as symmetrical with labor and other interests bearing on policy making. It has not yet generally recognized that business interests occupy a special place in imprisoned policy making.

More indirectly the market has taken hold of our thinking in social science in ways that cripple us, though a more complete account of what has happened to us would have to acknowledge the influence of professional economics as itself a major influence. For example, in regarding the market system as a piece of social machinery for organizing the nation's resources in response to individual wants expressed through purchases, economists have drifted into an ethics of preference. Insofar as possible, all ethical issues are settled by reference to individual preferences taken as given. Is X good or is X bad? All depends on the patterns of individual preferences.

Impressed both by the market as an institution and by the tidiness of economists' interpretation of it, many political scientists have adopted the ethic of preferences taken as given. Is this policy a good one? It depends on the patterns of individual political preferences, whatever they are. Is democracy a good thing? Yes, because it is a system for letting individual preferences, whatever they are, govern policy making. Democracy is a political market. Or as Schumpeter, who is a major source of this current of thought, put it: democracy is competitive politics.

What is wrong in this version of democracy as a market-like process in which individual preferences ideally prevail, as in an ideal market, is that the powerful and all-pervasive effect of politics on the formation of preferences is ignored. From at least Mill on to just before Schumpeter, so massive and persistent a process of preference

formation as is constituted by the political system itself was never ignored. In allowing the market to dominate our political thought since then, we have simplified our political theories, with some gains in clarity. But we have impoverished our thought by imprisoning it in an unsatisfactory model of preferences taken as given.

My main point, however, has been that market systems imprison policy. Those of us who live in those market-oriented systems that are called liberal democratic exercise significantly less control over policy than we have thought. And we are also less free than we may have thought. Such are the inevitable consequences of imprisonment. That our thinking is itself imprisoned is a separate phenomenon of importance. Given, however, the complexity of human thought and the impossibility of disentangling its sources, the second phenomenon cannot be so confidently argued as the first.

Again, I would like to leave a caution about inferences. What I have described constitutes serious disadvantages in making use of a market system. But the case for and against markets is extraordinarily complex, and my analysis is a long way from a case either for or against. It is also a long way from an answer to any question about what is to be done if the problems posed by my analysis are accepted as significant ones.

DISCUSSION QUESTIONS

1. How does the market system's imprisonment of the policy-making process contribute to the privileged position of business?

2. What does Lindblom mean when he says, "The prison is strong enough to incarcerate not only popular thought but professional thinking in the social sciences"?

3. From Lindblom's vantage point, why is the pluralist model of politics deficient?

DAN CLAWSON, ALAN NEUSTADTL, AND MARK WELLER

WHY DOES THE AIR STINK? CORPORATE POWER AND PUBLIC POLICY

How is economic power translated into political influence? Sociologists Dan Clawson, Alan Neustadtl, and Mark Weller examine the impact of corporate political action committees (PACS) on public policy. Uniquely drawing on interviews with PAC directors, they demonstrate how campaign contributions win "access" to members of Congress, resulting in loopholes and regulatory rules favorable to business. Clawson, Neustadtl, and Weller base their analysis of corporate PACS on a "field theory of power." Focus on this concept and consider its usefulness in understanding business "hegemony" in our political system. In a concluding section, the authors itemize the enormous public impact of private corporate power by providing a detailed list of decisions made by business companies in the United States. One implication of this analysis is that even if PACS were banned, business decisions would have a greater impact on our lives than most government decisions have, barring significant change in our economic system.

Everybody wants clean air. Who could oppose it? "I spent seven years of my life trying to stop the Clean Air Act," explained the vice president of a major corporation that is a heavy-duty polluter. Nonetheless, he was perfectly willing to make campaign contributions to members who voted for the act:

> How a person votes on the final piece of legislation often is not representative of what they have done. Somebody will do a lot of things during the process. How many guys voted against the Clean Air Act? But during the process some of them were very sympathetic to some of our concerns.

In the world of Congress and political action committees things are not always what they seem. Members of Congress all want to vote for clean air, but they also want to get campaign contributions from corporations, and they want to pass a law that business will accept as "reasonable." The compromise solution is to gut the bill by crafting dozens of loopholes. These are inserted in private meetings or in subcommittee hearings that don't get much (if any) attention in the press. Then the public vote on the final bill can be nearly unanimous. Members of Congress can reassure their constituents and their corporate contributors: constituents, that they voted

Source: Dan Clawson, Alan Neustadtl, and Mark Weller, *Dollars and Votes: How Business Campaign Contributions Subvert Democracy,* Philadelphia: Temple University Press, 1998, pp. 6–12, 21–26, and 188–191.

for the final bill; corporations, that they helped weaken it in private. Clean air, and especially the Clean Air Act of 1990, can serve as an introduction to the kind of process we try to expose.

The public strongly supports clean air, and is unimpressed when corporate officials and apologists trot out their normal arguments—"corporations are already doing all they reasonably can to improve environmental quality," "we need to balance the costs against the benefits," "people will lose their jobs if we make controls any stricter." The original Clean Air Act was passed in 1970, revised in 1977, and not revised again until 1990. Although the initial goal was to have us breathing clean air by 1975, the deadline has been repeatedly extended—and the 1990 legislation provides a new set of deadlines to be reached sometime in the distant future.

Corporations control the production process unless the government specifically intervenes. Therefore, any delay in government action leaves corporations free to do as they choose; business often prefers a weak, ineffective, and unenforceable law. The laws have not only been slow to come, but corporations have also fought to delay or subvert implementation. The 1970 law ordered the Environmental Protection Agency (EPA) to regulate the hundreds of poisonous chemicals that are emitted by corporations, but, as William Greider notes, "In twenty years of stalling, dodging, and fighting off court orders, the EPA has managed to issue regulatory standards for a total of seven toxics."

Corporations have done exceptionally well politically, given the problem they face: The interests of business are diametrically opposed to those of the public. Clean air laws and amendments have been few and far between, enforcement is ineffective, and the penalties minimal. On the one hand, corporations *have* had to pay *billions for clean-ups;* on the other hand, the costs to date are a small fraction of what would be needed to actually clean up the environment.

This corporate struggle for the right to pollute takes place on many fronts. The most visible is public relations: the Chemical Manufacturers

Association took out a two-page Earth Day ad in the *Washington Post* to demonstrate its concern; coincidentally, the names of many of the corporate signers of this ad appear on the EPA's list of high-risk producers. Another front is expert studies that delay action while more information is gathered. The federally funded National Acid Precipitation Assessment Program took ten years and $600 million to figure out whether acid rain was in fact a problem. Both business and the Reagan administration argued that nothing should be done until the study was completed. Ultimately, the study was discredited: The "summary of findings" minimized the impact of acid rain, even though this did not accurately represent the expert research in the report. But the key site of struggle was Congress. For years, corporations successfully defeated legislation. In 1987 utility companies were offered a compromise bill on acid rain, but they "were very adamant that they had beat the thing since 1981 and they could always beat it," according to Representative Edward Madigan (Republican-Illinois). The utilities beat back all efforts at reform through the 1980s, but their intransigence probably hurt them when revisions finally came to be made.

The stage was set for a revision of the Clean Air Act when George Bush, "the environmental president," was elected, and George Mitchell, a strong supporter of environmentalism, became the Senate majority leader. But what sort of clean air bill would it be? "What we wanted," said Richard Ayres, head of the environmentalists' Clean Air Coalition, "is a health based standard— one-in-1-million cancer risk," a standard that would require corporations to clean up their plants until the cancer risk from their operations was reduced to 1 in a million. "The Senate bill still has the requirement," Ayres said, "but there are forty pages of extensions and exceptions and qualifications and loopholes that largely render the health standard a nullity." Greider reports, for example, "According to the EPA, there are now twenty-six coke ovens that pose a cancer risk greater than 1 in 1000 and six where the risk is greater than 1 in 100. Yet the new clean-air bill will give the steel industry another thirty years to deal with the problem."

This change from what the bill was supposed to do to what it did do came about through what corporate executives like to call the "access" process. The principal aim of most corporate campaign contributions is to help corporate executives gain "access" to key members of Congress and their staffs. In these meetings, corporate executives (and corporate PAC money) work to persuade the member of Congress to accept a predesigned loophole that will sound innocent but effectively undercut the stated intention of the bill. Representative John D. Dingell (Democrat-Michigan), who was chair of the House Committee, is a strong industry supporter; one of the people we interviewed called him "the point man for the Business Roundtable on clean air." Representative Henry A. Waxman (Democrat-California), chair of the subcommittee, is an environmentalist. Observers had expected a confrontation and contested votes on the floor of the Congress.

The problem for corporations was that, as one Republican staff aide said, "If any bill has the blessing of Waxman and the environmental groups, unless it is totally in outer space, who's going to vote against it?" But corporations successfully minimized public votes. Somehow, Waxman was persuaded to make behind-the-scenes compromises with Dingell so members, during an election year, didn't have to side publicly with business against the environment. Often the access process leads to loopholes that protect a single corporation, but for "clean" air most of the special deals targeted not specific companies but entire industries. The initial bill, for example, required cars to be able to use carefully specified, cleaner fuels. But the auto industry wanted the rules loosened, and Congress eventually incorporated a variant of a formula suggested by the head of General Motors' fuels and lubricants department.

Nor did corporations stop fighting even after they gutted the bill through amendments. Business pressed the EPA for favorable regulations to implement the law: "The cost of this legislation could vary dramatically, depending on how EPA interprets it," said William D. Fay, vice president of the National Coal Association, who headed the hilariously misnamed Clean Air Working Group, an industry coalition that fought to weaken the legislation. As one EPA aide working on acid rain regulations reported, "We're having a hard time getting our work done because of the number of phone calls we're getting" from corporations and their lawyers.

Corporations trying to get federal regulators to adopt the "right" regulations don't rely exclusively on the cogency of their arguments. They often exert pressure on a member of Congress to intervene for them at the EPA or other agency. Senators and representatives regularly intervene on behalf of constituents and contributors by doing everything from straightening out a social security problem to asking a regulatory agency to explain why it is pressuring a company. This process—like campaign finance—usually follows rules of etiquette. In addressing a regulatory agency, the senator does not say, "Lay off my campaign contributors or I'll cut your budget." One standard phrasing for letters asks regulators to resolve the problem "as quickly as possible within applicable rules and regulations." No matter how mild and careful the inquiry, the agency receiving the request is certain to give it extra attention; only after careful consideration will they refuse to make any accommodation.

Soft money—unregulated megabuck contributions—also shaped what happened to air quality. Archer Daniels Midland argued that increased use of ethanol would reduce pollution from gasoline; coincidentally, ADM controls a majority of the ethanol market. To reinforce its arguments, in the 1992 election ADM gave $90,000 to Democrats and $600,000 to Republicans, the latter supplemented with an additional $200,000 as an individual contribution from the company head, Dwayne Andreas. Many environmentalists were skeptical about ethanol's value in a clean air strategy, but President Bush issued regulations promoting wider use of ethanol; we presume he was impressed by the force of ADM's 800,000 Republican arguments. Bob Dole, the 1996 Republican presidential candidate, helped pass and defend special breaks for the ethanol industry; he not only appreciated ADM's Republican contributions, but presumably approved of the more than $1 million they gave to the American Red Cross during the period when it was headed by his wife, Elizabeth Dole. What about the post-1994 Republican-controlled Congress, defenders of the free market and opponents of government giveaways? Were they ready to end this subsidy program, cracking down on corporate welfare as they did on people welfare? Not a chance. In 1997, the Republican chair of the House Ways and Means Committee actually attempted to eliminate the special tax breaks for ethanol. Needless to say, he was immediately put in his place by other members of the Republican leadership, including Speaker Newt Gingrich and most of the Senate, with the subsidy locked in place for years to come, in spite of a General Accounting Office report that "found that the ethanol subsidy justifies none of its political boasts." The Center for Responsive Politics calculated that ADM, its executives and PAC, made more than $1 million in campaign contributions of various types; the only thing that had changed was that in 1996, with a Democratic president, this money was "divided more or less evenly between Republicans and Democrats."

The disparity in power between business and environmentalists looms large during the legislative process, but it is enormous afterward. When the Clean Air Act passed, corporations and industry groups offered positions, typically with large pay increases, to congressional staff members who wrote the law. The former congressional staff members who now work for corporations both know how to evade the law and can persuasively claim to EPA that they know what Congress intended. Environmental organizations pay substantially less than Congress and can't afford large staffs. They are seldom able to become involved in the details of the administrative process or to influence implementation and enforcement.

Having pushed Congress and the Environmental Protection Agency to allow as much pollution as possible, business then went to the Quayle council for rules allowing even more pollution. Vice President J. Danforth Quayle's council, technically known as the "Council on Competitiveness," was created by President Bush specifically to help reduce regulations on business. Quayle told the *Boston Globe* "that his council has an 'open door' to business groups and that he has a bias against regulations." During the Bush administration, this council reviewed, and could override, all regulations, including those by the EPA setting the limits at which a chemical was subject to regulation. The council also recommended that corporations be allowed to increase their polluting emissions if a state did not object within seven days of the proposed increase. Corporations thus have multiple opportunities to win. If they lose in Congress, they can win at the regulatory agency; if they lose there, they can try again at the Quayle Council (or later equivalent). If they lose there, they can try to reduce the money available to enforce regulations, or tie the issue up in the courts, or plan on accepting a minimal fine.

The operation of the Quayle council probably would have received little publicity, but reporters discovered that the executive director of the Council, Allan Hubbard, had a clear conflict of interest. Hubbard chaired the biweekly White House meetings on the Clean Air Act. He owned half of World Wide Chemical, received an average of more than $1 million a year in profits from it while directing the Quayle council, and continued to attend quarterly stockholder meetings. According to the *Boston Globe,* "Records on file with the Indianapolis Air Pollution Control Board show that World Wide Chemical emitted 17,000 to 19,000 pounds of chemicals into the air" in 1991. At that time the company did "not have the permit required to release the emissions," was "putting out nearly four times the allowable emissions without a permit, and could be subject to a $2,500-a-day penalty," according to David Jordan, director of the Indianapolis Air Pollution Board.

This does not, however, mean that business always gets exactly what it wants. In 1997, the Environmental Protection Agency proposed tough new rules for soot and smog. Business fought hard to weaken or eliminate the rules: hiring experts (from pro-business think tanks) to attack the scientific studies supporting the regulations and putting a raft of lobbyists ("many of them former congressional staffers," the *Washington Post* reported) to work securing the signatures of 250 members of Congress questioning the standards. But the late 1990s version of these industry mobilizations adds a new twist—creating a pseudo-grassroots campaign. For example, business, operating under a suitably disguised name (Foundation for Clean Air Progress), paid for television ads telling farmers that the EPA rules would prohibit them from plowing on dry windy days, with other ads predicting the EPA rules "would lead to forced carpooling or bans on outdoor barbecues—claims the EPA dismisses as ridiculous." Along with the ads, industry worked to mobilize local politicians and business executives in what business groups called a "grass tops" campaign.

Despite a massive industry campaign, EPA head Carol Browner remained firm, and President Clinton was persuaded to go along. Of course, industry immediately began working on ways to undercut the regulations with congressional loopholes and exceptions—but business has suffered a defeat, and proponents of clean air (that is, most of the rest of us) had won at least a temporary and partial victory. And who leads the struggles to overturn or uphold these regulations? Just as before, Dingell and Waxman; Republicans "are skittish about challenging" the rules publicly, "so they gladly defer to Dingell as their surrogate." Dingell's forces have more than 130 cosponsors (about one-third of them Democrats) for a bill to, in effect, override the EPA standards.

In business-government relations most attention becomes focused on instances of scandal. The real issue, however, is not one or another scandal or conflict of interest, but rather the *system* of business-government relations, and

especially of campaign finance, that offers business so many opportunities to craft loopholes, undermine regulations, and subvert enforcement. Still worse, many of these actions take place beyond public scrutiny.

•　　•　　•

WHAT IS POWER?

Our analysis is based on an understanding of power that differs from that usually articulated by both business and politicians. The corporate PAC directors we interviewed insisted that they have no power.

> If you were to ask me what kind of access and influence do we have, being roughly the 150th largest PAC, I would have to tell you that on the basis of our money we have zero. . . . If you look at the level of our contributions, we know we're not going to buy anybody's vote, we're not going to rent anybody, or whatever the clichés have been over the years. We know that.

The executives who expressed these views clearly meant these words sincerely. Their statements are based on roughly the same understanding of "power" that is current with political science, which is also the way the term was defined by Max Weber, the classical sociological theorist. Power, in this common conception, is the ability to make someone do something against their will. If that is what power means, then corporations rarely have any in relation to members of Congress, nor does soft money give the donor power over presidents. As one senior vice president said to us: "You certainly aren't going to be able to buy anybody for $500 or $1,000 or $10,000—it's a joke." Soft money donations of a million dollars might seem to change the equation, but we will argue they do not: Just as $10,000 won't buy a member of Congress, $1,000,000 won't buy a president. In this regard we agree with the corporate officials we interviewed: A corporation is not in a position to say to a member of Congress, "Either you vote for this bill, or we will defeat your bid for reelection." Rarely do they even say: "You vote for this bill or you won't get any money from us."

This definition of power as the ability to make someone do something against their will is what Steven Lukes calls a "one-dimensional" view of power. A two-dimensional view recognizes the existence of nondecisions: A potential issue never gets articulated or, if articulated by someone somewhere, never receives serious consideration. For example, in 1989 and 1990 one of the major political battles, and a focus of great effort by corporate PACs, was the Clean Air Act. Yet twenty or thirty years earlier, before the rise of the environmental movement, pollution was a nonissue: it simply was not considered, although its effects were, in retrospect, of great importance. In one of Sherlock Holmes stories, the key clue is that the dog didn't bark. A two-dimensional view of power makes the same point: The most important clue in some situation may be that no one noticed power was exercised—because there was no overt conflict.

Even this model of power is too restrictive, however, because it still focuses on discrete decisions and nondecisions. Tom Wartenberg calls these "interventional" models of power, and notes that, in such models "the primary locus of power . . . is a specific social interaction between two social agents." Such models do not recognize "the idea that the most fundamental use of power in society is its use in structuring the basic manner in which social agents interact with one another." Wartenberg argues, instead, for a "field theory" of power that analyzes social power as a force similar to a magnetic field. A magnetic field alters the motion of objects susceptible to magnetism. Similarly, the mere presence of a powerful social agent alters the social space for others and causes them to orient themselves toward the powerful agent. For example, one of the executives we interviewed took it for granted that "if we go see the congressman who represents [a city where the company has a major plant], where 10,000 of our employees are also his constituents, we don't need a PAC to go see him." The corporation is so important in that area that the member

has to orient himself in relation to the corporation and its concerns. In a different sense, the very act of accepting a campaign contribution changes the way a member relates to a PAC, creating a sense of obligation, a need to reciprocate. The PAC contribution has altered the member's social space, his or her awareness of the company and wish to help it, even if no explicit commitments have been made.

BUSINESS IS DIFFERENT

Power, we would argue, is not just the ability to force someone to do something against their will; it is most effective (and least recognized) when it shapes the field of action. Moreover, business's vast resources, influence on the economy, and general legitimacy place it on a different footing from other campaign contributors. Every day a member of Congress accepts a $1,000 donation from a corporate PAC, goes to a committee hearing, proposes "minor" changes in a bill's wording, and has those changes accepted without discussion or examination. The changes "clarify" the language of the bill, legalizing higher levels of pollution for a specific pollutant, or exempting the company from some tax. The media do not report on this change, and no one speaks against it. On the other hand, if a PAC were formed by Drug Lords for Cocaine Legalization, no member would take their money. If a member introduced a "minor" wording change to make it easier to sell crack without bothersome police interference, the proposed change would attract massive attention, the campaign contribution would be labeled a scandal, the member's political career would be ruined, and the changed wording would not be incorporated into the bill. Drug Lords may make an extreme example, but approximately the same holds true for many groups: At present, equal rights for gays and lesbians could never be a minor and unnoticed addition to a bill with a different purpose.

Even groups with great social legitimacy encounter more opposition and controversy than business faces for proposals that are virtually without public support. One example is the contrast between the largely unopposed commitment of tens or hundreds of billions of dollars for the savings and loan bailout, compared to the sharp debate, close votes, and defeats for the rights of men and women to take *unpaid* parental leaves. The classic term for something non-controversial that everyone must support is "a motherhood issue," and while it costs little to guarantee every woman the right to an *un*paid parental leave, this measure nonetheless generated intense scrutiny and controversy—going down to defeat under President Bush, passing under President Clinton, and then again becoming a focus of attack after the 1994 Republican takeover of Congress. Few indeed are the people publicly prepared to defend pollution or tax evasion. Nevertheless, business is routinely able to win pollution exemptions and tax loopholes. Although cumulatively some vague awareness of these provisions may trouble people, most are allowed individually to pass without scrutiny. *No* analysis of corporate political activity makes sense unless it begins with a recognition of this absolutely vital point. The PAC is a vital element of corporate power, but it does not operate by itself. The PAC donation is always backed by the wider power and influence of business.

Corporations are unlike other "special interest" groups not only because business has far more resources, but also because its acceptance and legitimacy. When people feel that "the system" is screwing them, they tend to blame politicians, the government, the media—but rarely business. In terms of campaign finance, while much of the public is outraged at the way money influences elections and public policy, the issue is almost always posed in terms of politicians, what they do or don't do. This is part of a pervasive double standard that largely exempts business from criticism. We, however, believe it is vital to scrutinize business as well.

We did two dozen radio call-in shows after the appearance of our last book, *Money Talks*. On almost every show, at least one call came from someone outraged that members of Congress had recently raised their pay to $125,100. (For 1998, it will be about $137,000.) Not a single person even mentioned corporate executives' pay.

Business Week calculated that in 1996 corporate CEOs were paid an average of $5.8 million (counting salary, bonuses, and stock option grants), or more than 200 times the average worker's pay, and more than 40 times what members of Congress are paid. More anger is directed at Congress for delaying new environmental laws than at the companies who fight every step of the way to stall and subvert the legislation. When members of Congress do favors for large campaign contributors, anger is directed at the senators who went along, not at the business owner who paid the money (and usually initiated the pressure). The public focuses on the member's receipt of thousands of dollars, not on the business's receipt of millions (or hundreds of millions) in tax breaks or special treatment. It is a widely held belief that "politics is dirty." But little public comment and condemnation is generated when companies get away—quite literally—with murder. This disparity is evidence of business's success in shaping public perceptions. Lee Atwater, George Bush's 1988 campaign manager, saw this as a key to Republican success:

> In the 1980 campaign, we were able to make the establishment, insofar as it is bad, the government. In other words, big government was the enemy, not big business. If the people think the problem is that taxes are too high, and the government interferes too much, then we are doing our job. But, if they get to the point where they say that the real problem is that rich people aren't paying taxes, . . . then the Democrats are going to be in good shape.

We argue that corporations are so different, and so dominant, that they exercise a special kind of power, what Antonio Gramsci called hegemony. Hegemony can be regarded as the ultimate example of a field of power that structures what people and groups do. It is sometimes referred to as a worldview, a way of thinking about the world that influences every action, and makes it difficult to even consider alternatives. But in Gramsci's analysis it is much more than this, it is a culture and set of institutions that structure life patterns and coerce a particular way of life. Susan Harding gives the example of relations between whites and blacks in the South prior to the 1960s. Black inferiority and subservience were not simply ideas articulated by white racists, they were incorporated into a set of social practices: segregated schools, restrooms, swimming pools, restaurants; the black obligation to refer to white men as "Mister"; the prohibition on referring to black men as "Mister"; the use of the term "boy" for black males of any age and social status; the white right to go to the front of any line or to take the seat of any African American, and so on. Most blacks recognized the injustice and absurdity of these rules, but this did not enable them to escape, much less defy, them. White hegemony could not be overthrown simply by recognizing its existence or articulating an ideal of equality; black people had to create a movement that transformed themselves, the South, and the nation as a whole.

Hegemony is most successful and most powerful, when it is unrecognized. White hegemony in the South was strong but never unrecognized and rarely uncontested. White southerners would have denied, probably in all sincerity, that they exercised power: "Why our nigras are perfectly happy that's the way they want to be treated." But many black southerners would have vigorously disputed this while talking to each other. In some sense, gender relations in the 1950s embodied a hegemony even more powerful than that of race relations. Betty Friedan titled the first chapter of *The Feminine Mystique* "The Problem That Has No Name," because women literally did not have a name for, did not recognize the existence of, their oppression. Women as well as men denied the existence of inequality or oppression, denied the systematic exercise of power to maintain unequal relations.

We argue that today business has enormous power and exercises effective hegemony, even though (perhaps because) this is largely undiscussed and unrecognized. *Politically,* business power today is similar to white treatment of blacks in 1959—business may sincerely deny its power, but many of the groups it exercises power over recognize it, feel dominated, resent this, and fight the power as best they can. At least until

very recently, *economically,* business power was more like gender relations in 1959: Virtually no one saw this power as problematic. The revived labor movement is beginning to change this, and there are signs that a movement is beginning to contest corporate power. Nonetheless, if the issue is brought to people's attention, many still don't see a problem: "Well, so what? How else could it be? Maybe we don't like it, but that's just the way things are."

Hegemony is never absolute. African Americans and women both were (and are) forced to live in disadvantaged conditions, but simultaneously fought for dignity and respect. Unusual individuals always violated conventions and tested limits. A hegemonic power is usually opposed by a counterhegemony. Thus, while children in our society are taught to compete with each other to earn the praise of authority figures, and while most children engage in this process much of the time, it is also true that the "teacher's pet" is likely to face ostracism. We hope this book makes a small contribution to weakening business hegemony and to developing a counterhegemony.

• • •

The primary power of the wealthy is not exercised by individuals or even by families. Power in our society is based in institutions, not individuals, and the power of wealth is channeled through corporations. There are more than 200,000 industrial corporations in the United States, but all companies are *not* created equal: The 500 largest industrials control three-quarters of the sales, assets, and profits of *all* industrial corporations. More than 250 of these companies had revenues of more than $5 billion. Similarly, in the service sector, 500 firms control a disproportionate share of the resources. The dominance of these corporations means that a handful of owners and top executives, perhaps one-hundredth of one percent of the U.S. population, or 25,000 individuals, have the power to make decisions that have a huge impact on all of our lives. Collectively these people exercise incalculable power, making decisions with more impact on most of our lives than those made by the entire elected government.

Consider for a moment those decisions that virtually everyone in our society agrees should be made by business. Consider, for this exercise, only those decisions on which there is broad bipartisan political agreement; exclude anything that would generally be considered ethically or legally dubious and anything where a significant fraction of elected officials dispute business's right. Exclude, as well, any actions that are taken only through business's influence on government, and confine your attention to the decisions made in operating businesses. Remember that any decision made by "business" is primarily determined by the 25,000 individuals at the top of the corporate ladder, since their companies control about three-quarters of *all* corporate sales, assets, employees, and profits.

BUSINESS DECISIONS

What are some of these decisions? A brief and partial list indicates their scope:

Decisions about Employment

- the number of people employed.
- when to have layoffs.
- the number of hours people work.
- when work begins in the morning and ends in the afternoon.
- whether to phase out full-time jobs and replace them with part-time, lower-wage, no-benefits jobs. In 1997, UPS workers and the Teamsters Union successfully contested the company's increasingly heavy reliance on part-timers, but it was big news that a union even attempted to raise the issue, much less that they were able to win.
- whether or not there is overtime, and whether it is compulsory.
- whether to allow flextime and job-sharing.
- the skill level of the jobs. Does the company make an effort to use lots of skilled workers paid good wages or is it always trying to de-skill positions and replace skilled workers with unskilled?
- the educational (and other) requirements for employment. Are certain educational levels *necessary* in order to be hired, or are they simply helpful? Are exconvicts or former mental patients eligible for all jobs or only some? What about the handicapped?
- whether the firm de facto discriminates in favor of men and whites or makes an active effort to recruit and promote minorities and women.
- workers' rights on the job. For example, do they have free speech? A worker at a Coca-Cola plant was given a three-day suspension (without pay) because his wife brought him a lunch with a soda from Burger King, at a time when Burger King sold Pepsi. It is totally legal to penalize an employee for this or many other such actions.
- job safety. In one of the most extreme examples, a worker was killed while performing a dangerous task. Almost immediately thereafter another worker was ordered to do the same job and refused because he said conditions were unsafe and had not been remedied. The company fired him for this refusal, and the Supreme Court upheld the firing.
- (within limits) whether or not a union is recognized; whether the union and the workers are treated with dignity and respect; how bitterly and viciously the union is resisted.

Investment Decisions

- decisions about whether to expand a plant, and if so, which plant to expand.
- whether to merge the corporation and "downsize" workers. Recently, a number of corporations have laid off thousands of employees, blighting communities and individual lives, at the same time giving huge bonuses to the top executives.
- whether to contract out jobs.
- whether to close down a plant; when and how to do so. Virtually no one questions a com-

pany's absolute right (in the United States, not in Europe) to shut down if it chooses to do so, no matter what the effect on the workers and communities.

- where to open new plants. The company has every right to bargain for the best deal it can get. Deals can include tax abatements and implicit agreements to ignore labor or pollution laws.

Product and Marketing

- the products produced, including whether to introduce a new product and whether to discontinue an old stand-by.
- the design, both functional and aesthetic.
- the relative attention to different considerations: in a new car, how important is styling? sex appeal? fuel efficiency? safety? durability?
- the quality of the goods produced. Are they made to last, with high standards throughout, or are they just made to look good in the store and for the first month of use?
- the price for which goods are sold.
- the character of the advertising used to promote the product. Does it stress the significant features of the product, or distract through sex and extraneous symbols?
- the amount spent on advertising—90 percent of the commercials on prime time television are sponsored by the nation's 500 largest corporations.
- the places where ads appear—in left-wing journals? in right-wing journals? on television? on which programs?

Community and Environment

- the level of pollution in the workplace: air, heat, noise, chemicals, and so on.
- the level of pollution in the outside environment. Beginning in the 1970s, for pollution both in the workplace and in the larger community, the government set maximum limits for a few items, but companies are completely free to do better than these standards.

No government regulation prevents companies from setting and meeting tougher standards of their own devising. For example, in July 1991, a railroad tanker car derailed, tumbled into the Sacramento River, ruptured, and spilled pesticide. The pesticide was not listed as a regulated substance, and therefore the railroad was not required to carry it in a double-hulled tanker, though it could have chosen to do so. Though the pesticide was unregulated, it *was* strong enough to kill virtually all the fish in the river, formerly famous for its trout.

- the degree of consideration for the community: Does the company make an effort to be a good neighbor? Does it contribute to local charities? Support local initiatives?

This by no means exhausts the list of decisions that companies are allowed to make. Not only allowed to make, but expected and, in many cases, required to make. There is some regulation of business decisions at the margin, with possible regulation for issues such as: Can a company pull up stakes and leave town with no more than a day's notice? Can it dump raw wastes in the river? Can it make dubious claims in its advertising? For the most part, however, corporations are free to make decisions about their economic operations.

If the government fails to act, big business can do as it wishes.

DISCUSSION QUESTIONS

1. Consider the discussion of hidden versus blatant power and relate this to the manner in which business exercised its privileged position through the Clean Air Act negotiations.
2. What comparisons may be drawn, if any, between white hegemony (prior to the 1960s) and corporate hegemony today?
3. If corporations that are so central to the structure of our economy do constitute a "field of power," can their hegemony be reconciled with our "democracy"?

4 JOHN BELLAMY FOSTER

GLOBAL ECOLOGY AND THE COMMON GOOD

Sociologist John Bellamy Foster questions the efficacy of much of contemporary environmentalism. He argues that proponents of a "new ecological morality" too often blame individual behavior for our environmental problems while downplaying or neglecting outright the root cause of global degradation: the "global treadmill of production." By focusing on individual consumer choices, or looking to socially responsible business people for leadership, conventional environmentalists offer a relatively comforting way out of our ecological crisis. Foster sees this as a dangerous false comfort. For the treadmill of production—which he likens to a giant squirrel cage—is driven by the six-point logic of our corporate capitalist economic structure, a structure which renowned sociologist C. Wright Mills considered to be the "structural immorality" embedded in our way of life. In short, we need to confront the paradox that our way of life undermines our way of life. Foster asks us to resist the treadmill of production through social movements aimed at creating a "true moral revolution," a revolution that transforms our thinking about the relationship between capitalist economic practices and the environment. Ponder the possibility that anything less than a new ethic of the common good, which inextricably connects environmental values to social justice, may well not be sufficient to save the earth from ecological calamity.

Over the course of the twentieth century, human population has increased more than threefold and gross world product perhaps twentyfold. Such expansion has placed increasing pressure on the ecology of the planet. Everywhere we look—in the atmosphere, oceans, watersheds, forests, soil, etc.—it is now clear that rapid ecological decline is setting in.

Faced with the frightening reality of global ecological crisis, many are now calling for a moral revolution that would incorporate ecological values into our culture. This demand for a new ecological morality is, I believe, the essence of Green thinking. The kind of moral transformation envisaged is best captured by Aldo Leopold's land ethic, which says we abuse land because we regard it as

Source: John Bellamy Foster, "Global Ecology and the Common Good," *Monthly Review*, vol. 46, February 1995, pp. 1–10. Copyright © 1995 by *Monthly Review*. Reprinted by the author and *Monthly Review*.

a commodity belonging to us. When we begin to see land as a community to which we belong, we may begin to use it with love and respect.

Yet behind most appeals to ecological morality there lies the presumption that we live in a society where the morality of the individual is the key to the morality of society. If people as individuals could simply change their moral stance with respect to nature and alter their behavior in areas such as propagation, consumption, and the conduct of business, all would be well.

What is too often overlooked in such calls for moral transformation is the central institutional fact of our society: what might be called the global "treadmill of production." The logic of this treadmill can be broken down into six elements. First, built into this global system, and constituting its central rationale, is the increasing accumulation of wealth by a relatively small section of the population at the top of the social pyramid. Second, there is a long-term movement of workers away from self-employment and into wage jobs that are contingent on the continual expansion of production. Third, the competitive struggle between businesses necessitates on pain of extinction the allocation of accumulated wealth to new, revolutionary technologies that serve to expand production. Fourth, wants are manufactured in a manner that creates an insatiable hunger for more. Fifth, government becomes increasingly responsible for promoting national economic development, while ensuring some degree of "social security" for at least a portion of its citizens. Sixth, the dominant means of communication and education are part of the treadmill, serving to reinforce its priorities and values.

A defining trait of the system is that it is a kind of giant squirrel cage. Everyone, or nearly everyone, is part of this treadmill and is unable or unwilling to get off. Investors and managers are driven by the need to accumulate wealth and to expand the scale of their operations in order to prosper within a globally competitive milieu. For the vast majority, the commitment to the treadmill is more limited and indirect: they simply need to obtain jobs at liveable wages. But to retain those jobs and to maintain a given standard of living in these circumstances it is necessary, like the Red Queen in *Through the Looking Glass,* to run faster and faster in order to stay in the same place.

In such an environment, as the nineteenth-century German philosopher Arthur Schopenhauer once said, "A man can do what he wants. But he can't want what he wants." Our wants are conditioned by the kind of society in which we live. Looked at in this way, it is not individuals acting in accordance with their own innate desires, but rather the treadmill of production on which we are all placed that has become the main enemy of the environment.

Clearly, this treadmill leads in a direction that is incompatible with the basic ecological cycles of the planet. A continuous 3 percent average annual rate of growth in industrial production, such as obtained from 1970 to 1990, would mean that world industry would double in size every twenty-five years, grow sixteenfold approximately every century, increase by 250 times every two centuries, 4,000 times every three centuries, etc. Further, the tendency of the present treadmill of production is to expand the output of raw materials and energy because the greater this flow—from extraction through the delivery of final products to consumers—the more opportunity there is to realize profits. In order to generate profits, the treadmill relies heavily on energy-intensive, capital-intensive technology, which allows it to economize on labor inputs. Yet increased output and more substitution of energy and machines for labor mean a more rapid depletion of high-quality energy sources and other natural resources, and a larger amount of wastes dumped into the environment. It is unlikely therefore that the world could sustain many more doublings of industrial output under the present system without experiencing a complete ecological catastrophe. Indeed, we are already overshooting certain critical ecological thresholds.

Matters are made worse by the tendency in recent decades to move from "gross insults" to the environment to "microtoxicity." As synthetic products (like plastic) are substituted for natural ones (like wood and wool), the older pollutants associated with nineteenth-century industrialization are being replaced by more hazardous pollutants such as those resulting from chlorine-related (organochlorine) production—the source of DDT, dioxin, Agent Orange, PCBs, and CFCs. The degree of toxicity associated with a given level of output has thus risen fairly steadily over the last half century.

It would seem, then, that from an environmental perspective we have no choice but to resist the treadmill of production. This resistance must take the form of a far-reaching moral revolution. In order to carry out such a moral transformation we must confront what the great American sociologist C. Wright Mills called "the higher immorality." The "higher immorality" for Mills was a "structural immorality" built into the institutions of power in our society—in particular the treadmill of production. "In a civilization so thoroughly business-penetrated as America," he wrote, money becomes "the one unambiguous marker of success . . . the sovereign American value." Such a society, dominated by the corporate rich with the support of the political power elite, is a society of "organized irresponsibility," where moral virtue is divorced from success, and knowledge from power. Public communication, rather than constituting the basis for the exchange of ideas necessary for the conduct of a democracy, is largely given over to "an astounding volume of propaganda for commodities . . . addressed more often to the belly or to the groin than to the head or the heart." The corrupting influence that all of this has on the general public is visible in the loss of the capacity for moral indignation, the growth of cynicism, a drop in political participation, and the emergence of a passive, commercially centered existence. In short, the higher immorality spells the annihilation of a meaningful moral and political community.

Manifestations of this higher immorality—in which money divorced from all other considerations has become the supreme reality—are all around us. In 1992 alone U.S. business spent per-

haps $1 trillion on marketing, simply convincing people to consume more and more goods. This exceeded by about $600 billion the amount spent on education—public and private—at all levels. Under these circumstances we can expect people to grow up with their heads full of information about saleable commodities, and empty of knowledge about human history, morality, culture, science and the environment. What is most valued in such a society is the latest style, the most expensive clothing, the finest car. Hence, it is not surprising that more than 93 percent of teenage girls questioned in a survey conducted in the late 1980s indicated that their favorite leisure activity was to go shopping. Not long ago *Fortune* magazine quoted Dee Hock, former head of the Visa bank card operation, as saying, "It's not that people value money more but that they value everything else so much less—not that they are more greedy but that they have no other values to keep greed in check."

"Our social life is organized in such a way," German environmentalist Rudolf Bahro has observed, "that even people who work with their hands are more interested in a better car than in the single meal of the slum-dweller on the southern half of the earth or the need of the peasant there for water; or even a concern to expand their own consciousness, for their own self-realization."

Reflecting on the growing use of pesticides in our society, Rachel Carson wrote that this was indicative of "an era dominated by industry, in which the right to make money, at whatever cost to others, is seldom challenged."

Given the nature of the society in which we live, one must therefore be wary of solutions to environmental problems that place too much emphasis on the role of individuals, or too little emphasis on the treadmill of production and the higher immorality that it engenders. To be sure, it is necessary for individuals to struggle to organize their lives so that in their consumption they live more simply and ecologically. But to lay too much stress on this alone is to place too much onus on the individual, while ignoring institutional facts. Alan Durning of the Worldwatch

Institute, for example, argues that "we consumers have an ethical obligation to curb our consumption, since it jeopardizes the chances for future generations. Unless we climb down the consumption ladder a few rungs, our grandchildren will inherit a planetary home impoverished by our affluence."

This may seem like simple common sense but it ignores the higher immorality of a society like the United States in which the dominant institutions treat the public as mere consumers to be targeted with all of the techniques of modern marketing. The average adult in the United States watches 21,000 television commercials a year, about 75 percent of which are paid for by the 100 largest corporations. It also ignores the fact that the treadmill of production is rooted not in consumption but in production. Within the context of this system it is therefore economically naive to think that the problem can be solved simply by getting consumers to refrain from consumption and instead to save and invest their income. To invest means to expand the scale of productive capacity, increasing the size of the treadmill.

Even more questionable are the underlying assumptions of those who seek to stop environmental degradation by appealing not to individuals in general but to the ethics of individuals at the top of the social pyramid and to corporations. Thus in his widely heralded book, *The Ecology of Commerce,* Paul Hawken argues for a new environmental ethic for businesspeople and corporations. After advocating an ambitious program for ecological change, Hawken states, "Nothing written, suggested, or proposed is possible unless business is willing to embrace the world we live within and lead the way." According to Hawken, "the ultimate purpose of business is not, or should not be, simply to make money. Nor is it merely a system of making and selling things. The promise of business is to increase the general well-being of humankind through service, a creative invention and ethical philosophy."

Thus he goes on to observe that, "If Dupont, Monsanto, and Dow believe they are in the synthetic chemical production business, and cannot change this belief, they and we are in trouble. If they believe they are in the business to serve people, to help solve problems, to use and employ the ingenuity of workers to improve the lives of people around them by learning from the nature that gives us life, we have a chance."

The central message here is that business people merely have to change the ethical bases of their conduct and all will be well with the environment. Such views underestimate the extent to which the treadmill of production and the higher immorality are built into our society. Ironically, Hawken's argument places too much responsibility and blame on the individual corporate manager—since he or she too is likely to be a mere cog in the wheel of the system. As the great linguistics theorist and media critic Noam Chomsky has explained, "The chairman of the board will always tell you that he spends his every waking hour laboring so that people will get the best possible products at the cheapest possible price and work in the best possible conditions. But it is an institutional fact, independent of who the chairman of the board is, that he'd better be trying to maximize profit and market share, and if he doesn't do that, he's not going to be chairman of the board any more. If he were ever to succumb to the delusions that he expresses, he'd be out."

To be successful within any sphere in this society generally means that one has thoroughly internalized those values associated with the higher immorality. There is, as economist John Kenneth Galbraith has pointed out, a "culture of contentment" at the top of the social hierarchy; those who benefit most from the existing order have the least desire for change.

Resistance to the treadmill of production therefore has to come mainly from the lower echelons of society, and from social movements rather than individuals. This can only occur, to quote the late German Green Party leader Petra Kelly, if ecological concerns are "tied to issues of economic justice—the exploitation of the poor by the rich." Behind every environmental struggle of today there is a struggle over the expansion of the global treadmill—a case of landless workers or villagers who are compelled to destroy nature in order to survive, or of large corporations that seek to expand profits with little concern for the natural and social devastation that they leave in their wake. Ecological development is possible, but only if the economic as well as environmental injustices associated with the treadmill are addressed. An ecological approach to the economy is about having enough, not having more. It must have as its first priority people, particularly poor people, rather than production or even the environment, stressing the importance of meeting basic needs and long-term security. This is the common morality with which we must combat the higher immorality of the treadmill. Above all we must recognize the old truth, long understood by the romantic and socialist critics of capitalism, that increasing production does not eliminate poverty.

Indeed, the global treadmill is so designed that the poor countries of the world often help finance the rich ones. During the period from 1982 to 1990, the Third World was a "net exporter of hard currency to the developed countries, on average $30 billion per year." In this same period Third World debtors remitted to their creditors in the wealthy nations an average of almost $12.5 billion per month in payments on debt alone. This is equal to what the entire Third World spends each month on health and education. It is this system of global inequity that reinforces both overpopulation (since poverty spurs population growth) and the kind of rapacious development associated with the destruction of tropical rain forests in the Third World.

For those with a pragmatic bent, much of what I have said here may seem too global and too abstract. The essential point that I want to leave you with, however, is the notion that although we are all on the treadmill, we do not all relate to it in the same way and with the same degree of commitment. I have found in my research into the ancient forest struggle in the

Northwest—and others have discovered the same thing in other settings—that ordinary workers have strong environmental values even though they may be at loggerheads with the environmental movement. In essence they are fighting for their lives and livelihoods at a fairly basic level.

We must find a way of putting people first in order to protect the environment. There are many ways of reducing the economic stakes in environmental destruction on the part of those who have little direct stake in the treadmill itself. But this means taking seriously issues of social and economic inequality as well as environmental destruction. Only by committing itself to what is now called "environmental justice" (combining environmental concerns and social justice) can the environmental movement avoid being cut off from those classes of individuals who are most resistant to the treadmill on social grounds. The alternative is to promote an environmental movement that is very successful in creating parks with Keep Out! signs, yet is complicit with the larger treadmill of production. By recognizing that it is not people (as individuals and in aggregate) that are enemies of the environment but the historically specific economic and social order in which we live, we can find sufficient common ground for a true moral revolution to save the earth.

DISCUSSION QUESTIONS

1. Why does Foster believe that appealing generally to individual morality, or specifically to the ethics of business leaders, is an inadequate response to the global ecological crisis?

2. Why does Foster argue that environmental responses to the "treadmill of production" must be linked to issues of economic justice?

3. Reflecting on Foster's article, how might you be inspired to rethink the concept of "progress"?

CHAPTER (2)

Ideology and Political Culture

Politics is "in here"—within ourselves—as well as "out there," inside of government institutions. Each of us perceives the world by way of an *ideology*, a socially produced and culturally reinforced mental map made up of values, beliefs, and assumptions about why the world is the way it is and what, if anything, should be done about it. Rooted in the history and culture of our society, political ideology has a taken-for-granted naturalness about it such that we are usually not conscious of its grip on us. When left unchallenged, our received ideology impedes our capacity for independent thought and serves as a powerful force for social control. One of the goals of a liberal education should be to see our underlying beliefs and values for what they are, and to understand the selectiveness of our ideology in what it discloses and affirms, and in what it conceals and denies. The readings in this chapter address the nature and limitations of American political culture and ideology.

Any number of interpreters of U.S. history have identified *liberalism* as the dominant and unrivaled American ideology. Cut off from European brands of aristocratic conservatism on one hand, and working-class socialism on the other, Americans emphasized the values of individualism, private property, the free market, and limited government that had emerged in seventeenth- and eighteenth-century English thought, most notably in John Locke's *Second Treatise of Government* (1690). In this classical sense, liberalism is a broad set of ideas that encompasses both "liberal" and "conservative" positions today, a point that helps explain how limited our spectrum of political viewpoints actually is. As it developed out of the shadows of the feudal era, liberalism seemed to represent a great advance in human freedom. But given the interdependent nature of our increasingly multicultural world, how well do liberal individualism and the private market economy it legitimates prepare us for confronting the challenges of the twenty-first century?

WHAT IS THE AMERICAN DREAM?

In this selection, political scientist Jennifer Hochschild examines the four basic tenets of the American dream. The dream is rooted in a variation of philosopher John Locke's fantasy frontier, a state of nature where anyone is almost guaranteed to be able to achieve any success with enough personal determination. Hochschild discusses the myriad of ways American history and popular culture have portrayed the "almost-promise" of success, and the equally haunting power of the fear of failure. Having articulated the virtues of the American dream and its ascendance to the level of a seductive ideology, she then assesses the flaws inherent in the dream's four key tenets. Particularly troubling is the nightmarish quality of the dream for those who fail to achieve it, who are subsequently devalued by society and who, often, devalue themselves. Hochschild finds that the dream, taken as a whole, is overly (and unnecessarily) individualistic, fixated on an extremely narrow definition of "success," and analytically deceptive in that it encourages an emphasis on traits of individuals rather than political, economic, and social structures. Moreover, our political culture offers few alternative ideologies against which to evaluate the strengths and weakness of our own. Thus, the individually focused, nonstructural tendencies of the ideology of the American dream make it that much harder for U.S. citizens to fully understand themselves and the political world they inhabit.

"In the beginning," wrote John Locke, "all the world was *America*." Locke was referring specifically to the absence of a cash nexus in primitive society. But the sentence evokes the unsullied newness, infinite possibility, limitless resources that are commonly understood to be the essence of the "American dream." The idea of the American dream has been attached to everything from religious freedom to a home in the suburbs, and it has inspired emotions ranging from deep satisfaction to disillusioned fury. Nevertheless, the phrase elicits for most Americans some variant of Locke's fantasy—a new world where anything can happen and good things might. . . .

Source: Jennifer L. Hochschild, *Facing Up to the American Dream: Race, Class and the Soul of the Nation,* Princeton, NJ: Princeton University Press, 1995, pp. 15–38.

THE MEANING OF SUCCESS

The American dream consists of tenets about achieving success. Let us first explore the meaning of "success" and then consider the rules for achieving it.

People most often define success as the attainment of a high income, a prestigious job, economic security. My treatment is no exception. But *pace* President Reagan, material well-being is only one form of accomplishment. People seek success from the pulpit to the stage of the Metropolitan Opera, from membership in the newest dance club to membership in the Senate. Success can be as amorphous and encompassing as "a right to say what they wanta say, do what they wanta do, and fashion a world into something that can be great for everyone."

Different kinds of success need not, but often do, conflict. A classic plot of American family sagas is the children's rejection of the parents' hard-won wealth and social standing in favor of some "deeper," more meaningful form of accomplishment. The rejection may be reversed, as Cotton Mather sadly reported:

> There have been very fine settlements in the north-east regions; but what is become of them? . . . One of our ministers once preaching to a congregation there, urged them to approve themselves a religious people from this consideration, "that otherwise they would contradict the main end of planting this wilderness"; whereupon a well-known person, then in the assembly, cryed out, "Sir, you are mistaken: you think you are preaching to the people at the [Plymouth] Bay; our main end was to catch fish."

Mather "wished that something more excellent had been the main end of the settlements in that brave country," but the ideology of the American dream itself remains agnostic as to the meaning of "something more excellent."

A definition of success involves measurement as well as content. Success can be measured in at least three ways, with important normative and behavioral consequences. First, it can be *absolute*. In this case, achieving the American dream implies reaching some threshold of well-being, higher than where one began but not necessarily dazzling. As Bruce Springsteen puts it, "I don't think the American dream was that everybody was going to make . . . a billion dollars, but it was that everybody was going to have an opportunity and the chance to live a life with some decency and some dignity and a chance for some self-respect."

Second, success can be *relative*. Here achieving the American dream consists in becoming better off than some comparison point, whether one's childhood, people in the old country, one's neighbors, a character from a book, another race or gender—anything or anyone that one measures oneself against. Relative success implies no threshold of well-being, and it may or may not entail continually changing the comparison group as one achieves a given level of accomplishment. A benign version of relative success is captured by James Comer's "kind of competition . . . we had . . . going on" with "the closest friends that we had":

> When we first met them, we had a dining room and they didn't. They went back and they turned one of their bedrooms into a dining room . . . After that we bought this big Buick car. And we came to their house and they had bought another car. She bought a fur coat one year and your dad bought me one the next. But it was a friendly thing, the way we raced. It gave you something to work for, to look forward to. Every year we tried to have something different to show them what we had done, and they would have something to show us.

William Byrd II articulated a more malign version in 1736: slaves "blow up the pride, and ruin the industry of our white people, who seeing a rank of poor creatures below them, detest work for fear it should make them look like slaves."

Success can, alternatively, be *competitive*—achieving victory over someone else. My success implies your failure. Competitors are usually people, whether known and concrete (opponents in a tennis match) or unknown and abstract (all other applicants for a job). *U.S. News and World Report*, in an article celebrating "SUCCESS! The Chase Is Back in Style Again," graphically illustrates the relationship among competitors in the business world. An opponent may, however, be entirely impersonal. John Henry, "the steel-drivin' man," is famed for beating a machine, and Paul Bunyan for taming the primeval forest.

TENETS OF SUCCESS

> The American dream that we were all raised on is a simple but powerful one—if you work hard and play by the rules you should be given a chance to go as far as your God-given ability will take you.
> —President Bill Clinton,
> speech to Democratic
> Leadership Council, 1993

In one sentence, President Clinton has captured the bundle of shared, even unconsciously presumed, tenets about achieving success that make up the ideology of the American dream. Those tenets answer the questions: *Who* may pursue the American dream? In *what* does the pursuit consist? *How* does one successfully pursue the dream? *Why* is the pursuit worthy of our deepest commitment?

The answer to "who" in the standard ideology is "everyone, regardless of ascriptive traits, family background, or personal history." The answer to "what" is "the reasonable anticipation, though not the promise, of success, however it is defined." The answer to "how" is "through actions and traits under one's own control." The answer to "why" is "true success is associated with virtue." Let us consider each rule in turn.

Who May Pursue Success?

The first tenet, that everyone may always pursue their dream, is the most direct connotation of Locke's "in the beginning. . . ." But the idea extends beyond the image of a pristine state of nature waiting for whoever "discovers" it. Even in the distinctly nonpristine, nonnatural world of Harlem or Harlan County, anyone can pursue a dream. A century ago, one moved to the frontier to hide a spotted past and begin afresh; Montana frontierswomen "never ask[ed] women where they come from or what they did before they came to live in our neck of the woods. If they wore a wedding band and were good wives, mothers, and neighbors that was enough for us to know."

But seldom, say Americans, does one need to take such dramatic steps; fewer than one-fifth see race, gender, religion, or class as very important for "getting ahead in life." Even two-thirds of the poor are certain that Americans like themselves "have a good chance of improving our standard of living," and up to three times as many Americans as Europeans make that claim. In effect, Americans believe that they can create a personal mini-state of nature that will allow them to slough off the past and invent a better future.

What Does One Pursue?

The second tenet, that one may reasonably anticipate success, is less straightforward. "Reasonable anticipation" is far from a guarantee, as all children on the morning of their birthday know. But "reasonable anticipation" is also much more than simply longing; most children are fairly sure of getting at least some of what they wish for on their birthday. On a larger scale, from its inception America has been seen by many as an extravagant birthday party:

> Seagull: A whole countrie of English is there, man, . . . and . . . the Indians are so in love with 'hem that all the treasure they have they lay at their feete . . . Golde is more plentiful there than copper is with us. . . .

Why, man, all their dripping pans and their chamberpots are pure golde; and all the chaines with which they chaine up their streets are massie golde; all the prisoners they take are fettered in golde; and for rubies and diamonds they goe forthe on holy dayes and gather 'hem by the sea shore to hang on their childrens coats.

Presumably few Britons even in 1605 took this message literally, but the hope of abundant riches—whether material, spiritual, or otherwise—persists.

Thus Americans are exhorted to "go for it" in their advertisements as well as their commencement addresses. And they do; three-quarters of Americans, compared with only one-third of Britons, West Germans, and Hungarians (and fewer Dutch), agree that they have a good chance of improving their standard of living. Twice as many Americans as Canadians or Japanese think future generations of their nationality will live better than the present generation.

How Does One Pursue Success?

The third premise, for those who do not take Seagull literally, explains how one is to achieve the success that one anticipates. Ralph Waldo Emerson is uncharacteristically succinct on the point: "There is always a reason, *in the man,* for his good or bad fortune, and so in making money." Other nineteenth-century orators exhorted young men to

Behold him [a statue of Benjamin Franklin], . . . holding out to you an example of diligence, economy and virtue, and personifying the triumphant success which may await those who follow it! Behold him, ye that are humblest and poorest . . . —lift up your heads and look at the image of a man who rose from nothing, who owed nothing to parentage or patronage, who enjoyed no advantages of early education, which are not open,—a hundredfold open,—to yourselves,

who performed the most menial services in the business in which his early life was employed, but who lived to stand before Kings, and died to leave a name which the world will never forget.

Lest we smile at the quaint optimism (or crude propaganda) of our ancestors, consider a recent advertisement from Citicorp Bank. This carefully balanced group of shining faces—young and old, male and female, black, Latino, Nordic, and Asian—all gazing starry-eyed at the middle distance over the words "THE WILL TO SUCCEED IS PART OF THE AMERICAN SPIRIT" conveys the message of the third tenet in no uncertain terms.

This advertisement is well aimed; surveys unanimously show Americans' strong support for rewarding people in the marketplace according to their talents and accomplishments rather than their needs, efforts, or simple existence. And Americans mostly believe that people are in fact rewarded for their acts. In 1952 fully 88 percent of Americans agreed that "there is plenty of opportunity and anyone who works hard can go as far as he wants"; in 1980, 70 percent concurred.

Comparisons across space yield the same results as comparisons across time. In a 1973 survey of youth in ten nations, only Swedes and British disagreed more than did Americans that a man's [sic] future is "virtually determined" by his family background. A decade later only 31 percent of Americans agreed that in their nation "what you achieve in life depends largely on your family background," compared with over 50 percent of Austrians and Britons, and over 60 percent of Italians. Most pointedly, half of American adolescents compared with one-fourth of British adolescents agreed in 1972 that "people get to be poor . . . [because] they don't work hard enough."

Americans also believe more than do Europeans that people ought not to be buffered from the consequences of their actions, so long as they have a fair start in life. Thus up to four times as many more Americans think college opportunities should be increased, but roughly half as many think the government should reduce the income disparity between high- and low-income citizens, or provide jobs or income support for the poor.

Why Is Success Worth Pursuing?

Implicit in the flows of oratory and survey responses is the fourth tenet of the American dream, that the pursuit of success warrants so much fervor because it is associated with virtue. "Associated with" means at least four things: virtue leads to success, success makes a person virtuous, success indicates virtue, or apparent success is not real success unless one is also virtuous.

That quintessential American, Benjamin Franklin, illustrates three of these associations: the *Autobiography* instructs us that "no Qualities were so likely to make a poor Man's Fortune as those of Probity & Integrity." Conversely, "Proverbial Sentences, chiefly such as inculcated Industry and Frugality," are included in *Poor Richard's Almanack* as "the Means of procuring Wealth and thereby securing Virtue, it being more difficult for a Man in Want to act always honestly, as . . . *it is hard for an empty Sack to stand upright.*" Finally, mere wealth may actually impede true success, the attainment of which requires a long list of virtues: "Fond *Pride of Dress,* is sure a very Curse; E'er *Fancy* you consult, consult your Purse"; "A Ploughman on his Legs is higher than a Gentleman on his Knees"; and "Pride that dines on Vanity sups on Contempt."

Americans have learned Franklin's lessons well: they distinguish between the worthy and unworthy rich, as well as the deserving and undeserving poor. For example, most Americans characterize "yuppies" as people who "play fashionable games" and "eat in trendy restaurants," and on the whole they enjoy watching such forms of conspicuous consumption. But they also characterize yuppies as selfish, greedy, inclined to flaunt their wealth, and imbued with a false sense of superiority. These traits they mostly find unacceptable. Overall, Americans overwhelmingly deplore the 1980s sentiment of "making it fast while you can

regardless of what happened to others." This is not simply a reaction against the Reagan years. In surveys throughout the 1970s, four in ten Americans deemed honesty to be the most important quality for a child to learn, compared with 2 percent proclaiming that a child should try hard to succeed. Virtually all Americans require that their friends be "honest" and "responsible"—core components of the third and fourth tenets.

Americans also focus more on virtue than do citizens of other nations, at least in their self-descriptions. A survey of youth in ten nations found that more Americans than people in any other country described their chief goal in life as "sincerity and love between myself and others," and in only one other nation (the Philippines) did more youth seek "salvation through faith." Conversely, only in Sweden did fewer youths seek "money and position," and only in three other countries did fewer seek "freedom from restrictions." More Americans than Europeans gain strength from religion, report prayer to be an important part of their daily life, and agree that there are universally applicable "clear guidelines about what is good or evil." In short, "this country succeeds in living a very sinful life without being deeply cynical. That is the difference between Europe and America, and it signifies that ethics *means* something here."

The American Dream as Fantasy

We must beware reducing the dream to its components; as a whole it has an evocative resonance greater than the sum of its parts. The theme of most Walt Disney movies boil down to the lyrics in *Pinocchio:* "When you wish upon a star, makes no difference who you are, your dreams come true." It is no coincidence that Disney movies are so durable; they simply update Locke's fantasy. And the global, amorphous vision of establishing a city upon the hill, killing the great white whale, striking a vein of gold, making the world safe for democracy—or simply living a life of decency and dignity—underlies all analyses of what success means or what practices will attain it.

Virtues of the American Dream

Combining the amorphous fantasy or the more precise tenets of the American dream with the various meanings of success shows the full richness—and seductiveness—of the ideology. If one measures success absolutely and accepts a wide array of indicators of success, the ideology portrays America as a land of plenty, and Americans as "people of plenty." This is the great theme of one of the most powerful children's sagas ever written in America, the *Little House in the Big Woods* series. Decades (and nine volumes) of grasshopper plagues, ferocious blizzards, cheating and cowardly railroad bosses, even hostile Indians cannot prevent Pa and his girls from eventually "winning their bet with Uncle Sam" and becoming prosperous homesteaders. In the words of one of Pa's songs:

> I am sure in this world there are plenty
> of good things enough for us all. . . .
> It's cowards alone that are crying
> And foolishly saying, "I can't."
> It is only by plodding and striving
> And laboring up the steep hill
> Of life, that you'll ever be thriving,
> Which you'll do if you've only the will.

If success is measured competitively and defined narrowly, however, the ideology portrays a different America. Hard work and virtue combined with scarce resources produce a few spectacular winners and many dismissible losers. This is the theme of John Rockefeller's turn-of-the-century Sunday school address:

> The growth of a large business is merely a survival of the fittest. . . . The American Beauty rose can be produced in the splendor and fragrance which bring cheer to its beholder only by sacrificing the early buds which grow up around it. This is not an evil tendency in business. It is merely the working out of a law of nature and a law of God.

The *Little House* series has sold well over four million copies; Americans prefer the self-image of universal achievement to that of a few stalwarts triumphing over weaker contenders. What matters most, however, is not any single image but rather the elasticity and range of the ideology of the American dream. People can encourage themselves with soft versions, congratulate themselves with harder ones, and exult with the hardest, as their circumstances and characters warrant.

Thus the American dream is an impressive ideology. It has for centuries lured people to America and moved them around within it, and it has kept them striving in horrible conditions against impossible odds. Most Americans celebrate it unthinkingly, along with apple pie and motherhood; criticism typically is limited to imperfections in its application. But like apple pie and motherhood, the American dream turns out upon closer examination to be less than perfect. Let us look, then, at flaws intrinsic to the dream.

Flaws in the Tenets of the American Dream

The First Tenet

The first tenet, that everyone can participate equally and can always start over, is troubling to the degree that it is not true. It is, of course, never true in the strongest sense; people cannot shed their existing selves as snakes do their skin. So the myth of the individual mini-state of nature is just that—a fantasy to be sought but never achieved.

Fantasies are fine so long as people understand that that is what they are. For that reason, a weaker formulation of the first tenet—people start the pursuit of success with varying advantages, but no one is barred from the pursuit—is more troubling because the gap between ideological claim and actual fact is harder to recognize. As a factual claim, the first tenet is largely false; for most of American history, women of any race and men who were Native American, Asian, black, or poor were barred from all but a narrow range of "electable futures." Ascriptive constraints have arguably been weakened over time, but until recently no more than about a third of the population was able to take seriously the first premise of the American dream.

This flaw has implications beyond the evident ones of racism and sexism. The emotional potency of the American dream has made people who *were* able to identify with it the norm for everyone else. White men, especially European immigrants able to ride the wave of the Industrial Revolution (and to benefit from the absence of competition from the rest of the population) to comfort or even prosperity, are the epitomizing demonstration of America as the bountiful state of nature. Those who do not fit the model disappear from the collective self-portrait. Thus the irony is doubled: not only has the ideal of universal participation been denied to most Americans, but also the very fact of its denial has itself been denied in our national self-image.

This double irony creates deep misunderstandings and correspondingly deep political tensions. Whites increasingly believe that racial discrimination is slight and declining, and blacks increasingly believe the opposite. But this form of racial conflict is not unique. For example, surveys show that more women than men believe that women are discriminated against in employment and wages, in "being able to combine family and work," and in their overall chance to pursue their dreams. Similarly, regardless of when the survey was conducted, more men than women believe that women are better off now than a decade earlier with regard to these issues. Not surprisingly, bitter disagreements about the need for affirmative action, policies to stem sexual harassment, family leave policies, and the like ensue.

The Second Tenet

The flaws of the second tenet of the American dream, the reasonable anticipation of success, stem from the close link between anticipation and expectation. That link presents little problem so long as there are enough resources and opportunities that everyone has a reasonable chance of having some expectations met. Indeed, panegyrics to the American dream always expound on the bounty and openness of the American continent. Governor James Glen typified eighteenth-century entrepreneurs of colonization by promising that

> Adventurers will be pleased to find a Change from Poverty and Distress to Ease and Plenty; they are invited to a Country not yet half settled, where the Rivers are crowded with Fish, and the Forests with Game; and no Game-Act to restrain them from enjoying those Bounties of Providence, no heavy Taxes to impoverish them, nor oppressive Landlords to snatch the hard-earned Morsel from the Mouth of Indigence, and where Industry will certainly inrich them.

Three centuries later, the message was unchanged:

> All my life I am thinking to come to this country. For what I read in the magazines, and the movies. . . . I would have a beautiful castle in the U.S. I will have a thousand servant. I will have five Rolls-Royces in my door. . . . We thinking everybody has this kind of life. . . . I have this kind of dream.

These fantasies are innocuous so long as resources roughly balance dreams for enough people enough of the time. But if they do not—worse yet, if they used to but do no longer—then the dream rapidly loses its appeal. The circumstances that cause resources no longer to balance dreams vary, from an economic downturn to a rapid increase in the number of dreamers to a narrowing of the grounds on which success is publicly recognized. The general point, however, always holds: no one promises that dreams will be fulfilled, but the distinction between the right to dream and the right to succeed is psychologically hard to maintain and politically always blurred. It is especially hard to maintain because the dream sustains

Americans against daily nightmares only if they believe that they have a significant likelihood, not just a formal chance, of reaching their goals.

In short, the right to aspire to success works as an ideological substitute for a guarantee of success only if it begins to approach it. When people recognize that chances for success are slim or getting slimmer, the whole tenor of the American dream changes dramatically for the worse.

The general problem of scarcity varies depending on how people measure success and how broadly they define possible goals. It is most obvious and acute for those focused on competitive success in only a few arenas; by definition resources and opportunities are insufficient to satisfy all dreamers in such a case. But it may be more problematic for those who measure success relatively or who admit a wide array of outcomes into their picture of success. After all, there are more such people and they have no a priori reason to assume that many will fail.

The problem of scarcity may be most devastating, however, for people anticipating absolute success or for people willing to see success almost anywhere. They, after all, have the least reason to expect failure. Losers of this type have an unmatched poignancy: "I don't dream any more like I used to. I believed that in this country, we would have all we needed for the decent life. I don't see that any more."

Conversely, the availability of resources and opportunities may shape the kind of success that Americans dream of. If resources are profoundly scarce (as in a famine) or inherently limited (as in election to the presidency), people almost certainly envision competitive success in that arena. If resources are moderately scarce, people will be concerned about their position relative to that of others, but will not necessarily see another's gain as their loss. When resources and opportunities seem wide open and broadly defined—anyone can achieve salvation, get an "A" on the exam, claim 160 acres of western prairie—people are most free to pursue their idiosyncratic dreams and to measure their achievement by their own absolute standard.

This logic suggests a dynamic: as resources become tighter or success is more narrowly defined, Americans are likely to shift their understanding of success from absolute to relative to competitive. Before the 1980s, claims one journalist, "there was always enough to go around, plenty of places in the sun. It didn't even matter much about the rich—so long as everyone was living better, it seemed the rich couldn't be denied their chance to get richer." But "today [in 1988] that wave [of prosperity] has crested.... Now when the rich get richer, the middle class stagnates—and the poor get decidedly poorer. If left unchecked, a polarization of income ... is likely to provoke consequences that will affect America's politics and power, to say nothing of its psyche."

The risks of anticipating success do not stop with anticipation. Attaining one's dreams can be surprisingly problematic. From William Shakespeare to William Faulkner, writers have limned the loneliness of being at the top, the spiritual costs of cutthroat competition, the shallowness of a society that rewards achievement above all else. Alexis de Tocqueville characteristically provides one of the most eloquent of such admonitions:

> Every American is eaten up with longing to rise.... In America I have seen the freest and best educated of men in circumstances the happiest in the world; yet it seemed to me that a cloud habitually hung on their brow, and they seemed serious and almost sad even in their pleasures. The chief reason for this is that ... [they] never stop thinking of the good things they have not got.... They clutch everything but hold nothing fast, and so lose grip as they hurry after some new delight.

The obsession with ever more material success threatens the body politic as well as the individual soul:

> When the taste for physical pleasures has grown more rapidly than either education or experience of free institutions, the time

comes when men are carried away and lose control of themselves at sight of the new good things they are ready to snatch. . . . There is no need to drag their rights away from citizens of this type; they themselves voluntarily let them go. . . . The role of government is left unfilled. If, at this critical moment, an able and ambitious man once gets power, he finds the way open for usurpations of every sort.

Not only nineteenth-century romantics cautioned against the failures of success. Today psychotherapists specialize in helping "troubled winners" or the "working wounded," for whom "a life too much devoted to pursuing money, power, position, and control over others ends up being emotionally impoverished." In short, material—and perhaps other forms of—success is not all it's cracked up to be, even (or especially) in a nation where it is the centerpiece of the pervasive ideology.

The problems of success, however, pale beside the problems of failure. Because success is so central to Americans' self-image, and because they expect as well as hope to achieve, Americans are not gracious about failure. Others' failure reminds them that the dream may be just that—a dream, to be distinguished from waking reality. Their own failure confirms that fear. As Zora Neale Hurston puts it, "there is something about poverty that smells like death."

Furthermore, the better the dream works for other people, the more devastating is failure for the smaller and smaller proportion of people left behind. In World War II, members of military units with a high probability of promotion were less satisfied with advancement opportunities than members of units with a much lower probability of promotion, because failure to be promoted in the former case was both more salient and more demonstrably a personal rather than a systemic flaw. The "tunnel effect" is a more nuanced depiction of this phenomenon of relative deprivation. The first stage is one of relative gratification, in which others' success enhances one's own well-being. After all, drivers in a traffic jam in a tunnel are initially pleased when cars in the adjacent lane begin to move "because advances of others supply information about a more benign external environment; receipt of this information produces gratification; and this gratification overcomes, or at least suspends, *envy.*" At some point, however, those left behind come to believe that their heightened expectations will not be met; not only are their hopes now dashed, but they are also worse off than when the upward mobility began. "Nonrealization of the expectation ['that my turn to move will soon come'] will at some point result in my 'becoming furious.'" And one is still stuck in the tunnel. In short, the ideology of the American dream includes no provision for failure; a failed dream denies the loser not only success but even a safe harbor within which to hide the loss.

The Third Tenet

Failure is made more harsh by the third premise of the American dream—the belief that success results from actions and traits under one's own control. Logically, it does not follow that if success results from individual volition, then failure results from lack of volition. All one needs in order to see the logical flaw here is the distinction between necessary and sufficient. But that distinction is not obvious or intuitive, and in any case the psychologic of the American dream differs from strict logic. In the psychologic, if one may claim responsibility for success, one must accept responsibility for failure.

Americans who do everything they can and still fail may come to understand that effort and talent alone do not guarantee success. But they have a hard time persuading others. After all, they are losers—why listen to them? Will we not benefit more by listening to winners (who seldom challenge the premise that effort and talent breed success)?

The Fourth Tenet

Failure, then, is unseemly for two reasons: it challenges the blurring between anticipation and promise that is the emotional heart of the American dream, and people who fail are presumed to lack talent or will. The coup de grace comes from the fourth tenet of the dream, the association of success with virtue. By the psychologic just described, if success implies virtue, failure implies sin.

American history and popular culture are replete with demonstrations of the connection between failure and sin. In the 1600s, indentured servants—kidnapped children, convicts, and struggling families alike—were described by earlier immigrants as "strong and idle beggars, vagabonds, egyptians, common and notorious whoores, theeves, and other dissolute and lousy persons." Nineteenth-century reformers concurred: fallen women are typically "the daughters of the ignorant, depraved, and vicious part of our population, trained up without culture of any kind, amidst the contagion of evil example, and enter upon a life of prostitution for the ratification of their unbridled passions, and become harlots altogether by choice."

Small wonder that in the late twentieth century even the poor blame the poor for their condition. Despite her vivid awareness of exploitation by the rich, an aging cleaning woman insists that many people are poor because they "make the money and drink it all up. They don't care about the kids or the clothes. Just have a bottle on that table all the time." Losers even blame themselves: an unemployed factory worker, handicapped by a childhood accident, "wish[es] to hell I could do it [save money for his children]. I always said for years, 'I wanna get rich, I wanna get rich.' But then, phew! My mind doesn't have the strong will. I say, 'Well, I'm *gonna* do it.' Only the next day's different." These people are typical. In 1985, over 60 percent of poor people but only 45 percent of the nonpoor agreed that "poor young women often have babies so they can collect welfare." Seven years later, the same proportions of poor and well-off agreed that welfare recipients "are taking advantage of the system."

The equation of failure with evil and success with virtue cannot be attributed to poor educa-tion or low status. College students "who learned that a fellow student had been awarded a cash prize as a result of a random drawing were likely to conclude that he had in fact worked especially hard." In another experiment, subjects rated a presumed victim of electric shocks who was randomly selected to receive compensation for her pain more favorably than a victim who would not be compensated. "The sight of an innocent person suffering without possibility of reward or compensation motivated people to devalue the attractiveness of the victim in order to bring about a more appropriate fit between her fate and her character." Devaluing losers allows people to maintain their belief that the world is fundamentally just, even when it patently is not.

Losers are obviously harmed by the association of success with virtue. But the association creates equally important, if less obvious, problems for winners. Fitzwilliam Darcy, in Jane Austen's *Pride and Prejudice,* epitomizes the defect of pride: if I believe that virtue produced my success, or that success has made me even more virtuous, I am likely to become insufferably smug. That may not bother me much, but the fact that people around me feel the same way will. In addition, this equation raises the stakes very high for further rounds of endeavor. If I continue to win, all is well; if I falter, I lose my *amour propre* as well as my wealth or power. Alternatively, if I recognize that I partly owe my success to lying to a few clients, evading a few taxes, cheating a few employees, then I am likely to feel considerable guilt. This guilt might induce reform and recompense, but it may instead induce drinking to assuage the unease, persecuting other nonvirtuous winners, striving to show that losers are even more sinful, or simple hypocrisy.

These problems intensify when patterns of group success rather than the idiosyncrasies of individual success are at issue. When members of one group seem disproportionately successful, that group acquires a halo of ascribed virtue. Consider a 1907 article by Burton J. Hendrick on "The Great Jewish Invasion" in *McClure's Magazine.* The author's name, the publication, the date, and the title all lead one to expect an (at best, thinly veiled) anti-Semitic diatribe. The first few pages seem to confirm that expectation, with their claims that "the real modern Zion, greater in numbers and wealth and power than the old, steadily gathers on Manhattan Island," and that "the Jews are active, and invariably with success, in practically every business, professional, and intellectual field. The New Yorker constantly rubs shoulders with Israel." These feats are all the more "remarkable" because "the great mass of its [New York's] Jews are not what are commonly regarded as the most enlightened of their race" since they come from eastern Europe. After all, "no people have had a more inadequate preparation, educational and economic, for American citizenship."

Yet the article goes on to describe in careful and admiring detail how these dirt-poor, ignorant, orthodoxly non-Christian immigrants work, save, cooperate, sacrifice for their children—and end up wealthy beyond anyone's wildest imaginings. Nor are they merely money-grubbers; Russian Jews are "individualist[s]," the "city's largest productive force and the greatest contributor to its manufacturing wealth," demonstrating "intense ambition," abstinence, and foresight. In his highest accolade, Mr. Hendrick even insists that the Russian Jew's

> enthusiasm for America knows no bounds. He eagerly looks forward to the time when he can be naturalized. . . . The rapidity with which the New York Jew adopts the manners and trappings of Americans almost disproves his ancient heritage as a peculiar people. . . . Better than any other element, even the native stock, do they meet the two supreme tests of citizenship: they actually go to the polls, and when once there, vote independently.

In short, in one generation the east European Jewish immigrant has gone from an unassimilable, bovine drag on the American spirit to the epitome of all the American virtues. Nothing succeeds like success.

The contemporary equivalent of Mr. Hendrick's amazing Jews are Southeast Asians. A century ago, Chinese and Japanese immigrants could hardly be derogated enough. Now newspapers have a seemingly endless supply of rags-to-riches stories about destitute boat people whose daughter became the high school valedictorian a scant five years later and is now a pre-med student at Stanford. Such success is inevitably attributed to hard work, self-discipline, family support, and refusal to follow the bad example set by American-born peers. This portrayal is so ubiquitous that spokespeople for Asian immigrants feel impelled to insist publicly that not *all* Asians escape poverty, crime, and discrimination, and that even the successful pay a heavy emotional cost.

It would be churlish to argue that excessive praise is as bad as racism or ethnic slurs. But newly anointed groups are too often used to cast aspersions on some despised group that has not managed to fulfill the American dream. In Burton Hendrick's case, the main negative reference group is the Irish, who drink and gamble, yield their productive jobs to Jews, and—worst of all—band together in labor unions, in the "Irish vote," and in political party machines. In the case of immigrant Asians, the usual (if slightly more subtle) message is "Why can't African Americans do the same thing? At least they speak English when they start school." This dynamic adds yet another component to the nightmare of a failed American dream. Members of a denigrated group are disproportionately likely to fail to achieve their goals; they are blamed as individuals (and perhaps blame themselves) for their failure; and they carry a further stigma as members of a nonvirtuous (thus appropriately denigrated) group.

This effect of the fourth tenet can be taken a further, and most dangerous, step. For some Americans always, and for many Americans in some periods of our history, virtuous success has been defined as the dominance of some groups over others. This phenomenon extends the idea of competitive success from individual victories to collective hierarchies. If women are weak and emotional, it is *right* for men to control their bodies and wealth; if blacks are childlike pagans, it is *right* for whites to ensure their physical and spiritual survival through enslavement and conversion; if citizens of other nations refuse to recognize the value of capitalism and free elections, it is *right* for Americans to install a more enlightened government in their capitol. I find it hard to present these sentiments with a straight face, but they have arguably done almost as much as the American dream to shape Americans' beliefs, practices, and institutions.

FLAWS IN THE AMERICAN DREAM TAKEN AS A WHOLE

Atomistic Individualism

Not only each tenet, but also the ideology of the American dream as a whole, is flawed. One problem stems from the radical individualism often associated with the dream (although the ideology entails nothing that prohibits groups from pursuing collective success). Achievers mark their success by moving away from the tenement, ghetto, or holler of their impoverished and impotent youth, thus speeding the breakup of their ethnic community. This is a bittersweet phenomenon. The freedom to move up and out is desirable, or at least desired. But certainly those left behind, probably those who leave, and arguably the nation as a whole lose when groups of people with close cultural and personal ties break those ties in pursuit of or after attaining "the bitch-goddess, success." The line between autonomy and atomism is hard to draw.

American culture is full of stories about the mixed effects of success on communities and their residents. A Polish-American folk song tells of a man who emigrated to America, worked for three years in a foundry, returned home with "gold and silver," but found that "my children did

not know me, for they fled from me, a stranger." The emancipated children may be as pained as the abandoned parents, as illustrated by the five brothers who complained to the *Jewish Daily Forward* in 1933:

> Imagine, even when we go with our father to buy something in a store on Fifth Avenue, New York, he insists on speaking Yiddish. We are not ashamed of our parents, God forbid, but they ought to know where it's proper and where it's not. If they talk Yiddish among themselves at home, or to us, it's bad enough, but among strangers and Christians? Is that nice?

Only irresponsible romanticism permits the wish that peasants and villagers would opt for tradition rather than opportunity. It is surely significant that across the world and throughout centuries, they almost never do. But one can still regret what is lost. And Thomas Hooker's warning cannot be shrugged off: "For if each man may do what is good in his owne eyes, proceed according to his own pleasure, so that none may crosse him or controll him by any power, there must of necessity follow the distraction and desolation of the whole."

Narrowing "Success"

William James followed his comment on "the moral flabbiness born of the exclusive worship of the bitch-goddess, success" with the less well-known observation that "that—with the squalid cash interpretation put on the word success—is our national disease." It was at best indecorous for a man as wealthy and prestigious as William James to castigate others' pursuit of wealth or inattentiveness to philosophy. But his concern is warranted. The American dream is susceptible to having the open-ended definition of success, which can equally include salvation or writing the great American novel, narrowed to wealth, job status, or power. Well-educated women (not to speak of men) are embarrassed to admit that they would rather raise happy children than practice corporate law; environmentalists worry that the value of a beautiful forest cannot be monetized and therefore will not be considered in regulatory decisions. Even high school seniors, for whom "having lots of money" has become increasingly important over the past two decades, overwhelmingly and increasingly agree that "people are too much concerned with material things these days."

Sometimes market values colonize, rather than submerge, other values. Economists designing environmental regulations assign monetary value to a stand of redwood trees, thereby cheapening (note the metaphor) the meaning of the primeval forest in the eyes of environmentalists. Some feminists seek to enhance the status of women by calculating the wages due to housework and including them in the gross national product; other feminists see this move as turning loving wives and mothers into calculating *homo economici*. The problem in these and similar cases is not that the assignment of monetary worth is too high or low, but that the very process of assigning monetary worth reduces an array of values to a single thin one.

Only sentimentalism allows one to value the purity of artistic poverty over the sordidness of corporate wealth unless one made the choice after experiencing both states. But it is a serious flaw in the American dream if those who envision success in artistic or religious or altruistic terms must defend their vision as well as fight to achieve their chosen goals. Nothing in the ideology requires reducing success to money and power, but the ideology is so vulnerable to the reduction that that point must count as an internal flaw, not merely as grounds for an external attack.

The Ideology as Deception

I have argued that the American dream need not be individualistic in the narrow sense, given that one can under its rubric pursue success for one's family or community as well as for oneself. But it is highly *individual,* in that it leads one to focus on people's behaviors rather than on economic processes, environmental constraints, or political structures as the causal explanation for social orderings. That focus is not itself a flaw; it is simply an epistemological choice with methodological implications for the study of American politics. But to the degree that the focus carries a moral message, it points to a weakness at the very heart of the dream.

The idea of the blank slate in the first tenet, the almost-promise of success of the second, the reliance on personal attributes in the third, the association of failure with sin in the fourth—all these elements of the dream make it extremely difficult for Americans to see that everyone cannot simultaneously attain more than absolute success. Capitalist markets require some firms to fail; elections require some candidates and policy preferences to lose; status hierarchies must have a bottom in order to have a top. But the optimistic language of and methodological individualism built into the American dream *necessarily* deceive people about these societal operations. We need not invoke hypocrites out of Mark Twain or "blue-eyed white devils" in order to understand why some people never attain success; hypocrisy or bias only enter the picture in determining *who* fails. But our basic institutions are designed to ensure that some fail, at least relatively, and a dream does nothing to help Americans cope with or even to recognize that fact.

Few Alternative Visions

All ideologies are designed to put the best possible face on the social structure within which they operate, and all privilege some values over others. So all the flaws I have described, damning though they may seem, must themselves be judged in light of the comparable flaws of other ideological formations. That point is intended to soften slightly the critique of the American dream, but it also raises a final problem with it.

Americans have few alternative ideologies against which to measure the distinctive virtues and flaws of the American dream. Alternatives are not completely absent: Thoreau's *Walden* has long been recognized as a sharp political challenge couched in a literary classic. "Country-party" or labor republicanism, Protestant fundamentalism, and ascriptive Americanism similarly have deep roots and on occasion strong adherents and powerful institutional manifestations. But most Americans honor these alternative visions more in the breach than in the observance, if then. *Walden* is read by more students majoring in English than in political science. "Small is beautiful" and "social limits to growth" are slogans for a few, but warnings to many more. And many possible visions—within-class solidarity and cross-class warfare, a military or theocratic polity pursuing collective glory, small cooperative enterprises living lightly on the land—are barely visible in the American political spectrum. In short, the political culture of the U.S. is largely shaped by a set of views in which the American dream is prominent, and by a set of institutions that make it even more prominent than views alone could do.

Tocqueville assured his readers that "up to now the Americans have happily avoided all the reefs I have just charted." Some Americans continue, 150 years later, to sail free, and perhaps they always will. But some have wrecked, and some have never gotten anywhere near the boat. For those afloat, the ideology of the American dream is a vindication, a goad to further efforts, a cause for celebration—and also grounds for anxiety, guilt and disillusionment. For the shipwrecked and drifters, the dream is a taunt, a condemnation, an object of fury—and also grounds for hope; renewed striving, and dreams for one's children.

DISCUSSION QUESTIONS

1. According to Hochschild, what are the key tenets of success in the American dream, and in what ways might the American definition of success be considered narrow?

2. In what sense is the American dream a "fantasy"? How is this fantasy reinforced by American life and culture?

3. What does Hochschild mean by "atomistic individualism" and why does she consider it a flaw? Compare her argument on this point with the case made by Robert Bellah and his co-authors in the next selection.

Robert N. Bellah, Richard Madsen, William M. Sullivan, Ann Swidler, and Steven M. Tipton

6

LIBERAL INDIVIDUALISM AND THE CRISIS OF CITIZENSHIP

Sociologist Robert Bellah and his four collaborators suggest that the exaggerated importance placed on individualism in America undermines citizenship and a strong sense of political community. Drawing on in-depth interviews with middle-class Americans for their much-discussed 1985 book Habits of the Heart, *the authors contend that most of us are unable to find in political participation and public involvement elements of a good life. But this withdrawal into private pursuits leaves politics under the domination of those with the power and money to assert their organized interests. Writing more than a decade after the original publication of* Habits of the Heart, *Bellah draws on Robert Putnam's concept of "social capital" to argue that Americans face both a personal crisis and a social crisis that he calls a "crisis of civic membership." This crisis has been exacerbated by the success of "neocapitalism," an ideology that sees markets and privatization as the solutions to social problems. In contrast, Bellah calls for a revival of civic- and community-oriented discourses that historically have been subordinate to liberal-capitalist individualism and asks us to critically question the materialistic basis of our notion of a just society.*

How ought we to live? How do we think about how to live? Who are we, as Americans? What is our character? These are questions we have asked our fellow citizens in many parts of the country. We engaged them in conversations about their lives and about what matters most to them, talked about their families and communities, their doubts and uncertainties, and their hopes and fears with respect to the larger society. We found them eager to discuss the right way to live, what to teach our children, and what our public and private responsibilities should be, but also a little dismayed by these subjects. These are important matters to those to whom we talked, and yet concern about moral questions is often relegated to the realm of private anxiety, as if it

Source: Robert N. Bellah, Richard Madsen, William M. Sullivan, Ann Swidler, and Steven M. Tipton, *Habits of the Heart: Individualism and Commitment in American Life,* Updated Edition, Berkeley and Los Angeles: University of California Press, 1996, pp. xli–xliii, xi, and xvi–xxvi.

would be awkward or embarrassing to make it public. We hope this book will help transform this inner moral debate, often shared only with intimates, into public discourse. In these pages, Americans speak with us, and, indirectly, with one another, about issues that deeply concern us all. As we will see, many doubt that we have enough in common to be able mutually to discuss our central aspirations and fears. It is one of our purposes to persuade them that we do.

The fundamental question we posed, and that was repeatedly posed to us, was how to preserve or create a morally coherent life. But the kind of life we want depends on the kind of people we are—on our character. Our inquiry can thus be located in a longstanding discussion of the relationship between character and society. In the eighth book of the *Republic,* Plato sketched a theory of the relationship between the moral character of a people and the nature of its political community, the way it organizes and governs itself. The founders of the American republic at the time of the Revolution adopted a much later version of the same theory. Since for them, as for the Americans with whom we talked, freedom was perhaps the most important value, they were particularly concerned with the qualities of character necessary for the creation of a free republic.

In the 1830s, the French social philosopher Alexis de Tocqueville offered the most comprehensive and penetrating analysis of the relationship between character and society in America that has ever been written. In his book *Democracy in America,* based on acute observation and wide conversation with Americans, Tocqueville described the mores—which he on occasion called "habits of the heart"—of the American people and showed how they helped to form American character. He singled out family life, our religious traditions, and our participation in local politics as helping to create the kind of person who could sustain a connection to a wider political community and thus ultimately support the maintenance of free institutions. He also warned that some aspects of our character—what he was one of the first to call "individualism"—might eventually isolate Americans one from another and thereby undermine the conditions of freedom.

The central problem of our book concerns the American individualism that Tocqueville described with a mixture of admiration and anxiety. It seems to us that it is individualism, and not equality, as Tocqueville thought, that has marched inexorably through our history. We are concerned that this individualism may have grown cancerous—that it may be destroying those social integuments that Tocqueville saw as moderating its more destructive potentialities, that it may be threatening the survival of freedom itself. We want to know what individualism in America looks and feels like, and how the world appears in its light.

We are also interested in those cultural traditions and practices that, without destroying individuality, serve to limit and restrain the destructive side of individualism and provide alternative models for how Americans might live. We want to know how these have fared since Tocqueville's day, and how likely their renewal is.

While we focus on what people say, we are acutely aware that they often live in ways they cannot put into words. It is particularly here, in the tension between how we live and what our culture allows us to say, that we have found both some of our richest insights into the dilemmas our society faces and hope for the reappropriation of a common language in which those dilemmas can be discussed.

Taking our clue from Tocqueville, we believe that one of the keys to the survival of free institutions is the relationship between private and public life, the way in which citizens do, or do not, participate in the public sphere. We therefore decided to concentrate our research on how private and public life work in the United States: the extent to which private life either prepares people to take part in the public world or encourages them to find meaning exclusively in the private sphere, and the degree to which public life fulfills our private aspirations or discourages us so much that we withdraw from involvement in it.

•   •   •

THE CRISIS OF CIVIC MEMBERSHIP

The consequences of radical individualism are more strikingly evident today than they were even a decade ago, when *Habits of the Heart* was published. In *Habits* we spoke of commitment, of community, and of citizenship as useful terms to contrast to an alienating individualism. Properly understood, these terms are still valuable for our current understanding. But today we think the phrase "civic membership" brings out something not quite captured by those other terms. While we criticized distorted forms of individualism, we never sought to neglect the central significance of the individual person or failed to sympathize with the difficulties faced by the individual self in our society. "Civic membership" points to that critical intersection of personal identity with social identity. If we face a crisis of civic identity, it is not just a social crisis, it is a personal crisis as well.

One way of characterizing the weakening of the practices of social life and civic engagement that we have called the crisis of civic membership is to speak of declining social capital. Robert Putnam, who has brought the term to public attention recently, defines social capital as follows: "By analogy with notions of physical capital and human capital—tools and training that enhance individual productivity—'social capital' refers to features of social organization, such as networks, norms, and trust, that facilitate coordination and cooperation for mutual benefits." There are a number of possible indices of social capital; the two that Putnam has used most extensively are associational membership and public trust.

Putnam has chosen a stunning image as the title of a recent article: "Bowling Alone: America's Declining Social Capital." He reports that between 1980 and 1993 the total number of bowlers in America increased by 10 percent, while league bowling decreased by 40 percent. Nor, he points out, is this a trivial example: nearly 80 million Americans went bowling at least once in 1993, nearly a third more than voted in the 1994 congressional elections and roughly the same as claim to attend church regularly. But Putnam uses bowling only as a symbol for the decline of American associational life, the vigor of which has been seen as the heart of our civic culture ever since Tocqueville visited the U.S. in the 1830s.

In the 1970s dramatic declines in membership began to hit organizations typically associated with women, such as the PTA and the League of Women Voters, in what has often been explained as the result of the massive entry of women into the workforce. In the 1980s falling membership struck traditionally male associations, such as the Lions, Elks, Masons, and Shriners, as well. Union membership has dropped by half since its peak in the middle 1950s. We all know of the continuing decline in the numbers of eligible voters who actually go the polls, but Putnam reminds us that the number of Americans who answer yes when asked whether they have attended a public meeting on town or school affairs in the last year has fallen by more than a third since 1973.

Almost the only groups that are growing are the support groups, such as twelve-step groups, that Robert Wuthnow has recently studied. These groups make minimal demands on their members and are oriented primarily to the needs of individuals: indeed, Wuthnow has characterized them as involving individuals who "focus on themselves in the presence of others," what we might call being alone together. Putnam argues that paper membership groups, such as the AARP (American Association of Retired Persons), which has grown to gargantuan proportions, have few or no civic consequences, because their members may have common interests but they have no meaningful interactions. Putnam also worries that the Internet, the electronic town meeting, and other much ballyhooed new technological devices are probably civically vacuous, because they do not sustain civic engagement. Talk radio, for instance, mobilizes private opinion, not public opinion, and trades on anxiety, anger, and distrust, all of which are deadly to civic culture. The one sphere that seems to be resisting the general trend is religion. Religious membership and church attendance have remained fairly constant after the decline from the religious boom of the

1950s, although membership in church-related groups has declined by about one-sixth since the 1960s.

What goes together with the decline of associational involvement is the decline of public trust. We are not surprised to hear that the proportion of Americans who reply that they trust the government in Washington only some of the time or almost never has risen steadily, from 30 percent in 1966 to 75 percent in 1992. But are we prepared to hear that the proportion of Americans who say that most people can be trusted fell by more than a third between 1960, when 58 percent chose that alternative, and 1993, when only 37 percent did?

The argument for decline in social capital is not one that we made in *Habits of the Heart*. *Habits* was essentially a cultural analysis, more about language than about behavior. We worried that the language of individualism might undermine civic commitment, but we pointed to the historically high levels of associational membership in America and the relative strength of such memberships here compared with those in other advanced industrial nations. Whether there has really been such a decline is still controversial, but we are inclined to believe that tendencies that were not yet entirely clear in the early 1980s when *Habits* was written are now discernible and disconcerting.

We believe that the culture and language of individualism influence these trends but that there are also structural reasons for them, many of which stem from changes in the economy we have already mentioned. The decline in social capital is evident in different ways in different classes. For example, the decline in civic engagement in the overclass is indicated by their withdrawal into gated, guarded communities. It is also related to the constant movement of companies in the process of mergers and breakups. Rosabeth Kanter has recently suggested some of the consequences of this movement:

For communities as well as employees this constant shuffling of company identities is confusing and its effects profound. Cities and towns rely on the private sector to augment public services and support community causes. There is a strong "headquarters bias" in this giving: companies based in a city tend to do more for it, contributing $75,000 a year on average more to the local United Way, than companies of similar size with headquarters elsewhere.

Kanter points out that the departure of a corporate headquarters from a middle-sized city can tear holes in the social fabric of that city. Not only are thousands of jobs lost but so is the civic leadership of the corporate executives. Local charities lose not only money but board members.

Corporate volatility can lead to a kind of placelessness at the top of the pyramid: "Cut loose from society the rich man can play his chosen role free of guilt and responsibility," observes Michael Lewis. "He becomes that great figure of American mythology—the roaming frontiersman. These days the man who has made a fortune is likely to spend more on his means of transportation than on his home: the private jet is the possession that most distinguishes him from the rest of us. . . . The old aristocratic conceit of place has given way to glorious placelessness." The mansions of the old rich were certainly expressions of conspicuous consumption, but they also encouraged a sense of responsibility for a particular place (city, state, region) where they were located. Wendell Berry has spoken of "itinerant professional vandals," who are perhaps not too different from Reich's "symbolic analysts," attached to no place at all and thus tempted to act more like an oligarchy than an establishment.

Moving to the opposite end of the income spectrum, Lee Rainwater, in his classic book *What Money Buys*, shows that poverty—income insufficient to maintain an acceptable level of living—operates to deprive the poor not only of material capital but of social capital as well. In traditional hierarchical societies, low levels of material well-being can be associated with established statuses that confer the benefits of clientship. In our kind of society, with its fundamentally egalitarian ideology and its emphasis on individual self-reliance, status—even personal identity—of those not-so-distant ancestors was one of vulnerable subordination, of being kicked around by people who told them what to do. Owning one's own home, taking vacations wherever one wants, being free to decide whom to see or what to buy once one has left the workplace— these are all freedoms that are especially cherished by those whose ancestors have never had them. The modest suburb is not the open frontier but it is, under the circumstances, a reasonable facsimile thereof.

Among the many ironies in the lives of at least a significant number of these middle Americans, however, is that labor union membership had much to do with their attainment of relative affluence and its attendant independence; yet for many of them the labor union has become one more alien institution from which they would like to be free. Middle Americans not only are suspicious of government, according to Gans, they don't like organizations of any kind. Relative to the upper middle class (the lower echelons of what we have been calling the overclass), they are not joiners, belonging to only one or two associations at the most, the commonest being a church. While continuing to identify strongly with the nation, they are increasingly suspicious of politics, which they find confusing and dismaying. Their political participation declines steadily.

As a consequence of tendencies that Gans is probably right in asking us to understand, middle Americans are today losing the social capital that allowed them to attain their valued independence in the first place. Above all this is true of the decline of the labor movement. This decline stems from legislative changes in the last twenty years that have deprived unions of much of their power and influence, and from congressional refusal since 1991 to raise the minimum wage from $4.25 an hour. But, as we see in France and other European countries, where loyalty to labor unions has survived, such attacks can be turned back. In America, union meetings, even where there are unions, are attended by 5 percent of the members at most. Lacking the social capital that union membership would provide, anxious-class Americans are vulnerable in new ways to the arbitrary domination they thought they had escaped. One may lose even one's home and one's recreational vehicle if one's job is downsized and the only alternative employment is at the minimum wage.

The decline of social capital in America becomes particularly distressing if we consider what has happened to our political participation. In *Voice and Equality* Sydney Verba and his colleagues have recently given us a comprehensive review of political participation in the United States. Although the data concerning trends over time are not unambiguous, they do indicate certain tendencies. During the last thirty years the average level of education of the American public has risen steadily, but the level of political participation, which is usually associated with education, has not. This fact can be taken as an indication that, controlling for education, political participation has declined. Even more significant is the nature of the changes. Political party identification and membership have declined, while campaign contributions and writing to congresspersons have increased. Both of these growing kinds of activities normally take place in the privacy of one's home as one writes a check or a letter. Verba and his associates note that neither generates the personal satisfactions associated with more social forms of political participation.

Further, making monetary contributions correlates highly with income and is the most unequal form of participation in our society. The increasing salience of monetary contributions as a form of political participation, as well as the general tendency for political participation to correlate with income, education, and occupation, leads to the summary conclusion of *Voice and Equality:*

Meaningful democratic participation requires that the voices of citizens in politics be clear, loud, and equal: clear so that public officials know what citizens want and need, loud so that officials have an incentive to pay attention to what they hear, and equal so that the democratic ideal of equal responsiveness to the preferences and interests of all is not violated. Our analysis of voluntary activity in American politics suggests that the public's voice is often loud, sometimes clear, but rarely equal.

Although unequal levels of education, occupation, and income favor the originally advantaged in securing the resources for political participation, there is one significant exception. Verba and his associates note that:

[o]nly religious institutions provide a counterbalance to this cumulative resource process. They play an unusual role in the American participatory system by providing opportunities for the development of civic skills to those who would otherwise be resource-poor. It is commonplace to ascribe the special character of American politics to the weakness of unions and the absence of class-based political parties that can mobilize the disadvantaged—in particular, the working class—to political activity. Another way that American society is exceptional is in how often Americans go to church—with the result that the mobilizing function often performed elsewhere by unions and labor or social democratic parties is more likely to be performed by religious institutions.

To summarize the relationship of the decline of social capital to political participation we might consider how this relationship works out in the several social classes. Overall, with the exception of the activities centered in religious institutions, political participation has shifted away from those forms that require civic engagement to those that are essentially private, and above all to that of making monetary contributions. The unequal voice to which Verba and his associates point is an indication that the anxious class is seriously under-represented and the underclass scarcely represented at all. Even in the overclass, participation has shifted from more active forms of engagement to the more isolated forms of check- and letter-writing. Finally, Verba and his associates point out that the increasing importance of money in political life contributes to public cynicism: "In short, a participatory system in which money plays a more prominent role is one unlikely to leave either activists or the citizenry at large feeling better about politics."

INDIVIDUALISM AND THE AMERICAN CRISIS

Most Americans agree that things are seriously amiss in our society—that we are not, as the poll questions often put it, "headed in the right direction"—but they differ over why this is so and what should be done about it. We have sought for answers in the structural problems that we have described under the rubrics of the crisis in civic membership and the decline of social capital. What are some of the other explanations? Perhaps the most widespread alternative explanation locates the source of our problems in a crisis of the family. The cry that what our society most needs is "family values" is not one to be dismissed lightly. Almost all the tendencies we have been describing threaten family life and are often experienced most acutely within the family. Being unemployed and thus unable to get married or not having enough income to support an existing family due to downsizing or part-timing, along with the tensions caused by these conditions, can certainly be understood as family crisis. But why is the crisis expressed as a failure of family values?

It is unlikely that we will understand what is going on here unless we once again take into account the culture of individualism. If we see unemployment or reduced income because of downsizing as a purely individual problem rather than a structural problem of the economy, then we will seek to understand what is wrong with the unemployed or underemployed individual. If we also discern that such individuals are prone to have children out of wedlock, to divorce, or to fail to make child support payments, we may conclude that the cause is weakened family values. In *Habits of the Heart* we strongly affirmed the value of the family, and in both *Habits* and *The Good Society* we argued for renewed commitment to marriage and family responsibilities. But to imagine that problems arising from failures rooted in the structure of our economy and polity can primarily be traced to the failings of individuals with inadequate family values seems to us sadly mistaken. It not only increases the level of individual guilt, it also distracts attention from larger failures of collective responsibility.

The link between cultural individualism and the emphasis on family values has a further consequence. Families have traditionally been supported by the paid labor of men. Failure to support one's family may be taken as an indication of inadequate manhood. It is easy to draw the conclusion that if American men would only act like men, then family life would be improved and social problems solved. Some such way of thinking undoubtedly lies behind the movement known as Promise Keepers, as well as the Million Man March of 1995. While we share many of the values of these movements, we are skeptical that increased male responsibility will prove to be an adequate solution to our deep structural economic and political problems or even that it will do more than marginally diminish the severe strains on the American family. The notion that if men would only be men then all would be well in our society seems to us a sad cultural delusion.

Another common alternative explanation of our difficulties is to explain them as the failure of community. This is indeed valid, we believe, but only if our understanding of community is broad and deep enough. In many current usages of the term, however, community means face-to-face groups formed by the voluntary efforts of individuals. Used in this way, failure of community as the source of our problems can be interpreted to mean that if only more people would volunteer to help in soup kitchens or Habitat for Humanity or Meals on Wheels, then our social problems would

be solved. As in the case of family values, *Habits of the Heart* strongly affirms face-to-face communities and the valuable contributions voluntary groups can make to society. But we do not believe that the deep structural problems that we face as a society can be effectively alleviated by an increase in devotion to community in this narrow sense. We would agree that an increase in the voluntary commitments of individuals can over the long haul increase our social capital and thus add to the resources we can bring to bear on our problems. But to get at the roots of our problems these resources must be used to overcome institutional difficulties that cannot be directly addressed by voluntary action alone.

We see another difficulty in emphasizing a small-scale and voluntaristic understanding of community as the solution to our problems. As we noted in discussing the work of Verba and his colleagues, voluntary activity tends to correlate with income, education, and occupation. "Joiners" are more apt to be found in the overclass than in the underclass or the anxious class, again with the significant exception of religious groups. This means that voluntary activities are less often designed to help the most deprived, though we don't want to overlook those that are, than to serve the interests of the affluent. This is particularly true of political voluntarism, as Verba and his associates have shown conclusively. Thus, dismantling structures of public provision for the most deprived in hopes that the voluntary sector will take over is misguided in three important respects. First, the voluntary sector has by no means the resources to take up the slack, as churches, charities, and foundations have been pointing out repeatedly in recent years. The second reason is that our more affluent citizens may feel they have fulfilled their obligation to society by giving time and money to "making a difference" through voluntary activity without taking into account that they have hardly made a dent in the real problems faced by most Americans. The third reason is that, as we noted, the voluntary sector is disproportionately run by our better-off citizens and a good many voluntary activities do more to protect the well-to-do than the needy.

There is another sense of community that also presents difficulties if we think the solution to our problems lies in reviving community, and that is the notion of community as neighborhood or locality. *Habits of the Heart* encourages strong neighborhoods and supports civic engagement in towns and cities. But residential segregation is a fact of life in contemporary America. Even leaving aside the hypersegregation of urban ghettos, segregation by class arising from differential housing costs is becoming increasingly evident in suburban America. Thus it is quite possible that in "getting involved" with one's neighborhood or even with one's suburban town one will never meet someone of a different race or class. One will not be exposed to the realities of life for people in circumstances different from one's own. One may even succumb to the natural human temptation to think that people who are different, particularly those lower in social status, are inferior. The anxious class does not want itself to be confused with the underclass. One of the least pleasant characteristics of the overclass, including its lower echelons in the educated upper middle class, is that they do not want to associate with middle Americans, with "Joe Six-Pack" and others who lack the proper cultural attributes. Even in the underclass, those who are not on welfare look down on those who are, and those who are on the dole briefly look down on those on it for a long time. Under such circumstances an exclusive emphasis on neighborhood solidarity could actually contribute to larger social problems rather than solving them.

What the explanations of our social problems that stress the failure of family values or the failure of community have in common is the notion that our problems are individual or in only a narrow sense social (that is, involving family and local community), rather than economic, political, and cultural. A related feature that these common explanations of our troubles share is

hostility to the role of government or the state. If we can take care of ourselves, perhaps with a little help from our friends and family, who needs the state? Indeed, the state is often viewed as an interfering father who won't recognize that his children have grown up and don't need him anymore. He can't help solve our problems because it is in large measure he who created them.

In contrast, the market, in this mindset, seems benign, a mostly neutral theater for competition in which achievement is rewarded and incompetence punished. Some awareness exists, however, that markets are not neutral, that some people and organizations have enormous economic power and are capable of making decisions that adversely affect many citizens. From this point of view big business joins big government as the source of problems rather than their solution. Still, in America more than in most comparable societies, people are inclined to think that the market is fairer than the state.

INDIVIDUALISM AND NEOCAPITALISM

The culture of individualism, then, has made no small contribution to the rise of the ideology we called neocapitalism in chapter 10 of *Habits*. There we drew a picture of the American political situation that has turned out not to be entirely adequate. We suggested that the impasse between welfare liberalism and its counter-movement, neocapitalism, was coming to an end and that two alternatives, the administered society and economic democracy, were looming on the scene. As it turned out, this incipient pair of alternatives did not materialize, or at least they are enduring a long wait. Instead, neocapitalism has grown ever stronger ideologically and politically. Criticism of "big government" and "tax-and-spend liberalism" has mounted even as particular constituencies, which in the aggregate include most citizens, favor those forms of public provision that benefit them in particular, while opposing benefits they do not receive.

We do not believe we were wrong in seeing ten years ago the severe strains that the neocapitalist formula was creating for the nation. Today those strains are more obvious than ever. But we clearly underestimated the ideological fervor that the neocapitalist position was able to tap—ironically for us, because so much of that fervor derives from the very source we focused on in our book: individualism. The neocapitalist vision is viable only to the degree to which it can be seen as an expression—even a moral expression—of our dominant ideological individualism, with its compulsive stress on independence, its contempt for weakness, and its adulation of success.

DISCUSSION QUESTIONS

1. Bellah and his coauthors contend that the ideology of individualism—the foundation of our political beliefs—may well have grown "cancerous." Explain this disease in our belief system. Do you agree that this may be a serious problem today?

2. What is "social capital" and how does its depletion contribute to the "crisis of civic membership"?

3. Why do authors believe that explanations of our social problems that stress the failure of family values or the failure of community are inadequate?

7

POWER OF MAJORITY OPINION IN AMERICA OVER THOUGHT

"Habits of the heart" is a phrase taken from Alexis de Tocqueville, the Frenchman whose 1835 classic Democracy in America *reflects on his observations in the U.S. during the Jacksonian period. While he was generally enthusiastic about American democracy, Tocqueville was troubled by several dimensions of our public life. In this selection he argues that there is little true freedom of thought in America, despite the existence of liberal democratic principles and institutions. During Tocqueville's time, public discussion took place within narrow limits established by the majority, and those who moved beyond its bounds could expect to be ignored and ostracized. Tocqueville draws an important distinction between control over people exercised by autocratic rulers who use brute force and the subtler techniques of control he saw in operation in America. Are Tocqueville's explorations of American culture antiquated, or are his observations about thought control relevant today?*

It is in the examination of the exercise of thought in the United States that we clearly perceive how far the power of the majority surpasses all the powers with which we are acquainted in Europe. Thought is an invisible and subtle power that mocks all the efforts of tyranny. At the present time the most absolute monarchs in Europe cannot prevent certain opinions hostile to their authority from circulating in secret through their dominions and even in their courts. It is not so in America; as long as the majority is still undecided, discussion is carried on; but as soon as its decision is irrevocably pronounced, everyone is silent, and the friends as well as the opponents of the measure unite in assenting to its propriety. The reason for this is perfectly clear: no monarch is so absolute as to combine all the powers of society in his own hands and to conquer all opposition,

Source: Alexis de Tocqueville, *Democracy in America,* New York: Random House/Vintage Books, 1945, pp. 273–277.

as a majority is able to do, which has the right both of making and of executing the laws.

The authority of a king is physical and controls the actions of men without subduing their will. But the majority possesses a power that is physical and moral at the same time, which acts upon the will as much as upon the actions and represses not only all contest, but all controversy.

I know of no country in which there is so little independence of mind and real freedom of discussion as in America. In any constitutional state in Europe every sort of religious and political theory may be freely preached and disseminated; for there is no country in Europe so subdued by any single authority as not to protect the man who raises his voice in the cause of truth from the consequences of his hardihood. If he is unfortunate enough to live under an absolute government, the people are often on his side; if he inhabits a free country, he can, if necessary, find a shelter behind the throne. The aristocratic part of society supports him in some countries, and the democracy in others. But in a nation where democratic institutions exist, organized like those of the United States, there is but one authority, one element of strength and success, with nothing beyond it.

In America the majority raises formidable barriers around the liberty of opinion; within these barriers an author may write what he pleases, but woe to him if he goes beyond them. Not that he is in danger of an auto-da-fé, but he is exposed to continued obloquy and persecution. His political career is closed forever, since he has offended the only authority that is able to open it. Every sort of compensation, even that of celebrity, is refused to him. Before making public his opinions he thought he had sympathizers; now it seems to him that he has none any more since he has revealed himself to everyone; then those who blame him criticize loudly and those who think as he does keep quiet and move away without courage. He yields at length, overcome by the daily effort which he has to make, and subsides into silence, as if he felt remorse for having spoken the truth.

Fetters and headsmen were the coarse instruments that tyranny formerly employed; but the civilization of our age has perfected despotism itself, though it seemed to have nothing to learn. Monarchs had, so to speak, materialized oppression; the democratic republics of the present day have rendered it as entirely an affair of the mind as the will which it is intended to coerce. Under the absolute sway of one man the body was attacked in order to subdue the soul; but the soul escaped the blows which were directed against it and rose proudly superior. Such is not the course adopted by tyranny in democratic republics; there the body is left free, and the soul is enslaved. The master no longer says: "You shall think as I do or you shall die"; but he says: "You are free to think differently from me and to retain your life, your property, and all that you possess; but you are henceforth a stranger among your people. You may retain your civil rights, but they will be useless to you, for you will never be chosen by your fellow citizens if you solicit their votes; and they will affect to scorn you if you ask for their esteem. You will remain among men, but you will be deprived of the rights of mankind. Your fellow creatures will shun you like an impure being; and even those who believe in your innocence will abandon you, lest they should be shunned in their turn. Go in peace! I have given you your life, but it is an existence worse than death."

Absolute monarchies had dishonored despotism; let us beware lest democratic republics should reinstate it and render it less odious and degrading in the eyes of the many by making it still more onerous to the few.

Works have been published in the proudest nations of the Old World expressly intended to censure the vices and the follies of the times: Labruyère inhabited the palace of Louis XIV when he composed his chapter upon the Great, and Molière criticized the courtiers in the plays that were acted before the court. But the ruling power in the U.S. is not to be made game of. The smallest reproach irritates its sensibility, and the slightest joke that has any foundation in truth renders it indignant; from the forms of its language up to the solid virtues of its character, everything must be made the subject of encomium. No writer, whatever be his eminence, can escape paying this tribute of adulation to his fellow citizens. The majority lives in the perpetual utterance of self-applause, and there are certain truths which the Americans can learn only from strangers or from experience.

If America has not as yet had any great writers, the reason is given in these facts; there can be no literary genius without freedom of opinion, and freedom of opinion does not exist in America. The Inquisition has never been able to prevent a vast number of anti-religious books from circulating in Spain. The empire of the majority succeeds much better in the United States, since it actually removes any wish to publish them. Unbelievers are to be met with in America, but there is no public organ of infidelity. Attempts have been made by some governments to protect morality by prohibiting licentious books. In the U.S. no one is punished for this sort of books, but no one is induced to write them; not because all the citizens are immaculate in conduct, but because the majority of the community is decent and orderly.

In this case the use of the power is unquestionably good; and I am discussing the nature of the power itself. This irresistible authority is a constant fact, and its judicious exercise is only an accident. . . .

.   .   .

The tendencies that I have just mentioned are as yet but slightly perceptible in political society, but they already exercise an unfavorable influence upon the national character of the Americans. I attribute the small number of distinguished men in political life to the ever increasing despotism of the majority in the United States.

When the American Revolution broke out, they arose in great numbers; for public opinion then served, not to tyrannize over, but to direct the exertions of individuals. Those celebrated men, sharing the agitation of mind common at that period, had a grandeur peculiar to themselves, which was reflected back upon the nation, but was by no means borrowed from it.

In absolute governments the great nobles who are nearest to the throne flatter the passions of the sovereign and voluntarily truckle to his caprices. But the mass of the nation does not degrade itself by servitude; it often submits from weakness, from habit, or from ignorance, and sometimes from loyalty. Some nations have been known to sacrifice their own desires to those of the sovereign with pleasure and pride, thus exhibiting a sort of independence of mind in the very act of submission. These nations are miserable, but they are not degraded. There is a great difference between doing what one does not approve, and feigning to approve what one does; the one is the weakness of a feeble person, the other befits the temper of a lackey.

In free countries, where everyone is more or less called upon to give his opinion on affairs of state, in democratic republics, where public life is incessantly mingled with domestic affairs, where the sovereign authority is accessible on every side, and where its attention can always be attracted by vociferation, more persons are to be met with who speculate upon its weaknesses and live upon ministering to its passions than in absolute monarchies. Not because men are naturally worse in these states than elsewhere, but the temptation is stronger and at the same time of easier access. The result is a more extensive debasement of character.

Democratic republics extend the practice of currying favor with the many and introduce it into all classes at once; this is the most serious reproach that can be addressed to them. This is especially true in democratic states organized like the American republics, where the power of the majority is so absolute and irresistible that one must give up one's rights as a citizen and almost abjure one's qualities as a man if one intends to stray from the track which it prescribes.

In that immense crowd which throngs the avenues to power in the United States, I found very few men who displayed that manly candor and masculine independence of opinion which frequently distinguished the Americans in former times, and which constitutes the leading feature in distinguished characters wherever they may be found. It seems at first sight as if all the minds of the Americans were formed upon one model, so accurately do they follow the same route. A stranger does, indeed, sometimes meet with Americans who dissent from the rigor of these formulas, with men who deplore the defects of the laws, the mutability and the ignorance of democracy, who even go so far as to observe the evil tendencies that impair the national character, and to point out such remedies as it might be possible to apply; but no one is there to hear them except yourself, and you, to whom these secret reflections are confided, are a stranger and a bird of passage. They are very ready to communicate truths which are useless to you, but they hold a different language in public.

DISCUSSION QUESTIONS

1. Tocqueville said, "I know of no country in which there is so little independence of mind and real freedom of discussion in America." Why might such observations be made, and to what extent are they true?

2. In what manner does Tocqueville argue that the rule of the majority thought in America is more tyrannical than the rule of monarchs?

3. According to Tocqueville, what elements of American ideology contribute to narrowing the range of debate in American politics?

ROBERT JENSEN

THE GREATEST NATION ON EARTH

Since the terrorist attacks of September 11, 2001, journalism professor and political activist Robert Jensen has been the leading voice in the effort to rethink the notion of patriotism in the United States. His perspective begins with the simple and honest recognition of our place in the world: U.S. citizens are citizens of the empire. His book Citizens of the Empire *lays bare the reality of global empire that underlies the pursuit of U.S. foreign policy regardless of which party occupies the White House, and regardless of the flowery principles offered in the name of justifying the exercise of power. The following selection addresses one of the three key political slogans that frame public discussion of the U.S. role in the world—the common invocation that the United States is the greatest nation on earth. Jensen contends that while this rhetorical principle permeates our political discourse, and appears as an unassailable truth because of its ubiquity, "any claim to being the greatest nation is depraved and dangerous, especially when made in the empire." He proceeds to unravel the many strands of this assertion of greatness, pointing out with clear examples the moral dangers of such claims. His argument will not be familiar to you and may, in fact, make you angry. Such a reaction underscores the power of ideology and cultural indoctrination that forms the analytic heart of Chapter 2. His call for us to imagine a political world where all people are valued equally presents us with a challenge—a challenge to take our professed values seriously enough to apply them uniformly in a balanced way, for "if we are to be a moral people, everything about the United States, like everything about any country, needs to be examined and assessed." In the post 9-11 world, such questioning is an essential prerequisite for the humility needed to begin the process of building a truly safe world, free from fear and terror. For this task, hollow sloganeering and "patriotic" sound bites will not do. Only a frank assessment of who we are and what we believe in offers the hope that we can move forward along with the rest of humanity.*

Source: Robert Jensen, *Citizens of the Empire: The Struggle To Claim Our Humanity,* San Francisco: City Lights Books, 2004, pp. 1–17.

In any debate, the person who has the power to set the framework and define the terms has an enormous advantage. Part of the struggle for the antiwar movement, and those taking critical positions more generally, is to avoid being trapped in the rhetoric of the dominant culture.

Especially since 9/11, through the wars in Afghanistan and Iraq, there have been three crucial rhetorical frameworks that have been difficult to challenge in public. All of them are related, but each has to be deconstructed separately. First is the assertion that the United States is the greatest nation on earth. Second is the claim that one must support the troops because they defend our freedom. Third is the assumption that patriotism is a positive value. Anyone who challenges any of these in public in the contemporary United States risks being labeled irrelevant, crazy, or both. But all three claims must be challenged if there is to be progressive political change.

My critique does not dictate a single political strategy for dealing with these rhetorical frameworks in public. With different audiences and in different situations, different strategies will be appropriate. But it is crucial to be clear about why these ideas are dangerous. Embedded in each are moral and political assertions and assumptions that have to be resisted, which should make progressive political people cautious about buying into the frameworks at all. I will suggest that it's important not just to criticize the dominant culture's version of each claim but to step back and critique the framework itself.

·   ·   ·

One of the requirements for being a mainstream American politician, Republican or Democrat, is the willingness to repeat constantly the assertion that the United States is "the greatest nation on earth," maybe even "the greatest nation in history." At hearings for the House Select Committee on Homeland Security on July 11, 2002, Texas Republican Dick Armey described the United States as "the greatest, most free nation the world has ever known." California Democrat Nancy Pelosi declared that America is "the greatest country that ever existed on the face of the earth." Even other nations that want to play ball with the United States have caught on. When George W. Bush visited our new favored ally in the Persian Gulf, Qatar, the *Al-Watan* newspaper described it as "A visit by the president of the greatest nation."

I want to offer a different assessment: Any claim to being the greatest nation is depraved and dangerous, especially when made in the empire.

SIGN OF PATHOLOGY

Imagine your child, let's call him Joe, made the declaration, "I am the greatest ten-year-old on earth." If you were a loving parent, interested in helping your child develop into a decent person, what would you say? Let's assume you believe Joe to be a perfectly lovely boy, maybe even gifted in many ways. Would you indulge him in that fantasy? Most of us would not.

Instead, you would explain to Joe that however special he is, he is one of millions of ten-year-olds on the planet at that moment, and that—if there were a measure of greatness that could take into account all relevant attributes and abilities—the odds are against Joe coming out on top. But more important than that, you would explain to Joe that people are a wonderfully complex mix of many characteristics that are valued differently by different people, and that it would be impossible to make any sensible assessment of what makes one person the greatest. Even if you reduced it to a single item—let's say the ability to solve mathematical problems—there's no imaginable way to label one person the greatest. That's why people have so much fun arguing about, for example, who is the greatest hitter in baseball history. There's no way to answer the question definitively, and no one really expects to ever win; the fun is in the arguing.

Now, if Joe makes it to adulthood and continues to claim he is the greatest, we would come to one of two conclusions (assuming he's not saying it just to hype the sales of his book or sell tickets to some event): Either he is mentally unstable or he's an asshole. That is, either he believes it because there's something wrong with him cognitively and/or emotionally, or he believes it because he's an unpleasant person. It's painfully obvious that the best evidence that Joe is not the greatest is his claim to be that, for we can observe that throughout history people who have something in them that we might call "greatness" tend not to proclaim their own superiority.

So, we would want to put the brakes on young Joe's claim to greatness as soon as possible because of what tends to happen to people who believe they are the greatest: They lose perspective and tend to discount the feelings and legitimate claims of others. If I am so great, the reasoning goes, certainly my view of the world must be correct, and others who disagree with me—because they lack my greatness—must simply be wrong. And if they are wrong, well, I'm certainly within my rights as the greatest to make sure things turn out the way that I know (by virtue of my greatness) they should. The ability to force others to accept the decisions of those with greatness depends, of course, on power. If Joe takes positions in society that give him power, heaven help those below him.

All these observations are relevant to national assertions of greatness. Such claims ignore the complexity of societies and life within them. Even societies that do great things can have serious problems. We are all aware that a person with admirable qualities in one realm can have quite tragic flaws in another. The same is true of nations. Constant claims to being the greatest reveal a pathology in the national character. Crucially, that pathology is most dangerous in nations with great economic or military power (which tend to be the ones that most consistently make such claims). That is, the nations that claim to be great are usually the ones that can enforce their greatness through coercion and violence.

Nothing in this argument denies the ways that children or nations sometimes do great things. It is rather the claim to uniqueness in one's greatness that is at issue.

WHAT IS GREATNESS

Let's assume, for the sake of discussion, that determining which nation on earth is the greatest would be a meaningful and useful enterprise. On what criteria would we base the evaluation? And how would the United States stack up? In other words, what is greatness?

We might start with history, where we would observe that the histories of nation-states typically are not pretty. At best, it's a mixed bag. The United States broke away from a colonial power ruled by a monarch, espousing the revolutionary political ideal of democratic rights for citizens. Even though the Founding Fathers' definition of "citizen" was narrow enough to exclude the vast majority of the population, that breakthrough was an inspirational moment in human history. That's why, when declaring an independent Vietnam in 1945, Ho Chi Minh borrowed language from the U.S. Declaration of Independence.

But from the beginning the new American experiment was also bathed in blood. The land base of the new nation was secured by a genocide that was almost successful. Depending on the estimate one uses for the pre-contact population of the continent (the number of people here before Columbus)—12 million is a conservative estimate—the extermination rate was from 95 to 99 percent. That is to say, by the end of the Indian wars at the close of the nineteenth century, the European invaders had successfully eliminated almost the entire indigenous population (or the "merciless Indian Savages" as they are labeled in the Declaration of Independence). Let's call that the first American holocaust.

The second American holocaust was African slavery, a crucial factor in the emergence of the textile industry and the industrial revolution in the United States. Historians still debate the number of Africans who worked as slaves in the New World and the number who died during the process of enslavement in Africa, during the Middle Passage, and in the New World. But it is safe to say that tens of millions of people were rounded up and that as many as half of them died in the process.

Some would say greatness is not perfection but the capacity for critical self-reflection, the ability to correct mistakes, the constant quest for progressive change. If that were the case, then a starting point would be honest acknowledgment of the way in which the land base and wealth of the nation had been acquired, leading to meaningful attempts at reparations for the harm caused along the way. Have the American people taken serious steps in that direction on these two fundamental questions regarding indigenous and African peoples? Is the privilege of running casinos on reservation land a just resolution of the first holocaust? Are the Voting Rights and Civil Rights Acts an adequate solution to the second? Can we see the many gains made on these fronts, yet still come to terms with lingering problems?

And what of the third American holocaust, the building of the American empire in the Third World? What did the nation that finally turned its back on slavery turn to?

—The Spanish-American War and the conquest of the Philippines, at a cost of at least 200,000 Filipino lives.

—The creation of a U.S.-dominated sphere in Central America backed by regular military incursions to make countries safe for U.S. investment, leading to twentieth-century support for local dictatorships that brutalized their populations, at a total cost of hundreds of thousands of dead and whole countries ruined.

—The economic and diplomatic support of French efforts to recolonize Vietnam after World War II and, after the failure of that effort, the U.S. invasion of South Vietnam and devastation of Laos and Cambodia, at a cost of 4 million Southeast Asians dead and a region destabilized.

We could list every immoral and illegal U.S. intervention into other nations, which often had the goal of destroying democratically elected governments, undermining attempts by people to throw off colonial rule, or ensuring that a government would follow orders from Washington. But the point is easily made: Subjecting claims of American greatness to historical review suggests a more complex story. The United States has made important strides in recent decades to shed a brutal racist history and create a fairer society at home, though still falling short of a truly honest accounting and often leaving the most vulnerable in seemingly perpetual poverty. At the same time, U.S. policy abroad has been relentlessly barbaric.

Such an examination would lead to some simple conclusions: The United States was founded on noble principles that it has advanced and, often at the same time, undermined. As the United States has emerged as a world power with imperial ambitions—and we rest now at a place where commentators from all points on the political spectrum use the term "empire" to describe the United States, often in a celebratory fashion—we have much to answer for. Historically, empires are never benevolent, and nothing in history has changed that should lead to the conclusion that the United States will be the first benevolent empire. Unless, of course, one believes that God has a hand in all this.

WHAT'S GOD GOT TO DO WITH IT?

During the 2000 presidential campaign, George W. Bush was trying to recover from his association with the painfully public bigotry of Bob Jones University. On matters of racism, it's impossible—even for politicians—to make claims about America's heroic history. But in remarks at the Simon Wiesenthal Center and the Museum of Tolerance, Bush said, "For all its flaws, I believe our nation is chosen by God and commissioned by history to be the model to the world of justice and inclusion and diversity without division."

This invocation of a direct connection to God and truth—what we might call the "pathology of the anointed"—is a peculiar and particularly dangerous feature of American history and the "greatest nation" claims. The story we tell ourselves goes something like this: Other nations throughout history have acted out of greed and self-interest, seeking territory, wealth, and power. They often did bad things in the world. Then came the United States, touched by God, a shining city on the hill, whose leaders created the first real democracy and went on to be the beacon of freedom for people around the world. Unlike the rest of the world, we act out of a cause nobler than greed; we are both the model of, and the vehicle for, peace, freedom, and democracy in the world.

That is a story that can be believed only in the United States by people sufficiently insulated from the reality of U.S. actions abroad to maintain such illusions. It is tempting to laugh at and dismiss these rhetorical flourishes of pandering politicians, but the commonness of the chosen-by-God assertions—and the lack of outrage or amusement at them—suggests that the claims are taken seriously both by significant segments of the public and the politicians. Just as it has been in the past, the consequences of this pathology of the anointed will be borne not by those chosen by God, but by those against whom God's-chosen decide to take aim.

What stance on these matters would leaders who took seriously their religious tradition take? Scripture, for those who believe it to be an authority, is—as is typical—mixed on these matters. But certainly one plausible reading of that text would lead one not to claims of greatness but of humility. As one of the Old Testament prophets, Micah, put it: "What does the Lord require of you but to do justice, and to love kindness, and to walk humbly with your God?" (Micah 6:8).

In the second presidential debate on October 11, 2000, Bush himself made this point. When asked how he would try to project the United States around the world, Bush used the word "humble" five times:

> It really depends upon how our nation conducts itself in foreign policy. If we're an arrogant nation, they'll resent us, if we're a humble nation but strong, they'll welcome us. And our nation stands alone right now in the world in terms of power, and that's why we've got to be humble and yet project strength in a way that promotes freedom.
>
> We're a freedom-loving nation. And if we're an arrogant nation, they'll view us that way, but if we're a humble nation, they'll respect us.

> I think the United States must be humble and must be proud and confident of our values, but humble in how we treat nations that are figuring out how to chart their own course.

Although all available evidence suggests Bush and his advisers (or any other U.S. president, for that matter) were not serious about pursuing a foreign policy based in humility, his comments were sensible. Humility, it is important to remember, does not mean humiliation; it is a sign of strength, not weakness. It means recognizing that the United States is one nation among many; that the only way to security is to work together democratically with other nations; and that multilateral institutions must be strengthened and we must be willing to accept the decisions of such bodies, even when they go against us.

In other words, the exact opposite of the path that the Bush administration has pursued.

BLAME AMERICA FIRST?

When one points out these kinds of facts and analyses, which tend to get in the way of the "greatest nation" claims, a standard retort is, "Why do you blame America first?" Though it is a nonsensical question, the persistence and resonance of it in the culture requires a response.

First, it should not be controversial that when assessing the effects of actions, one is most clearly morally responsible for one's own actions. Depending on the circumstances, I may have obligations to act to curtail someone else's immoral behavior, but without question I have an obligation to curtail my own immoral behavior. In some circumstances, if someone else's immoral behavior is so egregious that the harm it does to others requires immediate intervention and such intervention is feasible in the real world, then there can be cases in which I have cause to temporarily put on hold an assessment of my own behavior to stop the greater evil. But such cases are rare, and the human tendency to rationalize our own bad behavior should give us pause whenever we claim that the greater good requires us to focus on the mistakes other people make before we tackle our own.

So, in place of the common phrase "judge not and ye shall not be judged," perhaps the rule should be "invite judgment of yourself by others, come to judgment about your behavior, commit to not repeating immoral behavior, repair to the degree possible the damage done by previous immoral acts, and keep an eye on others to help them in the same process."

There is no reason that the same logic that applies to us as individuals should not apply to us collectively as citizens of a nation. From such a vantage point, the emptiness of the accusation that one shouldn't "blame America first" becomes clear. America should be blamed first, if and when America is blameworthy. If the United States has engaged in behavior that cannot be morally justified—such as the invasion of another country to overthrow its legally elected democratic government for the self-interested material gain of some segment of U.S. society—whom else should we blame? Because people often use the term "blame" in a way to redirect accountability (when Johnny blames Joey for breaking the toy, we suspect that Johnny actually had something to do with the accident himself), the phrase is designed to divert people from an honest assessment. A better formulation would be, "Why do you hold America accountable first?" In that case, the obvious answer—we should hold America accountable first when America is responsible—is somewhat easier for a reasonable person to see.

That does raise the question, of course, of who is a reasonable person. We might ask that question about, for example, George H. W. Bush, the father. In 1988, after the U.S. Navy warship *Vincennes* shot down an Iranian commercial airliner in a commercial corridor, killing 290 civilians, the then-vice president said, "I will never apologize for the United States of America. I don't care what the facts are."

Whether the firing was an understandable reaction to the misidentification of the Iranian aircraft (as apologists claim), a deliberate act to send Iran a message about U.S. intentions in the region (as some suspect), or the responsibility primarily of a hyperaggressive, trigger-happy commander (as others argue), Bush's declaration is an extraordinarily blunt admission that he does not adhere to even minimal moral standards. The grotesqueness of the episode was only compounded by the fact that Bush later awarded the ship's commander a Legion of Merit award for "exceptionally meritorious conduct in the performance of outstanding service." We could call it the "blame America never" approach.

THE FACTS MATTER

My position does not lead to a blanket denunciation of the United States, our political institutions, or our culture. I simply put forward the proposition that facts matter. If we are to be moral people, everything about the United States, like everything about any country, needs to be examined and assessed. People often tell me, "You assume that everything about the United States is bad." But, of course, I do not assume that; it would be as absurd as the assumption that everything about the United States is good. After a lecture in which I outlined some of the important advances in the law of free speech in the United States but was also critical of contemporary U.S. foreign policy, someone in the audience asked, "Is there anything about America that you like?" Yes, I said, there is much I like—for example, the advances in the law of free speech that I just spent considerable time describing and celebrating. For some reason, honest assessments of both the successes and failures of the United States are seen as being hypercritical and negative.

The facts do matter, of course. And the "greatest nation on earth" mantra tends to lead us to get the facts wrong. Take the question of foreign aid. One would assume that the greatest nation on earth, which also happens to be the wealthiest nation on the planet with the largest economy, gives generously to nations less fortunate. And, in fact, many Americans do assume that. Unfortunately, it's wrong. Political journalist William Finnegan summarizes the polling data:

Americans always overestimate the amount of foreign aid we give. In recent national polls, people have guessed, on average, that between 15 and 24 percent of the federal budget goes for foreign aid. In reality, it is less than 1 percent. The U.N. has set a foreign-aid goal for the rich countries of .7 percent of gross national product. *A few countries have attained that modest goal, all of them Scandinavian. The U.S. has never come close, indeed, it comes in dead last, consistently, in the yearly totals of rich-country foreign aid as a percentage of GNP.* In 2000, we gave .1 percent. President Bush's dramatic proposal, post-September 11, to increase foreign aid to $15 billion looks rather puny next to the $48 billion increase in this year's $379 billion military budget.

So, on this count, are the Scandinavian nations the greatest on earth? They also seem to have the edge on us in providing health care to their citizens. H ere's the assessment of two prominent U.S. medical researchers:

The absence of universal access in the United States is a global scandal. No other highly industrialized country has so many citizens totally without access to even the most rudimentary health care. Consider these facts: there are almost twice as many people in the U.S. without access to health care than the entire population of Scandinavia where access is a universal right.

One might think that the greatest nation on earth would not leave its most vulnerable citizens without reliable access to health care. There will be, of course, disagreement on how to best achieve that, but it seems not to be a serious goal among the dominant political players in the United States. So, we score higher on legal guarantees of freedom of speech but lower on guarantees of health care compared with other developed countries. Our history and contemporary foreign policy suggest that self-interest and greed usually trump concern for human rights and democracy.

Yet the existence of a democratic process at home—the product of much struggle by the forces interested in progressive change—should leave us with hope that we can change the course of that policy through long-term, dedicated efforts. But to do that, honest reflection on the record is required. And it matters. It really matters. It is one thing for small and powerless nations to have delusions of grandeur; they can't do much damage outside their own borders. It is quite another thing for the nation with the most destructive military capacity in the history of the world—and a demonstrated willingness to use it to achieve self-interested goals—to play the "greatest nation on earth" game. To the degree that the game diminishes people's ability to assess facts, reach honest conclusions, and take moral action based on those conclusions, it increases the risk of people everywhere. It makes it easier for leaders to justify wars of conquest and mask the reasons for those wars. It's easy for a vice president to say, as Dick Cheney did in a speech in 2002:

America is again called by history to use our overwhelming power in defense of our freedom. We've accepted that duty, certain of the justice of our cause and confident of the victory to come. For my part, I'm grateful for the opportunity to work with the president who is making us all proud upholding the cause of freedom and serving the greatest nation on Earth.

DISCUSSION QUESTIONS

1. Discuss the ways in which you've been raised to buy in to the notion that we live in the greatest country in the world. How does this process work? Is it healthy for us as free thinkers?
2. Explain the many dangers that Jensen sees arising from the constant assertion of America's "greatness." How does Jensen respond to potential critics of his thesis?
3. Explain how a person in a foreign country might respond to Jensen's perspective about America's claims of greatness?

Constitutional and State Structures

Few, if any, American documents are worshiped as much as the Constitution. Political leaders across the ideological spectrum pay tribute to the 1787 parchment and its twenty-seven amendments as the bedrock of our political institutions and the sentry of our civil liberties. Not without reason, many Americans see more than 200 years of constitutional government as a unique achievement in the modern world. Former President Ronald Reagan, for his part, discerned in the Founders' creation "a sureness and originality so great that I can't help but perceive the guiding hand of God, the first political system that insisted that power flows from the people to the state, not the other way around." But does the U.S. Constitution deserve such veneration?

Taken together, the articles in this chapter offer an analysis of the U.S. Constitution and the state it helped to establish that challenges this posture of self-congratulation. Familiar features like the separation of powers, checks and balances, and federalism are related to the Framers' concerns about democratic threats to property rights and to their vision of a new political economy energized by men of commerce and finance. These articles suggest that the Constitution has been irrelevant or even an obstacle to democratic advances and that, at the least, we should avoid making the document a patriotic fetish.

9

AMERICAN EXCEPTIONALISM AND THE POLITICS OF FRAGMENTATION

Joshua Cohen and Joel Rogers situate the Constitution within the broader context of the "exceptional" nature of the American state, which lacks the class-based politics that characterizes other advanced capitalist democracies. They argue that the basic structures of our polity, including its constitutional framework, encourage fragmentation among people of ordinary means and raise their costs of collective action. When this pattern becomes entrenched, popular control of public policy is constrained and the inequalities flowing from the economy are difficult to challenge. Students may want to focus on two aspects of Cohen and Rogers's piece. First, locate the six historical factors that, in their view, have contributed to the fragmentation of democratic politics. Second, consider their claim that the "essence of politics is collective action." Doesn't this cut across the grain of our "look out for number one" culture? Perhaps the ideology of liberal individualism, one of the focal points of articles in Chapter 2, is itself a factor that limits meaningful democratic action.

The essence of politics is collective action—different people acting together for the achievement of common aims. There are many conditions for such action—including common interests, an awareness of those interests, a willingness to cooperate with one another, and the ability to sustain the costs of that cooperation.

On all these dimensions and others, the structure of the U.S. political system tends to constrain collective action by people of ordinary means. Most importantly, *American political conflict and bargaining is extremely fragmented.* Instead of bringing people together, the basic structures of American politics tend to keep them separate and divided, while encouraging the pursuit of narrower interests. This division raises the costs of coordination. Its effects are most sharply pronounced among those who have few resources to begin with—that is, among those whose "strength is in numbers," and not in their wallets.

Reflecting these tendencies to fragmentation, ordinary people in the U.S. are among the most politically disorganized in the world. Most strikingly, perhaps, the U.S. is virtually unique among advanced industrial capitalist democracies in never having had a labor party or socialist movement of

Source: Joshua Cohen and Joel Rogers, *Rules of the Game: American Politics and the Central America Movement,* Boston: South End Press, 1986, pp. 4–16.

significant strength and duration. To this day, conventional political debate here is not marked by the sort of class-based cleavages and terms ("workers" versus "capitalists") characteristic of the political systems of Italy, France, Germany, England, and indeed most of [the] advanced industrial world. This peculiar absence of class politics in the U.S.—one instance of the general fragmentation of the U.S. political system—is called "American exceptionalism."

... What generates these conditions in the first place? As might be expected, the answer is that over the course of U.S. history many factors have contributed, and that the importance of particular factors, and their interaction with others, has shifted over the course of U.S. history. Such historical variation and political complexity pose severe problems in providing an adequate rendering of American exceptionalism—problems which, we should emphasize, we do not pretend to solve here. These important complexities aside, however, there are six basic factors which can be identified as having contributed throughout *all* of U.S. history. Reinforcing one another, and given varied political expression, they have always been central to producing, and reproducing, the politics of fragmentation.

CONSTITUTIONAL DESIGN

The basic founding document of the U.S., the Constitution, mandates a fragmented government structure. This has permitted, within a single nation, considerable political experimentation, particularly at the local level, and has helped ensure certain limits on the abuse of centralized powers. But the clear effect of constitutional fragmentation has also been to limit the potential for political cooperation among people of ordinary means, and this was something that the architects of the constitutional system, the "founding fathers," clearly recognized and desired.

In *The Federalist Papers,* for example, James Madison explained that a fragmented system would help cure "the mischiefs of faction," whose

most common source was the distribution of property ownership:

> Those who hold and those who are without property have ever formed distinct interests in society. Those who are creditors, and those who are debtors, fall under a like discrimination. ... The regulation of these various and interfering interests forms the principal task of modern legislation and involves the spirit of party and faction in the necessary and ordinary operations of government.

Madison was particularly concerned that a "majority faction" composed of those owning little property might come together to challenge inequalities in wealth and income. He saw two ways to prevent its formation:

> Either the existence of the same passion or interest in a majority at the same time must be prevented, or the majority, having such coexistent passion or interest, must be rendered, by their number and local situation, unable to concert and carry into effect schemes of oppression.

In the constitutional scheme they eventually agreed upon, Madison and the other framers accordingly sought both to prevent majorities from forming common programs, and to impose barriers to the implementation of those programs, should they be formed. The most straightforward way this was done was by weakening and dividing the American state.

The Constitution, for example, mandates a *separation of powers* at the national level. The legislative, executive, and judicial functions are each assigned to distinct branches of government, and each branch is given powers to block the activities of the other two. While the power of the judiciary to curtail Congressional or Presidential action is great, probably the most important separation and source of blockage is that between executive and legislative authority. In contrast to parliamentary systems of representation, where the leader of the dominant party (or coalition of parties) in the legislature is also the chief executive of government, the U.S. Constitution mandates separate elections for Congress and the Presidency. This has commonly meant that the President comes from a party that does not command a majority within the legislature. Such differences between the executive and the legislature typically generate barriers to concerted national policy—except of course in those cases (foreign affairs being the source of most examples) where "bipartisan consensus" obtains between the major parties.

Additionally limiting the effectiveness of the national government, and limiting the potential for the emergence of majoritarian factions, is the principle of *federalism*. This means that public power is shared between the national government and the states. By contrast with "unified" governments, where subnational units are extensions of a central authority, the United States is a "divided" government, in which the states enjoy powers independent of the Federal government. Competing with the Federal government and one another, the fifty states produce wide variations in policy on basic issues, and reinforce political diversity and division. . . .

Even within national government, moreover, federalism shapes the perspective and interests of Congress. Candidates for Congress are not selected by national parties, but by state and local organizations. Members are then elected by local constituencies, and to stay in Congress they must satisfy the interests of those constituencies. Local interests are thus represented both in state governments and the national legislature. In fact, aside from the Presidency (and even there the case is ambiguous), there is no Federal office or body whose members are selected by exclusively national criteria. As House Speaker Tip O'Neill often points out, in the U.S. "*all* politics is local politics."

One effect of this is to immensely complicate the consideration of national issues, and to introduce yet additional barriers in generating coherent national policies. A closely related effect is the *discouragement* of attempts at such national

coordination, and the *encouragement* of a local or regional orientation in political action. This orientation, in turn, tends to solidify differences and divisions among people located in different places.

GEOGRAPHY AND NATURAL RESOURCES

In comparative terms, the United States has always been an enormous country, larger at its founding than all other countries of the time except Russia, and today, more than 200 years later, still larger than all countries but the Soviet Union, Canada, and China. Early on, the framers recognized that sheer size, like constitutional divisions, would tend to impose barriers to the existence and formation of mischievous majority factions. Rejecting the received wisdom in political theory, *The Federalist Papers* extolled the virtues of a "large commercial republic." Size would encourage a diversity of interests, and that diversity would in turn pose barriers to the existence and coordination of any stable popular majority.

In addition to encouraging diversity, the great size of the land, which for long periods had an open frontier, helped to provide a safety valve for social unrest. Those who did not like it in one place—and were not slaves—could simply leave. The widespread availability of free or very cheap land, moreover, facilitated widespread land *ownership*. This helped confirm Americans' status as a race of independent and free (white) men, and provided a ballast of popular support for a private property regime.

The repeated acquisition of new land helped prolong the period of an open frontier. Even after the rate of acquisition slowed, however, and even after the frontier was closed, the U.S. would also enjoy comparatively low population densities. Combined with the sheer size of the country, the sparse settlement of the land in turn meant that its different inhabitants could afford to operate in relative isolation from one another. This in turn encouraged extremely diverse, and largely uncoordinated, forms of political organization, giving further substance to the constitutional fragmentation of American politics.

Political fragmentation was also encouraged by America's strategic isolation. For most of its history—at least from the peace with Britain that concluded the War of 1812 to the Japanese attack on Pearl Harbor in 1941—the U.S. enjoyed a long unbroken period of strategic isolation, during which thousands of miles of ocean provided a bar to credible attack from abroad. It could thus develop without much concern for the activities of other nations, and could afford the highly decentralized political system that more threatened nations could not.

Finally, in addition to being big and isolated, the U.S. enjoyed (and continues to enjoy) tremendous advantages of climate and natural resources. Even leaving aside the productive activities of men and women, it is truly the richest nation on earth. Virtually all of the country is located in the temperate zone, which is ideal for agriculture and industry. Early settlers found vast deposits of timber and basic minerals, some of the best farmland on earth, apparently limitless water resources for farming and industry, and extended systems of lakes and rivers that eased the flow of trade. Once these resources were taken from their Native American owners, this was an almost perfect setting for economic development, which proceeded quickly.

By providing the basis for a comparatively high standard of living, these natural endowments tended to discourage efforts at collective organization along class lines. Throughout almost all of American history, and even after they had changed from a race of independent farmers to a population of wage and salary workers, ordinary people in the U.S. were paid more, and lived far better, than their counterparts in Western Europe and the rest of the developed world. In this relatively affluent environment, and especially given all the other social and political incentives to seek private gains, the appeal of collective organization was diminished. As the German economist Werner Sombart once overstated the point, "Socialist utopias came to nothing on roast beef and apple pie."

UNEVEN ECONOMIC DEVELOPMENT

The very rapid emergence of the U.S. as a major economic power concealed tremendous differences within the U.S. in the level and scope of economic activity. It was only after the Civil War that capitalism was firmly established as the exclusive mode of economic production in the U.S., and only after World War II, with the industrial development of the South, that it was possible to speak of a truly national industrial economy. This unevenness, combined with the tremendous diversity of American economic activity, encouraged different and competing interests in different regions of the country. An incalculably large part of American politics—from immigration to energy policy—is and always has been concerned with managing these differences.

Like so many other dynamics of American politics, this phenomenon of regional diversity was most dramatically highlighted by the Civil War. In that effort, infant industry and finance in the Northeast and Midwest joined with independent farming interests to crush the plantation South, initiating a period of economic and political subordination that would last well into the twentieth century. The long deflation that followed the war (like most major wars, it had been paid for by printing money) eventually ignited the great agrarian protest movement of the Populists, which drew particular strength from independent farmers in the South, Midwest, and West. But within a generation of the close of the war predominantly Northeastern industrial and financial interests had crushed the Populists as well, and were busy rolling back political organization, and even electoral participation, among the dependent classes.

Such dramatic events aside, and even after the great levelling of regional differences that has occurred over the past forty years, uneven and diverse economic development tends to fragment U.S. politics. Among elites, the enduring vitality of regional splits is evident in phenomena like the "Sagebrush Rebellion," which pits Western business interests against the Northeast in a battle over environmental regulation and Federal land management in the West. Among nonelites, it is evident in the difficulties northern workers have encountered from their southern counterparts in responding to "runaway" shops down South. Regional economic differences continue to slow concerted national responses to problems, and to divide ordinary people with potentially shared interests from one another.

RACISM

The first black slaves were brought to America in the early 1600s. By the time of the Declaration of Independence in 1776, slavery was established in all thirteen colonies. Oppressive relations between whites and blacks in America are as old as the country itself.

The history since is familiar, or should be. Shortly after the Revolution, the "First Emancipation" began in New England, as state after state abolished slavery, or phased it out. The most substantial black populations, however, were located in the South, and this "emancipation" stopped at Virginia. Growing tensions between the slave and non-slave states, which were importantly tensions between a precapitalist plantation economy and the imperatives of free capitalist development, eventually erupted in the Civil War. Ostensibly the war freed the slaves, but with the collapse of "radical" efforts to reconstruct the South in the postwar period, an elaborate system of oppressive and segregationist race relations was soon reestablished.

It would not be until well into the twentieth century—when the combined push of the mechanization of southern agriculture, and the pull of labor-starved northern industry in World War II, brought millions of blacks north—that racism began to be seriously addressed on a national scale. And it would not be until the 1960s, and only then under the pressures of massive protest and civil disobedience, that the major legal components of discrimination would be broken down. The fight over *de facto* discrimination—in housing, education, employment, and other essentials—continues, and blacks and whites in this country continue to live very different sorts of lives.

Volumes have been written on American racism. Suffice it to say here that there is no more persistent form of division in American politics, and none more debilitating to popular democratic politics. In the pre-Civil War period, the small number of "freemen" who trickled North were almost universally excluded from early worker organizations. In the late nineteenth century, each of the great attempts at forging classwide ties in labor failed to confront the race question, giving force to endless employer strategies of "divide and conquer" between antagonistic racial groups. In the twentieth century, at the peak of worker organization immediately after World War II, the failure to press the issue of racial equality by organizing the South defined the limits of labor's national power for a generation, and hastened its decline. And even today, 120 years after the close of the Civil War, racial animosity and fear, and the forms and habits of political association based on them, continue to impede the construction of a truly popular democratic coalition. The racial and ethnic tensions which marked the Rainbow Coalition's effort in 1984 provide ample evidence on this point.

ETHNIC AND RELIGIOUS DIVISIONS

At least until the turn of the twentieth century, the great natural wealth of the U.S., along with its rapid economic development and low population density, produced chronic labor shortages. The solution to this problem was provided by immigrant labor.

Over 1820–1830, only a little over 150,000 immigrants came to the U.S. Three decades later, over 1851–1860, the inflow had risen to 2.6 million. By 1881–1890, as the U.S. entered a peak phase in industrialization, the number doubled to 5.2 million. And at its high point, over 1901–1910, it rose to 8.7 million, or better than 10 percent of the resident population. In today's terms, that would amount to roughly 25 million new workers over the course of the 1980s.

Given all the other constraints on popular action, the fact that the population of the U.S. was comprised of people from diverse cultural backgrounds—while surely one of the appealing features of American society—contributed to the general fragmentation of U.S. politics and the weakness of worker organization within it. Coming to a vast land, with a decentralized political structure, successive waves of immigrants took up residence in communities that were often isolated from one another, and developed political commitments and organizations peculiar to individual locales. The deeply ethnic character of much local American politics—Slavs in the Midwest, Irish in Boston, Jews in New York—can be traced to this experience. The fact that the system was sufficiently porous and diffuse to permit such localized expressions, in turn, tended to consolidate patterns of organizational isolation along ethnic grounds. The myth of the American "melting pot" was only that—a myth. In all sorts of ways, immigrants found that they could preserve ethnic identities in the new land. But the maintenance of these diverse identities also tended to undermine attempts to forge alliances among workers that cut across ethnic differences.

Complementing the barriers of language and custom, and immensely important throughout American politics, were the deep religious splits with which ethnic divisions were commonly associated. In part because Americans never had to struggle for land or political rights against an entrenched church, the U.S. has always been a deeply religious country, and throughout its history religion has often served as an organizing metaphor for political action. Popular support for the Revolutionary War, for example, was fueled by the "First Great Awakening" of Protestant religious fervor; and black churches have long supplied the backbone of struggles for civil rights.

Even more often, however, religious differences have served to undermine or distort popular democratic politics. The arrival of waves of Irish Catholic immigrants in the 1850s, for example, led to the nativist backlash of the "Know Nothing" movement, and helped trigger the realignment of political parties that issued in the modern Republican and Democratic parties. This divided workers along Protestant/Catholic lines, reflected not only in the parties but in all manner of popular organizations. And just as the U.S. was entering the second great phase of industrialization in the late nineteenth century, a tidal wave of new immigrants from southern and eastern Europe introduced yet additional divisions into emergent worker organizations. Ably exploited by employers, ethnic and religious cleavages repeatedly wrecked efforts at working class solidarity.

STATE REPRESSION

Despite the many structural barriers to their coordination, ordinary Americans have often banded together to attempt to improve their condition. With some rare and notable exceptions, these efforts have met with physical violence, imprisonment, brutally applied court sanctions, or more subtle forms of harassment and intimidation sponsored by the state. Such state repression makes for a long history, coextensive with the history of the United States. It runs roughly from the 1786 suppression of the protests of indebted farmers in Massachusetts (Shays's Rebellion), through the labor injunctions that helped wreck worker organizations in the late nineteenth century, to the Reagan administration's surveillance of Central America activists, and prosecution of church groups offering sanctuary to refugees from U.S. policies in that region.

Over the last 200 years, there have been too many government sponsored shootings, beatings, lynchings, police spies, agents provocateurs, goons, scabs, rigged trials, imprisonments, burglaries, and illegal wiretaps to permit easy summary here. Once again we only note the obvious. By raising the costs of political action to individuals—in money, physical pain, imprisonment, or the destruction of their personal lives—repression makes it less likely that individuals will be willing to engage in collective political activity at all. And this is especially true for those individuals, comprising the most obvious mischievous faction, who can least afford those costs, since they have little "property" or other resources of their own.

Over the course of U.S. history, these six basic factors—constitutional design, geography and natural resources, uneven economic development, racism, ethnic and religious divisions, and state repression—have repeatedly constrained popular democratic action in the U.S. As indicated earlier, appreciating the interaction of these different factors at different times would require discussion of the peculiarities of particular circumstances and periods, and of the ways in which these divisions were themselves institu-tionalized and given political expression. This, again, we cannot do here. What is important to recognize, however, is that these sources of divisions are enduring and ongoing features of U.S. politics, and not merely of historical interest. They operate now, as well as having operated in the past.

DISCUSSION QUESTIONS

1. Cohen and Rogers state that "ordinary people in the United States are among the most politically disorganized in the world." What evidence of this do the authors provide and how does that relate to the issue of "American exceptionalism"?

2. Have the six basic factors contributing to American exceptionalism been equally important in U.S. history? Which are most important today?

KENNETH M. DOLBEARE AND LINDA MEDCALF

THE DARK SIDE OF THE CONSTITUTION

In a wide-ranging essay, written for the constitutional bicentennial in 1987, Kenneth Dolbeare and Linda Medcalf explore what they call the "dark side" of the Constitution, critically examining its meaning and values while relating them to contemporary political ills. Writing in the spirit of historian Charles Beard, whose 1913 book An Economic Interpretation of the Constitution *was a path-breaking critical study, they detail the Framers' concern for the protection of property, placing their fear of democracy in the context of such threatening events as Shays's Rebellion among farmers in western Massachusetts. The Constitution is read in light of the top-down model of political economy espoused by Alexander Hamilton and initially implemented during his tenure as Treasury Secretary in the 1790s. Dolbeare and Medcalf argue that current problems like policy gridlock, low voter turnout, and the general lack of political responsiveness are direct results of the hegemony of Hamiltonian principles in the twentieth century, and outline measures that might help to reverse the de-democratization of American politics.*

The golden glow of the Constitution's bicentennial celebration—already well launched—threatens to blind us all at a time when Americans most need to see clearly. We do not refer to the harmless factual errors and the merely misleading exaggerations that accompany this latest patriotic spectacular. Our national myopia is far more serious. In the midst of institutional paralysis, an urgent but unaddressed policy agenda, and the protracted withdrawal of the American public from "public" affairs, we continue to celebrate the Constitution as an unrivaled political achievement. When we most need

to critically examine our fundamental structures, we embark on a laudatory extravaganza—and do so with full scholarly support.

But, from its inception, there has been a dark side to the United States Constitution that accounts in part for many of the acknowledged ills of contemporary American politics. Low voter turnout, lack of confidence in government, the decline of the political parties, institutional deadlock and indecisiveness, the pervasiveness of protest, frustration, and resentment—all these can be traced to the deliberate anti-democratic design of our founding document and the way it

Source: Kenneth M. Dolbeare and Linda Medcalf, "The Dark Side of the Constitution." *The Case Against the Constitution: From the Antifederalists to the Present,* Kenneth M. Dolbeare and John F. Manley, eds., Armonk, NY: M.E. Sharpe, 1987, pp. 120–124, 126–133, and 136–141.

was completed by Alexander Hamilton's nation-building program.

In effect, the Framers, and Alexander Hamilton in particular, wrought too well. Their chief ambition—a strong and stable political economy insulated from popular control—is now threatened by the consequences of the very methods chosen to achieve that goal 200 years ago.

There is no news in the point that the men of 1787 sought to protect property and contain democracy. They have more than amply testified to this themselves. It is only later celebrants who have sought to make the Framers into "realistic" architects of a neutral political system; the Framers, and their opponents, knew better. But the celebrants have written history, and held office, in a country where democracy became a vital symbol. It became increasingly necessary to change the definition of democracy, in order to fit the reality of the limitations on popular impact that the Framers so artfully designed. Just as the proponents of the Constitution preempted the label "Federalist," turning it into its opposite, the celebrants of the Constitution worked similar magic with the word "democracy."

Alexander Hamilton's vital contributions to the development of a strong central government have been noted often, although by a minority of commentators. The crucial contract clause, several key Federalist essays, ratification in New York, and the various programs on credit, funding, the bank, and manufacturing are all recognized as major contributions to the development of the new nation. However, these are usually seen episodically, as independent events or specific isolated achievements in a context evolving in response to many other initiatives. Few have adequately appreciated Hamilton's grand design in its entirety, understood it as an agenda partially completed by the convention and partially by Hamilton later, or recognized its full realization in our twentieth-century history and contemporary situation. Instead, the utterly unrealized Jeffersonian image, more consistent with our attachment to "democracy," has dominated our national self-conception and our national rhetoric.

Inherent in Hamilton's grand design is a set of political implications with profound importance. He created an intricate central government machine that encouraged and rewarded behavior appropriate to his vision of a national commercial-financial-industrial economy—the entrepreneurial, productive, growth-oriented behavior that was to define our economic, political, and cultural life and identity for centuries. It was our first "industrial policy," incubating capitalism as a crucial by-product.

Hamilton also insulated the machine against the possibility that popular majorities or political chicanery might alter the outcomes he deemed essential to the creation of a great nation. In the process, by building upon the dark side of the Constitution, the Framers' property-protecting provisions and fear of democracy, Hamilton succeeded in almost completely removing the *substance* of public policy from popular hands. We live amidst the consequences today.

In this paper, we first review briefly the Framers' intentions and actions regarding the protection of property, both absolutely and from the interference of popular majorities. We shall see, as have many historians and political scientists before us, that the Framers were both class conscious and thorough in their efforts.

Then we explore Hamilton's grand design, its political implications, and the protection he added to assure that his system would be insulated in multiple ways against popular impact. Hamilton wove a web that deliberately deflected popular preferences away from the most sensitive and crucial areas of public policy—financial affairs, and the nature and distribution of wealth in the country. More specifically, he developed major expansive constitutional doctrines and set up the power of judicial review. One of the most important and intended results was the ensuing heavy reliance upon the law and the courts as decision makers, and a governing role for the legal profession. This erected an ostensibly neutral and objective shield that first obscured what was happening and then made it seem natural and inevitable.

Finally, we show how this system, in its twentieth-century maturity, has come to threaten the very political stability and productive national economy that were the Framers' and Hamilton's goals. What the more knowingly purposeful defenders of this system did when faced with the inescapable prospect of popular participation was *first* to build a maze of multiple limits on the effects of that participation, and *second,* to remove the substance of key policies into another, more remote, decision-making system. What its subsequent defenders have done is to triumphantly label the result "democracy."

Ironically, the great republican experiment has been converted into something like what the Framers feared almost as much as democracy— an absolutist monarchy complete with ongoing baronial struggles for court power and privilege, subject only to the occasional disturbance of crowds running in the streets. In the discouraging character and prospects of our contemporary politics, therefore, we have not experienced the *perversion* of the Framers' intent so much as we have seen the *fulfillment* of the dark side of the Constitution.

I. THE FRAMERS' CONSTITUTION

The Framers' Attitudes

As is well known, only a few of the delegates to the convention of 1787 were distinguished by concern for the rights and goals of popular majorities. Most of these dropped out or ended up among the Antifederalists in opposition to ratification. The general attitude of the main body of Framers can be summarized in the phrase "too much democracy." As James Madison put it in *Federalist No. 10:*

> Complaints are everywhere heard from our most considerate and virtuous citizens, equally the friends of public and private faith and of public and personal liberty, that our governments are too unstable, that the public good is disregarded in the conflicts of rival parties, and that measures are too

often decided, not according to the rules of justice and the rights of the minor party, but by the superior force of an interested and overbearing majority.

Or, as Hamilton wrote in *Federalist No. 15:* "There are material imperfections in our national system and . . . something is necessary to be done to rescue us from impending anarchy."

Concerns focused on "a rage for paper money, for an abolition of debts, for an equal division of property, or for any other improper or wicked project." All these improper projects and unjust legislation, of course, sprang from the state legislatures, where "men of more humble, more rural origins, less educated, and with more parochial interests" held sway. Even Jefferson could not support such an excess: "173 despots would surely be as oppressive as one," he wrote. "An *elective despotism* was not the government we fought for." Shays's Rebellion was much on the delegates' minds, and for many, provided the final straw. As Gordon Wood points out:

> Finally, when even Massachusetts with its supposedly model constitution [one of the less democratic of the states] experienced popular excesses, including Shays' Rebellion and the subsequent legislative "tyranny" of Shaysite sympathizers, many leaders were ready to shift the arena of constitutional change from the states to the nation.

The Framers' contemporaries were well aware of the backgrounds and biases of those who drafted our founding document. The Antifederalist writings of the period are full of accusations on this count. According to Jackson Turner Main, "the criticism that the Constitution favored the few at the expense of the many was almost universal." In the words of one prominent Antifederalist: "It changes, totally changes, the form of your present government. From a well-digested, well-formed democratic, you are at once rushing into an aristocratic government." The late Herbert Storing, who collected and edited the Antifederalist writings, called this "the underlying theme of a vast quantity of the specific criticism by the Anti-Federalists of the proposed Constitution."

"The Federal Farmer," a prominent opponent of the Constitution, argued that the state conventions should revise and amend the proposed Constitution as needed, before ratification. Otherwise, the liberty of free men will be lost to those who "avariciously grasp at all power and property." An aristocratic group had

> taken the political field, and with its fashionable dependents, and the tongue and the pen, is endeavouring to establish in great haste, a politer kind of government. . . . The fact is, these aristocrats support and hasten the adoption of the proposed constitution, merely because they think it is a stepping stone to their favorite object. I think I am well founded in this idea; I think the general politics of these men support it, as well as the common observation among them.

In addition, the Federal Farmer asserted,

> This system promises a large field of employment to military gentlemen, and gentlemen of the law; and . . . it will afford security to creditors, to the clergy, salarymen and others depending on money payments.
>
> [Once] power is transferred from the many to the few, all changes become extremely difficult; the government, in this case, being beneficial to the few, they will be exceedingly artful and adroit in preventing any measures which may lead to a change.

"Centinel," in his letters in opposition, was even more forceful, terming the effort to foist the Constitution on unsuspecting citizens "a most daring attempt to establish a despotic aristocracy among freemen, that the world has ever witnessed." He added:

> From this investigation into the organization of this government, it appears that it is devoid of all responsibility or accountability to the great body of the people, and that so

far from being a regular balanced government, it would be in practice a *permanent ARISTOCRACY.*

The Lure of the New Economy

As early as 1785, Hamilton and others had more in mind than merely the containment of democracy. They began to envision a new kind of commercial economy that would replace production for one's own use with production for sale elsewhere. Trade, transportation, and accompanying financial opportunities would be vastly expanded on a national scale. Eventually, such a national market and exchange system would penetrate parochial communities and replace the almost subsistence-level agricultural economies characteristic of all but the seacoast towns and cosmopolitan centers of the time.

But there would be no national commercial economy unless the Articles of Confederation could be replaced by some more powerful central government. That central government would not only put the brakes on the pernicious projects of the local majorities, but would protect the "property"—the contracts, bonds, paper, credit, etc.—essential to a commercial economy. Such a government would defend the hard money that made for a sound economy, promote the national market through uniform laws and otherwise overcome state protectionism, use import regulations both for taxes and to protect American goods against British competition, and establish sound credit in the international commercial community.

There were two prospective opponents whose interests would be directly damaged by such a new government. One was the mass of heavily indebted back-country farmers still stirred by the Revolutionary dream of equality and individual rights. The other was the state legislatures whose support the farmers sought in their struggle against their creditors and others of the "better people," and which would have had ample institutional reasons to be opposed to any strengthening of the center. An adequate new government would have to control both these threats.

The public campaign for the new government began with the call to the Annapolis Convention in 1786, though its origins are visible much earlier in the correspondence and speeches of advocates. A rather full reform proposal came from Hamilton as early as September 3, 1780, in his letter to James Duane, in which he stated that "The first step must be to give Congress powers competent to the public exigencies." In its call for the Annapolis Convention, the Virginia Legislature was more specific:

> To take into consideration the *trade* and *commerce* of the United States; to consider how far an uniform system, in their commercial intercourse and regulations, might be necessary to their common interest and permanent harmony, and to report to the several States such an act relative to this great object, as when unanimously ratified by them, would enable the United States, in Congress assembled, effectually to provide for the same.

As is well known, the Annapolis Convention was attended by only twelve delegates from five states. Among them was Alexander Hamilton, who seized the opportunity to issue the call for the constitutional convention, as follows:

> Your Commissioners cannot forbear to indulge an expression of their earnest and unanimous wish, that speedy measures may be taken, to effect a general meeting of the States, in a future Convention, for the same and such other purposes, as the situation of public affairs, may be found to require. . . .
>
> In this persuasion your Commissioners submit an opinion, that the Idea of extending the powers of their Deputies, to other objects, than those of Commerce . . . will deserve to be incorporated into that of a future Convention. . . .
>
> That there are important defects in the system of the Federal Government is acknowledged by the Acts of all those States, which have concurred in the present Meeting; That the defects, upon a closer examination, may be found greater and more numerous, than even these acts imply, is at least so far probable . . . as may reasonably be supposed to merit a deliberate and candid discussion. . . .
>
> Your Commissioners . . . beg leave to suggest their unanimous conviction, that it may essentially tend to advance the interests of the union, if the States, by whom they have been respectively delegated, would themselves concur, and use their endeavours to procure the concurrence of the other States, in the appointment of Commissioners, to meet at Philadelphia on the second Monday in May next, to take into consideration the situation of the United States, to devise such further provisions as shall appear to them necessary to render the constitution of the Federal Government adequate to the exigencies of the Union. . . .

Shays's Rebellion, that heroic and desperate act by a handful of farmers, is surely the dominant symbol of the period and in many ways the real source of the Constitution. It was the frightening, triggering event that caused a particular selection of delegates to be appointed by their legislatures, induced them to spend a hot summer at an uncertain task in Philadelphia, and provided the context for their work and its later reception. For Hamilton and his cause, it was a godsend. For the convention, it was the ever present threat that led to acceptance of several of the preventive provisions of the Constitution.

For us, Shays's Rebellion may serve to synthesize and express the two streams of thinking that led to the Constitution. The need to protect property and contain democracy could hardly be made more compelling. The need for a powerful central government that could protect commercial interests against citizens, if necessary, is indelibly clear. The basic principles that would have to be enforced in order to prevent such incidents were precisely those that would help to build the new national commercial economy.

The Framers' Constitution responds to both of these concerns, but leaves a substantial part of the second less explicit, and thus subject to Hamilton's later completion in the first administration. While there was little or no disagreement about the need to protect property and contain democracy, some delegates (particularly from the South) certainly would have had reservations about the new national economy and its implications for central government power if they had fully realized what was happening. The convention avoided potential conflict by leaving some provisions incomplete or undefined, in effect passing the responsibility to the first Congress.

In effect, several Framers (Hamilton central among them) were calling for the country—or at least its decisive elites—to make a crucial choice. The choice they advocated was to move from the current mostly agricultural economy (large plantations in the South, and small farms throughout the country) to a national commercial economy in which trade and finance would be dominant. They did not make this call openly, of course, and perhaps some of them did not grasp its totality or significance. Small wonder that their opponents did not see and oppose their design in explicit ways.

The Constitution as Synthesis

The Constitution's many provisions limiting the potential impact of popular majorities are too well known to require extensive comment. They range broadly from the design of basic structures, to methods of constituting the government, to limits on its powers. Examples in each category are separation of powers and checks and balances, the various forms of insulating elections, and prohibitions against specific acts that might impinge upon property rights.

More interesting and perhaps less familiar—at least in their totality as a means of instituting a new economy—are the several provisions that create and defend the new national commercial economy through central government power. Many of these provisions were unselfconsciously promoted under the rubric of "protection of property." They were meant to insure that "the rules of justice and the rights of the minor party," as Madison said, would be maintained, even in the face of the "superior force of an interested and overbearing majority." Many do double duty as limits on popular majorities, *but that is exactly the point.* The new economy *necessitated* a national political system in which commercial and financial interests were assured that new and potentially unpopular rules and practices would nevertheless be enforced reliably and consistently—and, it was hoped, be accepted under the more widespread acceptance of the necessity of protection for property rights.

The powers granted to the Congress in Article I, Section 8 and denied to the states in Section 10 amount to the framework for a new fiscal and commercial public policy. Congress gains the power to declare what shall constitute money and to control its value, while the states are forbidden to coin money, emit bills of credit, or allow anything but gold and silver coin in payment of debts. As a result, the states (and their "too democratic" legislatures) were prevented from issuing paper money or defining what might serve as legal tender for the payment of debts, and the gold and silver preferred by bankers and creditors would continue as the basis of the economy.

The Congress also acquired effective taxing powers, and with them the potential to become a creditworthy engine of economic development. Paying existing debts would make it possible to borrow more, to stabilize the currency, and to encourage investment and expansion in various ways. Vital among these tax powers was the power to impose duties and imposts. These are not only the easiest way to collect taxes, but also a means to manage access to the American market—whether to protect infant American industries or to open up other nations' markets. By contrast with the new powers of Congress and the past practice of the states alike, the states were firmly and completely excluded from all such powers (except for the strictly limited purposes of inspections).

The centrality of the famous "commerce clause" to the creation of the new national economy can hardly be debated, even if the question of exclusivity remains at issue today. Hamilton and some of the Framers would undoubtedly have preferred that the mere presence of this provision be understood to preclude the states from acting in the field of interstate commerce at all. But it is not a serious obstacle to their ends that the states be allowed to employ their police or regulatory powers in this area when the Congress has not fully occupied the field or acted in ways that conflict with such state legislation. More important to the creation of the new economy were the requirements for uniformity on the part of national laws pertaining to commerce.

Finally, the contract clause must be appreciated as something more than a prohibition that would assure creditors against any future Shays-type rebellions. Article I, Section 10 includes the prohibition against state laws impairing the obligations of contract as one of a long series of limitations starting with "No states shall. . . ." Clearly, this would render unconstitutional and void any state law that changed the terms of repayment of any existing private contract. By making such contracts into fixed "givens" of economic life, it also tended to discourage popular majorities from seeking redress of economic grievances from their state legislatures.

In Hamilton's hands, the clause applied equally to *public* contracts, so that state legislatures would lose the long-standing sovereign privilege of changing or withdrawing prior grants or franchises. Stability and predictability would be assured, but at the cost of legislative responsiveness to shifting popular preferences.

As Forrest McDonald has shown, this clause may also be distinguished as having been inserted in the Constitution through something like a Hamiltonian coup. At least we know that the convention had twice rejected the principle, and that it was re-inserted by the five-member Committee of Style at the last moment and (apparently) accepted without argument by a weary convention. McDonald makes the case that Hamilton was the only one of the five to grasp the potential in such a clause and therefore must have brought about its last-minute inclusion almost single-handedly.

These primarily economic provisions only sketch the outline of the Framers' intent. They do not by any means constitute the Constitution's entire commitment to the support of the new commercial economy. There are many other provisions that, when taken together, add up to some extensive buttressing of that economy. These include the privileges and immunities of state citizens (to do business in other states), full faith and credit requirements (so that contracts could be enforced and debtors pursued), authorization for a federal court system (for some of the same purposes), and the guarantee and supremacy clauses.

In the United States of the 1780s, it would have been politically difficult, if not impossible, to devise a government that was not, at the least, republican. The Framers had to devise a document with at least the appearance of some democracy, and which could be defended as "republican." Thus, the Constitution does have "democratical" features. However, between the fear of the majority and the desire to protect the newly developing property of the commercial classes, the Framers found it necessary to create a document with a darker side, as we have outlined.

The spare and often ambiguous language of the Constitution was ideally suited to Hamilton's interpretation and expansion. It is Hamilton's interpretations, such as that involving the necessary and proper clause and the creation of the bank, and his expansions, such as in the development of the power of judicial review, that really brought the new national commercial economy into life in the Constitution.

The Framers sketched an outline, but Hamilton made it real. Commercial property and its developing economic relations were protected, and, by the completion of Hamilton's program, removed from the public policy agenda. The ability to change the economy, to deal with substantive public policy issues such as the distribution of wealth and fiscal and monetary measures, was effectively removed from popular control. The "majority" was now contained.

II. Hamilton's Grand Design and Legislative Programs

As a constitutional architect of vision and purpose, no American compares with Alexander Hamilton. From his earliest critiques of the Articles to the legal cases he argued after leaving the Cabinet, Hamilton pursued a single comprehensive image of a future economy and a government that would promote and defend it. If one person can be singled out, surely Hamilton—not Madison—was the primary driving force behind the origin, character, and ultimate meaning of the American Constitution.

Hamilton's Federalist essays are widely known for their emphasis on the weakness of the Articles and the contrasting need for energy in government, taxing powers to maintain that government's creditworthiness, a strong executive, direct application of national laws to individuals, and the like. All of these reflect characteristic Hamiltonian principles, and together they indicate a direction for the new system.

But the Hamiltonian design comes into its clearest focus from two other major sources which represent the main thrust of his efforts to complete the work of the convention. The first of these is the set of Reports and accompanying legislation and opinions that Hamilton authored as Secretary of the Treasury. The other is *Federalist No. 78* and its argument for the power of judicial review, a bold and in many respects original expansion of central government power which helped to raise the courts, the law, and the legal profession to a governing role unprecedented then and unequaled elsewhere today.

·   ·   ·

What Hamilton demonstrated in these Reports was a clear conception of the national government's capacity to serve as the manipula-

tor of an array of carrots and sticks that would move the economy in desirable directions. Hamilton was also clear about who should determine what those desirable directions might be, and who should benefit from such purposeful action. Men of commercial foresight and experience, and probably of property, should hold such powers, and use them for mutual—and hence national—benefit. Most of all, no such system could tolerate significant popular involvement or impact.

Hamilton's design, let us acknowledge, was intended to build national strength and grandeur, on the model of the British Empire he so much admired. In practical terms, it added up to a new set of legal concepts, new financial principles and methods at the national level, and a new overall developmental role for the national government. His incipient commercial-financial economy (soon to emerge, with industrialization, as capitalism) required changing a number of key legal principles long established in the pre-commercial common law. It required creative use of the national debt, deliberate management of the currency, purposeful industrial policy, and conscious inducements in the form of grants of rights to the vast lands inexpensively acquired by the national government through treaties and conquest.

Most of all, Hamilton's design required insulation against reactions from all sides, and particularly against popular efforts to change the patterns of wealth distribution that this design would accomplish. Hamilton's answer to this compelling need was twofold.

First, as we have just seen, he placed the reins of power as far from the people as he could—in a centrally guided financial and development system that would be as hard to identify as it would be to reach and change. Hamilton's system had an early demonstration while he was Secretary of the Treasury, and was legitimated by Jefferson's failure to demolish it while in office. But it was visible only in isolated pieces—growing, merging, self-validating pieces like the restoration and refinement of the Bank, the development of the tariff and internal improvements and the income tax, the vigorous use of judicial review, the triumph of the legal profession—until its full flowering in the Progressive-New Deal Era.

Hamilton stood for an economy that would be dynamic, responsive to opportunities, and oriented to long-term growth. That economy required far-sighted elites to assure that the government would offer incentives for development, stabilize its context, and control its excesses. Government could also serve by providing a means of deflecting or absorbing popular complaints. For all of these goals, the government had to be big, powerful, highly centralized, and removed from the people—but apparently highly responsive to them. Herbert Croly aptly named the twentieth-century version of Hamilton's design "a Hamiltonian government for Jeffersonian ends." Thus the two ever-contending strands of American political thought—our two major images of the desirable American political economy—came to an ultimate merger. Together, they gave credence to labeling Hamilton's national government with the venerable Jeffersonian symbol of "democracy."

The *second* means by which Hamilton sought insulation from popular impact was through transferring as much policymaking as possible into the far less visible and apparently neutral and mechanical hands of courts and lawyers. This strategy encompassed not only the usual and often discretionary law-enforcing role of courts, but more significantly a deliberate law-changing function and—most important of all—a major policymaking role for the Supreme Court at least equal to that of the other branches.

·　　·　　·

The effect of Hamilton's various efforts in this area was to raise courts, the law, and the legal profession into a covert policy-making system representing his best hope of protecting the national economy from popular interference. He was apparently willing to pay the price of the law's rigidities and tendency toward backward-looking in order to insulate the economy and its distribution patterns in this way. But the price paid by the

people—and ultimately by the constitutional system itself—has yet to be calculated.

III. THE CONSEQUENCES OF THE DARK SIDE

Any list of the basic problems of current American politics would surely include institutional deadlock, the decline of the political parties, domination by special interests, the multiplicity and complexity of issues, television's role in diverting attention away from public policy, and the deplorable levels of knowledge and interest on the part of most citizens. For each problem, there are one or more standard explanations.

Most of the explanations (and prescriptions for improvement when the situation is not deemed totally hopeless) take one of two forms. The first involves a focus on specific causal factors, i.e., the effects of incumbency, patterns of campaign contributions, the candidate focus of the media, and so forth. The second is more or less an inventory of the incurable failures of the American people: low and declining turnout at elections, ignorance and self-interestedness, an enduring spectator orientation, apparent manipulability by money and media, and an inability to grasp and act on issues.

These standard explanations amount to a massive exercise in blaming the victim. More important, the situation is actually *worse,* and much more fundamental, than generally suggested. We have no quarrel with the list of problems. If anything, we would lengthen and deepen any such list, and would predict that many others will soon be doing so. The United States is already beginning to emerge from the self-congratulatory stupor of the early 1980s. Realism will be in vogue again by the next recession.

Many of the problems of our politics have their origins in the deliberate design of the Constitution, particularly as it was developed by Hamilton. The problems are *real*. The people's response to them is *rational*. What is missing is recognition that the roots of the problem lie in Hamilton's very success.

Today's national government is highly centralized, a huge and distant bureaucracy related in a merely episodic manner to gridlocked and unresponsive policy-making institutions. The web of special interests is a pragmatic answer, albeit one that represents only the most powerful few. Media and money call the tune for parties and candidates. People may quite rationally decide not to study issues or to participate in such a system.

What has brought about this set of problems and popular response? One absolutely fundamental cause is Hamilton's successful removal of the substance of policy from popular reach. The major pieces of Hamilton's design—the financial system and the legal system—were put in place in the late 1700s and early 1800s by Hamilton and his followers. They became fully integrated and coherently employed in the Progressive Era, from which the rise of the truly centralized Hamiltonian state can be dated.

These two major pieces of Hamilton's design, however, had more than proved their value in the nineteenth century. Each served effectively to obscure unpopular basic national policies from visibility, displace and eventually absorb popular complaints within apparently neutral and objective machines, and frustrate even quite determined popular movements. As Morton Horwitz has shown, the legal system took on its economic role as covert redistributor and allocator of financial burdens as early as the 1820s and 1830s. As opponents of the Bank alleged from the start, and as Goodwyn, Sharkey and others have shown with respect to the financing of the Civil War, the financial system effectively enriched the wealthy while putting the burden on the working and later the middle classes.

When the high point of judicial review was reached in the early 1890s and successfully defended in the election of 1896, the full Hamiltonian legal system was in place. The Supreme Court's power was confirmed; the multitude of state courts were encouraged; and the governing role of an increasingly elite and corporate-oriented Bar was further legitimated. Passage of the Federal Reserve Act offered a final financial link and means of leverage for the same corporate banking-legal community.

Once this system was consolidated in the First World War, participation could actually be encouraged because there was little chance that popular majorities could do much damage. If the basic defenses erected by the Framers did not work, then surely Hamilton's system would divert and absorb popular efforts until they were harmless. Nevertheless, the "better people" were still fearful, not just because of the near-success of labor and the Populists in the 1890s, but also because of the growing ranks of immigrants. Thus, deliberate repression sought to discourage lower class opposition and electoral participation for a decade or more, just as Hamilton's system was crystallizing. A newly refurbished ("democratic") rationalizing ideology was soon bolstered by powerful new means of communication and indoctrination.

The net result of all these efforts was dramatic decline in electoral turnout in the twentieth century.

Women were added to the eligible electorate in 1920, and blacks and many immigrants had been effectively subtracted in the previous decades, so that turnout percentages are not strictly comparable. However, it is still a shock to realize that elections in the 1880s and 1890s generally had turnout levels over 70 percent and often exceeding 80 percent. Today, when women have had 60 years of experience with the franchise and a whole new generation of black voters has entered the active electorate, we count ourselves lucky to attract more than half of the eligible electorate to the polls.

Where have all the voters gone? They have caught on that the system is rigged. Popular majorities' efforts to change either the distribution of wealth and power or the basic policies that seem necessary to maintain that structure of wealth and power simply don't seem possible. To be sure, decades of accomplishment by the ideological defenders and celebrants of this system have encouraged Americans to accept it as "democracy." Americans learn to want or, more likely, consider inevitable whatever is produced, to settle for various diversionary satisfactions, and/or to fear change and even suspect that those who do seek change must have self-interested and unpatriotic motives. These are ideological rationalizations for the central fact that the Hamiltonian Constitution excludes people from directly affecting important public policy outcomes.

This is not to say that there is no history of popular impact on government, or that the Supreme Court is merely a tool of the corporations. Either such caricature of our argument would be silly. What is important is that popular impact, such as it is, can be made effective only in very limited ways through the electoral process. For the most part, it must come through disruption—riots, massive strikes, demonstrations involving the threat of violence, and other attacks on the social order itself. What does it mean for a popular government that its people are politically effective only when they threaten to destroy it?

The Supreme Court has made many decisions, particularly in the middle years of this century, that advanced basic democratic rights. But that was a result of judicial appointments, not an attribute of the institution. The Supreme Court has, and can, and may well again, make precisely the opposite kinds of decisions. What does it mean for a popular government that its basic policies can be set by a transitory majority drawn from a body of nine life-appointed lawyers?

What we are saying is that the Framers' two major goals are threatened today by the success with which Hamilton and his followers implemented those goals. We do not have a stable political economic system, and we do not have the capacity to make the choices necessary to assure a strong and successful American political economy.

Our political system works by fits and starts. It is neither responsive nor accountable and it lacks solid grounding in the body of its people. It sits and waits for the next crisis. Unfortunately, to solve that crisis, it may have to transform itself into something that will be *very* difficult to rationalize as "democracy."

We have not addressed the great issues of nuclear war, planetary survival, or even American economic viability in a drastically changing world economy—not because the people don't care, but because there is no linkage between the people's felt needs and their policymakers. No such basic policies can be implemented, even if policymakers were to concur, without the sustained support of some major portion of the people.

To solve our problems, or merely to fulfill the Framers' goals in the wholly different conditions of our times, we will have to come to terms with Hamilton's Constitution in a realistic manner. Perhaps the best way to honor the Framers' work is not to join in obfuscating celebrations, but to act as they did under like circumstances.

We might start by critically exploring the ways in which today's analogue of the Articles of Confederation is defective in achieving goals that are necessary and desirable for the *future*. Obviously, like the Framers, we would have to address basic principles of social order and purpose—if we have not completely forgotten how to do so. (That we *have* forgotten is strongly suggested by the nature of the proposals currently offered for constitutional "reform.")

Curing the defects of Hamilton's Constitution may not be possible, for many reasons. It may be that patterns of material advantage, or the depth of the problems we face, or the sheer size of the country, make it practically impossible. Or our situation may be even worse: perhaps generations of structural deflection—of elites as well as of the general public—from considering the Constitution in a realistic manner has made it impossible for us to do so now. Decades of cultural lowering of the criteria of democracy may have made it impossible for us to recapture its fuller definition and potential.

If there is a route out of our crisis, it lies in deliberately reversing Hamilton's strategy. That is, we must seek to re-engage the people in their government, and particularly in ways that enable them to have direct impact on the substance of important public policies. Without regard to what might be "realistic" or "practical" in light of today's power distribution, or to questions of strategy, the kinds of measures to which consideration might be given are of the following order:

a. Radical decentralization, perhaps to some regional system, reserving only a few global functions for the national government, to put government within reach of the people;

b. Removing the incumbent character of the national government by putting limits on the number of terms that Representatives and Senators can serve;

c. Reducing the role of money by requiring free television time for public affairs issues, party deliberations and arguments, and candidates' presentations;

d. Sharply contracting the policy-making role of courts and lawyers by transferring jurisdiction of constitutional and major policy issues to openly political forums;

e. Instituting mechanisms for direct action— the old initiative and referendum in modern form, with encouragement and provision of educational opportunities and some screen for levels of information;

f. Making registration immediate and eligibility for voting open to all, if necessary by decentralized computer access;

g. Reviving the parties by starting at the local and state levels and providing a series of thresholds through which, by showing increasing levels of popular participation, parties might increasingly acquire control over campaign funding and nominations;

h. Overhauling the public education system to make public affairs a vital and exciting part of the curriculum, welcome controversy, and set future-oriented public service once again at the center of the aspirations of all citizens.

These suggestions are only a start, intended to illustrate the combined fundamental-and-electoral level at which rethinking must begin. They are easily caricatured, and of course they are not "realistic." The point is that institutional tinkering will not suffice.

When problems such as we have described are real, remedies must be radical; that is the lesson the Framers taught in 1787. Only when the people are re-engaged in a government within their reach will Hamilton's damage be undone. At that point, we can proceed to build upon his successes, and seek to truly achieve the stable political system and productive economy that were his vision for the new nation. Only the bright hope of a new twenty-first-century vision can finally transcend the dark side of our much-celebrated eighteenth-century Constitution.

DISCUSSION QUESTIONS

1. According to Dolbeare and Medcalf, how is the dark side of the Constitution related to Alexander Hamilton's model of political economy?

2. To what extent are the current problems of American politics rooted in the design of our Constitution and to what extent do they have other causes?

DANIEL LAZARE

THE CONSTITUTION, THE SUPREME COURT, AND THE DECLINE OF AMERICAN DEMOCRACY

In his thought-provoking 1996 book The Frozen Republic, *journalist Daniel Lazare highlighted the disjuncture between public faith in the wisdom of our Founding Fathers, and public unease and suspicion that their late eighteenth century constitutional handiwork was not up to the political challenges we face today. Lazare rooted this dilemma in our religiously-inspired adherence to the belief that the Framers crafted a perfect plan for all-time. In this excerpt from his 2001 book* The Velvet Coup, *Lazare relates the landmark Bush-Gore election of 2000 to his fundamental critique of the constitutional system. For Lazare the fiasco in Florida following the election "was not a fluke, but a breakdown of systemic proportions." Problems stemming from antiquated and patchwork counting procedures and the lack of a national election agency were compounded by the Electoral College, an eighteenth-century mechanism that multiplies opportunities for failure. "The only way the system could re-establish control was through a thinly veiled judicial coup d'état—which of course was no solution at all," Lazare argues, referring to the Supreme Court's 5–4 decision in* Bush v. Gore. *Among the most telling arguments in the majority opinion was the correct claim that citizens have no constitutional right to vote for president. This premodern, antidemocratic belief shaped the Constitution of 1787 and the electoral system that flows from it. "Rethinking the Constitution as a whole means rethinking the United States as a whole, something Americans have never dared to do," Lazare claims. Clearly the challenge of soberly rethinking our constitutional system and entering the world of modern democracy is a large one. Are we up to the task?*

Source: Daniel Lazare, *The Velvet Coup: The Constitution, the Supreme Court, and the Decline of American Democracy.* London and New York: Verso, 2001, pp. 1–13.

"In or about December 1910," wrote Virginia Woolf, "human nature changed." Close to a century later, we can be considerably more precise as to when American politics underwent a similar transformation. It was at 2:30 in the morning, Central Standard Time, on November 8, 2000, as Democratic presidential candidate Al Gore's motorcade was pulling into War Memorial Plaza in downtown Nashville. There, before TV cameras, reporters, and exhausted supporters, the vice president was expected to deliver the usual graceful exit speech conceding that his Republican opponent, Texas governor George W. Bush, had eked out a win in the Electoral College despite trailing in the popular vote. Under time-honored rules governing the election of every U.S. president since George Washington, Bush would soon take over the White House.

But then, farther back in the motorcade, an aide's Skytel pager began to vibrate. It was a message from a top Gore strategist back at campaign headquarters named Michael Whouley, whose job that night was to monitor the Florida results. Not so fast, Whouley advised. Where Bush had previously been ahead by 50,000 votes, the latest returns had cut his lead to just 6,000. With a number of precincts as yet uncounted, Florida's twenty-five electoral votes were back in play. Forty-five minutes earlier, Gore had called Bush in Austin to let him know that a formal concession was imminent. Now he picked up the phone to say the opposite.

"Circumstances have changed dramatically since I first called you," he told his opponent. "The state of Florida is too close to call."

"Are you saying what I think you're saying?" replied a stunned George W. "Let me make sure that I understand. You're calling back to retract that concession?"

"Don't get snippy about it!" Gore shot back according to an account pieced together by the *Washington Post*. If Bush prevailed in the final count, he would offer his full support. "But I don't think we should be going out making statements with the state of Florida still in the balance." When Bush protested that his brother, Florida governor Jeb Bush, had personally assured him that the Sunshine State was all locked up, Gore replied that he didn't believe that Jeb was the controlling legal authority in such matters.

Everyone knows, supposedly, what happened next. If Jeb was not the controlling legal authority, then no one was. Over the next few days, Americans watched in astonishment as a country judge in Tallahassee, the Florida Supreme Court, the Florida state legislature, and then the U.S. Supreme Court wrestled over what to do with some 14,000 votes in three counties that were still in dispute. It was monumental foul-up, all the pundits agreed, the equivalent of a four-car head-on collision at a four-way stop sign. Yet no single person or thing was to blame. With the popular vote a dead heat, the Florida tally was crucial. Yet because of an unusual number of election day glitches having to do with butterfly ballots, hanging chads, and whatnot, the Florida tally was indeterminate. The entire political system seemed frozen as a consequence. Newspapers printed detailed accounts of how a similar deadlock between Rutherford B. Hayes and Samuel J. Tilden had caused the 1876 presidential election to wind up in Congress. Yet doomsday forecasters pointed out that this time things could be even messier since, thanks to a constitutional quirk, the House would be in Republican hands as of January 1 while the Senate would be in Democratic. Who would the next president be as of January 20? No one could say. Perhaps Bill Clinton would agree to stay on in the interim. Perhaps, suggested the wits at *Saturday Night Live*, Bush and Gore would agree to share the Oval Office like Oscar and Felix in *The Odd Couple*. Late-night comics had a field day.

But then came the Supreme Court's infamous December 12 ruling, at which point the laughter stopped. The ruling, an unsigned mass of contradictions and absurdities, left court watchers aghast. After halting the Florida recount several days earlier, "The Supremes" had then decided to terminate it altogether on the grounds that the vote counting process had run out of time thanks to a deadline imposed by the Florida state legislature, which had never wanted a recount in the first place. Such reasoning was transparently partisan. Clearly, Republican justices had awarded victory to a Republican candidate so as to insure that control of the court would remain in Republican hands. Yet the Democrats were powerless to do anything about it. The Supreme Court was the highest authority in the land; there was no one left to appeal to. The only comfort they could find was in the thought that, after stealing the presidency in 2000, Republicans would no doubt get their comeuppance in the next round of congressional elections and certainly in the presidential election in 2004. Once voters had given the Republicans what they had coming to them, the Democrats would take back what was rightfully theirs, the electoral process would get back on track, and American democracy would resume its normal course of onward and ever upward. Having triumphed once again, the republic would emerge "more perfect" by virtue of having survived another test.

This is the official version, one that sees the events of November-December 2000 as *sui generis* and therefore unreflective of the true state of American democracy. Butterfly ballots, hanging chads, the November 22 "bourgeois riot" aimed at cutting short the Miami recount—the combination was a million-to-one event that was unlikely to ever occur again. Yet the official version is flawed. Narrow as it might have seemed in the wee hours of November 8, Gore's lead in the popular vote was not razor thin. To the contrary, by the time all the absentee ballots had been counted, it had grown to a healthy 540,000 votes, a margin of victory greater than Richard M. Nixon's in 1968 and five times that of John F. Kennedy in 1960. The results in Florida were also not the photo finish that they were portrayed as being. Had all the ballots there been accurately and honestly counted, a statistical analysis by the *Miami Herald* found that Gore would have carried the state by some 23,000 votes. Proportionally, this was a bit less than his lead nationally, 0.38 percent versus 0.5. But it was still hardly microscopic.

Indeed, in international terms, it was hard to know what all the fuss was about. In parliamentary democracies, election officials engage in far finer calibrations in distributing legislative seats according to each party's share of the national vote. When a handful of votes can determine whether a party gains a toehold in the national assembly or is shut out, the allowable margin of error is much less. Yet if Poland and the Czech Republic can accurately tabulate the results for a dozen or more parties at a time, why did the American system have such inordinate trouble tabulating them for just two? If the honesty of election officials in those countries is rarely called into question, why were the results in Florida so dubious that the two parties were immediately at each other's throat?

The answer is that the great unraveling that began on November 7 was not a fluke, but a breakdown of systemic proportions. The problems that the American electoral apparatus faced were ones that any competent system should have been able to handle. Yet, as the pressure mounted, the machinery froze. Thanks to a variety of factors—lackluster candidates, content-less campaigns, a tuned-out electorate, both sides' use of super-sophisticated marketing techniques that were increasingly canceling each other out—election results might reasonably have been expected to be growing narrower rather than broader. This would suggest that the country would need a more finely tuned tallying system. Yet thanks to aging voting machines, ill-trained and ill-paid election workers, and a hyper-fragmented political structure resulting in literally tens of thousands of state and local contests being decided on the same day, the U.S. was winding up with one that was less accurate rather than more. The Electoral College, unchanged since the eighteenth century, added yet another layer of uncertainty. In a pool of 100 million voters, glitches and counting errors could be expected to offset one another to a degree and "wash out" of the final tally. But by dividing the presidential race into fifty smaller state contests, the Electoral College multiplied the chances that an individual mishap could end up having serious reverberations. Rather than reducing the opportunities for failure, it expanded them. As a consequence, the election chaos that erupted in three or four Florida counties was enough to put the state race in doubt and hence the entire national election.

But this was not all. Once the dispute wound up in the hands of the state legislature and the courts, the system froze up again. At the very least, the United States should have had some national election agency capable of taking charge of the process and sorting things out. In India, to cite just one example, an all-powerful election commission sets the dates for elections, arranges for security at thousands of polling places, distributes the ballots, and then takes responsibility for gathering and counting them up—no small task in a country of more 600 million voters, sixteen major language groups, and a dozen-and-a-half major parties. Yet because the authors of the U.S. Constitution had made no such provision back in 1787, Americans two centuries later were at a loss over what to do. As former White House counsel Lloyd Cutler cracked a bit irreverently: "The boys in the powdered wigs didn't get this one right. They didn't anticipate anything like this ever happening, so we find ourselves in a kind of political wilderness"—a wilderness, one might add, from which Americans were unable to find their way out. Indeed, the more judges, local election commissioners, and state legislators tried to intervene, the more the general level of anger and confusion rose. Ultimately, it was left to a former *New York Times* executive editor named Max Frankel to argue on the *Times* op-ed page that although the outcome was "ugly, unfair, confusing or wrong," things might have been worse: there could have been blood in the streets. But the words rang hollow. Rather than settling the dispute peacefully and democratically, the American political system had compounded the problem in such a way as to bring the nation to the brink of an explosion. The only way the system could re-establish control was through a thinly veiled judicial coup d'état—which, of course, was no solution at all.

"The U.S. may be the most technologically advanced country, but our electoral system is any

day better," observed M.S. Gill, India's chief election commissioner, on the heels of the Florida fiasco. But, then, scores of other electoral systems around the globe are better as well. As a joke making the rounds of the Third World had it, perhaps next time it would be up to Haiti (or Russia, Serbia, Mozambique, etc.) to send observers to the United States to see to it that the governor of Florida did not again steal the election on his brother's behalf. In parts of the world where the natives are used to hanging their heads in shame whenever Jimmy Carter or Madeleine Albright lectures them on their democratic shortcomings, the schadenfreude was running at high tide.

But if America's performance was astonishing on one level, it was quite un-astonishing on another. Mechanisms like the Electoral College, which give state and local officials enormous leeway in determining how elections are to be conducted, date from the late eighteenth century when the infant United States consisted of scattered farms, plantations, and homesteads interspersed with a few coastal cities. It was a decentralized electoral system befitting a decentralized, homespun republic. But two centuries later, America is anything but decentralized. Thanks to round-the-clock cable newscasts, instant polling, and the Internet, information no longer takes weeks to travel by coach or schooner. Instead, it takes just nanoseconds to flash from coast to coast. Such a society needs election methods suitable for a new age, yet as of the year 2000 it was still making do with the same old mechanisms. The results were like traveling on a two-century-old stagecoach between Trenton and Philadelphia. The wonder was not that it took so long, but that the contraption made it at all.

The world's greatest democracy as a teetering old stagecoach—surely there is some mistake? Yet while the United States persists in thinking about itself as the newest of the new, it is in fact the oldest of the old, a polity dating from the days of the French monarchy, the Venetian republic, and the Holy Roman Empire. All those entities have long since vanished, yet the U.S. constitutional system staggers on. In other countries, mechanisms of government are viewed in modern terms as no less fallible than the beings who made them. They are machines that must be repaired, updated, and revamped from time to time in order to remain in good working order. Despite its reputation for practicality, though, the attitude in the U.S. is almost defiantly premodern. Rather than people like ourselves, the constitutional system, Americans persist in believing, was made by a race of giants that was infinitely superior. As no less a constitutional authority than Bill Clinton observed in mid-November, "Our Founders may not have foreseen every challenge in the march of democracy, but they crafted a Constitution that would"—this at a time when the constitutional system was verging on a nervous breakdown. Yet because the system was deemed to be superhuman, Americans were no more inclined to tamper with it than to tamper with, say, the *Mona Lisa.* On those rare occasions when they did approach the sacred temple and offer some modestly worded constitutional amendment, they did so only according to rules established by the Constitution itself, thereby underscoring their subservience.

Americans see their Constitution as something akin to "the ark of the covenant, too sacred to be touched," as Jefferson once observed. The flipside of religious veneration, however, is a feeling of passive helplessness whenever the machinery goes awry. Rather than making the necessary repairs, the only thing Americans feel they can do under such circumstances is cross themselves and hope the machinery will somehow fix itself. As Kay Bailey Hutchison, a Republican Senator from Texas, observed following the Supreme Court's velvet coup: "Now is the time to bring our country together and begin the orderly transition of power that has occurred in our nation for more than two hundred years. The Constitution has triumphed once again." But in the United States, the Constitution is always triumphant because it would be sacrilegious to view it any other way. Republican mobs in Miami, incompetent election officials, self-serving Supreme Court justices— such things merely *look* like symptoms of political breakdown. But if one truly *believes* in an omniscient Constitution, then one knows they are not.

Yet rather than triumphing in November– December 2000, the Constitution merely endured. Rather than proving its omniscience, its performance proved the opposite, i.e. that any device created by fallible beings is itself fallible and hence prone to breakdown and decay.

Unfortunately, the Constitution's performance also proved something else. Despite what it says in the high-school civics texts, the United States is not a democracy. What it is, rather, it is an eighteenth-century republic that has come to resemble a democracy in certain respects, but which at its core remains stubbornly pre-democratic. In stating on December 12 that the individual citizen has no constitutional right to vote for president, the Supreme Court's five-member conservative majority was merely stating what was obvious to anyone who had actually read Article II, which is that the power to choose members of the Electoral College lies with the individual state legislatures rather than the people at large. Yet it couldn't help but come as a shock to the millions of Americans who have come to regard voting in presidential elections as a fundamental democratic right. Now the Supreme Court wished to inform them that such a right did not exist. While the United States might look like a democracy and sometimes even act like one, it was fundamentally a holdover from the days when not even the most radical politicians believed that the people should be free to run the government as a whole.

Civil libertarians who define democracy as a series of "thou shall not's"—thou shall not abridge freedom of speech, thou shall not abridge freedom of the press, and so forth—miss the boat. As important as such liberties may be, modern democracy must be understood first and foremost in terms of the *positive* freedom of the people as a whole to exert effective control over the whole of society. A people's freedom to reshape their entire environment is the freedom on which all others rest. Yet a society in which an unelected judiciary lightly tosses aside the results of a popular election because it would take too much time to tally up the vote is one in which the people's impotence is all too apparent.

The Gore-Bush Presidential Election has thus emerged as the great divide. Where Americans were formerly inclined to see the Supreme Court as a neutral body devoted to a concept of the law as a force greater than politics, they now see that it as no less baldly political than any other institution in Washington. Where previously they had looked upon the Electoral College as a harmless relic from another era, they now see that it is not harmless at all, but a serious infringement on the people's right of self-government. But while it is certainly welcome that American eyes have opened at least a crack to the true nature of their ruling institutions, the process would be incomplete if it did not lead to a reexamination of the document from which all these institutions derive, i.e. the U.S. Constitution. The Electoral College is an essential part of a structure assembled more than two centuries ago with utmost rigor and care. The House and Senate, the presidency, the arduous amending process outlined in Article V—these were not items that the Founders lightly tossed onto the table like a deck of playing cards, but elements that they honed and crafted in such a way as to fit together as tightly as pieces in a jigsaw puzzle. If institutions like the Electoral College have resisted reform all these years, it is because Americans sense, not incorrectly, that they are integral to the overall design and that removing them would throw the entire machinery out of whack. As one constitutional scholar put it in the early 1990s, changing the Electoral College might be a good idea, "But it would take a constitutional amendment to change it. And people start to worry that when you tinker with the system, who knows what we'll be left with?" Since tinkering would necessitate rethinking the entire structure, Americans have preferred to leave well enough alone.

But now that the constitutional machinery has been thrown out of whack regardless, Americans may no longer have that option. They increasingly find themselves forced to tackle a problem that previous generations have repeatedly put off. Rethinking the Constitution in the twenty-first century is no easy task. Indeed, it is no less revolutionary than rethinking the solar system was in the sixteenth. Americans do not merely live under the Constitution; they live *in* the Constitution, inhabiting its recesses, shaping their lives according to its needs and dictates, absorbing its logic and making it their own. There is nothing in American society that does not bear the Constitution's stamp in one way or another; if this sounds dogmatic, it is because an entire legal and political system that derives from a single 4,400-word document is itself dogmatic. Rethinking the Constitution as a whole means rethinking the United States as a whole, something Americans have never dared to do.

This means learning to view a great deal else differently as well. Take history, an area in which American attitudes are surprisingly complex. Supposedly, Americans are great believers in progress, the idea that people are capable of learning from experience and improving their condition from one year to the next. As much as Americans may admire the ingenuity of a Benjamin Franklin or a Robert Fulton, they know that science and technology have advanced far beyond what those eighteenth-century pioneers could have imagined. But for all their belief in scientific progress, they believe the opposite in terms of constitutional development. Rather than progress and advancement, Americans consider it an article of faith that it is impossible to advance beyond the wisdom of the Founders. As Clinton put it in 1997 in a televised "town hall" meeting in Akron, Ohio:

> We live in a country that is the longest-lasting democracy in human history, founded on the elementary proposition that we are created equal by God. That's what the Constitution says. And we have never lived that way perfectly, but the whole history of America is in large measure the story of our attempt to give more perfect

meaning to the thing we started with—the Constitution and the Bill of Rights.

Leaving aside the fact that nowhere does the Constitution state that "we are created equal by God"—the statement is a paraphrase of the Declaration of Independence—this accurately sums up a concept of American history in which "we the people" are constantly circling back to the principles that made them great in the first place. Just as Edmund Burke described a nation as a partnership "between those who are living, those who are dead, and those who are to be born," constitutional development in the United States involves a similar kind of intergenerational partnership between the Framers and those following in their wake. Rather than improving government, Americans see their mission as remaining true to ideas that were present at the creation. Indeed, if Clinton is any authority, the idea is not merely to remain true, but "to give more perfect meaning" to ideas that preceded them by more than two centuries.

But how does one give more perfect meaning to something that was perfect to begin with? Are such efforts superfluous? Or could it be that the Founders' teachings were not perfect after all and that it is the job of subsequent generations to fill in the blanks they left behind? If so, it is a task that Americans feel they must undertake without ever admitting to themselves that is what they are up to. They must deny that the Founders were in any way imperfect and insist that they represented an unsurpassable peak of human wisdom that "we the living" can barely hope to comprehend. Yet they must fix problems that the Founders created. While human knowledge may advance in some areas, any thought of advancing beyond an eighteenth-century level in political science is forbidden.

But if Americans are to come to grips with the Constitution, they must say goodbye to such pre-modern beliefs. They must recognize that progress is not confined to the technological realm, but is something that must take place across the board if it is to take place at all. The lesson of the 2000 presidential election is that the United States is not the most perfect government on earth, but one of the most antique. Its constitutional machinery is woefully obsolete due to generations of neglect. It must be rethought from top to bottom if it is to be hauled into the world of modern democracy.

DISCUSSION QUESTIONS

1. How does Lazare justify his claim that the contested outcome of the 2000 presidential election in Florida was not a fluke, but a reflection of basic flaws in our electoral and constitutional system?

2. Lazare argues that the American belief in progress is at odds with the assumption that the eighteenth-century Constitution is nearly or completely perfect and should not be altered. What explains this attitude of reverence towards the Constitution? Is it akin to religious fundamentalism?

12 HOWARD ZINN

SOME TRUTHS ARE NOT SELF-EVIDENT

Writing during the bicentennial celebrations of 1987, historian and political scientist Howard Zinn makes a case that the Constitution is of minor importance in determining the degree of justice, liberty, and democracy in our society. While not denying the symbolic and moral weight of the Constitution, Zinn contends that social movements and citizen action have been far more significant in the realization of democratic values over the course of American history. He provides examples from the areas of racial equality, freedom of speech, economic justice, sexual equality, and questions of war and peace to support his claim that a "mere document" like the Constitution "is no substitute for the energy, boldness, and concerted action of the citizens."

This year [1987] Americans are talking about the Constitution but asking the wrong questions, such as, Could the Founding Fathers have done better? That concern is pointless, 200 years after the fact. Or, Does the Constitution provide the framework for a just and democratic society today? That question is also misplaced, because the Constitution, whatever its language and however interpreted by the Supreme Court, does not determine the degree of justice, liberty or democracy in our society.

The proper question, I believe, is not how good a document is or was the Constitution but, What effect does it have on the quality of our lives? And the answer to that, it seems to me, is, Very little. The Constitution makes promises it cannot by itself keep, and therefore deludes us into complacency about the rights we have. It is conspicuously silent on certain other rights that all human beings deserve. And it pretends to set limits on governmental powers, when in fact those limits are easily ignored.

I am not arguing that the Constitution has no importance; words have moral power and principles can be useful even when ambiguous. But, like other historic documents, the Constitution is of minor importance compared with the actions that citizens take, especially when those actions are joined in social movements. Such movements have worked, historically, to secure the rights our human sensibilities tell us are self-evidently ours, whether or not those rights are "granted" by the Constitution.

Let me illustrate my point with five issues of liberty and justice:

First is the matter of racial equality. When slavery was abolished, it was not by constitutional fiat but by the joining of military necessity with

Source: Howard Zinn, "Some Truths Are Not Self-Evident." *The Nation,* vol. 245, no. 3, 1–8 August 1987, pp. 87–88.

the moral force of a great antislavery movement, acting outside the Constitution and often against the law. The Thirteenth, Fourteenth and Fifteenth Amendments wrote into the Constitution rights that extra-legal action had already won. But the Fourteenth and Fifteenth Amendments were ignored for almost a hundred years. The right to equal protection of the law and the right to vote, even the Supreme Court decision in *Brown v. Board of Education* in 1954 underlining the meaning of the equal protection clause, did not become operative until blacks, in the fifteen years following the Montgomery bus boycott, shook up the nation by tumultuous actions inside and outside the law.

The Constitution played a helpful but marginal role in all that. Black people, in the political context of the 1960s, would have demanded equality whether or not the Constitution called for it, just as the antislavery movement demanded abolition even in the absence of constitutional support.

What about the most vaunted of constitutional rights, free speech? Historically, the Supreme Court has given the right to free speech only shaky support, seesawing erratically by sometimes affirming and sometimes overriding restrictions. Whatever a distant Court decided, the real right of citizens to free expression has been determined by the immediate power of the local police on the street, by the employer in the workplace and by the financial limits on the ability to use the mass media.

The existence of a First Amendment has been inspirational but its protection elusive. Its reality has depended on the willingness of citizens, whether labor organizers, socialists or Jehovah's Witnesses, to insist on their right to speak and write. Liberties have not been given; they have been taken. And whether in the future we have a right to say what we want, or air what we say, will be determined not by the existence of the First Amendment or the latest Supreme Court decision but by whether we are courageous enough to speak up at the risk of being jailed or fired, organized enough to defend our speech against offi-

cial interference and can command resources enough to get our ideas before a reasonably large public.

What of economic justice? The Constitution is silent on the right to earn a moderate income, silent on the rights to medical care and decent housing as legitimate claims of every human being from infancy to old age. Whatever degree of economic justice has been attained in this country (impressive compared with others, shameful compared with our resources) cannot be attributed to something in the Constitution. It is the result of the concerted action of laborers and farmers over the centuries, using strikes, boycotts and minor rebellions of all sorts, to get redress of grievances directly from employers and indirectly from legislators. In the future, as in the past, the Constitution will sleep as citizens battle over the distribution of the nation's wealth, and will be awakened only to mark the score.

On sexual equality the Constitution is also silent. What women have achieved thus far is the result of their own determination, in the feminist upsurge of the nineteenth and early twentieth centuries, and the more recent women's liberation movement. Women have accomplished this outside the Constitution, by raising female and male consciousness and inducing courts and legislators to recognize what the Constitution ignores.

Finally, in an age in which war approaches genocide, the irrelevance of the Constitution is especially striking. Long, ravaging conflicts in Korea and Vietnam were waged without following Constitutional procedures, and if there is a nuclear exchange, the decision to launch U.S. missiles will be made, as it was in those cases, by the President and a few advisers. The public will be shut out of the process and deliberately kept uninformed by an intricate web of secrecy and deceit. The current Iran/*contra* scandal hearings before Congressional select committees should be understood as exposing not an aberration but a steady state of foreign policy.

It was not constitutional checks and balances but an aroused populace that prodded Lyndon

Johnson and then Richard Nixon into deciding to extricate the United States from Vietnam. In the immediate future, our lives will depend not on the existence of the Constitution but on the power of an aroused citizenry demanding that we not go to war, and on Americans refusing, as did so many G.I.s and civilians in the Vietnam era, to cooperate in the conduct of a war.

The Constitution, like the Bible, has some good words. It is also, like the Bible, easily manipulated, distorted, ignored and used to make us feel comfortable and protected. But we risk the loss of our lives and liberties if we depend on a mere document to defend them. A constitution is a fine adornment for a democratic society, but it is no substitute for the energy, boldness and concerted action of the citizens.

DISCUSSION QUESTIONS

1. What is Zinn's main point about the relationship of the Constitution to political change and the expansion of democracy?
2. Identify the five issues of justice and liberty discussed by Zinn and explain how each relates to his main point about the Constitution.

POLITICS AND INSTITUTIONS

The formal institutions of the U.S. government exercise considerable influence over all of us. They touch our lives in many ways, quite independently of whether or not we want them to. Americans remain uneasy about the impact of government institutions. Surveys conducted since the 1960s reveal an erosion of trust in all government institutions. Americans generally do not trust the federal government to "do the right thing." One survey found that "an environment in which a majority of Americans believe that most people can't be trusted breeds attitudes that hold all politicians as corrupt, venal, and self-serving, and government action as doomed to failure."

While recognizing widespread public distrust, government nonetheless does matter. Congress, for example, has the authority to spend more than $2.4 trillion in fiscal year 2005. This is a staggering sum of money. And it undoubtedly is the case that the expenditure of those funds, not to mention the taxes levied to create the budget in the first place, will have an impact on us, whether we drive on federally subsidized roads, work in federally regulated workplaces, receive Social Security payments, or, perhaps in your case, receive federal loans to attend college. Notwithstanding debates over the social and moral implications of the nation's budgetary priorities, and recognizing the often exaggerated nature of protests from conservatives against the alleged evils of "big government," the fact remains that we *have* a large and active national government. It makes good sense to try to understand it.

The five chapters in Part II examine key political institutions and processes and the three branches of the federal government: the mass media, political parties and elections, as well as Congress, the presidency, and the courts—the three cornerstones of the Constitutional separation of powers. Although conventional political science texts include discussions of these institutional "nuts and bolts," we locate them against the backdrop of the structure of power analyzed in Part I. Thus we are stressing that political processes and government institutions do not make decisions in a vacuum; policymakers operate within the confines of economic and ideological boundaries that sharply limit the range of the possible.

We contend that your capacity to see the system clearly depends on your willingness to focus *first* on the structure, and *second* on the processes and institutions. That is why we have organized the book this way. This distinction between primary and secondary focus may seem like hairsplitting, but actually it is crucial. Mainstream accounts of American politics downplay or ignore outright the deeper structural concerns, thus amplifying the institutions. To do so is to give analytic priority to the parts of government that are most directly accountable to the public, which in turn makes the system appear fairer and more democratic than it really is. Such a conventional focus on institutions also offers hope that if we can just elect the candidate with the best personality or the right party affiliation, our political problems can be effectively addressed with minimal, if any, changes.

While relatively comforting, we believe this hope is not warranted. Significant progress in meeting the needs of the people requires questioning the structure itself. This obviously confronts you with a less comfortable and more daunting task, but it rests on an honest admission of what lies ahead for the student who seeks to interpret, and perhaps change, the political world we inhabit. In the final analysis, then, do our political institutions and the policy process deserve careful scrutiny? Absolutely. Part II will help you in this regard, but always be critically aware of the playing field where the clash of institutions takes place.

4

Mass Media and Politics

As a looming presence in contemporary America, the mass media are inescapable. Indeed Americans are eager consumers of media products and spend countless hours in contact with some form of media. Enhanced by technological breakthroughs of the late twentieth century, cable TV and the Internet allow access to more sources of information than ever before. Certainly the media have the potential to serve democratic ends by providing citizens with high quality electoral and policy information, as well as by acting as a watchdog over government and other powerful institutions. In practice, however, the mass media, driven by corporate profit imperatives, all too often contribute to cynicism, depoliticization, and a truncated and illusory view of the way the world works. The result, in the words of communications scholar Robert W. McChesney, is a "rich media" and a "poor democracy." Articles in this chapter provide the analytical tools to critically dissect the role of the mass media in politics today.

(13)

IT'S THE MEDIA, STUPID

During the 1992 presidential election, candidate Bill Clinton's campaign team hung a now-famous sign in their headquarters that read "It's the economy, stupid." The sign served as a reminder to link all discussions of policy issues to the faltering economy, thereby constantly connecting issues to a central critique of President George Bush's handling of the economy. In this article, Robert McChesney, a media scholar and activist, and John Nichols, a journalist, similarly seek to draw constant attention to the central importance of connecting all discussions about reforming American democracy to the need for media reform. They begin by emphasizing the important connection between the free flow of information and a healthy democratic society. Then they out-line the problem in straightforward terms: by 2000, fewer than ten giant media con-glomerates dominated the mass media of the United States, with firms like Disney, AOL-Time Warner, SONY, and GE leading the way. This level of corporate control over what we see and hear as "news" guarantees that the values of profit-maximizing and commercialism will guide the U.S. media system, to the detriment of news that truly informs the public on the crucial issues of the day. The result is news that does not challenge the world-view of elite interests, nor offer a broad range of competing per-spectives, thus greatly diminishing the quality of democracy. Or as the authors put it, corporate media has fanned the flames of a "crisis for democracy." To address this cri-sis, McChesney and Nichols offer an ambitious agenda for media reform aimed at strengthening democratic participation and citizenship. For the authors contend that what is needed in the twenty-first century is nothing short of a "broad crusade for democratic renewal in America."

Participatory self-government, or democracy, works best when at least three criteria are met. First, it helps when there are not significant dis-parities in economic wealth and property owner-ship across the society. Such disparities undermine the ability of citizens to act as equals.

Second, it helps when there is a sense of commu-nity and a notion that an individual's well-being is determined to no small extent by the commu-nity's well-being. This provides democratic politi-cal culture with a substance that cannot exist if everyone is simply out to advance narrowly

Source: Robert W. McChesney, *Corporate Media and the Threat to Democracy.* New York: Seven Stories Press, 1997, pp. 5–7; Robert W. McChesney and John Nichols, *It's the Media, Stupid.* New York: Seven Stories Press, 2000, pp. 21–25, 27–39, 110–115, and 119–120.

defined self-interests, even if those interests might be harmful to the community as a whole. Third, democracy requires that there be an effective system of political communication, broadly construed, that informs and engages the citizenry, drawing people meaningfully into the polity. This becomes especially important as societies grow larger and more complex, but has been true for all societies dedicated toward self-government. While democracies by definition must respect individual freedoms, these freedoms can only be exercised in a meaningful sense when the citizenry is informed, engaged, and participating. Moreover, without this, political debate can scarcely address the central issues of power and resource allocation that must be at the heart of public deliberation in a democracy. As James Madison noted, "A popular government without popular information, or the means of acquiring it, is but a prologue to a farce or a tragedy, or perhaps both."

These three criteria are related. In nondemocratic societies those in power invariably dominate the communication systems to maintain their rule. In democratic societies the manner by which the media system is structured, controlled and subsidized is of central political importance. Control over the means of communication is an integral aspect of political and economic power. In many nations, to their credit, media policy debates have been and are important political issues. In the U.S., to the contrary, private commercial control over communication is often regarded as innately democratic and benevolent, and therefore not subject to political discussion. Government involvement with media or communication is almost universally denigrated in the U.S. as a direct invitation to tyranny, no matter how well intended. The preponderance of U.S. mass communications is controlled by less than two dozen enormous profit-maximizing corporations, which receive much of their income from advertising placed largely by other huge corporations. But the extent of this media ownership and control goes generally unremarked in the media and intellectual culture, and there appears to be little sense of concern about its dimensions among citizenry as a whole.

•   •   •

It was the rainiest, wettest, coldest April morning Washington had seen in a long time. And still they came—thousands of mostly young activists determined to mount a non-violent but noisy protest outside the spring 2000 meetings of the World Bank and the International Monetary Fund (IMF). As they reached a key intersection near the World Bank building, they were blocked by armed battalions of riot police and National Guardsmen. The authorities stood their ground, but the Mobilization for Global Justice activists refused to back down.

This was the sort of standoff to which even the most jaded television assignment editors dispatched their crews—despite the fact that the weather made for some fogged-up camera lenses. On the street, a reporter for one Washington television station pulled aside a young woman who was soaking wet, and announced to the cameraman that it was time to do a live shot. When the signal came that they were on air, the reporter started to make small talk with the activist about the miserable weather. "I really want to talk about the policies of the World Bank and the IMF," the young woman said. "Their structural adjustment policies are causing real harm in specific countries around the world . . ." The reporter pulled the microphone back, looked to the camera and said, "Well, everybody has an opinion. Let's go back to the anchor desk."

That same afternoon, as young people who had attended teach-ins, listened to debates and read literature and books in preparation for the demonstration continued to face down the police in the streets, conservative commentator Tony Snow was attacking the protestors on Washington radio as ignorant and uninformed. The next morning, *The Wall Street Journal* referred to them as "Global Village Idiots." The supposedly liberal *Washington Post* and *New York Times* editorial pages both dismissed the protests as not much more than a waste of police resources and everyone else's time. And, despite the fact that at least 150 activists were still in jail, and that people in Washington, across the nation and indeed, around the world, were buzzing about a new era of activism, television news programs went back to broadcasting the usual mix of commercials and vapid "news you can use."

Molly Ivins put it rather succinctly when she observed, a few days later, that "for reasons unclear to me, the mainstream media seem to have decided that anyone who questions any aspect of globalization is an extremist nut, despite the rather obvious fact that global poverty is growing under the kind auspices of the World Bank, the International Monetary Fund, and the World Trade Organization."

In our view, the reasons for this are clear. The closer a story gets to examining corporate power the less reliable our corporate media system is as a source of information that is useful to the citizens of a democracy. And on issues like the global capitalist economy, the corporate media are doubly unreliable, because they rank as perhaps the foremost beneficiaries of Wall Street-designed trade deals like NAFTA, and of the machinations of the three multilateral agencies developed to shape the global economy to serve corporate interests: the World Bank, the IMF and the World Trade Organization (WTO). Moreover, almost all the favored mainstream sources for coverage of global economic affairs are strident advocates for a corporate-driven vision of globalization. Thus, corporate journalists—even those low enough on the pecking order to be dispatched to stand in the rain on a Washington street corner—generally will find arguments against the status quo incomprehensible.

Just as the media dropped the ball in Washington in April 2000, it blew a chance to cover an even more dramatic story of citizens speaking truth to power in the fall of 1999, when the WTO met in Seattle. As one of the most significant challenges to global economics in decades was playing out—a challenge so powerful that the

WTO meetings were actually shut down for a time and ultimately failed to launch a new round of trade liberalization, a challenge so intense that President Clinton felt compelled to assert his agreement on a variety of issues with those protesting in the streets—the broadcast media treated the story as an event of secondary importance. There was no round-the-clock coverage, as was seen only four months earlier when John F. Kennedy Jr.'s fatal plane crash reshaped the broadcast schedules of CNN, the Fox News Channel, and every other cable TV news service for two full weeks. During the WTO meetings and demonstrations—which dealt with arguably the most important political issues of our age—no attempt was made to provide comprehensive coverage. One night, as demonstrators filled the streets of Seattle and ministers of finance battled through the night over the most fundamental questions of how the global economy would be structured, as the President of the U.S. hunkered down in a hotel surrounded by armed troops, the Fox News Channel interrupted its scheduled programming for a live special report . . . not from Seattle, but from the scene of the latest doings of the parents of JonBenet Ramsey.

What happened in Seattle sums up the crisis for democracy that occurs when the media system is set up primarily to maximize profit for a handful of enormous self-interested corporations. An Orwellian disconnect is created. The news required for a functional democracy—the news that empowers citizens to act in their own interest and for the good of society—is discarded to make way for the trivial, sensational, and salacious. How many Americans have come home from a school board meeting, a city council session, a local demonstration or a mass national rally to discover the vital issues they had just addressed are being ignored or distorted? The flow of information that is the lifeblood of democracy is being choked by a media system that every day ignores a world of injustice and inequality, and the growing resistance to it. . . .

Back in 1992, Bill Clinton's campaign strategists hung a sign in the war room of their Little

Rock headquarters that read, "It's the economy, stupid." The point of the sign was to remind campaign workers to circle every discussion of election issues around to the subject of the sagging economy. In many senses, this book is like that sign. We are here to argue that it's time to point out the connections between media reform and democratic renewal. To sound a wake up call reminding us that access to communications is a non-negotiable demand in a democratic society, and that scoring real victories for labor, the environment, and social justice will be made all the more possible by opening up the democratizing the media. Meanwhile, when the corporate press comes looking for a soundbite on what the ruckus is all about, tell them, "It's the media, stupid."

·   ·   ·

Americans devour media at a staggering rate; in 1999 the average American spent almost twelve hours per day with some form of media. We are also in the midst of an unprecedented technological revolution—based around digital technologies, typified by the Internet—that looks to weave media and electronic communication into nearly every waking moment of our lives. In conventional parlance, these developments are presented as benign; they are all about liberating individuals, investors, and consumers from the constraints of time and space while offering a cornucopia of exciting new options and possibilities. This, however, is a superficial and misleading perspective on what is happening. Indeed, when one lifts the hood, so to speak, to see what is driving the media revolution, a very different picture emerges. It is instead a world where highly concentrated corporate power is pulling the strings to dominate our existence so as to maximize return to shareholders, and to protect the corporation's role—and corporate power in general—from being subjected to the public scrutiny and political debate it so richly deserves. It is a poison pill for democracy.

Yet in our American democracy the issue of media barely registers. The structures of our media, the concentration of its ownership, the role that it plays in shaping the lives of our children, in commercializing our culture, and in warping our elections, has been off-limits. When we examine the reality of media in the year 2000, however, it becomes clear that this circumstance must shift. The case for making media an issue is made, above all, by a survey of the contemporary media landscape.

In 2000, the U.S. media system is dominated by fewer than ten transnational conglomerates: Disney, AOL-Time Warner, News Corporation, Viacom, Seagram (Universal), Sony, Liberty (AT&T), Bertelsmann, and General Electric (NBC). Their media revenues range from roughly $8 billion to $30 billion per year. These firms tend to have holdings in numerous media sectors. AOL-Time Warner, for example, ranks among the largest players in film production, recorded music, TV show production, cable TV channels, cable TV systems, book publishing, magazine publishing, and Internet service provision. The great profit in media today comes from taking a movie or TV show and milking it for maximum return through spin-off books, CDs, video games, and merchandise. Another twelve to fifteen firms, which do from $2 or $3 billion to $8 billion per year in business, round out the system. These firms—like Comcast, Hearst, New York Times, Washington Post, Cox, Advance, Tribune Company, Gannett—tend to be less developed conglomerates, focusing on only two or three media sectors. All in all, these two dozen or so firms control the overwhelming percentage of movies, TV shows, cable systems, cable channels, TV stations, radio stations, books, magazines, newspapers, billboards, music, and TV networks that constitute the media culture that occupies one-half of the average American's life. It is an extraordinary degree of economic and social power located in very few hands.

It has not always been this way. Much of this concentration has taken place in the past few decades, as technology and market imperatives made concentration and conglomeration far more attractive and necessary. Today it is impossible for the small, independent firm to be anything but a marginal player in the industries mentioned above. Most important, the flames of media concentration were fanned by a collapsing commitment on the part of the federal government to serious antitrust prosecution, a diminution of the federal standards regarding fairness, and government "deregulation," most notably the 1996 Telecommunications Act. Congressional approval of the Telecommunications Act, after only a stilted and disengaged debate, was a historic turning point in media policy making in the United States, as it permitted a consolidation of media and communication ownership that had previously been unthinkable.

A surface survey of the statistics regarding media ownership, while deeply disturbing in what it reveals, fails to convey the full depth of the concentration of media ownership. Not only are media markets dominated by a handful of conglomerates with "barriers to entry," making it nearly impossible for newcomers to challenge their dominance, but they are also closely linked to each other in a manner that suggests almost a cartel-like arrangement. Some of the largest media firms own parts of the other giants; Liberty, for example, is the second largest shareholder in News Corporation and among the largest shareholders in AOL-Time Warner. Moreover, the media giants employ equity joint ventures—where two competing firms share ownership in a single venture—to an extent unknown almost anywhere else in the economy. These joint ventures work to reduce competition, lower risk, and increase profits. By 1999 the nine largest media giants had an equity join venture with six, on average, of the other eight giants; often a media giant would have multiple joint ventures with another firm. In sum, this is a tightly knit community of owners, dominated by some of the wealthiest individuals in the world. Indeed, thirteen of the hundred wealthiest individuals in the world—all of whom are worth over $4 billion—are media magnates.

Such concentration of media ownership is clearly negative by any standard that cherishes free speech and diversity in the marketplace of ideas. But concentration in media ownership is not the sole cause of the problems with the media, and in some cases it is not a significant factor at all. Concentration is important to a large extent because it magnifies the limitations of a commercial media system, and makes those limitations less susceptible to redress by the market. But this sounds very abstract, so let's cut to the bone: the problem with concentrated media is that it accentuates the two main problems of commercial media, hypercommercialism and denigration of public service. These are really two sides of the same coin. As massive media corporations are better able to commercially carpet bomb society, their ability or willingness to provide material with editorial and creative integrity declines. It is not that the individuals who run these firms are bad people; the problem is that they do destructive things by rationally following the market cues they are given. We have a media system set up to serve private investors first and foremost, not public citizens.

No better example of how this process works can be found than in the U.S. radio industry. Since deregulation of ownership in 1996, some one-half of U.S. stations have been sold. A few massive giants, owning hundreds of stations—as many as eight in each market—have come to dominate the industry. As profits shoot through the roof, low-budget standardized fare has nearly eliminated the local content, character, and creativity that were once features of this relatively inexpensive electronic medium. "A huge wave of consolidation has turned music stations into cash cows that focus on narrow playlists aimed at squeezing the most revenue from the richest demographics," the trade publication *Variety* observed in 1999. "Truth be told, in this era of megamergers, there has never been a greater need for a little diversity on the dial."

The radio example points to the one other crucial group, aside from media owners, that gets treated with love and affection by corporate media executives: the corporate advertising community. Businesses spent some $214 billion in the U.S. on advertising in 1999—some 2.4 percent of the GDP—and almost all of this money ended up in the hands of some media firm. Though journalists and civics teachers bristle at the notion, those media that depend upon advertising for the lion's share of their income—radio, TV, newspapers, magazines—are, in effect, part of the advertising industry. Throughout the 1990s the media giants used their market power to pummel their customers with ads and to bend over backward to make their media attractive to Madison Avenue. By 1999 the four major TV networks, for example, were providing nearly sixteen minutes per hour of commercials during prime time, an enormous increase from just a decade earlier. A conglomerate like Time Warner was able to sign a $200 million advertising deal with General Motors that "crosses most of the entertainment company's divisions," so that "GM will have a first-look option on all automobile marketing opportunities within Warner Bros. operations." Not content with traditional advertising, media firms are now working on "virtual ads," whereby "a marketer's product can be seamlessly inserted into live or taped broadcasts." With ads so inserted during actual programs, viewers will be unable to avoid the commercials through zapping. Advertising has also been plugged into new venues, such as video games. But this does not capture the full spread of commercialism. In television, for example, the new growth area for revenues is selling merchandise that is shown on its programs. It barely caused a ripple when Tommy Hilfiger hired the Viacom-owned cable channel VH1, rather than an ad agency, to produce a series of TV ads, because VH1 is so effective at selling. In sum, the entire U.S. media experience increasingly resembles an infomercial.

Nowhere is the commercial marination of the American mind more apparent than in the case of children, where the advertising assault was increased exponentially in the 1990s. There are now four full-time cable channels (owned by the four largest U.S. media firms) bombarding children with commercial programming twenty-four hours per day. Advertisers have targeted the youth market as arguably the most important in the nation. Girls between the ages of seven and fourteen spend some $24 billion per year and influence parental decisions worth another $66 billion. Commercial indoctrination of children is crucial to corporate America. One study revealed that when eight-year-olds were shown two pictures of identical shoes, one with the Nike logo and the other with the Kmart logo, they liked both equally. The response of twelve-year-olds was "Kmart, are you kidding me?" This desire to indoctrinate fuels the commercial drive into education and suggests that the moral foundation for coming generations may be resting on a dubious base. Nobody knows what the exact consequence of this commercial blitzkrieg upon children will be, but the range of debate extends from "pretty bad" to "absolutely terrible." The only thing we know for certain is that the media giants and advertisers who prosper from it do not care and cannot care. It is outside their frame of reference.

In this light, it is worth considering the status of the long-standing conflict between "church and state" in media; this refers to the ability of journalists and creative workers to conduct their affairs without having output determined by what serves the immediate interests of advertisers, or owners for that matter. In conventional wisdom, the U.S. media system has been at its best when the divider between "church and state"—especially though not exclusively in journalism—has been pronounced and respected. That way media users can regard the articles and news and entertainment programs they read, see, and hear in the media as reflecting the best judgment of media workers, not the surreptitious bribe of a commercial interest. Nowhere has the collapse of editorial integrity been more pronounced than in magazine publishing. As the late Alexander Liberman, legendary editorial director of Condé Nast, noted in 1999, advertisers "have too much power. They determine, if not specifically, then generally what magazines are now." A series of scandals in the late 1990s affirmed what has been suspected: Advertisers have tremendous control over the editorial copy in U.S. magazines, and editors who are discomfited by this had best find employment elsewhere. "They're glitz bags," Norman Mailer said of magazines in 1999. "They are so obviously driven by the ads that the ads take prominence over the stories."

Hollywood films have so thoroughly embraced commercial values that *Variety* now writes of the "burgeoning subfield of Product Placement Cinema." Conglomerate control of films and music and television (all of the TV networks, all of the main studios but the floundering MGM, and all four of the firms that dominate the U.S. music scene are owned by the eight largest media firms) has opened the floodgates to commercialism and has proven deadly for creativity. "A movie studio is part of this huge corporate cocoon," Peter Bart, editor of *Variety* and former head of Paramount, writes, "and therefore, theoretically, a studio should be willing to take bigger risks because one bad movie . . . won't erode the value of the [parent company's] shares. But the way it works out, the studios are if anything more risk averse. They are desperate to hedge their bets. It's the nature of bureaucratic self-protection. . . . The pressure is reflected in the sort of movies that get made . . . the sort of pablum that studios chewed on for ten years, that's gone through endless rewrites, has been pretested by endless focus groups, and is successful—if insipid." Or as an executive at Time Warner's "independent" studio New Line Pictures puts it, "We're very marketing-driven as a company. I'm instructed not to greenlight a project if I can't articulate how to sell it." As Bart concludes, this is "not exactly a recipe for art."

This said, we are not attempting to make a blanket indictment of everything produced by the corporate media system. We are not suggesting that every article or broadcast segment is foul, nor that they are all tainted, nor even that some material that is tainted cannot also be good. There are extremely talented people employed in the commercial media system, and the pressure to satisfy audiences does indeed sometimes promote excellent fare. But corporate and commer-

cial pressures greatly undermine the overall quality of the system and skew it in ways that are not at all the result of audience demand. In the world of corporate media, the key is to attract the preferred target audience while spending as little money as possible. In the battle for consumer attention, this strongly promotes a rehashing of tried-and-true formulae, as well as the use of sex, violence, and what is termed "shock" or "gross-out" fare. In a world where people are surrounded by innumerable media options (albeit owned by numerable firms), sex and violence are proven attention getters.

Corporate control and hypercommercialism are having what may be their most devastating effects in the real of journalism. There is no need to romanticize the nature of U.S. professional journalism from the middle of the century into the 1980s; in many respects it was deeply flawed. Yet whatever autonomy and integrity journalism enjoyed during that time of Bob Woodward, Carl Bernstein, and *Lou Grant* is now under sustained and unyielding attack by corporate owners in the hunt for profit. No more striking evidence for this exists than the results of a 1999 Pew Research Center poll of journalists concerning their profession. Until the 1990s, journalists tended to be stalwart defenders of the media system, and most scholarship emphasized journalists' hypersensitivity to criticism of their field. No more. The Pew poll found that "at both the local and national level, majorities of working journalists say the increased bottom-line pressure is hurting the quality of coverage." "This past year," David Halberstam wrote in 1999, "has been, I think, the worst year for American journalism since I entered the profession forty-four years ago." Bob Woodward, the Watergate investigator who has enjoyed one of the most successful and prestigious media careers of the era, says that in these days of hypercommercialism and hypercompetition, "No one is the keeper of the conscience of journalism."

The brave new world of corporate journalism manifests itself in many ways. The primary effects of tightened corporate control are a serious reduction in staff, combined with pressure to do vastly less expensive and less controversial lifestyle and feature stories. Where there is "news," it often takes the form of canned crime reports that foster unrealistic and unnecessary fears. This is the magic elixir for the bottom line. Sometimes the new world of corporate journalism is typified by blatant corporate censorship of stories that might hurt the image of the media owner. But the maniacal media baron as portrayed in James Bond films or profiles of Rupert Murdoch is far less a danger than the cautious and compromised editor who seeks to "balance" a responsibility to readers or viewers with a duty to serve his boss and the advertisers. In media today, even among journalists who entered the field for the noblest of reasons, there is an internalized bias to simply shy away from controversial journalism that might enmesh a media firm in a battle with powerful corporations or government agencies. True, such conflicts have always been the stuff of great journalism, but they can make for very bad business, and in the current climate business trumps journalism just about every time.

The most common and noticeable effect of the corporate noose on journalism is that it simply allows commercial values to redirect journalism to its most profitable position. So it is that relatively vast resources are deployed for news pitched at a narrow business class, and suited to their needs and prejudices; it is predominant in newspapers, magazines, and television. Likewise, news for the masses increasingly consists of stories about celebrities, royal families, athletes, natural disasters, plane crashes, and train wrecks. Political coverage is limited to regurgitating what some politician says, and "good" journalism is practiced when a politician from the other side of the aisle is given a chance to respond. But that is not journalism; it is stenography. Perhaps the strongest indictment of corporate journalism is that the preponderance of it would be compatible with an authoritarian political regime. So it is that China has few qualms about letting most commercial news from the

U.S. inside its borders; it can see that this low caliber of journalism is hardly a threat to its rule. It is the BBC, with its regrettable penchant for covering politics seriously, that draws the commissar's ire.

There is also intense pressure for journalism to contribute immediately and directly to the bottom line. One Tennessee TV station received adverse publicity for offering to do TV news "puff pieces" on local businesses in exchange for $15,000 payments. It is important to note, however, that the mistake made by that Tennessee station was not the spirit of the offer—it well reflects the pattern across the news media—but, rather, the baldness of it. Firms also use the news to hype their other programming, as in 1996 when *NBC Nightly News* made the Summer Olympics its most covered news story that year, even though none of the other networks had the Olympics ranked on their top-ten lists. Why? Because NBC was airing the Olympics that summer—and reaping the attendant financial rewards. The fall of 1999 saw a huge debate erupt in newspaper circles after the *Los Angeles Times* devoted the entire editorial space in an edition of its 164-page Sunday magazine to articles, photos and graphics describing downtown Los Angeles' new Staples Center sports arena. The newspaper did not reveal at the time of the magazine's publication, however, that it would be dividing the $2 million in revenues generated by the section with the owners of the arena. So dark was the scenario that the former publisher of the *L.A. Times,* Otis Chandler, sent a letter to the staff describing the new management's move as "unbelievably stupid and unprofessional."

Above all, however, the *L.A. Times* was blatant. It allowed the corrupting linkage between advertisers and the media to be clearly identified. More often than not, a measure of subtlety keeps controversies under wraps.

In addition to triviality and craven commercialism, the willingness or capacity of U.S. journalism to challenge elite assumptions or to question the status quo—never especially great in the best of times—has shriveled. So it was, for example, that the preponderance of media coverage of the 1999 war in Kosovo lamely reflected elite opinion in the U.S., when even the rudimentary application of traditional journalism standards would point to severe discrepancies in the official story line.

All told, this creates a crisis for democracy. Alexis de Tocqueville rightly celebrated the role that a free and diverse media plays not only in greasing the wheels of electoral systems but in maintaining the very structures of civil society. The nineteenth-century surveyor of the American public landscape went so far as to say of news organizations, "They maintain civilization." Who would seriously attempt to make such a statement about today's media?

· · ·

What is necessary, in the end, is for media reform to be advanced as part of a progressive platform for democratic reform across society. The foundation of a broader progressive platform will be the demand for social justice and an attack upon social inequality and the moral stench of a society operated purely along commercial lines. In the U.S. today, the richest one percent of the population has as much money to spend as the poorest 100 million Americans, double the ratio for just twenty years earlier. The political system reinforces this inequality by being, as is now roundly acknowledged, a plaything for big business where the interests of the balance of society have been pushed to the margins if not forgotten. The corporate media system reinforces this inequality and rule of the market and limits the possibility of democratic reform. In sum, media reform is inexorably intertwined with broader democratic reform; they rise and fall together.

Hence we return to the point that emerged forcefully in the analysis of media reform around the world: the importance of political parties to provide necessary leadership and to force the issue into the political arena. In the U.S., both the Republican and Democratic Parties, with only a

few prominent exceptions, have been and are in the pay of the corporate media and communication giants. It is unlikely that any breakthroughs can be expected there until much spadework is done. The logical place to begin that spadework ought to be the small parties and factions of the left in America, the New Party, the Greens, the Labor Party, Democratic Socialists of America, Americans for Democratic Action, and U.S. Action. In our view, all of these groups need to incorporate media reform issues into their platforms and their visions. Ideally, these organizations, which have remarkably similar stances on a host of issues, might adopt a shared vision—perhaps as a step toward building the sort of labor, left, green, feminist, people of color coalitions seen in New Zealand's Alliance Party, Iceland's Alliance, and other Third Left groupings. In Wisconsin, already, the Greens and New Party activists are working together on joint projects. In Washington, D.C., the Greens have merged with the D.C. Statehood Party.

Sadly, however, these new left parties have dropped the ball concerning media so far, with only one or two exceptions. As U.S. Rep. Bernie Sanders, the Vermont independent who is the only socialist member of the U.S. House of Representatives, and who has made media reform a central issue for over a decade has noted: "This is an issue that is absolutely vital to democracy, and that only the left can address. The New Party, the Green Party, the Labor Party, progressive Democrats should be all over this issue. But, for most of the left, it's not even on the agenda." This has to change, and change soon, both for the sake of media reform and for the sake of these parties and progressive politics in the United States. It is difficult for us to imagine a better place to build trust and cooperation across these left groupings than with a shared response to media, which has been so devastatingly dismissive of third-party initiatives, save those of billionaire hot dogs Ross Perot and Donald Trump.

Who would contribute to the shaping of a progressive media reform platform. Ideally, it would be shaped as similar platforms in Sweden, Finland, Canada, and other lands have been. Local and national groups working on media reform would participate. There would also be significant input from media unions, such as the Newspaper Guild, the National Writers Union, and the American Federation of Television and Radio Artists. We believe these groups could get the ball rolling by coming together in support of a set of basic principles not unlike those advanced by Britain's Campaign for Press and Broadcast Freedom.

There is every reason to believe that these groups could ultimately agree on an agenda that calls for basic reforms, such as:

- Expansion of funding for traditional public-service broadcasting with an eye toward making it fully non-commercial and democratically accountable. In particular, substantial new funding should be provided for the development of news and public affairs programming that will fill the gap created by the collapse of serious newsgathering by the networks and their local affiliates.
- Development of non-commercial, community-run, public-access television and radio systems that are distinct from public-service broadcasting and that are deeply rooted in local communities. As part of this initiative, the federal government should remove barriers to the development of microradio initiatives. Seed money, similar to that provided by government and foundations for economic development in low-income and minority communities, should be targeted toward groups seeking to develop microradio.
- Setting far stricter standards for commercial broadcasters in exchange for granting them broadcast licenses. For example, why not ban or strictly limit advertising on childrens' programs and on news broadcasts? Why not take a percentage of the broadcasters' revenues and set it aside for creative people and journalists to control time set aside for children's shows and newscasts? Why not make a condi-

tion of receiving a broadcast license that the broadcaster will not carry any paid political advertising during electoral campaigns? And that they will provide free time to all, liberally defined, viable candidates?

- Creation of a broad initiative to limit advertising in general, using regulation and taxation to prevent commercial saturation.
- Reassertion of anti-trust protections in order to limit the amount of media that can be owned by one firm. Why not, for example, limit radio stations to one per owner? The benefits of concentrated ownership accrue entirely to owners, not to the public. Make it government policy to encourage diversity of ownership and diversity of editorial opinions, as was intended by the First Amendment. There should, as well, be a reassertion of traditional restrictions on cross-ownership of media within particular communities.
- Renewing the commitment of the U.S. government to develop incentives aimed at encouraging and protecting minority ownership of broadcast and cable outlets.
- Promotion of newspaper and magazine competition through the use of tax deductions or subsidies. One approach might allow taxpayers to deduct the cost of a limited number of newspaper and magazine subscriptions—as some professionals and academics now do. Such an initiative would boost the circulations of publications from across the ideological spectrum, but would be particularly helpful to publications that target low-income, working-class, and elderly citizens, as well as students. Significantly lowered postal fees for nonprofit publications that have minimal advertising might also be appropriate.
- Strengthen the position of media unions by encouraging the development of a stronger role for workers in determining the editorial content of news publications and broadcast news. As in European countries, union protections in the U.S. should be strengthened in order to assure that working journalists

are free to perform their duties with an eye toward serving the public interest.

- Develop a new national program of subsidies for film and cultural production, particularly by members of ethnic and racial minority groups, women, low-income citizens, and others who frequently have a hard time finding market support for their artistic expressions.
- Use tax breaks and subsidies to promote creation of publishing and production cooperatives and other arts and culture vehicles designed to provide non-commercial outlets for writers and artists to bring meaningful, controversial, and substantive work to mass audiences. One proposal put forth by economist Dean Baker would let any American redirect $150 from their tax payments to any nonprofit medium of their choice. This could funnel as much as $25 billion into nonprofit media and create a very healthy competition among new and revitalized outlets for democratic and cultural expression. All this could be done without any government official gumming up the works.

In combination, these proposals would go a long way toward creating a strong democratic sector on the rapidly commercializing Internet, as every medium today has a web component almost by definition. By the same token, media reformers must demand that there be formal hearings and public deliberations on the future of digital communication systems. At present the crucial technical decisions are being made quietly behind closed doors to the benefit of the corporate community. That has to be stopped.

.   .   .

We believe that a media reform movement with clear goals and a clear strategy for achieving them will be a fundamental building block of a broad crusade for democratic renewal in America—a bold, powerful and ultimately successful initiative that has the potential to make this nation's promise for democracy real. It will be a movement that takes an issue too long neglected and pushes that concern to the center of the national debate. It will be a movement that gives us an answer to the powers-that-be who seek constantly to divert us from issues of consequence. It will be a movement that empowers us to respond to their distractions and deceits by laughing in their faces and saying: "It's the media, stupid."

DISCUSSION QUESTIONS

1. Identify and reflect on McChesney and Nichols's three criteria of participatory self-government.
2. In what ways do the consolidation of corporate control over the media and growing media commercialism represent a threat both to democracy and to journalism?
3. Identify the key elements of McChesney and Nichols's progressive media reform agenda. How might support for this agenda be built?

NEWS CONTENT AND ILLUSION: FOUR INFORMATION BIASES THAT MATTER

Debates about the quality of news coverage in the United States often revolve around assertions that the mass media are either too liberal or too conservative, depending on the politics of the critic. In this article, taken from his popular book News: The Politics of Illusion, *political scientist W. Lance Bennett argues that this liberal versus conservative controversy about journalistic bias is a "dead-end debate." Rather than focusing on the ideological slant of the news, Bennett asks us to consider "universal information problems" that lead journalists to frame stories in such a way that familiar political narratives come to replace hard-hitting investigative coverage. These "information biases" transcend ideology, debasing the quality of public information while contributing to the transformation of news into a "mass-produced consumer product." The four characteristics of the news include personalization, dramatization, fragmentation, and the authority-disorder bias. They developed as an outgrowth of the connection between evolving communications technologies and the profit motive that drives the corporate media. Taken together, while these four traits heighten the dramatic tension of news reports, they also feed the public's disenchantment with the news, accentuating already rampant public cynicism and furthering the distance between citizens and their leaders. Ultimately, Bennett contends, democracy is weakened by the way news stories are presented—the information biases inherent in the dominant news format—regardless of any ideological tilt that may or may not actually exist. Coupled with the forgoing analysis of McChesney and Nichols, the troubling issue we are left to ponder is whether our cherished notion of the "free press" retains any semblance of reality in the twenty-first century.*

It is a writer's obligation to impose narrative. Everyone does this. Every time you take a lump of material and turn it into something you are imposing a narrative. It's a writer's obligation to do this. And, by the same token, it is apparently a journalist's obligation to pretend that he never does anything of the sort. The journalist claims to believe that the narrative emerges from the lump of material, rises up and smacks you in the face like marsh gas.

—Nora Ephron

Source: W. Lance Bennett, *News: The Politics of Illusion,* 5th edition. New York: Longman, 2003, pp. 41–50 and 75–76.

When George W. Bush announced his presidential candidacy a breathtaking seventeen months before the 2000 presidential election, he did so on a movie-set stage in Iowa, surrounded by bales of hay and a shiny red forklift behind him. The day's news coverage anointed him the front-runner. As if to prove their point, reporters noted that Bush attracted by far the greatest press entourage, even though three other prominent candidates were also campaigning in the state that day. Mr. Bush wittily acknowledged that news organizations have choices about where they assign reporters, as he took the microphone on his campaign plane shortly after it took off for Iowa that morning. He quipped to the crowd of reporters on board: "Thanks for coming. We know you have a choice of candidates when you fly, and we appreciate you choosing Great Expectations." Great Expectations was the nickname he gave the plane as part of a larger spin effort to defuse the typical pattern of news building up expectations about candidates only to dramatize their next fall. Mr. Bush again played flight attendant when he asked the reporters to "Please stow your expectations securely in your overhead bins, as they may shift during the trip and can fall and hurt someone—especially me."

This campaign 2000 story was written more in an entertainment format than as a means to deliver serious political information; it was personality-centered, well-scripted, and set as a comedy scene in which Mr. Bush played a flight attendant doing the pre-takeoff announcement. The story was also artificial in the sense of being disconnected from larger questions about the race, the issues, or Mr. Bush's qualifications for being president. Most importantly, there was no clear basis on which the Washington press had decreed him the front-runner. True, the ability to deliver clever lines may be some qualification for being president, but the readers of the news story would be unable to know if Mr. Bush uttered that monologue spontaneously or if it was scripted as part his advisors' communication strategy to win over a skeptical press pack. Perhaps, in the mediated reality of contemporary politics, the distinction between an innate ability to think on one's feet and learning to deliver a scripted performance no longer matters.

A closer look at this front-runner story and the campaign news that surrounded it reveals one tangible political condition mentioned in passing that might explain why journalists granted Mr. Bush the early lead: money. Mr. Bush had already set a record for early campaign fund-raising. Raising the largest amount of money makes a candidate front-runner in the eyes of political insiders, as well as in the story lines of the prominent national journalists who cover politics from the perspectives of insiders. Pegging the political fortunes of candidates to the sizes of their war chests is not an idle measure of potential electoral success. It is money, after all, that indicates the strength of business and interest group belief that a candidate will support their political goals. And it takes money to bring a candidate's political messages to voters who are more expensive to reach than ever before. Yet one of the reasons that people are hard to reach is that they tend not to trust politicians or the journalists who cover them. And one of the reasons that people mistrust the political establishment is money. Both polls and public interest groups often identify money as one of the ills of politics.

The insider view that politics is bitter, partisan, personalized, manipulative and money-driven may be a defensible perspective (it is the inside view, after all), but this does not make it the only choice that news organizations have about how to cover government. This is not to argue that topics such as money should be ignored in campaign coverage. To the contrary, the question is how news organizations decide to play those topics in their stories.

Consider the choices that news organizations have in how to frame a campaign story in which money is a potential plot element. *Framing involves choosing a broad organizing theme for selecting, emphasizing, and linking the elements of a story such as the scenes, the characters, their actions, and supporting documentation.* For example the framing of the previous story might have been shifted from the *horse race* to the *money chase,* with a serious investigation of the interests to which Mr. Bush and the other candidates might be indebted. Yet the above story and hundreds more that followed it throughout the campaign told the tale of the horse race one more time. In the horse race plot, money is generally left poorly developed in the background, requiring us to decode the reasons why George W. Bush may be the leading candidate. Also typical of many political stories, this dramatized news fragment was implicitly negative. Money has become a code for what ails our public life, a disruptive or disordering principle in the democratic order of things.

The opening of the Bush presidential campaign thus displayed the information biases of many political news stories: (1) it was personality oriented, (2) with dramatic staging and scripting, (3) that left it fragmented or disconnected from underlying political issues and realities (such as Mr. Bush's issue positions or other qualifications for being named the leading candidate), and (4) its implicit message (about money in this case) is typically negative, suggesting threats to the normal order of things. The result is that while people may tune in to news for its entertainment value, they also find reason in many stories to doubt or dismiss politics in general.

This communication system appears to contribute to a public that is increasingly cynical and disillusioned with politics and government. The paradox is that journalists complain about the over-scripted campaigns, and, more generally, the staged events they cover, but they seem unable to find other ways to write stories or to replace the cynical tone with perspectives that might help citizens become more engaged. As a result of these and other factors, large numbers of people actively avoid politics, while watching the media spectacle with a mixture of disbelief and disapproval. Meanwhile more people escape from public affairs and political participation into ever more personalized media worlds that one observer has likened to the gated communities and suburban enclaves into which many people have physically migrated in society.

Let's move from the opening story of the 2000 election to the dramatic conclusion. To make a long story short, the *Bush as front-runner* story (with minor variations) swept through the news media for a time until it was replaced by other campaign *horse race* dramas, often with Mr. Gore as front-runner, each creating an episode to advance a long running story that must (if we are to call it news) continue to develop. Thus Mr. Bush and Democratic front-runner Al Gore jockeyed through the primaries, walked through heavily-scripted conventions, see-sawed through the debates, and finally headed to the finish line in one of the closest contests in American history. In an unexpected twist, the story was jarred from its predictable ending (an election night winner) because the electoral vote count was so close that it did not decide the result. The dispute over a handful of votes in Florida was eventually ended by a Supreme Court ruling that left many on both sides angry at the process that determined the result.

Did this photo finish in the presidential horse race of 2000 draw a large crowd of excited spectators? Hardly. The voter turnout reached a new modern era low beneath 50 percent. Continuous weekly polling of voters by *The Vanishing Voter,* a Harvard project led by Thomas Patterson and Marvin Kalb, revealed that a majority of voters did not become interested in the election until after it was over and the dispute in Florida broke out.

The point here is not to place the blame for civic disengagement on the news media. Journalists complained throughout the campaign that they had little to work with. How much more could they say about Al Gore's woodenness or George Bush's feeble grasp of foreign policy? Yet this begs the question: Why were journalists acting like movie critics giving barely passing reviews to all those poorly-scripted and repetitively-acted political performances? Why was there so little innovative coverage that might stimulate citizen engagement with the election either on the level of the candidates (for example, the political and economic interests that they represented) or on the level of stirring involvement beyond the momentary act of voting in the most important democratic ritual in the civic culture?

It is remarkable that the leading news organizations not only converged in their horse race and campaign strategy coverage, but they stuck with those narrative choices in the face of clear voter disinterest. Even in the final weeks of the contest, stories with standardized dramatized framings such as the *horse race,* the *war room,* and other military metaphors outnumbered stories on all the issues in the race, combined, by a wide margin. For example, a study of *The Washington Post* and *The New York Times* in the final two weeks of the campaign showed that dramatized framings of the race or the strategic conflict outnumbered all policy issue stories by a margin of 69 to 45 in the *Post,* while the *Times'* melodrama-to-issue gap was even greater at 93 to 63. *Consider the possibility that the choices of such narrative framings of politics contain information biases that are far more serious and at the same time more difficult for the average person to detect than ideological biases.*

A DIFFERENT KIND OF BIAS

This [article] takes a close look at news content. The concern is with information biases that make news hard to use as a guide to citizen action because they obscure the big picture in which daily events take place, and, in addition, they often convey a negative or cynical tone about politics that undermines citizen motivation for digging deeper to learn more or to become engaged. . . . Most debates about journalistic bias are concerned with the question of ideology. For example, does the news have a liberal or conservative, a Democratic or Republican, drift? To briefly review the argument, some variations in news content or political emphasis may occur, but they can seldom be explained as the result of journalists routinely injecting their partisan views into the news. To the contrary, the avoidance of political partisanship by journalists is reinforced, among other means, by the professional ethics codes of journalists, by the editors

who monitor their work, and by the business values of the companies they work for.

Another important point to recall is that people who see a consistent ideological press bias (that is, across most stories or over extended periods of time) are seeing it with the help of their own ideology. This generalization is supported by opinion research showing that people in the middle see the press as generally neutral, whereas those on the left complain that the news is too conservative, and those on the right think the news has a left-leaning bias. There are at least two ironies in this ongoing and inherently unresolvable debate about ideological bias. First, even if neutrality or objectivity could be achieved, citizens with strong views on particular issues would not recognize it. Second, even if the news contained strong ideological or issue biases, people with a point of view (who are most likely to detect bias in the first place) would be well equipped to defend themselves against such biases. Indeed many nations favor a partisan press system as the best way to conduct public debates and to explore issues. . . .

So, many Americans are caught up in dead-end debates about a kind of news bias that is at once far less systematic and much less dangerous than commonly assumed. In the meantime, and this may be the greatest irony of all, these preoccupations with the politics of journalists detract attention from other information bias that really are worth worrying about. A more sensible approach to news bias is to look for those universal information problems that hinder the efforts of citizens, whatever their ideology, to take part in political life.

The task [of this article] is to understand the U.S. public information system at a deeper level than the endless debates over ideological bias. Fortunately most of the pieces to the news puzzle are right in front of us. For all of its defects, the news continues to be largely a public production, with government press offices, media organizations, and popular tastes all available for inspection. . . .

In turning to the workings of this system, it is important to understand that the news biases examined here have evolved over a long period of time. Their roots can be traced to the transition from a partisan to a commercial press in the 1800s. . . . It is thus helpful to think of the biases that we see at any point in time as historical products of the changing system of relations between people, press, and politicians. These relations continually shape and construct news and contribute to its evolving forms.

FOUR INFORMATION BIASES THAT MATTER: AN OVERVIEW

Our expectations about the quality of public information are rather high. Most of us grew up with history books full of journalistic heroism exercised in the name of truth and free speech. We learned that the American Revolution was inspired by the political rhetoric of the underground press and by printers' effective opposition to the British Stamp Act. The lesson from the trial of Peter Zenger has endured through time: *the truth is not libelous.* The goal of the history book journalists was as unswerving as it was noble: to guarantee for the American people the most accurate, critical, coherent, illuminating, and independent reporting of political events. Yet Peter Zenger would probably not recognize, much less feel comfortable working in, a modern news organization.

Like it or not, the news has become a mass-produced consumer product, bearing little resemblance to history book images. Communication technologies, beginning with the wire services and progressing to satellite feeds and digital video, interact with corporate profit motives to create generic, "lowest-common-denominator" information formats. Those news story formulas often lack critical perspectives and coherent or useful organizing principles. . . . The illusions of coherence, diversity, and relevance have been achieved through packaging the news to suit the psychological tastes of different segments of the market audience. It is necessary to look beyond ideology and the packaging of our favorite news source in order to see the remarkable similarities that run through most mainstream news content. In particular, there are four characteristics of news that stand out as reasons why public information in the United States does not do as much as it could to advance the cause of democracy: *personalization, dramatization, fragmentation,* and the *authority-disorder bias.*

PERSONALIZATION

If there is a single most important flaw in the American news style, it is the overwhelming tendency to downplay the big social, economic, or political picture in favor of the human trials, tragedies, and triumphs that sit at the surface of events. For example, instead of focusing on power and process, the media concentrate on the people engaged in political combat over the issues. The reasons for this are numerous, from the journalist's fear that probing analysis will turn off audiences to the relative ease of telling the human-interest side of a story as opposed to explaining deeper causes and effects.

It is easy for the news audience to react for or against the actors in these personalized human-interest stories. When people are invited to take the news personally, they can find a wide range of private, emotional meanings in it, however, the meanings inspired by personalized news may not add up to the shared critical and analytical meanings on which a healthy democracy thrives. Personalized news encourages people to take an egocentric rather than a socially concerned view of political problems. The focus on personalities encourages a passive spectator attitude among the public. Moreover, the common media focus on flawed political personalities at the center of mistakes and scandals invites people to project their general anger and frustration at society or in their private lives onto the distant symbolic targets of politics. Either way, whether the focus is on sympathetic heroes and victims or hateful scoundrels and culprits, the media preference for personalized human-interest news creates a "can't-see-the-forest-for-the-trees" information bias that makes it difficult to see the big (institutional) picture that lies beyond the many actors crowding center stage who are caught in the eye of the news camera.

The tendency to personalize the news would be less worrisome if human-interest angles were used to hook audiences into more serious analysis of issues and problems. Almost all great literature and theater, from the Greek dramas to the modern day, use strong characters to promote audience identifications and reactions in order to draw people into thinking about larger moral and social issues. American news often stops at the character development stage, however, and leaves the larger lessons and social significance, if there is any, to the imagination of the audience. As a result, the main problem with personalized news is that the focus on personal concerns is seldom linked to more in-depth analysis. What often passes for analysis are opaque news formulas such as "he/she was a reflection of us," a line that was used in the media frenzies that followed the deaths of Britain's Princess Diana and America's John Kennedy, Jr. Even when large portions of the public reject personalized news formulas, as in the case of the year-long journalistic preoccupation with whether President Clinton's personal sexual behavior undermined his leadership, the personalization never stops. This systematic tendency to personalize situations is one of the defining biases of news.

DRAMATIZATION

Compounding the information bias of personalization is a second news property in which the aspects of events that are reported tend to be the ones most easily dramatized in simple "stories." As noted above, American journalism has settled overwhelmingly on the reporting form of stories or narratives, as contrasted, for example, to analytical essays, political polemics, or more scientific-style problem reports. Stories invite dramatization, particularly with sharply drawn actors at their center.

News dramas emphasize crisis over continuity, the present over the past or future, conflicts and relationship problems between the personalities at their center, and the impact of scandals on personal political careers. News dramas downplay complex policy information, the workings of government institutions, and the bases of power behind the central characters. Lost in the news drama (*melodrama* is often the more appropriate term) are sustained analyses of the persistent problems of our time, such as inequality, hunger, resource depletion, population pressures, environmental collapse, toxic waste, and political oppression. Serious though such human problems are, they just are not dramatic enough on a day-to-day level to make the news.

Important topics do come up, of course, such as when natural disasters strike, nuclear waste contaminates air or water supplies, or genocide breaks out in a distant land. Chronic conditions generally become news only when they reach astounding levels that threaten large-scale cataclysm through famine, depression, war, or revolution. But then the stories go away, again leaving the origins of and the solutions for those problems little-discussed in all but the biggest of stories. Most of these seemingly sudden "crises" are years in the making: deforestation that worsens flooding, neglected nuclear dumps festering in the Arctic or in Washington State, or bandit governments in African nations undermining the hope for civil society. With a steady flow of information provided by experts and issue advocacy organizations, these stories could be kept in the news as reminders to publics and politicians that there may be more important things than the glitzy media event of the day or the routine political skirmishing in Washington.

Crises, not the slow buildups to them, are the perfect news material, meaning that they fit neatly into the dramatization bias. The "crisis cycle" portrayed in the news is classic dramatic fare, with rising action, falling action, sharply drawn characters, and, of course, plot resolutions. By its very definition, a crisis is something that will subside on its own or reach dramatic closure through clean-up efforts or humanitarian relief operations. Unfortunately the crisis cycles that characterize our news system only reinforce the popular impression that high levels of human difficulty are inevitable and therefore acceptable. Crises are resolved when situations return to "manageable" levels of difficulty. Seldom are underlying problems treated and eliminated at their source. The news is certainly not the cause of these problems, but it could become part of the solution if it substituted illumination of causes for dramatic coverage of symptoms.

As in the case of personalization, dramatization would not be a problem if it were used mainly as an attention-focusing device to introduce more background and context surrounding events. Drama can help us engage with the great forces of history, science, politics, or human relations. When drama is used to bring analysis into mind, it is a good thing. When drama is employed as a cheap emotional device to focus on human conflict and travail, or farce and frailty, the larger significance of events becomes easily lost in waves of immediate emotion. The potential advantages of drama to enlighten and explain are sacrificed to the lesser tendencies of melodrama to excite, anger, and further personalize events. Thus the news often resembles real-life soap operas, only with far more important consequences than the ones on entertainment TV.

One of the things that makes the news dramatic—indeed, that may even drive news drama—is the use of visuals: photos, graphics, and live-action video. These elements of stories not only make the distant world seem more real, they make the news more believable. In many ways, particularly for television, the pictures may not only tell the stories but help editors and reporters decide which stories to tell and how to tell them.

In principle, there is nothing wrong with the emphasis on sights in news production. In fact one might argue that thinking visually is the best way to engage the senses more fully in communicating about society and politics. Yet there is often a tension between not reporting important stories that are hard to picture and reporting possibly unimportant stories simply because they offer great visual images. . . . The economics of audience attention often shade editorial decisions in the direction of starting with the pictures and then adding the words.

It is important to worry about the bases of such editorial decisions because in many ways they distinguish between good and bad uses of news drama. When stories are selected more for visuals than for larger political significance and context, the scripting of the story may bend information rather badly to suggest that the pictures do, in fact, reflect the larger situation. And since there is more than a grain of truth to the old adage that "seeing is believing," people may be compelled to see aspects of society that simply are not there or that are not there in the ways they are dramatically portrayed in the news. The visually graphic coverage of crime on TV is an example of this. . . . At the very least, the selection of news stories primarily because they offer dramatic images is one of several important reasons why the news is often so fragmented or disconnected from larger political or economic contexts that would provide other ways to tell the story.

FRAGMENTATION

The emphasis on personal and dramatic qualities of events feeds into a third information characteristic of the news: the isolation of stories from each other and from their larger contexts so that information in the news becomes fragmented and hard to assemble into a big picture. The fragmentation of information begins by emphasizing individual actors over the political contexts in which they operate. Fragmentation is then heightened by the use of dramatic formats that turn events into self-contained, isolated happenings. The fragmentation of information is further exaggerated by the severe space limits nearly all media impose for fear of boring readers and viewers with too much information.

Thus the news comes to us in sketchy dramatic capsules that make it difficult to see the causes of problems, their historical significance, or the connections across issues. It can even be difficult to follow the development of a particular issue over time as stories rise and fall more in response to the actions and reactions of prominent public figures than to independent reporting based on investigation of events. In addition, because it is difficult to bring historical background into the news, the impression is created of a world of chaotic events and crises that appear and disappear because the news picture offers little explanation of their origins.

THE AUTHORITY-DISORDER BIAS

Passing for depth and coherence in this system of personalized, dramatized, and fragmented information is a fourth news tendency in which the authoritative voices of officials take center stage in many political news dramas to interpret the threatening and confusing events that threaten the order of social life. There is bias in placing so much news focus on the largely emotional questions of Who's in charge? and Will order be restored? (As opposed, for example, to What is the problem?, Why is it a problem?, What are the alternative explanations beyond the official ones?, and What can citizens do to make the situation better?)

It may be tempting to say that government, after all, is centrally about authority and order, so why shouldn't these concerns be central preoccupations of the news? The problem comes when journalists build themes about authority and order into the news as core dramatic emotional plot elements, rather than letting them pass through the news gates more formally when they arise in public debate, much the way partisan political views are generally reported. Instead, the focus on authority and order is often driven by considerations of what makes for bigger, more dramatic, more emotional stories.

Whether the world is returned to a safe, normal place, or the very idea of a normal world is called in question, the news is preoccupied with order, along with related questions of whether authorities are capable of establishing or restoring it. It is easy to see why these generic plot elements are so central to news: They are versatile

and tireless themes that can be combined endlessly within personalized, dramatized, and fragmented news episodes. When the dramatic balance between order and disorder is not a plausible focus for an event, the news quickly turns the plot pair around and challenges authority itself, perhaps by publicizing the latest scandal charge against a leader or by opening the news gates to one politician willing to attack another.

In the past, it could be argued that the news more often resolved the authority-order balance in favor of official pronouncements aimed at "normalizing" conflicted situations by creating the appearance of order and control. A classic scenario of politics, according to political scientist Murray Edelman, is for authorities to take central stage to respond to crises (sometimes after having stirred them up in the first place) with emotionally reassuring promises that they will be handled effectively. Today's authorities still play out their parts, but the news increasingly finds ways to challenge either the pronouncements of officials or the presumption of order in society, or both. In short, the biggest change in portrayals of authority and order in the news . . . is that the dominant news focus has shifted away from trusted authorities providing reassuring promises to restore chaotic situations to a state of order or normalcy. Such stories continue to appear, of course, but the growing news trend is to portray unsympathetic, scheming politicians who often fail to solve problems, leaving disorder in their wake.

What is the evidence for the proposition that news is more negative and less likely to paint reassuring pictures of the return to normalcy following dramatic crises and scandals? . . . For reasons having more to do with the news business than with external realities, the following changes have been charted in news content in recent years:

- increased levels of mayhem (crime, violence, accidents, health threats, freeway chases, and other images of social chaos)

- greater volume of criticism of government, politicians, and their policies, and less focus on the substance of policies
- higher journalistic tone of cynicism and negativity.

Many of these order-challenging news patterns are relatively subtle, reflecting the "hidden hand" of economic decisions within news organizations. For example, ... the news recorded great increases in crime stories in the 1990s during a period in which officially reported rates of most violent crimes actually declined. This suggests that images of social disorder may be based on little more than choosing stories for their attention-getting effects. Images of disorder can be further amplified through subtle emphases in news writing. For example, is the traditional American family *threatened* by the increase in single-parent and two-working-parent households, or is the family in America simply *changing* in these ways as part of the normal course of social change?

The reason for thinking about authority and order as separable but related aspects of many news stories is that they are often set at odds with each other to create the dramatic tension in stories. Thus it would be too simple to say that authorities are almost always challenged and that disorder most often prevails. As news organizations take greater dramatic license with news plots, the two elements are mixed to achieve the greatest dramatic effect. A classic news plot represents authorities such as police, fire, and health officials as forces of good battling to restore order against social evils such as crime, violence, or disease. In one variation on this formula, crime or the latest health threat may seem to be running out of control, but officials appear in the news to tell us how we can be safe. Given the levels of mayhem and disorder in much of the news, the presence of at least some reassuring line of authority is a necessary dramatic counterpoint. Moreover, the question of what actually happened in a particular incident is often unclear at the time that news teams arrive. So we encounter the familiar news formula that goes: "The police aren't exactly sure what happened here yet, but their investigation is in progress, and we expect a report soon."

When authorities are anchoring a scene, dramatic speculation about levels of disorder may soar in news scripts. A typical example comes from a local newscast in Orlando, Florida, where Channel 6 announced an "exclusive" and promised a report from their "live truck" at the scene. The newscast opened with the anchor describing "A shocking scene in a Lake Mary neighborhood tonight. A home surrounded by crime-scene tape. A death police are calling 'suspicious.'" As the anchor spoke, the screen flashed the words "Neighborhood Shocker." Cut to the reporter live from the scene who further dramatized the death of a sixty-six-year-old woman by saying that police did not know what happened. As if to document this claim, the reporter interviewed a police officer who said that there were no signs of violence, forced entry, or robbery. Although this statement could easily have supported either an order or a disorder plot for the story, the local news format clearly favored playing the murder mystery/shocker plot. The reporter announced that the police planned an autopsy the next day and did not know what they would find. The live feed ended with the reporter saying that, in the mean time, they "want to keep a very tight lid on what happened. . . . Live in Lake Mary, Nicole Smith, Channel 6 News." The next day, it turned out that the woman had died naturally of a heart attack. So much for the "Neighborhood Shocker." As one observer noted, "Journalism Shocker" would have been a more appropriate on-screen warning.

By contrast, other dramatic plot formulas challenge authority either by focusing on alleged personal failings of politicians or by finding examples of government failures. The political poster story of the 1990s was about wasteful government spending. Many news organizations, both local and national, have run prominent features on "How government is wasting your tax dollars." The lure of such dramatic accounts over more representative news descriptions is illustrated in a *Los Angeles Times* investigative series on government spending on computers in different agencies. Even though the investigation turned up many positive examples of taxpayer dollars well spent, here is how the story opened:

WASHINGTON—After pumping $300 billion into computer systems in the last two decades, the federal government has compiled a record of failure that has jeopardized the nation's welfare, eroded public safety and squandered untold billions of dollars.

Whether or not most events fit the authority-disorder plot, it is easy enough to make them fit. A news show with a regular feature on government waste will, of course, find some alleged example of waste every time the feature is scheduled. Also, since there are few features on good things the government is doing, examples of government thrift (other than those forced by budget cuts) are less likely to be news.

·   ·   ·

Consider the picture so far: Each day news consumers are bombarded by dozens of compartmentalized, unrelated dramatic capsules. Some emotional satisfaction can be derived from forming strong identifications with or against the actors who star in these mini-dramas. But what about facts? What about knowledge and practical information? Unless the consumer has an existing interest or perspective on the subject, recalling facts from the news resembles a trivia game played alone. Most people cannot remember three-fourths of the stories in a TV news broadcast immediately after watching it, and information recall about the remembered quarter is sketchy at best.

Communication scholars have developed considerable empirical support for these four information biases in the news. There is now a sizable literature that reads like an inventory of these problems. The tendencies toward personalization, dramatization, and fragmentation have all been remarkably enduring over time, although they may have become more exaggerated with the economic pressures of the business. . . . While the focus on authority and order is also an enduring defining feature of the news, the shifting balance from order to mayhem and the unreflectively negative tone toward officials has left many observers puzzled and concerned. Indeed many politicians say they have left government because of the relentlessly negative media scrutiny, while others have surrounded themselves by legions of media consultants and handlers. At the same time that many journalists criticize their own product in these terms, they confess being helpless to change it under the current system of profit- and ratings-driven business values.

DISCUSSION QUESTIONS

1. Identify and explain the four information biases that Bennett explores. How do these biases affect what we see and hear as news? Can you think of ways any recent news stories have been influenced by these four biases?

2. In what way(s) is the quality of democracy imperiled by the continued consumption of news framed by information biases? Do you think that citizens would feel a stronger attachment to the political world if the news they received delved more honestly, analytically, and historically into the problems we face as a society?

MARK CRISPIN MILLER

THE MEDIA AND THE BUSH DYSLEXICON

Media scholar Mark Crispin Miller develops a diagnosis and a sharp critique of a new national disorder that he describes as a collective version of dyslexia. According to Miller, many Americans are unable to read correctly the disturbing political signs in front of them because the media machine increasingly serves as a propaganda conduit for the right-wing political forces, and thus is unable to offer interpretations consistent with the unsettling truths it allows us to glimpse. Today's culture of TV is a "bizarre postmodern form" wherein "the falseness of the spectacle before us is a sort of open secret, obvious to any viewer who wants to see it and, strangely, all the more deceptive for that fact." Miller's critique is meant to cut through the cynicism and hypocrisy purveyed by the media by setting the record straight so that we can distinguish truth from lies in ways that matter. In pursuit of this goal, Miller provides an entertaining, if depressing, account of the way in which the new dynamics of the media served George W. Bush in the campaign of 2000. All too many television chatterers denigrate both substantive political discussion and attention to the historical record because of a thinly-veiled, antidemocratic contempt for the ability of citizens to evaluate public debate over policy issues. Miller's coruscating account of the performance of the press in 2000, an account supported by the press' largely servile coverage of President Bush's first term, should go a long way towards retiring the myth of the "liberal media."

Far from merely goofing on this president, this [article] is meant to shed some light on propaganda in our time. The *Dyslexicon* attempts to give the lie to that enormous wave of propaganda—a joint production of the GOP and major media—whereby George W. Bush was forced on us as president, and then, after his inauguration, hailed almost universally for his amazing charm, his democratic ease, his rare ability to be all things to all Americans, and so on. Our experience of this transparent coup has been disorient-

ing from the start. On the one hand, TV has clearly shown the truth about him—with his own inadvertent help, since Bush is strangely frank about himself. His body language bellows his uninterest, his distraction, his uneasiness, his callousness; and he tends to blurt out all or part of what he's really thinking, even as he's trying to lie about it (a linguistic struggle that intensifies his incoherence). Meanwhile, his handlers and the mainstream media all keep on trying to play the revelations down, forever countering the

Source: Mark Crispin Miller, *The Bush Dyslexicon: Observations on a National Disorder.* New York: W. W. Norton, 2002, pp. 3–4, 60–73, and 75–76.

obvious with lots of upbeat spin and tactful silence. Thus TV keeps on sending us an eerie double message, by showing us one thing and telling us another. Those who want to buy the pitch prefer the latter, naturally, while those who just can't buy it feel as if they must be going crazy, what with all those smooth authoritative voices claiming that this man *should* be our president—when we can see, and have seen all along, that that is simply not the case.

Thus we are the victims of a strange new national disorder. It is as if the U.S. body politic were itself afflicted with a corporate version of dyslexia. The individual dyslexic cannot learn to read because he is unable, for whatever reasons, to translate letters into sounds. Because he can't decode those printed symbols for their phonic content, the writing on the page can make no sense to him. Today our body politic is comparably disabled, although it isn't written language that's the problem. The head that drives that body forward is, of course, the media machine—the busy neural network of producers, editors, anchors, journalists, and pundits, all subtly guided by the propagandists of the right. While it has no trouble scanning press releases or providing copy for the TelePrompTers, that swift, collective mind is fatally dyslexic when it comes to doping out the very spectacle that it presents to us. Unable to perceive the glaring daily evidence of absolute hypocrisy and cynical manipulation, it cannot read the writing on the wall—which, meanwhile, is crystal clear to many of the rest of us. The dyslexics at the top may be extremely savvy, yet they lack (to quote Orwell again) that all-important knowledge "in the bones" whereby we try, down here, to make our way. Seeing that it's all gone wrong yet always hearing, from on high, that everything is perfectly all right, we each feel—whether we can read or not—as helpless and perplexed as any undiagnosed dyslexic faced with street signs, menus, newspapers, and exams.

Against all that, *The Bush Dyslexicon* is meant to set the record straight: to remind us of the truth that TV shows us, even as it keeps on lying about it—much like the president himself, who, unless he knows his script by heart, often tells the truth despite himself, and does it most transparently when he is lying. (In this he is much like his dad, as we shall see.) By thus corroborating what TV so viscerally conveys, the [article] may also help dispel the great myth of "the liberal media"—a preposterous notion (or Big Lie) that Rush Limbaugh and his screaming brethren have long since sold to millions of Americans. And, more subtly, by pointing out the truths that television has revealed to us, this [article] may also shed some light on the bizarre postmodern form that propaganda often takes today, here in the culture of TV—wherein the falseness of the spectacle before us is a sort of open secret, obvious to any viewer who wants to see it and, strangely, all the more deceptive for that fact.

·　　·　　·

WHAT YOU SEE IS WHAT YOU GET

If Bush had won legitimately, we could say that we'd gotten the president that we deserve. His "message" having played well on TV, and the audience having picked him by a clear majority (both electoral *and* popular), he would be the people's choice, and there would be no ambiguity about it. But the situation now is highly complicated—and not just because of the shenanigans in Florida and on the Supreme Court. For Bush owes his unlikely victory not only to those party flacks and goons who forced the issue, nor only to the Rehnquist Five, but also to TV. Although he never played well on the medium per se, TV was very, very good to him, because the network that controls the medium—from above, and from the anchor desks and pundit chairs—embraced him, and implicitly endorsed him, for several reasons.

First of all, there is the great extrinsic factor of the media's corporate ownership, the top managers and major shareholders preferring the aggressively big-merger-friendly GOP to the less-aggressively big-merger-friendly Democrats. Al Gore had many champions in Hollywood, of course, including all the top pro-Clinton heavyweights from Michael Eisner on down. A tough New Democrat somewhat to Clinton's right, Gore was never threatening to the interests of the corporate media, for all his pulpit thumping with Joe Lieberman. (Indeed, even Rupert Murdoch was a quiet Gore supporter, the Democrats having used the Staples Center—40 percent owned by News Corporation—as a gift for their convention.) Nevertheless, the media's parent companies will do much better, and clean up much faster, now that they have Bush to play with, since he's for corporate concentration above all (literally), nor will his FCC—now chaired by Colin Powell's son, Michael, an adamant free-marketeer—discuss even the feeblest sort of regulation, whereas Powell's predecessor, Bill Kennard, did try now and then. (Under Bush, we will soon see the final merger of newspaper chains with media corporations—a move that Gore would not have made without a lot of prior shilly-shallying.) The media-corporate bias toward the governor was evident, for example, in MSNBC's decision to show repeatedly, throughout the five-week civil war in Florida, its dubious hail-Caesar documentary on Desert Storm—an obvious stroke of pro-Bush programming, certainly approved, if not dictated, by the network's corporate Dad and Mom: General Electric (a huge defense contractor, likely to do well from NMD) and Microsoft (whose antitrust woes Governor Bush did not approve of and will surely end).

Certainly such bias at the top does not translate directly into bias on camera. The influence is for the most part atmospheric rather than direct, the smartest, most ambitious employees inferring how the wind blows from on high and suiting up accordingly. This is true of all large corporations (including universities), but such impact is especially momentous in the culture industries, from which we tend to garner all we know about the world. In TV's case, the problem is compounded by the rightist conquest of the news divisions—a sweep that Nixon long ago envisioned and took some steps to realize, bullying the networks into mere cheerleading. ("ABC and CBS have improved considerably over the past couple of months since my visit with them," Chuck Colson reported to Bob Haldemen in late 1970.) The system once assailed by Spiro Agnew (his tirades penned by William Safire and Pat Buchanan) as pro-Red is now solidly right wing, its frequent talking heads including Ollie North, Bob Novak, Peggy Noonan, William Bennett, George Will, Tucker Carlson of the *Weekly Standard,* Rich Lowry of the *National Review,* Alan Simpson, William Kristol, John Sununu, Paul Gigot, Ed Rollins, David Frum, David Brooks, Linda Chavez, Andrew Sullivan, John McLaughlin, Tony Blankley, Armstrong Williams, John Reilly and the whole prime-time ménage at Fox, John Fund of the *Wall Street Journal, Time's* paranoid Hugh Sidey, and Reagan Democrat Chris Matthews. (Mary Matalin has gone back to work directly for the Bush machine.) Opposing that dark legion are a few wan pseudoliberals, like Bob Beckel and Bill Press, some genuine articles like Eleanor Clift, Mark Shields, Joe Conason, and Robert Reich, and here and there some true—and very lonely— people of the left, such as Katrina van den Heuvel of the *Nation,* the provocative Christopher Hitchens, Jim Hightower, and (on weekends) Jeff Cohen. Otherwise, TV's punditocracy (like radio's and like the brain trust in the think tanks) is firmly on the right—i.e., not conservative but *radical* in its support for private privilege and, to some extent, a theocratic state.

Always well armed with Bush/Cheney's talking points, that chorus worked efficiently to change the subject when the governor's incapacities came up—which was not often. And their canned views were generally seconded by those nervous nellies who worked with them—the anchors and reporters who, although not necessarily on the right themselves, could not afford to seem unsympathetic. Certainly the national press corps in D.C. is, on economic matters, largely to the right of the American majority—a fact documented by Fairness and Accuracy in Reporting— because those members of the Fourth Estate are in some pretty high tax brackets and would therefore benefit from a return to Reaganomics. And yet even the moderates and liberals of the press deferred to the pro-Bush consensus, for their careers depend on such compliance. What mainly drives them is a general fear of seeming "liberal"— as countless rightists (many of them *in* the media) have long been charging, notwithstanding the abundant counterevidence, from TV's long love affair with Ronald Reagan to the coverage of the 1988 campaign to the news divisions' loud huzzahs for Operation Desert Storm to the journalistic drives to make "Whitewater," "Filegate," "Travelgate," and "Chinagate" look like worthwhile stories and not propaganda fabrications. The media's refusal during the recent coup to call a spade a spade reflected the anxiety of those professionals, who all keep bending over backward not to be accused of "liberal bias." Such a tag would be a killer in the corporate news biz, since it would mean that you'd have no more *access* to those inside players who tell you what the news should be.

And yet there is another, deeper reason for TV's support of Governor Bush. On the one hand, as we have noted here, he is not telegenic unless his turns are very tightly choreographed, when he sticks closely to his script and shows no tension or bewilderment. It is worth noting here that Bush's incapacity is so apparent that it was gently conceded by his own supporters, once he had the job sewed up. "He has made sure that he has a high-powered team around him to make up for any deficiencies, though I'm not saying he has big deficiencies," said the GOP's Robert Michel vis-à-vis the president-select's impending cabinet. And William Safire, in a piece on the relationship between Don Rumsfeld at the Department of Defense and Colin Powell at the Department of State, offered this not-comforting conclusion: "What happens in those crises when State and Defense disagree? Bush can consult Dick Cheney or get George Shultz on the phone or, in due course, trust his own judgment."

And yet while Bush per se plays badly on the medium, the TV system as we know it is his natural ally—because both it and he are all about mere "message." Both of them, in other words, are all *about* TV and nothing else. This is nothing

new for him, a calculating sort from way, way back, but on TV it was not ever thus. For many years— indeed, from McLuhan's day—both observers and practitioners of campaign propaganda entertained the question of exactly where to find the proper balance between word and image, argument and spectacle, issue and impression. The comfortable assumption was that those two categories were entirely separate, fixed, both resilient and both perfectly amenable to expert handling by the news professionals who, if they were sober, civic-minded and meticulous enough, could strike the crucial balance, at once instructing and entertaining their audience.

But now there is very little place for "substance"—indeed, for any rational discourse— on TV (or throughout the other large commercial media), for formal, political, and economic reasons. As the networks have developed it, the medium is far too speedy, loud, disjunctive, and sensational to permit even the resonance, much less the discussion, of a complex sentence (never mind an idea). Furthermore, the heavy pressure of the advertisers forbids the airing of whatever issues might be either too depressing or too complicated, or too threatening, for the venue's crucial atmosphere of light festivity—a nonstop pseudo-carnival that never can slow down, or someone might lose money. Into this tightly regulated riot of commercial propaganda every politician has to fit his/her own propaganda "message"—and, if s/he's lucky, also has to fit him- or her*self,* looking "nice" enough (with just the right amount of self-effacing humor) and sounding "clear" enough (without alarming anyone) to keep from coming off as "stiff," "robotic," "wooden," or in any other way ridiculous. All "political" success has everything to do with such smooth integration—which by and large leaves out telling truth or making sense.

Thus Bush belongs here in the culture of TV. He fits in, not despite his open calculation and the utter superficiality of his (overt) concerns, but because of them. Such defects don't disturb the pundits of today, most of whom—whatever medium they work in—cannot even see what's wrong with Bush, so steeped are they themselves in TV's trivial world-view. Our president's most calculating predecessors weren't so lucky, their overconcentration on mere spin arousing strong objections back in those less TV-saturated days.

For example, Emmet John Hughes, one of Eisenhower's top assistants, was blown away by Nixon's straining effort to project a natural identity. Hughes quotes from Nixon's account, in *Six Crises,* of his resolution following his first debate with JFK: "I went into the second debate *determined* to do my best to *convey . . . sincerity. . . .* If I succeeded in this, I felt my 'image' would take care of itself." Hughes—who added those italics—found the contradiction there amazing and yet typical: "Only the most shallow exercise in self-scrutiny could conclude with such a resolve to appear 'sincere.' Yet it was characteristic of the candidate, the politician, and the man." Like his mentor, George H. W. Bush conceived "sincerity" as a performance. "I can't be as good as Ronald Reagan on conviction," he confessed during the 1988 campaign. "There's nobody like him at conveying what it is like to strongly feel patriotism and love of country." Just as it marks his son's, such ingenuous theatricality marked much of that failed president's public speech—a selfreflexiveness that many journalists noted at the time. "Bush is always telling you how to look at what he is doing, or what the impression is that he is trying to create," Meg Greenfield wrote in *Newsweek* back when George I was king. That tendency got lots of laughs when Bush, in the middle of a campaign speech in New Hampshire, accidentally read one of his stage directions: "Message: I care." And yet he did that all the time, and quite deliberately: "We have—I have—want to be positioned in that I could not possibly support David Duke because of the racism and because of the bigotry and all of this." Such dim transparency amounted almost to a kind of honesty, as Michael Kinsley wrote in 1992: "What these tics share is a clear view of the mind at work. Bush's mental processes lie close to the surface."

Our new President Bush is also endlessly explaining what the "theme" or "message" is—but in the new millennium our journalists don't seem to notice it. While Bush's comic flubs did get some press, his constant commentary on his own self-presentation raised no qualms or questions. "I think probably the best thing I've done is interface with the press," he told *Brill's Content* in September 2000. "They get to see the human—that I'm a human person, that I've got feelings, I care, I've got priorities. It gives them a better sense of who I am as a person. . . . I think the more somebody gets to know a person, the more likely it is they'll be able to write an objective story." The entire interview went like that, the candidate discoursing at great length on what a dandy job he had been doing keeping the whole press corps off the subjects of his record, his sponsors, his affiliations, and his ultimate intentions—and the *Brill's* reporter, Seth Mnookin, played right along, asking Bush no question that might spoil the mood of chummy candor. As any journalist should know, "the more somebody gets to know a person" the *less* likely it is that he or she will write objectively about him. If Mnookin had been listening to the candidate instead of watching him, he might have asked Bush to explain the meaning of "objectively" or, for that matter, what his "feelings" really had to do with anything, or what he meant by that all-too-familiar "message," "I care."

By now, the mainstream press has quite forgotten the important differences between what's on TV and (what we might call) reality. Instead of trying to interrogate the photo op, asking what it *isn't* saying or how it's fiddling with the truth, journalists—or those who have been granted the appropriate credentials—often actively *collaborate* with those who set up the picture so as to help the audience discern the proper "theme." When Bush presented certain choices for his cabinet, he was asked helpfully if his "diverse" selection might not indicate "a message that you're sending to America." "You bet," replied the president-select without missing a beat: "That people who work hard and make the right decisions in life can achieve anything they want in America."

At another such unveiling two weeks later, Bush was once again assisted big-time by the press: "You've now named a cabinet that is very diverse in terms of gender and ethnicity and experience in the private sector and the federal government. What does your cabinet say, do you think, about your management style, about how you intend to make decisions as president?" "It says I'm not afraid to surround myself with strong and competent people," Bush shot back, and then expanded on that "theme" by adding that he knows "how to recruit people and how to delegate, how to align authority and responsibility, how to hold people accountable for results and how to build a team of people." It was a memorable lesson, which Bush concluded with a stirring pledge: "And that's exactly what we're going to do."

The journalists' collusion has extended well beyond such servile prompting. On TV itself, the eternal "expert" nattering on "politics" deals mainly—and often exclusively—with what some still call "image" but what is really just TV. The networks' journalistic stars go on and on and on about the politicians' failure or success at pleasing—or at not displeasing—viewers. Reflexive and impressionistic, such interminable yakking tells us nothing, dwelling on details of bearing, posture, voice, and makeup, instead of dealing with what anybody did, said, or failed to say. And yet such discourse is not merely empty. By reducing all discussion to the level of the taste test, wherein "likeability" is all that counts, it tacitly discredits all intelligent discussion, while favoring those figures who can rile us without challenging or, as it were, taxing us. In other words, it is not just TV itself that works against the rational position but those never-ending propagandists *on* TV who *tell* us who is likeable and who is not. That influence will work on those inclined already to agree with it, especially when it manages to get in the last word.

Thus TV functioned after each of the debates. On CNN, for example, after the third encounter on October 17, Bob Novak got the ball rolling by suggesting that "there might have been a defeat for Gore on the likeability factor. I haven't seen all the numbers, but I understand he didn't do well on credibility or likeability." Of course, the wish was father to that thought, as Novak is among the steeliest of commandos, saying nothing that will not advance the Cause: cutting taxes. From there Jeff Greenfield took the ball and ran a long way with it, wondering whether "Gore's clear decision to be aggressive, to try to define very sharp differences," might make him seem "assertive and tough minded" or "rude and smug"—although "we're going to have to wait forty-eight hours or so to find out." He then moved on to Bush, who "clearly was trying to stage a conversation with both the people here and to [*sic*] the country, and, in effect, to say: Look, I'm a regular, soft-spoken guy. And Al Gore just wants this too much." *Time*'s Tamala Edwards then weighed in: Gore had learned the "lesson" that he can't "out-soften George Bush on compassion and talking about his heart" and therefore worked this time to "strike a contrast." She seemed, however, to differ with Bob Novak: "In this forum, where he was answering questions and being that aggressive, it will be interesting to see whether or not it plays as [if] he was a little terrier running out and trying to answer this person's question versus standing back and saying: You know, let me talk down to you [*sic*]." Bill Schneider then talked for what seemed like a week about a snap poll CNN had done just then. Novak summed up: "I don't think it's a win for Al Gore." And as for Bush: "I don't think that Governor Bush is very good in this kind of a format. . . . But I don't think he hurt himself."

That Novak would admit that much about the governor's inane performance confirms how bad it really was. Bush was vague on the details of his own voucher plan, his own position on the Patient's Bill of Rights, and on affirmative action, among other issues, while Gore was certain—and relentless. It was at that third debate that Bush's various evasive tactics were most blatant—crying out that he was being attacked, using ancient lines that didn't answer ("Well, you know, it's hard to make people love one another; I wish I knew the law because I'd darn sure sign it," he said regarding the accountability of schools), and at one point even needing Jim Lehrer to rescue him from Gore's persistent inquisition. Nevertheless, the "analysts" at CNN said not one word about the *substance* of the candidates' exchange but just kept harping on the general "statements" that the candidates were putatively "trying" to make about themselves, through their tone and body language.

Although a waste of time, that postdebate bull session was at least not strongly biased, nor was its anti-intellectualism too pronounced. On ABC there was a far more noxious session on the subject of the third debate. We will do well to reproduce that episode in its entirety because it captures perfectly the barbarous synergy between the right and TV news, each feigning populism for its own elitist purposes. It took place two weeks before Election Day 2000, on the October 22 broadcast of *This Week* with Sam Donaldson and Cokie Roberts, joined by George Will and George Stephanopoulos. The topic was the Dingell-Norwood bill, which would provide a patient's bill of rights, including the right to sue your HMO. In the debate, Bush had claimed to be in favor of a patient's bill of rights, and Gore then challenged him to say if he would back that piece of legislation.

[Donaldson:] Well, talk about the message. I mean, remember during the last debate, Gore kept talking about "the Dingell-Norwood bill, the Dingell-Norwood bill." And we thought, as a public service, we'd just show you who Dingell and Norwood are. Let us tell you about them. Representatives Dingell and Norwood introduced the Patient's Bill of Rights favored by Gore and the House of Representatives. John Dingell, from Michigan, is the longest-serving Democrat in the House. His father, who was a House member before him, was a sponsor of Social Security in the 1930s

and pioneered the idea of national health insurance back in 1943. Charlie Norwood, from Georgia, a Republican, is a dentist. He served in Vietnam and was first elected to the House in 1994 as part of the Republican revolution.

So that's who Dingell and Norwood are. Now I'll tell you—

[Stephanopoulos:] But the important—

[Roberts:] Yeah, but—

[Donaldson:] But there's a guy named Greg Ganske who's also on the bill. It's actually the Dingell-Norwood-*Ganske* bill!

[Stephanopoulos:] But the import—the *important* point—

[Donaldson:] But I don't have time to start telling you about him!

[Roberts:] He's from Iowa!

[Stephanopoulos:] The important point there is that George Bush didn't answer the question about the Dingell-Norwood bill, which is a patient's bill of rights that allows people to—the right to sue.

[Roberts:] Actually, I don't think that *is* the important point there.

[Stephanopoulos:] Why not?

[Roberts:] Because that's not what comes across when you're watching the debate. What comes across when you're watching the debate is this guy from *Washington* doing *Washington-speak*.

[Stephanopoulos:] But it's—

[Roberts:] And you know, it's having an effect not just at the presidential level but at the congressional level, as well. Because the Republicans did a very smart thing, which is that they voted for *their* version of a Patient's Bill of Rights, and they voted for *their* version of prescription drug coverage. So they get to go out and tout all these issues, and then the Democrats are left saying, "But you didn't do *Dingell* and *Norwood!*"

[Stephanopoulos:] Well, then they—but what gets lost there—wait a second, what gets *lost* there is that George Bush *did* oppose a patient's bill of rights in the state of Texas. And he did—and he's *not* for the Dingell-Norwood bill.

[Roberts:] It was lost because Al Gore didn't *say* it.

[Stephanopoulos:] Yeah, well, he did say it, actually, in the course of the debate.

[Donaldson:] This is very cerebral. George Will, you are, but it doesn't be—helping Gore [*sic*].

[Will:] It's not helping Gore in part because people find him overbearing and off-putting and all the rest. But also the fact—I think the issues are beginning to break, finally, for George W. Bush. The reports in the papers are that—that Gore is going to stress Social Security from now on. I think he's going to find that when p—I'm surprised that Bush hasn't been stressing his plan to allow people to invest a portion of their Social Security taxes in the stock market. Since 1992, Sam, the number of Americans with—owning stocks, largely through mutual funds, has doubled. Two-point-two million more Americans joined the stock-holding ranks last year alone. And I think you're going to find, and he's going to find, that it helps.

THE POWER OF FORGETTING

Amid all that sparkling repartee, Stephanopoulos's earnest efforts to *recall* and *explain* could not go anywhere—and neither could the issue of the Patient's Bill of Rights, a total bore as far as Sam and Cokie were concerned (and, in George Will's eyes, a portent of Communism). Stephanopoulos's colleagues couldn't possibly relate to Dingell-Norwood since they're far too wealthy to concern themselves with HMOs and therefore wouldn't ever need to sue one. However, Stephanopoulos's problem wasn't just the privileged superciliousness of his particular co-workers but the heavy anti-democratic bias of the entertainment system that employs them all.

The partnership of Donaldson and Will reflects the perfect union of two complementary probusiness forces. On the one hand, there is the incessant upscale emphasis of ABC News, which, like every other TV news division (and newsmagazine and national newspaper), is an advertising medium pitched at shoppers and investors and therefore devoid of labor coverage—unless a strike should inconvenience the commuters—and serious consumer news. (Case in point: The born-again anti-consumerist John Stossel does his let's-be-fair-to-agribusiness "exposés" on ABC.) On the other hand, we have, in Will, the outright plutocratic presence of the GOP, which doesn't want too many of the natives getting restless—or voting. Although Dingell-Norwood is not even slightly leftist (Charlie Norwood [R.-Ga.] was a Gingrich ally), the issue of the Patient's Bill of Rights, with its allowance for litigation by the masses, was just a bit too Bolshevik for the gang on ABC. And so the effervescent Sam and Cokie laughed it off, and the grave Will deftly changed the subject—to the stock market and all those glad Americans who own a piece of it, which upbeat subject Sam and Cokie and both Georges all discussed until the next commercial.

Thus that broadcast, in its light-hearted way, attempted to preserve the status quo by getting everybody to *forget* a democratic possibility and just go back to sleep. Whether they work brutally or entertainingly—or both—*all* anti-democratic forces see the people as extremely thick and basically oblivious—and work on them accordingly. "The receptivity of the great masses is very limited, their intelligence is small, but their power of forgetting is enormous," Hitler wrote. As that example will remind us, the effort to exploit the masses' feeble memory can be violently crude, with just one party taking over all the nation's media, its hooligans attacking dissidents, and all contrary books turned into "furnace fodder." Here in the United States, the mass forgetfulness is by and large more peaceably exploited, as those in power—economic or political—don't just overwhelm the audience with their own propaganda or send thugs to trash books and beat up writers. Rather, those powers rely on the media to carry out such labors for them—and to do it with finesse, hyping the authorities and killing off the opposition without violence (and without having to be told). This is a distinction that our president understands. Asked by Mnookin if there "should be some kind of redress in the courts" when writers such as Hatfield publish "rumors and gossip," Bush first answered that there should ("Yeah, I would hope so at some point"), then came up with a subtler, smarter answer:

> Well, I don't know that, I don't know that question [sic]. . . . I think there ought to be some—I think the press corps ought to self-police, and I think there ought to be—in order to enhance the integrity of the press corps, it seems like to me [sic] that when they catch, when they catch these fraudulent acts, these scurrilous attacks, they ought to rise up in indignation, and I don't know if that—you know, I think that maybe might have occurred when they started condemning this guy for writing the story.
>
> There's a little—you know there's kind of a deep—in the consciousness of the press corps there's still this gotcha element. It seems like it's improving.

It did improve, as we have seen, with the mainstream press consistently forgetting all the governor's weaknesses and thereby urging us to do the same. And yet the telejournalists' oblivious work on his behalf throughout the race was nothing by comparison with what they managed after his inauguration. Once installed, and having made the proper "unifying" gestures at his swearing-in, Bush was born-again again, as all of his past history went straight down the memory hole. Not only was his record utterly forgotten—and with it all his ultrarightist ties—but so was the chicanery in Florida, and so was all the party's brazen postelection propaganda, and so was the Supreme Court's arbitrary and unprecedented move to choose the nation's president. Once Bush had been enthroned, it was as if all that had never happened, so ravishing were his new clothes. On CNBC's *Hardball* just a week into the Bush regime, Chris Matthews gave historian Robert Dallek and *USA Today* reporter Doris Page his view on why the Democrats had "lost": Gore did not blast Clinton for his Oval Office dalliance back in '96 (Matthews meant '98), and Gore/Lieberman's campaign was too left-wing. Page tried politely to remind her bumptious host that Gore had actually not lost the national vote, and there even was some question as to whether he had lost in Florida; but Matthews was unfazed by those reminders—or, rather, couldn't hear them, but kept explaining why the Democrats had "lost" while Page and Dallek sat there, their perplexity apparent through their smiles.

Such forgetfulness, it seems, should not be quite so easy in the culture of TV. After all, there's so much stuff on tape, and so much of that is all so readily available—at least to those of us who can afford to be on-line—that journalists have no excuse for blanking out on what occurred, say, twenty years ago or even just last week (as long as what occurred was televised). Equipped with such an archive, journalists could do a lot to fight the institutional tendency to prettify our past. Indeed, unless they do such crucial work, that tendency will soon take over absolutely, hiding our whole history in a fog of fragrant myth. Certainly the videos can shed no light on matters too complex to have been televised (e.g., the savings and loan scandals of the 1980s) or that were largely hidden from the public (e.g., Iran-Contra) or that took place long, long ago, before the dawn of television. A grasp of history requires, of course, a knack for understanding things that were complex *and* secretive *and* happened long ago (e.g., Prescott Bush's business dealings with the Nazis). And yet there's still a great deal that the videos can teach us if we bother to look closely at them. They tell us much that books cannot—about the character of certain men and certain times.

• • •

Thus TV's news stars, and the many pundits to their right, kept urging us, and urge us now, to lighten up and join the party—or at least let the winners party on. In other words, they want us to forget what TV has itself made clear to us, thereby moving the majority to vote *against* that party. TV revealed the candidate's unsuitability (although he claimed to be "more suited") and revealed his constant calculation (which he kept imputing to his adversary). TV showed us how thin-skinned he really is—despite the endless hype about his "likeability"—and even that sadistic streak, which stood out most when he was trying to show his "lighter side." Moreover, TV had already shown us what the movement backing him is really all about—the crazy hatred and fanatical resolve on full display throughout the great mock epic of the failed impeachment (which Governor Bush was always very careful never to bring up). That same crusading madness was apparent on TV throughout the postelection crisis—a spectacle not easy to forget, whatever TV's newsmen say, and however charming this new president can be behind closed doors.

Given all that TV had to show us, it seems a little strange that, in the culture of TV, it takes a book to emphasize the obvious. And yet this book is only doing what TV did all along, despite the efforts of its managers: urging you, through all of Bush's "themes" and "messages," his half-truths and his slick, distracting lines, his endless shots at "them" for being "calculating," devious, and "irresponsible," to look who's talking.

DISCUSSION QUESTIONS

1. What parallels does Miller draw between the problems encountered by an individual with dyslexia and the collective disorder the U.S. public faces today? How do the mass media contribute to this collective form of dyslexia?

2. One of the most common criticisms of the mass media is that they display a "liberal bias." Why does Miller reject this perspective? What evidence does he provide to refute the liberal media thesis, and how compelling do you find it?

3. In the election of 2000, how did the downplaying of "substance" in media coverage work to the advantage of George W. Bush and to the detriment of Al Gore? How does Miller interpret the October 22, 2000, discussion from ABC's This Week show?

INA HOWARD

MEDIA POWER SOURCES: TV SETS THE AGENDA

Even in the age of the Internet, most Americans continue to get the bulk of their news from the television networks. In this article Ina Howard, the former U.S. research director of the media watchdog group Media Tenor International, takes a straightforward approach to analyzing the content of the big three network evening news shows throughout 2001, including ABC World News Tonight, CBS Evening News, *and* NBC Nightly News. *Bear in mind that the other major news network not covered in the study,* Fox News Channel, *actually is more conservative than the other three. Her results dispel the widespread conservative position that the networks represent a liberal news bias in terms of story selection and sources quoted. Far from a liberal bias, what Howard found in her comprehensive analysis is that the news is heavily weighted toward sources that "favored the elite interests that the corporate owners of these shows depend on for advertising revenue, regulatory support and access to information." In every analytic category—partisan balance, gender issues, race and minority issues, and the choice of "experts"—the news shows overwhelmingly amplified the voices of those who supported political and economic elites with power, while muffling or ignoring outright the voices of those who might pose a serious challenge to powerful interests. We ask you to consider Howard's analysis in light of our nation's commitment to "free thinking" and lively discourse.*

On an average weeknight, *ABC World News Tonight, CBS Evening News,* and *NBC Nightly News* are tuned in by approximately one-quarter of television-viewing homes in the U.S.—about two-thirds of the U.S. public that claims to follow current events regularly. In 22 minutes the newscasts deliver snapshots of national and international news that not only frame current events for the public, but influence story selection at local affiliate stations, at radio outlets, and in print media. In addition to putting topics on the nation's agenda, the networks help set the range of debate on those issues by selecting sources who ostensibly represent the interests and opinions of the population.

In this role as agenda setters and debate arbiters, the networks' broadcasts profoundly affect the democratic process. While conservatives

Source: Ina Howard, "Power Sources: On Party, Gender, Race and Class, TV News Looks to the Most Powerful Groups." *Extra!*, vol. 15, no. 3, May–June 2002, pp. 11–14.

from Spiro Agnew to Bernard Goldberg have accused the news media of using this influence to promote liberal ideals, a comprehensive analysis of the sources used on the big three networks' evening news shows in 2001 suggests otherwise.

Instead of a liberal bias, the study found, source selection favored the elite interests that the corporate owners of these shows depend on for advertising revenue, regulatory support, and access to information. Network news demonstrated a clear tendency to showcase the opinions of the most powerful political and economic actors, while giving limited access to those voices that would be most likely to challenge them.

On the partisan level, the news programs provided a generous platform for sources from the Republican Party—the party in power in the White House for almost the entire year—while giving much less access to the opposition Democrats, and virtually no time to third party or independent politicians. Based on the criterion of who got to speak, the broadcast networks functioned much more as venues for the claims and opinions of the powerful than as democratic forums for public discussion or education.

PARTISAN IMBALANCE

This study was based on data compiled by Media Tenor Ltd., a nonpartisan, German-based media analysis firm with an office in New York City. During 2001, for each report on *ABC World News Tonight, NBC Nightly News,* and *CBS Evening News,* Media Tenor researchers coded the topic, time period, location, protagonists, and detailed source information (including partisan affiliation, gender, and race or nationality, when determinable). If special programming pre-empted the news shows' broadcast in New York City, transcripts were analyzed when available. For this study, data was analyzed for the time period between January 1 and December 31, 2001, which included 14,632 sources in 18,765 individual reports.

In 2001, the voices of Washington's elite politicians were the dominant sources of opinion on the network evening news, making up one in three Americans (and more than one in four of all sources) who were quoted on all topics throughout the year. Of sources who had an identifiable partisan affiliation, 75 percent were Republican and only 24 percent Democrats. A mere 1 percent were third-party representatives or independents.

The three networks varied only slightly in their selection of partisan sources. CBS had the most Republicans and the fewest Democrats (76 percent vs. 23 percent); NBC (75 percent vs. 25 percent) and ABC (73 percent vs. 27 percent) were marginally less imbalanced. CBS had the most independents (1.2 percent), followed by ABC (0.7 percent) and NBC (an almost invisible 0.2 percent).

Small as they are, these latter figures may overstate the presence of independent politicians on the nightly news. Sen. James Jeffords, the centrist Vermont Republican who broke with his party in May (giving Democrats control of the Senate), made up 83 percent of the independent sources who were quoted throughout the year, suggesting that networks highlighted independent politicians mainly when they impacted the fates of the two major parties. The only avowedly anti-establishment independent who appeared in 2001, Ralph Nader, made up 3 percent of independent or third-party sources—0.03 percent of all politicians quoted.

Although the attacks of September 11 exacerbated the tilt toward Republicans, the difference was pronounced beforehand as well. Prior to the attacks Republicans made up 68 percent, Democrats 31 percent and independents 1 percent of partisan sources. Afterward, Republican sources surged to 87 percent, with Democrats (13 percent) and independents (0.1 percent) falling even further behind.

DISPELLING "DEMOCRATIC BIAS"

While these figures ought to dispel the persistent notion that network news has a liberal or pro-Democratic bias, they do not in themselves necessarily prove a conservative or Republican bias.

Rather, they may reflect the networks' definition of news that prioritizes the actions and opinions of the executive branch. Members of the Bush administration (and Clinton administration, for the pre-inauguration period in January), including the president, vice president, cabinet members, and official spokespeople, made up 17 percent of all U.S. sources and 62 percent of all partisan sources. When these are set aside, the remaining partisan sources showed a rough parity between the two major parties, with 51 percent Republicans, 48 percent Democrats and 2 percent third-party members or independents appearing as sources.

This breakdown suggests that in 2001 there was a strong advantage on the nightly news for the party that held the White House; after the administration had its say, there was roughly one source from its own party to defend it for every representative from the opposition party that might criticize it. Unfortunately, complete data do not exist from 2000 or earlier to determine whether the same ratio held true during a Democratic administration.

The leading topics on which partisan sources were quoted, however, suggest that the disparities in sourcing could indicate a more substantial bias than mere reverence for the presidency. Partisan sources from both parties were most likely to appear in stories on domestic politicking, such as speeches or debates in Congress. After that area of coverage, however, their next most common appearances were qualitatively very different: Republicans appeared in reports on the widely supported war in Afghanistan, while 12 percent of the reports in which Democrats were quoted focused on corruption and scandals, with Democrats in most cases defending themselves or other party members. Republicans, by contrast, were presented in such reports in only 1 percent of their total appearances. By focusing so much on largely nonpolitical scandals (e.g., Chandra Levy, White House gifts) involving the party out of power, the networks bolstered the Republican image—not only by showcasing Democratic "character" questions, but by reserving the vast majority of

Republican quotes for more dignified policy discussions, thereby disassociating the party from the "dirty politics" of scandal-mongering.

The top individual sources on the news reflect the emphasis given to the administration at the expense of the opposition. George W. Bush alone made up 9 percent of all sources and 33 percent of partisan sources, putting him far ahead of any other individual voice for the year. The next most common sources were Al Qaeda leader Osama bin Laden (2 percent), former President Bill Clinton, Secretary of State Colin Powell, Attorney General John Ashcroft, Defense Secretary Donald Rumsfeld, Palestinian Authority President Yassir Arafat, Vice President Dick Cheney, Senate Majority Leader Tom Daschle and New York mayor Rudolph Giuliani (with 1 percent each). Clinton faded from prominence shortly after the Bush inauguration (80 percent of his appearances occurred in the first four months of the year), leaving Daschle as the only other top 10 source from the domestic opposition party. The remaining top U.S. sources were all members of the Bush administration, with the exception of the Republican mayor of New York (89 percent of whose appearances occurred after September 11).

WOMEN'S RESTRICTED ROLE

After U.S. politicians, "unclassified citizens"—a category that can be used as a proxy for ordinary Americans—were the most common individual type of source, providing 20 percent of all quotes. While it's valuable to hear the voices of ordinary citizens on the nightly news, the context in which most of their soundbites appeared makes it unlikely that their viewpoints did much to shape the nation's political debate: They were more often presented in human interest stories, crime reports and entertainment news than in all "hard" news topics combined, leaving discussion of most policy issues to "expert" political and economic elites.

While women made up only 15 percent of total sources, they represented more than double that share—40 percent—of the ordinary citizens in the news. This reflects a tendency to quote men as the vast majority of authoritative voices while presenting women as non-experts; women made up only 9 percent of the professional and political voices that were presented. More than half of the women (52 percent) who appeared on the news were presented as average citizens, whereas only 14 percent of male sources were.

The balance was roughly equal among networks. NBC, with 18 percent, had slightly more female sources (of whom 53 percent were non-authorities), while ABC and CBS both presented 14 percent (of whom 48 percent and 55 percent, respectively, were ordinary citizens).

Even in coverage of gender-related policies (which made up 0.2 percent of coverage), women made up only 43 percent of the sources. On such issues as equal opportunity, gender equality and discrimination, partisan sources made up 24 percent of the total; 71 percent of these were Republicans and 29 percent Democrats. All of these partisan sources were men. Women were presented as non-expert citizens 77 percent of the time in gender stories. Men, by contrast, spoke as experts in their fields 100 percent of the time in such stories.

Ordinary citizens (all women) made up 33 percent of sources on gender policies, followed by George W. Bush (17 percent), company representatives (10 percent, all men), Alan Greenspan (10 percent), soldiers (7 percent, all men), writers (7 percent, half men, half women), and other groups that each constituted 3 percent or less of the total. In keeping with other areas of coverage, white Americans clearly dominated the quoted sources, making up 89 percent of sources for whom race was determinable.

Two women from the Middle East represented the only non-U.S. women quoted on issues of gender policy. It's noteworthy that the Taliban's oppression of women did not become a topic for the evening news in 2001 until First Lady Laura Bush "introduced" the long-recognized problem during the U.S. bombing of Afghanistan in mid-November.

RACIAL UNDERREPRESENTATION

The racial balance of all sources was firmly tilted toward the historically most powerful segment of society as well. Among U.S. sources for whom race was determinable, whites made up 92 percent of the total, blacks 7 percent, Latinos and Arab-Americans 0.6 percent each, and Asian-Americans 0.2 percent. (According to the 2000 census, the U.S. population is 69 percent non-Hispanic white, 13 percent Hispanic, 12 percent black and 4 percent Asian.) A single source who appeared on NBC (7/26/01) was the only Native American identified as appearing on the nightly news in 2001—0.008 percent of total sources.

Among all sources, white Americans constituted 67 percent of the total, followed by Middle Easterners (9 percent), black Americans (5 percent) and Northern Europeans (mostly British) at 3 percent. No other racial or regional group made up more than 2 percent of the total.

The networks presented a remarkably similar distribution of races among U.S. sources. On all three networks, 92 percent of racially categorized U.S. sources were white, while 7 percent were black. Latinos were the next most quoted sources on all networks (0.6 percent on NBC, 0.5 percent on ABC and 0.7 percent on CBS) followed by Arab-Americans (0.6 percent, 0.5 percent and 0.7 percent respectively) and Asian-Americans (0.2 percent, 0.3 percent and 0.3 percent respectively).

As with the network's presentation of women as non-experts, racial minorities were disproportionately presented as ordinary citizens rather than as authorities or experts. Non-white U.S. sources made up 16 percent of average citizens and 11 percent of expert sources. When race, gender and nationality are considered together, white American men clearly dominated the evening news, making up 62 percent of all sources, far ahead of the next most commonly quoted sources: white American women (12 percent), Middle Eastern men (6 percent), black American men (4 percent) and Northern European men (2 percent).

Even on racial issues like affirmative action, racism and asylum policy (which made up 0.9 percent of overall coverage), the majority group was still afforded far greater opportunity to televise their opinions than the populations most directly affected by those issues. White Americans made up 68 percent of sources on such stories, followed by residents of Latin America (14 percent), African-Americans (7 percent), U.S. Latinos and people of the Middle East (3 percent each).

Among U.S. sources quoted on minority policies, whites made up 87 percent, far ahead of blacks (8 percent), Latinos (4 percent) and Asians (1 percent). Even in reports specifically on racism, 59 percent of quoted sources were white Americans, 29 percent were African-Americans, and 6 percent were Asian-Americans, with no Arab-Americans, Latinos, Native Americans or other minority groups quoted at all.

Of partisan sources quoted in racial stories, 84 percent were Republicans, a group so dominant that they made up more than one in four overall sources on these issues throughout the year. Democrats made up the remainder, with no independents or third party representatives quoted at all.

WHO ARE THE EXPERTS?

After ordinary citizens, the next largest categories of sources on the nightly news were various professional or expert voices of industry, science and government. The most common among these were corporate representatives, providing 7 percent of all sources, along with economists and academics, also at 7 percent; the visibility of these categories reflects the networks' heavy coverage of business and financial stories. The economists were unlikely to provide perspectives that challenged the corporate spokespersons, since they generally came from major investment banks such as Goldman Sachs and Morgan Stanley, from conservative think tanks such as the

Heritage Foundation, or from elite business schools such as those at Princeton and Stanford.

Non-partisan government employees and officials—such as Environmental Protection Agency representatives, National Security Council spokes-persons and mail carriers (especially in the midst of the Anthrax attacks)—were the next most quoted sources (6 percent). Medical doctors provided 5 percent of soundbites, reflecting the nightly news' interest in health issues. No other professional or social group provided more than 4 percent of the total.

Representatives of non-governmental organizations, which might have provided an alternative perspective to the U.S. government, business community or establishment experts, made up only 3 percent of the sources. Not all of these were from organizations that were likely to challenge the status quo, however; groups represented ranged from the United Nations and Human Rights Watch to the Christian Coalition and the National Rifle Association.

Organized labor was granted even less access to the airwaves. Even as the country lost 2.4 million jobs in 2001, union representatives made up less than 0.2 percent of sources on the evening news, making company representatives 35 times more likely to be heard.

This lack of interest in labor was reflected not only in sourcing but in topic selection: The unemployment rate, layoffs, strikes, wage levels, workplace discrimination and all other labor issues combined were only 1 percent of total coverage. By contrast, other business and economic issues made up 14 percent of the total. Product reports alone were twice as likely to appear on the news as labor-related stories, making up 2 percent of overall coverage. Even on labor stories, union representatives were rarely heard, making up a mere 2 percent of quoted sources. This was far behind corporate and business association representatives (26 percent), economists (19 percent) and politicians from the major parties (15 percent). Of the partisan sources presented on labor issues, 89 percent were Republicans and 11 percent were Democrats.

DISCUSSION QUESTIONS

1. One of the assumptions underlying a democratic society is that the mass media are supposed to serve a vital role as a forum for diverse ideas, exposing the people to the wide range of information they need to make informed decisions, and providing one way for the people to monitor what leaders do. Given the results of the study Howard presents, how well do you think the media fulfill this key assumption of a democracy? In what ways might the news be different if a broader range of parties were given coverage, and if women, minorities, and non-traditional "experts" had a greater voice?

2. Recall the argument made by Tocqueville in Article No. 7. How might he view the analysis offered by Howard? Tocqueville highlighted what he termed "formidable barriers around the liberty of opinion." Are the barriers today as formidable? Explain.

CHAPTER 5

Parties and Elections

Elections and voting in America today reveal a wide gap between democratic ideals of citizen participation in the substantive discussion of issues and the realities of low voter turnout, the ascendancy of image and emotional manipulation in campaigns, and the distorting impact of big money. In principle, a broad franchise and regular elections (in which competing parties offer distinct approaches to important problems) should provide citizens with a link to government officials. This link should ensure responsiveness to public concerns and a measure of control over public policy. Indeed, many Americans have seen the very existence of elections and the right to vote as proof of the democratic nature of our political system. But many others are aware of the discrepancy between ideals and reality. This gap was underscored by the disputed presidential election of 2000. Readings in this chapter will help you understand this gap and what might be done to bridge it.

FRANCES FOX PIVEN AND RICHARD A. CLOWARD

WHY AMERICANS STILL DON'T VOTE

Political scientist Frances Fox Piven and sociologist Richard A. Cloward have written a series of widely discussed books on the relationship between lower class and working class political action and the development of the U.S. welfare state. In this updated 2000 version of their much-discussed 1988 study Why Americans Don't Vote, *Piven and Cloward continue their analysis of the connection between electoral politics and the political behavior of nonaffluent Americans. They begin with the apparent paradox that while voting is central to democracy, and Americans consider their nation to be model of democracy, the United States ranks at the bottom in terms of voter turnout rates when compared to other industrial democracies. Moreover, voters are significantly different than nonvoters, with the latter generally being poorer and less well educated. Piven and Cloward then look at explanations for nonvoting, exploring the history of the franchise. The right to vote historically has been contested in the United States, and the early part of the twentieth century witnessed the demobilization of vast numbers of people who might have used the vote to alter the political and economic direction of the nation in a time of great national upheaval. Thus through the reintroduction of poll taxes and literacy tests, the design of cumbersome voter registration requirements, and the decline of party efforts to mobilize new voters, the active electorate began to shrink. This skewing of the electorate toward better-off voters and away from lower-class voters intensified at the end of the twentieth century through increased business mobilization to shape the substance of public policy. Now more than ever, the existence of very high levels of nonvoting tilts public policy even further toward elite interests. Finally, Piven and Cloward discuss the complex relationship between electoral participation and social movement-building, seeing both voting and protest mobilization as necessary for a reinvigoration of democracy in a nation where the two major political parties essentially have little or nothing to offer lower-status citizens.*

Source: Frances Fox Piven and Richard A. Cloward, *Why American's Still Don't Vote: And Why Politicians Want It That Way.* Boston: Beacon Press, 2000, pp. 2–17.

The right to vote is the core symbol of democratic politics. Of course, the vote itself is meaningless unless citizens have other rights, such as the right to speak, write, and assemble; unless opposition parties can compete for power by offering alternative programs, cultural appeals, and leaders; and unless diverse popular groupings can gain some recognition by the parties. And democratic arrangements that guarantee formal equality through the universal franchise are inevitably compromised by sharp social and economic inequalities. Nevertheless, the right to vote is the feature of the democratic polity that makes all other political rights significant. "The electorate occupies, at least in the mystique of [democratic] orders, the position of the principal organ of governance."

Americans generally take for granted that ours is the very model of democracy. Our leaders regularly proclaim the United States to be the world's leading democracy and assert that other nations should measure their progress by the extent to which they develop electoral arrangements that match our own. At the core of this self-congratulation is the belief that the right to vote is firmly established here. But in fact the United States is the only major democratic nation in which the less-well-off, as well as the young and minorities, are substantially underrepresented in the electorate. Only about half of the eligible population votes in presidential elections, and far fewer vote in off-year elections. As a result, the United States ranks at the bottom in turnout compared with other major democracies. Moreover, those who vote are different in politically important respects from those who do not. Voters are better off and better educated, and nonvoters are poorer and less well educated. Modest shifts from time to time notwithstanding, this has been true for most of the twentieth century and has actually worsened in the last three decades. In sum, the active American electorate overrepresents those who have more and underrepresents those who have less.

Despite the central role that political scientists typically assign to electoral processes in shaping politics, some scholars deny that important political consequences follow from the constriction of the electorate. In one variant of this argument, nonvoting is defined as a kind of voting, a tacit expression of satisfaction with the political status quo. Since many people abstain and are apparently satisfied, the size of the nonvoting population actually demonstrates the strength of the American democracy. Of course, no one has offered an adequate explanation of why this "politics of happiness" is consistently concentrated among the least well-off.

Another variant of the no-problem position asserts that mass abstention contributes to the health of a democratic polity not because it is a mark of satisfaction but because it reduces conflict and provides political leaders with the latitude they require for responsible governance. A functioning democracy, the argument goes, requires a balance between participation and nonparticipation, between involvement and noninvolvement. The "crisis of democracy" theorists of the 1970s, for example, reasoned that an "excess" of participation endangered democratic institutions by "overloading" them with demands, especially economic demands. This rather Olympian view of the democratic "functions" of nonvoting fails, of course, to deal with the decidedly undemocratic consequences of muffling the demands of some groups in the polity and not others.

A bolder but kindred argument fastens on the characteristics of nonvoters—especially their presumed extremism and volatility—to explain why their abstention is healthy for the polity. To cite a classic example, [Seymour Martin] Lipset points to evidence that nonvoters are more likely to have antidemocratic attitudes. Similarly, George Will, writing "In Defense of Nonvoting," says that "the fundamental human right" is not to the franchise but "to good government"; he points to the high turnouts in the late Weimar Republic as evidence of the dangers of increased voter participation, an example often favored by those who make this argument. Will's point of view is reminiscent of the arguments of nineteenth-century reformers who proposed various methods of *reducing* turnout—by introducing property qualifications on the vote, for example—in order to improve the quality of the electorate. Consider, for example, the *New York Times* in 1878: "It would be a great gain if people could be made to understand distinctly that the right to life, liberty, and the pursuit of happiness involves, to be sure, the right to good government, but not the right to take part, either immediately or indirectly, in the management of the state."

THE CONTESTED VOTE

American history has been marked by sharp contests over the question of who may vote, the conditions under which they may vote, or just which state offices they may vote for, and how much some votes will weigh in relation to other votes. These questions were hard fought because they were a crucial dimension of struggles for political advantage.

The United States was the first nation in the world in which the franchise began to be widely distributed, a historical achievement that helps to explain the democratic hubris we display to this day. That achievement occurred at a time when the hopes of peasants, artisans, and the urban poor everywhere in the West were fired by the essential democratic idea, the idea that if ordinary people had the right to participate in the selection of state leaders, their grievances would be acted upon. That hope was surely overstated, as were the fears of the propertied classes that the extension of the vote would give the "poor and ignorant majority" the power to "bring about a more equitable distribution of the good things of this world." Nevertheless, the large possibilities associated with democracy help to explain why the right of ordinary people to vote was sharply contested. And if the franchise was ceded earlier in the United States, it was because post-Revolutionary elites has less ability to resist popular demands. The common men who had fought the Revolution were still armed and still insurgent. Moreover, having severed their connection with England, American men of property

were unprotected by the majesty and military forces of a traditional state apparatus.

The political institutions that developed in the context of an expanded suffrage did not remedy many popular grievances. Still, a state influenced by political parties and elections did not merely replicate traditional patterns of class domination either. It also reflected in some measure the new social compact embodied in the franchise. Contenders for rulership now needed votes, and that fact altered the dynamics of power, modestly most of the time, more sharply some of the time, as we will point out in the pages that follow. In the early nineteenth century, the electoral arrangements that forced leaders to bid for popular support led to the gradual elimination of property, religious, and literacy qualifications on the franchise and to the expansion of the number of government posts whose occupants had to stand for election. By the 1830s, virtually all white men could vote. And, for a brief period after the Civil War, black men could as well. As the century wore on and the political parties developed systematic patronage operations to win elections, wide voting rights meant that common people received at least a share of the largesse, distributed in the form of Civil War pensions, friendly interventions with the courts or city agencies, and sometimes county or municipal poor relief—a reflection, if somewhat dim, of the electoral compact.

But at the beginning of the twentieth century, a series of changes in American electoral arrangements—such as the reintroduction of literacy tests and poll taxes, the invention of cumbersome voter registration requirements, and the subsequent withering of party efforts to mobilize those who were confronted by these barriers—sharply reduced voting by the northern immigrant working class and virtually eliminated voting by blacks and poor whites in the South. By World War I, turnout rates had fallen to half the eligible electorate and, despite some rises and dips, they have never recovered.

The purging of lower-strata voters from the electorate occurred at precisely that time in our history when the possibilities of democratic electoral politics had begun to enlarge. Indeed, we think it occurred *because* the possibilities of popular influence were expanding. First, as the economy industrialized and nationalized, government intervened more, so that at least in principle, the vote bore on a wide range of issues that were crucial to economic elites. Of course, government policies had always played a pivotal role in economic development: policies on tariff and currency, slavery, immigration and welfare, internal improvements, and the subsidization of the railroads had all shaped the course of American development. But as the twentieth century began, the scale and penetration of government activity, especially regulatory activity, grew rapidly. It grew even more rapidly during the Great Depression.

Second, government's expanding role in the economy came to influence popular political ideas, and popular organizational capacities, in ways that suggested a new potential for popular struggle and electoral mobilization. Thus, a more pervasively and transparently interventionist state undermined the old laissez-faire idea that economy and polity necessarily belonged to separate spheres and encouraged the twentieth-century idea that political rights include economic rights, particularly the right to protection by government from the worst instabilities and predations of the market.

Expanded state activities created new solidarities that became the basis for political action, including action in electoral politics. For example, government protection of the right to collective bargaining, ceded in response to mass strikes, reinforced the idea that workers had rights, promoted the unionization of millions of industrial workers, and made possible a large role for unions in electoral politics; Social Security reinforced the idea that government was responsible for economic well-being and promoted the organization of millions of "seniors" and the disabled; increased expenditures on social services nourished the growth of a voluntary sector that contracted to provide these services; and the enormous expansion of public programs gave rise to a vast network of public employee organiza-

tions, which were naturally keenly interested in electoral politics and had the organizational capacity to express that interest. In other words, new and expanded state activities gave rise to new political understandings and new political forces, and to the possibility that these new understandings and forces would become an influence in electoral politics.

But while the enlarged role of government and the new popular ideas and solidarities that resulted created the possibility that electoral politics would become a major arena for the expression of working- and lower-class interests, that possibility was only partly realized. One reason was that vast numbers of those who might have been at the vortex of electoral discontents were, for all practical purposes, effectively disenfranchised at the beginning of the twentieth century. In Western Europe, the pattern was virtually reversed. There working-class men were enfranchised at the beginning of the twentieth century, and their enfranchisement led to the emergence of labor or socialist or social democratic parties that articulated working class interests and ultimately exerted considerable influence on the policies and political culture of their nations. In the United States, by contrast, the partial disenfranchisement of working people during the same period helps explain why no comparable labor-based political party developed here, and why public policy and political culture remained more narrowly individualistic and property-oriented.

The costs of exclusion were also indirect, for exclusion helped to sustain the distinctive southern system. Southern states had been especially aggressive in promulgating legal and administrative barriers to the vote, arrangements that of course disfranchised blacks, and most poor whites as well, and ensured that the quasi-feudal plantation system and the regular use of terror on which it depended would remain unchallenged within the South. But the consequences went beyond the South to the nation as a whole. Southern representatives always wielded great influence in national politics, largely as a result of the terms of the sectional compromise through which a nation had been formed in 1789. The compromise not only guaranteed the "states' rights" through which the southern section managed their own affairs before the Civil War, and afterwards as well. It also laid out the several arrangements that guaranteed the South enduring predominance in national politics, including the three-fifths rule, which weighted slaves, a form of property, in allocating representation in the Congress, and a system of allocating representation to the states in the electoral college and in the Senate without regard to population. After the Civil War, and especially after the election of 1896, party competition disappeared from the South, and the subsequent disfranchisement of blacks and poor whites made its reemergence unlikely, with the consequence that unfailingly reelected southern congressmen gained the seniority that permitted them to dominate congressional committees.

If the peculiar development of the South was made possible by disfranchisement, southern representatives used their large influence in national government to steadfastly resist any federal policies that threatened the southern system. In particular, they vigorously resisted the labor and welfare policies that might have nourished the development of working-class politics during the New Deal and thereafter, as a matter of sectional and class interest and also as a matter of ideology. National welfare and labor policies were weakened as a result, and, even then, southern states were often granted exemption from coverage, with the further consequence that the South with its low wages and draconian labor discipline became—and remains today—a haven for industries eager to escape from the unionized workforces and more liberal state policies in the non-South.

The South also illustrates the important political consequences that followed from the expansion of the franchise. Consider, for example, the impact of the Twenty-fourth Amendment of 1964 and the Voting Rights Act of 1965, which together eliminated poll taxes, literacy tests, and voter-registration obstructions that had kept blacks and many poor whites from the polls. In the aftermath of these reforms, both black and white voter participation rose sharply, and as it did, state and local policies became less discriminatory. More important, once politicians had to face blacks at the polls, the age-old use of violence against blacks, which had been the linchpin of southern apartheid, declined sharply, signaling the inevitable transformation of the southern system.

We do not mean by these comments to overstate the importance of the ballot. Voters have limited ability to affect policy, and that limited influence is tempered by other influences. In the United States, a weak party system penetrated by moneyed interest groups and a strong laissez-faire culture were and are constraints on the political influence of the less-well-off, no matter the shape of the electorate. Nevertheless, a full complement of lower-strata voters would have at least moderated the distinctively harsh features of American capitalist development in the twentieth century. Corporate predations against workers and consumers probably would have been curbed more effectively. Enlarged electoral influence from the bottom might have blocked public policies that weakened unions and inhibited their ability to organize. And an effectively enfranchised working class almost surely would have prodded political leaders to initiate social welfare protections earlier and to provide more comprehensive coverage in a pattern more nearly resembling that of Western Europe. Not least important, the enfranchisement of blacks and poor whites would have prevented the restoration of the caste labor system in the South after Reconstruction and the development of a one-party system whose oligarchical leaders wielded enormous power in national politics for most of the twentieth century. The influence of the South, in turn, effectively countered what influence the working-class electorate in the North, its strength reduced by disfranchisement, was able to exert. And finally, the exclusion from electoral politics of large sectors of the working class, as well as the rural poor of the South, precluded the emergence of a political party that could have stimulated greater class consciousness among American workers and the poor by articulating their interests and cultural orientations. In other words, the distinctive pattern of American political development at least partly stems from the fact that the United States was not a democracy, in the elementary sense of an effective universal suffrage, during the twentieth century.

The politics of the closing decades of the twentieth century also illustrate the pivotal role of a skewed electorate. Numerous commentators have pointed out that beginning in the 1970s and continuing through the 1980s and 1990s, American corporations mobilized for politics with a focus and determination rare in the American experience. True, large corporations had always maintained a political presence to guard their particular firm and sector interests in legislative and bureaucratic spheres. However, the economic instabilities of the 1970s and the sagging and uncertain profits that resulted spurred business leaders to coordinate their efforts and to develop a broad legislative program calling for tax and regulatory rollbacks, cuts in spending on social programs, a tougher stance toward unions, and increases in military spending. The scale of this agenda demanded a new and broad-ranging political mobilization, including the creation of an extensive infrastructure of business associations, policy institutes, and think tanks that functioned as lobbying and public relations organizations.

During the same years that business leaders were organizing to break the constraints of post–World War II public policies, and especially the constraints of the regulatory and social policy expansion of the 1960s, the Christian Right movement was emerging. The movement was also a reaction to the politics of the 1960s, albeit less to the public policies of the decade than to the cultural assaults on traditional sexual and family mores with which the sixties movements were associated. This late-twentieth-century revival movement turned out to be, at least during the 1970s and 1980s, an opportunity for newly politicized corporate leaders. Business

organization and money are of course themselves formidable political resources, especially when campaign contributions are coordinated to achieve party influence as they began to be in the 1970s. But elections are ultimately won by voters at the polls, and the Christian Right provided the foot soldiers—the activists and many of the voters—who brought a business-backed Republican party to power.

These several developments came together in the election of 1980, shortly before the reform efforts recounted here began. Reagan's victory was made possible by the coordination of business campaign contributions on the one hand, and on the other the voter registration and mobilization efforts of the growing Christian Right with a network of fundamentalist churches at its base. However achieved, the election made it possible for the new Republican-business-fundamentalist alliance to claim that their agenda was in fact demanded by the American people. Among other things, Reagan was said to have tapped deep popular resentments against the public policies that were singled out for attack, as well as vast popular support for tax cuts and a military buildup. In fact, postelection polls showed that Reagan won not because of his campaign broadsides against big government but because of popular discontent with the Carter administration's policies, especially anger over high unemployment. Americans believe that presidents are responsible for the state of the economy, and by that criterion, Carter had failed.

But the truncated electorate may have mattered even more than the formidable corporate campaign mobilization, the surge of activism among Christian fundamentalists, and Carter's failure to manage the "political business" cycle. The underrepresentation of working and poor people, whose living standards were the target of much of the business program, helped to explain the weakness of political opposition to the Reagan administration's agenda during the 1980 campaign and thereafter. Elections were being won in the teeth of public opposition to the programmatic goals of the victors, and one reason was simply that the electorate did not represent the public. The 1980 evidence was clearcut. Polls showed that voters tilted toward Reagan by 52 percent over Carter's 38 percent. But nonvoters, who were nearly as numerous, tilted toward Carter by 51 percent over 37 percent. In a close study of that particular election, Petrocik concluded that the "margin for Ronald Reagan in 1980 was made possible by a failure of prospective Carter voters to turn out on election day."

To be sure, over the course of the next decade and more, a dominant conservative regime did succeed in promoting a conservative swing in public opinion and in the Democratic party. Nevertheless, fast-forward to 1994, the year of another historic victory, the takeover of the House of Representatives by the same Republican-business-fundamentalist coalition, with the fundamentalists now even more prominent and more assertive. The data repeat the pattern of 1980: while the Democrats won only 47 percent of the actual vote, they scored 58 percent among non-voters, according to the National Election Studies, a percentage-point spread sufficient to throw the election to them. In a definitive study of that election, Joel Lefkowitz concludes that "Republicans won, then, not because more potential voters preferred their party, but because more of those who preferred Republicans voted." In sum, nonvoting is important not merely for the intellectual queries it suggests but for its role in patterning American politics.

MOVEMENTS AND ELECTORAL PARTICIPATION

With their voting numbers depleted and without a labor party, whatever influence poor and working-class people have exerted in American politics has depended mainly on the emergence of mass insurgency. Protest movements dramatized the issues that parties detached from a lower class base could ignore, galvanized broad public attention to those issues, and threatened to cause the dissensus that parties dependent on broad coalitions feared. In *Poor People's Movements* (1977),

we argued that it was when political discontent among the lower classes "breaks out of the confines of electoral procedures that the poor may have some influences." Our view, in brief was that working-class people sometimes exercised power when they mobilized in mass defiance, breaking the rules that governed their participation in the institutions of a densely interdependent society. As evidence for this thesis, we summoned our studies of the role of protest movements of the 1930s and 1960s in winning major reforms. Consistently, the virtual absence of large-scale protest during the 1980s made it possible to initiate domestic policies that dramatically increased the bias of public policy against working-class and lower-class groups.

But the electoral context matters, nevertheless, for it is a crucial influence on the emergence and success of movements in contemporary democracies. This point needs a little explaining, because movements and voting are sometimes treated simply as conflicting and alternative forms of political expression. The bearing of each on the other is, however, multifaceted; some aspects of electoral politics undermine movements, as many observers have emphasized. But other aspects of electoral politics are crucial to the growth and success of movements.

On the one hand, there are features of a vigorous and inclusive electoral politics that tend to suppress collective protest. Electoral arrangements promulgate powerful meanings and rituals which define and limit the appropriate forms of political action. The very availability of the vote and the ritual of the periodic election are like magnets attracting and channeling popular political impulses. Other forms of collective action, and especially defiant collective action, are discredited precisely because voting and electioneering are presumably available as the normative ways to act on political discontent. In addition to constraining the forms of popular political action, the electoral system tends to restrict the goals of popular politics, and even the orientations of popular political culture, to the political alternatives generated by the dominant parties. Further, involvement in electoral politics can weaken the solidarities which undergird political movements, a development which takes its most extreme form under clientelist or machine modes of appealing to voters. And finally, electoral political institutions can seduce people away from any kind of oppositional politics. People are hypnotized by the circuses of election campaigns, while their leaders are enticed by the multiple opportunities to gain positions in the electoral representative system. In short, involvement in electoral politics can channel people away from movement politics. . . .

However, we think the bearing of electoral politics on movement politics is more complex and multifaceted than these simple oppositions suggest. Electoral politics also constitutes the principal environment of contemporary movements, and aspects of that environment nurture rather than suppress movements. After all, the idea of popular rights associated with democratic electoral arrangements encourages the belief that change is possible, and by the efforts of ordinary people. This is the implication of the very core democratic idea, the idea that ordinary people have the right to participate in governance by choosing their rulers. Furthermore, movements may also gain protection from electoral politics, since the anticipation of adverse voter reactions often restrains state leaders from resorting to repression as a way of dealing with political defiance.

Some electoral conditions are more conducive to movements than others. Movements tend to arise when electoral alignments become unstable, usually as a result of changes in the larger society that generate new discontents or stimulate new aspirations and thus undermine established party alliances. Electoral volatility is particularly associated with large-scale economic change, especially change that generates widespread hardship. When the allegiance of key voter blocs can no longer be taken for granted, contenders are likely to raise the stakes in electoral contests by employing campaign rhetoric that acknowledges grievances and gives voice to

demands as a way of building majorities. In other words, movements are more likely to emerge when a climate of political possibility has been created and communicated through the electoral system.

Movements also win what they win largely as a result of their impact on electoral politics. The issues raised when masses of people become defiant sometimes break the grip of ruling groups on political interpretations so that new definitions of social reality, and new definitions of the possible and just, can be advanced. In turn, these issues and understandings, raised and communicated by masses of defiant people, activate and politicize voters and sometimes attract new voters to the polls who alter electoral calculations. It is in fact mainly by their ability to galvanize and polarize voters, with the result that electoral coalitions fragment or threaten to fragment, that protest movements score gains in electoral-representative systems. When political leaders issue new rhetorical appeals to attract or hold voters or go on to make policy concessions, it is to cope with threats of electoral defection and cleavage or to rebuild coalitions when faced with the threat or reality of electoral defections. In this way, the electoral system not only protects and nourishes movements but also yields them leverage on state leaders. The influence of voters is also enhanced, for movements activate electoral constituencies and make their allegiance conditional on policy responses. In short, the life course of contemporary movements can be understood only in relation to the electoral environment in which they emerge and on which they have an impact.

There is broad historical confirmation for this aspect of the relationship between movements and electoral politics. In the 1930s, striking industrial workers were able to force a wavering New Deal administration to support government protection for collective bargaining. The strike movement had so antagonized business groups as to eliminate any possibility that the New Deal could recover their support, and it also threatened to put at risk the votes of the working class, on which the New Deal depended.

Similarly, in the 1950s and 1960s, the southern civil rights movement forced national Democratic leaders to throw their weight behind legislation that would dismantle the southern caste system and strike down the procedures by which blacks and most poor whites had been disfranchised. The reason is that the civil rights movement simultaneously precipitated defections among southern whites to the Republican party and jeopardized the votes of growing numbers of blacks in the cities of the border states and the North.

Thus, while a vigorous electoral politics probably dampens the tendency to protest, electoral politics is nevertheless also critical to movement success. When we wrote *Poor People's Movements* (1977) it was in part to specify some of the ways in which this was so, if only because earlier analyses of protest movements tended to ignore their electoral environment. But there was one major feature of the American electoral system with which we did not deal. We did not call attention to the distinctive pattern of lower-strata exclusion in the United States or explore its implications for the emergence and evolution of protest movements.

How, then, did the twentieth-century history of massive nonvoting by poorer and minority people bear on the fate of movements in American politics? At first glance, one might expect large-scale nonvoting to reduce the effectiveness of the electoral system in absorbing discontent and suppressing movements. However, the methods by which people are made into nonvoters matter. When whole categories of people are denied the vote as a matter of acknowledged state policy—as southern blacks were—their exclusion may well strengthen their collective identity, provoke their indignation, and legitimate defiant forms of political action. But in the United States, the formal right to the franchise has been virtually universal, a condition much celebrated in the political culture. Only those who are aliens, felons, not yet of age, or undomiciled are denied the vote as a matter of acknowledged policy. At the same time, the effectiveness of the franchise for the bottom strata has been reduced by the failure of the parties to make the appeals and deploy the outreach strategies that would mobilize these voters and by residual procedural obstructions embedded in the voting process. This pattern of demobilization and obstruction was selective in that it was more likely to reduce voting by the poor and unlettered than by the better-off and educated. Still, entire categories of the population were not legally denied the franchise, and the administrative methods by which the exercise of the franchise is impeded remained obscure and indeed seemed to be the fault of the nonvoters themselves, of their apathy or poor education. Under these circumstances, the *idea* that voting and elections provided the means for acting on political grievances remains largely intact, even though the means were not in fact available to tens of millions of people. The demobilization of large sectors of the American electorate was thus secured at less cost to the legitimacy of electoral processes as the prescribed avenue for political change than would otherwise have been the case.

At the same time, the constriction of the electorate weakened the complementarities between electoral politics and protest movements. The interactions between movements and the electoral context that encouraged the growth of movements and sometimes led to movement victories depended on the existence of voter constituencies inclined to be responsive to the appeals of protesters. Thus protests from below were more likely to arise in the first place when contenders for office were forced to employ rhetoric that appealed to less-well-off voters and thus gave courage to the potential protesters. Such movements were more likely to grow when they were at least somewhat safe from the threat of state repression because political leaders were constrained by fear of adverse reactions by working-class or lower-class or minority voters. Finally, protesters were more likely to win when the issues they raised stirred support among significant numbers of these voters, threatening to lead to voter defections. The complementary dynamic between movements and electoral politics thus depended both on the composition and orientation of movements and on the composition and orientation of significant blocs in the electorate. In other words, the sharp under-representation of poor and minority people in the American electorate created an electoral environment that also weakened their ability to act politically through movements. This is another important way in which massive nonvoting has shaped American politics.

DISCUSSION QUESTIONS

1. Early in their article, Piven and Cloward cite several scholarly arguments that contend that widespread nonvoting has few, if any, negative political consequences. What do you make of these arguments?

2. According to Piven and Cloward, how has the underrepresentation of the less wealthy been reinforced in the United States? Why is the historical timing of electoral exclusion important?

3. To what extent do you think low voter turnout weakens U.S. democracy? Explain.

4. Piven and Cloward contend that electoral politics and protest movements are complementary forms of political activity. Explain the dynamic interplay between voting and mass protest.

MICAH L. SIFRY

FINDING THE LOST VOTERS

Election campaigns usually focus on reaching "likely voters," citizens who vote regularly. In this article political analyst Micah L. Sifry challenges the view that the American electorate is a stable, predictable mass. He contends that this calculation ignores discouraged voters—"potential participants who have been turned off or pushed out by an increasingly money-driven and manipulative electoral process." These potential voters are drawn to candidates who come from "outside the box" and who convey a populist message and style. As examples of such populist candidates, who have successfully mobilized discouraged voters, Sifry points to former Minnesota Governor Jesse Ventura, the late Minnesota Senator Paul Wellstone, Vermont Congressman Bernie Sanders, and Illinois Congressman Jesse Jackson Jr. Sifry discusses alternative approaches to electoral politics at greater length in his 2002 book Spoiling for a Fight: Third-Party Politics in America.*

Al Garcia is one frustrated Democratic campaign manager. A criminal defense lawyer by trade and a twenty-year veteran of Minnesota politics, he ran two candidates for the state assembly in 1998. Both were in Anoka County, ground zero of the Jesse Ventura vote. One candidate, Jerry Newton, a decorated Vietnam veteran and small-business owner, fiscally conservative but very supportive of public schools and the environment, lost badly to a far-right pro-lifer as the voters who turned out for Ventura voted for Republican state representatives down the ballot. Garcia's other candidate, Luanne Koskinen, an incumbent with strong labor backing, barely held onto her office. Garcia's problems were hardly unique: Ventura voters across the state ended up costing Democrats control of the state assembly.

Over lunch last winter at Billie's, a popular Anoka County restaurant, Garcia delivered his postmortem: Democrats had gotten whipped because they hadn't reached out to new voters—and there had been a lot of them. "At 7:45 in the morning on Election Day," Garcia recalled, "I'm number 250 at my polling place in Coon Rapids [a city in Anoka County]. Six people were registering to vote, and they had already registered eighty people. At 8:00 p.m. you still had lines of people waiting to vote. When the first Coon Rapids numbers came in, I got a chill. Humphrey 120, Coleman 35, Ventura 340. The election was over."

And why had his candidates fared so poorly? "We were too focused on the regular voters," Garcia said. "If you hadn't voted in two out of the last four elections, you didn't get anything from

Source: Micah L. Sifry, "Finding the Lost Voters." *The American Prospect,* vol. 11, no. 6, 31 January 2000, pp. 23–27.

Luanne or Jerry." Targeting likely voters, of course, is standard practice in most campaigns these days. But Garcia said he'd known that strategy wouldn't be enough.

"I could sense it coming," he said. "My wife told me early on that she would support Ventura, and she hates politics. All my legal clients were supporting Jesse, from the first-time DWI offenders to the major dope dealers! And he was pulling at me, in my gut. I'm a blue-collar guy who grew up in north Minneapolis. My dad's a dockworker, my mother's a waitress. Like the folks in Anoka. And he was saying things that average people could connect with."

Garcia said he'd wanted his candidates to do the same thing. "The number-one issues in Anoka are taxes, wages, and traffic. That's what we wanted to focus on." But he'd been hamstrung by centralized campaign effort run out of the House Democratic Caucus. "They had a $15,000 mail program—half of our budget—that we were forced to buy into or lose our field worker and party funds. Six out of the nine pieces they mailed were on education, even though we said that wasn't our top concern. And they mailed to too small a target group, and they wouldn't let us change it."

Campaigns at all levels of American politics these days are focused narrowly on "likely voters," people who vote regularly. Eric Johnson, campaign manager to Hubert "Skip" Humphrey, the losing Democratic candidate for governor, admitted as much after the election. "We didn't see Ventura coming because our polling screened out unlikely voters," he told *The Wall Street Journal*. All four of Minnesota's major polling organizations also failed to project Ventura's victory because they factored out these voters.

The assumption governing the typical political campaign is that the American electorate is a stable, predictable mass—or, worse, that they're apathetic and easily manipulated. Ventura's victory is just the latest and loudest explosion of that piece of conventional wisdom.

Indeed, politicians are making a huge mistake when they focus only on "likely voters." A large subset of the "unlikely voters" filtered out

by pollsters and left out of campaign targeting efforts might be better described as *discouraged* voters—potential participants who have been turned off or pushed out by an increasingly money-driven and manipulative electoral process.

Many of these citizens, people who are disproportionately downscale and correspondingly attracted to working-class issues and symbols, can be remotivated to turn out. A central question is whether more Democrats will take their campaigns to these voters or, by failing to do so, will continue to create opportunities for outsiders ranging from Jesse Ventura to Bernie Sanders to Patrick Buchanan.

APATHY OR INDEPENDENCE?

Public trust in government has been declining steadily over the past four decades. The authoritative surveys conducted biennially since the 1950s by the University of Michigan's National Election Studies (NES) have found that large majorities of Americans, across all demographic groups, don't believe "you can trust the government in Washington to do what is right just about always [or] most of the time." Similarly, most people think "the government is pretty much run by a few big interests looking out for themselves." According to the NES, the percentage agreeing that "people like me don't have any say about what the government does" rose from 31 percent in 1952 to 53 in 1996. This is a strong statement of disaffection.

But some Americans still feel better represented than others. People are more likely to believe that they "don't have any say" if they are black rather than white, are poor rather than well-off, have a limited education compared to a college diploma or postgraduate degree, or work in blue-collar jobs rather than white-collar or professional fields. For example, 62 percent of people with a high school diploma said they don't have any say in what government does, compared to 40 percent of those with more education. And about 56 percent of those in the bottom two-thirds of the national income distribution felt left out, compared to 38 percent in the top twentieth.

A similar pattern applies to how Americans think about the major political parties. In general, polls find that between 50 and 60 percent of the population believes there are "important differences in what the Republicans and Democrats stand for." But in 1996, while most people in the top income brackets believed that there were significant differences between the parties, 50 percent of people in the bottom sixth of income distribution thought there was no difference. Similarly, 59 percent of those with less than a high school education and 40 percent of those with a high school diploma said there was no difference between the parties, compared to just 25 percent of those with at least some college education. Overall, blue-collar workers were almost twice as likely as professionals to believe party distinctions were meaningless.

Among active voters, the trend is away from the major parties and toward independence. From 1990 to 1998, while the number of voters registered as independent or third-party increased approximately 57 percent, the number of registered Republicans dropped by almost 5 percent and the number of Democrats by almost 14 percent, according to data collected from state agencies by the Committee for the Study of the American Electorate. Voters' political preferences—a looser definition than party registration—showed the same trend. The proportion of people identifying themselves as independents increased from 23 percent in 1952 to an average of 35 percent in the 1990s, according to the NES. Independent voters are somewhat more likely to be of lower income, education, age, and occupational status than hard-core party partisans (though this variation is tempered by the strong Democratic loyalties of many blacks). And 41 percent of people under the age of 29 self-identify as independents, according to a 1999 Gallup poll.

Independents are the most volatile of active voters, with a marked tendency to support candidates who come from "outside the box." All the exit polls going back to George Wallace's 1968 presidential candidacy show that voters who identify themselves as independents are about twice as likely as other voters to support third-party candidates. In Minnesota in 1998, Ventura won with 37 percent overall, but got 52 percent of the independents.

As the National Voter Registration Act of 1993 (known as the motor-voter law) brings more voters onto the registration rolls, this trend toward electoral volatility seems likely to strengthen. In Florida, the numbers of registered Republicans, Democrats, and nonaffiliates/third-party registrants each rose by about 500,000 in the first two years of the law's implementation. Since 1996, however, the number of major party registrants has declined slightly, while the number of non-major party registrants has risen another 250,000. The same thing has happened in California, where the number of major party registrants has held steady since 1996, while the number of non-major party registrants has risen about 300,000.

Of course, rising voter alienation and disaffection from the two major parties does not prove that a different kind of political engagement is possible. After all, as measures of political alienation have risen, turnout in national and state elections has declined. But are citizens really just signaling their apathy when they fail to vote? Or are they more specifically alienated from the Democratic and Republican establishments and their candidates? In fact, a significant number of nonvoters look a lot like politically active independent voters.

It is difficult to find data that distinguishes those abstainers who are principled or angry and those who are merely indifferent, but it does exist. In May of 1996, the League of Women Voters released a poll that showed nonvoters were no more distrustful of the federal government than regular voters. Active voters were, however, far more likely to see significant differences between the parties on major issues, to believe that elections mattered and that their votes made a difference. The poll also suggested that efforts to mobilize voters were highly important: About three-quarters of voters said they had been contacted by a candidate or party, compared with less than half of the nonvoters.

But this says little about the actual political preferences of novoters. More answers can be found in two little-noticed surveys, one conducted in the summer of 1983 by ABC News, and the second done after the election of 1996 by Republican pollster Kellyanne Fitzpatrick. ABC News polled more than 2,500 voting-age Americans and then compared highly likely voters (people who were registered to vote who said they always vote) with very unlikely voters (people who were not registered to vote and gave little inclination that they were planning to vote in the next election). The Fitzpatrick poll compared a sample of 800 voters with one of 400 nonvoters. Together, the two surveys reveal some telling points.

First, about a third of the nonvoters aren't apathetic. Rather, they're angry and feel shut out by the choices offered. When asked by ABC why they didn't vote in the 1980 presidential election, 36 percent of the nonvoters gave a political reason such as "None of the candidates appealed to me." Thirty-eight percent of the nonvoters in the Fitzpatrick poll didn't vote in the 1996 because they "did not care for any of the candidates" or were "fed up with the political system" or "did not feel like the candidates were interested in people like me."

Second, nonvoters tilt toward liberalism. In the ABC News poll, 60 percent of the nonvoters who said they had voted in 1980 recalled choosing either Jimmy Carter or John Anderson; only 30 percent said they had voted for Ronald Reagan. Considering that after an election, voters tend to "recall" voting for the winner, this is a striking finding. Sixty-seven percent of nonvoters said they had voted for the Democratic candidate for the House of Representatives, compared to 52 percent of regular voters. In the Fitzpatrick poll, just 38 percent of nonvoters identified as conservatives, compared to 48 percent of the voting public. And while 17 percent of voters called themselves liberals, 22 percent of nonvoters chose that label. (A *New York Times*/CBS News poll found that those who were not planning to vote in the 1998 election preferred Democrats for Congress by 49 percent to 27 percent; likely voters, on the other hand, were evenly split between Republicans and Democrats.)

HOW TO REACH DISCOURAGED VOTERS

"Low turnout is the compound consequence of legal and procedural barriers intertwined with the parties' reluctance to mobilize many voters, especially, working-class and minority voters," says Frances Fox Piven, who along with her husband Richard Cloward wrote *Why Americans Don't Vote* and built the movement that passed the motor-voter law. "I've come to the conclusion that party competition takes the form of demobilizing, not mobilizing, voters, because new voters threaten incumbents, raise new issues, or create the incentive to raise new issues," she adds. "You need mavericks, outsiders to try to mobilize newvoters—nobody else wants to take that risk."

"Nonvoters matter a lot," agrees pollster Stanley Greenberg, "though most candidates act as if they don't. . . . There's no questions that you can change the shape and size of the electorate, though that is more true for presidential elections than for individual, even statewide, campaigns." For example, turnout increased by 5.5 percent in the three-way presidential race of 1992. "There's reason to believe that the populist economic issues that Clinton was raising and the independent-libertarian issues that Perot was raising were at work there," Greenberg argues. "By comparison, in 1994, conservative definitions of the issues brought in more rural, conservative portions of the electorate while the health care reform failure led many noncollege women to drop out." Pollster John Zogby agrees: "If there's a strong independent candidate in the race, you begin to see the numbers of undecided voters in those groups who often don't vote—younger voters, registered independents—start to decline in our surveys, a sign they are planning to vote."

Representative Jesse Jackson, Jr., points to his father's 1984 and 1988 campaigns as proof that discouraged voters can be effectively mobilized.

Indeed, the number of Democratic primary voters rose from 18 million in 1984 to nearly 23 million in 1988, with Reverend Jackson's total share rising by 3.4 million. "If you're able to tap into the people who aren't consciously involved in politics or following it," the younger Jackson says, "and show how everything they do has something to do with politics—that shirt they wear, the stop sign, the taxes they pay, the schools they attend, the police officer on their street . . . you can inspire them and give them reason to participate."

It takes a certain kind of candidate, message, and campaign to reach these voters. "You're not going to be able to cater to traditional economic forces that have significant influence," says Jackson. "You have to have some relationship to them, but you can't be seen as beholden to them. You have to be seen as a real American; you have to be someone who can look the press right in the face and tell them exactly how it is. You have to be Beattyite, almost Bulworthian."

Not many American politicians are trying to run this kind of campaign or can convincingly pull it off. However, there are a number of successful examples that predate Jesse Ventura. What seems to matter most is that the candidate have a populist message and style—someone who wants to empower ordinary people versus the establishment, who is blue collar as opposed to button-down, who favors effective government on behalf of the interests of average working people, and who supports sweeping efforts to clean up politics and reform the electoral process itself.

Those were Paul Wellstone's attributes in 1990, when he came from nowhere—had been a college professor and progressive activist—to win the Minnesota Senate race. Not only did Wellstone draw more votes than the Democratic candidate in the previous Senate contest; more voters came out in 1990 than did in 1988, a presidential election year. (According to Francis Fox Piven, Wellstone attributed his victory in part to the increased number of poorer voters on the rolls, thanks to the earlier passage of a state-level, agency-based voter registration system.) Some-

thing similar happened in 1998 with Iowan Tom Vilsack, who waged a successful underdog run for governor and raised the Democratic vote total nearly 20 percent over the previous gubernatorial race. And activists in Washington State argue that their 1998 ballot initiative to raise the state minimum wage to the highest level in the country had a similar effect—drawing more votes than any other item or candidate on the ballot and bringing in enough new voters to swing control of the both houses of the state legislature back to the Democratic column.

In 1990, Bernie Sanders, the former socialist mayor of Burlington, won Vermont's lone seat in Congress as an independent. He ran on issues like national health care, tax fairness, environmental activism, addressing the needs of the poor, and involving working people in the political process. In his first try for Congress in 1988, he came close, drawing 37.5 percent of the vote. Two years later, he won a solid victory with 56 percent of the vote. In both races, the total vote was way up—13 percent higher—compared to the previous election cycle.

And while Sanders did well in his breakthrough victory in 1990 with the college-educated, alternative life-style types who have moved up to Vermont in the past generation, his strongest support actually came from the poor conservative hill towns and farm communities of the state's "Northeast Kingdom." For example, Sanders's strongest showing statewide came in the county of Orleans, where he pulled 62 percent of the vote. A rural county on the border of Canada that voted solidly for George Bush in 1988, Orleans had a median household income in 1990 of $22,800, about $7,000 less than the state average. Only 14.2 percent of Orleans's residents were college graduates. The standard of living was low, with homes worth on average just $66,500, compared to $95,600 statewide. Nearly 15 percent of Orleans's residents were living under the official poverty line, 4 percent more than in the rest of the state.

And then there is Jesse Ventura, a socially liberal, fiscally conservative, pro-campaign finance reform, anti-establishment candidate with a working-class style, who hit discouraged voters—as well as disaffected Democrats and Republicans—on the bull's-eye. His campaign deliberately targeted "unlikely voters" by focusing his public appearances in an "Independent Belt" of bedroom communities to the north and west of Minnesota's Twin Cities, and by placing his offbeat TV ads not on the nightly news shows but on Fox programs like *The Simpsons* and *The X-Files,* and on cable TV wrestling programs. Helped by same-day voter registration, his candidacy drastically boosted turnout, and most of those new voters pulled his lever. He won a near-majority of 18- to 44-year olds, the heart of political independents.

In several other ways, Ventura's vote corresponded with those groups least satisfied with the existing political choices. Far more self-identified liberals than conservatives voted for him. Women voted for him almost as much as men. In the high-income professional suburbs, Ventura did poorly. In the less affluent suburbs, he did very well. Turnout in many of these blue-collar districts was over 70 percent, with as many as 20 percent of the total registering on Election Day. Many rank-and-file union members swung to Ventura as well. "I could tell going into the election," said Doug Williams, head of an electrical workers' union. "I was getting requests for information on him from my members. People were wearing his T-shirts and bumper stickers—people who hadn't really participated before."

People think Ventura won because he was a celebrity. But his early name recognition in Minnesota, while high for a third-party candidate, only gave him a chance to get the voters' attention. It's what he said and how he said it that made him a contender. "The voters saw Jesse as someone who's an outsider who's going to change things," said Ed Gross, who worked on voter targeting for the Ventura campaign. "Watching the TV debates, they saw two 'suits' and one 'nonsuit'—and most of them don't wear suits. Not only that, one of the 'suits' has worked for the other, and they both were owned by big money."

Gross recognized the dynamic from the 1990 and 1996 Wellstone campaigns for Senate, on which he had also worked. "I told Ventura, in a lot of ways, to the voters, you are a Wellstone. And voters went for Wellstone because they want to have a connection. They've felt disconnected for a long time. They want to feel like the guy up there knows how they live." In the end, they latched onto Ventura with enthusiasm. And the strength of his campaign—which succeeded in a state with one of the lowest unemployment rates in the country—stands as a warning to both of the major parties: This could happen to you.

RAISING TURNOUT, REVIVING POLITICS

As the barriers to voter registration have fallen with the gradual implementation of motor-voter, the pool of potential voters has grown. According to the Federal Election Commission, the total number of registered voters rose from 129 million in 1994 to 151 million in 1998, an increase of 8 percent of the total voting-age population. But politicians haven't caught on. "Candidates aren't yet campaigning to those voters," says Linda Davidoff, the former executive director of Human SERVE, the nonprofit organization set up by Priven and Cloward to spearhead the motor-voter drive. "[But] motor-voter is laying the groundwork for poorer people to participate differently. There's an enormous opportunity here for candidates who get the picture and campaign to the potential voter," she says.

Jesse Jackson, Jr. is one politician who understands very well the new potential of reaching out to discouraged voters. One of the keys to his first race, in which he beat a veteran Democratic legislator backed by the Daley political machine in a special election to fill Mel Reynolds's seat, was his energetic campaign to register young voters. "He set up voter registration tables during local college registration," says Frank Watkins, his press secretary, "and we kept a record of those people and sent them a personal letter just before the election." Jackson registered about 6,500 new voters—5,000 of whom lived in his district. It's likely that many of them made his winning margin of 6,000 votes.

Despite Jackson's evident success and personal energy (even though he's in a safe district, he's continued to work to turn out more voters, winning more votes than almost any other member of Congress), there's been little interest from the Democratic Party establishment in helping him spread his message of increasing political participation. "We went to the DNC and showed them how we did it," Watkins says, "and they sat there and looked at us like we were crazy. They'd rather focus on raising more and more money to spend on advertising to fewer and fewer people."

Obviously, going after the discouraged voters involves taking some risks, and it may be especially hard to do so in states that close their registration rolls weeks before Election Day. And there is a deeper challenge: convincing these citizens that voting really can matter again. Noting that outward expressions of populist anger seem to have declined in recent years, pollster John Zogby points to despair about politics as the explanation. "In one of my focus groups, a guy in Cleveland said, 'I'm now in the third of a series of lousy jobs. I lost my good job in '85. I was angry before. But now it's not going to happen. Government can't do anything. And my vote doesn't matter at all.' He had downsized his expectations," Zogby concludes. Piven agrees: "The sense that politics is so corrupt, combined with neoliberal rhetoric that argues that government can't do anything, tends to demobilize people."

The ultimate challenge then for anyone seeking to connect with discouraged voters is to restore their hope while not denying that they have good reason to be cynical. What is fascinating and exciting about each of the handful of populist victories of the last decade—by Jackson, Sanders, Wellstone, and Ventura—is that in every case, their success raised expectations about politics across the country. Hope, it seems, can be contagious; we need to keep it alive.

DISCUSSION QUESTIONS

1. Why does Sifry think it is a mistake to think that discouraged voters are apathetic about politics and therefore unreachable?

2. According to Sifry, what sorts of appeals and candidates might reach the lost voters and bring them to the polls?

19

ARLIE HOCHSCHILD

LET THEM EAT WAR

In the past decade political commentators have often identified upscale "wired work-ers" or suburban "soccer moms" as the key swing group in the electorate. In this arti-cle, sociologist Arlie Hochschild examines white, blue-collar men as a key voting bloc. Following up on the analysis of Joel Rogers and Ruy Teixeira in their much-discussed book America's Forgotten Majority *(2000), Hochschild looks at the political identity of the so-called "Nascar Dads" in the Bush years. She searches for explanations of higher than average support for President Bush among this group, despite concerns over job security, wages, health, and safety. She argues that Bush has carried on a long-standing Republican politics of dispacement, whereby blue-collar fears of economic decline come to focus on an assortment of convenient enemies, in this case "evildoers" abroad. Hochschild's provocative analysis was written in the fall of 2003. We ask you to consider its validity in light of the presidential election of 2004, and what we learned about the voting choices of white, blue-collar men.*

[In late 2003] George W. Bush was sinking in the polls, but a few beats on the war drum could reverse that trend and re-elect him in 2004. Ironi-cally, the sector of American society now poised to keep him in the White House is the one which stands to lose the most from virtually all of his policies—blue-collar men. A full 49% of them and 38% percent of blue-collar women told a January 2003 Roper poll they would vote for Bush in 2004.

In fact, blue-collar workers were more pro-Bush than professionals and managers among whom only 40% of men and 32% of women, when polled, favor him; that is, people who reported to Roper such occupations as painter, furniture mover, waitress, and sewer repairman were more

likely to be for our pro-big business president than people with occupations like doctor, attor-ney, CPA or property manager. High-school grad-uates and dropouts were more pro-Bush (41%) than people with graduate degrees (36%). And people with family incomes of $30,000 or less were no more opposed to Bush than those with incomes of $75,000 or more.

We should think about this. The blue-collar vote is huge. Skilled and semi-skilled manual jobs are on the decline, of course, but if we count as blue-collar those workers without a college degree, as Ruy Teixeira and Joel Rogers do in their book *Why the White Working Class Still Matters*, then blue-collar voters represent 55% of

Source: Arlie Hochschild, "Let Them Eat War," *TomDispatch.com*, 2 October 2003. Available online at: http://www.nationinstitute.org/tomdispatch/

all voters. They are, the authors note, the real swing vote in America. "Their loyalties shift the most from election to election and in so doing determine the winners in American politics."

This fact has not been lost on Republican strategists who are now targeting right-leaning blue-collar men, or as they call them, "Nascar Dads." These are, reporter Liz Clarke of the *Washington Post* tells us, "lower or middle-class men who once voted Democratic but who now favor Republicans." Nascar Dads, commentator Bill Decker adds, are likely to be racing-car fans, live in rural areas, and have voted for Bush in 2000. Bush is giving special attention to steel-workers, autoworkers, carpenters and other building-trades workers, according to Richard Dunham and Aaron Bernstein of *Business Week,* and finding common cause on such issues as placing tariffs on imported steel and offering tax breaks on pensions.

We can certainly understand why Bush wants blue-collar voters. But why would a near majority of blue-collar voters still want Bush? Millionaires, billionaires for Bush, well, sure; he's their man. But why pipe fitters and cafeteria workers? Some are drawn to his pro-marriage, pro-church, pro-gun stands, but could those issues override a voter's economic self-interest?

Let's consider the situation. Since Bush took office in 2000, the U.S. has lost 4.9 million jobs (2.5 million net), the vast majority of them in manufacturing. While this cannot be blamed entirely on Bush, his bleed-'em-dry approach to the non-Pentagon parts of the government has led him to do nothing to help blue-collar workers learn new trades, find affordable housing, or help their children go to college. The loosening of Occupational Health and Safety Administration regulations has made plants less safe. Bush's agri-cultural policies favor agribusiness and have put many small and medium-sized farms into bank-ruptcy. His tax cuts are creating state budget shortfalls, which will hit the public schools blue-collar children go to, and erode what services they now get. He has put industrialists in his environmental posts, so that the air and water will grow dirtier. His administration's disregard for the severe understaffing of America's nursing homes means worse care for the elderly parents of the Nascar Dad as they live out their last days. His invasion of Iraq has sent blue-collar children and relatives to the front. Indeed, his entire tap-the-hornets'-nest foreign policy has made the U.S. arguably less secure than it was before he took office. Indeed, a recent series of polls revealed that most people around the world believe him to be a greater danger than Osama bin Laden. Many blue-collar voters know at least some of this already. So why are so many of them pro-Bush anyway?

WONDERING ABOUT THE NASCAR DAD

Among blue-collar voters, more men than women favor Bush, so we can ask what's going on with the men. It might seem that their pocketbooks say one thing, their votes another, but could it be that, by some good fortune, blue-collar men are actually better off than we imagine? No, that can't be it. About a fifth of them had household incomes of $30,000 or less; 4 in 10 between $30,000 and $75,000; and 4 in 10 $75,000 or more. Among the poorest blue-collar families (with household incomes of $30,000 or less) a full 44% were pro-Bush. Perhaps even more strik-ingly, $75,000-plus Nascar Dads are more likely to favor Bush than their income-counterparts who hold professional and managerial jobs.

Even if poor blue-collar men were pro-Bush in general, we might at least assume that they would oppose Bush's massive program of tax cuts if they thought it favored the rich? If we did, then we'd be wrong again. "Do you think this tax plan benefits mainly the rich or benefits everyone?" Roper interviewers asked. Among blue-collar men who answered, "Yes, it benefits mainly the rich," 56% percent nonetheless favored the plan. Among blue-collar men with $30,000 or less who answered "yes" and who believed that yes, this tax cut "benefits mainly the rich," a full 53% favored it. This far exceeds the 35% of people who make

$75,000 or more, knew the tax cut favored the rich, and still supported it.

So, what's going on? Should we throw out the classic Clinton-era explanation for how we all vote: "It's the economy, stupid"? Not right away. Maybe the blue-collar man who favors that tax cut is thinking "the economy stupid" but only in the short term. He badly needs even the small amounts of money he'll get from a tax cut to repair his car or contribute to the rent. But then many working-class men labor decade after decade at difficult jobs to secure a future for their children. So if they think long term as a way of life, why are they thinking short-term when it comes to their vote?

One possibility is that the Nascar Dad is not well informed; that indeed, like the rest of us, he's been duped. For example, he may have fallen for the Karl Rove-inspired bandwagon effect. "Bush is unbeatable," he hears, or "Bush has a $200,000,000 re-election fund. Get with the winner." It makes you a winner too, he feels. This might account for some blue-collar Bush support, but it doesn't explain why the Nascar Dad would be more likely to be taken in by the bandwagon effect than the professional or managerial dad. Anyway, most blue-collar men would seem to be no less likely than anyone else to vote their conscience, regardless of whom they think will win, and that's not even counting those who root for the underdog as a matter of principle.

But another kind of manipulation could be going on. A certain amount of crucial information has gone missing in the Bush years. As has recently become clear, information that would be of great interest to the Nascar Dad has been withheld. With jobs disappearing at a staggering rate, the Bureau of Labor Statistics ended its Mass Layoff Tracking Study on Christmas Eve of 2002, thanks to this administration. And although Congressional Democrats managed to get funding for the study restored in February of 2003, the loss of 614,167 jobs in those two months was unannounced.

Conveying the truth in a misleading manner is, of course, another way of manipulating people.

As the linguist George Lakoff astutely observes, the term "tax relief" slyly invites us to imagine taxes as an affliction and those who propose them as villains. If we add in such distortions to the suppression of vital information, the Nascar Dad who listens to Rush Limbaugh on the commute home, turns on *Fox News* at dinner, and is too tired after working overtime to catch more than the headlines is perhaps a man being exposed to only one side of the political story.

But then Nascar Dad could always turn the radio dial. He could do a google search on job loss on his kid's computer. He could talk to his union buddies—if he's one of the 12% who are still unionized—or to his slightly more liberal wife. It could be he knows perfectly well that he's being lied to, but believes people are usually being lied to, and that Bush is, in this respect, still the better of two evils. But how could that be?

Maybe it's because Bush fits an underlying recipe for the kind of confident, authoritative father figure such dads believe should run the ship of state as they believe a man should run a family. Republican rhetoric may appeal to the blue-collar man, Lakoff suggests, because we tend to match our view of good politics with our image of a good family. The appeal of any political leader, he believes, lies in the way he matches our images of the father in the ideal family. There are two main pictures of such an ideal American family, Lakoff argues. According to a "strict father family" model, dad should provide for the family, control mom, and use discipline to teach his children how to survive in a competitive and hostile world. Those who advocate the strict father model, Lakoff reasons, favor a "strict father" kind of government. If an administration fits this model, it supports the family (by maximizing overall wealth). It protects the family from harm (by building up the military). It raises the children to be self-reliant and obedient (by fostering citizens who ask for little and speak when spoken to). The match-up here is, of course, to Bush Republicans.

Then there is the "nurturing parent family" model in which parents don't simply control their children but encourage their development. The government equivalent would be offering services to the citizenry, funding education, health, and welfare, and emphasizing diplomacy on a global stage. The core values here are empathy and responsibility, not control and discipline and the match up is to the pro-public sector Dean/Kucinich Democrats. Studies have shown that blue-collar ideals are closer to the strict father than to the nurturing parent model. But that's been true for a very long time, while the blue-collar vote sometimes goes left as in the 1930s, and sometimes goes right as it's doing now. So we can't simply pin the pro-Bush Nascar Dad vote on a sudden change in blue-collar family ideals.

APPEALING TO THE "FORGOTTEN AMERICAN"

Maybe, however, something deeper is going on, which has so far permitted Bush's flag-waving and cowboy-boot-strutting to trump issues of job security, wages, safety, and health—and even, in the case of Bush's threats of further war—life itself. In an essay, "The White Man Unburdened," in a recent *New York Review of Books,* Norman Mailer recently argued that the war in Iraq returned to white males a lost sense of mastery, offering them a feeling of revenge for imagined wrongs, and a sense of psychic rejuvenation. In the last thirty years, white men have taken a drubbing, he notes, especially the three quarters of them who lack college degrees. Between 1979 and 1999, for example, real wages for male high-school graduates dropped 24%. In addition, Mailer notes, white working class men have lost white champs in football, basketball and boxing. (A lot of white men cheer black athletes, of course, whomever they vote for.) But the war in Iraq, Mailer notes, gave white men white heroes. By climbing into his jumpsuit, stepping out of an S–3B Viking jet onto the aircraft carrier *USS Abraham Lincoln,* Bush posed as—one could say impersonated—such a hero.

Mailer is talking here about white men and support for the war in Iraq. But we're talking about something that cuts deeper into emotional life, and stretches further back into the twin histories of American labor and Republican presidencies. For Republicans have been capturing blue-collar hearts for some time now. In the summer of 1971, Jefferson Cowie tells us in a recent essay, Richard Nixon worked out a semi-clandestine "blue-collar strategy." Nixon instructed Jerome Rosow of the Department of Labor to draw up a confidential report, only 25 copies of which were circulated. One of them got into the hands of a *Wall Street Journal* reporter who exposed it under the banner, "Secret Report Tells Nixon How to Help White Workingmen and Win Their Votes."

As the article noted, "President Nixon has before him a confidential blueprint designed to help him capture the hearts and votes of the nation's white working men—the traditionally Democratic 'forgotten Americans' that the Administration believes are ripe for political plucking." According to close advisor, H. R. Haldeman, Nixon's plan was to maintain an image as "a tough, courageous, masculine leader." The never-ending Nixon tapes actually catch Nixon talking with aides Haldeman and Ehlichman about an episode in the popular television show "All in the Family" in which the working-class Archie Bunker confronts an old buddy, a former football player who has just come out of the closet as gay. Nixon then recounts on tape how civilizations decline when homosexuality rises, and concludes, "We have to stand up to this." Nixon sought to appeal to the blue-collar man's straightness (at least he still had that), his superiority over women (that, too), and his native-born whiteness (and that). As Cowie sums it up, "It was neither the entire working class nor its material grievances on which the administration would focus; rather it was the 'feeling of being forgotten' among white male workers that Nixon and his advisors would seek to tap."

Until Nixon, Republicans had for a century written off the blue-collar voter. But turning Marx on his head, Nixon appealed not to a desire for real economic change but to the distress caused by the absence of it. And it worked as it's doing again now. In the 1972 contest between

Nixon and McGovern, 57% of the manual worker vote and 54% of the union vote went to Nixon. (This meant 22- and 25-point gains for Nixon over his 1968 presidential run.) After Nixon, other Republican presidents—Ford, Reagan, and Bush Sr.—followed in the same footsteps, although not always so cleverly.

Now George Bush Jr. is pursuing a sequel strategy by again appealing to the emotions of male blue-collar voters. Only he's added a new element to the mix. Instead of appealing, as Nixon did, to anger at economic decline, Bush is appealing to fear of economic displacement, and offering the Nascar Dad a set of villains to blame, and a hero to thank—George W. Bush.

Let's begin by re-imagining the blue-collar man, for we do not normally think of him as a fearful man. The very term "Nascar Dad" like the earlier term "Joe Six Pack" suggests, somewhat dismissively, an "I'm-alright-Jack" kind of guy. We imagine him with his son, some money in his pocket, in the stands with the other guys rooting for his favorite driver and car. The term doesn't call to mind a restless house-husband or a despondent divorcee living back in his parents' house and seeing his kids every other weekend. In other words, the very image we start with may lead us away from clues to his worldview, his feelings, his politics and the links between these.

Since the 1970s, the blue-collar man has taken a lot of economic hits. The buying power of his paycheck, the size of his benefits, the security of his job—all these have diminished. As Ed Landry, a 62-year-old-machinist interviewed by Paul Solman on the *Lehrer News Hour* said, "We went to lunch and our jobs went to China." He searched for another job and couldn't find one. He was even turned down for a job as a grocery bagger. "I was told that we'd get back to you. Did they?" Solman asked. "No. I couldn't believe it myself. I couldn't get the job." In today's jobless recovery, the average jobless stint for a man like Landry is now 19 weeks, the longest since 1983. Jobs that don't even exist at present may eventually open up, experts reassure us, but they aren't opening up yet. In the meantime, three out of every four available jobs are low-level service jobs.

A lot of workers like Ed Landry, cast out of one economic sector, have been unable to land a job even at the bottom of another.

For anyone who stakes his pride on earning an honest day's pay, this economic fall is, unsurprisingly enough, hard to bear. How, then, do these blue-collar men feel about it? Ed Landry said he felt "numb." Others are anxious, humiliated and, as who wouldn't be, fearful. But in cultural terms, Nascar Dad isn't supposed to feel afraid. What he can feel though is angry. As Susan Faludi has described so well in her book *Stiffed,* that is what many such men feel. As a friend who works in a Maine lumber mill among blue-collar Republicans explained about his co-workers, "They felt that everyone else—women, kids, minorities—were all moving up, and they felt like they were moving down. Even the spotted owl seemed like it was on its way up, while he and his job, were on the way down. And he's angry."

STRUTTING THE POLITICAL FLIGHT DECK

But is that anger directed downward—at "welfare cheats," women, gays, blacks, and immigrants—or is it aimed up at job exporters and rich tax dodgers? Or out at alien enemies? The answer is likely to depend on the political turn of the screw. The Republicans are clearly doing all they can to aim that anger down or out, but in any case away from the rich beneficiaries of Bush's tax cut. Unhinging the personal from the political, playing on identity politics, Republican strategists have offered the blue-collar voter a Faustian bargain: We'll lift your self-respect by putting down women, minorities, immigrants, even those spotted owls. We'll honor the manly fortitude you've shown in taking bad news. But (and this is implicit) don't ask us to do anything to change that bad news. Instead of Marie Antoinette's "let them eat cake," we have—and this is Bush's twist on the old Nixonian strategy—"let them eat war."

Paired with this is an aggressive right-wing attempt to mobilize blue-collar fear, resentment and a sense of being lost—and attach it to the fear of American vulnerability, American loss. By doing so, Bush aims to win the blue-collar man's identification with big business, empire, and himself. The resentment anyone might feel at the personnel officer who didn't have the courtesy to call him back and tell him he didn't have the job, Bush now redirects toward the target of Osama bin Laden, and when we can't find him, Saddam Hussein and when we can't find him . . . And these enemies are now so intimate that we see them close up on the small screen in our bedrooms and call them by their first names.

Whether strutting across a flight deck or mocking the enemy, Bush with his seemingly fearless bravado—ironically born of class entitlement—offers an aura of confidence. And this confidence dampens, even if temporarily, the feelings of insecurity and fear exacerbated by virtually every major domestic and foreign policy initiative of the Bush administration. Maybe it comes down to this: George W. Bush is deregulating American global capitalism with one hand while regulating the feelings it produces with the other. Or, to put it another way, he is doing nothing to change the causes of fear and everything to channel the feeling and expression of it. He speaks to a working man's lost pride and his fear of the future by offering an image of fearlessness. He poses here in his union jacket, there in his pilot's jumpsuit, taunting the Iraqis to "bring 'em on"—all of it meant to feed something in the heart of a frightened man. In this light, even Bush's "bad boy" past is a plus. He steals a wreath off a Macy's door for his Yale fraternity and careens around drunk in Daddy's car. But in the politics of anger and fear, the Republican politics of feelings, this is a plus.

There is a paradox here. While Nixon was born into a lower-middle-class family, his distrustful personality ensured that his embrace of the blue-collar voter would prove to be wary and distrustful. Paradoxically, Bush, who was born to wealth, seems really to like being the top gun talking to "regular guys." In this way, Bush adds to Nixon's strategy his lone-ranger machismo.

More important, Nixon came into power already saddled with an unpopular war. Bush has taken a single horrific set of attacks on September 11, 2001, and mobilized his supporters and their feelings around them. Unlike Nixon, Bush created his own war, declared it ongoing but triumphant, and fed it to his potential supporters. His policy—and this his political advisor Karl Rove has carefully calibrated—is something like the old bait-and-switch. He continues to take the steaks out of the blue-collar refrigerator and to declare instead, "let them eat war." He has been, in effect, strip-mining the emotional responses of blue-collar men to the problems his own administration is so intent on causing.

But there is a chance this won't work. For one thing, the war may turn out to have been a bad idea, Bush's equivalent of a runaway plant. For another thing, working men may smell a skunk. Many of them may resent those they think have emerged from the pack behind them and are now getting ahead, and they may fear for their future. But they may also come to question whether they've been offered Osama bin Laden as a stand-in for the many unfixed problems they face. They may wonder whether their own emotions aren't just one more natural resource the Republicans are exploiting for their profit. What we urgently need now, of course, is a presidential candidate who addresses the root causes of blue-collar anger and fear and who actually tackles the problems before us all, instead of pandering to the emotions bad times evoke.

DISCUSSION QUESTIONS

1. Identify key facts about the economic and demographic profile of blue-collar workers, as presented by Hochschild. In what ways have their living conditions become more strained in recent years?

2. According to Hochschild, in what ways does Bush's "war on terrorism" provide the "Nascar Dads" with a positive sense of identity? Why would Hochschild regard this identity as based on a process of "displacement"?

LANI GUINIER

AFTER THE DELUGE: ELECTORAL REFORM IN THE WAKE OF THE ELECTION OF 2000

In the wake of the historic presidential election of 2000—with the outcome hanging in the balance for well over a month after election day, rampant charges of fraud and disenfranchisement, a national split between the popular vote winner and the Electoral College winner, and the ultimately decisive role played by the U.S. Supreme Court in stopping the Florida recount—a cry has gone up for all manner of election law reform. In this post-election analysis, Harvard law professor and long-time electoral reform advocate Lani Guinier weighs in on the side of a major overhaul of the electoral system. Guinier urges Americans to seize this rare opportunity to see the nation's electoral flaws under the glaring media spotlight and address many basic questions about how we vote. She examines the nation's extremely low voter turnout rate, the class and race-based nature of who votes, the often antiquated mechanics of voting procedures, the equally antiquated Electoral College, and the winner-take-all system of allocating electoral votes. In each area she identifies the need for major changes if we are to seriously strive to be a nation that fulfills the still-elusive promise of democracy—a promise that declares that every vote, and every voter, counts. Moreover, she sees a role for an active and engaged citizenry to call for substantial reform and to monitor the electoral process at the grassroots level, thus helping to reinvigorate civic life. Guinier's perspective suggests that there are many lessons to be learned from the controversy that has raged over the first U.S. presidential election of the twenty-first century. It remains to be seen how attentive we are as students of democracy.

For years many of us have called for a national conversation about what it means to be a multiracial democracy. We have enumerated the glaring flaws inherent in our winner-take-all form of voting, which has produced a steady decline in voter participation, underrepresentation of racial minorities in office, lack of meaningful competition and choice in most elections, and the general failure of politics to mobilize, inform and inspire half the eligible electorate. But nothing changed. Democracy was an asterisk in political debate, typically encompassed in a vague reference to "campaign finance reform." Enter Florida.

Source: Lani Guinier, "Making Every Vote Count." *The Nation,* vol. 271, no. 18, 4 December 2000, pp. 5–7.

The fiasco there provides a rare opportunity to rethink and improve our voting practices in a way that reflects our professed desire to have "every vote count." This conversation has already begun, as several highly educated communities in Palm Beach experienced the same sense of systematic disfranchisement that beset the area's poorer and less-educated communities of color. "It felt like Birmingham last night," Mari Castellanos, a Latina activist in Miami, wrote in an e-mail describing a mammoth rally at the 14,000-member New Birth Baptist Church, a primarily African-American congregation in Miami. "The sanctuary was standing room only. So were the overflow rooms and the school hall, where congregants connected via large TV screens. The people sang and prayed and listened. Story after story was told of voters being turned away at the polls, of ballots being destroyed, of NAACP election literature being discarded at the main post office, of Spanish-speaking poll workers being sent to Creole precincts and vice-versa. . . . Union leaders, civil rights activists, Black elected officials, ministers, rabbis and an incredibly passionate and inspiring Marlene Bastiene—president of the Haitian women's organization—spoke for two or three minutes each, reminding the assembly of the price their communities had paid for the right to vote and vowing not to be disfranchised ever again."

We must not let this once-in-a-generation moment pass without addressing the basic questions these impassioned citizens are raising: Who votes, how do they vote, whom do they vote for, how are their votes counted and what happens after the voting? These questions go to the very legitimacy of our democratic procedures, not just in Florida but nationwide—and the answers could lead to profound but eminently achievable reforms.

Who votes—and doesn't? As with the rest of the nation, in Florida only about half of all adults vote, about the same as the national average. Even more disturbing, nonvoters are increasingly low-income, young and less educated. This trend persists despite the Voting Rights Act, which since 1970 has banned literacy tests nationwide as prerequisites for voting—a ban enacted by Congress and unanimously upheld by the Supreme Court.

We are a democracy that supposedly believes in universal suffrage, and yet the differential turnout between high-income and low-income voters is far greater than in Europe, where it ranges from 5 to 10 percent. More than two-thirds of people in America with incomes greater than $50,000 vote, compared with one-third of those with income under $10,000. Those convicted of a felony are permanently banned from voting in Florida and twelve other states. In Florida alone, this year more than 40,000 ex-felons, about half of them black, were denied the opportunity to vote. Canada, on the other hand, takes special steps to register former prisoners and bring them into full citizenship.

How do they vote? Florida now abounds with stories of long poll lines, confusing ballots and strict limitations on how long voters could spend in the voting booth. The shocking number of invalid ballots—more ballots were "spoiled" in the presidential race than were cast for "spoiler" Ralph Nader—are a direct result of antiquated voting mechanics that would shame any nation, let alone one of the world's oldest democracies. Even the better-educated older voters of Palm Beach found, to their surprise, how much they had in common with more frequently disfranchised populations. Given how many decisions voters are expected to make in less than five minutes in the polling booth, it is common sense that the polls should be open over a weekend, or at least for twenty-four hours, and that Election Day should be a national holiday. By highlighting our wretched record on voting practices, Florida raises the obvious question: Do we really want large voter participation?

Whom do they vote for? Obviously, Florida voters chose among Al Gore, George Bush and a handful of minor-party candidates who, given their status as unlikely to win, were generally ignored and at best chastised as spoilers. But as many voters are now realizing, in the presidential race they were voting not for the candidates whose name they selected (or attempted to select) but for "electors" to that opaque institution, the Electoral College. Our constitutional framers did some things well—chiefly dulling the edge of winner-take-all elections through institutions that demand coalition-building, compromise and recognition of certain minority voices—but the Electoral College was created on illegitimate grounds and has no place in a modern democracy.

As Yale law professor Akhil Reed Amar argues, the Electoral College was established as a device to boost the power of Southern states in the election of the President. The same "compromise" that gave Southern states more House members by counting slaves as three-fifths of a person for purposes of apportioning representation (while giving them none of the privileges of citizenship) gave those states Electoral College votes in proportion to their Congressional delegation. This hypocrisy enhanced the Southern states' Electoral College percentage, and as a result, Virginia slaveowners controlled the presidency for thirty-two of our first thirty-six years.

Its immoral origins notwithstanding, the Electoral College was soon justified as a deliberative body that would choose among several candidates and assure the voice of small geographic areas. But under the Electoral College, voters in small states have more than just a voice; indeed their say often exceeds that of voters in big states. In Wyoming one vote in the Electoral College corresponds to 71,000 voters; in Florida, one electoral vote corresponds to 238,000 voters. At minimum we should eliminate the extra bias that adding electors for each of two senators gives our smallest states. As Robert Naiman of the Center for Economic and Policy Research reports, allowing each state only as many electors as it has members in the House of Representatives would mean, for example, that even if Bush won Oregon and Florida, he would have 216 and Gore would have 220 electoral votes.

Today its backers still argue that the Electoral College is necessary to insure that small states are not ignored by the presidential candidates. Yet the many states—including the small ones—that weren't close in this election were neglected by both campaigns. Some of the nation's biggest states, with the most people of color, saw very little presidential campaigning and get-out-the-vote activity. Given their lopsided results this year, we can expect California, Illinois, New York, Texas and nearly all Southern states to be shunned in the 2004 campaign.

How are their votes counted? The presidency rests on a handful of votes in Florida because allocation of electoral votes is winner-take-all—if Gore wins by ten votes out of 6 million, he will win 100 percent of the state's twenty-five electoral votes. The ballots cast for a losing candidate are always "invalid" for the purposes of representation; only those cast for the winner actually "count." Thus winner-take-all elections underrepresent the voice of the minority and exaggerate the power of one state's razor-thin majority. Winner-take-all is the great barrier to representation of political and racial minorities at both the federal and the state level. No blacks or Latinos serve in the U.S. Senate or in any governor's mansion. Third-party candidates did not win a single state legislature race except for a handful in Vermont.

Given the national questioning of the Electoral College sparked by the anomalous gap between the popular vote and the college's vote in the presidential election, those committed to real representative democracy now have a chance to shine a spotlight on the glaring flaws and disenfranchisement inherent in winner-take-all practices and to propose important reforms.

What we need are election rules that encourage voter turnout rather than suppress it. A system of proportional representation—which would allocate seats to parties based on their proportion of the total vote—would more fairly reflect intense feeling within the electorate, mobilize more people to participate and even encourage those who do participate to do so beyond just the single act of voting on Election Day. Most democracies around the world have some form of proportional voting and manage to engage a much greater percentage of their citizens in elections. Proportional representation in South Africa, for example, allows the white Afrikaner parties and the ANC to gain seats in the national legislature commensurate with the total number of votes cast for each party. Under this system, third parties are a plausible alternative. Moreover, to allow third parties to run presidential candidates without being "spoilers," some advocate instant-runoff elections in which voters would rank their choices for President (see box on next page). That way, even voters whose top choice loses the election could influence the race among the other candidates.

Winner-take-all elections, by contrast, encourage the two major parties to concentrate primarily on the "undecideds" and to take tens of millions of dollars of corporate and special-interest contributions to broadcast ads on the public airwaves appealing to the center of the political spectrum. Winner-take-all incentives discourage either of the two major parties from trying to learn, through organizing and door-knocking, how to mobilize the vast numbers of disengaged poor and working-class voters. Rather than develop a vision, they produce a product and fail to build political capacity from the ground up.

What happens after the voting? Our nation is more focused on elections now than it has been for decades; yet on any given Sunday, more people will watch professional football than voted this November. What democracy demands is a system of elections that enables minor parties to gain a voice in the legislature and encourages the development of local political organizations that educate and mobilize voters.

Between elections, grassroots organizations could play an important monitoring role now unfulfilled by the two major parties. If the Bush campaign is right that large numbers of ballots using the same butterfly format were thrown out in previous elections in Palm Beach, then something is wrong with more than the ballot. For those Democratic senior citizens in Palm Beach, it was not enough that their election supervisor was a Democrat. They needed a vibrant local organization that could have served as a watchdog, alerting voters and election officials that there were problems with the ballot. No one should inadvertently vote for two candidates; the same watchdog organizations should require ballot-counting machines like those in some states that notify the voter of such problems before he or she leaves the booth. Voters should be asked, as on the popular TV quiz show, "Is that your final answer?" And surely we cannot claim to be a functioning democracy when voters are turned away from the polls or denied assistance in violation of both state and federal law.

Before the lessons of Florida are forgotten, let us use this window of opportunity to forge a strong pro-democracy coalition to rally around "one vote, one value." The value of a vote depends on it being fairly counted but also on its counting toward the election of the person the voter chose as her representative. This can happen only if we recognize the excesses of winner-take-all voting and stop exaggerating the power of the winner by denying the loser any voice at all.

DISCUSSION QUESTIONS

1. In what ways does Lani Guinier see democracy being compromised by current electoral laws and practices in the United States?

2. How did the communities affected by the electoral fiasco in Florida react to the situation following the 2000 presidential election? What role does Guinier see communities potentially playing in the fight to reform electoral law?

3. What is your reaction to Guinier's proposals, especially with regard to the Electoral College?

WHAT IS INSTANT RUNOFF VOTING?

IRV is a ranked ballot method of voting that results in a winner chosen by a majority of the voters. The voters rank the candidates in order of preference. Each voter has one vote which counts for the highest preferred candidate that can use it. The term "Instant Runoff Voting" was coined because the method of transferring votes from defeated candidates to continuing candidates is just like a runoff election except that it is accomplished on one ballot. It is also known as Single Transferable Vote (single winner version), Alternative Vote, and Majority Preferential Vote.

Rank the candidates in order of preference—your first choice and your runoff choices

	1st choice	2nd choice	3rd choice
John	❏	❏	❏
Bill	❏	❏	❏
Frank	❏	❏	❏

How are the votes counted in IRV?

First choices are counted. If no candidate receives a majority, the candidate with the fewest votes is defeated, and those votes are transferred to the next ranked candidate on each ballot. The votes are recounted. The process continues until one candidate has a majority of the votes and is declared the winner.

	1st Choices	Instant Runoff	Final Results
John	35	+16	51 winner
Bill	20	−20	
Frank	45	+4	49
Total	100		
Winning Threshold 50%+1=	51		

Instant Runoff Example

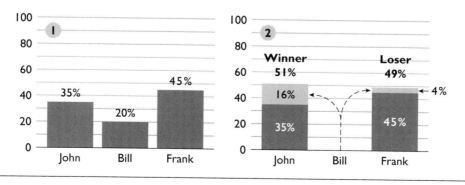

CHAPTER 6

Congress

Congress has frequently been described as the world's foremost legislative body, but its performance often disappoints Americans. Polls show consistently that we have less confidence in the legislative branch than in either the presidency or the judiciary. Ironically, the legislature is the first branch of government discussed in the Constitution, and there is no doubt that most of the Framers intended Congress to be the primary policy-making institution. In the nineteenth century, with the exception of several periods of strong presidential leadership, the Congress did in fact exert this kind of primacy in our political system. But in the twentieth century, and particularly since the 1930s, increased assertion of presidential power has left the Congress as a reactive and fragmented body, though still with the power to block presidential initiatives.

Former Speaker of the House of Representatives Thomas P. "Tip" O'Neill used to say that all politics is local. Part of the problem with Congress is the mismatch between its local orientation and the increasingly national and international imperatives placed on the U.S. state to secure the domestic health and worldwide expansion of corporate capitalism. Members of Congress, especially in the House, are elected to represent states and districts with specific social needs, economic characteristics, and local power structures. Overlaying this local orientation and contributing to congressional indecision are weak party structures, the impact of campaign contributions, the typically great advantages for incumbents seeking reelection, and the ubiquitous impact of interest groups on policy-making. All of these pressures make it difficult for Congress to set an independent agenda for attaining the public good through taking on the myriad social and economic problems facing America. And these pressures are exacerbated by the bitter partisan divide in Congress after the elections of 2000, 2002 and 2004.

JOHN C. BERG

CONGRESS AND BIG BUSINESS

Political scientist John Berg frames this chapter with an article that places Congress within the context of a theory of society that views class structure, the needs of corporate capitalism, and our dominant liberal ideology as basic structural determinants that set the boundaries of debate on policy issues. Following in the tradition of Philip Brenner's pathbreaking 1983 book The Limits and Possibilities of Congress, *Berg analyzes how congressional politics can be seen as part of the larger ongoing social conflict in America. Contrary to the principles of pluralist theory (see our Introduction), this conflict privileges the interests of one key participant—giant multinational corporations—who exercise dominating class power, or "hegemony." Berg uses several examples to illustrate how and why Congress protects corporate interests with a swiftness and effectiveness that other classes and groups do not enjoy. He then details three ways in which corporate hegemony is built into the structure of Congress: through the legal system of the country, governmental separation of powers, and the power of specific congressional committees. Big business certainly does not win all the time, but the rules of the game are skewed so that their overall interests dominate policy debates and outcomes regardless of the party and personalities of congressional leaders.*

Money talks. Everyone knows that. It talks a lot to Congress. Well-heeled lobbyists, political action committees (PACs), expense-paid junkets, multi-million-dollar campaigns, and juicy honoraria are abiding elements of American political lore. Everyone knows, too, that the rich do better than other people at getting their opinions heard and their interests accommodated by legislators. Average citizens, political scientists, and the members of Congress themselves join in bewailing the excessive importance of money in politics.

Congressional politics is part of the fundamental social conflict in America. Congress is one arena in which this conflict takes place, but it is not an independent arena. Forces outside Congress influence what goes on inside it; in particular, if the Marxist theory is correct, Congress is influenced heavily by the economic structure of our society. Those who dominate the American economy dominate Congress as well. But Congress is also the most democratic part of our national government. Thus, oppressed social

Source: John C. Berg, *Unequal Struggle: Class, Gender, Race, and Power in the U.S. Congress.* Boulder, CO: Westview Press, 1994, pp. 31–34 and 37–44.

groups have found it the most permeable part of the state, often seeking to use congressional politics to advance their cause. . . .

We can see the effect of economic structure when we compare the way Congress handles different issues. In 1977, with the nation suffering from an energy shortage that restricted economic growth, hurt the balance of trade, inflated the cost of living, and forced many poor people to go without heat in winter, President Jimmy Carter presented a comprehensive national energy plan to Congress. After two years of hearings, backroom negotiations, and public debate, Congress managed to pass only one part of the plan: It removed price controls from natural gas, thus making energy even more expensive.

In 1989 the wreck of the oil tanker Exxon *Valdez* killed thousands of waterfowl, fish, marine mammals, and plants, threatened the ecological balance of Prince William Sound, and infuriated the public. Individual members of Congress responded with thousands of dramatic public speeches; but it was sixteen months before Congress as a legislative body managed to pass a bill raising the limits on liability of negligent oil shippers from $150 to $1,200 per ton of oil. Although the final bill was considered a victory by environmental lobbyists, several concessions had to be made to the oil industry before it could be passed. Double-hull requirements for oil tankers were deferred until 2010 (and to 2015 for most barges and for ships unloading offshore to lighters), oil companies shipping oil in tankers owned by others were exempted, and state governors lost any power to determine when a cleanup was complete.

In the early 1980s a large number of savings and loan associations—known as thrift institutions, or simply "thrifts"—began to lose money; by 1987 many were in danger of failing. The Federal Savings and Loan Insurance Corporation (FSLIC), which insured thrift deposits of $100,000 or less, warned that it might not be able to pay all the claims. Congress gave the FSLIC another $10 billion in 1987, but otherwise did nothing until after the 1988 election. Then, in early 1989,

Congress moved with remarkable speed to enact a complicated—and expensive—reorganization plan for the thrift industry. President George Bush proposed a plan on February 6 and signed a new law on August 9. The S&L Bailout—as it became known—would cost $50 billion by the end of 1991, and at least $110 billion by 1999; some of the money would be paid to the holders of insured accounts, but much of it would be used to subsidize healthier, more profitable banks and thrifts in taking over unhealthy ones.

In this case Congress acted not only quickly but ingeniously. Since the passage of the Gramm-Rudman-Hollings Deficit Reduction Act (GRH) in 1985, new spending programs had been difficult to create. The bill deftly evaded this problem. It simply labeled $30 billion "off-budget" and assigned the remaining $20 billion to a fiscal year that had already begun—and which therefore had already passed the GRH test.

One could argue that Congress acted so quickly and smoothly in the savings and loan case because it simply had to. The nation faced a crisis, and failure to act would have had unthinkable consequences. However, this line of thought leads to further questions. What is a crisis? What sort of consequences are unthinkable? In 1991 a cholera epidemic broke out in Peru, threatening to spread throughout South and Central America; it was expected to be hard to stop because the projected cost of the necessary sanitary improvements was prohibitive—$200 billion over twelve years, or about the same as the savings and loan bailout.

Closer to home, it has been argued that American public education is in crisis. Millions of young people fail to complete high school; millions more graduate unable to read, to multiply fractions, or to understand the basic nature of atoms and molecules. These consequences are unthinkably tragic, but they are happening, and Congress has not found the will to prevent them.

Marxists use the concept of *hegemony* to explain the differences between these two crises. Hegemony refers to the dominating power of a social class (or part of one) whose class interests have come to be widely accepted as equivalent to the interests of society as a whole. The United States today is dominated in this way by the giant multinational corporations.

·   ·   ·

The American economy is not just capitalist; it is dominated by a small number of gigantic capitalist corporations. In 1988, the 500 largest industrial corporations in the United States—the so-called Fortune 500—had total sales of over $2 trillion. One-fifth of this amount, $402,183,000,000, was produced by just five companies: General Motors (GM), Ford, Exxon, International Business Machines (IBM), and General Electric (GE). In the same year, there were about 3.5 million corporations, and 14 million nonfarm proprietorships and partnerships, in the United States. The three major automobile makers alone employed 1,270,000 people, had assets of $356 billion, and earned profits of $11.2 billion. The ten largest commercial banks—all but one of them located in New York City—had assets of $860 billion, with nearly one-quarter of that, $207 billion, held by one bank, New York's Citicorp.

These giants are so big that the rest of the country needs them to be healthy. When Chrysler Corporation, only the third largest automobile maker, faced possible bankruptcy, the federal government stepped in to save it. It stepped in again to avert the failure of Chicago-based Continental Bank Corporation, the fourteenth largest commercial bank. As this practice has become more common, it has acquired a name, the "too big to fail" doctrine. It is one example of *hegemony.*

When Charles E. ("Engine Charlie") Wilson went from president of General Motors to secretary of defense in the Eisenhower administration, he told a Senate committee that he was not worried about any possible conflict of interest because he had always believed that "what was good for our country was good for General Motors, and vice versa. The difference did not exist. Our company is too big. It goes with the welfare of the country."

In the largest sense, Wilson was dead wrong. GM has been a cumbersome, inefficient enterprise that has contributed greatly to a whole range of national problems, from low productivity to air pollution to worker alienation. But in the short run—that is, given that GM already existed—Wilson was right. GM's huge labor force, its annual sales, and its impact as a customer on other major industries were so great that a failure of GM—or of another giant corporation—might well have plunged the whole economy into recession.

CORPORATE HEGEMONY

Until sometime in the early 1970s the giant financial and industrial corporations were able to dominate America and much of the rest of the world. This domination gave them a sense of security and led some to conclude that they were more interested in stability than in profits. Since that time, however, their dominance has been threatened by growing international competition. The best-known example is the auto industry, in which the big three U.S. automakers have lost market share to Japanese and European competitors both at home and abroad; but the same thing has occurred in many other industries as well.

This new global competition has changed both the composition and the interests of the hegemonic bloc. By reviving the emphasis on profits it has reinforced the dominance of finance capital over industrial corporations. Such once-mighty giants as IBM have learned that Wall Street would rather shift its investments to other companies and industries than support them in fighting to preserve their corporate position. The willingness of many corporations to accept high wages and benefits and a certain amount of government regulation is likewise falling before international competitive pressure. These changes in the economic position of U.S. big business have had important political results; but the basic division between hegemonic and nonhegemonic sectors of the capitalist class remains.

Politics and ideology tend to reflect economics. Thus, the state (including Congress) tends to further the interests of the giant corporations; and public debate tends to be carried on in terms that incorporate those interests—as in 1990, when President Bush referred to protection of Exxon's oil supplies in the Persian Gulf as a defense of "our way of life." This is not automatically so. The nonhegemonic classes can and do organize themselves to contend for political power, and to change the terms of public discourse. But they find it harder to win; and unless they succeed in changing the economic structure as well, such political and ideological reforms are likely to be only temporary. Let us look at some concrete examples.

The crisis in the savings and loan industry threatened to destabilize the whole financial system, endangering giant banks along with small thrift institutions. It thus struck at the heart of corporate hegemony. The nature of this hegemony is missed by much left rhetoric. For example, Manning Marable has written recently:

Is it right for a government to spend billions and billions for bailing out fat cats who profited from the savings and loan scam while millions of jobless Americans stand in unemployment lines desperate for work? Is it fair that billions of our dollars are allocated for the Pentagon's permanent war economy to obliterate the lives of millions of poor people from Panama to Iraq to Grenada to Vietnam, while two million Americans sleep in the streets and 37 million Americans lack any form of medical coverage?

The policies Marable decries are indeed neither right nor fair; but even those members of Congress who agree with this characterization fear that allowing the savings and loan industry to collapse, or (more debatably) cutting the military budget, would send even more millions to the unemployment lines or into the streets. For this reason, debate within Congress about the savings and loan crisis has centered on who should take the blame, not on whether to act.

By contrast, the crisis in education strikes at the U.S. working class, and cholera threatens workers and peasants in other countries. Millions of lives may be blighted, neighborhoods destabilized, and great human suffering caused, but most members of Congress still see a solution as optional—something we certainly ought to do if we can just find the money. Even the advocates of school reform find it useful to base their arguments on the need of capitalism for a more skilled labor force.

This is the theory of hegemony in its bare bones. Hegemonic interests are privileged in that Congress and the state act quickly and effectively to protect them; they find it more difficult to promote other interests that are equally vital in human terms. But students of politics must ask how this privilege is maintained. What is it about our political system—what is it about Congress—that makes it more responsive to hegemonic interests than to others?

In fact, the interests of the great corporations are well entrenched in the structure of American government. This structure is itself the product of past political struggles, dating back at least to the drafting of the Constitution. Some of these struggles have been won by the working class, farmers, and petty bourgeoisie; by women; by racial minorities; and by other democratizing forces. But on the whole, the trend has been toward the kind of state envisioned by Alexander Hamilton, a state dedicated to furthering business interests.

Corporate hegemony is built into the structure of Congress on at least three levels. First, it has become part of our basic legal order. Second, it is built into the separation of powers, which places the most crucial decisions outside of Congress's reach. Finally, it is part of the internal structure of Congress itself. The end result of decades of conflict is that Congress finds it easy to act on behalf of corporate interests and difficult to act against them. These structural features are reinforced by the nature of the American electoral system, and by the weakness of anticapitalist ideology.

Americans think of our legal order as founded on individual rights. However, the meaning of these rights has been transformed since the U.S. Constitution was first written. On the one hand, rights have been broadened and extended in such a way that the universalistic language of the Declaration of Independence is now applied to the propertyless, to women, and to the descendants of slaves, none of whom had been included at first. On the other hand, the language of rights has been applied to big business, becoming a fundamental restraint on the power of Congress and other democratic institutions to regulate business in the public interest.

Perhaps the most important business victory was the extension of individual civil rights to corporations. Today this extension has become such a basic feature of our legal system that we tend not to notice it, but it came about only in the latter half of the nineteenth century. Through a combination of state and federal legislation and Supreme Court decisions, two legal doctrines became firmly established. First, corporations—which had been conceived of originally as quasi-state agencies chartered by the state in order to achieve an important public purpose, such as building a bridge or a canal, settling Massachusetts Bay, or conquering India—were transformed into a means of concentrating capital without exposing its individual owners to excessive risk, for the sole purpose of making money.

Second, these corporations gained the status of *persons* under the law, and as such won the legal rights granted to persons by the Fourteenth Amendment. This amendment had been designed to give federal protection to the freed slaves; but the Supreme Court ignored this purpose for seventy years, while using the amendment to protect corporations from government regulation. The Court has since backed away from some of its more extreme interpretations, but the basic legal structure of corporate rights continues to place many possible policies beyond the bounds of congressional or state legislative action.

Most recently, the Supreme Court has extended freedom of expression to corporate persons. The Court ruled in 1975 that the First Amendment applied to commercial advertising and, in 1980, extended it to cover political advocacy by businesses. A constitutional provision intended to protect human democracy and individualism thereby became a barrier to attempts to protect democratic discourse from the domination of capital.

The interests of giant corporations are also built into the operation of the constitutional separation of powers. Those who study the making of public policy know that the balance of power between Congress and the president varies with the issue at hand. The executive branch has the largest role in foreign policy, military action, and the regulation of the national economy. The president can order military action, recognize foreign governments, or sign Executive Agreements without congressional approval. Even when funds must be appropriated by Congress, he has considerable discretion to divert them to other purposes—and, as the Iran-*contra* case showed, he also has the *de facto* ability to exceed that discretion. He and his appointees also play the major role in attempts to regulate the national economy.

Congress, for its part, wields more detailed control over such issues as aid to education, environmental protection, housing, health, and welfare. In these areas, presidentially appointed officials must work with specific mandates and finite appropriations from Congress, and important issues are often decided by Congress, in committees or by floor amendments.

Some of these differences are rooted in the Constitution, whereas others have emerged since—as with the creation of the Federal Reserve System; but in general, those policy areas that are more vital to the interests of the great corporations are further removed from the influence of Congress.

Nonhegemonic classes and groups have better access to Congress than to the president and his inner cabinet, but this access does not give them proportional influence over those matters most important to the hegemonic fraction. The president can invade Grenada or Panama, go to war with Iraq, or sponsor terrorist attacks in Nicaragua, and Congress finds it hard to restrain him. The Federal Reserve system sets the nation's monetary policy, a key determinant of the fate of our economy, with little accountability to Congress or even to the president. In the case of foreign affairs, Congress's power is limited by the Constitution, which makes the president commander in chief of the armed forces; but it has been unable to resist the erosion of its own power to declare war. The United States fought both the Korean and Vietnam wars without formal declarations of war by Congress, and in the case of Vietnam the fighting continued long after Congress had turned against it. Finding itself unable to stop a war that was under way, Congress passed the War Powers Act of 1974; but this act has proved ineffective, having often been ignored by the president. However, the regulation of banking and currency are powers assigned to Congress; its loss of influence in these areas is the result of its own past decisions to create and maintain the Federal Reserve System. As a result, Congress must try to manage the economy—if it wishes to try at all—by raising or lowering federal taxes and spending, tools that are difficult to wield and uncertain in their effect. The powers to regulate interest rates and the money supply have proven more effective, but they have been removed from Congress and given to the Federal Reserve Board and the Federal Open Market Committee. In both cases, political struggles of the past have helped form structures that bias the political struggles of today.

The class basis of the separation of powers, and its changes over time, merit further study. As a simple approximation we could say that hegemonic interests dominate the presidency, whereas the influence of other social forces is confined to Congress. But hegemony operates within Congress as well. Congress has been unable to stop presidents from encroaching on its traditional powers partly because the interests that dominate the presidency also control the main levers of power within Congress.

Decisionmaking in each house of Congress is formally democratic, usually by majority vote. Yet small groups of members have always possessed the greatest share of power over decisions. Such power can come from control over the flow of bills to the floor, as with the party leaderships and the House Rules Committee; or from control over important legislative subject matter, as with the appropriations, tax-writing, and budget committees. The Appropriations, Rules, and Ways and Means committees in the House are called "exclusive committees"—because they are so important that their members are not supposed to serve on other standing committees at the same time (a rule often broken, as it happens). The House Budget Committee is a special case; it is formed of selected representatives from other committees, and its chair, rather than being chosen by seniority, is elected by the House and considered a member of the House leadership. The Senate also recognizes certain committees as having extra importance: Appropriations, Budget, Finance (the Senate equivalent of House Ways and Means), and Foreign Relations (given special importance in the Senate because of that body's treaty ratification power). For ease of reference, all of these will be referred to from now on as *hegemonic committees.*

Both party leadership and hegemonic committee positions are almost always held by members who have incorporated the hegemonic ideology into their own outlooks. Several studies have shown that positions of power go to those members who have a "responsible legislative style," one of the essential elements of which is a willingness to put what is conceived of as the national interest ahead of narrow constituency interests.

For hegemonic committees, congressional leaders also prefer to pick members who come from seats that are relatively safe, so that they will be less subject to popular pressure on controversial decisions. There is also some self-selection of members. Richard Fenno, in a famous study of House committees, found that representatives were most likely to seek seats on the Ways and

Means or Appropriations committees if they were more interested in achieving power as an end in itself than in promoting specific policies. Given the structure of American society, such power can best be pursued by choosing to side with big business.

These selection procedures do not work perfectly. However, potentially dissident committee members find themselves outnumbered and face strong pressure not to rock the boat. If they cooperate with hegemonic interests, they can use their committee positions to win significant benefits for their districts or for other interests they support; but if they come to be seen as troublemakers, such benefits are much harder to come by. Generally such pressures are enough to keep potential dissidents in line.

The hegemonic faction does not dominate Congress through sheer force; its power is maintained only by the tacit, and sometimes open, support of a majority of the members, who could vote to change the structure at any time. One of the strengths of Congress is that its leaders understand this contingency and act consciously to maintain their support. "Responsibility" includes "reciprocity" and "accommodation"—the willingness of a member of Ways and Means, for example, to serve as a voice for interests in his or her region that want particular concessions in the tax code, and to cooperate with members from other regions with like interests. The willingness to grant such concessions from time to time provides the solid foundation for the Ways and Means Committee's ability at other times to gain acceptance of an omnibus tax bill under a closed rule.

As Fenno observes, the power of the hegemonic committees is reinforced by institutional pride. House members want the Ways and Means Committee to be strong, because its power is, to some extent, theirs as well.

In addition to a generalized willingness to be accommodating, hegemony within Congress can involve specific accommodations of particular groups. For example, the Rayburn-McCormack leadership of the House Democrats—whose successors, known as the Austin-Boston Axis, remained in control of the House Democratic leadership through the 1980s—won and maintained power on the basis both of a moderate New Deal ideology and of a very specific agreement that amendments to the tax code that were regarded unfavorably by Southwestern oil interests would not be allowed on the floor. The oil industry has since been forced to fight harder for its interests, but it continues to be well represented in the House and Senate tax-writing committees, and still receives tax treatment more favorable than that accorded to most other industries. This arrangement is a reflection of the central position of the oil companies in the American economy—their inclusion in the hegemonic bloc—but it is not an automatic result of that economic importance. Rather, it is the consequence of a series of political victories by which the representatives of the oil companies have gained control of some of the levers of congressional power.

These three structural factors—the basic legal order, the division of powers among the branches of government, and the power of the hegemonic committees within Congress—provide the terrain on which pluralist conflict takes place. This conflict is fought out with the usual weapons of democratic politics—namely, votes and money; but the giant corporations enter the battle already in possession of the commanding heights and are therefore much more likely to win.

DISCUSSION QUESTIONS

1. What situations constitute a crisis to the U.S. Congress? According to what interests are crisis situations determined?
2. What evidence does Berg provide that corporations use our political system to exercise their hegemony? Relate this argument to Article 3 by Clawson, Neustadtl, and Weller by comparing the authors' perspectives on corporate hegemony.

(22)

DEMOCRACY ON DRUGS: HOW A BILL REALLY BECOMES A LAW

There's an old adage in politics that goes like this: The two things you shouldn't see in the process of being made are sausage and legislation. The following selection is a report from Common Cause, a Washington-based nonpartisan citizens' lobbying organization that offers a window into the legislative process. It does not present us with a sanitized picture; it shows us the dirt and the blood. In late November of 2003 the House and Senate handed President Bush a huge legislative victory by passing a bill establishing a voluntary prescription drug program under Medicare, one of the centerpieces of the President's domestic agenda. The bill passed 220–215 in the House and 54–44 in the Senate. The Common Cause study chronicles a tale of deceit, manipulation, strong arm tactics, procedural violations, secrecy and favoritism toward the pharmaceutical industry—all undertaken by the Republican leadership of Congress in the pursuit of private corporate profit under the guise of the public interest of the 40 million Medicare beneficiaries. So heavy-handed were the Republican tactics that in the fall of 2004 House Majority Leader Tom Delay (R-TX) was officially admonished by the House Ethics Committee for his efforts to strong arm Rep. Nick Smith (R-MI) into changing his vote against the bill. The Medicare prescription drug saga belies the neat and tidy legislative flow charts that grace standard high school and college American government textbooks. And as Common Cause points out, the sum total of irregularities and shenanigans involved in this story raises troubling questions about the democratic process and its promise of fairness and accountability. "From start to finish, the $535 billion Medicare bill . . . has been a study in shutting out opposing voices and suppressing the flow of vital information." The result was a give-away to pharmaceutical companies with negligible, if any benefits for the elderly. Students of government might be left wondering: is this any way to run a legislature?

INTRODUCTION

Our Constitution reflects the over-arching concern of the Founding Fathers that the rights of the minority be jealously preserved and protected, even in the presence of a strong majority. From start to finish, the $535 billion Medicare bill passed by Congress and signed by President

Source: Common Cause, *Democracy on Drugs. The Medicare/Prescription Drug Bill: A Study in How Government Shouldn't Work.* Washington, D.C.: Common Cause, May 18, 2004.

Bush late in 2003 has been a study in shutting out opposing voices and suppressing the flow of vital information.

This Common Cause report chronicles a series of incidents, large and small, that add up to a consistent effort by the Administration and Congressional leadership to bypass or undermine the rules and laws that are in place to ensure that our government works in an open and accountable manner and that all voices are heard on critical public policy issues.

The Medicare bill is the product of a process that included:

- Charges of bribery, delayed votes, inappropriate cabinet member lobbying and censoring of C-SPAN cameras.
- The Administration misleading Congress by withholding its own cost estimates for the prescription drug legislation—estimates that greatly exceeded what the President was telling the public. A career civil servant being threatened with his job if he told Congress the truth.
- Congressional Members excluded from the House-Senate conference committee that finalized the bill. Only a "coalition of the willing" was invited to participate.
- A principal author of the bill was forced to step down as head of a powerful House committee after it was reported that he was negotiating a $2 million a year lobbying job with the drug industry while he was moving the proposal through his committee. And a key Administration official involved in pushing the legislation was also offered lucrative private sector healthcare jobs.
- The drug industry showered Congress with campaign contributions and spent millions of dollars on highly paid lobbyists who swarmed Capitol Hill while the bill was being considered.
- A propaganda campaign waged by the Department of Health and Human Services. The Administration paid people to pose as journalists in television segments that praised the benefits of the new Medicare law, and spent

tens of millions of dollars on a campaign promoting the new program.

CHARGES OF BRIBERY ON THE HOUSE FLOOR

"directly or indirectly, corruptly gives, offers or promises anything of value to any public official . . . with intent to influence any official act."
—U.S. Code. Title 18 Sec. 201.
"Bribery of public officials"

At the break of dawn on Nov. 22, 2003, Representative Nick Smith (R-MI) was about to cast his vote against a Medicare/prescription drug bill so flawed and controversial that the Republican House leadership held the vote open for three hours while they pressured their own Republican colleagues to vote for the bill. Votes in the House typically are open for 15 minutes.

Strong-arming Members of the House to vote with the leadership is routine business, but what went on in those early morning hours appears to have slid over the line from political pressure to outright bribery.

A Nov. 23, 2003 column written by Rep. Smith appearing on his website reads:

I was targeted by lobbyists and the congressional leadership to change my vote, being a fiscal conservative and being on record as a no vote. Secretary of Health and Human Services Tommy Thompson and Speaker of the House Dennis Hastert talked to me for a long time about the bill and about why I should vote yes. Other members and groups made offers of extensive financial campaign support and endorsements for my son Brad who is running for my seat. They also made threats of working against Brad if I voted no.

On Dec. 1, 2003, in a radio interview with Kevin Vandenbroek of WKZO in Kalamazoo, Mich., Rep. Smith said:

They started out by offering the carrot, and they know what's important to every member, and what's important to me is my family and my kids. And I've term-limited myself, and so Bradley my son is running for [my congressional seat] and so the first offer was to give him $100,000-plus for his campaign and endorsement by national leadership. And I said No, I'm gonna stick to my guns on what I think is right for the constituents in my district.

Since Rep. Smith went public with his allegations, he has made several attempts to modify his original statement. Speaking to David Frownfelder of the *Daily Telegram* in Adrian, Mich. Rep. Smith said:

I was told there would be aggressive, substantial support for my son, Brad [in his race for Congress] if I could vote yes on the bill. There were offers of endorsements and so maybe a member [of Congress] sitting close by said, 'Boy that really could be big money.' Tens of thousands or hundreds of thousands. But never was I offered any exact amount of money in exchange for my vote. Technically, in the legal description that I later reviewed on what a bribe is, probably it didn't meet the legal description of a bribe.

Censoring C-SPAN

C-SPAN cameras perched above the House floor have for 25 years allowed the public to see for themselves how their representatives are carrying on the public's business. But the night of the vote on the prescription drug bill, the House leadership censored the public's view of the chamber.

In an interview on the 25th anniversary of C-SPAN's television coverage of Congress, the head of C-SPAN, Brian Lamb, noted that the congressional leadership has always controlled the cameras in the House and Senate chambers, generally focused on whoever is speaking, but also panning across the chamber to show activity on the floor.

Lamb pointed out how the leadership's control of the cameras can subvert C-SPAN's studiously nonpartisan, objective coverage of Congress. Lamb said:

You saw what happened in the middle of the night over the vote on Medicare on the floor of the House of Representatives, when they controlled the cameras. And I noticed that the camera wasn't moving from—it usually moves constantly from side to side. For almost the entire two or three hours that they had it open, the camera was showing the Democratic side. And that's where people don't get a fair shot.

In other words, the Republican leadership of the House intentionally diverted the C-SPAN cameras away from the Republican side of the House floor. Consequently, there is no visual record of who was talking to who that night while votes were sought by the leadership.

HHS Secretary on the House Floor

Rep. Smith said he was pressured during the three-hour vote by his own House leadership, but also, to his surprise, by the Department of Health and Human Services (HHS) Secretary Tommy Thompson, who made an unusual appearance on the House floor that night.

While House rules allow federal department heads to be in the House chamber, it is rare for such an official to be lobbying for legislation being considered by the House. According to *National Journal's CongressDaily*, Secretary Thompson defended the fact that he had broken House customs by lobbying members on the House floor during the final, three-hour roll call vote on the Medicare reform bill. "I spent five months working on this bill. I think it was only proper my being on the floor," Thompson said. But it appears Thompson's activities that night were a sharp departure from House customs.

MISLEADING CONGRESS AND WITHHOLDING PIVOTAL INFORMATION

"No government official should ever be muzzled from providing critical information to Congress."

—Senator Chuck Grassley (R-IA)
Senate Finance Committee Chairman

In 1997, Rep. Bill Thomas (R-CA) added language to the Balanced Budget Act conference report citing the importance of access by Congress to the estimates of HHS chief actuary (then, as now, Richard Foster). Some of that language in the conference report reads as follows:

It is important to emphasize that the Senate Committee on Finance, the House Committee on Ways and Means, and the House Committee on Commerce all rely on their ability to seek estimates and other technical assistance from the Chief Actuary, especially when developing new legislation.... The process of monitoring, updating and reforming the Medicare and Medicaid programs is greatly enhanced by the free flow of actuarial information from the Office of the Actuary to the committees of jurisdiction in the Congress.... When information is delayed or circumscribed by the operation of an internal Administration clearance process or the inadequacy of actuarial resources, the Committees' ability to make informed decisions based on the best available information is compromised.

Flying in the face of this statement, Foster, who has been the chief auditor in HHS for several years, said that he was threatened with dismissal if he released his official estimate of the cost of the prescription drug bill. His estimate added $156.5 billion to the estimated cost and likely would have led to several conservative Republicans voting against the bill.

In a public statement, Foster said:

For many years my office has provided technical assistance to the administration and Congress on a nonpartisan basis. But in June 2003, the Medicare administrator, Tom Scully, decided to restrict the practice of our responding directly to Congressional requests and ordered us to provide responses to him so he could decide what to do with them. There was a pattern of withholding information for what I perceived to be political purposes, which I thought was inappropriate.

Foster has said that he gave analyses in June 2003 to the White House and the Office of Management and Budget—which were not shared with Congress—predicting that prescription drug benefits being drafted on Capitol Hill would cost about $156 billion more than President Bush said he wanted to spend. Since Congress passed the Medicare bill, the Administration has revised its estimated 10-year cost of the program to $534 billion. Its original estimate was $395 billion.

Foster, the government's chief analyst of Medicare costs, says that he was warned repeatedly by his former boss, Thomas A. Scully, the Medicare administrator for three years, that he would be dismissed if he replied directly to legislative requests for information about prescription drug bills pending in Congress. In an email released by Foster, Scully's assistant, Jeffrey Flick, instructed the actuary to answer Republican queries regarding provisions in the Medicare bill but was warned—in bold font—not to provide information for Democratic requests "with anyone else until Tom Scully explicitly talks with you—authorizing release of information. The consequences for insubordination are extremely severe," Flick wrote in bold type. Interviews with federal officials, including Foster and Scully, make clear that the actuary's numbers were circulating within the Administration, and possibly among some Republican supporters of the bill on Capitol Hill, throughout the second half of last year, as Congress voted on the prescription drug bill, first in June and again in November.

At a hearing on Feb. 10, Secretary Thompson told lawmakers as much. Thompson said, "we knew all along" that the administration's cost estimates would be higher, but said he did not have a final figure until Dec. 24, 2003, after the bill was already signed into law.

On April 26, the Congressional Research Service issued a letter on the legality of Scully's decision to withhold information from Congress. Its conclusions read in part as follows:

> . . . actions which purposefully result in the transmission of knowingly false information to the United States Congress, and actions that involving the intentional and active prevention of the communication of accurate information to Congress in derogation of Federal law or responsibilities, might in certain circumstances involve activities which constitute violations of federal criminal provisions. . . . The issuance by an officer or employee in a department or agency of the Federal Government of a "gag order" on subordinate employees, to expressly prevent and prohibit those employees from communicating directly with Members or committees of Congress, would appear to violate a specific and express prohibition of federal law.

CONFERENCE COMMITTEE LOCKOUT

"This meeting is only open to the coalition of the willing."

—Rep. Bill Thomas (R-CA)
Chairman of the House Ways and Means Committee

When the House and Senate each passed their own version of the Medicare bill, the Republican leadership at first followed routine procedure by appointing a 17-member conference committee to work out the differences between the two pieces of legislation. Seven Democrats were appointed to the committee. However, only two of those Democrats, Senators Max Baucus (MT) and John Breaux (LA), were included in the closed-door meetings that had actually produced the final legislation. Why? Because they were among the few Democrats who would not raise significant objections to the bill. According to conference members from both parties, when the bill was made available to the rest of the committee, they were given just one hour to review the 678-page document before they voted.

The ranking Democrat on the Ways and Means Committee, Rep. Charles Rangel (NY), was among the members of the original conference committee. However, he was excluded from the closed-door meetings. He arrived uninvited to one meeting, and Rep. Thomas, the conference chairman, stopped substantive discussion of the legislation until Rep. Rangel left.

Democrats and others have complained the tactics like those employed during the conference on the Medicare bill are becoming more common. Similar lockouts were staged during crucial conference committee meetings on huge energy and transportation bills. More and more the role of the full conference committee is perfunctory while the details of the legislation are hammered out in closed meetings that include only a small coterie handpicked by the party leadership.

SCULLY CASHES IN

In December 2003, as the ink of the President's signature was drying on the Medicare bill, Thomas A. Scully, the government official responsible for Medicare, announced that he was leaving the government for lucrative healthcare jobs in the private sector. He joined Alston & Bird, a law firm that represents hospitals, drug manufacturers and other companies in the health care industry. Scully also accepted a job with Welsh, Carson, Anderson & Stowe, a New York investment firm specializing in telecommunications and health care.

Surprisingly, even though federal law generally bars presidential appointees such as Scully from discussing possible employment with firms involved in matters handled by those officials, Scully obtained a waiver from the HHS ethics officer so that he could negotiate with potential employers while he helped write the Medicare law. These jobs did not just drop into his lap in December. He had apparently been negotiating with healthcare-related firms at the same time he was helping the Administration push the controversial prescription drug legislation through Congress, which directly affected those industries.

Apparently in response to criticism of Scully's waiver, the White house ordered federal agencies to cease issuing ethics waivers for senior Administration appointees that would allow them to pursue jobs with private companies while influencing federal policies that could affect those companies. A memo issued on Jan. 6, 2004 by the White House Chief of Staff stated that, effective immediately, such waivers could only be approved by the White House.

TAUZIN NEGOTIATES PhRMA JOB WHILE NEGOTIATING PRESCRIPTION DRUG BILL

As Medicare chief Scully was job searching while also helping pass the drug legislation, a powerful Member of Congress was also looking for a new job.

The Pharmaceutical Research and Manufacturers Association (PhRMA), the trade group for name-brand drug producers, reportedly offered Representative Billy Tauzin (R-LA) the top position at PhRMA and a compensation package that "would be the biggest deal given to anyone at a trade association," around $2 million a year, according to *The Washington Post*. The offer came just two months after Rep. Tauzin helped negotiate a $534 billion Medicare prescription drug bill widely viewed as a boon to pharmaceutical companies, which stand to make

billions in profits while avoiding government price restrictions.

In February 2004, Common Cause called on Tauzin to resign his chairmanship of the powerful House Energy and Commerce Committee, saying "Even if your job negotiations with PhRMA began after your work on the Medicare bill was over, as you have reportedly said, it leaves one wondering whether you were trying to please PhRMA and what PhRMA may have promised you in return."

Tauzin denied there were any dealings with industry in exchange for his work on the bill, but he stepped down from the chairmanship of the House Energy and Commerce Committee in early February, while negotiations over the PhRMA lobbying post continued. The job remains open and Tauzin may still be eligible if it remains open at the end of his term.

DRUG INDUSTRY MONEY UNDERMINED THE PROCESS

As the Congressional fight on prescription drugs loomed, the drug industry drew up plans for raising millions of dollars to defeat efforts to reduce drug prices. The financial stakes were huge and the industry began to spend enormous amounts of money on campaign spending, lobbying, and advertising to influence the outcome of the legislation.

No group epitomized this more than PhRMA. PhRMA not only had a tremendous stake in the bill, but also turned out to be a major winner. The law prohibits the federal government from negotiating for lower drug prices and prohibits the reimportation of prescription drugs that are produced in the U.S. but sold for significantly less in other countries, which would also bring down the price of drugs.

PhRMA increased its yearly budget 23 percent to $150 million in anticipation of the upcoming Medicare fight. While PhRMA's interests range from international policy to local initiatives, industry protection in the Medicare reform bill was its top priority. According to published reports, PhRMA planned to spend $1 million for an "intellectual echo chamber of economists—a standing network of economists and thought leaders to speak against federal price control regulations through articles and testimony, and to serve as a rapid response team." Says one PhRMA document, "Unless we achieve enactment this year of market-based Medicare drug coverage for seniors, the industry's vulnerability will increase in the remainder of 2003 and in the 2004 election year."

PhRMA is well known as one of Washington's most powerful lobbying forces. The trade group alone spent $16 million on lobbying in 2003, according to federal lobby disclosure reports filed with the Senate Office of Public Records. Including lobbying spent by all of PhRMA's companies, the group spent at least $72.6 million lobbying in 2003—or roughly $135,701 per member of Congress.

PhRMA has capitalized on hiring former Members of Congress and their staffs as part of its lobbying army. According to reports, PhRMA lobbyists include former Reps. Vic Fazio (D-CA), Vin Weber (R-MN) and Bill Paxon (R-NY). Other drug industry lobbyists include David W. Beier, former domestic policy advisor for Vice President Al Gore; Dave Larson, former health policy advisor to Senator Bill First (R-TN); and Edwin A Buckham, former chief of staff to Rep. Tom DeLay.

The industry maintains a constant presence among policymakers. For example, in the weeks following the House and Senate's passage of their respective Medicare bills in June, pharmaceutical companies organized parties for congressional staffers that worked on the legislation. According to *The Washington Post*, the drug company Johnson & Johnson planned a cocktail party near the Capitol. The invitations read, "In recognition of your part in the historic passage of Medicare drug bills by both houses of Congress . . . " After Common Cause sent letters to Senate conferees and House leaders stating that attendance by staff members to the party could violate congressional ethics rules, the leadership discouraged their staff from going and the party was later cancelled. Congressional staff still had the opportunity, however, to attend a "Rooftop Rendezvous" thrown by PhRMA and hospital trade groups.

HHS PROPAGANDA CAMPAIGN

Once legislation passes Congress and is signed into law by the President, it is the job of the executive branch to implement the new law, including informing the public of the effect or the benefits of the new law. HHS, charged with implementing the new prescription drug law, immediately launched a multi-million dollar campaign promoting the new prescription drug benefit under the guise of public service advertising.

Early this year, HHS created a TV ad designed to educate the public on the new drug benefits, but many criticized the ads as being political advertisements for the Administration that mislead the public about the facts of the new program. Adding to the concern about politicization of the prescription drug program was a contract for $9.5 million for producing and distributing the ads that went to a partisan media company, National Media, Inc.

HHS has also produced videos that were sent to broadcasters around the country touting the new program. The videos feature hired "reporters" who appear to be delivering straight news stories, but do not identify the government as the producer. Two videos end with the voice of a woman who says, "In Washington, I'm Karen Ryan reporting." The "reporter" in the commercial is reading from a script written by HHS.

The General Accounting Office (GAO) is now investigating these 'fake video news' clips. The GAO will determine if they constitute illegal "covert propaganda." Federal law prohibits the use of federal money for "publicity or propaganda purposes" not authorized by Congress.

CONCLUSION

Posted on Congressional websites is a document called "How Our Laws Are Made." [http://thomas.loc.gov/home/lawsmade.toc.html]. No one really believes the process meticulously detailed in the document is followed exactly—legislating is a messy process. But the laws, rules and procedures cited in the document are there to ensure that democratic principles are not empty words in the Constitution, but inform the way our government operates on a daily basis.

This report has told a tale of the rush to pass a thinly supported prescription drug bill that was a prime political goal of the Administration. In that rush, supporters showed disregard for the law, congressional rules, and other procedures and customs. We must reform and strengthen some of those laws and rules and, perhaps more importantly, those public officials must be held accountable. Americans must be assured that democracy is not just another word, but an integral part of how our government operates.

DISCUSSION QUESTIONS

1. What are the various ways the Republican leadership of Congress and the executive branch undermined the legislative process in pursuit of a Medicare and prescription drug reform bill? How is democracy threatened by such tactics?

2. Why do you think there is such a gulf between the appearance and reality of how a bill becomes a law within the U.S. Congress? Would the quality of citizenship be improved if the truth were more widely known? Explain.

SENATOR JAMES JEFFORDS (I-VT) AND
REPRESENTATIVE BARBARA LEE (D-CA)

COURAGE IN CONGRESS: TWO DISSENTERS EXPLAIN THEIR ACTIONS

Although they often carry important policy implications, the votes of individual members of Congress seldom entail great political risk. There are times, though, when both the policy stakes and the symbolic implications are enormous, when constituents back home will remember what you've done and vote accordingly. The politically charged year of 2001 offered times of great personal and political crisis. On May 24, Vermont's junior senator, Jim Jeffords, rocked the political world by announcing what had been rumored for weeks: he would leave his lifelong home in the Republican Party and become an Independent. Prior to his announcement, the Senate was split evenly, with Democrats and Republicans each holding 50 seats. Since the Constitution gives the vice president the deciding vote in a tie-break situation, President George W. Bush's vice president, Dick Cheney, gave the GOP control of the Senate. After Jeffords's earthquake, the Democratic Party gained control of the Senate by a count of 50-49-1. Widely known in Vermont as an honest but unpolished speaker, Senator Jeffords returned to his home state to deliver his "Declaration of Independence," what was almost universally hailed as the greatest speech of his career, and one that instantly made him a celebrity—praised by many as a hero, but also condemned by many within his party as a traitor. The first selection below is the text of the Senator's declaration. Less than four months later, on September 11, the United States was plunged into a frenzy of fear following a terrorist attack on the twin towers of the World Trade Center in New York and the Pentagon in Washington, D.C. In the wake of these chilling assaults, Congress rushed to respond to a world seemingly gone mad. Congresswoman Barbara Lee represents the 9th Congressional District in California, which includes Alameda, Berkeley, and Oakland. On September 14, Lee stood before her colleagues in the House of Representatives and voted against a bill granting President Bush broad authority to use "all necessary and appropriate force" to respond to the terrorist attacks. With polls suggesting that roughly 90 percent of Americans favored the use of force, Lee cast the controversial lone vote against this grant of executive

Sources: James Jeffords, "Statement of Senator Jeffords: Declaration of Independence," May 24, 2001, available on line at http://jeffords.senate.gov/declaration_of_independence.html. Barbara Lee, "Why I Opposed the Resolution to Authorize Force," *San Francisco Chronicle*, September 23, 2001, available online at http://www.commondreams.org/views01/0923-04.htm.

power. The measure passed the House 420-1 (or, as some put it, "420-Lee"), and the Senate approved it 98-0. In the second piece below, Rep. Lee explains the reasoning behind her lonely stance in an op-ed in the San Francisco Chronicle. *Both brief selections remind us that despite Congress generally being held in low esteem, lawmaking does at times require acts of personal conscience and political courage.*

Senator James Jeffords, 24 May 2001

Anyone who knows me, knows I love the State of Vermont.

It has always been known for its independence and social conscience. It was the first state to outlaw slavery in its constitution. It proudly elected Matthew Lyon to Congress, despite his flouting of the Sedition Act. It sacrificed a higher share of its sons to the Civil War than perhaps any other state in the Union.

I recall Vermont Senator Ralph Flanders' dramatic statement almost 50 years ago, helping to bring to a close the McCarthy hearings, a sorry chapter in our history.

Today's chapter is of much smaller consequence, but I think it appropriate that I share my thoughts with my fellow Vermonters.

For the past several weeks, I have been struggling with a very difficult decision. It is difficult on a personal level, but it is even more difficult because of its larger impact on the Senate and the nation.

I've been talking with my family, and a few close advisors, about whether or not I should remain a Republican. I do not approach this question lightly. I have spent a lifetime in the Republican Party, and served for 12 years in what I believe is the longest continuously held Republican seat in the U.S. Senate. I ran for re-election as a Republican just last fall, and had no thoughts whatsoever then about changing parties.

The party I grew up in was the party of George Aiken, Ernest Gibson, Ralph Flanders, and Bob Stafford. These names may not mean much today outside Vermont. But each served Vermont as a Republican Senator in the 20th century.

I became a Republican not because I was born into the party but because of the kind of fundamental principles that these and many other Republicans stood for: moderation, tolerance, and fiscal responsibility. Their party, our party, was the party of Lincoln.

To be sure, we had our differences in the Vermont Republican Party. But even our more conservative leaders were in many ways progressive. Our former governor, Deane Davis, championed Act 250, which preserved our environmental heritage. And Vermont's Calvin Coolidge, our nation's 30th president, could point with pride to our state's willingness to sacrifice in the service of others.

Aiken and Gibson and Flanders and Stafford were all Republicans. But they were Vermonters first. They spoke their minds—often to the dismay of their party leaders—and did their best to guide the party in the direction of our fundamental principles.

For 26 years in Washington, first in the House of Representatives and now in the Senate, I have tried to do the same. But I can no longer do so.

Increasingly, I find myself in disagreement with my party. I understand that many people are more conservative than I am, and they form the Republican Party. Given the changing nature of the national party, it has become a struggle for our leaders to deal with me, and for me to deal with them.

Indeed, the party's electoral success has underscored the dilemma I face within my party.

In the past, without the presidency, the various wings of the Republican Party in Congress have had some freedom to argue and ultimately to shape the party's agenda. The election of President Bush changed that dramatically. We don't live in a parliamentary system, but it is only natural to expect that people such as myself, who have been honored with positions of leadership, will largely support the president's agenda.

And yet, more and more, I find I cannot. Those who don't know me may have thought I took pleasure in resisting the president's budget, or that I enjoyed the limelight. Nothing could be further from the truth. I had serious, substantive reservations about that budget, and the decisions it sets in place for today and the future.

Looking ahead, I can see more and more instances where I will disagree with the President on very fundamental issues: the issues of choice, the direction of the judiciary, tax and spending decisions, missile defense, energy and the environment, and a host of other issues, large and small.

The largest for me is education. I come from the state of Justin Smith Morrill, a U.S. Senator who gave America the land grant college system. His Republican Party stood for opportunity for all, for opening the doors of public school education to every American child. Now, for some, success seems to be measured by the number of students moved out of public schools.

In order to best represent my state of Vermont, my own conscience, and the principles I have stood for my whole life, I will leave the Republican Party and become an Independent. Control of the Senate will soon be changed by my decision. I will make this change and will caucus with the Democrats for organizational purposes, once the conference report on the tax bill is sent to the President.

My colleagues, many of them my friends for years, may find it difficult in their hearts to befriend me any longer. Many of my supporters will be disappointed, and some of my staffers will see their lives upended. I regret this very much. Having made my decision, the weight that has been lifted from my shoulders now hangs on my heart.

But I was not elected to this office to be something that I am not. This comes as no surprise to Vermonters, because independence is the Vermont way. My friends back home have supported and encouraged my independence even when they did not agree with my decisions. I appreciate the support they have shown when they have agreed with me, and their patience when they have not. I will ask for that support and patience again, which I understand will be difficult for a number of my friends.

I have informed President Bush, Vice President Cheney, and Senator Lott of my decision. They are good people with whom I disagree. They have been fair and decent to me. I have also informed Senator Daschle of my decision. Three of these four men disagreed with my decision, but I hope each understood my reasons. And it is entirely possible that the fourth may well have second thoughts down the road.

I have changed my party label, but I have not changed my beliefs. Indeed, my decision is about affirming the principles that have shaped my career. I hope the people of Vermont will understand it. I hope, in time that my colleagues will as well. I am confident that it is the right decision.

REPRESENTATIVE BARBARA LEE, 23 SEPTEMBER 2001

On September 11, terrorists attacked the United States in an unprecedented and brutal manner, killing thousands of innocent people, including the passengers and crews of four aircraft.

Like everyone throughout our country, I am repulsed and angered by these attacks and believe all appropriate steps must be taken to bring the perpetrators to justice.

We must prevent any future such attacks. That is the highest obligation of our federal, state and local governments. On this, we are united as a nation. Any nation, group or individual that fails to comprehend this or believes that we will tolerate such illegal and uncivilized attacks is grossly mistaken.

Last week, filled with grief and sorrow for those killed and injured and with anger at those who had done this, I confronted the solemn responsibility of voting to authorize the nation to go to war. Some believe this resolution was only symbolic, designed to show national resolve. But I could not ignore that it provided explicit authority, under the War Powers Resolution and the Constitution, to go to war.

It was a blank check to the president to attack anyone involved in the Sept. 11 events—anywhere, in any country, without regard to our nation's long-term foreign policy, economic and national security interests, and without time limit. In granting these overly broad powers, the Congress failed its responsibility to understand the dimensions of its declaration. I could not support such a grant of war-making authority to the president; I believe it would put more innocent lives at risk.

The president has the constitutional authority to protect the nation from further attack and he has mobilized the armed forces to do just that. The Congress should have waited for the facts to be presented and then acted with fuller knowledge of the consequences of our action.

I have heard from thousands of my constituents in the wake of this vote. Many—a majority—have counseled restraint and caution, demanding that we ascertain the facts and ensure that violence does not beget violence. They understand the boundless consequences of proceeding hastily to war, and I thank them for their support.

Others believe that I should have voted for the resolution—either for symbolic or geopolitical reasons, or because they truly believe a military option is unavoidable. However, I am not convinced that voting for the resolution preserves and protects U.S. interests. We must develop our intelligence and bring those who did this to justice. We must mobilize and maintain an international coalition against terrorism. Finally, we have a chance to demonstrate to the world that great powers can choose to fight on the fronts of their choosing, and that we can choose to avoid needless military action when other avenues to redress our rightful grievances and to protect our nation are available to us.

We must respond, but the character of that response will determine for us and for our children the world that they will inherit. I do not dispute the president's intent to rid the world of terrorism—but we have many means to reach that goal, and measures that spawn further acts of terror or that do not address the sources of hatred do not increase our security.

Secretary of State Colin Powell himself eloquently pointed out the many ways to get at the root of this problem—economic, diplomatic, legal and political, as well as military. A rush to launch precipitous military counterattacks runs too great a risk that more innocent men, women, children will be killed. I could not vote for a resolution that I believe could lead to such an outcome.

DISCUSSION QUESTIONS

1. In making their courageous stands, did Senator Jeffords and Representative Lee face identical political risks? Explain the similarities and any potential differences.
2. Identify the reasons behind the actions taken by the Senator and the Representative. How do these reasons stand up to the claims of some of their opponents, who blast them for being "traitors" to their party (Jeffords) and their country (Lee)?

WILLIAM F. GROVER

CONGRESS AND MOVEMENT-BUILDING: BERNIE SANDERS AND THE CONGRESSIONAL PROGRESSIVE CAUCUS

Elected in 1990 as the first authentic congressional independent in forty years, and reelected each year through 2004, Vermont congressman Bernie Sanders is the longest-serving Independent in the history of the U.S. Congress. In this article political scientist William Grover assesses the performance and prospects of Sanders, a democratic socialist, and his attempt to "change the conversation" in Congress. Grover explores Sanders's agenda that promised a progressive voice for the advocacy of issues important to ordinary Vermonters and all Americans, especially poor and working-class people. He examines the constraints Sanders faced in his early years as an outsider on the inside of this conventional institution and reflects upon the prospects for Sanders's future in the twenty-first century Congress. Special attention is paid to the Congressional Progressive Caucus, which Sanders helped found and chaired for many years. With fifty-five members, the Progressive Caucus plans an active leadership role in the fight against Republican and conservative Democratic initiatives. Whether Sanders and liberal Democratic members can continue to be effective advocates for ordinary Americans remains to be seen as they continue to confront the Republican administration of President George W. Bush and a Congress controlled by GOP majorities. But the key to this fight rests on two factors: their ability to forge coalitions within Congress and their willingness to build and sustain alliances with broader grassroots social movements beyond Washington.

As the year 2005 unfolds, it would appear that the outlook for progressive politics in the United States is bleak. After two terms of rightward policy drift and mounting scandal under Democrat Bill Clinton, the administration of President George W. Bush moved the national political agenda even further in a conservative direction, with war and tax breaks for the wealthy as his rallying cries. Taking office amid the still swirling winds of controversy following an intensely disputed presidential election of 2000, which ended with the decisive intervention of

Source: Revised and updated by the author from William F. Grover, *Creating New Political Priorities: Bernie Sanders and the Congressional Progressive Caucus.* Copyright © 1999 by William F. Grover.

the U.S. Supreme Court, Bush's Republican Party increased its majorities in both the House and the Senate in the elections of 2004. As if ongoing GOP control of the executive and legislative branches wasn't enough, back-to-back presidential defeats have left the Democratic Party with numerous unanswered questions. The 2000 defeat of Al Gore left a bitter taste in the mouths of many liberals and progressives, who blamed Gore's defeat not on his lifeless and uninspiring candidacy, but on the candidacy of progressive Green Party member and renowned consumer advocate Ralph Nader. But the even more decisive defeat of Senator John Kerry in 2004 has prompted deep soul-searching and considerable self-doubt within the Democratic Party. Considering these two electoral losses, progressives are thus left asking themselves an old and familiar question: What is to be done?

In the wake of these political upheavals on the national political scene, what options are open to U.S. progressives? And more specifically, what do these political currents portend for the U.S. Rep. Bernie Sanders (I-VT), an avowed democratic socialist and the longest-serving independent in the history of Congress? Beyond Sanders's personal political fortunes, which appear bright, how will the increasingly conservative climate affect the Congressional Progressive Caucus he co-founded and chaired for many years? Can progressive-minded politicians still swim in political waters now even more strongly controlled by the forces of reaction, punitive domestic social policy and global corporate power? While no one can be sanguine about the prospects for satisfactory answers to these questions from a progressive perspective, the political and economic difficulties we face bring opportunities as well as dangers. This article explores these possibilities with an eye toward analyzing the prospects for rethinking a progressive agenda in the face of what might appear to be a rather dismal political landscape. And as a highly visible voice for progressive change in the U.S., Congressman Bernie Sanders figures to play a prominent role in such rethinking, especially with his rising status among House Democratic Party leaders and his leadership of the Congressional Progressive Caucus.

"CHANGING THE CONVERSATION": SANDERS'S ROLE AS AN INDEPENDENT

In a sense, of course, there is nothing really "new" about the conservatism of Congress—the current 109th Congress (2005–2006) or any other. The structural primacy accorded business interests, especially the massive weight of corporate hegemony, is an enduring feature of our capitalist democracy, and Congress as an institution operates within an arena demarcated by these leading interests. In a nation that thinks of itself as the most vibrant democracy imaginable, but where in fact the political and economic options publicly discussable among "serious" thinkers span the spectrum from A to B—where what Noam Chomsky has referred to as the bounds of thinkable thought are so tightly drawn—it comes as no surprise that Congress reflects and reproduces this anemic version of what passes for political debate.

One of Sanders's goals when he was first elected to Congress was to expand the range of debate both within the House of Representatives and within the nation as a whole. He offered this succinct political self-conception following his initial congressional electoral victory in 1990:

> I have a vision, which I think is quite different than most members of Congress. I want to change the conversation, to raise issues that are not being talked about, to provide a voice inside the building [the Capitol] that is not always heard. I want to make people feel they're part of the process, part of a movement.

Now in his eighth term, Sanders has not abandoned his goal of changing the conversation, although he has a more realistic idea of how much any one member can accomplish. His political endurance on Capitol Hill can be attributed to many factors, one of which is his ability to adjust to the basic operational realities of how the House works. One reality is the importance of the relatively mundane conventional functions all members perform. Changing the political conversation entails working tirelessly within one's district to educate citizens, writing "Dear Colleague" letters on the Hill, lobbying fellow members, writing op-ed pieces in local and national papers, writing books, crafting legislation, amending bills in committee, doing other committee work, joining and forming caucuses, writing press releases, endlessly making speeches—the list is as long as it is dull. Repetition of what you stand for is common to all of this. And the sheer volume of overlapping congressional responsibilities in Washington and back at home, leaves members with precious little time to think clearly about the connection between the minutia of daily workloads and the bigger picture. The key difference between Sanders and other members, then, rests not on means, but on **ends**.

Before we explore Sanders's political ends, though, we need to look briefly at another contextual reality of life on Capitol Hill, the dilemma involved in the interplay of leadership and numbers. The Republicans now control the House by virtue of what Ross Baker characterizes as the power of "raw numbers." As the majority party, the GOP controls all of the House committees and sets the rules for debate on all bills that come to the floor. Despite the efforts of the mass media to build up suspense on impending floor votes with a breathtaking narrative format to the story of the day, the fact of the matter is that on most social and economic issues in particular, the Republicans will win. The legislative problems for the minority—the Democrats, and Sanders as the sole Independent—are compounded by deep fissures within the Democratic party on economic budgetary matters. The leverage exercised by fiscally conservative Democrats within the party is considerable. Dubbed "Boll Weevils" in the early years of the Reagan presidency, (now called "Blue Dogs"), the members (nominally led by Rep. Charles Stenholm, D-TX), coalesced in the 104th Congress into a caucus known as the Coalition, with whom the Clinton White House worked closely on issues that can be pursued from the vantage point of conservative "New Democrats." The prospects for liberal economic initiatives, let alone progressive ones, are dramatically reduced to near zero. Economic and budgetary discourse thus proceeds from the assumption that priorities such as cutting social programs, balancing the budget, "getting tough" on crime and increasing defense spending are givens.

Beyond these difficulties, Sanders confronts another normal constraint of the legislative process: the, at best, murky fit between issues you care deeply about and the votes you actually cast on those issues as framed (often mangled) into the form of legislation. Compromise happens every day. Votes seldom can be "pure" in any meaningful sense. Members almost always compromise because of the nature of the process, especially since the Rules Committee limits the number of amendments offered and the length of debate time on the floor. And of course debates are framed, and bills are drafted, by influential members and committees outside the reach of Congressman Sanders, or any other single member. Therefore, it is extremely difficult to be completely "right" on a vote, regardless of the ideology of the member. Tradeoffs are many, and choices are rarely as clear as a member would like. Indeed, from Sanders's radical vantage point outside the two party system, the choices often are dismal, although with Republican priorities shaping the current legislative agenda, being "right" on economic and social issues from a progressive perspective is easier—simply vote "no."

But positive action remains extremely difficult, unless coalitions with Democrats and at least some Republicans can be worked out in unusual circumstances. Such coalitions have been part of Sanders's leadership strategy since the Republican resurgence of 1994. His opposition to budget subsidies and tax breaks to corporations (known as "corporate welfare") as part of the Congressional Progressive Caucus's "Corporate Responsibility Act," drew the attention of some powerful fiscal conservatives like House Budget Committee Chair John Kasich (R-OH) and analysts at the Cato Institute. Kasich and others came to the realization that in order to balance the federal budget in accord with the Republican principles, hundreds of billions of dollars would have to be found—and not simply from cutting welfare programs for the poor, Social Security and Medicare—or that bottom line would be out of reach. "You're going to see some odd coalitions on that," Sanders commented on a potential alliance against corporate welfare. "It's going to scare the hell out of the big business Democrats and the Republicans." Obviously "sleeping with the enemy" would be only an occasional event, since Sanders and other progressive-minded Democrats bitterly opposed the balanced budget provision of the Contract to which Kasich and others were wed.

Taking into account, then, these tactical realities of the legislative process, Sanders's goal of broadening the nation's political debate and "changing the conversation" comes into sharper focus. Sanders steadfastly maintains his "outsider" approach to Congress, even while occupying a position on the inside of this conventional institution. The hallmarks of his outsider approach are an intense commitment to class-based politics, a fundamental critique of the two-party system and a socialist ideology that questions the roots of the U.S. political economy. He insists on the importance of wearing the socialist label because of the value he places on the principles involved, especially when issues of class come into play. Moreover, he is adamant about not being a member of either major political party. He never would shift to one of the major parties, as other "independents" have done in the past, even though he does vote with the Democrats the vast majority of the time. Nor does he shy away from criticizing the Democrats, sometimes harshly, as was clear in the floor debate over a version of the 1993 tax bill. While sharply decrying the persistent income and wealth inequalities

exacerbated by the economic programs of Republican Presidents Reagan and Bush, to the detriment of middle income and working class Americans, Sanders delivered these typically feisty remarks about class warfare:

> What our Republican friends are upset about is that for the last fifteen years their side has been winning this war, and that we should concede. It is not that I want to identify with the Democrats, who threw in the towel years ago. As the only Independent in this body, what I concede and congratulate my Republican friends about is "You won." Reaganomics and the trickle-down theory was a fraud, but you got enough of the Democrats to go along with you.

This is not the rhetoric of a traditional legislative insider. And Speaker Newt Gingrich's rise to power in 1994 with Republican control of the House and the policy dominance of the Contract With America only reinforced the need for Sanders to maintain his class message in defense of the needs of ordinary people, especially poor and working class Americans:

> To me what is lacking in American politics is a strong enough focus on the needs of working people. Class warfare is currently being practiced on working people by corporate America—which is represented by Gingrich and his friends here [in Congress].

Sanders worked tirelessly to lead congressional opposition to the ten-point Republican Contract, as always advocating for a comprehensive Canadian-style single-payer national health care system, full funding basic human needs for children, the elderly and the poor, dramatic cuts in the defense budget, redistribution of income and wealth, expansion of workers' rights and improvements in the quality of democracy and citizen participation.

Nor was Sanders delicate in his belief that Congress would not play a major role in fighting for social justice and equality until more progressive voices are elected, as evidenced in this statement about projections of massive incumbent losses in the 1992 election. While acknowledging the efforts of a few dozen House colleagues who work hard on behalf of progressive issues, he welcomed talk of large turnover as a result of voter anger over scandals in the legislature and disgust with the political process generally, saying, "We need to throw out many, many hundreds of members of Congress from both parties." Obviously the 1994 electoral swing resulting in GOP control of the House is not what he had in mind. Still, many analysts agreed with Garrison Nelson's observation that "there is no way Sanders will ever be considered a member of the club."

Sanders's experience with his role in the House for eleven years has challenged two pieces of conventional wisdom. The first is the assumption that without a major party affiliation, a member is effectively marginalized to the point of being a non-factor. Within our bicameral structure, the Senate—with its smaller size and internal arrangements that favor the efforts of individual Senators and render party leadership much more problematic—would be more hospitable to a maverick independent. The House, by contrast, is far more formal and tied to majority party control. Yet like any member, and probably more than most, Congressman Sanders benefits from the oft-noted individualization of Congress. The decline of parties over the past forty years, the rising importance of television as a medium of political communication and other factors have made all members—Representatives and Senators alike—more "independent" in the sense of being less bound to party dictates. Sanders even had his own talk show on C-Span, which served as a platform from which he advocated progressive causes and critiqued the Contract With America. While certainly not negating the influence of parties, this general increase in congressional free agent status opens up wider spaces for progressive voices to maneuver politically.

The second assumption—more a creature of Vermont state politics, but also prevalent on the Hill in Sanders's first few months—was that Bernie Sanders is a political loner who can't work well with others. A quote from Rep. Barney Frank (D-MA) about Sanders's early abrasiveness and difficulty adjusting to congressional life found its way into print in several news stories. But by the summer of 1991, Frank had modified his view: "He [Sanders] now fits in. He's very much an outsider, but not an outsider in the sense that he is isolated." The shift evident in the following quotes also captures a change in Sanders's thinking about his role, and reflects his skill as a politician who wants to make an impact within Congress. As Congressman-elect in 1990, Sanders had this to say about the body he was about to join:

> Many of these congressmen are being bought and sold by large corporations. I walk in there and I'm going to meet these guys. Ninety-eight percent get reelected. They have a great thing going in Congress. Will I get a standing ovation when I walk out on the floor? 'Bernie! You're the guy we've been waiting for. Thank you for telling the American people to throw us out en masse. Boy, have we been anxious to hear that.' I understand they're not going to say that. I know I'm going to have to fight every day.

At the outset of his second term in 1993, his earlier position had been tempered, at least in his public statements: "The way this institution works is that you have to have friends." The change in attitude can be attributed, at least in part, to his surprise at the fact that he was able to find a few dozen liberal Democratic Members who shared parts of his vision of changing the nation's budgetary priorities, and a handful who more generally thought quite a lot like him. The House Progressive Caucus (now known as the Congressional Progressive Caucus, or CPC), which Sanders convened in 1991 with Ron Dellums (D-CA), Maxine Waters (D-CA), Lane Evans (D-IL) and Peter DeFazio (D-OR), has in the 107th Congress (2001–2002) grown into a coalition of some fifty-five progressive members—many drawn from overlapping membership in the Congressional Black Caucus and increasingly from new Hispanic Members—that has forged unity on the need to push legislative proposals in a leftward direction and to articulate a progressive vision far beyond that.

One early example of the Progressive Caucus's efforts to influence President Clinton's programs occurred in 1993 during the budget reconciliation debate in August. With the President's budget plan in doubt, Sanders and eight other Caucus members met with the president to urge him to stick with the more progressive tendencies of his program in terms of funding social programs, taxing the wealthy, job creation and other areas in future legislation. Sanders also led the Progressive Coalition in its meeting with then-House Speaker Thomas Foley (D–WA), Vice President Al Gore and Budget Director Leon Panetta. The Progressives made it clear that they would not support the final version of the budget bill if the "children's initiative" was removed or if Medicare was cut more deeply. Given the 218–216 margin of victory on the final vote, Sanders and his group had a significant impact.

While these kinds of meetings (and subsequent Progressive Caucus meetings with White House officials in 1997 over the administration's balanced budget plans) can be seen as pure atmospherics, they do indicate that the kinds of progressive ideas Sanders and his colleagues champion did gain a hearing. It could be argued, of course, that with tight vote margins in the closely divided House, every individual member and group is important. But on these economic issues, the Progressive Caucus gained a new level of public notoriety. The expansion of social programs and rearguard actions to minimize the level of damage done to existing social programs obviously do not represent the ideal policy objective of Sanders. But given the circumstances of this particular case, the result reasonably can be construed as at least a short-term legislative "victory."

Whether the Progressive Caucus can become an established agenda-setter, or at least an agenda-shaper, with the ability to influence a long-term vision for public policy in the House, remains to be seen. One thing is certain, though: with Republicans controlling Congress and Democrats grappling with deep fissures within the party, Sanders clearly has gotten a higher leadership profile—both in the House and as a national spokesperson for progressive ideas—than most observers thought possible. His larger political impact will rest on the **symbolic** value of being a socialist advocate for expanding the range of debate from the narrow mainstream liberal-conservative spectrum on a host of policy issues. But of course he must be **substantively** important as well. He must be able to point to some tangible legislative accomplishments. Lofty long-range objectives alone are not enough. For as the adage goes, people don't eat in the long run. The role Rep. Sanders plays, then, can be seen as a dynamic and precarious combination of symbol and substance.

REASSESSING SANDERS'S PROSPECTS IN THE HOUSE

In an earlier article written midway through Sanders's second term, I explored three issues on which might turn Sanders's prospects for maintaining this balance as an outsider working from inside a conventional political institution. Three key factors seemed important then, and it is useful to revisit them now to see how Republican dominance in Congress has affected Sanders's prospects.

1. **Who's in the White House?** By any standard, Sanders was one of, if not the strongest, most articulate Bush-bashers during his first term in the 102nd Congress. He delivered countless scathing critiques of Reaganomics and the shared economic priorities of Republican rule during the Reagan-Bush years. The Democratic Party was more than happy to give him the debate time needed on the floor to pound a Republican president, and to share party information with his office on any legislative matter—especially since they also could count on his vote more

than 90 percent of the time. He initially was paired with two relatively ideologically sympathetic committee Chairs: Rep. Henry Gonzales (D-TX) on the Banking, Finance and Urban Affairs Committee, and Rep. John Conyers (D-MI) on the Government Operations Committee. The working relationship Sanders maintained with both of them personally, and with Committee staff, was very cordial. Although he was not allowed to join the Democratic Caucus (which he initially thought would be important for seniority status and information purposes), in his first term it was quite easy for him to find out how policy debates were taking shape behind those doors. He was not frozen out of the information loop.

As the 103rd Congress began, the House Democratic Steering and Policy Committee granted Sanders "standing" in his committees, effectively allowing him to accrue seniority like a Democrat, albeit without joining the Democratic Caucus. This unprecedented treatment for an Independent was a major victory for Sanders, and by seating him above their own freshmen, indicated the Democrats clearly were taking him more seriously. He was treated like the least senior second-term Democrat for the purpose of recognition and seating in committee. The trickier issue of allowing him to chair a subcommittee was deferred. At the start of the 104th Congress, Gingrich decided not to change Sanders's committee assignments, (although they were renamed Banking and Financial Services, and Government Reform and Oversight), and his standing with the Democratic Party was not altered.

I previously thought that future treatment of Sanders would depend on how he handles the current occupant of the White House. It is one thing to denounce George Bush and the legacy of President Reagan within an institution controlled by the other party. But when Bill Clinton came to office, I wondered how much criticism Democratic leaders would tolerate. Early indications were favorable for Sanders, as he used his voice respectfully to encourage the new President to play to the populist instincts that encompassed part of his winning presidential campaign strategy in 1992. Clinton's aforementioned dealings with the Progressive Caucus attest to that. Moreover, Sanders had a personal meeting with Clinton in June of 1993 to encourage him to travel around the country to get a feel for the realities of life from the perspective of working-class people and the poor. As Sanders wrote in *The Nation* before he visited the President:

> The politics of yesterday, the backroom deals with Congressional leaders, will not work. Clinton must get out of Washington and rally the American people against the greed and self-interest of a ruling elite that is causing massive suffering for tens of millions of working people.

However well-developed Clinton's populist instincts, Sanders conceded in his article that it is doubtful this cautious, moderate Democrat is likely to begin lashing out against corporate greed and the ruling elite like an emboldened Franklin Roosevelt in 1936, much less a Eugene Debs. And subsequent administration positions on a range of social and especially economic issues make it clear that Clinton's instincts are not that far removed from those of Republicans; Jesse Jackson has dubbed Clinton's embrace of a balanced budget plan and other issues on his domestic agenda "Republican Lite."

At least in the short-term, then, Sanders— far from alienating all Democrats—actually served as a rallying voice for the more progressive-minded of them. As one analyst put it, "Sanders's brand of class-struggle politics now alienates fewer liberals, and his socialist label is no longer automatically anathema to many mainstream Dems." Certainly this could be a transitory attraction, resting only on the belief of some Democrats that the party could be saved by coalescing around progressive issues. On this view, Sanders's larger agenda is of no use to the party, with Barney Frank (D-MA), a relatively inactive Progressive Caucus member, serving as an example of this position. A Progressive Caucus staffer put it this way: "Many of our members are more progressive first and Democrats second, and Barney's clearly a Democrat first."

One point does seem certain, though, and that is that Sanders's standing in the eyes of Democrats did not depend on how much he criticized their own President. Many of them rushed to disown Clinton. In fact, on an issue like the 1994 health care reform battle, Sanders's unflinching advocacy of a single-payer approach with lots of grass roots support looks very good compared with Clinton's confusing and bureaucratic "managed competition" model, which did nothing to challenge the entrenched power of the insurance industry, pharmaceutical companies and hospitals. It thus appears that the relationship between Sanders's efficacy within Congress as an Independent and the party affiliation of the President is not terribly relevant. With George W. Bush now in the White House, he may even have an expanded role as a progressive voice.

2. **What Is "Effectiveness?"** A second issue I raised was the question of how best to measure the "effectiveness" of a Representative—progressive or otherwise? Surely the need for a certain amount of political pragmatism, even radical pragmatism, cannot be discounted. If, for example, as a socialist mayor of Burlington, you can't get the streets plowed after a February snowstorm, then your socialist vision is pretty irrelevant to people's lives. Any politician has to "deliver" and Sanders is no different. What standard of evaluation should we use when assessing Congressman Sanders?

Analysts often heavily favor legislative work as the yardstick against which to measure the effectiveness of a member of Congress. The crafty inside deal-maker who can work the levers of power—within and outside the committee structure—is seen as the paragon of a legislative "workhorse." On this model, specialization in committee work and passing bills are what counts. This legislative style offers tangible, quantifiable proof of one's efficacy. But members could choose to play other roles that are just as legitimate, or play several roles with different priorities.

Focusing on constituent service, for example, could rightly occupy the bulk of a legislator's time, and this certainly is a key function of a Representative, including Sanders. In Sanders's case, the style and substance of the "outsider" maverick who forcefully articulates a progressive ideological position is a basic part of his conception of his job. Posing alternatives to status quo policy positions of the major parties is another way of defining one's role within the institution and is no less legitimate than any other possible role. It is perhaps a noisier role than the quiet, hardworking member who toils on legislation behind the scenes, but that image has ceased to represent the reality of congressional life for many politicians. Indeed, much of Newt Gingrich's appeal to fellow Republicans came from his ability to mobilize his party to have a combative, vociferous, ideologically conservative national vision, even though he had virtually no impact on legislation during his many years in the minority party. And from a more critical point of view, one could look at the mass of legislation passed each session and ask if much of it—whether carefully crafted by adroit insiders or not—really will improve peoples' lives or begin to get to the root of our nation's ills. Fundamentally, the most important question should involve ends. What does a Representative or Senator really stand for?

For better or worse, though, the legislative "workhorse" conception still dominates the way legislators, the press, scholars and the public assess congressional activity. The impact this has on one's evaluation of Sanders will depend on the extent to which the traditional "pork" measurement is applied to his efforts. If "effectiveness" for him is determined by the number of projects he secures in his district (as an At Large Member, the whole state of Vermont is his district), then he may not fare as well as a Republican might in his position. The narrow "pork" measurement would seem always to favor a member of the majority party, especially if he or she sits on the Appropriations Committee. Here **particularized** benefits to one's district are what matters.

If, by contrast, the broader measurement of **collective** or **generalized** benefits is applied, then Sanders may be evaluated much more favorably. Although much more difficult to achieve, working on behalf of programs that confer benefits generally to large numbers of people—or to everyone—is much more in keeping with Sanders's ethic of socialism. Though obviously politically embattled, the model of Social Security serves as an example of a collective benefit (compared to, say, a dam or post office for one's district). Sanders does place great emphasis on such collective programs, as his advocacy of single-payer national health care demonstrates. He also fought for his "Workplace Democracy Act," introduced in June of 1997, to comprehensively reform and strengthen labor laws protecting workers' rights. This is an updated legislative vehicle for his advocacy of a "Workers' Bill of Rights" to improve living standards for American workers, which have fallen precipitously over the past thirty years. Fashioning a comprehensive plan for conversion from a military to a civilian economy would constitute another example. The point is that programs to deliver collective benefits aim at the high goal of universality—which is, of course, one of the drawbacks to such a strategy. They are

harder to enact. But if successful, they can offer a progressive alternative to problems that continue to defy the more piecemeal efforts of the two major parties. As in the case of single-payer national health care, a more generalized approach also can redefine the "problem" and the "solution" in ways that can challenge the normal market assumptions about business power to which both parties are wed. In turn, this opens up the possibility of what Andre Gorz called "non-reformist" reforms—achievable reforms that open the door for deeper structural reform of the system itself. One might call this "progressive effectiveness," relying less on insider legislative craftwork (although this aspect would not be wholly absent) and more on mobilizing popular pressure on Congress.

3. **Walking the Line: Outsider, Insider Or What?**
Ultimately, Congressman Sanders walks a tightrope now as he did upon my earlier assessment. By the nature of his job, he must; any progressive politician does. He exists in the real world of actual politics, and in that world there is a very delicate balance between being an "outsider" and being an "insider." As long as he remains the lone progressive Independent in the House, if he is too strident, too much of an uncompromising socialist, too "right," if you will, he will reduce and perhaps eliminate his chances of getting anything done. On the other hand, if he moves too far in the direction of making coalitions with Democrats and, occasionally Republicans, he risks being seen as a "sellout," just like any other politician. He would lose his distinctive identity. An isolated voice crying in the wilderness, or just another bastard who sold out—either way it's not an appealing choice.

Sanders must strive to retain the "give 'em Hell, Bernie!" spirit that pervades the electoral climate in Vermont, remaining honestly different in the eyes of voters by what they see him doing with his political skills. The environmental trends within Congress may actually be working in his favor on this point. The traditional congressional "folkways" (what legendary House Speaker Sam Rayburn once termed "getting along by going along") no longer dominate. The norm of extended apprenticeship in specialized committee work has yielded to the more prevalent norm of policy entrepreneurship. Deference to party leaders, while not absent, is not the firm rule. This dimension of the evolution of the House would suggest that nothing institutionally should restrain him from continuing to walk an independent line.

Sanders blurred this line considerably in 1999, though, by making an insider deal with House Minority Leader Richard Gephardt (D-MO). Sanders was seriously considering challenging moderate Vermont Republican Jim Jeffords for his Senate seat. In recognition of Sanders's loyalty to the Democratic Party on most votes in the House, and fearing that a Republican might win Sanders's House seat if he took on Jeffords, Gephardt urged Sanders to stay in the House. With the House so closely divided between Republicans and Democrats, Gephardt needed to preserve every vote he could get. He promised Sanders that if the Democrats regained control of the House in the 2000 elections, Sanders would be rewarded with a seat on the coveted Appropriations Committee. Sanders opted to run for reelection, savoring a possible seat on Appropriations over the tough challenge of unseating an incumbent Senator. Unfortunately for him, the Democrats fell short of retaking the House. Moreover, at the presidential level Sanders did not support his long-time friend and political ally, Green Party candidate Ralph Nader, opting instead to endorse Democrat Al Gore's ultimately unsuccessful campaign as the "lesser of two evils." Taking into account these two political decisions, some progressives criticized Sanders as an opportunist, charging him

with seeking to join the conversation rather than change it. His willingness to cut deals with Democratic Party leaders—even if pursued for the goal of having a direct progressive impact on the nation's priorities—raises important questions about his status as a true independent. The answer to these questions may rest less on what committee assignment he obtains, or what deals he cuts, and more on his role in long-term progressive movement-building.

THE CONGRESSIONAL PROGRESSIVE CAUCUS AND "THE CONVERSATION"

As a democratic socialist Sanders's instincts always have been toward movement-building—forging links of solidarity with other progressives. It has been part of the air he has breathed for the past thirty years of toiling in the cold political wilderness of Vermont. As a former four-term mayor of Burlington, the State's largest city, Sanders amassed an enormous debt to Burlington's Progressive Coalition, which he helped found, and the thousands of other volunteers who make his political life possible. It should come as no surprise, then, that he would make the establishment of a Congressional Progressive Caucus (CPC) one of his first tasks upon being elected to Congress in 1990.

Initially called the House Progressive Caucus, the CPC fits most clearly into what Susan Webb Hammond has characterized within her typology as constituency-oriented caucuses with a national orientation. And it successfully survived the Republican attack on caucuses after the 1994 elections, when Legislative Service Organizations were abolished and Congressional Member Organizations were created in their place. During its formative early years, the CPC served two primary functions: to highlight President Bush's continuation of Reaganomics from the point of view of the victims of its class-based, trickle-down approach, and to try to accentuate whatever progressive possibilities could be found in President Clinton's agenda. Especially in the case of economic analysis, the CPC relied extensively on the Congressional Black Caucus Budget to deliver a comprehensive critique of the nation's warped budgetary priorities. The Democratically-controlled House always gave the CPC a respectful hearing, but then urged passage of leadership bills that fell far short of progressive hopes.

With the dawning of the GOP congressional reign, however, the CPC took on a much broader role, and articulated its vision with renewed vigor and urgency. Within the 104th Congress, for example, the Progressive Caucus led the fight against the GOP Contract With America, a leadership role made all the more visible by the slow reaction of House Minority Leader Gephardt. At the outset of the 104th Congress—and about a year before the Democratic leadership belatedly announced its "Families First" initiative—the CPC went on the offensive against the policy agenda of the Republican leadership. Rep. Cynthia McKinney (D-GA) sums up her view of the leadership role Sanders played in this struggle:

We [progressive Democrats] all owe Bernie because he gives us leadership. And he's always an unwavering anchor. That's the good part about being an Independent. He's not tied down to any particular party. He's not tied down to any political philosophy. He's only tied to what is right for the people. . . . Bernie is good for the caucus. Bernie is good for the Congress.

The irony here is worth noting. The socialist Sanders has played a key role in helping to breath life into McKinney's party since, in her view, "the Progressive Caucus actually leads the Democratic Caucus now since we have been placed in the minority." And electorally CPC members have done well in the face of conservative success nationally. Not one Caucus member was defeated in 1996 or 1998.

At the heart of the Caucus's strategy was an eleven-point response to the Republican "Contract." Called "The Progressive Promise: Fairness," the plan included legislation responding to what Sanders and others saw as the GOP's assault on ordinary Americans. As the plan's introduction declared:

Our plan shall be rooted in the principles of social and economic justice, non-discrimination and tolerance. It shall embody national priorities which reflect the interests and needs of all the American people, not just the wealthy and powerful.

Among other things, the plan called for the aforementioned end to corporate welfare (subsidies and tax breaks for the nation's wealthiest corporations), reform of labor laws, an increase in the minimum wage, dramatic cuts in the Pentagon and CIA budgets, single-payer health care, preservation of Social Security, Medicare and Medicaid and a $127 billion investment in the nation's physical infrastructure and environmental cleanup. The provision to end corporate welfare alone entailed some twenty-four separate bills.

The Progressive Caucus reintroduced its policy agenda in 1998 under the banner of the "Fairness Agenda," with an eye toward a revival of President Franklin Roosevelt's 1944 "Economic Bill of Rights." This was part of the Caucus's more aggressive attempt to develop a progressive vision that draws support from the larger progressive community around the country. The overall effort at progressive unity was begun in 1997 as part of what the Progressive Caucus called the Progressive Challenge, a cooperative arrangement between the Caucus and environmental, labor, women's and public interest organizations. The "Fairness Agenda" is the legislative expression of this new unity. Among its provisions are:

- More equitable budgetary priorities
- A broad expansion of workers' rights
- Promotion of a just and sustainable economy
- Real campaign finance reform based on public financing

- Social investment as a legislative priority
- Sustainable communities and environmental justice
- Civil rights and wage equity for all Americans, regardless of race, gender or sexual orientation
- A foreign policy that includes demilitarization, human rights and a "new internationalism"

With Republican control of the House, progressives had little hope of passing any of the bills attached to specific provisions of the Fairness Agenda, although they have won some interesting victories in coalition with Republicans, such as the aforementioned effort to draw attention to "corporate welfare." And in the fall of 1997 progressives won outright victories on bills banning the importation of goods made by child slave labor and shielding U.S. federal, state and local laws from adverse actions undertaken by the World Trade Organization as a prelude to the debate over "fast track" free trade policy. These unusual tripartisan left-right coalitions typically result from Representatives voting the same way for markedly different ideological and political reasons. Progressive Caucus members will continue to forge these coalitions whenever possible on an issue-by-issue basis. But realistically they should get swamped much more often than not by the combined weight of a unified Republican Party and conservative Democrats. However, the Progressive Promise and accompanying legislation will serve as a valuable educational tool for members who want to articulate an alternative course of action for their constituents and the nation as a whole.

Another iteration of the Progressive Challenge, Action Agenda 2001, was launched in the same spirit of the original Challenge. The campaign highlights similar themes: electoral reform and campaign finance (with heightened salience given the way the outcome of the 2000 election played out), universal health care, reform of drug policy and sentencing, an end to corporate-led globalization, closing the gap between the rich and poor, and a dramatic reduction in military spending. Public support has grown too, with the number of grassroots progressive organizations nationwide who have endorsed the agenda reaching more than 175.

The goal of these coalition efforts must be two-fold. First, in the short term, progressives simply must counter the continuation of policies inspired by Republican electoral successes from 1994 onward. This necessarily will involve defensive actions to protect what is left of the social safety net after twenty years of attacks on it. This is especially imperative for issues relating to children and the elderly, our most vulnerable citizens. While this represents a backward vision of sorts, Progressive Caucus members view it as important for the preservation of at least a minimum level of decency for millions of Americans. Over the longer term, a forward-looking progressive vision must emerge on a wide range of issues and from the need for collective or generalized benefits mentioned earlier. And this vision must articulate a future that speaks to the varied needs of the working class, women, the elderly, African Americans, Latinos/as and others left out of, or disaffected from, the trajectory of conservative and "New Democrat" politics in the 1990s.

The CPC "Progressive Promise," "Fairness Agenda," and "Agenda 2001" are just vehicles. Absent an effort to mobilize citizens to overcome their understandable cynicism about politics as usual, the CPC manifestos will be forgotten as just so many words. In an ironic sense, what progressives in the House need to do parallels what a young Newt Gingrich did after the 1980 election when—frustrated by the combined prospect of a Republican in the White House but an overwhelming Democratic majority in the House of Representatives—he organized a coalition of conservative, free-market Republicans around his vision of a GOP majority in the House. Called the Conservative Opportunity Society, these minority members fashioned the intellectual basis for what became the Republican Contract With America. Sanders and the CPC should want to nationalize congressional elections and policymaking, again much like Gingrich successfully did in 1994, but to different ends and with the real citizen empowerment that comes from political movements. And of course the task is that much harder for progressives because they have no national party to which they can turn. The Democrats who want the CPC to shore up the party's old New Deal coalition will not stand for a truly progressive party. And genuinely progressive Democrats who are uncomfortable or outraged with "New Democratic" politics will have serious decisions to make. In the end, progressive party-building must be embraced.

For this to occur, however, progressives need to keep the **idea** of parties alive. While it was tempting to be heartened polls repeatedly showing that majorities of Americans would like to see a third major political party, voters might be just as likely to give up on parties altogether and flirt with independents for congressional and presidential races. Sanders and other progressives must keep up the push for a national third party (the Green Party, the Labor Party, or otherwise) if a mass movement for alternative politics is to have a real chance to flourish. Without a vibrant sense of solidarity with others within an enduring institution, a progressive vision is not possible beyond an occasional isolated victory.

Social movements historically have depended upon a shifting and sometimes contested mix of outsiders and insiders to pursue their objectives. While we cannot be sanguine about the role Congress must play in facilitating transformative agendas, we should heed Berg's reminder that congressional insiders like Sanders "can succeed only if protest activity in Congress remains linked to a broad social coalition that develops and voices a vision of what it stands for." Progressive hopes thus lie well beyond the CPC and Sanders, although they can help create the language, and perhaps forge the political space, which will allow alternatives to grow. As Sanders has commented, "We're moving toward an oligarchic form of government in the U.S. today. We currently have the largest gap between the rich

and the poor—but that's outside the table of discussible issues." This view is shared by many Caucus members, such as Rep. Maurice Hinchey (D-NY), who also wants the Progressive Caucus to fight what he sees as the growth of "economic oligarchy." Putting such issues on the table is what movement-building is all about. Again, Sanders states: "Someone has to start talking about the fact that 1 percent of Americans own 40 percent of the wealth. If there is a future for the left it has to be to focus on basic class issues and corporate America." The Congressional Progressive Caucus can play a role in helping to sharpen that focus. But if it is truly to "change the conversation," it must do so as part of a broader effort. As Sanders has remarked:

> We [members of the Congressional Progressive Caucus] have to distinguish between what we can accomplish within Congress, which is not very much, and outside Congress, which may be a little more.

Maybe a little more. Maybe a lot more. But in the absence of grassroots organizing to augment work from within existing institutions, definitely nothing of lasting value can be accomplished. This point was driven home with passion and pain by Rep. Ron Dellums (D-CA) in 1997 when announcing his impending retirement from the House the following year. A Black Caucus and Progressive Caucus veteran, and twenty-eight-year champion of progressive causes in the House, Dellums made the following observation about the relationship between politicians and movements:

> I did not come here to become a politician. I came here to become a representative of a movement. The movement elects me, and goes home, and I have to keep going forward without a movement. I have maintained the integrity of these ideas, but where is the movement? The Republicans have had a contract for and on America. Where is the movement? Here is the nation

that gave the Congress of the United States to the Republicans for two elections in a row. Here is a Congress that has escalated the military budget, and we have been fighting for years to decrease the military budget. Where is the movement?

To be effective agenda-shapers in the future, progressives must heed the lessons of Dellums's long tenure in office and work together to unify the energies of citizen movements and their elected officials, "outsiders" and "insiders," if you will. Each avenue of organizational vitality is important; neither can afford to be overlooked. This is the only alternative strategy that makes sense if the pitfalls of Dellums's lament are to be

avoided in the political struggles of the twenty-first century.

DISCUSSION QUESTIONS

1. What features of Congress as an institution shape and constrain Sanders's independent role?

2. To what extent has Sanders been able to find common ground with other members of Congress in the Progressive Caucus? Are there any risks to working so closely with the Democratic Party leadership?

3. Why is it so important for members of the Progressive Caucus to have close ties with citizen groups around the country?

CHAPTER 7

The Presidency

The presidency has come to occupy the center stage of American government. Anyone who hopes to understand the American political system, especially as it has developed since the 1930s, must come to terms with the nature of the presidency. After World War II, the expansion of presidential power that began under President Franklin D. Roosevelt continued, and this growth was generally celebrated by scholars and other observers of the office, who saw in the president a personification of the American system of government. But in the 1960s and 1970s, abuses symbolized by Vietnam and Watergate and the downfalls of Lyndon Johnson and Richard Nixon, led to a more critical view of the "imperial presidency." Despite an upward trend in public trust in the presidency in the 1980s, the Iran-contra affair of 1986–1987, the impeachment and trial of President Bill Clinton in the late 1990s, and the hotly contested presidential election of 2000 call into question the ability of the presidency to resolve policy conflicts in an equitable and responsible way. This presidential challenge persists even after the post 9-11 "rally-'round-the-flag" response, which boosted George W. Bush's approval ratings to record levels.

As president during the Great Depression and World War II, Franklin D. Roosevelt established the model of strong executive leadership that was venerated in postwar America. Indeed, even Ronald Reagan expressed his admiration for Roosevelt's leadership style at the very time he was attempting to reverse the liberal turn in public policy inaugurated by the New Deal. Still, given the recurrent crises that have beset the presidency in the past 30 years, many recent explanations of the presidency emphasize that the chief executive is, or should be, limited in powers by the constitutional structure and is not the free agent in policy decisions that the FDR model of presidential power suggested. In our view it is no doubt important to put the president in the context of other government actors, but it is even more important to understand the interaction between the president and forces outside of government, such as the economy and the business community, social and political movements, and the role of the United States in the international political economy. The readings in this chapter should help you to put the presidency into context as the tenure of George W. Bush continues into his second term.

25 MICHAEL A. GENOVESE

THE LIMITS OF PRESIDENTIAL POWER

Political observers have commented frequently on the modern gulf between high public expectations of the American presidency and disappointing presidential performance. Michael Genovese, a scholar of the presidency, provides a deeper explanation of this gap by identifying two structural constraints that shape and limit presidential action. The first constraint is the economic framework of corporate capitalism. Drawing on the work of Charles Lindblom, whose analysis of the privileged position of business is featured in Chapter 1, Genovese notes that presidents who pursue reform agendas run the risk of losing business confidence. The need for business confidence has become an unexamined assumption of the modern presidency, an assumption with conservative implications for public policy and political change. Genovese also shows how the nature of the contemporary international economic system shapes presidential policy. Presidents operate in the context of global capitalism or "globalization," which involves powerful pressures towards market economies, open markets, free trade, and economic interdependence. Genovese contends that despite the superpower status of the United States and the benefits that derive from this status, economic globalism "takes power out of the hands of nations and places it in the hands of markets and corporations." Presidents are less free to pursue policies that do not succumb to the demands of the market.

Presidential politics operates within an economic framework of corporate capitalism. How does this reality shape and influence presidential behavior?

Two major functions of the modern capitalist state are (1) the stimulation of material accumulation and (2) the legitimization of the social order. The first function derives from the fact that the state is ultimately held responsible for meeting the material needs of the society; thus, at least in some minimal terms, economic deterio-

ration is blamed on presidents. But in this regard the capitalist state is "weak," in that it does not own the means of production; they are privately held and will not be put in operation unless a return (profit) on investment is foreseen. Thus, the capitalist state must use the carrot more than the stick, by helping the owning class in the accumulation of profit in order to promote production. Conversely, the owning class is in a strong position with presidents, who face the likelihood

Source: Michael Genovese, *The Presidential Dilemma: Leadership in the American System,* 2nd edition. New York: Longman, 2003, pp. 73–79.

of an "investment strike" if policy is seen to hurt profits. This gives business a privileged position and places the president in a position of some dependency on what is referred to as "business confidence." In order to govern effectively, presidents must please the business community, lest they face a decline in business confidence and a deterioration of the overall economy, thus leading to a decline in presidential popularity and power.

It is just this situation that Charles Lindblom—though not referring specifically to the presidency—discusses in his article "The Market as Prison." Lindblom argues that political regimes with market systems have built-in defense systems that automatically trigger punishment whenever there is an attempt to tamper with or alter the basic structures of such systems. This built-in punishing mechanism makes market systems resilient and highly resistant to change because attempts at change bring quick and sure punishment. As Lindblom writes, "Many kinds of market reform automatically trigger punishments in the form of unemployment or a sluggish economy." This punishment is not the result of any conspiracy on the part of business; it is simply a built-in by-product of market oriented systems. Lindblom writes:

Business people do not have to debate whether or not to impose the penalty. They need do no more . . . than tend to their own business, which means that, without thought of effecting a punishment on us, they restrict investment and jobs simply in the course of being prudent managers of their enterprises.

While Lindblom does not focus on the presidency in this context, he does discuss the notion that the economic system is highly resistant to change by political leaders. He describes the situation thus:

What about government officials? It is critical to the efficiency of automatic punishment that it be visited on them. For it is they who immediately or proximately decide to persist in policy changes or to

withdraw from such initiatives. The penalty visited on them by business disincentives caused by proposed policies is that declining business activity is a threat to the party and the officials in power. When a decline in prosperity and employment is brought about by decisions of corporate and other business executives, it is not they but government officials who consequently are retired from their offices.

That result, then, is why the market might be characterized as a prison. For a broad category of political/economic affairs, it imprisons policy making, and imprisons our attempts to improve our institutions. It greatly cripples our attempts to improve the social world because it afflicts us with sluggish economic performance and unemployment simply because we begin to debate or undertake reform.

Thus, with policy making being "imprisoned" in market-oriented systems, the leverage of presidents for reform is severely restricted by this self-regulating, self-punishing mechanism built into the system.

The other function, legitimization of the social order, derives from the need for the state to be seen as ruling in the interest of all, not in the interest of a dominant class. Welfare programs for the nonowning classes and entitlement programs for the middle class are examples of policies to satisfy this task. But when profits are squeezed, the revenues to support such programs become tight, and a crisis for the state can occur because it cannot reach an adequate balance between these contradictory goals.

Edward S. Greenberg develops the notion of the privileged position of business in policy making in these words:

Presidents must act in such a way that they maintain the confidence of business leaders and ensure an economic environment conducive to profitable investment. The president's popularity and thus much of his ability to effect a domestic program and foreign policy objectives is dependent on the state of the economy and the sense of well-being felt by the American people.

Since business people cannot be forced to make productive, job-creating investments in the American economy, government must induce them to do so. They are induced, in the main, by public policies that encourage and ensure profitability, especially among the most powerful economic actors and enterprises in the system. Thus, while no president can afford to respond to every whim of important business leaders, all his actions are bounded by the need to maintain "business confidence."

There is no active conspiracy on the part of business to "capture" the presidency. Rather, presidential success is intimately connected with business success. As presidential popularity rises and falls, in part due to economic conditions, presidents quickly learn that what is good for business is usually good for presidential popularity. When corporate capitalism gains, the president usually gains. Conversely, a sluggish economy is blamed on an administration's activities or lack thereof. Thus, the fate of the president is closely connected to fluctuations in the economy. Presidents help themselves by helping business.

In this way, presidents who do not have the confidence of business find themselves at a distinct political and economic disadvantage. As John Kennedy noted:

I understand better every day why Roosevelt, who started out such a mild fellow, ended up so ferociously antibusiness. It is hard as hell to be friendly with people who keep trying to cut your legs off . . . There are about ten thousand people in this country involved in this—bankers, industrialists, lawyers, publishers, politicians—a small group, but doing everything they can to say we are going into a depression because business has no confidence in the administration. They are starting to call me

the Democratic Hoover. Well, we're not going to take that.

But Kennedy recognized the other side of the business confidence coin as well, as he attempted to act as economic cheerleader:

This country cannot prosper unless business prospers. This country cannot meet its obligations and tax obligations and all the rest unless business is doing well. Business will not do well and we will not have full employment unless there is a chance to make a profit. So there is no long-run hostility between business and government. There cannot be. We cannot succeed unless they succeed.

Similarly, presidents who wish to pursue a reform agenda find themselves in a bind: "Do I sacrifice economic reforms for economic performance and personal popularity, or, do I play it safe and hope for incremental changes?" Which president would want to stir the embers of the market's self-punishing mechanism? Shortly after his election, Bill Clinton met with his top economic advisors to devise an economic stimulus package. After a lengthy discussion, a consensus was reluctantly arrived at that determined the first priority of the president: to rescue the bond market. Angry and frustrated that his reform agenda was being hijacked by the bond market, an exasperated Clinton threw his arms up in the air and said, "We've all become Eisenhower Republicans!" Which president could afford to stir the beast that will likely produce a sluggish economy and lower presidential popularity? Thus, presidential leverage in economic reform is severely limited by the invisible prison of the market.

Thomas Cronin, probably the most highly regarded of today's presidential scholars, begins to suggest a structural impediment in presidential choice vis-à-vis the business community when, in a lengthy reexamination of Richard Neustadt's *Presidential Power*, he chides Neustadt for failing "to take into account the degree to which presidents are almost invariably stabilizers or protectors of the status quo rather than agents of redistribution or progressive change." Cronin adds that "all our presidents have had to prove their political orthodoxy and their acceptability to a wide array of established powers, especially to corporate leaders."

Political scientist Bruce Miroff notes that presidential scholars remain firmly committed to a "progressive" interpretation of the presidency. But as Miroff writes, "The Presidency, even (perhaps especially) in liberal hands, is best understood as the chief stabilizer—and not the leading force for change—in American politics." No president has "sought to question, much less assault, corporate power and its extraordinary skewing of resources and rewards. The present structure of the American economy has been accepted by modern Presidents as a given of American life."

In line with Charles Lindblom's concerns, Miroff writes:

> Because of their acceptance of the prevailing social and economic order, even the more liberal of recent Presidents have had little novel or profound that they really wanted to achieve in domestic affairs. Their most controversial domestic proposals have envisioned only modest reforms. Basically, these Presidents have sought to patch up remaining holes in the New Deal, and to stabilize and rationalize the corporate economy. None have acknowledged more fundamental problems in American society; none have proposed anything that resembles a program of social and economic reconstruction. Contrary to the conventional view, it has not been an obstructionist Congress or an apathetic public that has kept Presidents since FDR from major domestic accomplishments as much as it has been the orthodoxy of their own domestic vision.

Presidents are thus constrained by the needs of corporate capitalism. They are in part imprisoned, limited in what they can do, by the requirements of accumulation and legitimization.

The United States is the world's only superpower. In fact, it is a hyper-power. With military might second to none, a massive economy, and cultural penetration to all parts of the globe (I defy you to go to any large city in any country in the world and not find a McDonalds, Starbucks, or a local kid wearing a New York Yankee baseball cap or a "23" basketball jersey), the United States is the hegemonic power, or "big kid on the block." But if we are so strong, why do we seem so weak? Why, at a time when there are no rivals to power, is our grip on international events so fragile and tenuous?

When the Soviet Union imploded—marking the end of the Cold War—analysts wondered what international regime would replace the old order. For a time policymakers groped for an answer. George Bush (the first), in response to the invasion of Kuwait by Iraq, developed a multinationalist coalition based on a "new world order." But as the Gulf War ended, Bush abandoned this promising approach to international order and stability.

It was not until the Clinton years that the parameters of the new regime would come into view. Called "globalization," it encompassed an international acceptance of global capitalism—market economies, open markets, free trade, and integration and interdependence. Building on the institutions designed to oversee, coordinate, and stabilize the international economy—the International Monetary Fund (IMF), the World Bank, and the General Agreement on Tariffs and Trade (GATT), now the World Trade Organization (WTO)—these institutions have helped create a more integrated international economy.

The promise of globalism is political (countries that are connected by common bonds will better cooperate) and economic (a rising tide lifts all boats, although critics might argue that the rising tide lifts all yachts!) Those opposing the rise of globalism fear the widening gap between rich and poor nations, environmental degradation, and a decline in worker's rights.

In this age of globalization, what role and power would be assumed by the United States? And what role and power would be assumed by the presidency? Globalism takes power out of the hands of nations and places it in the hands of the market and corporations. National sovereignty is diminished as the requirements of the global economy drive policy. Globalism demands that market forces shape policy. Thus governments must please the international market or decline.

The United States is the most powerful actor in this system, and draws benefits from its leadership position. But this new system inhibits the freedom of a president to choose. Bound by the demands of a global economy, and the need to develop multinational responses to a variety of problems, the president is less free to pursue policies he chooses and increasingly compelled to succumb to the demands of the market.

Globalism is a two-edged sword. It brings some economic benefits but imposes further lim-

its on choice. Non-Governmental Organizations (NGOs), international institutions, central banks, and market forces gain in power. Nations—and the U.S. president—lose power.

DISCUSSION QUESTIONS

1. How does Genovese use the theories of "accumulation" and "legitimization" to explain how the structure of our political economy imposes a squeeze on the office of president?

2. In what way does economic "globalization" place new limitations on the president's power? Has the international power of the American president changed as a result of the September 11, 2001, terrorist attacks?

BRUCE MIROFF

THE PRESIDENTIAL SPECTACLE

Public support has always been important to presidential governance, but modern presidents have "gone public" to an unprecedented degree in an attempt to shape public perceptions. Bruce Miroff, a political scientist who has written important books on the Kennedy presidency and on styles of presidential leadership, analyzes the relationship between the presidency and the public in a mass media age in which the presidency has assumed primacy in the political system. Drawing on cultural theory, Miroff argues that presidents actively shape public perceptions through the creation of images and the presentation of symbolic "spectacles." Miroff develops the notion of the presidency as spectacle through innovative case studies of Ronald Reagan, George H. W. Bush, Bill Clinton, and George W. Bush. Miroff's analysis of the "spectacular" nature of the presidency raises disturbing questions about American democracy. Popular sovereignty requires an accurate public understanding of the course and consequences of presidential action. But the presidential spectacle helps to obscure our understanding of actual presidential performance and relegates citizens to spectators at a performance.

One of the most distinctive features of the modern presidency is its constant cultivation of popular support. The Framers of the U. S. Constitution envisioned a president substantially insulated from the demands and passions of the people by the long duration of the term and the dignity of the office. The modern president, in contrast, not only responds to popular demands and passions but also actively reaches out to shape them. The possibilities opened up by modern technology and the problems presented by the increased fragility of parties and institutional coalitions lead presidents to turn to the public for support and strength. If popular backing is to be maintained, however, the public must believe in the president's leadership qualities.

Observers of presidential politics have come to recognize the centrality of the president's relationship with the American public. George Edwards has written of "the public presidency" and argued that the "greatest source of influence for the president is public approval." Samuel Kernell has suggested that presidential appeals for popular favor now overshadow more traditional methods of seeking influence, especially bargaining. Presidents today, Kernell argued, are "going

Source: Bruce Miroff, "The Presidential Spectacle." *The Presidency and the Political System,* 7th edition, edited by Michael Nelson, Washington, D.C.: CQ Press, 2003, pp. 278–302.

public," and he demonstrated their propensity to cultivate popular support by recording the mounting frequency of their public addresses, public appearances, and political travel. These constitute, he claimed, "the repertoire of modern leadership."

This new understanding of presidential leadership can be carried further. A president's approach to, and impact on, public perceptions is not limited to overt appeals in speeches and appearances. Much of what the modern presidency does, in fact, involves the projection of images whose purpose is to shape public understanding and gain popular support. A significant—and growing—part of the presidency revolves around the enactment of leadership as a spectacle.

To examine the presidency as a spectacle is to ask not only how a president seeks to appear but also what the public sees. We are accustomed to gauging the public's responses to a president with polls that measure approval and disapproval of overall performance in office and effectiveness in managing the economy and foreign policy. Yet these evaluative categories may say more about the information desired by politicians or academic researchers than about the terms in which most members of a president's audience actually view the president. A public that responds mainly to presidential spectacles will not ignore the president's performance, but its understanding of that performance, as well as its sense of the more overarching and intangible strengths and weaknesses of the administration, will be colored by the terms of the spectacle.

THE PRESIDENCY AS SPECTACLE

A spectacle is a kind of symbolic event, one in which particular details stand for broader and deeper meanings. What differentiates a spectacle from other kinds of symbolic events is the centrality of character and action. A spectacle presents intriguing and often dominating characters not in static poses but through actions that establish their public identities.

Spectacle implies a clear division between actors and spectators. As Daniel Dayan and Elihu Katz have noted, a spectacle possesses "a narrowness of focus, a limited set of appropriate responses, and . . . a minimal level of interaction. What there is to see is very clearly exhibited; spectacle implies a distinction between the roles of performers and audience." A spectacle does not permit the audience to interrupt the action and redirect its meaning. Spectators can become absorbed in a spectacle or can find it unconvincing, but they cannot become performers. A spectacle is not designed for mass participation; it is not a democratic event.

Perhaps the most distinctive characteristic of a spectacle is that the actions that constitute it are meaningful not for what they achieve but for what they signify. Actions in a spectacle are gestures rather than means to an end. What is important is that they be understandable and impressive to the spectators. This distinction between gestures and means is illustrated by Roland Barthes in his classic discussion of professional wrestling as a spectacle. Barthes shows that professional wrestling is completely unlike professional boxing. Boxing is a form of competition, a contest of skill in a situation of uncertainty. What matters is the outcome; because this is in doubt, we can wager on it. But in professional wrestling, the outcome is preordained; it would be senseless to bet on who is going to win. What matters in professional wrestling are the gestures made during the match, gestures by performers portraying distinctive characters, gestures that carry moral significance. In a typical match, an evil character threatens a good character, knocks him down on the canvas, abuses him with dirty tricks, but ultimately loses when the good character rises up to exact a just revenge.

It may seem odd to approach the presidency through an analogy with boxing and wrestling—but let us pursue it for a moment. Much of what presidents do is analogous to what boxers do—they engage in contests of power and policy with other political actors, contests in which the outcomes are uncertain. But a growing amount of presidential activity is akin to wrestling. The contemporary presidency is presented by the White House (with the collaboration of the media) as a series of spectacles in which a larger-than-life main character and a supporting team engage in emblematic bouts with immoral or dangerous adversaries.

A number of contemporary developments have converged to foster the rise of spectacle in the modern presidency. The mass media have become the principal vehicle for presidential spectacle. Focusing more of their coverage on presidents than on any other person or institution in American-life, the media keep them constantly before the public and give them unmatched opportunities to display their leadership qualities. Television provides the view most amenable to spectacle; by favoring the visual and the dramatic, it promotes stories with simple plot lines over complex analyses of causes and consequences. But other kinds of media are not fundamentally different. As David Paletz and Robert Entman have shown, American journalists "define events from a short-term, anti-historical perspective; see individual or group action, not structural or other impersonal long run forces, at the root of most occurrences; and simplify and reduce stories to conventional symbols for easy assimilation by audiences."

The mass media are not, to be sure, always reliable vehicles for presidential spectacles. Reporters may frame their stories in terms that undermine the meanings the White House intends to convey. Their desire for controversy can feed off presidential spectacles, but it also can destroy them. The media can contribute to spectacular failures in the presidency as well as to successful spectacles.

Spectacle has also been fostered by the president's rise to primacy in the American political system. A political order originally centered on institutions has given way, especially in the public mind, to a political order that centers on the person of the president. Theodore Lowi wrote, "Since the president has become the embodiment of government, it seems perfectly normal for mil-

lions upon millions of Americans to concentrate their hopes and fears directly and personally upon him." The "personal president" that Lowi described is the object of popular expectations; these expectations, Stephen Wayne and Thomas Cronin have shown, are both excessive and contradictory. The president must attempt to satisfy the public by delivering tangible benefits, such as economic growth, but these will almost never be enough. Not surprisingly, then, presidents turn to the gestures of the spectacle to satisfy their audience.

To understand the modern presidency as a form of spectacle, we must consider the presentation of the presidents as spectacular characters, their teams' role as supporting performers, and the arrangement of gestures that convey to the audience the meaning of their actions.

A contemporary president is, to borrow a phrase from Guy Debord, "the spectacular representation of a living human being." An enormous amount of attention is paid to the president as a public character; every deed, quality, and even foible is regarded as fascinating and important. The American public may not learn the details of policy formulation, but they know that Gerald Ford bumps his head on helicopter doorframes, that Ronald Reagan likes jellybeans, and that Bill Clinton enjoys hanging out with Hollywood celebrities. In a spectacle, a president's character possesses intrinsic as well as symbolic value; it is to be appreciated for its own sake. The spectators do not press presidents to specify what economic or social benefits they are providing; nor do they closely inquire into the truthfulness of the claims presidents make. (To the extent that they do evaluate the president in such terms, they step outside the terms of the spectacle.) The president's featured qualities are presented as benefits in themselves. Thus, John F. Kennedy's glamour casts his whole era in a romanticized glow, Ronald Reagan's amiability relieves the grim national mood that had developed under his predecessor, and George W. Bush's traditional marriage rebukes the cultural decay associated with Bill Clinton's sex scandals.

The president's character must be not only appealing but also magnified by the spectacle. The spectacle makes the president appear exceptionally decisive, tough, courageous, prescient, or prudent. Whether the president is in fact all or any of these things is obscured. What matters is that he or she is presented as having these qualities, in magnitudes far beyond what ordinary citizens can imagine themselves to possess. The president must appear confident and masterful before spectators whose very position, as onlookers, denies the possibility of mastery.

The most likely presidential qualities to be magnified will be those that contrast dramatically with the attributes that drew criticism to the previous president. Reagan, following a president perceived as weak, was featured in spectacles that highlighted his potency. The elder Bush, succeeding a president notorious for his disengagement from the workings of his own administration, was featured in spectacles of "hands-on" management. Clinton, supplanting a president who seemed disengaged from the economic problems of ordinary Americans, began his administration with spectacles of populist intimacy. The younger Bush, replacing a president notorious for personal indiscipline and staff disorder, presents a corporate-style White House where meetings run on time and proper business attire is required in the Oval Office.

Presidents are the principal figures in presidential spectacles, but they have the help of aides and advisers. The star performer is surrounded by a team. Members of the president's team can, through the supporting parts they play, enhance or detract from the spectacle's effect on the audience. For a president's team to enhance the spectacles, its members should project attractive qualities that either resemble the featured attributes of the president or make up for the president's perceived deficiencies. A team will diminish presidential spectacles if its members project qualities that underscore the president's weaknesses.

A performance team, Erving Goffman has shown, contains "a set of individuals whose intimate cooperation is required if a given projected definition of the situation is to be maintained." There are a number of ways the team can disrupt presidential spectacles. A member of the team can

call too much attention to himself or herself, partially upstaging the president. This was one of the disruptive practices that made the Reagan White House eager to be rid of Secretary of State Alexander Haig. A team member can give away important secrets to the audience; Budget Director David Stockman's famous confessions about supply-side economics to a reporter for the *Atlantic* jeopardized the mystique of economic innovation that the Reagan administration had created in 1981. Worst of all, a member of the team can, perhaps inadvertently, discredit the central meanings that a presidential spectacle has been designed to establish. Thus, revelations of Budget Director Bert Lance's questionable banking practices deflated the lofty moral tone established at the beginning of the Carter presidency.

The audience watching a presidential spectacle is, the White House hopes, as impressed by gestures as by results. Indeed, the gestures are sometimes preferable to the results. Thus, a "show" of force by the president is preferable to the death and destruction that are the results of force. The ways in which the invasion of Grenada in 1983, the bombing of Libya in 1986, and the seizing of the Panamanian dictator Manuel Noriega in 1989 were portrayed to the American public suggest an eagerness in the White House to present the image of military toughness but not the casualties from military conflict—even when they are the enemy's casualties.

Gestures overshadow results. They also overshadow facts. But facts are not obliterated in a presidential spectacle. They remain present; they are needed, in a sense, to nurture the gestures. Without real events, presidential spectacles would not be impressive; they would seem contrived, mere pseudoevents. However, some of the facts that emerge in the course of an event might discredit its presentation as spectacle. Therefore, a successful spectacle, such as Reagan's "liberation" of Grenada, must be more powerful than any of the facts on which it draws. Rising above contradictory or disconfirming details, the spectacle must transfigure the more pliant facts and make them carriers of its most spectacular gestures.

Presidential spectacles are seldom pure spectacles in the sense that a wrestling match can be a pure spectacle. Although they may involve a good deal of advance planning and careful calculation of gestures, they cannot be completely scripted in advance. Unexpected and unpredictable events will occur during a presidential spectacle. If the White House is fortunate and skillful, it can capitalize on some of these events by using them to enhance the spectacle. If the White House is not so lucky or talented, such events can detract from, or even undermine, the spectacle.

Also unlike wrestling or other pure spectacles, the presidential variety often has more than one audience. Its primary purpose is to construct meanings for the American public. But it also can direct messages to those whom the White House has identified as its foes or the sources of its problems. In 1981, when Reagan fired the air traffic controllers of the Professional Air Traffic Controllers' Organization (PATCO) because they engaged in an illegal strike, he presented to the public the spectacle of a tough, determined president who would uphold the law and, unlike his predecessor, would not be pushed around by grasping interest groups. The spectacle also conveyed to organized labor that the White House knew how to feed popular suspicions of unions and could make things difficult for a labor movement that became too assertive.

As the PATCO firing shows, some presidential spectacles retain important policy dimensions. One could construct a continuum in which one end represents pure policy and the other pure spectacle. Toward the policy end one would find behind-the-scenes presidential actions, including quiet bargaining over domestic policies (such as Lyndon Johnson's lining up of Republican support for civil rights legislation) and covert actions in foreign affairs (the Nixon administration's use of the CIA to "destabilize" a Socialist regime in Chile). Toward the spectacle end would be presidential posturing at home (law and order and drugs have been handy topics) and dramatic foreign travel (from 1972 until the 1989 massacre in Tiananmen Square, China was a particular presidential favorite). Most of the president's actions are a mix of policy and spectacle.

THE TRIUMPH OF SPECTACLE: RONALD REAGAN

The Reagan presidency was a triumph of spectacle. In the realm of substantive policy, it was marked by striking failures as well as significant successes. But even the most egregious of these failures—public exposure of the disastrous covert policy of selling arms to Iran and diverting some of the profits from the sales to the Nicaraguan contras—proved to be only a temporary blow to the political fortunes of the most spectacular president in decades. With the help of two heartwarming summits with Soviet leader Mikhail Gorbachev, Reagan recovered from the Iran-contra debacle and left office near the peak of his popularity. His presidency had, for the most part, floated above its flawed processes and failed policies, secure in the brilliant glow of its successful spectacles.

The basis of this success was the character of Ronald Reagan. His previous career in movies and television made him comfortable with and adept at spectacles; he moved easily from one kind to another. Reagan presented to his audience a multifaceted character, funny yet powerful, ordinary yet heroic, individual yet representative. He was a character richer even than Kennedy in mythic resonance.

Coming into office after a president who was widely perceived as weak, Reagan as a spectacle character projected potency. His administration featured a number of spectacles in which Reagan displayed his decisiveness, forcefulness, and will to prevail. The image of masculine toughness was played up repeatedly. The American people saw a president who, even though in his seventies, rode horses and exercised vigorously, a president who liked to quote (and thereby identify himself with) movie tough guys such as Clint Eastwood and Sylvester Stallone. Yet Reagan's strength was nicely balanced by his amiability; his aggressiveness was rendered benign by his characteristic one-line quips. The warm grin took the edge off, removed any intimations of callousness or violence.

Quickly dubbed the Great Communicator, Reagan presented his character not through eloquent rhetoric but through storytelling. As Paul Erickson has demonstrated, Reagan liked to tell tales of "stock symbolic characters," figures whose values and behavior were "heavily colored with Reagan's ideological and emotional principles." Although the villains in these tales ranged from Washington bureaucrats to Marxist dictators, the heroes, whether ordinary people or inspirational figures like Knute Rockne, shared a belief in America. Examined more closely, these heroes turned out to resemble Reagan himself. Praising the heroism of Americans, Reagan, as representative American, praised himself.

The power of Reagan's character rested not only on its intrinsic attractiveness but also on its symbolic appeal. The spectacle specialists who worked for Reagan seized on the idea of making him an emblem for the American identity. In a June 1984 memo, White House aide Richard Darman sketched a campaign strategy that revolved around the president's mythic role: "Paint RR as the personification of all that is right with or heroized by America. Leave Mondale in a position where an attack on Reagan is tantamount to an attack on America's idealized image of itself." Having come into office at a time of considerable anxiety, with many Americans uncertain (according to polls and interviews) about the economy, their future, and the country itself, Reagan was an immensely reassuring character. He had not been marked by the shocks of recent U.S. history—and he denied that those shocks had meaning. He told Americans that the Vietnam War was noble rather than appalling, that Watergate was forgotten, that racial conflict was a thing of the distant past, and that the U.S. economy still offered the American dream to any aspiring individual. Reagan (the character) and America (the country) were presented in the spectacles of the Reagan presidency

as timeless, above the decay of aging and the difficulties of history.

The Reagan team assumed special importance because Reagan ran what Lou Cannon has called "the delegated presidency." His team members carried on, as was well known to the public, most of the business of the executive branch; Reagan's own work habits were decidedly relaxed. Reagan's team did not contain many performers who reinforced the president's character, as did Kennedy's New Frontiersmen. But it featured several figures whose spectacle role was to compensate for Reagan's deficiencies or to carry on his mission with a greater air of vigor than the amiable president usually conveyed. The Reagan presidency was not free of disruptive characters— Alexander Haig's and James Watt's unattractive qualities and gestures called the president's spectacle into question. Unlike the Carter presidency, however, the Reagan administration removed these characters before too much damage had been done.

David Stockman was the most publicized supporting player in the first months of 1981. His image in the media was formidable. *Newsweek,* for example, marveled at how "his buzz-saw intellect has helped him stage a series of bravura performances before Congress," and acclaimed him "the Reagan Administration's boy wonder." There was spectacle appeal in the sight of the nation's youngest ever budget director serving as the right arm of the nation's oldest ever chief executive. More important, Stockman's appearance as the master of budget numbers compensated for a president who was notoriously uninterested in data. Stockman faded in spectacle value after his disastrous confession in the fall of 1981 that budget numbers had been doctored to show the results the administration wanted.

As Reagan's longtime aide, Edwin Meese III was one of the most prominent members of the president's team. Meese's principal spectacle role was not as a White House manager but as a cop. Even before he moved from the White House to the Justice Department, Meese became the voice and the symbol of the administration's tough stance on law-and-order issues. Although the president sometimes spoke about law and order, Meese took on the issue with a vigor that his more benign boss could not convey.

In foreign affairs, the Reagan administration developed an effective balance of images in the persons of Caspar Weinberger and George Shultz. Weinberger quickly became the administration's most visible cold war hard-liner. As the tireless spokesperson and unbudging champion of a soaring defense budget, he was a handy symbol for the Reagan military buildup. Nicholas Lemann noted that although "Weinberger's predecessor, Harold Brown, devoted himself almost completely to management, Weinberger . . . operated more and more on the theatrical side." His grim, hawklike visage was as much a reminder of the Soviet threat as the alarming paperback reports on the Russian behemoth that his Defense Department issued every year. Yet Weinberger could seem too alarming, feeding the fears of those who worried about Reagan's war-making proclivities.

Once Haig was pushed out as secretary of state, however, the Reagan administration found the ideal counterpoint to Weinberger in George Shultz. In contrast to both Haig and Weinberger, Shultz was a reassuring figure. He was portrayed in the media in soothing terms: low-key, quiet, conciliatory. In form and demeanor, he came across, in the words of *Time,* "as a good gray diplomat." Shultz was taken to be a voice of foreign policy moderation in an administration otherwise dominated by hard-liners. Actually, Shultz had better cold war credentials than Weinberger, having been a founding member of the hard-line Committee on the Present Danger in 1976. And he was more inclined to support the use of military force than was the secretary of defense, who reflected the caution of a Pentagon burned by the Vietnam experience. But Shultz's real views were less evident than his spectacle role as the gentle diplomat.

The Reagan presidency benefited not only from a spectacular main character and a useful team but also from talent and good fortune at enacting spectacle gestures. It is not difficult to find events during the Reagan years—the PATCO strike, the Geneva summit, the Libyan bombing, and others—whose significance primarily lay in their spectacle value. The most striking Reagan spectacle of all was the invasion of Grenada. Grenada deserves a close look, as it can serve as the archetypal presidential spectacle.

American forces invaded the island of Grenada in October 1983. Relations had become tense between the Reagan administration and the Marxist regime of Grenada's Maurice Bishop. When Bishop was overthrown and murdered by a clique of more militant Marxists, the Reagan administration began to consider military action. It was urged to invade by the Organization of Eastern Caribbean States, composed of Grenada's island neighbors. And it had a pretext for action in the safety of the Americans—most of them medical students—on the island. Once the decision to invade was made, U.S. troops landed in force, evacuated most of the students, and seized the island after encountering unexpectedly stiff resistance. Reagan administration officials announced that in the course of securing the island U.S. forces had discovered large caches of military supplies and documents, indicating that Cuba planned to turn Grenada into a base for the export of revolution and terror.

Examination of the details that eventually came to light cast doubt on the Reagan administration's claims of a threat to the American students and a buildup of "sophisticated" Cuban weaponry in Grenada. Beyond such details, there was sheer incongruity between the importance bestowed on Grenada by the Reagan administration and the insignificance that the facts seemed to suggest. Grenada is a tiny island, with a population of 100,000, a land area of 133 square miles, and an economy whose exports totaled $19 million in 1981. That U.S. troops could secure it was never in question; as Richard Gabriel has noted, "in terms of actual combat forces, the U.S. outnumbered the island's defenders approximately ten to one." Grenada's importance did not derive from the facts of the event or from the military, political, and economic implications of America's actions, but from its value as a spectacle.

What was the spectacle about? Its meaning was articulated by a triumphant President Reagan: "Our days of weakness are over. Our military forces are back on their feet and standing tall." Reagan, even more than the American military, came across in the media as "standing tall" in Grenada.

The spectacle actually began with the president on a weekend golfing vacation in Augusta, Georgia. His vacation was interrupted first by planning for an invasion of Grenada and then by news that the U.S. Marine barracks in Beirut had been bombed. Once the news of the Grenada landings replaced the tragedy in Beirut on the front page and television screen, the golfing angle proved to be an apt beginning for a spectacle. It was used to dramatize the ability of a relaxed and laid-back president to rise to a grave challenge. And it supplied the White House with an unusual backdrop to present the president in charge, with members of his team by his side. As Francis X. Clines reported in the *New York Times,*

> The White House offered the public some graphic tableaux, snapped by the White House photographer over the weekend, depicting the President at the center of various conferences. He is seen in bathrobe and slippers being briefed by Mr. Shultz and Mr. McFarlane, then out on the Augusta fairway, pausing at the wheel of his golf cart as he receives another dispatch. Mr. Shultz is getting the latest word in another, holding the special security phone with a golf glove on.

Pictures of the president as decision-maker were particularly effective because pictures from Grenada itself were lacking; the Reagan administration had barred the American press from covering the invasion. This move outraged the press but was extremely useful to the spectacle, which would not have been furthered by pictures of dead bodies or civilian casualties or by independent sources of information with which congressional critics could raise unpleasant questions.

The initial meaning of the Grenada spectacle was established by Reagan in his announcement of the invasion. The enemy was suitably evil: "a brutal group of leftist thugs." American objectives were purely moral—to protect the lives of innocent people on the island, namely American medical students, and to restore democracy to the people of Grenada. And the actions taken were unmistakably forceful: "The United States had no choice but to act strongly and decisively."

But the spectacle of Grenada soon expanded beyond this initial definition. The evacuation of the medical students provided one of those unanticipated occurrences that heighten the power of spectacle: When several of the students kissed the airport tarmac to express their relief and joy at returning to American soil, the resulting pictures on television and in the newspapers were better than anything the administration could have orchestrated. They provided the spectacle with historical as well as emotional resonance. Here was a second hostage crisis—but where Carter had been helpless to release captive Americans, Reagan had swiftly come to the rescue.

Rescue of the students quickly took second place, however, to a new theme: the claim that U.S. forces had uncovered and uprooted a hidden Soviet-Cuban base for adventurism and terrorism. In his nationally televised address, Reagan did not ignore the Iran analogy: "The nightmare of our hostages in Iran must never be repeated." But he stressed the greater drama of defeating a sinister Communist plot. "Grenada, we were told, was a friendly island paradise for tourism. Well, it wasn't. It was a Soviet-Cuban colony being readied as a major military bastion to export terror and undermine democracy. We got there just in time." Grenada was turning out to be an even better spectacle for Reagan: He had rescued not only the students but the people of all the Americas as well.

As the spectacle expanded and grew more heroic, public approval increased. The president's standing in the polls went up. *Time* reported that "a post-invasion poll taken by the *Washington Post* and ABC News showed that 63 percent of

Americans approve the way Reagan is handling the presidency, the highest level in two years, and attributed his gain largely to the Grenada intervention." Congressional critics, although skeptical of many of the claims made by the administration, began to stifle their doubts and chime in with endorsements in accordance with the polls. An unnamed White House aide, quoted in *Newsweek,* drew the obvious lesson: "You can scream and shout and gnash your teeth all you want, but the folks out there like it. It was done right and done with dispatch."

In its final gestures, the Grenada spectacle commemorated itself. Reagan invited the medical students to the White House, and, predictably, basked in their praise and cheering. The Pentagon contributed its symbolic share, awarding some eight thousand medals for the Grenada operation—more than the number of American troops that set foot on the island. In actuality, Gabriel has shown, "the operation was marred by a number of military failures." Yet these were obscured by the triumphant appearances of the spectacle.

That the spectacle of Grenada was more potent and would prove more lasting in its effects than any disconfirming facts was observed at the time by Anthony Lewis. Reagan "knew the facts would come out eventually," wrote Lewis. "But if that day could be postponed, it might make a great political difference. People would be left with their first impression that this was a decisive President fighting communism." Grenada became for most Americans a highlight of Reagan's first term. Insignificant in military or diplomatic terms, as spectacle it was one of the most successful acts of the Reagan presidency.

A SCHIZOID SPECTACLE: GEORGE H. W. BUSH

Time magazine accorded George Herbert Walker Bush a unique honor: it named him its "Men of the Year" for 1990. There were really two President Bushes, the magazine explained, a strong and visionary leader in international affairs and a fumbling and directionless executive at home. The split in Bush's presidency that *Time* highlighted was as evident in the realm of spectacle as in the realm of policy. The foreign affairs spectacle of the first Bush presidency featured a masterful leader, a powerhouse team, and thrilling gestures. The domestic spectacle featured a confused leader, a colorless team, and gestures of remarkable ineptitude. Together, they created a schizoid spectacle.

Critics could find much to fault in the substance of Bush's foreign policy, but as spectacle, his foreign policy leadership was a great triumph. The main character in the Bush administration's foreign policy spectacle was experienced, confident, decisively in charge. Bush seemed bred to foreign policy stewardship in a patrician tradition dating back to Theodore Roosevelt and Henry Stimson. He came across to the public as the master diplomat, successfully cajoling and persuading other world leaders through well-publicized telephone calls; in truth, he moved easily among international elites, obviously in his element. He was an even more triumphant spectacle character when featured in winning tableaux as commander in chief of Operation Desert Storm.

The foreign policy team made a superb contribution to the global side of the Bush spectacle. Not since the administration of Richard Nixon had a president's skill at diplomacy been so effectively magnified by his top civilian advisers; not since World War II had a commander in chief been blessed with such popular military subordinates. James Baker, Bush's one-time Houston neighbor and long-time political manager, was both courtly and canny as secretary of state. Richard Cheney was a cool, cerebral secretary of defense, with an air of mastery reminiscent of Robert McNamara. Colin Powell, chair of the Joint Chiefs of Staff, radiated dignity and authority as the highest-ranking African American in the history of the military and was almost universally admired. Gen. Norman Schwarzkopf was a feisty commander for Desert Storm—an appealing emblem for a military finally restored to glorious health after two decades of licking its Vietnam wounds.

More than anything else, military gestures produced exciting drama in the Bush foreign affairs spectacle. Panama was the prelude to the Persian Gulf War. It featured, in Manuel Noriega, a doubly immoral adversary—a drug smuggler as well as a dictator. The U.S. military operation to depose Noriega was swift and efficient, and a victorious outcome was assured once the Panamanian strongman was seized and transported to the United States to face drug-trafficking charges.

The Gulf War victory dwarfed Panama, not only as significant policy accomplishment but also as spectacle. Bush depicted Iraqi dictator Saddam Hussein as a second Hitler, a figure whose immense record of evil made Noriega look like a small-time thug. To be sure, Operation Desert Storm lacked the satisfying climax of destroying the evil adversary, but as a military display, it provided Americans with numerous scenes to cheer. The indisputable favorites were Defense Department videos of laser-guided bombs homing in on Iraqi targets with pinpoint accuracy. In the cinematic terms that President Reagan had made popular, Desert Storm was not the cavalry rescue of Grenada or the capture of the pirate captain in Panama; it was high-tech epic, the return of the American Jedi.

Bush's foreign policy spectacle was successful—perhaps too successful. Once the Soviet Union crumbled and Iraq was militarily humiliated, foreign policy seemed much less relevant to most Americans. According to Walter Dean Burnham, "In 1992 foreign policy issues and public concerns about them played the smallest role in any American presidential election since 1936." As Americans began to focus almost exclusively on the home front, they witnessed a domestic Bush spectacle utterly unlike the foreign affairs version.

The domestic Bush was an uncertain, awkward character, especially in the electorally decisive field of economic policy. Inheriting what he

had once derided as Reagan's "voodoo economics," Bush presided over an economic crisis when the policy's magic failed. In the face of this crisis, which was evident by the second year of his administration, Bush drifted, seemingly without a clue as to how to restore the economy to health. The only economic prescription he ever put forward with any conviction was a cut in the capital gains tax rate that would have most directly benefited wealthy investors. Comfortable dealing with the problems that beset international elites, Bush seemed ill at ease with the economic problems plaguing ordinary Americans.

Bush's economic team only magnified his weaknesses. His secretary of the treasury Nicholas Brady, and chairman of the Council of Economic Advisers, Michael Boskin, were pale, dim figures who barely registered in the public's consciousness. To the extent that anyone did notice them, they seemed to epitomize inaction. A more visible economic team member was the budget director, Richard Darman. But he was portrayed in the media as arrogant and abrasive, epitomizing the antagonism between the Bush White House and Capitol Hill that resulted in domestic policy gridlock.

It was through a series of small gestures, some intended and others inadvertent, that Bush's disengagement from the economic difficulties of ordinary people was most dramatically demonstrated. Touring a grocery store, the president expressed amazement at the electronic scanners that read prices. To those who stood by every week as these scanners recorded their food purchases, here was a president unfamiliar with how families struggled to pay their grocery bills. Visiting a suburban mall on the day after Thanksgiving (the busiest shopping day of the year) in 1991, Bush brought along reporters who publicized his purchases: athletic socks for himself, Christmas presents for his family. Bush's shopping expedition seemed designed to convey the message that Americans could lift themselves out of recession just by taking a few more trips to the local mall. The most telling gesture of disengagement came early in 1992 at a campaign stop in New Hampshire, when Bush blurted out a stage cue from one of his speechwriters: "Message: I care." The message that came through, instead, was that the president had to be prompted to commiserate with the economic woes of the American people.

Real economic fears and pains denied Bush reelection in 1992. But the fears and pains were made worse by the ineptitude of his domestic spectacle. A president who lacked not only a credible economic plan but also credible gestures that would communicate concern and effort to restore economic health went down to a landslide defeat, with 63 percent of the electorate voting against him. The schizoid spectacle of George Bush, triumphant in its foreign policy performance, disastrous in its domestic policy performance, was over.

A POSTMODERN SPECTACLE: BILL CLINTON

George Bush had two disparate spectacles; Bill Clinton had many. Clinton's was a postmodern spectacle. A postmodern spectacle, heretofore more familiar in popular culture than in presidential politics, features fleeting images and fractured continuity, surfaces without depths, personae rather than personalities. Characters in a postmodern spectacle do not succeed by capturing the lasting admiration or trust of their audience but by personifying artfully the changing fashions that fascinate it.

Depictions of Clinton by close observers in the media tended to agree on his shape-shifting presidential performance but to differ as to whether it should evoke moral indignation or neutral evaluation. One constantly caustic Clinton-watcher, *New York Times* columnist Maureen Dowd, has called the president "the man of a thousand faces." Other commentators prefer cool postmodern terms such as *makeover* and *reinvention,* the same words used to describe the diva of contemporary pop culture, Madonna.

Clinton's presidency had important elements of constancy, including the successful economic course first charted in 1993 and the president's underlying attachment to government as a potentially positive force in society. And the frequent changes during Clinton's two terms owed as much to the formidable political constraints he faced as to the opportunities for spectacle he seized. Moreover, historical precedents for Clinton's "mongrel politics" may be found in the administrations of presidents such as Woodrow Wilson and Richard Nixon, who also were accused of opportunistic borrowings from ideological adversaries in eras when the opposition party had established the reigning terms of political discourse. Nonetheless, Clinton's repeated redefinitions of himself and his presidency made these predecessors seem almost static by comparison. Sometimes awkwardly, sometimes nimbly, Clinton pirouetted across the presidential stage like no one before him.

Clinton's first two years in power were largely a failure of spectacle. The promising populist intimacy of the 1992 campaign quickly gave way to a spectacle of Washington elitism, of social life among the rich and famous (the infamous $200 haircut by a Beverly Hills stylist) and politics among the entrenched and arrogant (the cozy alliance with the Democratic congressional leadership). The new president seemed simultaneously immature (the undisciplined decision delayer aided by a youthful and inexperienced White House staff) and old-fashioned (the big-government liberal with his bureaucratic scheme to reform the health care system). The crushing rebukes that Clinton suffered in 1994—the failure of his health care plan even to reach the floor of either house of Congress and the Republican takeover of both houses in the midterm elections—showed how little he had impressed his audience. Yet a postmodern irony was at work for Clinton, for his defeats freed him. Not having to implement a large-scale health care plan, Clinton was able to dance away from the liberal label. Not having to link himself with his party's congressional leadership in a bid for legislative achievement, he was able to shift his policy stances opportunely to capitalize on the weaknesses of the new Republican agenda.

In his first two years Clinton lacked an important ingredient for many presidential spectacles: a dramatic foil. Bush had used Manuel Noriega and Saddam Hussein, but the post–cold war world was too uninteresting to most Americans to supply foreign leaders ripe for demonization. The hidden blessing of the 1994 elections for Clinton was that they provided him with a domestic foil of suitably dramatic proportions: Newt Gingrich. Gingrich was often compared to Clinton—and the comparison worked mostly in Clinton's favor. Shedding the taint of liberalism, Clinton pronounced himself a nonideological centrist saving the country from Gingrich's conservative extremism. Before, Clinton had talked and shown off too much in public; now, in comparison to the grandiose garrulousness of Gingrich, he seemed almost reticent—and certainly more mature. Attacked as too soft in his first two years, Clinton could turn the image of compassion into a strength by attacking a foil who proposed to reduce spending for seniors on Medicare and Medicaid and to place the children of welfare mothers in orphanages. Lampooned as spineless in his first two years, Clinton could display his backbone in winning the budget showdown with the Republicans in the winter of 1995–1996.

In a postmodern spectacle, a president can try on a variety of styles without being committed to any one of them. As the 1996 election season commenced (and as Gingrich fled the spotlight after his budget defeat), Clinton executed another nimble pirouette by emulating the patron saint of modern Republicans, Ronald Reagan. Clinton's advisers had him watch Reagan videotapes to study "the Gipper's bearing, his aura of command." His campaign team found a model for 1996 in the 1984 Reagan theme of "Morning in America," in which a sunny president capitalized on peace and prosperity while floating serenely above divisive issues. Like Reagan in 1984, Clinton presented himself in 1996 as the benevolent manager of economic growth, the patriotic commander in chief comfortable with military power, and the good father devoted to family values. Unlike Reagan, he added the images of the good

son protecting seniors and the good steward protecting the environment. Clinton's postmodern appropriation of Reagan imagery helped to block the Republicans from achieving their goal of a unified party government fulfilling Reagan's ideological dreams.

Clinton's postmodern spectacle shaped public impressions of his team. With a man of uncertain character in the White House, strong women in the cabinet draw special attention: Attorney General Janet Reno at the outset of his first term, Secretary of State Madeleine Albright at the outset of his second. But no members of Clinton's cabinet or staff have played as important supporting roles in his spectacle as his wife, Hillary, and his vice president, Al Gore. Hillary Rodham Clinton appears as an updated, postfeminist version of Eleanor Roosevelt, a principled liberal goad pressing against her husband's pragmatic instincts. Like Eleanor, she is a hero to the liberal Democratic faithful and a despised symbol of radicalism to conservative Republican foes. Al Gore's spectacle role was to be the stable and stolid sidekick to the quicksilver president. Even his much-satirized reputation as boring is reassuring when counterposed to a president who appeared all too eager to charm and seduce his audience.

A postmodern spectacle is best crafted by postmodern spectacle specialists. When Clinton's presidential image began taking a beating, he turned for help to image makers who previously had worked for Republicans but who were as ideologically unanchored as he was. In 1993 Clinton responded to plunging polls by hiring David Gergen, the White House communications chief during Ronald Reagan's first term. But the amiable Gergen could not reposition Clinton as a centrist nearly so well as Dick Morris, Clinton's image consultant after the 1994 electoral debacle. Morris had worked before for Clinton but also for conservative Republicans such as Senate Majority Leader Trent Lott. As a *Newsweek* story described him, Morris "was a classic mercenary—demonic, brilliant, principle-free." It was Morris's insight, as much as Clinton's, that rhetoric and gesture, supported by the power of the veto, could turn a seemingly moribund presidency after 1994 into a triumphant one in 1996.

The remarkable prosperity of Clinton's second term purchased an unusual stretch of calm (some called it lethargy) for his administration—until the Monica Lewinsky storm threatened to wreck it early in 1998. Numerous Americans of all political persuasions were appalled by Clinton's sexual escapades and dishonest explanations in the Lewinsky affair. But for Clinton-haters on the right, long infuriated by the successful spectacles of a character who symbolized (for them) the 1960s culture they despised, the Lewinsky scandal produced a thrill of self-confirmation: See, they proclaimed, his soul *is* the moral wasteland we always claimed it to be. The fact that the majority of Americans did not concur with conservative Republicans that Clinton's moral failures necessitated his ouster from the presidency only made his impeachment and conviction more urgent for the right. If strong support for Clinton in the polls indicated that the public was following him down the path toward moral hollowness, removing him became a crusade for the nation's soul, an exorcism of moral rot jeopardizing the meaning of the Republic.

But the moralistic fulminations of the right were no match for the power of spectacle. It was not spectacle alone that saved the Clinton presidency. Clinton was protected by prosperity and by Americans' preference for his centrist policies over the conservative alternatives. He was aided, too, by the inclination of most Americans to draw a line between public rectitude and private freedom. Nonetheless, Clinton's eventual acquittal by the Senate owed much to spectacle. To be sure, his own spectacle performance in the Year of Lewinsky was hardly his best. Perhaps no role so little suited Clinton as repentant sinner. But he was blessed by even worse performances from his adversaries. Just as Newt Gingrich was necessary to resuscitate Clinton from the political disaster of 1994, so was Kenneth Starr essential to his rescue from the personal disaster of 1998. Starr's self-righteous moralism disturbed most Americans more than Clinton's self-serving narcissism.

In the end, the shallowness of the postmodern spectacle that had characterized the Clinton presidency from the start supplied an ironic benefit in the Lewinsky scandal. Had Clinton possessed a stable, respected character, revelations of secret behavior that violated that character might have startled the public and shrunk its approval of his performance in office. His standing in the polls might have plummeted, as President Reagan's did after the disclosure that his administration was selling arms to terrorists. But a majority of Americans had long believed, according to the polls, that Clinton was not very honest or trustworthy, so his misbehavior in the Lewinsky affair came as less of a shock, and was quickly diluted by reminders of his administration's popular achievements and agenda. Postmodern spectacle is not about character, at least not in a traditional sense; it is about delivering what the audience desires at the moment. Personality, political talent, and a keen instinct for survival made Bill Clinton the master of postmodern spectacle.

FROM RECYCLED SPECTACLE TO WAR ON TERRORISM: GEORGE W. BUSH

After reaching the White House through one of the closest and most intensely disputed elections in the history of the presidency, George W. Bush began his administration with a recycled spectacle. Promising the novelty of a "compassionate conservatism" during the campaign, the Bush administration's original agenda mainly followed the familiar priorities of the Republican right. But its conservatism ran deeper than its policy prescriptions. In its characters, its styles, its gestures, the Bush administration was determined to reach back past the postmodern spectacle of Bill Clinton and restore the faded glories of contemporary conservatism by recycling them.

One fund of recycled images and themes upon which Bush drew was the Reagan style spectacle. As a presidential character, Bush enjoyed many affinities with Reagan. Bush presented himself as a Reagan-style nonpolitician whose sunny optimism and embracing bonhomie would brighten a harsh and demoralizing political environment. His principal prescriptions for the nation also recycled Reaganesque themes and gestures. Like Reagan, Bush rapidly pushed through Congress a massive tax cut that favored the wealthy in the guise of an economic stimulus, using "fuzzy math" to promise Americans the pleasure of prosperity without the pain of federal deficits. Like Reagan, Bush promoted a national missile defense that would use cutting edge (and still nonexistent) technology to restore the ancient dream of an innocent America invulnerable to the violent quarrels of the world. Even the Bush administration's most politically costly stance in its early months—presidential decisions favoring private interests over environmental protection—was couched in the Reagan claim of protecting the pocketbooks of ordinary citizens. Revising a Clinton rule that would mandate higher efficiency for central air conditioners, Bush's secretary of energy, Spencer Abraham, indicated that his goal was to save low-income consumers from having to pay more to cool their homes or trailers.

Recycled images and themes from his father's administration were equally evident in the early months of Bush's presidency. They were especially useful as emblems of the "compassionate" side of the new chief executive. Like his father, "W" trumpeted his conciliatory stance toward congressional opponents. Like his father, W set out to be an "education president." The recycling of paternal gestures also was apparent in his meetings with representatives of the groups that had opposed his election most strongly. Just as the father had met with Jesse Jackson after winning the White House, the son invited the Congressional Black Caucus. Neither Bush expected to win over African American voters through these gestures. Instead, each hoped to signal to moderate white voters that they were "kinder, gentler" conservatives who exuded tolerance and good will.

The new Bush administration also reached even farther back in time in its bid to dramatize its repudiation of Clinton's postmodern character and style. Two of the new administration's most important figures—Vice President Richard Cheney and Secretary of Defense Donald Rumsfeld—were prominent alumni of the Ford administration; Cheney and Rumsfeld represented Bush's "That '70s Show," although they no longer sported the sideburns and wide lapels of Ford's day. Leaping back before the hated 1960s, the Bush administration also evoked an even earlier time, as Cheney, echoing the 1950s theme of "our friend, the atom," praised nuclear energy as "the cleanest method of power generation we know." Maureen Dowd, the most savage yet perceptive critic of Clinton's postmodern character, has been no less troubled by the "retro" nature of the Bush spectacle. After watching Bush speak at his alma mater, Yale, Dowd wrote that the president "seemed like a throwback" and described him as "Eisenhower with hair."

Bush's presidential team draws upon Republican characters and themes of the past to provide a reassuringly mature, veteran cast in contrast to the youthful self-indulgence associated with the postmodern Clinton. It also drains some of the political danger out of the widespread doubts about Bush's lack of preparation and seriousness in the presidency. Initially, the most visible team member was the vice president, who played the role of the wise and experienced father to the reformed playboy son, even though Cheney is only five years older than Bush. But Cheney's time in the spotlight was cut short when jokes and cartoons proliferated about him being the real White House decision-maker. Once Cheney declined in visibility (although not in influence), various members of the Bush cabinet emerged to signal compassion or conservatism as the situation seemed to require. On the compassionate end of the spectrum, the most interesting figure was Secretary of State Colin Powell, conveying the warm image of moderation and multilateralism otherwise absent from the administration's approach to foreign affairs. On the conservative end, the most striking figure was Attorney General John Ashcroft, conveying the dour image of the Christian right's culture wars. The fundamental conservatism of the Bush spectacle was even evident in the first lady. As a demure traditional wife who eschews a political role, Laura Bush quietly renounces the feminist activism of Hillary Rodham Clinton.

Perhaps the most revealing spectacle gesture in the early months of the Bush presidency was the speech on stem-cell research on August 9, 2001. Speaking from his Texas ranch in his first televised address to the American public since his inauguration, Bush ended weeks of fevered media speculation by announcing that he would permit federal tax dollars to be used for research on existing stem-cell lines but not for research on lines established after August 9. Balancing the public's hope for miracle cures to an array of severe illnesses with the conservatives' insistence on preserving the life of embryos, Bush's decision was meant to epitomize compassionate conservatism. Yet the heart of the spectacle lay in the presentation of his decision more than in its substance. Reminiscent of Reagan at the launch of the Grenada spectacle, Bush's speech countered criticisms of a disengaged presidency by presenting a highly serious chief executive sacrificing his vacation time to make the gravest of decisions. A president under fire in the media as an intellectual lightweight who was the captive of his advisers was presented (by his advisers) as the real decision-maker, confronting a policy dilemma worthy of a moral philosopher. To make sure that the public grasped the gesture, the day after the speech, presidential communication director Karen Hughes provided the press with a detailed briefing on how Bush had wrestled with the decision. She portrayed the president, in the words of the *New York Times,* as "a soul-searching, intellectually curious leader."

Although the stem-cell speech was politically effective, by late summer of Bush's first year in office the recycled spectacle was wearing a bit thin. Polls revealed a downward drift in public approval, and media commentary suggested a policy drift after the enactment of the Bush tax program. In early August, word came from the White House that the fall would witness a new Bush focus on "values." Just as Bill Clinton, following the advice of Dick Morris, had turned to the rhetoric and gestures of values to overcome public unhappiness about his liberalism, so Bush was being urged to stress values to change the subject from his administration's increasingly unpopular conservatism. By early September, however, a sharp downturn in economic indicators had overshadowed the values campaign and redirected the Bush team's attention to the economy. On September 9, the *New York Times* reported that "as White House officials move to refocus President Bush's energies on the precarious economy, they are working to present him as a more commanding leader in what may be the most treacherous stretch of his first year in the White House."

As the Bush White House scrambled to adjust to changing political issues and fashions, it contemplated the same kind of reinventions that it had denounced in its postmodern predecessor. But the reinvention it was actually to undergo was completely unscripted. The terrorist attacks of September 11 and their aftermath hurled the Bush presidency into a crisis for which none of its previous images and gestures seemed particularly appropriate.

The terrorists who piloted hijacked airliners into the World Trade Center and the Pentagon meant to kill thousands of Americans, but they also had a twisted spectacle of their own in mind by striking at symbols of American capitalism and military might. In the person of Osama bin Laden, the attack on America has featured a demonic villain far more menacing that the Manuel Noriega or Saddam Hussein who served as foils for the first Bush presidency. No one has accused the younger Bush of exaggerating when he labeled bin Laden "the evil one." But if the ingredients for a drama of extraordinary proportions were readily available, the horror of September 11 seemed too elemental for the contrivances characteristic of spectacle. The spectacle with which the Bush presidency commenced had recycled conservative themes from the past five decades to portray him as the opposite of a narcissistic Clinton presiding over a self-indulgent society. The war on terrorism that began on September 11 offered Bush the chance to be the opposite of Clinton in a more novel and profound sense.

In the first weeks after the terrorist attacks, Bush at times seemed to leave behind the gestures of recycled spectacle and rise to this extraordinary occasion. His impressive speech to Congress on September 20 struck a delicate balance between a forceful response to terrorism, a compassionate response to tragedy, and a teaching of tolerance toward followers of the Islamic faith. Many observers were impressed by Bush's demeanor during the speech. Less stiff and more articulate than in prior national addresses, Bush appeared animated by the gravity of the crisis. His associates began to describe a transformation of the heretofore laid-back president. As Frank Bruni wrote in the *New York Times,* one Bush friend reported that Bush "clearly feels he has encountered his reason for being, a conviction informed and shaped by the president's own strain of Christianity." Of course, in an age of spectacle any characterization of the president from his aides and associates has been carefully "spun" for public consumption.

Although at times after September 11 Bush appeared a changed president, the habits of spectacle are too ingrained in the modern White House to allow the abandonment of its characteristic contrivances. Bush often turned the war on terror into a personal duel with bin Laden, playing the hero locked in mortal combat with the avatar of evil. Evoking Ronald Reagan doing his best Clint Eastwood imitation (and employing the title of a classic TV western starring Steve McQueen), Bush pledged that bin Laden would be hunted down: "There's an old poster out West, as I recall, that said 'Wanted: Dead or Alive.'" White House spectacle specialists, such as Karen Hughes, Ari Fleischer, and Karl Rove, worked furiously to stifle criticisms of their boss, using media-management techniques, as Dowd observed, to "spoon-feed the press the image of an In-Charge, Focused, Resolute President." At first, Bush's war on terrorism seemed to be fought most effectively on the terrain of television: the White House prevailed on the networks to edit bin Laden's videotapes before showing them, while arranging for the popular "America's Most Wanted" show to feature the administration's hunt for his accomplices.

With the unexpectedly swift success of the military campaign in Afghanistan, the delicate balance in Bush's initial response to September 11 gave way to a consistently martial tone. Paced by Secretary of Defense Rumsfeld, the Bush administration began to feature a spectacle of muscular globalism. In his State of the Union address in January 2002, the commander in chief previewed an expansion of the war on terror to combat "an axis of evil," composed of North Korea, Iran, and especially Iraq. Bush's dramatic phrase, which made headlines around the world, rhetorically called U.S. enemies on World War II and the cold war to amplify the peril from adversaries in the Middle East and Asia. In its emphasis on Iraq, it gestured toward the spectacular completion by the son of the mission in which the father had sadly fallen short. But as Bush looked to exemplary global crusades of the past to build support for an escalation of his own war on terror, messy modern realities, especially in the Middle East, began to complicate his strategy. As of this writing in April 2002, they threaten to call into question the crusading imagery of good versus evil that has become the central spectacle of the Bush presidency.

CONCLUSION

It is tempting to blame the growth of spectacle on individual presidents, their calculating advisers, and compliant journalists. It is more accurate, however, to attribute the growth of spectacle to larger structural forces: the extreme personalization of the modern presidency, the excessive expectations of the president that most Americans possess, and the voluminous media coverage that fixes on presidents and treats American politics largely as a report of their adventures. Indeed, presidential spectacles can be linked to a culture of consumption in which spectacle is the predominant form that relates the few to the many.

Spectacle, then, is more a structural feature of the contemporary presidency than a strategy of deception adopted by particular presidents. In running for the presidency, then carrying out its tasks, any contemporary chief executive is likely to turn to spectacle. Spectacle has become institutionalized, as specialists in the White House routinely devise performances for a vast press corps that is eager to report every colorful detail. Spectacle is expected by the public as the most visible manifestation of presidential leadership. A president who deliberately eschewed its possibilities would probably encounter the same kind of difficulties as a president who tried to lead by spectacle and failed.

Still, the rise of spectacle in the presidency remains a disturbing development. It is harmful to presidents, promoting gesture over accomplishment and appearance over fact. It is even more harmful to the public, since it obfuscates presidential activity, undermines executive accountability, and encourages passivity on the part of citizens. The presentation of leadership as spectacle has little in common with the kind of leadership that American democratic values imply.

DISCUSSION QUESTIONS

1. What examples does Miroff provide to support his view that the presidency as a spectacle "obfuscates presidential activity, undermines executive accountability, and encourages passivity on the part of citizens"?

2. Since the September 11, 2001, attacks, President George W. Bush has been preoccupied with the "war on terrorism." How has Bush invoked symbolic language to build support for this effort?

PRESIDENTIAL DYNASTIES

Political analyst Kevin Phillips is well-known for his attention to the role of economic and social inequality in political conflict and for his historical approach to understanding the cycles of U.S. politics. Both of these themes are featured prominently in his 2002 book Wealth and Democracy: A Political History of the American Rich. *Americans have faced the dangers of concentrated wealth and power on previous occasions, and we forget these episodes at our peril. In this article Phillips explores the soaring levels of inequality in recent decades—what he calls the "upper-tier hogging of the economic benefits"—and links this trend to the threat of political dynasty-building. Political elites of both parties are tempted to profit from corporate connections before, during, and after their terms in office. Phillips provides details of the close connections of the Bush family and both Bush administrations to the Texas-based Enron corporation. In his 2004 study* American Dynasty: Aristocracy, Fortune, and the Politics of Deceit in the House of Bush, *Phillips develops a book-length account of the thesis presented in this article. Americans have at times looked to presidential leadership to offset the distortion of democracy springing from unbridled wealth and power. If political and economic inheritance becomes a precondition for the presidency, the substance of democracy suffers. Phillips notes that the public climate of patriotism and the war on terrorism has tended to sideline those reforms in taxation, regulation, and campaign finance policy that are necessary to stem the dynastic tide.*

Maybe it's time for a new set of Fourth of July orations. Only at first blush is there silliness to the idea of the United States—the nation of the Minutemen, John and Samuel Adams and Thomas Jefferson—becoming a hereditary economic aristocracy. When you think about it, there is evidence for serious concern.

More than a decade ago, the United States passed France to have the highest inequality ratios of any major Western nation. More and more of the country's richest clans have been setting up family offices, captive trust companies and other devices to manage and entrench their swelling fortunes. The elimination of the inheritance tax being sought by the Bush Administration will only make that entrenchment easier.

Politically, we already have a dynasty at 1600 Pennsylvania Avenue: the first son ever to take

Source: Kevin Phillips, "Dynasties: How Their Wealth and Power Threaten Democracy." *The Nation,* vol. 275, no. 2, 8 July 2002, pp. 11–14.

the presidency just eight years after it was held by his father, with the same party label. This dynasticism also has its economic side: both Bushes, *père et fils,* having been closely involved with the rise of Enron, another first for a presidential family, more on which shortly.

If we lack an official House of Lords, there are Bushes, Tafts, Simons, Rockefellers, Gores, Kennedys and Bayhs out to create a kindred phenomenon. Laura Bush is the only wife of a 1996 or 2000 major-party presidential nominee who has not yet entertained seeking a U.S. Senate seat in her own right. The duchesses of Clinton, Dole and Gore have already considered (or acted).

A soft, blurry kind of cultural corruption has all but muted discussion. Dynasty is no longer a bad word, and in the wake of this semantic revision, the inheritance tax supported by presidents from Lincoln to FDR has been renamed the "death tax" by George II and may be heading toward extinction. Small-business men from Maine to San Diego are already dreaming of founding personal dynasties, built on lobsters-by-mail or Buick dealerships.

Progressive taxation—only a memory for most—died in the 1980s as regressive FICA taxes replaced income levies as the heaviest tax paid by a majority of American families. The First Amendment to the U.S. Constitution, in turn, is not far from being twisted by the courts to include fat-cat political donations within the protection of free speech. Cynics might suggest that George Orwell set his book *1984* two decades too early.

But democracy is being eroded more by money and its power than by skilled semantics. For want of insights and data often unobtainable from the corporate media, the public opinion vital to U.S. democracy has trouble remaining vigorous and informed. Many politicians are themselves part of the national economic elite, and others depend on that elite for campaign funding. History tells us that America overcame kindred problems in the Progressive era a century ago. The national will to do so again, however, is hardly clear.

The menace of economic and political dynastization is that it flies under the radar of the Americans who grew up believing that the democratic values of World War II and Franklin D. Roosevelt, carried by another leadership generation into the 1960s, would last forever. Instead, the 1980s and '90s ambulanced many of those values to an ideological emergency ward. But much of the liberal and progressive community—caught up in older micro-issues—has found the changing *über*-philosophy difficult to grasp.

A similar thing happened in the mid-to-late-nineteenth century, when aging Jeffersonians and Jacksonians remained lulled by the egalitarian implant of those earlier days, as well as by the post-1783 elimination of the British system of entail and primogeniture, which kept estates intact at death. Finally, in the 1880s, it became clear that the advent of large corporations, enjoying a long legal existence and constitutional rights equivalent to persons, had provided the framework for the rise of a new aristocracy. Hundred-year-old reforms and shibboleths had become irrelevant.

By this point, the average American had stopped believing the old Fourth of July speeches about how the forefathers had anticipated every danger. From Maine to California, citizens saw railroads taking control of state politics. Muckraking journalists began to employ a new descriptive term: *plutocracy.* As the trusts and monopolies flourished while America's largest fortunes grew tenfold and twentyfold between 1861 and 1901 thanks to stock values, it became clear that some critical safeguards were missing. Luckily, the need to bridle railroads, trusts and monopolies, and to tax the incomes and inheritances of the rich, voiced with increasing clarity by Theodore Roosevelt, Woodrow Wilson and the Progressives, brought significant results by 1914. FDR added further reforms during the New Deal years.

As of 2002, alas, old New Deal memories and 60 cents will get you a candy bar. The transformation of the U.S. economy and its supporting politics since the 1960s has been staggering; and especially so since the 1980s, with the growth of financialization, wealth concentration, economic elitism and dynastization. Millionaires' income tax rates dropped so fast in the 1980s, for example, while those of people in the middle rose with FICA increases, that in 1985 the two almost met.

Back in 1937, an economics writer named Ferdinand Lundberg wrote about how "America's Sixty Families" (and another hundred lesser clans) owned a huge chunk of U.S. business through their corporate stock holdings. Six decades later, the current "overclass" probably begins with the largely overlapping quarter-million "deca-millionaires" ($10 million and up) and the quarter-million Americans with incomes in excess of $1 million a year. But for sticklers, the 2000 equivalent of the rich families of 1937 could be the roughly 5,000 clans having assets of $100 million or more.

Today, following the havoc of the biggest two-year major market debacle since 1929, many of the Internet fortunes are gone, while the established rich are very much with us and, by and large, sleeker than ever. This was also true in 1937, parenthetically, when researcher Lundberg's discourse paid hardly any attention to the nouveau-riche aviation, radio, motion picture and electric gadget fortunes of the Roaring Twenties. Most had shriveled or vanished between 1929 and 1932. The old money was back on top.

So it is again, although a third of the tech billionaires of 1999 have kept billionaire status, a much better ratio than in 1929–32. Nevertheless, what is striking in the current lists is the entrenchment of established families through the good offices of the Dow Jones and the S&P 500. The top 1 percent of Americans own about 40 percent of the individually owned exchange-traded stock in the United States, and own an even higher ratio of other financial and corporate instruments.

The median U.S. family, depending on the calculus, has only $6,000 or $9,000 of stock, a benefit overshadowed during the 1990s because its debt level rose by a good deal more. The financialization of America since the 1980s—by which I mean the shift of onetime savings deposits into mutual funds, the focus on financial instruments,

the giantization of the financial industry and the galloping preoccupation of corporate CEOs with stock options instead of production lines—has been a major force for economic polarization. This is because of its disproportionate favoritism to the top income and wealth brackets. The never-ending stream of 1980s and '90s bailouts of banks, S&Ls, hedge funds, foreign currencies and (arguably) stock markets by the Federal Reserve has been another prop.

The upper-tier hogging of the economic benefits of the 1990s can be approached from a number of directions, but hardly anyone controverts that the top 1 percent made out like bandits. The *New York Times,* for example, reported that 90 percent of the income gain going to the top fifth of Americans went to the top 1 percent, who are only a twentieth of that top fifth. Some scholars bluntly contend that attention should focus on the top one-tenth of 1 percent, because these are the raw capitalists and money-handlers, not the high-salaried doctors, lawyers and Cadillac dealers.

In 1935, Franklin Roosevelt proclaimed that "the transmission from generation to generation of vast fortunes by will, inheritance or gift is not consistent with the ideals and sentiments of the American people," but politics became friendlier to wealth in the 1960s and '70s, and positively effusive in its courtship during the 1980s and '90s. Over the past two decades, the same soaring costs of seeking office that drove middle-class office-seekers to sell their souls to big contributors also made dynastic heirs appealing to political parties that were looking for self-funding nominees or those whose famous names gave them a built-in fundraising edge. Two billionaires, Ross Perot and Donald Trump, actually sought the presidency or talked about it during the 1990s.

The number of U.S. senators with serious multimillion-dollar fortunes, in the meantime, has begun to approach the high set back in the early 1900s, when senators were appointed by state legislatures to whom money spoke easily and powerfully. This ended in 1913, when the

Seventeenth Amendment to the Constitution provided for popular election of senators, although the submergence of politics in today's money culture has accomplished somewhat the same thing, despite popular election.

As for Presidents, nineteenth- and twentieth-century White House service was not much of a pathway to getting rich. Most had government pensions and some other income, but few who didn't come to Washington rich left that way unless they inherited. What seems to have happened over the past twenty years, however, is that several Presidents—George H. W. Bush and the Hamptons-craving Bill Clinton—have decided to swim with the money culture. While Clinton was governor of Arkansas, wife Hillary held a number of corporate directorships. Now Clinton's post-White House speechmaking and deal-seeking looks perfectly normal in an ethically loose sort of way.

The first Bush administration probably represents the critical transition, both in the grabby behavior of family members and in the gravitation of top officeholders toward political investment banking, scarcely camouflaged lobbying and defense contract involvement. These practices, indeed, were vaguely reminiscent of the Whig grandees who ruled eighteenth-century England under the first George I and the first George II. One even gets the sense that the Bushes and their entourage came to see this kind of profiteering as their due, much like the families and associates of Walpole, Pelham and Newcastle.

George H. W. Bush's father and grandfather, investment bankers at old white-shoe firms, both had high reputations, but erosion soon set in. Even as the senior Bush was seeking a second term in 1992, the newspapers buzzed with the financial and deal-making escapades of his brothers and sons.

The most interesting Bush family involvement is with Enron. Over the twentieth-century emergence of modern government ethics, no presidential family has had a parallel relationship. As a senator, Lyndon Johnson buddied with Texas companies like Brown & Root, but its fingerprints on his presidency weren't all that notable. Geor-

gia's Jimmy Carter was close to his home-state corporate giant, Coca-Cola, and Richard Nixon brought the Pepsi-Cola account to his law firm during the 1960s.

Episode by episode, none of the Bushes' Enron involvement seems to be illegal. Before 2000–01, moreover, the ties weren't overwhelming in any one national administration. However, the only way that a chronicler can seriously weigh the Enron-Bush tie is by a yardstick the American press has never really employed: the unseemliness of a sixteen- or seventeen-year interaction by the members of an American political dynasty in promoting and being rewarded by a single U.S. corporation based in its home state.

Enron was organized in 1985, and within a year or two, Vice President Bush was chairing the Reagan administration's energy deregulation task force and his son George W., through one of his succession of minor energy companies, had an oil-well deal with Enron Oil & Gas. The first Bush administration saw passage of the Energy Policy Act of 1992, which obliged utility companies to transmit energy shipped by Enron and other marketers, while the Bush-appointed Commodity Futures Trading Commission created a legal exemption allowing Enron to begin trading energy derivatives. Enron chief Ken Lay, one of Bush Senior's top election contributors, was made chair of the President's Export Council.

Several years later, when George W. became governor of Texas, Lay asked him to receive visiting dignitaries from places Enron hoped to do business with, and by the time Bush got to the White House, Enron was his biggest contributor. Former Enron officials, advisers and consultants wound up getting several dozen positions in the new administration, including White House economic adviser, Secretary of the Army and U.S. Trade Representative. These were important to Enron on issues ranging from energy policy to its ambition to open up foreign markets by bringing exports of energy and water services under the WTO trade framework.

Had Bush tried to bail out Enron in November or December of 2001, his personal and dynastic ties to the company would have come under intense scrutiny. Without that bailout, most of the Washington press corps has been content to leave alone the much larger story—the apparent seventeen-year connection between the Bush dynasty and Enron.

Even without such information, it seems clear, counting campaign contributions, consultancies, joint investments, deals, presidential library and inaugural contributions, speech fees and the like, that the Bush family and entourage collected some $8 million to $10 million from Enron over the years, which is more than changed hands in Harding's Teapot Dome scandal. Depending on some still-unclear relationships, it could be as high as $25 million.

Obviously, this sort of dynastic financial outreach is not confined to Republicans. When Bill Clinton left the White House in a glare of unfavorable publicity over his last-minute pardons, especially that of fugitive financier Marc Rich, some of the focus was on money paid to or arrangements made by his wife's two brothers. Nor is it confined to Presidents. Texas Senator Phil Gramm and his wife, Wendy, got themselves referred to in *Barron's Financial Weekly* as "Mr. and Mrs. Enron" for his legislative work on the company's behalf at the same time that she was taking home money and company stock as an Enron director.

Because the dynastic aspect of American wealth and politics has been growing much faster than public (and press) appreciation of its ballooning significance, much of this record has received little attention. The neglect, however, is something that American democracy cannot afford. If Americans still believe in what Franklin Roosevelt said back in 1935 about the unacceptability of inherited wealth and power—and frankly, even if few have thought about it—a whole new political, ethical and economic agenda calls out for immediate and vocal embrace.

It's easy to limn broad outlines—further reform of campaign finance (perhaps including a constitutional amendment), federal tax changes, maintenance of the federal inheritance tax (certainly on estates over $3 million or so) and regulatory overhauls to curb the widespread corporate abuses pushed into the spotlight by Enron, Tyco and the accounting and brokerage firms. Still, a century ago, and then again in the early 1930s, the critical impetus for Americans' insistence on reform came from stock-market crashes and deep economic downturns. In 2002, we have had the first but not yet the second—and since 9-11, antiterrorism has been a rallying point, with patriotism offered to the electorate in lieu of economic concern.

As for economic and political dynastization, the United States is not the first republic to tilt in this direction. Rome did, and in the eighteenth century even the once proudly middle-class Dutch Republic let many of its offices become hereditary. Let's hope Americans do not also allow political and economic inheritance to displace democracy.

DISCUSSION QUESTIONS

1. Phillips claims that the United States has the highest inequality ratio of any Western nation? What evidence does Phillips provide of growing economic inequality? How do recent trends follow the patterns of earlier periods of American history?

2. What connections does Phillips reveal between the Bush family and the top rungs of corporate wealth and power? How significant do you think are the ties between the Enron corporation and George W. Bush in terms of the policy approach of the current Bush administration?

JOSEPH G. PESCHEK

THE BUSH PRESIDENCY AND THE POLITICS OF CONSERVATIVE DOMINATION

In the presidential campaign of 2000 George W. Bush presented himself as a "compassionate conservative." Given the closeness of the election, which was determined by a 5-4 decision of the U.S. Supreme Court to halt the vote recount in Florida, some commentators expected Bush as president to govern from the inclusive center. Political scientist Joseph G. Peschek argues that the Bush presidency has been characterized by a politics of conservative domination with few, if any, concessions to centrist moderation. Bush's right-turn is clear in the area of foreign policy. Peschek contends that Bush's foreign policy, as it unfolded in the year after September 11, was rooted in much more than a response to the threat of terrorism by Osama bin Laden and his al Qaeda network. The "Bush Doctrine" was based on an imperial strategy for American global dominance - military, political, and economic - that had been forged in conservative policy circles since the 1990s. Peschek explains that the Bush administrations persistent drive for "regime change" in Iraq was driven more by the goal of enhancing the strategic position of the United States in the Middle East and beyond than by concerns over Iraq's development of weapons of mass destruction. Bush's national security focus has functioned to obscure his highly contestable domestic record, particularly on economy policy, which above all serves the interests of business and the wealthy. Bush campaigned in 2004 as a "war president" and he interpreted his victory over John F. Kerry as a clear mandate for his conservative agenda. However public support for Bush's second term agenda is thin and precarious.

As George W. Bush began his second term as president, his agenda regarding national defense, the war on terrorism, economic policy, social issues, environmental regulation, and the federal judiciary was shaped by a politics of conservative domination. This marked a change from the expectations set by Bush during the election campaign of 2000, in which a moderate-sounding approach of "compassionate conservatism" was marketed. Foreign policy issues played only a minor role in 2000. In his contest with Al Gore, George W. Bush stated that America must be "humble in how we treat nations that are figuring out how to chart their own course." In the

Source: The author has written this article specifically for this edition of *Voices of Dissent.*

months after September 11, however, Bush's foreign policy took on an aggressive and far-from-humble tone, particularly towards Iraq, that went far beyond a response to the terrorist assaults of 2001. Bush's hawkish turn in foreign policy may be considered an integral component of the "politics of conservative domination" on which his presidency rests.

In this article I will examine Bush's first term as president from a critical perspective. First, I will discuss the nature of the Bush doctrine in foreign affairs and its core ideas of preventive war, unilateralism, hegemony, and market fundamentalism. Second, I will locate the sources of the Bush doctrine in the ideas of a conservative policy current that has been shaping the debate on post-Cold War foreign policy since the early 1990s. Third, I will critically examine Bush's policy towards Iraq in light of this emerging strategic doctrine and the interests that underpin it. Fourth, I will show how foreign policy and the war on terrorism have served to distract attention from the domestic agenda of the Bush administration which has systematically favored corporations and the wealthy Fifth, and finally, I will challenge the idea the Bush's victory in the presidential election of 2004 carried a mandate for him to move forward on his right-wing agenda. This article was completed shortly after the November 2004 elections. I encourage you to read it critically in light of subsequent political developments.

THE BUSH DOCTRINE: IMPERIAL AMERICA

Since World War II, most presidents have developed foreign policy "doctrines" that reveal their interpretations of the challenges facing the United States and the strategies by which they should be met. For example, the Truman Doctrine of 1947 shaped American Cold War strategy by identifying the containment of communism as the chief goal of foreign policy. In the first six months of his presidency, Bush championed an unapologetic, unilateralist approach to interna-

tional issues that included repudiation of U.S. support for the Anti-Ballistic Missile Treaty, the International Criminal Court, and the Kyoto environmental treaty on climate change and aggressive backing for the development of a National Missile Defense system.

In the year after September 11, the Bush administration put together the elements of a more far-reaching foreign policy doctrine based on unilateral action, pre-emptive military strikes, and prevention of the emergence of any strategic rivals to U.S. supremacy. Bush's grand strategy was formalized in a September 17, 2002 presidential report called *The National Security Strategy of the United States of America.* Maintaining a skeptical view of multilateral action and international treaties, the report argued for pre-emptive strikes against rogue states and terrorists, even if faced with international opposition, and for the maintenance of American military supremacy. In his introduction to the report, Bush contended that "America will act against such emerging threats before they are fully formed. . . . History will judge harshly those who saw the coming danger but failed to act. In the new world we have entered, the only path to peace and security is the path of action." While many commentators interpreted the national security strategy document as endorsing pre-emptive military action, it might more accurately be seen as attempting to legitimate the radical concept of preventive war, or a decision to attack now to prevent a real or potential adversary from becoming a substantial threat in the future. As author Rahul Mahajan comments, "Since such a justification could easily be used by any country to attack any other, it's long been understood in international legal circles that preventive war is completely illegitimate."

Such actions are described as "anticipatory" or "preemptive" in the report. They are justified by the nature of new adversaries, who cannot be deterred by conventional measures: "Given the goals of rogue states and terrorists, the United States can no longer rely on a reactive posture as we have in the past." The U.S. must be prepared to aggressively defend its interests on its own terms. If necessary it is legitimate for the U.S. to engage in a defensive first strike against governments that aid or harbor terrorists or pursue the development of weapons of mass destruction. "Traditional concepts of deterrence will not work against a terrorist enemy whose avowed tactics are wanton destruction and the targeting of innocents," the report stated. "America will act against such emerging threats before they are fully formed." The report made clear that the U.S. will act against its enemies even if it does not have international support: "While the U.S. will constantly strive to enlist the support of the international community, we will not hesitate to act alone." Additionally the report placed the U.S. off-limits to international law, asserting that the jurisdiction of the International Criminal Court "does not extend to Americans." Underlying the Bush doctrine is the notion that the U.S. must remain the unchallenged power in world affairs. "The United States possesses unprecedented—and unequaled—strength and influence in the world," the report began. Supremacy involves maintaining forces that "will be strong enough to dissuade potential adversaries from pursuing a military build-up in hopes of surpassing, or equaling, the power of the United States."

In the Bush Doctrine military strength is closely linked to an economic model that might be called "market fundamentalism." There is "a single sustainable model for national success: freedom, democracy, and free enterprise," the report contended. "The lessons of history are clear: market economies, not command-and-control economies with the heavy hand of government, are the best way to promote prosperity and reduce poverty." Seeking to "ignite a new era of global economic growth through free markets and free trade," the report advocated specific neoliberal policies such as "pro-growth legal and regulatory policies," "lower marginal tax rates," and "sound fiscal policies to support business activity."

Finally, the Bush report is based on the premise that the United States is the ultimate guarantor of universal values. The report declared that U.S. national security policy "will be based on a distinctly American internationalism that reflects the union of our values and our national interests." Seeking to make the world "not just safer, but better," the report asserted that the values of freedom "are right and true for every person, in every society—and the duty of protecting these values against their enemies is the common calling of freedom-loving people across the globe and across the ages. . . . The United States welcomes our responsibility to lead in this great mission." Journalist Hendrik Hertzberg described the perspective of the Bush report as "a vision of what used to be called, when we believed it to be the Soviet ambition, world domination."

This expansive doctrine of unilateral and preemptive military action and the maintenance of American military and economic supremacy was foreshadowed in several earlier presidential statements. On the night of September 11, 2001, Bush declared on national television, "We will make no distinction between the terrorists who committed these acts and those who harbor them." Four days later, Bush made clear that he did not want other countries setting conditions for the new war on terrorism. "At some point we may be the only ones left. That's okay with me. We are America," the president told his advisors. Addressing a joint session of Congress on September 20, 2001, Bush stated, "Every nation, in every region, now has a decision to make. Either you are with us, or you are with the terrorists. From this day forward, any nation that continues to harbor or support terrorism will be regarded by the United States as a hostile regime."

In his January 2002 state of the union address, Bush widened the war on terrorism when he identified an "axis of evil" involving Iran, Iraq, and North Korea. Maintaining that "our war on terrorism is only beginning," Bush warned the world that "America will do what is necessary to ensure our nation's security. We'll be deliberate, yet time is not on our side. I will not wait on events while dangers gather. I will not stand by as peril draws closer and closer. The United States of America will not permit the world's most dangerous regimes to threaten us with the world's most destructive weapons." In his speech at West Point in June 2002, the president bundled these post-9/11 statements into a proclamation of strategy. Bush called for pre-emptive attacks on countries that endanger the U.S., arguing that American security required "a military ready to strike at a moment's notice in any dark corner of the world." Rejecting as inadequate the Cold War doctrines of containment and deterrence, Bush said the United States must be "ready for preemptive action when necessary to defend our liberty." Speaking with self-described "moral clarity," Bush proclaimed that "America has no empire to extend or utopia to establish. We wish for others only what we wish for ourselves—safety from violence, the rewards of liberty, and the hope for a better life." Here again we see the Bush's administrations conflation of particular U.S. interests with universal values.

While the major implementation of the Bush Doctrine would come with the 2003 war on Iraq, it should be noted briefly that both the 2001 assault on the Taliban regime in Afghanistan and the Bush administration's nuclear weapons strategy also signaled imperial intentions. Although the U.S. military attack on Afghanistan in that began in October 2001 was in many ways understandable and predictable, it was carried out with little concern for diplomacy, multilateralism, and international law. Bush's approach was revealed in his September 20, 2001, address to Congress in which the president issued a set of demands on the Taliban, concluding, "These demands are not open to negotiation or discussion. The Taliban must act, and act immediately. They will hand over the terrorists or they will share in their fate." Assessments of the war in Afghanistan as just and successful need to consider the large number of civilian casualties and human rights abuses, the failure to apprehend Osama bin Laden, and the very partial consolidation of control over Afghanistan by the regime of Hamid Karzai.

With respect to nuclear weapons, the Bush administration revealed an expansive targeting strategy in the classified Nuclear Posture Review

(NPR) that was presented to Congress on January 8, 2002. The Defense Department was instructed to prepare contingency plans for the use of nuclear weapons against Russia, China, Iran, Iraq, North Korea, Libya, and Syria. According to the NPR, the Pentagon should be prepared to use nuclear weapons in an Arab-Israel conflict, in a war between China and Taiwan, in the event of an attack on South Korea by North Korea, and possibly in an attack by Iraq against Israel or its neighbors. The NPR also called for expansion of the U.S. nuclear arsenal by developing bunker-busting mini-nukes and nuclear weapons that reduce "collateral damage" and for planning to use nuclear weapons against chemical or biological attacks.

SOURCES OF THE NEW IMPERIUM

The Bush Doctrine reflects the ascendancy of a policy current of neoconservative ideologues and traditional national security hawks and unilateralists, including former officials of the Ronald Reagan and George H. W. Bush administrations. During the 2000 presidential campaign, several provided foreign policy advice to George W. Bush. At that time they called themselves the "vulcans" after the Roman god of fire and metal. Their worldview and policy objectives overlap with and are reinforced by pro-Israel hardliners and elements of the Christian Right. During the 1980s, this current supported the depiction of the Soviet Union as an "evil empire," the development of a national missile defense system ("Star Wars"), and political and military aid to anti-communist rebels such as the Nicaraguan *contras* and the Islamic *mujahedeen* in Afghanistan. After the Soviet Union imploded in 1991, foreign policy hawks and neo-conservatives refined their blueprints for American hegemony in a post-Cold War world. During the 1990s and into the years of the Bush II administration, they developed their goals and strategies through a network of groups, often funded by conservative foundations, such as the Project for a New American Century, the Center for Security Policy, the Jewish Institute for

National Security, and the American Enterprise Institute. They articulated their views in the pages of the *Weekly Standard, Wall Street Journal, National Review, Commentary,* and the *Washington Times,* as well as through syndicated columns by Charles Krauthammer, William Safire, and others.

Vice President Dick Cheney played a key role in supporting this policy current when he was Secretary of Defense in the first Bush administration. In 1992 a draft of a *Defense Policy Guidance* document from Cheney's Defense Department was leaked to the press. Written by Pentagon analysts Paul Wolfowitz (Bush's Deputy Secretary of Defense) and I. Lewis Libby (Cheney's chief-of-staff), the document laid out the rationale for an American first strike against any country deemed to threaten the security of the United States. It also established the goal of "deterring potential competitors from even aspiring to a larger regional or global role." While the global implications of the draft caused an uproar, leading to the document being rewritten and toned down, neo-imperial aspirations for seizing the "unipolar moment" on the post-Cold War world had been made plain.

During the 1990s key activists within this policy network, including columnist Robert Kagan and *Weekly Standard* editor William Kristol, formed the Project for a New American Century (PNAC), which won the support of many defense hawks, neoconservative intellectuals, and leaders of the Christian and Catholic Right. In its 1997 statement of principles, the PNAC stated that "a Reaganite policy of military strength and moral clarity may not be fashionable today. But it is necessary if the United States is to build on the successes of the past century and to ensure our security and our greatness in the next." In addition to Paul Wolfowitz and I. Lewis Libby, the signatories of this statement included such future Bush administration officials as Dick Cheney, Secretary of Defense Donald Rumsfeld, Zalmay Khalilzad, a former Unocal Corporation oil industry consultant who became special envoy to

Afghanistan, and Elliott Abrams, who was convicted for his part in the Reagan era Iran-contra affair and was named the Middle East affairs director for the National Security Council.

In 2000 PNAC published a 76-page document called *Rebuilding America's Defenses: Strategy, Forces, and Resources for a New Century* that has become a blueprint for Bush's foreign and defense policies. After noting that the PNAC plan "builds upon the defense strategy outlined by the Cheney Defense Department in the waning days of the Bush administration," the report states, "At present the United States faces no global rival. America's grand strategy should aim to preserve and extend this advantageous position as far into the future as possible." The PNAC report went on to urge such measures as large increases in military spending, the development of missile defense systems, the deployment of a new family of nuclear weapons, and facing up to "the realities of multiple constabulary missions that will require a permanent allocation of U.S. forces." These actions were necessary to "preserve Pax Americana" (an American peace) and a "unipolar 21st century."

PNAC and its allies have been the main advocates of an aggressive Bush Doctrine. During Bush's first term their main opponent was Secretary of State Colin Powell, who often adhered to a more moderate, less unilateralist approach to foreign policy. PNAC leaders expected the far-reaching changes in U.S. military policy they favored would have to come about slowly in the absence of "a catastrophic and catalyzing event like a new Pearl Harbor." As foreign policy analyst Chalmers Johnson puts it, "On September 11, 2001, they got their Pearl Harbor." Nine days later, on September 20, 2001, the PNAC sent a letter to President Bush advocating "a determined effort to remove Saddam Hussein from power in Iraq," a "large increase in defense spending," and staunch support for Israel and an end to U.S. support for the Palestinian Authority. The war on terrorism would be used to implement the pre-September 11 agenda of important elements of the Bush administration and the political and business interests that coalesce around them.

Neoconservatives see a close affinity between an imperial U.S. foreign policy and a hard-line interpretation of Israel's strategic interests. Under the Bush administration, U.S. policy in the Middle East coincides with the approach of Israeli Prime Minister Ariel Sharon. "This is the best administration for Israel since Harry Truman," said Thomas Neumann, executive director of the Jewish Institute for National Security Affairs. A number of leading neoconservative strategists have been involved with right-wing Israeli politics. Richard Perle, former chair of Bush's Defense Policy Board, led a 1996 study group that proposed to incoming Israeli Prime Minister Benjamin Netanyahu that he abandon the 1993 Oslo peace accords, reject the idea of land for peace, insist on Arab recognition of Israel's claim to biblical land, and focus on removing Saddam Hussein from power in Iraq. Aside from Perle, then at the American Enterprise Institute, the study group included David Wurmser, who became a special assistant to Undersecretary of State John Bolton, and Douglas J. Feith, named undersecretary of defense for policy. Of these men, Michael Lind writes, "Their admiration for the Israeli Likud party's tactics, including preventive warfare such as Israel's 1981 raid on Iraq's Osirak nuclear reactor, is mixed with odd bursts of ideological enthusiasm for 'democracy'." For neoconservatives in the Bush administration, part of the attraction of war against Iraq, perhaps followed by campaigns against other radical Arab forces, was "to guarantee Israel's security by eliminating its greatest military threats, forging a regional balance of power overwhelmingly in Israel's favor, and in general creating a more friendly atmosphere for Israel in the Middle East."

Southern Christian conservatives, who are an important base of support for the Bush administration, coloring its rhetoric and moral preoccupations, have played a supplemental role to the neoconservative current. They perhaps help to infuse Bush's foreign policy rhetoric with a strong sense of apocalyptic righteousness against the "evil ones" that Bush has targeted. As Kevin Phillips contends, "The idea that the de facto head of the Religious Right and the president of the United States can be the same person is a precedent-shattering circumstance that has barely crept into the national political discussion." Leaders of the Christian Right bolster near unconditional support for Israel in its struggle with the Palestinians. Bush's position on the Middle East increasingly dovetails with that of the hard-line Israeli leader Ariel Sharon. "Christian Zionists" have a biblically derived belief in the coming showdown with the forces of the Antichrist. Ironically, Protestant denominations that historically have been far from friendly to Jews are now among the most ardently pro-Israel forces in the United States. As political analyst Anatol Lieven puts it, for Christian fundamentalists, "the existence of the Israeli state is seen as a necessary prelude to the arrival of the Antichrist, the Apocalypse, and the rule of Christ and His Saints." Christian conservatives play important roles in many state Republican parties and provided George W. Bush with needed support in several key primary contests in 2000. The Christian Right has also influenced U.S. policy towards the United Nations, including American withdrawal from any programs that deal with family planning. The Christian Right has long hated the United Nations, both on nationalist grounds and because of their fears of world government by the Antichrist.

Finally we must note the role of business interests in influencing the Bush's defense and foreign policies. One need not resort to either economic reductionism or crude conspiracy theories to believe that profane economic interests help to determine the foreign policy approach of an administration as friendly to business as Bush's. Certainly massive increases in military spending will reward any number of business interests close to the administration in ways that have little to do with the war on terrorism. Consider the $396 billion defense spending request from President Bush in January 2002, four months after the terrorist attacks. Much of the weapons acquisition portion of this request—at least $21.2 billion—would go for big ticket items of the Cold War era. Another $9 billion would go for ballistic missile defense, leaving just $3.2 billion for the kind of precision munitions used in the war in Afghanistan. Thus at least 44 percent of the weapons funding in Bush's proposal had nothing to do with the war on terrorism, putting aside the question of the extent to which the use of military force will solve the problem of terrorist violence. According to defense spending expert Michelle Ciarocca, the increases in defense spending due to September 11 have allowed the Pentagon to avoid reform and transformation. Moreover the failure of policymakers and defense officials to cancel unnecessary weapons programs is, in large part, due to the undue influence exerted by the top defense contractors. According to a study by the World Policy Institute, 32 high administration officials were former arms company executives, consultants, or shareholders. The Center for Public Integrity found that of the 30 members of the Defense Policy Board, the government-appointed group that advises the Pentagon, at least nine had ties to companies that have won more than $76 billion in defense contracts in 2001 and 2002. Four members were registered lobbyists, one of whom represented two of the three largest defense contractors. The Bush years have seen the revitalization of what President Dwight D. Eisenhower called the military industrial complex.

WHY IRAQ?

In his January 29, 2002, State of the Union address, President Bush stated that the "war on terror is well begun, but it is only begun." He went on to identify three countries that constituted an "axis of evil." They were North Korea, Iran and Iraq. Linking them to weapons of mass destruction and the threat of terrorism, Bush asserted that "time is not on our side. The United States of America will not permit the world's most dangerous regimes to threaten us with the world's most destructive weapons." Throughout 2002 Bush kept up the drumbeats against Iraq and its leader Saddam Hussein, whom his father had compared unfavorably with Adolph Hitler. Ironically, while United Nations inspectors were finding little evidence that Iraq possessed weapons of mass destruction, it became clear in early 2003 that North Korea had enough plutonium and tested bomb technology for nuclear warheads and was working on missiles to deliver them. Amidst these developments, Secretary of State Powell said of the situation on the Korean peninsula, "Let's take this patiently. Let's take it with deliberation. Let's work with our friends and allies." Iraq was met with a very different approach. During 2002 President Bush won votes from the U.S. Congress and from the United Nations for possible action against Iraq, even as a burgeoning antiwar movement took shape in the United States and abroad. Certainly Bush and his team saw little need to defer to allied objections. As historian Donald Kagan, co-chair of the 2000 PNAC report, stated, "You saw the movie 'High Noon'? We're Gary Cooper." On March 17, 2003, the U.S. launched the second Persian Gulf war by attacking Iraq, leading to the downfall of Saddam Hussein's regime in April and the occupation of Iraq by thousands of American and allied forces.

What explains the focus on "regime change" in Iraq and the deprecation of non-military options? The Bush administration argued that war with Iraq was necessary to eliminate Saddam Hussein's arsenal of weapons of mass destruction, to diminish the threat of international terrorism, and to promote democracy in Iraq and the region. Little hard evidence was offered in support of the administration's claims about the dangers of Iraq. There also were clumsy attempts by Vice President Cheney and others to posit links between Iraq and the al Qaeda terrorist network. These claims have been completely discredited by numerous postwar investigations.

While it was clear that Saddam's regime was brutal, Iraq was arguably much more dangerous in both intentions and capabilities in the 1980s, when the United States saw Iraq as an ally in the struggle against Iran. According to the *Washington Post,* "The administrations of Ronald Reagan and George H.W. Bush authorized the sale to Iraq of numerous items that had both military and civilian applications, including poisonous chemicals and deadly biological viruses, such as anthrax and bubonic plague." Donald Rumsfeld, now Secretary of Defense, met with Saddam Hussein in December 1983 as a special presidential envoy and opened the way for the normalization of U.S.-Iraqi relations. According to recently declassified documents, Rumsfeld's meeting in Baghdad took place at a time when Iraq was using chemical weapons "almost daily" in its war with Iran, in defiance of international conventions. Little concern about American promotion of democracy in the Middle East can gleaned from the historical record.

According to journalist Bob Woodward, on the day after the September 11 attacks, Secretary Rumsfeld advocated that "Iraq should be a principal target in the first round in the war against terrorism." Hawks in the Bush administration saw an opportunity to implement their long-standing goal of attacking Iraq and deposing Saddam Hussein. But President Bush, sensitive to claims that public opinion was not ready for such a move, chose to focus U.S. military forces on Afghanistan. The ousting of the Taliban regime provided an opportunity to refocus on Iraq and implement the "Saddam Must Go" policy that hard-line activists had long advocated. In 2002 the Committee for the Liberation of Iraq, largely an offshoot of the Project for a New American Century, set up shop to rally public support for the invasion of Iraq.

Bush administration claims that Iraq possessed weapons of mass destruction were deflated after the war when no such weapons were found by the Iraq Survey Group, leading to resignation of chief weapons inspector David Kay in January 2004. While officials spoke of an "intelligence failure" and Kay stated "we were all wrong," it was clear that the buildup to the war had involved a massive propaganda campaign in which the intelligence process was thoroughly politicized. As Sidney Blumenthal contends, "The truth is that much of the intelligence community did not fail, but presented correct assessments and warnings, that were overridden and suppressed. On virtually every single important claim made by the Bush administration in its case for war, there was serious dissension. Discordant views—not from individual analysts but from several intelligence agencies as a whole—were kept from the public as momentum was built for a congressional vote on the war resolution." By early October of 2002, with votes on the use of force against Iraq pending both in Congress and in the United Nations, several press accounts noted pressure on CIA analysts to reach conclusions in line with administration goals. Most of the mainstream press, including the *New York Times,* remained submissive to official claims and relied on misinformation from Iraq opposition leader Ahmed Chalabi and other defectors.

The Pentagon-based Office of Special Plans (OSP), created shortly after the September 11 attacks to search for links between Iraq and terrorists, skirted routine intelligence filtering procedures. Directed by Abram Shulsky, the OSP worked with neoconservative political appointees in the National Security Council, the State Department and the office of the Vice President. As foreign policy analyst Tom Barry explains, "Convinced that the CIA, Defense Intelligence Agency (DIA), and the State Department would not provide them with type of alarmist threat assessments to justify a preventive war, they created their own tightly controlled intelligence operation at the top levels of the Pentagon bureaucracy."

If the official reasons for the aggressive stance towards Iraq can be refuted, what sort of alternative explanation makes sense? In my view, Iraq represents an opportunity to implement the broad imperial strategy underlying the Bush Doctrine. The administration dismissed options for the containment and deterrence of Iraq because these measures would not allow for the expansion of American power in the region. As Jay Bookman of the *Atlanta Journal-Constitution* wrote, "This war, should it come, is intended to mark the official emergence of the United States as a full-fledged global empire, seizing sole responsibility and authority as planetary policeman. It would be the culmination of a plan 10 years or more in the making, carried out by those who believe the United States must seize the opportunity for global domination, even if it means becoming the 'American imperialists' that our enemies always claimed we were." Writer and activist Tariq Ali makes a similar point: "The Iraq war is a demonstration occupation of a country not just for the Arab world or to appease Israel—that's a part of it—but the big game is to show the rest of the world who the United States is and what it's capable of doing."

The conquest of Iraq, and the American occupation that would follow it, would provide an opportunity to establish new U.S. bases in the Middle East and to obtain more reliable control over Iraq's vast oil supplies. In January 2003 the U.S. Department of Energy stated that by 2025, imports would account for about 70 percent of U.S. domestic demand, up from 55 percent in 2001. The United States, with only 2 percent of the world's known oil reserves, uses 25 percent of the world's annual output. Estimates from the Energy Department are that Iraq has as much as 220 billion barrels in "probable and possible" reserves, making the estimated total enough to cover U.S. annual oil imports at their current levels for ninety-eight years. However oil interests must be linked to broader U.S. geopolitical and geoeconomic goals to adequately explain the campaign against Iraq. As foreign policy analyst Michael Klare argues, an explanation of the real reason for the Bush administration's campaign to oust Saddam Hussein must include "the pursuit

of oil and the preservation of America's status as the paramount world power."

DOMINATING THE DOMESTIC AGENDA

From the standpoint of his political clout and political capital, foreign policy has in many ways served President Bush well. Most obviously it has bolstered his sense of legitimacy as president. Dimmed are recollections of the way in which he was, in effect, selected to be president by the Supreme Court in a highly controversial 5-4 decision in December 2000. Bush's approval ratings have been bolstered by the war on terrorism. Just before the September 11 attacks on New York and Washington, Bush's job approval rating was 51 percent, the lowest of his tenure to that point. By September 21, 2001, it had risen to 90 percent, a record for presidents in the Gallup poll, and remained in the high 80s through the end of 2001. This is the well-known "rally around the flag" phenomenon of American support for the president in a time of crisis.

During the congressional campaign of 2002, Bush used his political capital to help fellow Republicans by calling for support for his policies, especially the war on terrorism. The elections resulted in the recapture of the Senate by the Republicans and the widening of their majority in the House. Many commentators noted that Bush, who logged more than 10,000 miles on the campaign trail, attempted to nationalize the congressional elections around national security themes. Because of his success in doing so, Bush accrued political clout that enabled him to better implement his agenda of tax cuts, a conservative federal judiciary, and hawkish defense and foreign policies. Bush's agenda is more consistently conservative than that of any president since Herbert Hoover.

Bush's war on terrorism has served to displace and divert attention from potentially troublesome domestic conditions and policies. The "crime in the suites" scandals associated with the collapse of Enron and other corporate giants, and the relationship of key administration officials to discredited business leaders, have been less prominent in political discussion than they might have been. Bush's identification with business agendas has been consistent in tax legislation, immigration policy, regulatory decisions, and labor policies. Thomas Edsall of the *Washington Post* explained in a February 2004 article: "For three years, President Bush has been willing to anger environmentalists, civil libertarians of the right and left, unions, trial lawyers and conservative advocates of free markets. But one group that almost always comes out a winner when Bush sets policy is the business community, from Fortune 500 corporations to small, family-run companies."

Despite a modest recovery in 2004, Bush's record on the economy and economic policy in his first term conferred no bragging rights. As economist and *New York Times* columnist Paul Krugman pointed out, "An unusually large number of people have given up looking for work, so they are no longer counted as unemployed, and many of those who say they have jobs seem to be marginally employed. Such measures as the length of time it takes laid-off workers to get new jobs continue to indicate the worst job market in 20 years." Consumer debt hit record levels, resulting in soaring rates of consumer bankruptcy, mortgage foreclosure, car repossession, and credit card delinquency. Growing family financial instability left more and more workers insecure in the face of the jobless recovery. By October of 2004, Commerce Department data showed that the share of Gross Domestic Product consisting of wage and salary income fell for the 14th straight quarter, a decline unprecedented in the post-World War II era. Political scientist Jacob Hacker observed that "even as wages have become more unstable, the financial effects of losing a job have worsened, and the cost of things families need, from housing to education, has ballooned. Yet government and the private sector aren't just ignoring these problems, they are making them worse. Many programs for the poor, for example, have been substantially cut. And middle-class programs like Social Security have steadily eroded."

Bush's presidency saw the return of large federal budget deficits. In fiscal year 2004, the deficit was $413 billion, a $36 billion increase from fiscal year 2003, and a steep fall from the $236 billion budget surplus in 2000 The Bush administration offered assurances that it would cut the deficit in half by 2009. A report by the nonpartisan Congressional Budget Office disputed the claims of the Bush budget, and predicted that accumulated deficits over the next decade would total $1.9 trillion. Other analysts forecasts deficits of over $5 trillion from 2005 to 2014, assuming a continuation of current policies. Bush's budget for fiscal year 2005 omitted a number of likely or inevitable costs in taxes, defense spending, and other areas. When these missing costs are added, the Center on Budget and Policy Priorities (CBPP) demonstrated, the deficit for 2009 would be $400 billion to $435 billion, or 2.8 percent to 3.0 percent of GDP. "For the Administration to legitimately halve the deficit as a share of GDP by 2009 and continue to hold to its tax-cutting agenda, it would have to slash federal spending by an amount equal to the entire budget of the Department of Education or seven times the amount of the budget for environmental protection," the CBPP explained. Bush's budget called for real spending cuts in domestic discretionary programs that, if enacted by Congress, "would mark an unprecedented shift in federal priorities," according to the *Washington Post*. Programs subject to freezes or cuts at least through 2009 included low-income education programs, medical research, grants to local law enforcement agencies, and job training. In guns over butter fashion the proposed 2005 budget would raise spending for the military and domestic security to climb to record levels. 128 programs would be eliminated by 2010, nearly all of which serve the most vulnerable sections of American society: children, the poor, the sick, and those living in public housing.

Bush's tax policies seemed to be based on the view that the rich don't have enough money. In

2001 Bush succeeded in winning a $1.3 trillion tax cut, marketed as an economic stimulus plan, of which 36 percent went to the richest one percent of taxpayers, with an average annual income of $1.1 million. In January 2003, Bush unveiled a new economic stimulus plan with a ten-year price tag of $674 billion. The chief feature of the Bush plan, comprising over half the cost, was an end to the taxation of corporate dividends. While about half of all households hold stock, stock ownership is highly concentrated among the wealthy. According to political analyst Kevin Phillips, the top 1 percent of investors took 42 percent of stock market gains between 1989 and 1997, while the top 10 percent of the population took 86 percent. Many ordinary Americans hold stock only through 401K and other retirement accounts, but under Bush's plan income from this source would remain subject to taxation when withdrawn. Some 40 percent of the benefits of Bush's proposal would have gone to the top one percent of wealthy Americans. Less than 10 percent of this stimulant would have gone to the 80 percent of households earning less than $73,000 a year. As Kevin Phillips put it, though touted as an economic stimulant, "What this complicated proposal would stimulate is not the workaday economy but the already huge gap between the wealthiest Americans and everyone else."

Bush's tax plan was passed by Congress in May of 2003 with a scaled-down $350 billion price tag that masked the real costs. If its provisions were extended, as the White House and Congressional Republicans favored, the true cost over ten years could reach $1 trillion. 53 percent of all U.S. households were to receive a tax cut of $100 or less in 2003 from the bill. 36 percent of households were to receive no tax cut at all in 2003. On the other hand tax filers who made $1 million or more per year were to receive an average tax cut of $93,500. "Ninety-two million Americans will keep an average of $1,083 more of their own money," stated President Bush in introducing his plan. As journalist Hendrik Hertzberg commented, this claim is true "only in the sense that it is also true that if

Bill Gates happened to drop by a homeless shelter where a couple of nuns were serving soup to sixty down-and-outers dressed in rags, the average person in the room would have a net worth of a billion dollars. Average, yes; typical, no." Supporters of the Bush administration's policies accused critics of playing "class warfare" politics. Tax cuts deprive government of funds for domestic spending and thus serve to "starve the beast." At least three-fourths of the swing from surpluses to deficits under Bush can be attributed to a decline in revenues.

Growing budget and trade deficits, combined with other forms of external debt, led the International Monetary Fund (IMF) to issue a report in January 2004 warning that U.S. fiscal policies could destabilize international financial markets. IMF economists were concerned that within several years the U.S. would owe 40 percent of its total economy. Growing deficits could lead to higher interest rates within the U.S. and the rest of the world, choking growth, while a diminishing willingness of foreign investors to purchase U.S. assets might lead to rapid movements in exchange rates. Economic analyst Nick Beams noted, "The problem confronting central bankers and policymakers in the leading capitalist countries is that, while on the one hand world economic growth as a whole is more dependent than ever on the expansion of the U.S. economy, on the other this expansion itself generates ever-increasing levels of debt."

A MANDATE IN 2004?

By early 2004 there were signs of declining public support for the president's agenda. A *New York Times*/CBS News poll in January found Bush's overall job approval rating at 50 percent. Fewer than one in five respondents said Bush had eased their tax burden. Only 27 percent believed the tax cuts were good for the economy, while 17 percent said the tax cuts were bad and 51 percent said the tax cuts had not made much of a difference. The traditional Republican Achilles heel of perceived top-end bias was visible. 57 percent thought Bush generally favored the rich as opposed to the middle class and poor. 64 percent said they thought big business had too much influence on the Bush administration. By March a majority of Americans—57 percent—said they wanted the next president to steer the country away from the course set by Bush, according to a *Washington Post*/ABC News poll. Only 39 percent stated that they supported Bush's handling of the economy. Two-thirds of the poll respondents said that Bush cared more about protecting the interests of large business corporations than working people.

While 60 percent of Americans supported Bush's war on terrorism, doubts grew about the president's handling of Iraq. A February 2004 *Washington Post*/ABC News poll found that 47 percent of Americans approved of Bush's handling of the situation in Iraq, a steep decline. 54 percent of Americans though Bush exaggerated or lied about prewar intelligence. 52 percent believed that Bush was "honest and trustworthy," down from his peak of 71 percent in the summer of 2002, and his worst showing his the question was first asked in 1999. For the first time since the war in Iraq ended, a majority of Americans— 48 percent—said the war was worth fighting. Fifty percent said the war was not worth it.

Despite this weak support, which continued into the autumn, Bush was able to capture 51 percent of the popular vote and 286 electoral votes on November 2. The Bush campaign was able to portray John Kerry as a culturally elitist "flip-flopper" and as a danger to national security in such a way that Kerry's advantage over Bush on economic and other domestic issues was nullified. Bush combined strong support from those making over $200,000 with increased support from downscale, white working class voters in small town and rural areas. According to political analysts John B. Judis and Ruy Teixeira, "Bush recreated the Reagan-era coalition by combining Brooks Brothers and Wal-Mart, the upper class and the lower middle class. . . . reached these voters, who made up the bulk of his support, through opposition to

gay marriage and abortion and through patriotic appeal as the commander-in-chief in a war against terrorism that seamlessly unites Osama bin Laden with Saddam Hussein." These were voters most likely to accept the Bush administrations distorted claims about Iraq and weapons of mass destruction (WMD) and the connection between Iraq and the war on terrorism. A survey found that 72 percent of Bush supporters believed either that Iraq had actual WMD (47 percent) or a major program for making them (25 percent), despite the conclusion of the CIA's Iraq Survey Group that Saddam Hussein had dismantled his WMD programs after the 1991 Gulf war and did not reconstitute them.

After the election President Bush declared that because of his victory, and GOP gains in Congress, he had earned political capital in the election and that he intended to use it to pursue conservative, business-oriented tax, health care, and Social Security policies. However both the election results and post-election polls call into question Bush's claim of a mandate. According to journalist Ronald Brownstein, measured as a share of the popular vote, Bush's 2.9 percent edge over Kerry was the smallest margin of victory for a reelected president since 1828. A post-election CBS News/*New York Times* poll found Bush's overall approval rating at just 51 percent, with 54 percent feeling the country is going in the wrong direction. 57 percent disapproved of Bush's handling of the economy and 55 disapproved of his handling of Iraq. Less than a third thought that Bush's tax cuts since 2001 had been good for the economy and two-thirds thought that large corporations had too much influence on the Bush administration. By more than 2 to 1, the public thought that reducing the federal budget deficit should be a higher priority than cutting taxes. In many ways the American public was at odds with much of Bush's agenda. Still Bush's early post-election political appointments and policy statements appeared to signal renewed determination to consolidate conservative political gains and return the role of government to pre-New Deal, if not Social Darwinian, levels. Whether or not Bush can continue to find political success in advancing his conservative agenda by invoking a never-ending "war on terrorism" will form a large part of the story of his second term.

DISCUSSION QUESTIONS

1. Peschek argues that foreign policy and the war on terrorism has served to distract attention from Bush's weak domestic economic record. What evidence does Peschek provide to support this argument and how compelling do you find it?

2. Supporters of a new American empire argue that the global power of the U.S. is benign and motivated by high moral ideals, in contrast to previous world empires. To what extent do you agree or disagree with this claim?

3. What factors best explain why Bush won reelection in 2004? How do your responses pertain to another question about whether or not Bush has a popular "mandate" for his second term?

CHAPTER 8

Law and
the Courts

Law and courts play a central role in settling political conflicts in the United States, a point driven home by the Supreme Court decision that effectively decided the presidential election of 2000. In part this reflects the dominance of classic liberal thought in America, with its emphasis on resolving disputes through formal procedures. Certainly there is no denying we are a very litigious country, with a presence of lawyers and lawsuits that outstrips most, if not all, of the world's other nations. We also know that a good number of you, political science majors and students in political science courses, are on the road to law school. The articles in this chapter explore connections between law and politics in our legalistic culture, and depict courts and judges as *political* actors whose values and practices usually reinforce the structure of power discussed in Part I.

Because we have a written Constitution that declares itself to be the supreme law of the land, who is authorized to interpret that Constitution becomes a crucial question. In our system, courts, especially the Supreme Court, have assumed this power of judicial review. The 1787 Constitution provided for a separate judicial branch of government but left its powers unclear. In *Federalist Paper 78*, Alexander Hamilton, an advocate of a strong central union, argued for a judiciary with the power to declare acts of the other branches of government unconstitutional. Thomas Jefferson, in contrast, feared the antidemocratic nature of Hamilton's argument, especially because the Constitution exempts the Court from direct democratic control. Jefferson argued that all three branches of government, within their assigned spheres of power, have important constitutional roles to play. The Court, he reasoned, is not the sole arbiter of constitutional questions. And government, ultimately, is answerable to the people. Hamilton's position triumphed when the Supreme Court under John Marshall, who was chief justice from 1801 to 1835, asserted the power of judicial review in the historic *Marbury v. Madison* case of 1803.

CORPORATIONS, THE LAW, AND DEMOCRACY

In this article political scientist Carl Swidorski examines the role of the courts, especially the Supreme Court, in facilitating the development of a capitalist economy and enhancing corporate power. He views law as an arena of political, economic, and social struggles between groups and classes that have taken place throughout U.S. history. Swidorski examines key legal developments related to property rights in the nineteenth century. Next he turns to the transformation of economic doctrines by the Supreme Court to support an emerging corporate-administrative state during and after the New Deal of the 1930s. Swidorski critically examines the important issue of extending First Amendment free speech rights to corporations and the wealthy (see also the next article by Cass Sunstein). He concludes with a discussion of the implications of these developments for politics and democracy in the United States today.

Stocks are property, yes.
Bonds are property, yes.
Machines, land, buildings, are property, yes.
A job is property,
no, nix, nah nah.
(Carl Sandburg, *The People Yes*)

The more we reflect upon all that occurs in the United States, the more we shall be persuaded that the lawyers . . . form the most powerful . . . counterpoise to the democratic element. . . . The courts of justice are the visible organs by which the legal profession is enabled to control democracy . . .

(Alexis de Tocqueville, *Democracy in America*)

At the beginning of a new century, corporations enjoy a privileged legal position in the United States. Corporations can count on the law to protect their property rights and facilitate further transformations of the political economy to their advantage, such as the contemporary shift to a

Source: Adapted by the author from Carl Swidorski, "Corporations and the Law: Historical Lessons for Contemporary Practice." *New Political Science,* no. 28/29, Winter-Spring 1994, pp. 167–189.

globalized, capitalist economy. In conflicts between corporate economic rights and individual personal rights, the law generally favors corporate rights. Furthermore, over the past three decades, the Supreme Court has extended rights to corporations that previously had been primarily conceived of as individual political rights. These decisions have serious implications for democratic dialogue and government. As Ralph Nader and Carl Mayer state: "Equality of constitutional rights plus an inequality of legislated and de facto powers leads inevitably to the supremacy of artificial over real persons." This privileged position of corporations is primarily due to the crucial structural role corporations have played and continue to play in the U.S. economy. Ideological factors, such as the "normal" way of thinking about law, interrelate with these structural features. The way the law—the language of the state—"knows" society is an important dimension in understanding this privileged legal status.

Since the ratification of the U.S. Constitution in 1788, the development of the law has been a process of struggle among classes and groups with different interests, values, and visions. The social and economic assumptions underlying the Constitution primarily favored the property owning classes who dominated the writing and initial interpretation of the Constitution. As Supreme Court Justice William Paterson said in *Van Hornes's Lessee v. Dorrance* (1795): "The right of acquiring and possessing property, and having it protected, is one of the natural, inherent and inalienable rights of man," and preserving property "is a primary object of the social compact." But the framers' vision and that of their successors has always been contested. Reflecting on the historical development of the law, therefore, can help us understand broader political and economic developments and assess the possibilities for progressive politics today. The law is both an effect and a cause of other political, economic, and social forces—it helps constitute a society.

Structurally, corporations are the key economic institutions in society. Major decisions about what is produced by whom, when, where, and under what conditions, are largely controlled by corporations. Governments rely on corporations for revenue, job creation, and investment. Planning, to the degree it exists, is dominated by corporate decisions. Thus, governments are highly responsive to the needs and demands of corporations because the perceived success of our economy depends on ensuring a "favorable business climate."

Ideologically, the belief in the "rule of law" and its accompanying concepts of state neutrality, justice, equality before the law, and individual freedom often inhibits people from looking at the law as an arena of political and economic struggle. As Bertell Ollman points out, the law serves as a kind of "bourgeois fairy tale" in which "the struggle over the legitimacy of any social act or relationship is removed from the plane of morality to that of law. Justice is no longer what is fair but what is legal, and politics itself is transformed into the technical wranglings of lawyers and courts." This ideological function of law limits the examination of the role that the law has played in facilitating capitalist development and corporate power. Many scholars refuse to acknowledge the insight of Thomas Gray: ". . . [F]ederal courts have through most of the country's history been the guardians of wealth and property against the excesses of democracy." This ideological attachment to the "rule of law" also has had important effects on the political strategies chosen by liberal reformers and progressives, thus functioning to organize dissent into certain types of activity.

The law is an arena of political, economic, and social struggle that reflects and helps shape those struggles. Overall, the results of the class and group struggles in U.S. history have favored corporate power. It is hard to understand how anyone today could argue otherwise. Yet the process of struggle is important. Working people, women, African Americans, gays and lesbians, and others have used the law to fight for their rights and, at times, win important gains. Nonetheless, the fundamental contradiction between political democracy and economic exploitation remains embodied in the law, and corporate power has more often prevailed than not. As Brooks Adams said early in the twentieth century: "The capitalist . . . regards the constitutional form of government which exists in the United States, as a convenient method of obtaining his own way against a majority."

In this article I focus on the role of the courts, especially the Supreme Court, in facilitating the development of a capitalist economy and enhancing corporate power. First, I examine key legal developments related to property rights in the nineteenth century. I also survey the metamorphosis in property and related jurisprudential accommodations during the late nineteenth and early twentieth centuries. The second part of the article focuses on the transformation of economic doctrines by the Supreme Court to legitimate a consolidating corporate-administrative state during and after the New Deal. Within this context, I examine the attempt to extend property rights concepts to the poor and contrast this with the recrudescence of property protections for corporations and the wealthy beginning in the 1970s. I also look at the trend of extending First Amendment free speech rights to corporations and the wealthy. Finally, I conclude with a discussion of the implications of these developments for politics and democracy.

COURTS AND PROPERTY RIGHTS BEFORE THE NEW DEAL

There were three important dimensions of the relationship between the law, property rights, and capitalist development during this period. First, in the conflict between slave labor and free labor, legal decisions both protected the system of slavery and, at the same time, fostered the growth of a capitalist economy. Second, in the conflicts between labor and capital, the courts were hostile to the attempt of workers to act collectively. Finally, and most importantly, federal courts, state civil law courts, and legislatures incrementally developed the law to favor the interests of dynamic, entrepreneurial, commercial

capital over land-based, vested capital. The courts were the most influential economic policymakers during this period. It was their responsibility, in the words of Stephen Skowronek, "to nurture, protect, interpret, and invoke the state's prerogatives over economy and society as expressed in law."

Slavery was firmly written into the U.S. Constitution. James Ely states: "No other type of property received such detailed attention from the framers." Slaves were an important form of personal property and a major source of wealth for the antebellum South as well as for those Northern economic interests involved in the trans-Atlantic slave trade, the coastal cotton markets, and the manufacture of textiles. The courts protected this form of property. Individual slaves rarely won freedom in cases in which they contested their condition. The system of slavery itself was never seriously questioned by the federal courts. At the same time, courts recognized the power of states to limit the right of owners to maim and kill their slaves. These regulatory laws were passed not so much out of humanitarian concerns but rather because states recognized the value of slave property for the South's economy, and because states were responding to slave rebellions, sabotage, and other forms of collective actions by African Americans protesting their conditions. In this regard, these slave regulations were similar to much other economic regulation upheld by the courts during this period of time under the broad "police powers" of states to legislate for the health, safety, and welfare of the community.

The second major property rights issue of the period involved the conflict between organized labor and capital. After the Civil War, the courts' general hostility toward labor unions would be graphically demonstrated through their authorization of the widespread use of police and military force against striking and picketing workers, their use of the infamous labor injunction, and their hostility toward social welfare legislation that benefited working Americans. The judiciary used the labor injunction not just to control strikes and demonstrations but to limit the associative and expressive activities of workers and their unions. Over 4,300 injunctions were issued against the labor movement between 1880 and 1930, forbidding a wide variety of associative activities including picketing, striking, holding union meetings, communicating through the mail, saying specific words such as "scab" or "fair," and even supplying food to starving workers and their families. In addition to the use of the injunction, courts struck down social welfare laws such as those establishing minimum wages and maximum hours, requiring safe conditions at work, and forbidding child labor. Between 1900 and 1937, the judiciary ruled unconstitutional over two hundred state social welfare laws or laws regulating business on the grounds that they violated the "due process" or "equal protection" of corporations or individuals with property rights claims. Furthermore, between the 1880s and 1920s courts struck down almost three hundred labor laws aimed at protecting workers.

The third category of significant legal developments during this period was the efforts by the courts and legislatures to promote economic development and stimulate investment by favoring the dynamic use of property. J. Willard Hurst calls it "property in motion or at risk rather than property secure and at rest." State legislatures sold or gave away public lands; subsidized businesses; sponsored internal improvement projects, especially in transportation; and passed a variety of other forms of promotional legislation to stimulate commercial activities. States even went so far as to delegate their own governmental powers of eminent domain to business corporations. The Supreme Court under Chief Justice John Marshall (1801–1835) was especially sympathetic to business and propertied interests. Marshall was very committed to creating a national market and distrusted those state regulations that he feared would interfere with the productive use of economic resources. The contract clause was used to protect the nascent form of corporate organization from excessive state regulation, especially in the banking sector, as well as to limit the ability of states to provide relief to debtors and grant

exemptions from taxation. The Marshall Court also relied on a broad interpretation of the national commerce power to encourage the growth of a national market system particularly in transportation. Under Roger Taney (1836–1863), the Supreme Court continued this approach, although it was more inclined to permit states greater latitude in shaping economic policy that stimulated commercial activities and promoted competition. Also, corporations were constitutionally recognized as "persons" for the first time for the purpose of suing in diversity of citizenship cases in the federal courts.

State courts also played a major role in promoting economic growth through the legal system, instead of the tax system. Private law judges interpreting the common law promoted economic development and carried out a major transformation of the legal system. According to Morton Horwitz, their decisions "enabled emergent entrepreneurial and commercial groups to win a disproportionate share of wealth and power in American society." Judges came to view the ownership of property as conferring the right, and indeed obligation, to develop the property. Eminent domain was one of the most potent legal weapons used to further this process of redistributing "old" property for the benefit of the "new." Land was taken for the purposes of building roads, canals, and railroads. Compensation for these takings was limited because entrepreneurial groups resisted full compensation as a threat to low cost economic development. Another method of encouraging economic growth was changing the common law doctrines on liability to force those injured by economic activity to bear many of the costs of growth. Personal or property damage increasingly became seen as an inevitable cost of doing business, largely to be absorbed by the injured. Finally, the law of contract was transformed, ridding it of medieval concepts of fairness and shifting it to principles compatible with a market economy, such as *caveat emptor* (let the buyer beware).

The courts' role in fostering economic development for the advantage of the more powerful continued after the Civil War. Initially, the Supreme Court upheld broad use of government powers over the economy during the Civil War. Furthermore, courts upheld many state laws regulating the economy during the 1870s and 1880s. However, during the 1870s and 1880s, certain judges and lawyers conducted a vigorous campaign to develop the legal doctrine of laissez-faire constitutionalism to protect corporations from regulatory activity. A key decision was the 1886 *Santa Clara County v. Southern Pacific Railroad* ruling that corporations were "persons" within the meaning of the Fourteenth Amendment, having the same rights as natural persons. After this, the Supreme Court regularly struck down the state and national regulatory regulation that it felt to be unduly restrictive of property rights.

While the legal foundation of the corporate-administrative state was laid between 1900 and 1932, the Court's negative reaction to many of the New Deal programs reflected contradictory nineteenth century visions of free enterprise, competitive capitalism, and "free" labor. However, in 1937 the Court underwent a miraculous change of heart and mind and began to uphold regulatory schemes it had just recently rejected. By 1939, FDR had appointed a majority of the Court, and according to conventional wisdom, the new Roosevelt Court rejected those old economic doctrines that had been selectively used to defeat a great deal of regulatory legislation for over half a century. The Court supposedly washed its hands entirely of economic policy making and slowly took up a new agenda of individual political and civil rights. However, the conventional wisdom is substantially misplaced.

THE MODERN ROLE OF THE LAW: LEGITIMATING THE NEW CORPORATE-ADMINISTRATIVE STATE

The idealized conception of the modern Supreme Court as the guardian of individual rights and defender of transcendental constitutional values has been problematic even for some mainstream political scientists. To Robert Dahl the Court was a legitimator of the political system not a defender of rights. He argued that the Court had "used the protections of the Fifth, Thirteenth, Fourteenth, and Fifteenth Amendments to preserve the rights and liberties of a relatively privileged group at the expense of the rights and liberties of a submerged group, chiefly slaveholders at the expense of slaves, white people at the expense of colored people, and property holders at the expense of wage earners and other groups." Yet subsequent assessments of the Court by political scientists have tended to stress the Court's role as "guardian of the Constitution." Even mildly debunking analyses still assume the Court is democratic because it plays a vital legitimizing role in a fundamentally fair, pluralistic political system. However, a more realistic assessment of the role of law and the Supreme Court must place the change in the Court's agenda and doctrines within the context of the changes in the modern capitalist economy, especially the relationship among corporations, government, and organized labor.

After 1937, the Court transformed judicial doctrine to ratify the new social contract of big business, the state, and the unions. Under its terms unions became junior partners in return for recognition and protection of their right to organize, promises of higher wages and better working conditions, and various social programs. Government assumed important responsibilities for rationalizing the market and managing the economy. The new social contract did not challenge capitalism or seriously undermine corporate prerogatives. Instead, it used the expertise of the modern state to coordinate, guide, and supplement the functioning of the capitalist economy. The Court also attempted to manage social conflict by ensuring formal, but limited, representation for "legitimate" affected interests in the administrative agencies of the corporate-administrative state. To the degree racial minorities, women, the poor, consumers, and environmentalists transformed themselves into *organized* interests they became incorporated in varying degrees in the new social compact.

The symbol of the new judicial attitude in economic matters was the famous footnote number four of *U.S. v. Carolene Products* of 1938 that established the "double standard" for due process review. According to this doctrine, the Court would employ different levels of judicial scrutiny to personal or civil rights as opposed to traditional property rights. Legislative regulation of property would be presumed constitutional and subject only to minimal scrutiny to determine if there was a rational basis for the regulation. On the other hand, stricter judicial scrutiny would apply to individual rights under any of three conditions: 1) where fundamental rights were involved; 2) where laws restricted access to the political process; and 3) where governmental action was directed against "discrete and insular" minorities.

To mainstream analysts, the double standard symbolized a Court committed to protecting individual rights and abandoning its historical regard for property rights. However, as Michael McCann makes clear, the "result was nothing less than a significant qualitative transformation in the constitutional status of 'property' itself." Property in a corporate society was no longer perceived as a relatively unfettered domain of freedom or autonomy, but increasingly a set of relationships with the modern administrative state. The Court gradually realized that its dominant purpose was no longer the prevention of unauthorized intrusions on private property, but the assurance of "fair" representation for all organized interests in the corporate-administrative state. The courts adopted an idealized version of democratic elitism. The United States was seen as a pluralistic, liberal society in which all "legitimate" interests were guaranteed representation and the right to pursue their self-interests. The courts' principal functions were protecting individual political liberties to participate in the game of politics and ensuring that the rules of the game were fairly administered.

LABOR LAW AND CORPORATE CAPITALISM

Labor law offers a good illustration of the legal role in constructing an ideology and an institutional structure to support corporate capitalism. On the one hand, labor law is class-based and justifies hierarchy and domination in the workplace and the community. For example, the preeminent importance of capital mobility and ease of disinvestment is supported by the law. Communities surrounding a plant have few legally protected interests in decisions a company makes affecting that community. Employees do not have a legally recognized interest in the fruits of their labor or the management of a company, much less a right to a job. Management decision about operations and resource allocations, even unauthorized commands, must be obeyed pending completion of grievance procedures. The workplace, both physically and existentially, belongs to the employer and workers acquire no rights or entitlements there, unless contractually conceded. And even here, companies have maneuverability as evidence by the use of Chapter VI bankruptcy filings to avoid contractual obligations.

On the other hand, labor law reflects the contractions of the modern social contract. It both fosters and constricts worker self-expression. Workers are allowed to organize, and prior to the 1970s, this right was even protected by the National Labor Relations Board (NLRB). But at the same time, labor law tries to guide worker activity into narrow, institutionalized channels in which only "legitimate" conflict is permitted. Forms of worker activity such as wildcat strikes, sit-down strikes, and secondary boycotts are prohibited even under life-threatening conditions. Workers must go through the proper legal procedures to gain recognition as a union or to protest management practices. These administrative requirements moderate social conflict and prevent it from spilling over beyond acceptable boundaries.

Labor law also encourages, yet limits, employee participation in the workplace. Worker participation is facilitated but largely confined to wages and working conditions. The attempts of workers to influence the organization of the work process or decisions about investment, disinvestment, and long-range planning are restricted. The law recognizes a core of managerial prerogatives where decisions are not negotiable. The more important the issue is to employer control the fewer the legal bargaining rights for workers. Finally, labor law enhances the institutional interest of unions at the expense of their own members. In return, unions have accepted a role in preserving industrial peace and performing managerial and disciplinary functions in the workplace.

In sum, labor law reflects the priorities of corporate liberalism. It allows limited opportunities for working people to fight for their rights but increasingly, under this legal model, working people are losing. This legal framework sees conflict as interest-group based, not class-based. It assumes that economic growth is the primary social goal. Permissible conflict by "legitimate" interests is to be directed by the state into acceptable channels and resolved administratively or judicially. Many important societal decisions remain off the public agenda because they are the prerogatives of those who control the corporate-dominated private sphere. The Court has acknowledged this function of labor law in its decision in *First National Maintenance Corporation v. NLRB* of 1981:

> A fundamental aim of the National Labor Relations Act is the establishment and maintenance of industrial peace . . . Central to the achievement of this purpose is the promotion of collective bargaining as a method of defusing and channeling conflict between labor and management . . . In view of an employer's need for unencumbered decision making, bargaining over management decisions that have a substantial impact on the continued availability of employment should be required only if the benefit for labor-management relations and the collective bargaining process, outweighs the burden placed on the conduct of the business.

FREE SPEECH AND PROPERTY RIGHTS

First Amendment decisions of the last two decades provide a clear example of how the law poses a set of contradictions for those seeking fundamental change in the United States. The "Free Speech Tradition" embodies valuable, hard-won rights for Americans. Yet recent decisions of the Supreme Court show how the First Amendment can be interpreted to limit the rights supposedly contained within it. For example, the Court has shrunk the scope of the public sphere in decisions involving conflicts between freedom of expression and private property. It has refused to equate shopping centers with public streets or parks and allowed mall owners to restrict access to and expression in "private" spaces. The Court also has limited handbilling on a military base crisscrossed by public roads; permitted a city to allow the use of placard space on public buses for commercial advertising but not for political advertising; and limited press access to jails and pretrial hearings. These decisions suggest that while ownership of or access to property, especially the corporate controlled media, is necessary to effectively exercise one's speech and press rights. The law supports restrictions on such access.

Another series of decisions, dealing with commercial speech, has continued the historical pattern of increasing the constitutional protection of corporations as "persons" with individual rights. Prior to 1975 commercial advertising had not enjoyed full First Amendment protection. However, in *Bigelow v. Virginia* of 1975 the Court decided that commercial speech was protected, finding a public, consumer interest in such speech. A series of other decisions extended these "consumer rights," illustrating the contradictions involved when a liberal, market-based conception of personal liberties is used to interpret the First Amendment. Similar to the way in which the worker's "right to work" was used in the past to legally restrict trade union organizing and enhance corporate power, consumers' "rights to know" have become the basis for the empowerment of corporations and advertising agencies, not consumers. Even more significantly, the Court extended corporations free speech rights and the full protection of the First Amendment in *Consolidated Edison v. Public Service Commis-*

sion of 1980. A New York State Public Service Commission regulation prohibiting public utilities from enclosing statements of their views on public issues along with monthly bills was ruled an unconstitutional restriction of a corporation's free speech. Using the same logic, the Court also struck down a ban on utility advertising promoting the use of electricity.

Several related cases further demonstrate the Court's solicitude for expanding speech rights for corporations and the wealthy. In *Miami Herald Publishing Company v. Tornillo* of 1974, Florida's right-of-reply statute, compelling a newspaper to furnish cost-free reply space, was unanimously struck down as an abridgment of the paper's private property rights and its free speech rights to exclude access by third parties. The Court also invalidated a Massachusetts law forbidding corporations from spending corporate funds to influence public referenda (*First National Bank v. Belotti* of 1978). Finally, the 2000 presidential election illustrates the significance of two Court decisions dealing with campaign finance reform and third party access to the nation's voters through media. In 1976, the Court struck down provisions of the Federal Election Campaign Act that placed limits on the amount of money individuals could spend independently to support political candidates as well as limitations on the amount candidates could spend on their own campaigns (*Buckley v. Valeo*). Spending money was seen by the Justices as a form of protected speech, not just speech-related conduct. In 1998, the Court ruled that a decision by a state-operated television station to deny a third party candidate the right to participate in a televised congressional candidate debate did not violate the candidate's First Amendment rights or the public's rights to freedom of information (*Arkansas Educational Television Commission v. Forbes*). According to John Shockley: ". . . [T]he Court has in fact used the First Amendment to protect the influence of the wealthy in American politics, reshaping [the First] Amendment . . . into a means to afford both fundamental and exclusive protection to the wealthy in the political process."

Rather than seeing such decisions as victories for abstract principles of free speech, such as "consumers' rights," we should understand their class dimensions—they benefit the wealthy and corporations over ordinary citizens. These kinds of decisions reveal the structural character of class inequality embedded in U.S. constitutional law. As Michael McCann points out, they parallel "the older judicial activism not only in its substantive and economic character but also in its fundamental, if more subtle, embrace of ideas supporting uniquely capitalist forms of social organization against substantive egalitarian challenge . . . The Court still adheres to the established constitutional tradition of limiting concern for systemic socioeconomic inequalities to an individualistic, exchange-oriented logic of public goods allocation."

RECENT JUDICIAL TRENDS

Over the past decade, to the disappointment of many conservative legal scholars and judges, the Supreme Court has not issued any major decision that significantly challenges the constitutional principles on which the corporate-administrative state was established after 1937. After all, deregulation, privatization, and the legal changes needed for globalization have been carried out under that system through the legislative and executive branches without the need of any significant judicial involvement. Corporations have learned that they can use their power in legislatures, administrative agencies, political parties, the media, and the universities to accomplish their goals without having to rely on the kind of constitutional doctrines prevalent before 1937. Therefore, the courts have tinkered at the edges of constitutional property doctrine. Recent decisions in the area of federalism, limiting the national government's powers over the states, whether based on grounds of sovereign immunity or of narrower congressional power under the commerce clause and Fourteenth Amendment, may be indirectly beneficial to corporations, but they do not pose a major challenge to the legal foundations of the corporate-administrative state. Occasionally some Justices have hinted at the possibility of significantly changing the post-1937 system, but that is quite unlikely until the economic foundations of that system significantly change.

The judiciary also has been involved during the past two decades in reversing or limiting some of the reforms of the 1960s and 1970s in areas such as individual liberties, affirmative action, freedom of choice, and access to the courts. While many of these decisions have class dimensions and have negative implications for democracy, they also do not directly affect the corporate-administrative system of property that was able to survive, and even flourish, during the period when these liberal reforms were more firmly in place.

However, there is one other area—labor relations—in which the judiciary has played a significant role in protecting corporate power, especially since the Reagan administration. A 2000 report of Human Rights Watch concludes that workers in the U.S. lack the rights to organize, bargain, and strike supposedly guaranteed in the First Amendment's provision of freedom of association and expression, and in internationally recognized human rights norms. The report finds that employers are free to fire, harass, and intimidate with impunity workers trying to organize unions; to refuse to bargain with workers who successfully have stepped over the legal hurdles placed in the way of organizing; and to make the right to strike a travesty by permanently replacing strikers. Furthermore, the report states that millions of workers in the United States are denied coverage of the labor laws that do exist. While some of these principles have been in place since the passage of the Wagner Act in 1935, courts and the National Labor Relations Board have made matters much worse for the labor movement since the Reagan administration. In the process, they have demonstrated the normal, historical tendency of the law to support and facilitate the exercise of corporate power.

CONCLUSION

So what role does the law play in making anything really different as opposed to supporting the status quo or the kind of reforms that give us more of the same? First, we should not see the law cynically as merely an instrument of class oppression or ideological co-optation. Neither should we see it idealistically as fundamentally autonomous of economic power, and therefore, a principal means to bring about reform. This law can be, and to a degree has been, both a force for maintaining the status quo and an instrument of reform, even sometimes radical reform. However, those forces with the most political-economic power historically have been the most successful in using the law to promote their interests just as they have been in using the media, education, religion, and political parties. The law is one important arena of struggle we should not dismiss. Neither should we be unrealistic about its possibilities. The real issue is about the role law can play in contesting power—a very difficult proposition indeed, given the tendency of those who have power to hold onto it with all the forces at their disposal.

Second, with this realization, is a major issue of *how* the law can be used to contest power. To the degree that the law can be used within the established political process, judicial strategies for change are less desirable than legislative strategies. The historical record here seems clear. Throughout most of our history, the courts have been one of the most conservative institutions in society. Their patterns of recruitment, socialization, and decision-making all contribute to this. Judges are relatively insulated from public pressures and accountability; are non-representative of the larger population; and are socialized to "know" the law as a non-political, neutral process. Given this, few judges see their role as that of agents of social reform other than through helping adapt the system to necessary economic and political changes.

Too many baby-boomer liberals and legal reformers grew up with an idealized image of the

Warren Court as a liberal instrument of change that fostered the Civil Rights movement and tried to bring about other significant changes in U.S. politics until it was frustrated by the Nixon administration. To a minor degree this was true, but it is more mythology than history. The liberal record of the Warren Court contained more blemishes than is often acknowledged; the Warren Court operated within prevailing liberal, individualistic, market-oriented conceptions of society, which largely denied the reality of class or group solutions to social problems; and, to the degree it fostered progressive change, it was facilitating the development of the U.S. post-World War II political economy, just as courts had facilitated capitalist economic development previously. It is more accurate to see the Warren Court as an institution of legitimation and social conflict management than of progressive reform.

Over the last half-century, more reform, even if it was not fundamental, has been brought about through the legislative than the judicial process. For every *Brown v. Board of Education* or *Baker v. Carr* there are many more laws such as the National Labor Relations Act, Civil Rights Act of 1964, and Voting Rights Act of 1965. Quite often, even when progressive legislation is passed, the courts are more likely to interpret the legislation to limit, rather than enhance, the reforms instituted, as indicated by the courts' interpretation of civil rights, labor, and campaign finance reform legislation over the last twenty-five years. Therefore, to the degree people use the law as a vehicle for change, it should de-emphasize, judicial-based strategies.

If legislative legal strategies are more likely to be effective, then how do people participate in changing the law? While not completely dismissing the idea of changing the law by changing people's consciousness, I think language-based strategies are limited. Political activity, both inside and outside established political processes,

which leads to laws changing people's material reality, is more important, and in the process is more likely to affect people's consciousness. A law guaranteeing a sustainable income or national health care as a right of citizenship in a modern society can be much more effective in changing people's consciousness than attempts to do so through using language and persuasion to reconstitute their beliefs.

We must remember that a political-economic system dominated by large corporations will tend to have laws reflecting that power and protecting the property interests of those corporations. As Raymond Williams has stated:

> . . . Laws are necessarily the instruments of a particular social order. None can survive without them. But then what is at issue, in any conflict about particular law, is the underlying definition of the desired social order . . . To challenge that order is to challenge those laws.

Challenging that order necessitates challenging capitalism. Many people today do not want to talk about this. They hope to bring about progressive change by avoiding a discussion of the inherent, exploitative characteristics of capitalism. They seem to be hoping for some form of "friendly capitalism." But we need to move beyond capitalism if we are to create a decent, just, and humane world.

DISCUSSION QUESTIONS

1. In what ways does Swidorski's analysis challenge the notion of the neutrality of the law?
2. To what extent does Swidorski see a role for law and the courts in creating social change? Compare his views on this issue with those of Howard Zinn on the Constitution in Article 12.

CASS R. SUNSTEIN

IS FREE SPEECH THE ENEMY
OF DEMOCRACY?

In this provocative essay legal scholar and political theorist Cass R. Sunstein lays bare the flawed reasoning behind arguments that invoke freedom of speech to protect the current system of media ownership and campaign finance. Sunstein rejects libertarian views of the First Amendment as flawed in the same way as free market concepts of the economy are defective. He contends that we need a New Deal for speech that would extend some of the ideas of the economic New Deal of the 1930s to the political arena of the 1990s. Of course a regulated regime of expression sounds ominous to many Americans, even if its goal is to promote democratic deliberation. But many legal scholars and political analysts share Sunstein's view that the 1976 Buckley v. Valeo *Supreme Court decision, which rejected campaign spending limits as a violation of free speech rights, rests on outmoded legal reasoning. Sunstein's article, published in 1993, opens on a note of hope for democratic reform. Political developments since then, including passage of the much debated McCain-Feingold bill in 2002, show the difficulties of achieving reform, but Sunstein suggests some of the key changes in our political and legal thinking that may be necessary if we are to reclaim democracy.*

For the first time in twenty years, democratic reform is on the American political agenda. Indeed, there is reason to hope that the 1990s will be an important period of political renewal. The new administration and Congress are showing interest in regulations of campaign finance that would help reduce the influence of wealth on elections. Reformers are also exploring strategies for increasing public attention to political issues in campaigns and indeed in daily life. Proposals here range from diminishing the power of advertisers over programming content to encouraging greater network coverage of public issues and ensuring diversity in that coverage. Some even hold out the hope that—in the words of the Clinton/Gore campaign monograph, *Putting People First*—television might be turned from "a weapon of political assassination" into "an instrument of education."

Such proposals are extremely attractive. At a minimum, they could help to conform American practice to the best current approaches in West-

Source: Cass R. Sunstein, "Is Free Speech the Enemy of Democracy?" *Boston Review*, vol. 18, no. 2, March-April 1993.

ern Europe. More ambitiously, they could set new standards for promoting democratic goals and political deliberation.

These attractions notwithstanding, reform proposals face serious obstacles, and from an odd quarter. According to some analysts, there are high constitutional hurdles to regulating political contributions and expenditures or commercial broadcasting, even in the name of democratic reform. Some people argue that such efforts would inevitably violate the First Amendment prohibition on laws abridging freedom of speech and of the press. In short, they interpret the First Amendment as hostile to democratic renewal.

I think that this understanding of the First Amendment depends on a large mistake. It is precisely the mistake that fueled early constitutional objections to President Roosevelt's New Deal. In that earlier period, too, libertarianism was an important constitutional faith. And keepers of that faith—including a majority of the justices of the Supreme Court—argued that constitutional protections of liberty precluded democratic experimentation with the economy. In arriving at this conclusion, they identified the economic status quo with a system of constitutional freedom.

The 1930s New Deal for the economy ultimately triumphed over this economic libertarianism. The intellectual background of that triumph lay in the insistence by supporters of the New Deal on a simple point: that the economic status quo was a product of legal rules and political decisions and not simply free, individual market choices. Emphasizing the legal and political foundations of the economic status quo, the New Dealers rejected the identification of that status quo with genuine freedom and so dismissed the idea that new forms of regulation of the market would necessarily restrict liberty.

We now need a New Deal for speech, one that would extend some of the ideas of the economic New Deal to the political arena. A New Deal for speech would require a new understanding of freedom of expression. That understanding would draw a sharp distinction between a "marketplace of ideas" and a system of democratic deliberation.

It would be more self-consciously focused on our constitutional aspirations to democracy. In the name of those aspirations, it would reject our current system of regulation of expression and support a good deal of new government regulation of speech. But to proceed down this path we need first to embrace the key insight of the original New Deal about the legal-political foundations of "free markets." Applied to speech, that insight shows that our current "marketplace of ideas" is itself a system of regulation, not an untrammeled intellectual bazaar. So the choice we now face is not "leaving expression unregulated" or "regulating" it, but deciding among different systems of regulation, some of which serve the aims of democratic deliberation better than others.

POLITICS AND MARKETS

To understand what I have in mind, I need to say a little more about the original New Deal. From about 1905 to 1935, the Constitution was regularly invoked to prohibit efforts by states or the nation to address economic ills. For example, minimum wage and maximum hour laws were seen as unjustifiable exactions—"takings"—from employers for the benefit of employees and the public at large. Government must be neutral in general and between employers and employees in particular. It should respect their free choices. A violation of the neutrality requirement, thus understood, would count as a violation of the constitutional protection of liberty.

In practice, this meant that the Constitution prohibited government interference with the economic status quo—with existing distributions of economic rights and entitlements. In the pre-New Deal view, existing distributions marked the boundary not only between partisanship and neutrality, but between government action and inaction as well. When government protected existing distributions, it was not really acting at all, but only permitting free market choices to determine wages and hours. When the government altered the existing distributions—for example, imposing a minimum wage—it would be seen as "acting," thus raising constitutional doubts. The rallying cry "laissez-faire" captured such ideas. The fear of, and more importantly, the very conception of "government intervention" resulted from this basic approach.

The New Deal reformers insisted that this entire framework was built on fictions. President Roosevelt referred to "this man-made world of ours" and emphasized that "economic laws are not made by nature. They are made by human beings." The pre-New Deal framework treated the existing distribution of resources and opportunities as pre-political. It saw minimum wage and maximum hour laws as introducing government into an otherwise private or voluntary sphere. But the New Dealers claimed that legal rules of property, contract, and tort produced the set of entitlements that ultimately yielded market hours and wages. Those hours and wages were not part of a voluntary, law-free realm; they were an artifact of legal choices.

In fact, to the New Deal reformers, the very terms "free market," "regulation," and "government intervention" were misleading. The laissez-faire system itself required government allocations of legal rights, and government protection of those rights. In allocating those rights and providing that protection, the government was acting. The government did not "act" only when it disturbed existing distributions. The initial problem with the system of "laissez-faire" was therefore conceptual. The term itself was a conspicuous fiction.

The New Dealers, of course, were not interested in simply registering this conceptual point. Their principal aim was to reject the libertarian's a priori identification of markets with liberty, and to insist that we evaluate different regulatory systems pragmatically and in terms of their consequences for social efficiency and social justice. The New Dealers understood that in general, a market system—for property or for speech—promotes both liberty and prosperity; its inevitable origins in law do not undermine that fact. But the New Dealers thought that courts should respect democratic judgments about the need to limit free markets, and reject an easy resort to the Constitution to pre-empt those judgments. A democratic conclusion that free markets sometimes constrained liberty—embodied in a law calling for maximum hours or minimum wages—was plausible and entitled to judicial respect. Such regulations might be wise or unwise, but the Constitution should not serve as an obstacle.

CONSTITUTIONALISM, DEMOCRACY, AND SPEECH

These ideas have played astonishingly little role in the law of free speech. For purposes of speech, our current understandings of partisanship and neutrality, or government action and inaction, are identical to those that predate the New Deal. The chief failing of American thought with respect to free speech is that it has not taken the New Deal reformation seriously enough.

To understand the point, we need to have a sense of what a successful system of free expression should look like. I suggest that such a system must promote democratic goals, which have of course been a prime impetus behind our enthusiasm for a free speech principle. To promote those goals, the system should have two minimal features.

First, it should allow for *broad and deep public attention* to public issues. An absence of information and attention is a decisive problem for the system. Serious issues must be covered, and they must be covered in a serious way. Indeed, the mere availability of such coverage may not be enough if few citizens take advantage of it, and if most viewers and readers are content with programming that does not deal in depth with public issues.

Second, there must be public exposure to *an appropriate diversity of view.* The kind of diversity that counts as appropriate is, of course, controversial. I suggest only that a broad spectrum of opinion must be represented, that people must be allowed to hear divergent views, and that it is important to find not merely the conventional wisdom, but also challenges to the conventional wisdom from different perspectives. Without exposure to such perspectives, public deliberation will be far less successful, and the democratic system will be badly compromised.

A system of free markets in speech often fails on the relevant counts; regulatory reforms could make things better. I do not claim that speech rights should be freely subject to political determination, as are current issues of occupational safety and health, for instance. I do, however, insist that in some circumstances, policies that seem to involve government regulation of speech actually might promote the depth and diversity that are central to a system of free speech, and should not be treated as abridgments at all. I mean also to argue that what seems to be free speech in markets might, in some circumstances, amount to an abridgment of free speech.

It will be tempting to think that any such argument amounts to a bizarre plea for more government control of speech. But this criticism misses the point. Suppose, for example, that someone tries to get access to the airwaves to make a political statement. Suppose, too, that the networks, refused to allow the statement to air. If so, then the government's own grant of legal protection—rights of exclusive use—to the networks might itself be responsible for compromising democratic values. The exclusion of the would-be speaker is not simply a product of the choices of the networks. It is made possible by the law of civil and criminal trespass. If government changed the rules—if networks were required to present competing perspectives—then the networks would not be able to make the choices they now make.

Here, then, is the lesson of the New Deal for speech: The state is deeply implicated in, indeed responsible for, what we now count as "private" action in the marketplace of ideas. We cannot have markets without law. This is not an argument against markets, but we should judge the status quo and efforts at reform by their conse-quences, not by question-begging characterizations of "threats from government." Efforts to promote greater quality and diversity in broadcasting, for example, seek a new and better regulatory regime, not to replace freedom with "government intervention."

BROADCASTING, CITIZENSHIP, DEMOCRACY

If we wanted to increase the democratic character of our politics, we would explore many proposals for reform. I deal with broadcasting regulation in some detail; the area has obvious general importance, and it can serve as a case study having broad implications. I discuss some of these implications in the case of campaign finance regulation.

Regulation of Broadcasting

For much of its history, the Federal Communications Commission (F.C.C.) imposed the "fairness doctrine" on broadcast licensees. Among other things, the fairness doctrine required licensees to devote time to issues of public importance and to broadcast speech by people of diverse views.

The last decade witnessed a mounting constitutional assault on the fairness doctrine. One reason for the doctrine was the scarcity of licenses, but licenses are no longer scarce. The F.C.C. concluded in the 1980s that the fairness doctrine violates the First Amendment because it is an effort by government to prevent broadcasters from choosing what they say.

The Constitution does forbid any "law abridging the freedom of speech." But is the fairness doctrine such a law? An alternative view is that the fairness doctrine promotes "the freedom of speech" by broadening access to the airwaves and ensuring more diversity than the market provides. Perhaps this is true; perhaps not. Even to address this issue, however, we need first to reject the F.C.C.'s contention that the fairness doctrine represents impermissible government interference with an otherwise law-free and voluntary private sphere. Extending the insights of the New Dealers, we should assess the fairness doctrine by exploring the relationships between the goals of a system of free expression and various alternative regulatory systems.

Three assessments of these alternatives naturally suggest themselves. First, courts might decide that the current broadcast market—without requirements of fairness—is unconstitutional because the existing property rights produce little political discussion or exclude certain views. (Recall that exclusion is a product of law.) Pursuing this path, they might conclude that the fairness doctrine is not simply permissible, but actually mandated by the Constitution. I think that courts should be cautious about reaching this conclusion, in part because the issue turns on complex factual issues not easily within judicial competence. A second possibility is that fairness-style regulation of the market might be upheld if the legislature has made a considered judgment, based on a factual record, that the particular regulation will promote First Amendment goals. The third possibility is to invalidate government regulation of the market because it discriminates on the basis of the viewpoint of speakers, or actually diminishes either attention to public affairs or diversity of view.

The first lesson of the New Deal for speech is that judgments about the consistency of proposed regulations with the First Amendment must depend in large part on the facts. So let's consider some of them.

Some Facts

We now have a good deal of information on the content of broadcasting. For example, local television news devotes very little time to genuine news. Instead, coverage is principally devoted to movies, television programs, and sensationalized disasters. During a half-hour of news programming, no more than eight to twelve minutes involve news. Moreover, the stories themselves—which tend to focus on fires, accidents, and crimes—typically last for twenty to thirty seconds. Coverage of government tends not to describe the content of relevant policies, but instead focuses on brief "soundbites" or sensational and often misleading "human impact" anecdotes. In addition, there has been greater emphasis on "features" dealing with popular actors, or entertainment shows, or even the movie immediately preceding the news. Economic pressures seem to be pushing local news in this direction even if reporters might prefer to deal with public issues more seriously.

With respect to network news, the pattern is similar. Consider the coverage of presidential elections. In 1988, the average "soundbite" from the candidates was about ten seconds long, a dramatic contrast to the much longer and more substantive excerpts in the 1960s. In the same year, almost 60 percent of the national campaign coverage involved "horse race" issues—who was winning, who had momentum—while about 30 percent involved issues and qualifications. In 1992, there was a preliminary effort to counteract the "sound-bite" phenomenon, but by the end of the campaign, the average length of candidate statements was even smaller than in 1988—about eight seconds.

There is evidence as well of advertiser influence over programming content. No conspiracy theory appears plausible; but some recent events are disturbing. Advertisers have a large impact on local news programs, especially consumer reports. Advertisers appear especially reluctant to sponsor material that deals with controversial subjects or that endorses a controversial point of view. It is for this reason unlikely that a program taking (for example) a pro-life or pro-choice position could attract sponsors during primetime. Indeed, there are many examples of advertisers refusing to fund or withdrawing support from shows that do not create "a favorable buying atmosphere"—including shows that are politically controversial, that put businesses generally in an unfavorable light, or that are "depressing."

Educational programming for children, meanwhile, simply cannot acquire sponsors. In 1974, the F.C.C. concluded that "broadcasters have a special obligation to serve children," and thus pressured the industry to adopt codes calling for educational programs. But in 1981, the new F.C.C. Chair, Mark Fowler, rejected this approach. For Fowler, "television is just another appliance. It's a toaster with pictures." Shortly thereafter, network programming for children dramatically decreased, and programs based on products increased.

Correctives and the First Amendment

Regulatory strategies cannot solve all of these problems, but they could help with some of them.

For example, there appears to be a strong case for public provision of high quality programming for children, or for obligations, imposed by government on broadcasters, to provide such programming. The provision of free media time to candidates would be especially helpful, simultaneously providing attention to public affairs and diversity of view, while overcoming some of the distorting effects of "soundbites" and financial pressures.

More dramatically, government might require purely commercial stations to provide financial subsidies to public television or to commercial stations that agree to provide less profitable high quality programming. Or government might award subsidies or "points" to license applicants who promise to deal with serious questions or provide public affairs broadcasting even if unsupported by market demand.

Many steps might be taken to reduce the effects of advertising on program content. We might impose a tax on advertising proceeds from the newspaper or broadcasting industry as a whole and use the proceeds to subsidize circulation or programming. (Sweden does something of this sort.) The consequence should be to decrease the incentive to respond to advertising desires and to increase responsiveness to readers and viewers—while at the same time increasing attention to controversial issues.

It is worthwhile to consider more dramatic approaches as well. These might include rights of reply for both candidates and commentators, reductions in advertising on children's television, content review of children's television by nonpartisan experts, or guidelines in the form of recommendations designed to encourage attention to public issues and diversity of view.

Objections

Of course there may be problems with some of these proposals. One general objection is that in an era of cable television, the problems I have described disappear. People can always change the channel. Some stations even provide public affairs broadcasting around the clock. Both quality and diversity can be found as a result of the dazzling array of options made available by modern technology. Why should a foreclosure of expressive options not be viewed as an infringement on the freedom of speech?

The most basic response is that we should be extremely cautious about the use, for constitutional and political purposes, of the notion of "consumer sovereignty." Consumer sovereignty is the conventional economic term for the virtues of a free market, in which commodities are allocated through consumer choices, as measured through the criterion of private willingness to pay. Those who invoke free choice in markets are really insisting on consumer sovereignty as the governing free speech principle. But the constitutional conception of "sovereignty" is the relevant one for First Amendment purposes, and that conception has an altogether different character.

According to the constitutional conception of sovereignty, we should respect not private consumption choices, but the considered judgments of free and equal citizens. In a well-functioning polity, laws frequently reflect those judgments—what might be described as the convictions of the public as a whole. Those convictions can and often do call for markets themselves. But they might also diverge from consumption choices—a familiar phenomenon in such areas as environmental law, protection of endangered species, social security, and antidiscrimination law. Democratic aspirations should not be disparaged. And in the context at hand, the people, acting through their elected representatives, might well decide that democratic liberty, calling for quality and diversity of view in the mass media, is more valuable than consumer sovereignty.

A thought experiment may make the point more vivid. Imagine a regime in which there was extraordinary competition with respect to broadcasting—such astonishingly robust competition as to ensure 10,000, or 100,000, or 250 million separate stations. In the most extreme of these cases, each person would even be allowed to see or hear a station all her own. If technology progressed this far, and if the marketplace worked perfectly to satisfy consumer tastes, would our problems be solved? On the contrary, a system of this kind would not be anything to celebrate. It could well entail the elimination of a shared civic culture, which contemplates at least a degree of commonality among the citizenry. More importantly, it could fail to promote attention to public affairs and diversity of view. For those concerned with democratic goals, everything depends on the relationship between the robust marketplace and those goals; this issue cannot be resolved on an a priori basis, or through a belief in axiomatic connections between markets and liberty.

There are other, more familiar, objections as well. Most obviously, some new regulations might leave room for discretion and abuse in making decisions about quality and public affairs. The market, surrounded by existing property rights, may restrict speech; but at least it does not entail the sort of official approval or disapproval, or overview of speech content, that would be involved in the suggested New Deal.

But there are several responses to such objections. The current system itself creates serious obstacles to a well-functioning system of free expression, and government is responsible for that system. The absence of continuous government supervision should not obscure the point. Moreover, the right institutions could ensure that such decisions can be made in a nonpartisan way. Regulatory policies have helped greatly in the past. They are responsible for the very creation of local news in the first instance. They have helped increase the quality of children's television. Public television, which offers a wide range of high quality fare, owes its existence to governmental involvement. Nor is there any reason grounded in evidence—as opposed to market theology—to think that regulatory solutions of these sorts would inevitably be inferior to the current system.

Finally, any regulations would be subject to a degree of judicial scrutiny under the First Amendment. Government would be banned from favoring particular points of view. The free speech principle would be satisfied by a broad requirement that public affairs programming, or free time for candidates, be provided. It would be violated by a requirement that feminists, pro-lifers, or the Democrats in particular must be heard. And the legislature must generate a factual record to support any regulatory alternative to the existing regime.

Campaign Finance

Many people have argued for restrictions on campaign finance. In their view, such restrictions are an effort to promote political deliberation and political equality by reducing the distorting effects of disparities in wealth.

But some people have said that campaign finance laws violate the First Amendment and so lie beyond the legitimate reach of the democratic process. Indeed, some people claim that these laws unjustly take from rich speakers for the benefit of poor ones. It was on this rationale that the Supreme Court invalidated expenditure limits in the crucial 1976 case of *Buckley v. Valeo*. In the key passage, the Court said that "the concept that government may restrict the speech of some elements of our society in order to enhance the relative voice of others is wholly foreign to the First Amendment . . . ."

The *Buckley* Court issued several holdings. According to the Court, the government could constitutionally limit campaign *contributions*. Such contributions could create the appearance and even the reality of corruption, in the form of cash in return for political favors. But legal restrictions on campaign *expenditures* (by candidates themselves or by people acting in the interest of but independently of the candidate) would be unacceptable. Restrictions on expenditures fall in the category of unacceptable efforts to "restrict the speech of some elements . . . in order to enhance the relative voice of others." With its uneasy distinction between contributions and expenditures, *Buckley* has produced an exceptionally complex body of law. It has produced the current legal morass with respect to the status of political action committees (P.A.C.s). In the aftermath of *Buckley*, it is clear that serious constitutional issues are raised by any efforts to limit expenditures by or contributions to PACs.

The *Buckley* framework strikingly reflects pre-New Deal understandings. According to the Court, reliance on markets *is* governmental neutrality; letting the existing distributions determine political expenditures is the mark of government inaction; it does not constitute government action.

But it should now be clear that this is all a mistake. Elections based on existing distributions are actually subject to a regulatory system, made possible and constituted through law. That law consists not only of legal rules protecting the present distribution of wealth, but more fundamentally, of legal rules allowing candidates to buy speech through markets.

Efforts to redress economic inequalities, or to ensure that they do not translate into political inequalities, should not be seen as impermissible

redistribution, or as the introduction of government regulation where it did not exist before. Instead we should evaluate campaign finance laws pragmatically in terms of their consequences for the system of free expression. Much will depend on the particular regulation under discussion. My point is that here, as in the broadcasting context, market theology is operating to bar a serious look at the democratic effects of different regulatory systems. We should be entitled to examine such alternatives as full, or increased, public financing; flat caps on donations; and curbs on contributions to or expenditures by political action committees. These proposals raise serious issues about the nature of our commitment to political equality, indeed about our self-definition as a democratic system. They should not be foreclosed by reflexive resort to the Constitution.

·   ·   ·

These are simply a few examples of the sorts of questions that would arise if we were to focus our thinking about the First Amendment on issues of democratic self-government. We would see that there is a sharp difference between a marketplace of ideas and a system of democratic deliberation. I do not deny that a system of markets in speech has major advantages over other forms of regulation. But our current system of free expression does not sufficiently serve the democratic aspirations that underlie the First Amendment itself. It would therefore be a supreme irony if the First Amendment turns out to be an obstacle to such democratic experiments as campaign finance reform and improvements of the broadcasting market in the interest of political deliberation.

The most dangerous aspect of current free speech debates is that this very difference has become decreasingly visible; it sometimes seems as if deregulated markets *are* the system of free expression. Those who value a democratic conception of the First Amendment should insist that this is wrong—that free markets in speech have only a contingent and partial connection with free speech goals. We should not allow the First Amendment, the overarching symbol of our commitment to democratic self-governance, to be transformed into an obstacle to efforts to improve democratic deliberation. We should instead attempt to create a system of free expression that is both old and new—old in its emphatic reaffirmation of democratic aspirations; new in its willingness to adapt our practices to sustain those aspirations under changing social conditions.

DISCUSSION QUESTIONS

1. What analogy does Sunstein make between the New Deal's revolution in economic doctrine and the change he advocates in our interpretations of free expression and the First Amendment?

2. Sunstein claims that his proposals will further democracy. Critics might argue that he wants to limit liberty in a dangerous way. How would you assess these claims?

31 · PATRICIA J. WILLIAMS

THIS DANGEROUS PATRIOT'S GAME

In the aftermath of the September 11 bombings of the World Trade Center and the Pentagon, political leaders enacted a series of sweeping laws, which restricted traditional constitutional liberties in the name of enhanced security. Columnist and Columbia University law professor Patricia Williams offers her assessment of the cost and benefits of this darkened legal landscape in this probing selection. For Williams, the devastation of September 11 left in its wake many profound, long-term tests for America. These challenges stem from the need to balance our response to the threat of terrorism with the need to preserve the rights of citizens. From her perspective, the balance has tipped dramatically away from civil rights and freedoms, toward "the 'comfort' and convenience of high-tech totalitarianism." As a result, today we face "one of the more dramatic Constitutional crises in United States history." She explores this crisis as it impinges on three areas of constitutional protection: freedom of the press, freedom from unreasonable searches and seizures, and the right to due process of law (including the right to adequate counsel, the right to a speedy public and impartial trial, and the right against self-incrimination). In each area, of course, defenders of the shrinkage of civil liberties justify it in the name of fighting "terrorism," assuring us that only those justly suspected of being a terrorist, or aiding terrorists, need have any fear. But given the elastic nature of the term "terrorist" and the nation's history of abusing rights during the panic of wartime, Williams fears expansive use of executive and judicial power may go largely unchecked. As she explains, "A war against terrorism is a war of the mind, so broadly defined that the enemy becomes anybody who makes us afraid." She reminds us that rights exist as a ritualized legal process intended to ensure that "we don't allow the grief of great tragedies to blind us with mob fury, inflamed judgments and uninformed reasoning." An erosion of the tempering impact of legal rights strikes Williams as dangerous—indeed, perhaps a danger as great as terrorism itself.

Things fall apart, as Chinua Achebe put it, in times of great despair. The American nightmare that began with the bombing of the World Trade Center and the Pentagon, has, like an earthquake, been followed by jolt after jolt of disruption and fear. In the intervening three months, yet another airplane crashed, this time into a residential section of New York City. Anthrax contamination

---

Source: Patricia J. Williams, "This Dangerous Patriot's Game." *The Observer* (U.K.), 2 December 2001.

275

succeeded in closing, for varying lengths of time, all three branches of government. From the tabloids to *The New York Times,* major media outlets have had their centers of operation evacuated repeatedly. The United States Postal Service is tied in knots. Hundreds of anthrax hoaxes have stretched law enforcement beyond all capacity. Soldiers guard all our public buildings.

Around four thousand Americans have died in planes, collapsing buildings or of anthrax toxin since that morning in September; tens of thousands more have lost their jobs. Some 5000 Arab residents between the ages of 18 and 33 have been summoned for interrogation by the FBI. And twenty million resident aliens live suddenly subject to the exceedingly broad terms of a new martial law. Even while we try to follow the president's advice to pick ourselves up in time for the Christmas shopping season, punchdrunk and giddily committed to soldiering on as before, we know that the economic and emotional devastation of these events has only begun to register.

As the enormity of the destruction settles in and becomes less dreamlike, more waking catastrophe, American society begins to face those long-term tests that inevitably come after the shock and horror of so much loss. We face the test of keeping the unity that visited us in that first moment of sheer chaos. We face the test of maintaining our dignity and civility in a time of fear and disorder. Above all, we face the test of preserving the rights and freedoms in our Constitution and its Bill of Rights.

Few in the United States question the necessity for unusual civil measures in keeping with the current state of emergency. But a number of the Bush administration's new laws, orders and policies are deservedly controversial: the disregard for international treaties and conventions; strict controls on media reports about the war; secret surveillance and searches of citizens' computers; widespread ethnic profiling; indefinite detention of non-citizens; offers of expedited American citizenship to those who provide evidence about terrorists; and military tribunals with the power to try enemies in secret, without application of the usual laws of evidence, without right of appeal, yet with the ability to impose the death penalty. Opportunity for legislative or other public discussion of these measures has been largely eclipsed by the rapidity with which most of them have been pushed into effect. This speed, one must accede, is in large part an exigency of war. It is perhaps also because Mr. Bush has always preferred operating in a rather starkly corporate style. In any event, the president has attempted to enlarge the power of the executive to an unprecedented extent, while limiting both Congressional input as well as the check of the judiciary.

Overall, we face one of the more dramatic Constitutional crises in United States history. First, while national security mandates some fair degree of restraint, blanket control of information is in tension with the Constitution's expectation that freedom of a diverse and opinionated press will moderate the tyrannical tendencies of power. We need to have some inkling of what is happening on the battlefield in our name. On the domestic front, moreover, the First Amendment's protection of free speech, is eroded if even peaceful dissent becomes casually categorized as dangerous or unpatriotic, as it has sometimes been in recent weeks. This concern is heightened by the fact that the war has been framed as one against "terror"—against unruly if deadly emotionalism—rather than as a war against specific bodies, specific land, specific resources.

A war against terrorism is a war of the mind, so broadly defined that the enemy becomes anybody who makes us afraid. Indeed what is conspicuous about American public discourse right now is how hard it is to talk about facts rather than fear.

In a struggle that is coloured by a degree of social panic, we must be very careful not to allow human rights to be cast as an indulgence. There is always a certain hypnosis to the language of war—the poetry of the Pentagon a friend calls it—in which war means peace, and peace-mongering invites war. In this somewhat inverted system of reference, the bleeding heart does not beat within the corpus of law but rather in the bosom of those whose craven sympathies amount to naive and treacherous self-delusion. Everywhere one hears what, if taken literally, amounts to a death knell for the American dream: rights must be tossed out the window because "the constitution is not a suicide pact."

But accepting rational reasons to be afraid, the unalloyed ideology of efficiency has not only chilled free expression, but left us poised at the gateway of an even more fearsome world in which the "comfort" and convenience of high-tech totalitarianism gleam temptingly; a world in which our American-ness endures only with hands up so that our fingerprints can be scanned, and our nationalized-identity scrutinised for signs of suspicious behaviour.

This brings me to the second aspect of our Constitutional crisis—that is, the encroachment of our historical freedom from unreasonable searches and seizures. The establishment of the new Office of Homeland Security and the passage of the so-called USA Patriot Act has brought into being an unprecedented merger between the functions of intelligence agencies and law enforcement. What this means might be clearer if we used the more straightforward term for intelligence—that is, spying. Law enforcement agents can now spy on us, "destabilizing" citizens not just non-citizens.

They can gather information with few checks or balances from the judiciary. Morton Halperin, a defense expert who worked with the National Security Council under Henry Kissinger, was quoted, in *The New Yorker* magazine, worrying that if a government intelligence agency thinks you're under the control of a foreign government, "they can wiretap you and never tell you, search your house and never tell you, break into your home, copy your hard drive, and never tell you that they've done it." Moreover, says Halperin, upon whose own phone Kissinger placed a tap, "Historically, the government has often believed that anyone who is protesting government policy is doing it at the behest of a foreign government and opened counterintelligence investigations of them."

This expansion of domestic spying highlights the distinction between punishing what has already occurred and preventing what might happen in the future. In a very rough sense, agencies like the F.B.I. have been concerned with catching criminals who have already done their dirty work, while agencies like the CIA have been involved in predicting or manipulating future outcomes—activities of prior restraint, in other words, from which the Constitution generally protects citizens.

The third and most distressing area of Constitutional concern has been Mr. Bush's issuance of an executive order setting up military tribunals that would deprive even long-time resident aliens of the right to due process of law. The elements of the new order are as straightforward as trains running on time. The President would have the military try non-citizens suspected of terrorism in closed tribunals rather than courts. No requirement of public charges, adequacy of counsel, usual rules of evidence, nor proof beyond a reasonable doubt. The cases would be presented before unspecified judges, with rulings based on the accusations of unidentified witnesses. The tribunals would have the power to execute anyone so convicted, with no right of appeal. According to polls conducted by National Public Radio, *The Washington Post,* and ABC News, approximately 65 percent of Americans wholeheartedly endorse such measures.

"Foreign terrorists who commit war crimes against the United States, in my judgment, are not entitled to and do not deserve the protections of the American Constitution," says Attorney General John Ashcroft in defense of tribunals. There are a number of aspects of that statement that ought to worry us. The reasoning is alarmingly circular in Ashcroft's characterization of suspects who have not yet been convicted as "terrorists." It presumes guilt before adjudication. Our system of innocent-until-proven-guilty is hardly foolproof, but does provide an essential, base-line bulwark against the furious thirst for quick vengeance, the carelessly deadly mistake—albeit in the name of self-protection.

It is worrisome, too, when the highest prosecutor in the land declares that war criminals do not "deserve" basic constitutional protections. We confer due process not because putative criminals are "deserving" recipients of rights-as-reward. Rights are not "earned" in this way. What makes rights rights is that they ritualize the importance of solid, impartial and public consensus before we take life or liberty from anyone, particularly those whom we fear. We ritualize this process to make sure we don't allow the grief of great tragedies to blind us with mob fury, inflamed judgments and uninformed reasoning. In any event, Bush's new order bypasses not only the American Constitution but the laws of most other democratic nations. It exceeds the accepted conventions of most military courts. (I say all this provisionally, given that the Bush administration is urging the enactment of similar anti-terrorism measures in Britain, Russia, and that troublesome holdout, the European Union).

As time has passed since the order was published, a number of popular defenses of tribunals have emerged: we should trust our president, we should have faith in our government, we are in a new world facing new kinds of enemies who have access to new weapons of mass destruction. Assuming all this, we must wonder if this administration also questions whether citizens who are thought to have committed heinous crimes "deserve" the protections of American citizenship. The terrorist who mailed "aerosolised" anthrax spores to various Senate offices is, according to the FBI, probably a lone American microbiologist. Although we have not yet rounded up thousands of microbiologists for questioning by the FBI, I wonder if the government will be hauling them before tribunals—for if this is a war without national borders, the panicked logic of secret trials will surely expand domestically rather than contract. A friend observes wryly that if reasoning behind the order is that the perpetrators of mass death must be summarily executed, then there are some CEOs in the tobacco industry who ought to be trem-

bling in their boots. Another friend who works with questions of reproductive choice notes more grimly that that is exactly the reasoning used by those who assault and murder abortion doctors.

"There are situations when you do need to presume guilt over innocence," one citizen from Chattanooga told *The New York Times*. The conservative talk show host Mike Reagan leads the pack in such boundlessly-presumed guilt by warning that you might think the guy living next door is the most wonderful person in the world, you see him playing with his children, but in fact "he might be part of a sleeper cell that wants to blow you away." We forget, perhaps, that J. Edgar Hoover justified sabotaging Martin Luther King and the "dangerous suspects" of that era with similar sentiment.

In addition to the paranoia generated, the importance of the right to adequate counsel has been degraded. Attorney General Ashcroft's stated policies include allowing federal officials to listen in on conversations between suspected terrorists and their lawyers. And President Bush's military tribunals would not recognize the right of defendants to choose their own lawyers. Again, there has been very little public opposition to such measures. Rather, one hears many glib, racialized references to O.J. Simpson—who, last anyone heard, was still a citizen: "You wouldn't want Osama Bin Laden to have O.J.'s lawyer, or they'd end up playing golf together in Florida."

The tribunals also challenge the right to a speedy, public and impartial trial. More than 1000 immigrants have been arrested and held, approximately 800 with no disclosure of identities or location or charges against them. This is "frighteningly close to the practice of disappearing people in Latin America," according to Kate Martin, the director of the Center for National Security Studies.

Finally, there has been an ominous amount of public vilification of the constitutional right against self-incrimination. Such a right is, in essence, a proscription against the literal arm-twisting and leg pulling that might otherwise be necessary to physically compel someone to testify when they do not want to. It is perhaps a rather too-subtly-worded limitation of the use of torture.

While not yet the direct subject of official sanction, torture has suddenly gained remarkable legitimacy. Callers to radio programs say that we don't always have the "luxury of following all the rules"; that given recent events, people are "more understanding" of the necessity for a little behind-the-scenes roughing up. The unanimity of international conventions against torture notwithstanding, one hears authoritative voices—for example, Robert Litt, a former Justice Department official—arguing that while torture is not "authorized," perhaps it could be used in "emergencies," as long as the person who tortures then presents himself to "take the consequences."

Harvard Law School Professor Alan Dershowitz has suggested the use of "torture warrants" limited, he insists, to cases where time is of the essence. Most alarming of all, a recent CNN poll revealed that 45 percent of Americans would not object to torturing someone if it would provide information about terrorism. While fully acknowledging the stakes of this new war, I worry that this attitude of lawless righteousness is one that has been practiced in oppressed communities for years. It is a habit that has produced cynicism, riots and bloodshed. The always-urgently-felt convenience of torture has left us with civic calamities ranging from Abner Louima—a Haitian immigrant whom two New York City police officers beat and sodomized with a broom handle because they mistook him for someone involved in a barroom brawl—to Jacobo Timerman in Argentina to Alexander Solzhenitsyn in the Soviet Union—all victims of physical force and mental manipulation, all people who refused to speak or didn't speak the words their inquisitors wanted to hear, but who were 'known' to know something. In such times and places, the devastation has been profound. People know nothing so they suspect everything. Deaths are never just accidental. Every human catastrophe is also a mystery and

mysteries create ghosts, hauntings, "blowback," and ultimately new forms of terror. The problem with this kind of 'preventive' measure is that we are not mindreaders. Even with sodium pentathol, whose use some have suggested recently, we don't and we can't know every last thought of those who refuse to speak.

Torture is an investment in the right to be all-knowing, in the certitude of what appears "obvious." It is the essence of totalitarianism. Those who justify it with confident proclamations of "I have nothing to hide, why should they," overlap substantially with the class of those who have never been the persistent object of suspect profiling, never been harrassed, never been stigmatized or generalized or feared just for the way they look.

The human mind is endlessly inventive. People create enemies as much as fear real ones. We are familiar with stories of the intimate and wrong-headed projections heaped upon the maid who is accused of taking something that the lady of the house simply misplaced. Stoked by trauma, tragedy and dread, the creativity of our paranoia is in overdrive right now. We must take a deep collective breath and be wary of persecuting those who conform to our fears instead of prosecuting enemies who were and will be smart enough to play against such prejudices.

In grief, sometimes we merge with the world, all boundary erased in deference to the commonality of the human condition. But traumatic loss can also mean—sometimes—that you want to hurt anyone in your path. Anyone who is light-hearted, you want to crush. Anyone who laughs is discordant. Anyone who has a healthy spouse or child is your enemy, is undeserving, is frivolous and in need of muting.

When I served as a prosecutor years ago, I was very aware of this propensity among victims, the absolute need to rage at God or whoever is near—for that is what great sorrow feels like when the senses are overwhelmed. You lose words and thus want to reinscribe the hell of which you cannot speak. It is unfair that the rest of the world should not suffer as you have.

This is precisely why we have always had rules in trials about burdens of proof, standards of evidence, the ability to confront and cross-examine witnesses. The fiercely evocative howls of the widow, the orphan, the innocently wronged—these are the forces by which many a lynch mob has been rallied, how many a posse has been motivated to bypass due process, how many a holy crusade has been launched. It is easy to suspend the hard work of moral thought in the name of Ultimate Justice, or even Enduring Freedom, when one is blindly grief-stricken. "If you didn't do it then your brother did," is the underlying force of blood feuds since time began. "If you're not with us, you're against us," is the dangerous modern corollary to this rage.

I have many friends for whom the dominant emotion is anger. Mine is fear, and not only of the conflagration smouldering throughout the Middle East. I fear no less the risks closer to home: this is how urban riots occur, this is how the Japanese were interned during World War II, this is why hundreds of "Arab-looking" Americans have been attacked and harassed in the last weeks alone.

I hear much about how my sort of gabbling amounts to nothing but blaming the victim. But it is hardly a matter of condoning to point out that we cannot afford to substitute some statistical probability or hunch for actual evidence. We face a wrenching global crisis now, of almost unimaginable proportion, but we should take the risks of precipitous action no less seriously than when the grief with which we were stricken drove us to see evil embodied in witches, in Jews, in blacks or heathens or hippies.

Perhaps our leaders have, as they assure us, more intelligence about these matters than we the people can know at this time. I spend a lot of time praying that they are imbued with greater wisdom. But the stakes are very, very high. We cannot take an evil act and use it to justify making an entire people, an entire nation or an entire culture the corpus of "evil."

Give the government the power to assassinate terrorists, comes the call on chat shows.

Spare us a the circus of long public trials, say the letters to the editor.

I used to think that the most important human rights work facing Americans would be a national reconsideration of the death penalty. I could not have imagined that we would so willingly discard even the right of habeus corpus. I desperately hope we are a wiser people than to unloose the power to kill based on undisclosed "information" with no accountability.

We have faced horrendous war crimes in the world before. World War II presented lessons we should not forget, and Nuremburg should be our model. The United States and its allies must seriously consider the option of a world court. Our greatest work is always keeping our heads when our hearts are broken. Our best resistance to terror is the summoning of those principles so suited to keep us from descending into infinite bouts of vengeance and revenge with those who wonder, like Milton's Stygian Counsel.

Will he, so wise, let loose at once his ire,
Belike through impotence, or unaware,
To give his Enemies their wish, and end
Them in his anger, whom his anger saves
To punish endless. . . .

DISCUSSION QUESTIONS

1. Williams writes, "A war against terrorism is a war of the mind . . . ." Explain. In what way(s) might the constitutional crises engendered by the Patriot Act affect the minds of Americans?

2. The essay poses a distinction between a criminal justice system based on reason, as represented in rules of procedure, and a system rooted in collective fear, prejudice, and hatred. What are the differences? Is collective fear a threat to individual rights? To democracy?

3. Williams warns us against the temptations of "the 'comfort' and convenience of

high-tech totalitarianism." What are some contemporary examples of the technology of surveillance and control? How might these technologies collide with the basic values embodied in the First Amendment to the United States Constitution? The Fourth Amendment? The Fifth and Sixth Amendments?

R. CLAIRE SNYDER

NEO-PATRIARCHY AND THE ANTI-HOMOSEXUAL AGENDA

By 2004 same-sex marriage had perhaps equaled abortion as a contentious and divisive social issue in American politics. Even as lesbians and gay men wed legally in Massachusetts, a constitutional amendment to ban homosexual marriage was becoming a kind of political litmus test among conservatives. In this article political scientist R. Claire Snyder explores and criticizes opposition to same-sex marriage. In many ways the liberal principle of legal equality would seem to support the case for gay marriage. However an overlapping coalition of religious and political conservatives, "pro-family" activists, and political theorists have developed an antigay agenda powered by a rhetoric that "resonates with many of our most cherished cultural narratives and personal fantasies." Snyder, author of a forthcoming book on gay marriage finds that these arguments are "based on an idealized, inegalitarian heterosexual family with rigid gender roles." She argues that the antihomosexual agenda threatens valuable aspects of the liberal democratic tradition, including the separation of church and state, legal equality, and personal freedom. In this way Snyder demonstrates that the stakes in the battle debate over sexual orientation and marriage involve the core values of democracy itself.

Since the late 1990s a series of court decisions has raised the possibility that the civil right to marriage might soon be accorded to all citizens, not just to heterosexuals. Most significantly, in 2003 the Massachusetts Supreme Court ruled that denying same-sex couples access to civil marriage violates the state's constitution, which "forbids the creation of "second class citizens," and on May 17, 2004, Massachusetts began issuing marriage licenses to same-sex couples who reside in the state. In direct opposition to legal equality for lesbian and gay couples, conservative forces have mobilized across the country in "defense" of heterosexual-only marriage. The Massachusetts decision fuelled calls for the passage of the Federal Marriage Amendment, originally introduced in 2001, which states "Marriage in the United States shall consist only of the

Source: Revised and updated by the author from R. Claire Snyder, "Neo-Patriarchy and the Anti-Homosexual Agenda." *Fundamental Differences: Feminists Talk Back To Social Conservatives,* Cynthia Burack and Jyl J. Josephson, eds., Lanham, MD: Rowman and Littlefield, 2003, pp. 157–171.

union of a man and a woman. Neither this Constitution, nor the constitution of any State, shall be construed to require that marriage or the legal incidents thereof be conferred upon any union other than the union of a man and a woman." The Amendment would make permanent the 1996 Defense of Marriage Act (DOMA)—"no State shall be required to give effect to a law of any other State with respect to a same-sex 'marriage'"— which might be found to violate the Constitution's "full faith and credit clause." Even without the Amendment, however, DOMA prohibits the extension of federal benefits to legally married same-sex couples, thus denying those married in Massachusetts full equality before the law.

In their attempt to prevent the logical extension of liberal principles to lesbian and gay citizens, anti-homosexual activists have made common cause with a number of other reactionary movements that want to undo the progress of feminism and reestablish the patriarchal nuclear family as the dominant family form. This essay examines the interconnected arguments advanced by a number of conservative constituencies committed to the politics of neo-patriarchy, including the religious particularism of the Christian Right, the homophobic anti-feminism of Concerned Women for America, the "family values" of James Dobson, the Fatherhood movement spearheaded by David Blankenhorn, and the conservative democratic theory of William Galston. While the details of these arguments differ, all have a similar form and use the same authorities, and all are both homophobic and anti-feminist. Thus, all undermine the principles of liberal democracy, despite rhetorical assertions to the contrary.

LESBIAN/GAY CIVIL RIGHTS AND THE LOGIC OF LIBERALISM

Legal equality constitutes one of the most important founding principles of liberal democracy in the United States. While the equal rights of the Declaration of Independence were largely aspira-

tional at the time they were written, over the course of the twentieth century, American society has become increasingly imbued with a liberal public philosophy that values individual choice, civil rights, legal equality, and a "neutral state" that leaves individuals free to pursue their own vision of the good life in civil society and the private sphere without interference from the government.

The revolutionary principle of legal equality has been successfully used to justify progressive change. African-Americans utilized this principle during the Civil Rights Movement in their struggle to end segregation. While violently opposed by the Right at the time, the principle of color-blind law has been largely accepted by contemporary conservatives. The struggle for gender-blind law has also been largely successful. Although feminists lost the battle for the Equal Rights Amendment (ERA) during the 1970s, since that time the principle of legal equality for women has been implemented through the Courts, which are charged with following the logic of liberalism as they apply the principles of the Constitution to new areas. While progress has not been inevitable or without setbacks, overall the level of legal equality within American society has advanced over time.

Despite the compelling logic of philosophical liberalism, the American Right actively opposed the extension of legal equality in every instance. The Old Right was explicitly racist and violently fought to stop the extension of civil rights to African-Americans. By 1965, however, Gallup polls "showed that 52 percent of Americans identified civil rights as the 'most important problem' confronting the nation, and an astonishing 75 percent of respondents favored federal voting rights legislation.'" With explicit racism on the decline, in 1965 right-wing leaders began developing a more marketable message, "mainstreaming the ideological positions of the Old Right and developing winnable policies" that "highlighted a protest theme" against a wide range of cultural changes inaugurated by the new social movements of the 1960s. This "New Right" successfully created a coalition between cultural conservatives, including Christian fundamentalists, and anti-government, fiscal conservatives (*aka* neo-liberals).

Feminism constituted precisely the enemy the New Right needed to consolidate its base. Anti-feminism "provided a link with fundamentalist churches," focused "the reaction against the changes in child rearing, sexual behavior, divorce, and the use of drugs that had taken place in the 1960s and 1970s," and "mobilized a group, traditional homemakers, that had lost status over the two previous decades and was feeling the psychological effects of the loss." The conservative mobilization against feminism solidified the New Right during the 1970s and played a "very important" role in its success: the election of Ronald Reagan in 1980 and the rightward shift of American politics.

The women's movement and the lesbian/gay civil rights movement were linked theoretically and through common struggle, and the Right used this connection to its advantage. For example, Phyllis Schlafly's Eagle Forum argued that "militant homosexuals from all over America have made the ERA issue a hot priority. Why? To be able finally to get homosexual marriage licenses, to adopt children and raise them to emulate their homosexual 'parents,' and to obtain pension and medical benefits for odd-couple 'spouses.' . . . Vote *NO on 6! The Pro-Gay E.R.A.*" In its rise to power, the New Right successfully manipulated homophobia to increase opposition to gender equality and explicitly condemned all attempts to accord lesbians and gay men the equal protection of the law.

While the Christian Right continues to pose a serious threat to civil rights and has achieved unprecedented levels of power since 1980, the logic of liberalism in American society is hard to deny. While public opinion polls vary, support for same-sex marriage is particularly strong among young people who have come to age during an era of nearly hegemonic liberalism. A UCLA survey of first-year college students revealed that 58 percent of first year college students now "think gay

and lesbian couples should have the right to 'equal marital status,' i.e., civil marriage." Remarkably, of that 58 percent, half consider themselves conservative or "middle-of-the-road" in their political views. A poll of first year students at Ithaca College shows that "79 percent of Ithaca College freshmen agreed that same-sex marriage should be legal, compared to 59.3 percent nationwide." In the New Jersey poll an overwhelming 71 percent of those between 18 and 29 support the legalization of same-sex marriage, and in the New Hampshire poll, 70 percent of 17 to 29 year olds do. While the media widely publicized a Gallup poll conducted after the *Lawrence v. Texas* ruling striking down anti-homosexual sodomy laws that revealed some decline in support for same-sex unions, the decline was not evident among the young (18–29), 61 percent of whom "say they support legalizing same-sex 'marriage.'" Nevertheless, a coalition of religious, secular, and academic activists and organizations continue to oppose, and organize around their opposition to, the rights of gays and lesbians to marry or form civil unions.

RELIGIOUS PARTICULARISM AND THE ANTI-HOMOSEXUAL AGENDA

The Christian Right opposes legal equality for lesbians and gay men when it comes to marriage because it defines marriage as a sacred religious institution, and its particular version of Christianity views homosexuality as a particularly grave sin. According to the Family Research Council (FRC) marriage is "the *work of heaven and every major religion* and culture throughout world history." Concerned Women for America (CWA) proclaims "we believe that marriage is *a covenant established by God* wherein one man and one woman, united for life, are licensed by the state for the purpose of founding and maintaining a family." Focus on the Family (FOF) opposes even "civil unions" because they "would essentially legalize homosexual marriage and therefore undermine the *sanctity* of marriage." Indeed because of this religious worldview, all three groups have made opposition to same-sex marriage a centerpiece of their political agenda.

The Christian Right's vision of heterosexual marriage directly relates to its understanding of gender differences, which it bases on its particular interpretation of the Christian Bible. More specifically, this reading focuses on the second creation story in Genesis, in which God created Eve out of Adam's rib to be his helper and declared that the man and his wife would become "one flesh" (Genesis 18: 21–24), rather than on the first story in which "God created man in His image, in the image of God He created him; *male and female He created them*" (Genesis 1:26–27, emphasis added). Additionally, instead of reading the latter version as establishing gender equality at the origin, or even androgyny, as some religious scholars do, the Christian Right interprets it to mean "God's purpose for man was that there should be two sexes, male and female. Every person is either a 'he' or a 'she.' God did not divide mankind into three or four or five sexes." The Christian Right bolsters its interpretation with a few New Testament verses stating that woman is the "weaker vessel" (1 Peter 3:7), that man is "joined to his wife, and the two become one flesh" (Eph. 5:31–32), and that the "husband is the head of the wife" (1 Cor. 11:4; Eph. 5:23).

For the Christian Right, the Bible not only proclaims a natural gender hierarchy but also condemns homosexuality as a sin. It bases its interpretation on two sentences in Leviticus that proclaim "do not lie with a male as one lies with a woman; it is an abhorrence" (Leviticus 18:22) and "if a man lies with a male as one lies with a woman, the two of them have done an abhorrent thing; they shall be put to death" (Leviticus 20:13), completely ignoring the fact that the Ten Commandments did not include a prohibition on homosexuality. The Christian Right also stresses an interpretation of the Sodom and Gomorrah story (Genesis 18:16–19:29) that depicts the city's destruction as God's punishment for homosexuality, an interpretation that is highly contested by religious scholars. Finally, right-wing Christians justify their condemnation of lesbian and gay sex-

uality on three passages in Paul's writings—two words and two sentences total (I Corinthians 6:9–10, I Timothy 1:8–10, and Romans 1:26–27). They cannot base it on what Jesus said because he never even mentioned homosexuality. Although the meanings of all these passages have been debated at length by religious scholars, and no consensus exists as to their meanings, nevertheless, conservative Christians insist that God's will is as clear as it is specific: man and woman are naturally different, designed by God for heterosexual marriage and the establishment of the patriarchal family.

As far as their own religious rites are concerned, Christian Right churches certainly have the religious liberty to define marriage any way they see fit. However, when the faithful of the Christian Right ask the U.S. government and the governments of the states to restrict the right to civil marriage because of their particular interpretation of revealed religion, they violate the separation of church and state mandated by the First Amendment. Not all religions share the Christian Right's definition of marriage. For example, Reform Judaism not only favors civil marriage for gays and lesbians but also allows for religious unions, and many Muslims practice polygamy. In fact, even within Christianity, no clear consensus exists on the question of same-sex marriage. Nevertheless, despite the diversity of beliefs within America's religiously pluralistic society, the Christian Right group Alliance for Marriage has introduced a Federal Marriage Amendment that declares "Marriage in the United States shall consist only of the union of a man and a woman." Clearly this Amendment asks the federal government to establish one particular religious definition of marriage as the law of the land, thus violating the separation of church and state.

THAT '70S ARGUMENT: THE ANXIETY OF RIGHT-WING WOMEN

The Christian Right group Concerned Women for America, which claims to be the largest women's group in the country, consistently asserts that the struggle of lesbians and gay men for the right to marry is not an attempt to participate in the institution of marriage but rather an attempt to "undermine marriage" and destroy the family. In strictly logical terms this makes no sense. Aren't lesbians and gays actually *reinforcing* the legitimacy of marriage as an institution through their struggle for the right to marry? Indeed many within the LGBT community have criticized this struggle for doing precisely that and not much more. While same-sex marriage would not undermine the institution of marriage in general, it would undermine the *traditional patriarchal heterosexual vision of marriage* in particular, which is precisely what the Christian Right desperately wants to re-establish.

Concerned Women for America wants heterosexual marriage to maintain its privileged status in American society and to continue to function as the justification for special rights. This line of argumentation plays on a number of anxieties expressed by the first generation of New Right women who mobilized in opposition to the ERA and abortion rights during the 1970s. Status was a key concern for those women. "At the beginning of the contemporary women's movement, in 1968, women of all classes found themselves in something like the same boat." Most were homemakers and/or low-level employees. However, over the course of the next two decades "homemakers suffered a tremendous loss in social prestige" as "high-status women" began choosing careers over homemaking. Consequently, conservative homemakers—who, after all, had done the *right thing* for their time—now found themselves facing "status degradation," and they resented it. Twenty-five years later, the special status of heterosexual marriage is being threatened by lesbians and gays, and many right-wing women again feel diminished.

Opposed to government-sponsored family support, Christian Right women favor laws that force individual men to take responsibility for the children they father and for the mothers who bear those children. The '70s generation feared that the changes inaugurated by feminism—the ERA, reproductive freedom, no-fault divorce, and the loosening of sexual mores—would make it easier for men to get out of their familial commitments. As opposed to liberal feminist women who wanted the right to compete equally with men, many anti-feminist women did not have the educational level or job skills that would allow them to pursue satisfying careers if forced to work outside the home. They feared that the ERA would eliminate the traditional legal requirement for husbands to support their wives financially. Phyllis Schlafly told homemakers that the ERA would say "Boys, supporting your wives isn't your responsibility anymore." At the same time, the rise of "no-fault" divorce laws during this period further threatened the economic security of traditional "housewives." As Schlafly put it, "even though love may go out the window, the obligation should remain. ERA would eliminate that obligation." To this day, Christian Right women condemn no-fault divorce, which "allows one person to decide when a relationship can be severed," often catapulting women into poverty. While higher wages for women, safe and affordable childcare, and universal health insurance constitute a progressive solution to the problems caused by the fragility of marriage and callousness of deadbeat dads, right-wing women demand the return of a traditional patriarchal vision of marriage, ignoring the reality of social change.

In the 1970s, conservative women worried that if sex became widely available outside of marriage, they would have difficulty keeping their husbands interested in them. Kristen Luker's interviews with the first generation of "pro-life" women revealed the following insight:

> If women plan to find their primary role in marriage and the family, then they face a need to create a "moral cartel" when it comes to sex. . . . If many women are willing to sleep with men outside of marriage, then the regular sexual activity that comes with marriage is much less valuable an incentive to marry. . . . [For] traditional women, their primary resource for marriage is the promise

of a stable home, with everything it implies: children, regular sex, a "haven in a heartless world."

For the first generation of Christian Right women, the sexual liberation of many feminist women threatened to destabilize the marital bargain that many traditional women relied upon. Given the option, their husbands might abandon them for more exciting women.

Do today's Christian Right women fear that if given the choice their husbands might choose other men? Perhaps. After all, anti-gay activist Dr. Paul Cameron tells them that "the evidence is that men do a better job on men, and women on women, if all you are looking for is orgasm." If you want "the most satisfying orgasm you can get," he explains, "then homosexuality seems too powerful to resist. . . . It's pure sexuality. It's almost like pure heroin. It's such a rush." In opposition, "marital sex tends toward the boring" and generally "doesn't deliver the kind of sheer sexual pleasure that homosexual sex does." Although the American Psychological Association expelled Cameron for ethics violations in 1983, he still serves as an oft-quoted right-wing "expert" on homosexuality. In light of his comments, it would be understandable if Christian Right women feel anxious about their ability to keep their husbands interested in heterosexual marriage.

Fundamentally different, men and women come together to reproduce and remain coupled in order to rear their children. Because homosexuality severs the connection between sex and reproduction, CWA sees homosexual relationships as necessarily fleeting, as driven by sexual gratification alone. For example, Beverly LaHaye insists that "homosexual relationships are not only the antithesis to family, but also threaten its very core. It is *the compulsive desire for sexual gratification without lasting commitment,* the high rate of promiscuity, and the self-defined morality among homosexuals that sap the vitality of the family structure, making it something less than it was, is, and should be." Clearly the desire

of many gay and lesbian couples to marry and to raise children belies this argument. Nevertheless, Christian Right groups like CWA purposely depict the struggle for lesbian/gay civil rights in a reductive and patently distorted way in order to manipulate the anxieties of traditional women, secure their own special interests and advance their larger political agenda.

NEO-PATRIARCHY AND THE FATHERHOOD MOVEMENT

Joining the opposition to same-sex marriage are advocates of the fatherhood movement who seek to restore traditional gender roles and reestablish the patriarchal family as the dominant family form in America. Because no evidence exists that same-sex couples are less functional than heterosexual ones, or that their children are more likely to suffer negative effects, allowing same-sex couples to marry and have children would clearly undermine the myth that the patriarchal heterosexual family is the superior family form. Consequently, the fatherhood activists repeatedly assert that children need both a masculine father and a feminine mother in order to develop properly.

The fatherhood movement blames feminism and single mothers for the social problems caused by men and teenaged boys. While the packaging of their arguments varies slightly, advocates of this school of thought generally make a similar claim: Refusing to respect natural gender differences, feminists have pathologized masculinity and futilely attempted to change the behavior of men and boys. They have undermined the rightful authority of men as the head of the household, attempted to change the natural division of labor that exists between mothers and fathers, and propagated the idea that a woman can fulfill the role traditionally played by a man, thus rendering fathers superfluous to family life. Consequently, men have lost interest in fulfilling their traditional family responsibilities, and boys have no one to teach them how to become responsible men. Detached from the civilizing influence of the traditional patriarchal family, males increasingly cause a wide array of social problems, and everybody suffers.

Focus on the Family president James Dobson makes this argument from a Christian Right perspective. In *Bringing Up Boys,* he argues that traditional gender roles are natural and cannot be changed. He points to the continued power of men in society as evidence of their natural, "biochemical and anatomical," dominance. Dobson strongly opposes attempts to change the gender socialization of children and explicitly links this "unisex" idea to "the powerful gay and lesbian agenda," whose propagandists are teaching a revolutionary view of sexuality called "gender feminism," which insists that sex assignment is irrelevant. While Dobson sees this as dangerous for both sexes, it is particularly harmful for boys: "Protect the masculinity of your boys, who will be under increasing political pressure in years to come."

Dobson believes that a breakdown of traditional gender roles within the family fosters homosexuality in children. The prevention of homosexuality among boys requires the involvement of a properly masculine heterosexual father, especially during the early years. Dobson relies on the work of Dr. Joseph Nicolosi, a leading proponent of the Christian Right's "ex-gay" movement, who urges parents to monitor their children for signs of "prehomosexuality," so professionals can step in before it is too late. While "feminine behavior in boyhood" is clearly a sign, so is "nonmasculinity" defined as not fitting in with male peers. "The father," Nicolosi asserts, "plays an essential role in a boy's normal development as a man. The truth is, Dad is more important than Mom." In order to ensure heterosexuality, the father "needs to mirror and affirm his son's maleness. He can play rough-and-tumble games with his son, in ways that are decidedly different from the games he would play with a little girl. He can help his son learn to throw and catch a ball. . . . He can even take his son with him into the shower, where the boy cannot help but notice that Dad has a penis, just like his, only bigger."

Based solely on the work of Nicolosi, Dobson concludes, "if you as a parent have an effeminate boy or a masculinized girl, I urge you to get a copy [of Nicolosi's book] and then seek immediate professional help." Beware, however, of "secular" mental health professionals who will most certainly "take the wrong approach—telling your child that he is homosexual and needs to accept that fact." Instead, Dobson recommends a referral from either Exodus International, the leading organization of the ex-gay ministries, or the National Association for Research and Therapy of Homosexuality, "formed to oppose the 1973 decision by the American Psychological Association to no longer classify homosexuality as an emotional or mental disorder."

Dobson's emphasis on the important role played by fathers bolsters the arguments of the "fatherhood movement," which emerged during the 1990s. One of the first organizations to spearhead this movement was the Promise Keepers (PK), founded by Bill McCartney in 1990 as a "Christ-centered ministry dedicated to uniting men through vital relationships to become godly influences in their world." This organization wants to restore fathers to their rightful place at the head of the patriarchal family.

Institute for American Values president David Blankenhorn advances a similar agenda using secular arguments. His book *Fatherless America* (1995) and the follow-up volume *The Fatherhood Movement* (1999)—co-edited with Wade Horn (George W. Bush's Secretary of Health and Human Services) and Mitchell Pearlstein—blames the "declining child well-being in our society," not on growing levels of poverty, deteriorating public services, lack of safe and affordable childcare, the lower income of women, child abuse, racism or misogyny, but rather on fatherlessness. Fatherlessness, he tells us, is "the engine driving our most urgent social problems, from crime to adolescent pregnancy to child sexual abuse to domestic violence against women." While some conservatives argue that "the best anti-poverty program for children is a stable, intact family," Blankenhorn demands more: "a married father on the premises."

Like those on the Christian Right, Blankenhorn insists that children need not just two involved parents but more specifically *a male father and a female mother enacting traditional gender roles.* Citing two anthropologists, Blankenhorn claims that "gendered parental roles derive precisely from children's needs." During childhood "the needs of the child compel mothers and fathers to specialize in their labor and to adopt gender-based parental roles." Consequently, men and women should stick with traditional roles, Blankenhorn insists, even if this conflicts with their "narcissistic claims" to personal autonomy.

Like Dobson, Blankenhorn condemns attempts to equalize the roles of mothers and fathers in childrearing, and derides what he calls the new "like-a-mother father." While Blankenhorn barely mentions lesbians and gay men in his analysis, his argument clearly justifies an opposition to same-sex marriage. Obviously, his insistence that proper childhood development requires heterosexual parents who enact traditional gender roles implies that, in his view, homosexual couples cannot raise healthy children. In addition, however, Blankenhorn specifically advocates laws to prohibit unmarried women from accessing sperm banks. Perhaps he shares the fear of CWA that gender equality would mean that "lesbian women would be considered no different from men," especially once they get access to male seed. If that were to happen, where would that leave men?

"SEEDBEDS OF VIRTUE": WHAT LESSONS DOES THE PATRIARCHAL FAMILY TEACH?

Building directly on the body of literature outlined above, a growing number of right-wing activists, respectable scholars, and well-known political theorists have begun connecting the neo-patriarchal movement to the survival and revitalization of American democracy. This approach claims, in short, that liberal democracy requires virtuous citizens, and virtue is best learned at home in a traditional family with two married parents. The Institute for American Val-

ues sponsored a conference on this topic that resulted in the publication of *Seedbeds of Virtue: Sources of Competence, Character, and Citizenship in American Society* that Blankenhorn edited with Mary Ann Glendon who so strongly opposes same-sex unions that she helped draft both the Federal Marriage Amendment and a similar amendment to the Massachusetts constitution.

While many conservative thinkers support the "seedbeds of virtue" approach to justifying the patriarchal heterosexual family—many in exactly the same terms as the fatherhood movement—I will concentrate on the arguments advanced by political theorist William Galston, who served as Deputy Assistant to the President for Domestic Policy under Bill Clinton, a *Democratic* president. While Galston's defense of the family does not explicitly specify the patriarchal heterosexual family form in particular, one can only infer that he endorses that vision for several reasons. First, he makes arguments similar to those of the neo-patriarchalists *without any caveats.* Second, he explicitly praises Mary Ann Glendon and Jean Bethke Elshtain for having "already said nearly every thing that needs saying on [the subject of the family]." While Glendon works politically in opposition to same-sex marriage, Elshtain's scholarship specifically proposes "a normative vision of the family—mothers, fathers, and children" and claims that this particular family form "is not only *not* at odds with democratic civil society but is in fact, now more than ever, a prerequisite for that society to function." Third, Galston himself signs *A Call to Civil Society: Why Democracy Needs Moral Truths* that says the number one priority for American democracy should be "to increase the likelihood that more children will grow up with their two married parents."

In addition, the lack of explicit references to homosexuality should not be interpreted as a lack of homophobia. As Jean Hardisty has discovered, since the mid-1980s, Christian Right organizations have tended to "highlight the religious principles undergirding their anti-homosexual politics only when they are targeting other Christians. When organizing in the wider political arena, they frame their anti-gay organizing as a struggle for secular ends, such as 'defense of the family.'" Thus you get James Dobson in Christian Right circles, David Blankenhorn in secular circles, and William Galston in academic circles. Despite variations on the theme, one thing remains constant: the normative vision presented by these conservatives gives lesbians and gay men absolutely no place in family life, and, by extension, no place in democratic society.

Working from a firm foundation in the history of political thought, Galston argues that liberal democracy requires individuals who have the virtues necessary for life in a free society. The claim is simple: "that the operation of liberal institutions is affected in important ways by the character of citizens (and leaders), and that at some point, the attenuation of individual virtue will create pathologies with which liberal political contrivances, however technically perfect their design, simply cannot cope." Cataloguing the wide array of virtues necessary for liberal democracy, Galston only implies that the traditional family best teaches these virtues to youngsters; he never argues it explicitly.

An examination of how the particular virtues cited by Galston relate to the traditional family produces three different arguments. First, many of the virtues Galston emphasizes, while originally acquired in a family, do not require a patriarchal heterosexual family form in particular. For example, important virtues like civility, the work ethic, delayed gratification, adaptability, discernment, and "the ability to work within constraints on action imposed by social diversity and constitutional institutions" could certainly be instilled in children by any functional family, including one headed by same-sex parents. Galston makes no argument for the superiority of heterosexuals in fostering these characteristics in children, and such an argument is not supported by empirical evidence.

Second, the traditional patriarchal family could actually undermine a number of important

virtues extolled by Galston. For example, he argues that a liberal society is characterized by two key features—individualism and diversity. While children certainly need to learn independence, how does the traditional patriarchal family, in which wives are dependent upon their husbands' leadership and economic support, teach the virtue of independence to future *female* citizens? Galston must be focusing on boys only. Additionally, Galston cites "loyalty" as a central virtue for liberal democracy, defining it as "the developed capacity to understand, to accept, and to act on the core principles of one's society." This "is particularly important in liberal communities," he argues, because they "tend to be organized around abstract principles rather than shared ethnicity, nationality, or history." But if one of the fundamental principles of liberal democracy is legal equality for all citizens, again we must ask: What lessons does a child learn about equality growing up in a patriarchal nuclear family in which *men lead and women submit?* While the traditional family may provide certain benefits to children, it is unclear how it teaches them the universal principle of equality for all citizens, when this family form models gender inequality.

Third, a number of the democratic virtues Galston emphasizes could be undermined by the normative vision of the Christian Right. For example, Galston emphasizes "the willingness to *listen seriously to a range of views*" and the "willingness to set forth one's own views intelligibly and candidly as the basis of a *politics of persuasion rather than manipulation or coercion.*" This directly relates to the virtue of *tolerance.* While Galston stresses that tolerance does not mean a belief that all lifestyles are "equally good," it does mean that "the pursuit of the better course should be (and in some cases can only be) the consequence of *education or persuasion rather than coercion.*" While open-mindedness, tolerance, and non-coercion certainly constitute important virtues for any democratic society, they are not hallmarks of the Christian Right, especially when it comes to its anti-homosexual agenda.

CONCLUSION

The fight against the extension of civil rights to lesbians and gay men forms a central component of the larger battle against women's equality. While the rhetoric deployed by conservatives resonates with many of our most cherished cultural narratives and personal fantasies, their overarching agenda actually undermines our most precious political values, including the separation of church and state, legal equality and personal liberty. While liberal democracy has its limitations, its virtue is that it maximizes the freedom of all by allowing individuals to organize their personal lives as they see fit. While a liberal state may respond to the will of its citizens by providing a default set of legal entanglements that make it easier for individuals to establish families (i.e., civil marriage), it may not legitimately deny equal protection of the laws to particular groups of citizens, no matter how unpopular they are. The con-servative arguments against same-sex marriage, whether religious, secular, or academic, are all similarly structured and based on an idealized, inegalitarian heterosexual family with rigid gender roles. Justified by references to the well-being of children, these arguments are unsustainable when subjected to close scrutiny.

DISCUSSION QUESTIONS

1. Snyder argues that the founding principles of liberal democracy lend support to the struggle for equality of lesbians and gay men? How compelling do you find her argument?

2. Identify the leading arguments against homosexual equality and gay marriage? What are Snyder's arguments against each of these positions? Do you agree that these antigay perspectives serve to uphold rigid gender roles or "neo-patriarchy"?

PART  III

POLITICS AND VISION

Politics is everywhere. Although you may not think of yourself as a political person, you are surrounded by, bombarded by, and inescapably influenced by politics. There is no shelter from the storm.

We firmly believe that as citizens you have an enormous stake in the direction American politics takes in the twenty-first century. We further assume that you do not automatically agree that the direction we are heading is the direction we ought to take. If our assumption is correct, and your views are not cast in stone, you may want to question critically the possible future options open to us. Given the structural context we have sketched in Part I, and the discussion of political institutions in Part II, it follows that we think conventional political leaders lack the creative vision necessary to move us beyond status quo conceptions of "problems" and "solutions." In our judgment, we face a potentially stifling lack of national political imagination.

In Part III we offer you chapters that attempt to spark your interest and imagination on two fronts. First we look at some particularly important policy challenges involving issues of class and inequality, gender, race, and U.S. foreign policy. Our selection of these issues does not pretend to be exhaustive, but we do think these articles will give you a clearer sense of how an alternative critical perspective looks at difficult political questions.

After exploring these issues, we conclude with a chapter that amounts to a call for action. Government, corporate, and media elites routinely defend their behavior by saying they act with the peoples' best interests at heart. In their minds this may well be true, for they often equate their class interests and political interests with a broader public interest. We are quite skeptical of this equation. Nevertheless, there is a sense in which we are all indirectly responsible for the actions of political and economic elites, at least to the extent that we remain silent in the face of actions we find morally wrong.

We are implicated in behavior we oppose if we have the freedom to oppose that behavior but choose not to. This is especially true for those of us who have gone to college and presumably have had the time and resources to develop the skills to think critically in an academic environment where alternative information should be readily available. The final chapter of our anthology thus encourages you to take responsibility in a political world that too often fosters apathy and disengagement.

9

Political Challenges at Home and Abroad

We live in a changing world. Our values, ideologies, politics, society, economics, and the larger world outside America are being challenged and transformed, often in directions we only dimly understand. In the final chapter we stress that the shape of the future partly depends on choices we make and interpretations we reach. In this chapter we wish to indicate, without any attempt to be comprehensive, some of the major policy challenges facing Americans in the twenty-first century. By now it should be clear that we do not believe these challenges can be resolved on a humane and democratic basis unless we make far-reaching economic, political, and social changes. Confronted with crises, many of us react by withdrawing from politics or by hoping to muddle through. But opinion polls and other evidence convince us that millions of Americans have a sober-minded desire to comprehend and grapple with the dangers and opportunities we face. Each of the four readings in this chapter prepares us for the critical choices ahead.

FOR RICHER: CLASS INEQUALITY AND DEMOCRACY

"The rich get richer and the poor get poorer." How many times have you heard this sentiment expressed as if it is an unalterable fact of nature? In this article, Paul Krugman surveys the growing disparity in income and wealth that he believes has created a "new Gilded Age" in America. As a Professor of Economics and International Affairs at Princeton University and noted columnist for the New York Times, *Krugman has written exhaustively about the political, economic, and social impacts of inequality for decades. Alarmed by the "tectonic shifts" in the nation's political economy, he focuses keenly on "the astonishing concentration of income and wealth in just a few hands." This concentration has come very quickly by historical standards. Inequality was substantially reduced in the United States during the Great Depression and WW II era—a "Great Compression" that created a broadly middle-class society with social norms that set limits on inequality. With the unraveling of this postwar socioeconomic consensus, American politics has shifted sharply to the right, with party politics taking on a distinct tenor of divisiveness and rancor. In terms of public policy, the price of soaring inequality can be seen in social indicators and standards of living that do not stand up well when compared to Western European and Japanese democracies, despite well-financed propaganda campaigns to the contrary as orchestrated by conservative think tanks. Money buys more than just economic influence. It also buys political and intellectual influence, which accounts for the tilting of public discourse toward policies that actually enrich the top 1 percent (and above) of the population that already has been benefiting from this sea change in the landscape of the American political economy. In short, the growth in inequality is not the result of some imagined set of economic "laws." Rather, it is a result of pure political power wielded on behalf of the wealthy. In the early twenty-first century, then, our nation actually is moving forward by heading backwards—toward an economic profile more appropriate to the "plutocracy" of the late nineteenth and early twentieth centuries. Krugman finds the implications for democracy to be both chilling and disheartening.*

Source: Paul Krugman, "For Richer." *New York Times Magazine,* 20 October 2002.

THE DISAPPEARING MIDDLE

When I was a teenager growing up on Long Island, one of my favorite excursions was a trip to see the great Gilded Age mansions of the North Shore. Those mansions weren't just pieces of architectural history. They were monuments to a bygone social era, one in which the rich could afford the armies of servants needed to maintain a house the size of a European palace. By the time I saw them, of course, that era was long past. Almost none of the Long Island mansions were still private residences. Those that hadn't been turned into museums were occupied by nursing homes or private schools.

For the America I grew up in—the America of the 1950s and 1960s—was a middle-class society, both in reality and in feel. The vast income and wealth inequalities of the Gilded Age had disappeared. Yes, of course, there was the poverty of the underclass—but the conventional wisdom of the time viewed that as a social rather than an economic problem. Yes, of course, some wealthy businessmen and heirs to large fortunes lived far better than the average American. But they weren't rich the way the robber barons who built the mansions had been rich, and there weren't that many of them. The days when plutocrats were a force to be reckoned with in American society, economically or politically, seemed long past.

Daily experience confirmed the sense of a fairly equal society. The economic disparities you were conscious of were quite muted. Highly educated professionals—middle managers, college teachers, even lawyers—often claimed that they earned less than unionized blue-collar workers. Those considered very well off lived in split-levels, had a housecleaner come in once a week and took summer vacations in Europe. But they sent their kids to public schools and drove themselves to work, just like everyone else.

But that was long ago. The middle-class America of my youth was another country.

We are now living in a new Gilded Age, as extravagant as the original. Mansions have made a comeback. Back in 1999 this magazine profiled Thierry Despont, the "eminence of excess," an architect who specializes in designing houses for the superrich. His creations typically range from 20,000 to 60,000 square feet; houses at the upper end of his range are not much smaller than the White House. Needless to say, the armies of servants are back, too. So are the yachts. Still, even J.P. Morgan didn't have a Gulfstream.

As the story about Despont suggests, it's not fair to say that the fact of widening inequality in America has gone unreported. Yet glimpses of the lifestyles of the rich and tasteless don't necessarily add up in people's minds to a clear picture of the tectonic shifts that have taken place in the distribution of income and wealth in this country. My sense is that few people are aware of just how much the gap between the very rich and the rest has widened over a relatively short period of time. In fact, even bringing up the subject exposes you to charges of "class warfare," the "politics of envy" and so on. And very few people indeed are willing to talk about the profound effects—economic, social and political—of that widening gap.

Yet you can't understand what's happening in America today without understanding the extent, causes and consequences of the vast increase in inequality that has taken place over the last three decades, and in particular the astonishing concentration of income and wealth in just a few hands. To make sense of the current wave of corporate scandal, you need to understand how the man in the gray flannel suit has been replaced by the imperial C.E.O. The concentration of income at the top is a key reason that the United States, for all its economic achievements, has more poverty and lower life expectancy than any other major advanced nation. Above all, the growing concentration of wealth has reshaped our political system: it is at the root both of a general shift to the right and of an extreme polarization of our politics.

But before we get to all that, let's take a look at who gets what.

THE NEW GILDED AGE

The Securities and Exchange Commission hath no fury like a woman scorned. The messy divorce proceedings of Jack Welch, the legendary former

C.E.O. of General Electric, have had one unintended benefit: they have given us a peek at the perks of the corporate elite, which are normally hidden from public view. For it turns out that when Welch retired, he was granted for life the use of a Manhattan apartment (including food, wine and laundry), access to corporate jets and a variety of other in-kind benefits, worth at least $2 million a year. The perks were revealing: they illustrated the extent to which corporate leaders now expect to be treated like *ancien regime* royalty. In monetary terms, however, the perks must have meant little to Welch. In 2000, his last full year running G.E., Welch was paid $123 million, mainly in stock and stock options.

Is it news that C.E.O.s of large American corporations make a lot of money? Actually, it is. They were always well paid compared with the average worker, but there is simply no comparison between what executives got a generation ago and what they are paid today.

Over the past 30 years most people have seen only modest salary increases: the average annual salary in America, expressed in 1998 dollars (that is, adjusted for inflation), rose from $32,522 in 1970 to $35,864 in 1999. That's about a 10 percent increase over 29 years—progress, but not much. Over the same period, however, according to Fortune magazine, the average real annual compensation of the top 100 C.E.O.s went from $1.3 million—39 times the pay of an average worker—to $37.5 million, more than 1,000 times the pay of ordinary workers.

The explosion in C.E.O. pay over the past 30 years is an amazing story in its own right, and an important one. But it is only the most spectacular indicator of a broader story, the reconcentration of income and wealth in the U.S. The rich have always been different from you and me, but they are far more different now than they were not long ago—indeed, they are as different now as they were when F. Scott Fitzgerald made his famous remark.

That's a controversial statement, though it shouldn't be. For at least the past 15 years it has been hard to deny the evidence for growing inequality in the United States. Census data clearly show a rising share of income going to the top 20 percent of families, and within that top 20 percent to the top 5 percent, with a declining share going to families in the middle. Nonetheless, denial of that evidence is a sizable, well-financed industry. Conservative think tanks have produced scores of studies that try to discredit the data, the methodology and, not least, the motives of those who report the obvious. Studies that appear to refute claims of increasing inequality receive prominent endorsements on editorial pages and are eagerly cited by right-leaning government officials. Four years ago Alan Greenspan (why did anyone ever think that he was nonpartisan?) gave a keynote speech at the Federal Reserve's annual Jackson Hole conference that amounted to an attempt to deny that there has been any real increase in inequality in America.

The concerted effort to deny that inequality is increasing is itself a symptom of the growing influence of our emerging plutocracy (more on this later). So is the fierce defense of the backup position, that inequality doesn't matter—or maybe even that, to use Martha Stewart's signature phrase, it's a good thing. Meanwhile, politically motivated smoke screens aside, the reality of increasing inequality is not in doubt. In fact, the census data understate the case, because for technical reasons those data tend to undercount very high incomes—for example, it's unlikely that they reflect the explosion in C.E.O. compensation. And other evidence makes it clear not only that inequality is increasing but that the action gets bigger the closer you get to the top. That is, it's not simply that the top 20 percent of families have had bigger percentage gains than families near the middle: the top 5 percent have done better than the next 15, the top 1 percent better than the next 4, and so on up to Bill Gates.

Studies that try to do a better job of tracking high incomes have found startling results. For example, a recent study by the nonpartisan Congressional Budget Office used income tax data and other sources to improve on the census estimates. The C.B.O. study found that between 1979 and 1997, the after-tax incomes of the top 1 percent of families rose 157 percent, compared with only a 10 percent gain for families near the middle of the income distribution. Even more startling results come from a new study by Thomas Piketty, at the French research institute Cepremap, and Emmanuel Saez, who is now at the University of California at Berkeley. Using income tax data, Piketty and Saez have produced estimates of the incomes of the well-to-do, the rich and the very rich back to 1913.

The first point you learn from these new estimates is that the middle-class America of my youth is best thought of not as the normal state of our society, but as an interregnum between Gilded Ages. America before 1930 was a society in which a small number of very rich people controlled a large share of the nation's wealth. We became a middle-class society only after the concentration of income at the top dropped sharply during the New Deal, and especially during World War II. The economic historians Claudia Goldin and Robert Margo have dubbed the narrowing of income gaps during those years the Great Compression. Incomes then stayed fairly equally distributed until the 1970s: the rapid rise in incomes during the first postwar generation was very evenly spread across the population.

Since the 1970s, however, income gaps have been rapidly widening. Piketty and Saez confirm what I suspected: by most measures we are, in fact, back to the days of "The Great Gatsby." After 30 years in which the income shares of the top 10 percent of taxpayers, the top 1 percent and so on were far below their levels in the 1920s, all are very nearly back where they were.

And the big winners are the very, very rich. One ploy often used to play down growing inequality is to rely on rather coarse statistical breakdowns—dividing the population into five "quintiles," each containing 20 percent of families, or at most 10 "deciles." Indeed, Greenspan's speech at Jackson Hole relied mainly on decile data. From there it's a short step to denying that we're really talking about the rich at all. For example, a conservative commentator might concede, grudgingly, that there has been some increase in the share of national income going to the top 10 percent of taxpayers, but then point out that anyone with an income over $81,000 is in that top 10 percent. So we're just talking about shifts within the middle class, right?

Wrong: the top 10 percent contains a lot of people whom we would still consider middle class, but they weren't the big winners. Most of the gains in the share of the top 10 percent of taxpayers over the past 30 years were actually gains to the top 1 percent, rather than the next 9 percent. In 1998 the top 1 percent started at $230,000. In turn, 60 percent of the gains of that top 1 percent went to the top 0.1 percent, those with incomes of more than $790,000. And almost half of those gains went to a mere 13,000 taxpayers, the top 0.01 percent, who had an income of at least $3.6 million and an average income of $17 million.

A stickler for detail might point out that the Piketty-Saez estimates end in 1998 and that the C.B.O. numbers end a year earlier. Have the trends shown in the data reversed? Almost surely not. In fact, all indications are that the explosion of incomes at the top continued through 2000. Since then the plunge in stock prices must have put some crimp in high incomes—but census data show inequality continuing to increase in 2001, mainly because of the severe effects of the recession on the working poor and near poor. When the recession ends, we can be sure that we will find ourselves a society in which income inequality is even higher than it was in the late 90s.

So claims that we've entered a second Gilded Age aren't exaggerated. In America's middle-class era, the mansion-building, yacht-owning classes had pretty much disappeared. According to Piketty and Saez, in 1970 the top 0.01 percent of taxpayers had 0.7 percent of total income—that is, they earned "only" 70 times as much as the average, not enough to buy or maintain a mega-residence. But in 1998 the top 0.01 percent received more than 3 percent of all income. That meant that the 13,000 richest families in America had almost as much income as the 20 million poorest households; those 13,000 families had incomes 300 times that of average families.

And let me repeat: this transformation has happened very quickly, and it is still going on. You might think that 1987, the year Tom Wolfe published his novel "The Bonfire of the Vanities" and Oliver Stone released his movie "Wall Street," marked the high tide of America's new money culture. But in 1987 the top 0.01 percent earned only about 40 percent of what they do today, and top executives less than a fifth as much. The America of "Wall Street" and "The Bonfire of the Vanities" was positively egalitarian compared with the country we live in today.

UNDOING THE NEW DEAL

In the middle of the 1980s, as economists became aware that something important was happening to the distribution of income in America, they formulated three main hypotheses about its causes.

The "globalization" hypothesis tied America's changing income distribution to the growth of world trade, and especially the growing imports of manufactured goods from the third world. Its basic message was that blue-collar workers—the sort of people who in my youth often made as much money as college-educated middle managers—were losing ground in the face of competition from low-wage workers in Asia. A result was stagnation or decline in the wages of ordinary people, with a growing share of national income going to the highly educated.

A second hypothesis, "skill-biased technological change," situated the cause of growing inequality not in foreign trade but in domestic innovation. The torrid pace of progress in information technology, so the story went, had increased the demand for the highly skilled and educated. And so the income distribution increasingly favored brains rather than brawn.

Finally, the "superstar" hypothesis—named by the Chicago economist Sherwin Rosen—offered a variant on the technological story. It argued that modern technologies of communication often turn competition into a tournament in which the winner is richly rewarded, while the runners-up get far less. The classic example—which gives the theory its name—is the entertainment business. As Rosen pointed out, in bygone days there were hundreds of comedians making a modest living at live shows in the borscht belt and other places. Now they are mostly gone; what is left is a handful of superstar TV comedians.

The debates among these hypotheses—particularly the debate between those who attributed growing inequality to globalization and those who attributed it to technology—were many and bitter. I was a participant in those debates myself. But I won't dwell on them, because in the last few years there has been a growing sense among economists that none of these hypotheses work.

I don't mean to say that there was nothing to these stories. Yet as more evidence has accumulated, each of the hypotheses has seemed increasingly inadequate. Globalization can explain part of the relative decline in blue-collar wages, but it can't explain the 2,500 percent rise in C.E.O. incomes. Technology may explain why the salary premium associated with a college education has risen, but it's hard to match up with the huge increase in inequality among the college-educated, with little progress for many but gigantic gains at the top. The superstar theory works for Jay Leno, but not for the thousands of people who have become awesomely rich without going on TV.

The Great Compression—the substantial reduction in inequality during the New Deal and the Second World War—also seems hard to understand in terms of the usual theories. During World War II Franklin Roosevelt used government control over wages to compress wage gaps. But if the middle-class society that emerged from the war was an artificial creation, why did it persist for another 30 years?

Some—by no means all—economists trying to understand growing inequality have begun to take seriously a hypothesis that would have been considered irredeemably fuzzy-minded not long ago. This view stresses the role of social norms in setting limits to inequality. According to this view, the New Deal had a more profound impact on American society than even its most ardent admirers have suggested: it imposed norms of relative equality in pay that persisted for more than 30 years, creating the broadly middle-class society we came to take for granted. But those norms began to unravel in the 1970s and have done so at an accelerating pace.

Exhibit A for this view is the story of executive compensation. In the 1960s, America's great corporations behaved more like socialist republics than like cutthroat capitalist enterprises, and top executives behaved more like public-spirited bureaucrats than like captains of industry. I'm not exaggerating. Consider the description of executive behavior offered by John Kenneth Galbraith in his 1967 book, *The New Industrial State*. "Management does not go out ruthlessly to reward itself—a sound management is expected to exercise restraint." Managerial self-dealing was a thing of the past: "With the power of decision goes opportunity for making money. . . . Were everyone to seek to do so . . . the corporation would be a chaos of competitive avarice. But these are not the sort of thing that a good company man does; a remarkably effective code bans such behavior. Group decision-making insures, moreover, that almost everyone's actions and even thoughts are known to others. This acts to enforce the code and, more than incidentally, a high standard of personal honesty as well."

Thirty-five years on, a cover article in Fortune is titled "You Bought. They Sold." "All over corporate America," reads the blurb, "top execs were cashing in stocks even as their companies were tanking. Who was left holding the bag? You." As I said, we've become a different country.

Let's leave actual malfeasance on one side for a moment, and ask how the relatively modest salaries of top executives 30 years ago became the gigantic pay packages of today. There are two main stories, both of which emphasize changing norms rather than pure economics. The more optimistic story draws an analogy between the explosion of C.E.O. pay and the explosion of baseball salaries with the introduction of free agency.

According to this story, highly paid C.E.O.s really are worth it, because having the right man in that job makes a huge difference. The more pessimistic view—which I find more plausible—is that competition for talent is a minor factor. Yes, a great executive can make a big difference—but those huge pay packages have been going as often as not to executives whose performance is mediocre at best. The key reason executives are paid so much now is that they appoint the members of the corporate board that determines their compensation and control many of the perks that board members count on. So it's not the invisible hand of the market that leads to those monumental executive incomes; it's the invisible handshake in the boardroom.

But then why weren't executives paid lavishly 30 years ago? Again, it's a matter of corporate culture. For a generation after World War II, fear of outrage kept executive salaries in check. Now the outrage is gone. That is, the explosion of executive pay represents a social change rather than the purely economic forces of supply and demand. We should think of it not as a market trend like the rising value of waterfront property, but as something more like the sexual revolution of the 1960s—a relaxation of old strictures, a new permissiveness, but in this case the permissiveness is financial rather than sexual. Sure enough, John Kenneth Galbraith described the honest executive of 1967 as being one who "eschews the lovely, available and even naked woman by whom he is intimately surrounded." By the end of the 1990s, the executive motto might as well have been "If it feels good, do it."

How did this change in corporate culture happen? Economists and management theorists are only beginning to explore that question, but it's easy to suggest a few factors. One was the changing structure of financial markets. In his new book, "Searching for a Corporate Savior," Rakesh Khurana of Harvard Business School suggests that during the 1980s and 1990s, "managerial capitalism"—the world of the man in the gray flannel suit—was replaced by "investor capitalism." Institutional investors weren't willing to let a C.E.O. choose his own successor from inside the corporation; they wanted heroic leaders, often outsiders, and were willing to pay immense sums to get them. The subtitle of Khurana's book, by the way, is "The Irrational Quest for Charismatic C.E.O.s."

But fashionable management theorists didn't think it was irrational. Since the 1980s there has been ever more emphasis on the importance of "leadership"—meaning personal, charismatic leadership. When Lee Iacocca of Chrysler became a business celebrity in the early 1980s, he was practically alone: Khurana reports that in 1980 only one issue of Business Week featured a C.E.O. on its cover. By 1999 the number was up to 19. And once it was considered normal, even necessary, for a C.E.O. to be famous, it also became easier to make him rich.

Economists also did their bit to legitimize previously unthinkable levels of executive pay. During the 1980s and 1990s a torrent of academic papers—popularized in business magazines and incorporated into consultants' recommendations—argued that Gordon Gekko was right: greed is good; greed works. In order to get the best performance out of executives, these papers argued, it was necessary to align their interests with those of stockholders. And the way to do that was with large grants of stock or stock options.

It's hard to escape the suspicion that these new intellectual justifications for soaring executive pay were as much effect as cause. I'm not suggesting that management theorists and economists were personally corrupt. It would have been a subtle, unconscious process: the ideas that were taken up by business schools, that led to nice speaking and consulting fees, tended to be the ones that ratified an existing trend, and thereby gave it legitimacy.

What economists like Piketty and Saez are now suggesting is that the story of executive compensation is representative of a broader story. Much more than economists and free-market advocates like to imagine, wages—particularly at the top—are determined by social norms. What

happened during the 1930s and 1940s was that new norms of equality were established, largely through the political process. What happened in the 1980s and 1990s was that those norms unraveled, replaced by an ethos of "anything goes." And a result was an explosion of income at the top of the scale.

THE PRICE OF INEQUALITY

It was one of those revealing moments. Responding to an e-mail message from a Canadian viewer, Robert Novak of "Crossfire" delivered a little speech: "Marg, like most Canadians, you're ill informed and wrong. The U.S. has the longest standard of living—longest life expectancy of any country in the world, including Canada. That's the truth."

But it was Novak who had his facts wrong. Canadians can expect to live about two years longer than Americans. In fact, life expectancy in the U.S. is well below that in Canada, Japan and every major nation in Western Europe. On average, we can expect lives a bit shorter than those of Greeks, a bit longer than those of Portuguese. Male life expectancy is lower in the U.S. than it is in Costa Rica.

Still, you can understand why Novak assumed that we were No. 1. After all, we really are the richest major nation, with real G.D.P. per capita about 20 percent higher than Canada's. And it has been an article of faith in this country that a rising tide lifts all boats. Doesn't our high and rising national wealth translate into a high standard of living—including good medical care—for all Americans?

Well, no. Although America has higher per capita income than other advanced countries, it turns out that that's mainly because our rich are much richer. And here's a radical thought: if the rich get more, that leaves less for everyone else.

That statement—which is simply a matter of arithmetic—is guaranteed to bring accusations of "class warfare." If the accuser gets more specific, he'll probably offer two reasons that it's foolish to make a fuss over the high incomes of a few people at the top of the income distribution. First, he'll tell you that what the elite get may look like a lot of money, but it's still a small share of the total—that is, when all is said and done the rich aren't getting that big a piece of the pie. Second, he'll tell you that trying to do anything to reduce incomes at the top will hurt, not help, people further down the distribution, because attempts to redistribute income damage incentives.

These arguments for lack of concern are plausible. And they were entirely correct, once upon a time—namely, back when we had a middle-class society. But there's a lot less truth to them now.

First, the share of the rich in total income is no longer trivial. These days 1 percent of families receive about 16 percent of total pretax income, and have about 14 percent of after-tax income. That share has roughly doubled over the past 30 years, and is now about as large as the share of the bottom 40 percent of the population. That's a big shift of income to the top; as a matter of pure arithmetic, it must mean that the incomes of less well off families grew considerably more slowly than average income. And they did. Adjusting for inflation, average family income—total income divided by the number of families—grew 28 percent from 1979 to 1997. But median family income—the income of a family in the middle of the distribution, a better indicator of how typical American families are doing—grew only 10 percent. And the incomes of the bottom fifth of families actually fell slightly.

Let me belabor this point for a bit. We pride ourselves, with considerable justification, on our record of economic growth. But over the last few decades it's remarkable how little of that growth has trickled down to ordinary families. Median family income has risen only about 0.5 percent per year—and as far as we can tell from somewhat unreliable data, just about all of that increase was due to wives working longer hours, with little or no gain in real wages. Furthermore, numbers about income don't reflect the growing riskiness of life for ordinary workers. In the days when General Motors was known in-house as

Generous Motors, many workers felt that they had considerable job security—the company wouldn't fire them except in extremis. Many had contracts that guaranteed health insurance, even if they were laid off; they had pension benefits that did not depend on the stock market. Now mass firings from long-established companies are commonplace; losing your job means losing your insurance; and as millions of people have been learning, a 401(k) plan is no guarantee of a comfortable retirement.

Still, many people will say that while the U.S. economic system may generate a lot of inequality, it also generates much higher incomes than any alternative, so that everyone is better off. That was the moral *Business Week* tried to convey in its recent special issue with "25 Ideas for a Changing World." One of those ideas was "the rich get richer, and that's O.K." High incomes at the top, the conventional wisdom declares, are the result of a free-market system that provides huge incentives for performance. And the system delivers that performance, which means that wealth at the top doesn't come at the expense of the rest of us.

A skeptic might point out that the explosion in executive compensation seems at best loosely related to actual performance. Jack Welch was one of the 10 highest-paid executives in the United States in 2000, and you could argue that he earned it. But did Dennis Kozlowski of Tyco, or Gerald Levin of Time Warner, who were also in the top 10? A skeptic might also point out that even during the economic boom of the late 1990s, U.S. productivity growth was no better than it was during the great postwar expansion, which corresponds to the era when America was truly middle class and C.E.O.s were modestly paid technocrats.

But can we produce any direct evidence about the effects of inequality? We can't rerun our own history and ask what would have happened if the social norms of middle-class America had continued to limit incomes at the top, and if government policy had leaned against rising inequality instead of reinforcing it, which is what actually happened. But we can compare ourselves with other advanced countries. And the results are somewhat surprising.

Many Americans assume that because we are the richest country in the world, with real G.D.P. per capita higher than that of other major advanced countries, Americans must be better off across the board—that it's not just our rich who are richer than their counterparts abroad, but that the typical American family is much better off than the typical family elsewhere, and that even our poor are well off by foreign standards.

But it's not true. Let me use the example of Sweden, that great conservative *bete noire.*

A few months ago the conservative cyber-pundit Glenn Reynolds made a splash when he pointed out that Sweden's G.D.P. per capita is roughly comparable with that of Mississippi—see, those foolish believers in the welfare state have impoverished themselves! Presumably he assumed that this means that the typical Swede is as poor as the typical resident of Mississippi, and therefore much worse off than the typical American.

But life expectancy in Sweden is about three years higher than that of the U.S. Infant mortality is half the U.S. level, and less than a third the rate in Mississippi. Functional illiteracy is much less common than in the U.S.

How is this possible? One answer is that G.D.P. per capita is in some ways a misleading measure. Swedes take longer vacations than Americans, so they work fewer hours per year. That's a choice, not a failure of economic performance. Real G.D.P. per hour worked is 16 percent lower than in the United States, which makes Swedish productivity about the same as Canada's.

But the main point is that though Sweden may have lower average income than the United States, that's mainly because our rich are so much richer. The median Swedish family has a standard of living roughly comparable with that of the median U.S. family: wages are if anything higher in Sweden, and a higher tax burden is off-set by public provision of health care and generally better public services. And as you move further down the income distribution, Swedish

living standards are way ahead of those in the U.S. Swedish families with children that are at the 10th percentile—poorer than 90 percent of the population—have incomes 60 percent higher than their U.S. counterparts. And very few people in Sweden experience the deep poverty that is all too common in the United States. One measure: in 1994 only 6 percent of Swedes lived on less than $11 per day, compared with 14 percent in the U.S.

The moral of this comparison is that even if you think that America's high levels of inequality are the price of our high level of national income, it's not at all clear that this price is worth paying. The reason conservatives engage in bouts of Sweden-bashing is that they want to convince us that there is no tradeoff between economic efficiency and equity—that if you try to take from the rich and give to the poor, you actually make everyone worse off. But the comparison between the U.S. and other advanced countries doesn't support this conclusion at all. Yes, we are the richest major nation. But because so much of our national income is concentrated in relatively few hands, large numbers of Americans are worse off economically than their counterparts in other advanced countries. And we might even offer a challenge from the other side: inequality in the United States has arguably reached levels where it is counterproductive. That is, you can make a case that our society would be richer if its richest members didn't get quite so much.

I could make this argument on historical grounds. The most impressive economic growth in U.S. history coincided with the middle-class interregnum, the post-World War II generation, when incomes were most evenly distributed. But let's focus on a specific case, the extraordinary pay packages of today's top executives. Are these good for the economy?

Until recently it was almost unchallenged conventional wisdom that, whatever else you might say, the new imperial C.E.O.s had delivered results that dwarfed the expense of their compensation. But now that the stock bubble has burst, it has become increasingly clear that there was a price to those big pay packages, after all. In fact, the price paid by shareholders and society at large may have been many times larger than the amount actually paid to the executives.

It's easy to get boggled by the details of corporate scandal—insider loans, stock options, special-purpose entities, mark-to-market, round-tripping. But there's a simple reason that the details are so complicated. All of these schemes were designed to benefit corporate insiders—to inflate the pay of the C.E.O. and his inner circle. That is, they were all about the "chaos of competitive avarice" that, according to John Kenneth Galbraith, had been ruled out in the corporation of the 1960s. But while all restraint has vanished within the American corporation, the outside world—including stockholders—is still prudish, and open looting by executives is still not acceptable. So the looting has to be camouflaged, taking place through complicated schemes that can be rationalized to outsiders as clever corporate strategies.

Economists who study crime tell us that crime is inefficient—that is, the costs of crime to the economy are much larger than the amount stolen. Crime, and the fear of crime, divert resources away from productive uses: criminals spend their time stealing rather than producing, and potential victims spend time and money trying to protect their property. Also, the things people do to avoid becoming victims—like avoiding dangerous districts—have a cost even if they succeed in averting an actual crime.

The same holds true of corporate malfeasance, whether or not it actually involves breaking the law. Executives who devote their time to creating innovative ways to divert shareholder money into their own pockets probably aren't running the real business very well (think Enron, WorldCom, Tyco, Global Crossing, Adelphia . . .). Investments chosen because they create the illusion of profitability while insiders cash in their stock options are a waste of scarce resources. And if the supply of funds from lenders and shareholders dries up because of a lack of trust, the economy as a whole suffers. Just ask Indonesia.

The argument for a system in which some people get very rich has always been that the lure of wealth provides powerful incentives. But the question is, incentives to do what? As we learn more about what has actually been going on in corporate America, it's becoming less and less clear whether those incentives have actually made executives work on behalf of the rest of us.

INEQUALITY AND POLITICS

In September the Senate debated a proposed measure that would impose a one-time capital gains tax on Americans who renounce their citizenship in order to avoid paying U.S. taxes. Senator Phil Gramm was not pleased, declaring that the proposal was "right out of Nazi Germany." Pretty strong language, but no stronger than the metaphor Daniel Mitchell of the Heritage Foundation used, in an op-ed article in *The Washington Times*, to describe a bill designed to prevent corporations from rechartering abroad for tax purposes: Mitchell described this legislation as the "Dred Scott tax bill," referring to the infamous 1857 Supreme Court ruling that required free states to return escaped slaves.

Twenty years ago, would a prominent senator have likened those who want wealthy people to pay taxes to Nazis? Would a member of a think tank with close ties to the administration have drawn a parallel between corporate taxation and slavery? I don't think so. The remarks by Gramm and Mitchell, while stronger than usual, were indicators of two huge changes in American politics. One is the growing polarization of our politics—our politicians are less and less inclined to offer even the appearance of moderation. The other is the growing tendency of policy and policy makers to cater to the interests of the wealthy. And I mean the wealthy, not the merely well-off: only someone with a net worth of at least several million dollars is likely to find it worthwhile to become a tax exile.

You don't need a political scientist to tell you that modern American politics is bitterly polarized. But wasn't it always thus? No, it wasn't.

From World War II until the 1970s—the same era during which income inequality was historically low—political partisanship was much more muted than it is today. That's not just a subjective assessment. My Princeton political science colleagues Nolan McCarty and Howard Rosenthal, together with Keith Poole at the University of Houston, have done a statistical analysis showing that the voting behavior of a congressman is much better predicted by his party affiliation today than it was 25 years ago. In fact, the division between the parties is sharper now than it has been since the 1920s.

What are the parties divided about? The answer is simple: economics. McCarty, Rosenthal and Poole write that "voting in Congress is highly ideological—one-dimensional left/right, liberal versus conservative." It may sound simplistic to describe Democrats as the party that wants to tax the rich and help the poor, and Republicans as the party that wants to keep taxes and social spending as low as possible. And during the era of middle-class America that would indeed have been simplistic: politics wasn't defined by economic issues. But that was a different country; as McCarty, Rosenthal and Poole put it, "If income and wealth are distributed in a fairly equitable way, little is to be gained for politicians to organize politics around nonexistent conflicts." Now the conflicts are real, and our politics is organized around them. In other words, the growing inequality of our incomes probably lies behind the growing divisiveness of our politics.

But the politics of rich and poor hasn't played out the way you might think. Since the incomes of America's wealthy have soared while ordinary families have seen at best small gains, you might have expected politicians to seek votes by proposing to soak the rich. In fact, however, the polarization of politics has occurred because the Republicans have moved to the right, not because the Democrats have moved to the left. And actual economic policy has moved steadily in favor of the wealthy. The major tax cuts of the past 25 years, the Reagan cuts in the 1980s and the recent Bush cuts, were both heavily tilted toward the very well off. (Despite obfuscations, it remains true that more than half the Bush tax cut will eventually go to the top 1 percent of families.) The major tax increase over that period, the increase in payroll taxes in the 1980s, fell most heavily on working-class families.

The most remarkable example of how politics has shifted in favor of the wealthy—an example that helps us understand why economic policy has reinforced, not countered, the movement toward greater inequality—is the drive to repeal the estate tax. The estate tax is, overwhelmingly, a tax on the wealthy. In 1999, only the top 2 percent of estates paid any tax at all, and half the estate tax was paid by only 3,300 estates, 0.16 percent of the total, with a minimum value of $5 million and an average value of $17 million. A quarter of the tax was paid by just 467 estates worth more than $20 million. Tales of family farms and businesses broken up to pay the estate tax are basically rural legends; hardly any real examples have been found, despite diligent searching.

You might have thought that a tax that falls on so few people yet yields a significant amount of revenue would be politically popular; you certainly wouldn't expect widespread opposition. Moreover, there has long been an argument that the estate tax promotes democratic values, precisely because it limits the ability of the wealthy to form dynasties. So why has there been a powerful political drive to repeal the estate tax, and why was such a repeal a centerpiece of the Bush tax cut?

There is an economic argument for repealing the estate tax, but it's hard to believe that many people take it seriously. More significant for members of Congress, surely, is the question of who would benefit from repeal: while those who will actually benefit from estate tax repeal are few in number, they have a lot of money and control even more (corporate C.E.O.s can now count on leaving taxable estates behind). That is, they are the sort of people who command the attention of politicians in search of campaign funds.

But it's not just about campaign contributions: much of the general public has been convinced that the estate tax is a bad thing. If you try talking about the tax to a group of moderately prosperous retirees, you get some interesting reactions. They refer to it as the "death tax"; many of them believe that their estates will face punitive taxation, even though most of them will pay little or nothing; they are convinced that small businesses and family farms bear the brunt of the tax.

These misconceptions don't arise by accident. They have, instead, been deliberately promoted. For example, a Heritage Foundation document titled "Time to Repeal Federal Death Taxes: The Nightmare of the American Dream" emphasizes stories that rarely, if ever, happen in real life: "Small-business owners, particularly minority owners, suffer anxious moments wondering whether the businesses they hope to hand down to their children will be destroyed by the death tax bill, . . . Women whose children are grown struggle to find ways to re-enter the work force without upsetting the family's estate tax avoidance plan." And who finances the Heritage Foundation? Why, foundations created by wealthy families, of course.

The point is that it is no accident that strongly conservative views, views that militate against taxes on the rich, have spread even as the rich get richer compared with the rest of us: in addition to directly buying influence, money can be used to shape public perceptions. The liberal group People for the American Way's report on how conservative foundations have deployed vast sums to support think tanks, friendly media and other institutions that promote right-wing causes is titled "Buying a Movement."

Not to put too fine a point on it: as the rich get richer, they can buy a lot of things besides goods and services. Money buys political influence; used cleverly, it also buys intellectual influence. A result is that growing income disparities in the United States, far from leading to demands to soak the rich, have been accompanied by a growing movement to let them keep more of their earnings and to pass their wealth on to their children.

This obviously raises the possibility of a self-reinforcing process. As the gap between the rich and the rest of the population grows, economic policy increasingly caters to the interests of the elite, while public services for the population at large—above all, public education—are starved of resources. As policy increasingly favors the interests of the rich and neglects the interests of the general population, income disparities grow even wider.

PLUTOCRACY?

In 1924, the mansions of Long Island's North Shore were still in their full glory, as was the political power of the class that owned them. When Gov. Al Smith of New York proposed building a system of parks on Long Island, the mansion owners were bitterly opposed. One baron—Horace Havemeyer, the "sultan of sugar"—warned that North Shore towns would be "overrun with rabble from the city." "Rabble?" Smith said. "That's me you're talking about." In the end New Yorkers got their parks, but it was close: the interests of a few hundred wealthy families nearly prevailed over those of New York City's middle class.

America in the 1920s wasn't a feudal society. But it was a nation in which vast privilege—often inherited privilege—stood in contrast to vast misery. It was also a nation in which the government, more often than not, served the interests of the privileged and ignored the aspirations of ordinary people.

Those days are past—or are they? Income inequality in America has now returned to the levels of the 1920s. Inherited wealth doesn't yet play a big part in our society, but given time—and the repeal of the estate tax—we will grow ourselves a hereditary elite just as set apart from the concerns of ordinary Americans as old Horace Havemeyer. And the new elite, like the old, will have enormous political power.

Kevin Phillips concludes his book "Wealth and Democracy" with a grim warning: "Either democracy must be renewed, with politics brought back to life, or wealth is likely to cement a new and less democratic regime—plutocracy by some other name." It's a pretty extreme line, but we live in extreme times. Even if the forms of democracy remain, they may become meaningless. It's all too easy to see how we may become a country in which the big rewards are reserved for people with the right connections; in which ordinary people see little hope of advancement; in which political involvement seems pointless, because in the end the interests of the elite always get served.

Am I being too pessimistic? Even my liberal friends tell me not to worry, that our system has great resilience, that the center will hold. I hope they're right, but they may be looking in the rearview mirror. Our optimism about America, our belief that in the end our nation always finds its way, comes from the past—a past in which we were a middle-class society. But that was another country.

DISCUSSION QUESTIONS

1. Referring to the issue of income and wealth disparities in the United States, at one point Krugman observes that "even bringing up the subject exposes you to charges of 'class warfare,' the 'politics of envy' and so on." Given the importance he assigns to it, why do you think that class inequality is such a nonissue within the American political culture?

2. Compare and contrast Krugman's analysis with the critique offered by Robert Jensen in Article 8.

3. Identify the reasons behind the sharp rise in economic inequality in America over the past 30 years. What are the political impacts of inequality as they appear in Krugman's analysis? Assess the implications of these impacts on the quality of democracy in the United States.

BARBARA EHRENREICH

DOING IT FOR OURSELVES: CAN FEMINISM SURVIVE CLASS POLARIZATION?

Barbara Ehrenreich is a popular and prolific writer, feminist and social critic who often writes about the intersection of gender and class. In this article she contends that class polarization in America over the past three decades has created divisions among previously united feminists, with those in the top 20 to 30 percent of income earners (professional women) having significantly different lifestyles and consumption patterns than those in the bottom 40 percent (working class women). "Frequent-flying female executives" find themselves with little or nothing in common with "airport cleaning women." This class polarization has dampened the egalitarianism of the early feminist movement, dramatically weakening "the sense of shared conditions" that was vital to sisterhood. Ehrenreich examines the impact of class polarization on three core feminist issues—welfare, health care, and housework—finding that in each instance class differences now trump feminist solidarity. Only the issues of sexual harassment and violence against women have survived growing female class inequality. The solution to this gender-class dilemma does not lie in a retreat into conservative abandonment of the feminist project. Rather, Ehrenreich suggests that feminists reclaim the original radical feminist vision of the abolition of all forms of hierarchy, be they based on race, gender, or class. The problem, most fundamentally, from Ehrenreich's perspective is class inequality—among women, and between women and men. Challenging that class inequity should be the first priority of those seeking to fashion public policy for women and to revitalize the feminist movement.

Here's a scene from feminist ancient history: It's 1972 and about twenty of us are gathered in somebody's living room for our weekly "women's support group" meeting. We're all associated, in one way or another, with a small public college catering mostly to "nontraditional" students, meaning those who are older, poorer and more likely to be black or Latina than typical college students in this suburban area. Almost every level of the college hierarchy is represented—students of all ages, clerical workers, junior faculty members and even one or two full professors. There

Source: Barbara Ehrenreich, "Doing It for Ourselves: Can Feminism Survive Class Polarization?" *In These Times*, vol. 23, no. 26, 28 November 1999, pp. 10–12.

are acknowledged differences among us—race and sexual preference, for example—which we examine eagerly and a little anxiously. But we are comfortable together, and excited to have a chance to discuss everything from the administration's sexist policies to our personal struggles with husbands and lovers. Whatever may divide us, we are all women, and we understand this to be one of the great defining qualities of our lives and politics.

Could a group so diverse happily converse today? Please let me know if you can offer a present day parallel, but I tend to suspect the answer is "very seldom" or "not at all." Perhaps the biggest social and economic trend of the past three decades has been class polarization—the expanding inequality in income and wealth. As United for a Fair Economy's excellent book, *Shifting Fortunes: The Perils of the Growing American Wealth Gap,* points out, the most glaring polarization has occurred between those at the very top of the income distribution—the upper 1 to 5 percent—and those who occupy the bottom 30 to 40 percent. Less striking, but more ominous for the future of feminism, is the growing gap between those in the top 40 percent and those in the bottom 40. One chart in *Shifting Fortunes* shows that the net worth of households in the bottom 40 percent declined by nearly 80 percent between 1983 and 1995. Except for the top 1 percent, the top 40 percent lost ground too—but much less. Today's college teacher, if she is not an adjunct, occupies that relatively lucky top 40 group, while today's clerical worker is in the rapidly sinking bottom 40. Could they still gather comfortably in each other's living rooms to discuss common issues? Do they still have common issues to discuss?

Numbers hardly begin to tell the story. The '80s brought sharp changes in lifestyle and consumption habits between the lower 40 percent—which is roughly what we call the "working class"—and the upper 20 to 30, which is populated by professors, administrators, executives, doctors, lawyers and other "professionals." "Mass markets" became "segmented markets," with dif-

ferent consumer trends signaling differences in status. In 1972, a junior faculty member's living room looked much like that of a departmental secretary—only, in most cases, messier. Today, the secretary is likely to accessorize her home at Kmart; the professor at Pottery Barn. Three decades ago, we all enjoyed sugary, refined-flour treats at our meetings (not to mention Maxwell House coffee and cigarettes!) Today, the upper-middle class grinds its own beans, insists on whole grains, organic snacks, and vehemently eschews hot dogs and meatloaf. In the '70s, conspicuous, or even just overly enthusiastic, consumption was considered gauche—and not only by leftists and feminists. Today, professors, including quite liberal ones, are likely to have made a deep emotional investment in their houses, their furniture and their pewter ware. It shows how tasteful they are, meaning—when we cut through the garbage about aesthetics—how distinct they are from the "lower" classes.

In the case of women, there is an additional factor compounding the division wrought by class polarization: In the '60s, only about 30 percent of American women worked outside their homes; today, the proportion is reversed, with more than 70 percent of women in the work force. This represents a great advance, since women who earn their own way are of course more able to avoid male domination in their personal lives. But women's influx into the work force also means that fewer and fewer women share the common occupational experience once defined by the word "housewife." I don't want to exaggerate this commonality as it existed in the '60s and '70s; obviously the stay-at-home wife of an executive led a very different life from that of the stay-at-home wife of a blue-collar man. But they did perform similar daily tasks—housecleaning, childcare, shopping, cooking. Today, in contrast, the majority of women fan out every morning to face vastly different work experiences, from manual labor to positions of power. Like men, women are now spread throughout the occupational hierarchy (though not at the very top), where they encounter each other daily as unequals—bosses vs. clerical workers, givers of orders vs. those who are ordered around, etc.

Class was always an issue. Even before polarization set in, some of us lived on the statistical hilltops, others deep in the valleys. But today we are distributed on what looks less like a mountain range and more like a cliff-face. Gender, race and sexual preference still define compelling commonalities, but the sense of a shared condition necessarily weakens as we separate into frequent-flying female executives on the one hand and airport cleaning women on the other. Can feminism or, for that matter, any cross-class social movement, survive as class polarization spreads Americans further and further apart?

For all the ardent egalitarianism of the early movement, feminism had the unforeseen consequence of heightening the class differences between women. It was educated, middle-class women who most successfully used feminist ideology and solidarity to advance themselves professionally. Feminism has played a role in working-class women's struggles too—for example, in the union organizing drives of university clerical workers—but probably its greatest single economic effect was to open up the formerly male-dominated professions to women. Between the '70s and the '90s, the percentage of female students in business, medical and law schools shot up from less than 10 percent to more than 40 percent.

There have been, however, no comparable gains for young women who cannot afford higher degrees, and most of these women remain in the same low-paid occupations that have been "women's work" for decades. All in all, feminism has had little impact on the status or pay of traditional female occupations like clerical, retail, health care and light assembly line work. While middle-class women gained MBAs, working-class women won the right not to be called "honey"— and not a whole lot more than that.

Secondly, since people tend to marry within their own class, the gains made by women in the professions added to the growing economic gap between the working class and the professional-managerial class. Working-class families gained too, as wives went to work. But, as I argued in *Fear of Falling: The Inner Life of the Middle Class,* the most striking gains have accrued to couples consisting of two well-paid professionals or managers. The doctor/lawyer household zoomed well ahead of the truck driver/typist combination.

So how well has feminism managed to maintain its stance as the ground shifts beneath its feet? Here are some brief observations of the impact of class polarization on a few issues once central to the feminist project:

WELFARE

This has to be the most tragic case. In the '70s, feminists hewed to the slogan, "Every woman is just one man away from welfare." This was an exaggeration of course; even then, there were plenty of self-supporting and independently wealthy women. But it was true enough to resonate with the large numbers of women who worked outside their homes part time or not at all. We recognized our commonality as homemakers and mothers as we considered this kind of work to be important enough to be paid for—even when there was no husband on the scene. Welfare, in other words, was potentially every woman's concern.

Flash forward to 1996, when Clinton signed the odious Republican welfare reform bill, and you find only the weakest and most tokenistic protests from groups bearing the label "feminist." The core problem, as those of us who were pro-welfare advocates found, was that many middle- and upper-middle class women could no longer see why a woman should be subsidized to raise her children. "Well, I work and raise my kids— why shouldn't they?" was a common response, as if poor women could command wages that would enable them to purchase reliable childcare. As for that other classic feminist slogan—"every mother is a working mother"—no one seems to remember it anymore.

HEALTH CARE

Our bodies, after all, are what we have most in common as women, and the women's health movement of the '70s and early '80s probably brought together as diverse a constituency—at least in terms of class—as any other component of feminism. We worked to legalize abortion and to stop the involuntary sterilization of poor women of color, to challenge the sexism of medical care faced by all women consumers and to expand low-income women's access to care.

In many ways, we were successful: Abortion is legal, if not always accessible; the kinds of health information once available only in underground publications like the original *Our Bodies, Ourselves* can now be found in *Mademoiselle;* the medical profession is no longer an all-male bastion of patriarchy. We were not so successful, however, in increasing low-income women's access to health care—in fact, the number of the uninsured is far larger than it used to be, and poor women still get second-class health care when they get any at all. Yet the only women's health issue that seems to generate any kind of broad, cross-class participation today is breast cancer, at least if wearing a pink ribbon counts as "participation."

Even the nature of medical care is increasingly different for women of different classes. While lower-income women worry about paying for abortions or their children's care, many in the upper-middle class are far more concerned with such medical luxuries as high-tech infertility treatments and cosmetic surgery. Young college women get bulimia; less affluent young women are more likely to suffer from toxemia of pregnancy, which is basically a consequence of malnutrition.

HOUSEWORK

In the '70s, housework was a hot feminist issue and a major theme of consciousness-raising groups. After all, whatever else women did, we did housework; it was the nearly universal female occupation. We debated Pat Mainardi's famous essay on "The Politics of Housework," which focused on the private struggles to get men to pick up their own socks. We argued bitterly about the "wages for housework" movement's proposal that women working at home should be paid by

the state. We studied the Cuban legal code, with its intriguing provision that males do their share or face jail time.

Thirty years later, the feminist silence on the issue of housework is nearly absolute. Not, I think, because men are at last doing their share, but because so many women of the upper-middle class now pay other women to do their housework for them. Bring up the subject among affluent feminists today, and you get a guilty silence, followed by defensive patter about how well they pay and treat their cleaning women.

In fact, the $15 an hour commonly earned by freelance maids is not so generous at all, when you consider that it has to cover cleaning equipment, transportation to various cleaning sites throughout the day, as well as any benefits, like health insurance, the cleaning person might choose to purchase for herself. The fast-growing corporate cleaning services like Merry Maids and The Maids International are far worse, offering (at least in the northeastern urban area I looked into) their workers between $5 (yes, that's below the minimum wage) and $7 an hour.

In a particularly bitter irony, many of the women employed by the corporate cleaning services are former welfare recipients bumped off the rolls by the welfare reform bill so feebly resisted by organized feminists. One could conclude, if one was in a very bad mood, that it is not in the interests of affluent feminists to see the wages of working class women improve. As for the prospects of "sisterhood" between affluent women and the women who scrub their toilets—forget about it, even at a "generous" $15 an hour.

The issues that have most successfully weathered class polarization are sexual harassment and male violence against women. These may be the last concerns that potentially unite all women; and they are of course crucial. But there is a danger in letting these issues virtually define feminism, as seems to be the case in some campus women's centers today: Poor and working-class women (and men) face forms of harassment and violence on the job that are not sexual or even clearly gender-related. Being reamed out repeatedly by an obnoxious supervisor of either sex can lead to depression and stress-related disorders. Being forced to work long hours of overtime, or under ergonomically or chemically hazardous conditions, can make a person physically sick. Yet feminism has yet to recognize such routine workplaces experiences as forms of "violence against women."

When posing the question—"can feminism survive class polarization?"—to middle-class feminist acquaintances, I sometimes get the response: "Well, you're right—we have to confront our classism." But the problem is not classism, the problem is class itself: the existence of grave inequalities among women, as well as between women and men.

We should recall that the original radical—and, yes, utopian—feminist vision was of a society without hierarchies of any kind. This of course means equality among the races and the genders, but class is different: There can be no such thing as "equality among the classes." The abolition of hierarchy demands not only racial and gender equality, but the abolition of class. For a start, let's put that outrageous aim back into the long-range feminist agenda and mention it as loudly and often as we can.

In the shorter term, there's plenty to do, and the burden necessarily falls on the more privileged among us: to support working-class women's workplace struggles, to advocate for expanded social services (like childcare and health care) for all women, to push for greater educational access for low-income women and so

on and so forth. I'm not telling you anything new here, sisters—you know what to do.

But there's something else, too, in the spirit of another ancient slogan that is usually either forgotten or misinterpreted today: "The personal is the political." Those of us who are fortunate enough to have assets and income beyond our immediate needs need to take a hard look at how we're spending our money. New furniture—and please, I don't want to hear about how tastefully funky or antique-y it is—or a donation to a homeless shelter? A chic outfit or a check written to an organization fighting sweatshop conditions in the garment industry? A maid or a contribution to a clinic serving low-income women?

I know it sounds scary, but it will be a lot less so if we can make sharing stylish again and excess consumption look as ugly as it actually is. Better yet, give some of your time and your energy too. But if all you can do is write a check, that's fine: Since Congress will never redistribute the wealth (downward, anyway), we may just have to do it ourselves.

DISCUSSION QUESTIONS

1. According to Ehrenreich, in what ways have class differences among women complicated feminism since its revival in the 1970s?
2. How would you interpret Ehrenreich's comment that "the problem is not classism, the problem is class itself"?

BLACK AMERICA AND THE DILEMMA OF PATRIOTISM

Poet and attorney Brian Gilmore explores with sensitivity his complex reactions as a black American to the September 11 attacks. While he is obviously appalled and saddened by the attacks, Gilmore is concerned about the implications for black America of the call to unconditionally "stand by the man" and support the "war on terrorism" launched by President George W. Bush. Reflecting on statements made by the novelist Richard Wright during World War II, Gilmore explains that calls for Americans to close ranks during wartime have often served to remove the problems and grievances of black Americans from the political agenda. In the tradition of scholar and activist W. E. B. Du Bois, Gilmore explores black American "double consciousness" in a way that enables all Americans to comprehend the complexities of national identity. He helps us understand how a ritual like flying the flag has distinct meanings in different communities.

"I pledge my loyalty and allegiance, without mental reservation or evasions, to America. I shall through my writing seek to rally the Negro people to stand shoulder to shoulder with the Administration in a solid national front to wage war until victory is won."
—*Richard Wright (December 16, 1941)*

On the morning of September 11, I was driving down R Street in Washington on my way to a local foundation where I was working as a writer when I saw a huge cloud of smoke off in the distance. I had already heard that two hijacked planes had crashed into the twin towers of the World Trade Center in New York City. When I saw the huge cloud of smoke rising into the sky, I kind of figured it wasn't someone's house on fire. No more than a minute later, the radio reported that a plane had hit the Pentagon. I immediately pulled over and went inside the Washington Legal Clinic for the Homeless, where I once worked. Everyone there was distraught. Some people began crying. Others were speechless. Then the newscaster announced that the towers had collapsed with possibly thousands of people trapped inside. I told my former co-workers I was leaving.

"Where are you headed?"

"The racetrack," I answered.

Source: Brian Gilmore, "Stand by the Man: Black America and the Dilemma of Patriotisms." *The Progressive,* vol. 66, no. 1, January 2002, pp. 24–27.

My answer was knee-jerk but honest. I wasn't at all surprised at what happened that day because I have always suspected that there are people and nations and factions that do not like America. Oftentimes, Black America does not like America, but, for the most part, many of us remain quiet. We go along for the ride because it is what we are accustomed to doing. Our interests are tied to America. And if you want to know the most poignant truth of all: We really have no choice in the matter. Where are we to go? We are, though some of us forget sometimes, American, perhaps more so than anyone else.

But that is, of course, part of why I was headed to the racetrack. I wanted to pretend that the bombing hadn't happened. I also knew that all of us—every black American—would be called upon (like every other American) from that day forth until we were instructed otherwise, to stand by our man—Uncle Sam. Support the war unconditionally. One shouldn't even question the approach to solving the problem (as if there is only one way to fight this battle). Any other conduct during the war would be deemed un-American.

For black Americans, it has always been that way, no matter our position in society. We would be asked to do what we had always done without any promise of future benefit: to prove our unconditional love and loyalty for America. Drop any grievances or problems we have with our American condition for the time being, or maybe for a generation or so. I didn't want to deal with the bombings, and I definitely didn't want to deal with the culture of violence that the bombings had spawned.

I preferred simply to go look at the horses.

Days after the bombing, with all of those thoughts of my American self still bearing down on me, I read Richard Wright's statement on World War II that appears above. I found it in Michel Fabre's celebrated biography of Wright, *The Unfinished Quest of Richard Wright* (University of Illinois, 1993). I had been in search of statements by authors, black authors in particular, following Pearl Harbor. I wanted to know what they had to say as that attack became part of

us. This was war, and that was war back in 1941, and I knew they found themselves in a difficult spot. Before that war, Roosevelt had expressed some interest in being a friend of Black America, but he hadn't really gone that far. Most people even forget that Black America had planned a March on Washington in 1941 that was canceled at the last minute. The argument by black Americans that fighting against tyranny will make democracy for blacks more possible in America was strong even before the Japanese bombed Pearl Harbor; afterwards, it was overwhelming.

Before the September 11 attack, Black America was even more frustrated. The election and subsequent decision by the Supreme Court that propelled George W. Bush into office still burned in the souls of many black folks. In fact, I can't remember a day that went by in the last year that at least one of my black American friends or acquaintances didn't bring up the vote count irregularities among blacks in Florida and how they couldn't wait to vote Bush out of office in 2004.

Even more painfully, our issues, the issues that at least were on the table during the Clinton years (despite his failure to address them), weren't even being discussed anymore. The country was talking tax cuts; we were asking about job cuts. The country was talking education reform; we were asking about just getting an education for our children. Then there were the bigger fish that Clinton turned and ran from for eight years: reparations, racial profiling, police brutality, reforming "drug war" sentencing guidelines, black men disproportionately going to jail.

But when those planes plunged into the World Trade Center and the Pentagon on that blue, blue morning of September 11, 2001, not only was the black agenda taken off the table for the foreseeable future, the table itself was taken down.

That is why Richard Wright's statement struck a chord in me. I finally began to think clearly for the first time about the September 11 bombing. I began to put the attack into some sort of context without being "upset" or "angry" or full of guilt about my initial reaction of wanting to go to the racetrack. I finally knew where I was at that moment, right after I read that quote. I was where the average black American always seems to be in America—in that tragic Duboisian state of double consciousness.

What did the average African American say about the attack and what we should do? This is what I was hearing:

It was an awful thing.

Evil.

Kill the bastards.

Crush them.

Bomb them.

Kill them all.

Profile them Arabs.

Deport them all.

(Note: It was especially vexing to hear black people come on the radio following the bombing and basically call for racial profiling of Arab Americans and deportation. I assure you, this view was rampant. On one radio program based in Washington, D.C., caller after caller, black Americans, stated that "profiling" of Arab Americans was, in fact, needed and had to be done for the good of the nation.)

But that is just one side of the black American experience. Here is the other that I began to hear:

Don't we bomb people all the time?

And look how they treated us for so long.

Slavery.

Lynchings.

Second-class citizenship.

Segregation.

Not to mention the same old bullshit we still got to put up with in daily life.

We are arguing over an apology for slavery.

How can we forget any of it?

We the ones who are going to be over there fighting, too.

And after this war, what then? The same?

Two peoples always, it seems.

I could not get it out of my head that Wright had felt a need to make a statement in support of World War II. For one thing, he was a pacifist. And prior to December 7, 1941, he was badgering America about the need for social justice and equality for the Negro society. He was against any involvement in the war; he was more interested in addressing America's racial policies. Months before the war, on June 6, 1941, at a League of American Writers council meeting, Wright delivered a speech entitled "Not My People's War" that basically stated World War II was not a war black people should participate in because of how they are treated in society. Even after America's entry into that war, Wright remained focused on the improvement of conditions for America's black citizens.

Though he eventually volunteered to contribute to the war effort through writing, Wright's ambivalence was obvious. He supported the war for essentially the same naive reasons Frederick Douglass asked black people to fight with the Union in the Civil War: It was a chance for freedom and democracy. How could they continue to hold us down if we fought beside them against the true oppressors?

But though I was sure something drastic had to be done against terrorism, I couldn't support America's call for war against Afghanistan. I was against terrorism and violence, for sure, with every bone in my body. I abhorred the actions of the suicide bombers, which were so sick and so terribly destructive. Yet, I was sure that bombing a country that is hopelessly stuck in the medieval age would not solve anything. I was sure that as America began dropping bombs, we would become even more unsafe. I was more concerned about civil defense than revenge. I also could not get all that history out of my head about America and its black American people.

But still I wondered: Why wasn't I deeply depressed? This was a tragedy of epic proportions. The loss of human life was unfathomable. We were all attacked that day, too. Black America as well. Osama bin Laden issued a *fatwa* (holy war decree) years ago, and he said all Americans should be killed. Not white Americans, but all

Americans. That meant me and my wife and my daughter and the rest of my family and Americans of every race and ethnicity.

This wasn't the Iranian hostage crisis of 1979 and '80, when the captors, in a clever show of political solidarity, released the black American hostages from the U.S. Embassy. Whoever was responsible for the crashes of September 11 didn't give a damn who you were as a person; this was an attack on America. If the bombers of September 11, 2001, were acting upon bin Laden's *fatwa,* or whoever's order, black America was also a target.

A very good family friend, a schoolteacher, Lizzie Jones, a black American woman who was like a second mother to me, lost one of her best friends in one of the suicide crashes. Her friend was a schoolteacher. They had known each other for more than thirty years and had talked right before the bombing. Her friend was taking a student on a study trip sponsored by *National Geographic.* She told Ms. Jones she would be back on Saturday, and that she would tell her all about it. Her friend did not come back. She is gone. I saw Ms. Jones on television on the news speaking to her lost friend in spiritual phrases. I felt nauseous.

I am afraid for my daughter. She does not need to live in a world that is full of violence, death, and chaos. My sincere hope is that all of us now understand the real horror of mass violence of this magnitude. I know I do. No way should anyone suffer as we did on September 11, 2001. The frantic phone calls looking for friends and family members, the e-mails seeking out answers, the devastation, the catastrophic grief.

Chilean writer Ariel Dorfman refers to America now as "Unique No More." Dorfman says this is so because America has finally experienced what "so many other human beings" in "faraway zones, have suffered." Yes, we have felt it.

I am pretty sure that Richard Wright anguished over writing all the other words he wrote supporting entry into World War II. But he felt America in 1941 was still his country. America is my country, too, but it is much more complex than that. I don't mean just the place where I was born, but a place that is unequivocally my land and the land of my people without the enormous contradictions that create a strange dialogue, which can be summed up like this:

"But we ended slavery."

"But you allowed it to be legal for hundreds of years."

"We conquered Jim Crow and segregation."

"But it was legal for most of the twentieth century, and we had to almost burn the country down to get you to do it."

Today, I marvel at my friends who talk of their families coming to America from India or Nicaragua or my law school classmates who speak about their grandfather or grandmother's journey to America from Italy or Ireland or Greece in search of a better life in America. It is a magical story I don't have. That's why black Americans can never be whole in America, no matter how hard we try. How can we? We don't even have a past that can be defined, and the part that we know, the story that is passed to us regarding our country's relationship to us, is a complete tragedy. America is my country, yet my country, it seems, has never wanted me.

They were blowing their car horn. They were drunk. I was in Georgetown, and several young, white youths were hanging out of the windows of the car with a sign that read: "Honk, If You Love America." It was cute in a way to see such brash patriotism. Drivers began honking in response to the sign. This was September 16, and everyone was still in immense pain. The young drunks were trying to make themselves feel better and everyone else at the same time. I didn't honk my horn. I was in the Georgetown traffic jam, frozen and unable to do anything. I began looking around and realized that no one really would notice because so many cars were honking. Most of the people I saw honking their horns were white. I didn't see any black people around. I didn't honk. It was a disturbing moment for me because I wasn't standing by my man in one of his toughest times. I realized again (as I have been reminded many times since) that though I was and am an American, I didn't have what most Americans feel—that unique sense of belonging. The tragedy was a part of me but it was mostly about the victims, the injured, the dead. I knew I wasn't alone, either.

On the radio in the days after the bombing, I heard many black Americans state that they felt bad for the victims, they felt violated, and they felt that America had to do something, but then some would add at the end of their comments statements about not feeling that deep sense of patriotism that most Americans feel. The kind of emotion that pushes you to put your hand over your heart, take your hat off when the National Anthem is played. The "God Bless America" brand of patriotism. They were Americans, but not quite as American as white Americans. They cried for the victims but not necessarily for America.

In the days following the bombing, I was asked several times with strange looks: "Where is your flag?" I told some people I didn't have a flag. I told others that I simply could not lie to myself. It never dawned on me that I should fly a flag. I felt terrible for the victims. Awful. If the flag was for the victims, it should be flown, but I didn't fly a flag because I remembered the victims in other ways. For me, simply to resign myself to flying the flag was not enough. It was superficial, and it took the focus away from those who had died.

I spent much of my time in the days following the bombing riding through the city, looking at flags. I wanted to see who was flying them, and who wasn't. It would tell me something about America. I rode to upper Northwest first. This is the area of Washington where the affluent live, and I saw the American flag waving on nearly every street. On some streets you could tell that the neighbors probably had talked to each other

because nearly every house had a flag out front. There was a pride there that was impressive. Cars had flags, too. It made the streets look like there was going to be a July 4 parade.

Then I rode to my old neighborhood, where I grew up. The families there are less affluent, but they are doing fairly well, at least most of them. They've always wanted to be American. Black Americans live there mostly, some middle class, some working class, but the neighborhood has only small pockets of despair and is usually quiet except on hot summer nights. There were American flags flying up here, too, but not as many as in upper Northwest. My mother, who still lives there, had a tiny flag on her front door. You could barely see it. She said someone gave it to her.

Finally, I rode through the most economically depressed areas of Washington: the hood—Northwest, below Howard University, but above downtown—streets where crack and heroin continued to be sold and used as the tragedy unfolded. Drunks were laid out in the gutter, children ran the streets late at night, addicts came up to my car trying to sell stolen items. There was hardly a flag in sight.

DISCUSSION QUESTIONS

1. Why does Gilmore believe that the war on terrorism might in some ways undercut the interests and agenda of black America?

2. Compare Gilmore's reaction to September 11 with Richard Wright's comments about World War II that open this selection. What is it about the black experience in America that leads Gilmore to feel ambivalence about the call to rally around the flag?

(**36**)

THE UNITED STATES AND GLOBAL WARS OF TERROR

In this article, adapted from a lecture, world-renowned linguist, philosopher, and political activist Noam Chomsky situates the Bush response to the terrorist attacks of September 11, 2001, in historical perspective. For nearly 40 years Chomsky has been the leading critic of the hypocrisy, double standards, and support for state terror that marks U.S. foreign policy. The Bush "doctrine of preemption," announced on September 20, 2002 [see Article 28], explicitly extends a policy in place since the end of WWII. Chomsky points out that the United States consistently has inflicted violence and state terror on numerous nations, either directly or, more commonly, indirectly through economic and military support for client regimes who brutalize their own people to protect U.S. interests, as in the case of Columbia, Turkey, South Africa, Nicaragua, East Timor, Panama, and numerous other examples. In the Middle East specifically, U.S. and Israeli state terror sets the context for today's unrest, with disregard for international law and against the opposition of most of the rest of the world. Indeed, as he shows with ample reference to U.S. foreign policy elites, the United States simply does not acknowledge international law when it might inconveniently interfere with the unfettered U.S. pursuit of its objectives and power interests, a standard which would be criticized with ferocity in the United States if another nation adopted such an arrogant posture. Chomsky's work is driven by the hope that U.S. citizens would not stand for such duplicity and double standards if they were allowed to look at their nation's foreign policy record with an honest eye. As he writes: "A comparison of leading beneficiaries of U.S. military assistance and the record of state terror should shame honest people, and would, if it were not so effectively removed from the public eye." After surveying the dismal post-WWII record, which is marked by great continuity regardless of which political party controls the White House, Chomsky ends with a consideration of four key questions posed by the horrible tragedy of 9-11. His answers raise troubling questions about the moral standards our government applies to international affairs.

Source: Noam Chomsky, "Wars of Terror." *New Political Science,* vol. 25, no. 1, March 2003, pp. 113–127.

It is widely argued that the September 11 terrorist attacks have changed the world dramatically, that nothing will be the same as the world enters into a new and frightening "age of terror"—the title of a collection of academic essays by Yale University scholars and others, which regards the anthrax attack as even more ominous.

It had been recognized for some time that with new technology, the industrial powers would probably lose their virtual monopoly of violence, retaining only an enormous preponderance. Well before 9-11, technical studies had concluded that "a well-planned operation to smuggle WMD into the United States would have at least a 90 percent probability of success—much higher than ICBM delivery even in the absence of [National Missile Defense]." That has become "America's Achilles Heel," a study with that title concluded several years ago. Surely the dangers were evident after the 1993 attempt to blow up the World Trade Center, which came close to succeeding along with much more ambitious plans, and might have killed tens of thousands of people with better planning, the WTC building engineers reported.

On September 11, the threats were realized: with "wickedness and awesome cruelty," to recall Robert Fisk's memorable words, capturing the world reaction of shock and horror, and sympathy for the innocent victims. For the first time in modern history, Europe and its offshoots were subjected, on home soil, to atrocities of the kind that are all too familiar elsewhere. The history should be unnecessary to review, and though the West may choose to disregard it, the victims do not. The sharp break in the traditional pattern surely qualifies 9-11 as a historic event, and the repercussions are sure to be significant.

The consequences will, of course, be determined substantially by policy choices made within the United States. In this case, the target of the terrorist attack is not Cuba or Lebanon or Chechnya or a long list of others, but a state with an awesome potential for shaping the future. Any sensible attempt to assess the likely consequences will naturally begin with an investigation of U.S. power, how it has been exercised, particularly in the very recent past, and how it is interpreted within the political culture.

At this point there are two choices: we can approach these questions with the rational standards we apply to others, or we can dismiss the historical and contemporary record on some grounds or other.

One familiar device is miraculous conversion: true, there have been flaws in the past, but they have now been overcome so we can forget those boring and now-irrelevant topics and march on to a bright future. This useful doctrine of "change of course" has been invoked frequently over the years, in ways that are instructive when we look closely. To take a current example, a few months ago Bill Clinton attended the independence day celebration of the world's newest country, East Timor. He informed the press that "I don't believe America and any of the other countries were sufficiently sensitive in the beginning . . . and for a long time before 1999, going way back to the '70s, to the suffering of the people of East Timor," but "when it became obvious to me what was really going on . . . I tried to make sure we had the right policy."

We can identify the timing of the conversion with some precision. Clearly, it was after September 8, 1999, when the Secretary of Defense reiterated the official position that "it is the responsibility of the Government of Indonesia, and we don't want to take that responsibility away from them." They had fulfilled their responsibility by killing hundreds of thousands of people with firm U.S. and British support since the 1970s, then thousands more in the early months of 1999, finally destroying most of the country and driving out the population when they voted the wrong way in the August 30 referendum—fulfilling not only their responsibilities but also their promises, as Washington and London surely had known well before.

The U.S. "never tried to sanction or support the oppression of the East Timorese," Clinton explained, referring to the 25 years of crucial military and diplomatic support for Indonesian atrocities, continuing through the last paroxysm of fury in September. But we should not "look backward," he advised, because America did finally become sensitive to the "oppression": sometime between September 8 and September 11, when, under severe domestic and international pressure, Clinton informed the Indonesian generals that the game is over and they quickly withdrew, allowing an Australian-led UN peace-keeping force to enter unopposed.

The course of events revealed with great clarity how some of the worst crimes of the late twentieth century could have been ended very easily, simply by withdrawing crucial participation. That is hardly the only case, and Clinton was not alone in his interpretation of what scholarship now depicts as another inspiring achievement of the new era of humanitarianism.

There is a new and highly-regarded literary genre inquiring into the cultural defects that keep us from responding properly to the crimes of others. An interesting question no doubt, though by any reasonable standards it ranks well below a different one: Why do we and our allies persist in our own substantial crimes, either directly or through crucial support for murderous clients? That remains unasked, and if raised at the margins, arouses shivers of horror.

Another familiar way to evade rational standards is to dismiss the historical record as merely "the abuse of reality," not "reality itself," which is "the unachieved national purpose." In this version of the traditional "city on a hill" conception, formulated by the founder of realist IR theory, America has a "transcendent purpose," "the establishment of equality in freedom," and American politics is designed to achieve this "national purpose," however flawed it may be in execution. In a current version, published shortly before 9-11 by a prominent scholar, there is a guiding principle that "defines the parameters within which the policy debate occurs," a spectrum that excludes only "tattered remnants" on the right and left and is "so authoritative as to be virtually immune to challenge." The principle is that America is a "historical vanguard." "History has a discernible direction and destination. Uniquely among all the nations of the world, the United States comprehends and manifests history's purpose." It follows that U.S. "hegemony" is the realization of history's purpose and its application is therefore for the common good, a truism that renders empirical evaluation irrelevant.

That stance too has a distinguished pedigree. A century before Rumsfeld and Cheney, Woodrow Wilson called for conquest of the Philippines because "Our interest must march forward, altruists though we are; other nations must see to it that they stand off, and do not seek to stay us." And he was borrowing from admired sources, among them John Stuart Mill in a remarkable essay.

That is one choice. The other is to understand "reality" as reality, and to ask whether its unpleasant features are "flaws" in the pursuit of history's purpose or have more mundane causes, as in the case of every other power system of past and present. If we adopt that stance, joining the tattered remnants outside the authoritative spectrum, we will be led to conclude, I think, that policy choices are likely to remain within a framework that is well-entrenched, enhanced perhaps in important ways but not fundamentally changed: much as after the collapse of the USSR, I believe. There are a number of reasons to anticipate essential continuity, among them the stability of the basic institutions in which policy decisions are rooted, but also narrower ones that merit some attention.

The "war on terror" re-declared on 9-11 had been declared 20 years earlier, with much the same rhetoric and many of the same people in high-level positions. The Reagan administration came into office announcing that a primary concern of U.S. foreign policy would be a "war on terror," particularly state-supported international terrorism, the most virulent form of the plague spread by "depraved opponents of civilization itself" in "a return to barbarism in the modern age," in the words of the Administration moderate, George Shultz. The war to eradicate the plague was to focus on two regions where it was raging with unusual virulence: Central America and West Asia/North Africa. Shultz was particularly exercised by the "cancer, right here in our land mass," which was openly renewing the goals of Hitler's *Mein Kampf,* he informed Congress. The President declared a national emergency, renewed annually, because "the policies and actions of the Government of Nicaragua constitute an unusual and extraordinary threat to the national security and foreign policy of the United States." Explaining the bombing of Libya, Reagan announced that the mad dog Qaddafi was sending arms and advisers to Nicaragua "to bring his war home to the United States," part of the campaign "to expel America from the world," Reagan lamented. Scholarship has explored still deeper roots for that ambitious enterprise. One prominent academic terrorologist finds that contemporary terrorism can be traced to South Vietnam, where "the effectiveness of Vietcong terror against the American Goliath armed with modern technology kindled hopes that the Western heartland was vulnerable too."

More ominous still, by the 1980s, was the swamp from which the plague was spreading. It was drained just in time by the U.S. army, which helped to "defeat liberation theology," the School of the Americas now proclaims with pride.

In the second locus of the war, the threat was no less dreadful: Mideast/Mediterranean terror was selected as the peak story of the year in 1985 in the annual AP poll of editors, and ranked high in others. As the worst year of terror ended, Reagan and Israeli Prime Minister Peres condemned "the evil scourge of terrorism" in a news conference in Washington. A few days before Peres had sent his bombers to Tunis, where they killed 75 people on no credible pretext, a mission expedited by Washington and praised by Secretary of State Shultz, though he chose silence after the Security Council condemned the attack as an "act of armed aggression" (U.S. abstaining). That was only one of the contenders for the prize of major terrorist atrocity in the peak year of terror. A second was a car-bomb outside a mosque in Beirut that killed 80 people and wounded 250 others, timed to explode as people were leaving, killing

mostly women and girls, traced back to the CIA and British intelligence. The third contender is Peres's Iron Fist operations in southern Lebanon, fought against "terrorist villagers," the high command explained, "reaching new depths of 'calculated brutality and arbitrary murder'" according to a Western diplomat familiar with the area, a judgment amply supported by direct coverage.

Scholarship too recognizes 1985 to be a peak year of Middle East terrorism, but does not cite these events: rather, two terrorist atrocities in which a single person was murdered, in each case an American. But the victims do not so easily forget.

Shultz demanded that resort to violence to destroy "the evil scourge of terrorism," particularly in Central America. He bitterly condemned advocates of "utopian, legalistic means like outside mediation, the United Nations, and the World Court, while ignoring the power element of the equation." His administration succumbed to no such weaknesses, and should be praised for its foresight by sober scholars who now explain that international law and institutions of world order must be swept aside by the enlightened hegemon, in a new era of dedication to human rights.

In both regions of primary concern, the commanders of the "war on terror" compiled a record of "state-supported international terrorism" that vastly exceeded anything that could be attributed to their targets. And that hardly exhausts the record. During the Reagan years Washington's South African ally had primary responsibility for over 1.5 million dead and $60 billion in damage in neighboring countries, while the administration found ways to evade congressional sanctions and substantially increase trade. A UNICEF study estimated the death toll of infants and young children at 850,000, 150,000 in the single year 1988, reversing gains of the early post-independence years primarily by the weapon of "mass terrorism." That is putting aside South Africa's practices within, where it was defending civilization against the onslaughts of the ANC, one of the "more notorious terrorist groups" according to a 1988 Pentagon report.

For such reasons the U.S. and Israel voted alone against an 1987 UN resolution condemning terrorism in the strongest terms and calling on all nations to combat the plague, passed 153-2, Honduras abstaining. The two opponents identified the offending passage: it recognized "the right to self-determination, freedom, and independence, as derived from the Charter of the United Nations, of people forcibly deprived of that right . . . , particularly peoples under colonial and racist regimes and foreign occupation . . ."—understood to refer to South Africa and the Israeli-occupied territories, therefore unacceptable.

The base for U.S. operations in Central America was Honduras, where the U.S. Ambassador during the worst years of terror was John Negroponte, who is now in charge of the diplomatic component of the new phase of the "war on terror" at the UN. Reagan's special envoy to the Middle East was Donald Rumsfeld, who now presides over its military component, as well as the new wars that have been announced.

Rumsfeld is joined by others who were prominent figures in the Reagan administration. Their thinking and goals have not changed, and although they may represent an extreme position on the policy spectrum, it is worth bearing in mind that they are by no means isolated. There is considerable continuity of doctrine, assumptions, and actions, persisting for many years until today. Careful investigation of this very recent history should be a particularly high priority for those who hold that "global security" requires "a respected and legitimate law-enforcer," in Brzezinski's words. He is referring of course to the sole power capable of undertaking this critical role: "the idealistic new world bent on ending inhumanity" as the world's leading newspaper describes it, dedicated to "principles and values" rather than crass and narrow ends, mobilizing its reluctant allies to join it in a new epoch of moral rectitude.

The concept "respected and legitimate law-enforcer" is an important one. The term "legitimate" begs the question, so we can drop it. Perhaps some question arises about the respect for law of the chosen "law-enforcer," and about its reputation outside of narrow elite circles. But such questions aside, the concept again reflects the emerging doctrine that we must discard the efforts of the past century to construct an international order in which the powerful are not free to resort to violence at will. Instead, we must institute a new principle—which is in fact a venerable principle: the self-anointed "enlightened states" will serve as global enforcers, no impolite questions asked.

The scrupulous avoidance of the events of the recent past is easy to understand, given what inquiry will quickly reveal. That includes not only the terrorist crimes of the 1980s and what came before, but also those of the 1990s, right to the present. A comparison of leading beneficiaries of U.S. military assistance and the record of state terror should shame honest people, and would, if it were not so effectively removed from the public eye. It suffices to look at the two countries that have been vying for leadership in this competition: Turkey and Colombia. As a personal aside I happened to visit both recently, including scenes of some of the worst crimes of the 1990s, adding some vivid personal experience to what is horrifying enough in the printed record. I am putting aside Israel and Egypt, a separate category.

To repeat the obvious, we basically have two choices. Either history is bunk, including current history, and we can march forward with confidence that the global enforcer will drive evil from the world much as the President's speech writers declare, plagiarizing ancient epics and children's tales. Or we can subject the doctrines of the proclaimed grand new era to scrutiny, drawing rational conclusions, perhaps gaining some sense of the emerging reality. If there is a third way, I do not see it.

The wars that are contemplated in the renewed "war on terror" are to go on for a long time. "There's no telling how many wars it will take to secure freedom in the homeland," the President announced. That's fair enough. Potential threats are virtually limitless, everywhere, even at home, as the anthrax attack illustrates. We should also be able to appreciate recent comments on the matter by the 1996–2000 head of Israel's General Security Service (Shabak), Ami Ayalon. He observed realistically that "those who want victory" against terror without addressing underlying grievances "want an unending war." He was speaking of Israel-Palestine, where the only "solution of the problem of terrorism [is] to offer an honorable solution to the Palestinians respecting their right to self-determination." So former head of Israeli military intelligence Yehoshaphat Harkabi, also a leading Arabist, observed 20 years ago, at a time when Israel still retained its immunity from retaliation from within the occupied territories to its harsh and brutal practices there.

The observations generalize in obvious ways. In serious scholarship, at least, it is recognized that "Unless the social, political, and economic conditions that spawned al Qaeda and other associated groups are addressed, the United States and its allies in Western Europe and elsewhere will continue to be targeted by Islamist terrorists."

In proclaiming the right of attack against perceived potential threats, the President is once again echoing the principles of the first phase of the "war on terror." The Reagan-Shultz doctrine held that the UN Charter entitles the U.S. to resort to force in "self-defense against future attack." That interpretation of Article 51 was offered in justification of the bombing of Libya, eliciting praise from commentators who were impressed by the reliance "on a legal argument that violence against the perpetrators of repeated violence is justified as an act of self-defense"; I am quoting *NYT* legal specialist Anthony Lewis.

The doctrine was amplified by the Bush #1 administration, which justified the invasion of Panama, vetoing two Security Council resolutions, on the grounds that Article 51 "provides for the use of armed force to defend a country, to defend our interests and our people," and entitles the U.S. to invade another country to prevent its "territory from being used as a base for smuggling drugs into the United States." In the light of

that expansive interpretation of the Charter, it is not surprising that James Baker suggested a few days ago that Washington could now appeal to Article 51 to authorize conquest and occupation of Iraq, because Iraq may some day threaten the U.S. with WMD, or threaten others while the U.S. stands helplessly by.

Quite apart from the plain meaning of the Charter, the argument offered by Baker's State Department in 1989 was not too convincing on other grounds. Operation Just Cause reinstated in power the white elite of bankers and businessmen, many suspected of narcotrafficking and money laundering, who soon lived up to their reputation; drug trafficking "may have doubled" and money laundering "flourished" in the months after the invasion, the GAO reported, while USAID found that narcotics use in Panama had gone up by 400 percent, reaching the highest level in Latin America. All without eliciting notable concern, except in Latin America, and Panama itself, where the invasion was harshly condemned.

Clinton's Strategic Command also advocated "preemptive response," with nuclear weapons if deemed appropriate. Clinton himself forged some new paths in implementing the doctrine, though his major contributions to international terrorism lie elsewhere.

The doctrine of preemptive strike has much earlier origins, even in words. Forty years ago Dean Acheson informed the American Society of International Law that legal issues do not arise in the case of a U.S. response to a "challenge [to its] power, position, and prestige." He was referring to Washington's response to what it called Cuba's "successful defiance" of the United States. That included Cuba's resistance to the Bay of Pigs invasion, but also much more serious crimes. When Kennedy ordered his staff to subject Cubans to the "terrors of the earth" until Castro is eliminated, his planners advised that "The very existence of his regime . . . represents a successful defiance of the U.S., a negation of our whole hemispheric policy of almost half a century," based on the principle of subordination to U.S. will. Worse yet, Castro's regime was providing an "example and general stimulus" that might "encourage agitation and radical change" in other parts of Latin America, where "social and economic conditions . . . invite opposition to ruling authority" and susceptibility to "the Castro idea of taking matters into one's own hands." These are grave dangers, Kennedy planners recognized, when "The distribution of land and other forms of national wealth greatly favors the propertied classes . . . [and] The poor and underprivileged, stimulated by the example of the Cuban revolution, are now demanding opportunities for a decent living." These threats were only compounded by successful resistance to invasion, an intolerable threat to credibility, warranting the "terrors of the earth" and destructive economic warfare to excise that earlier "cancer."

Cuba's crimes became still more immense when it served as the instrument of Russia's crusade to dominate the world in 1975, Washington proclaimed. "If Soviet necolonialism succeeds" in Angola, UN Ambassador Daniel Patrick Moynihan thundered, "the world will not be the same in the aftermath. Europe's oil routes will be under Soviet control as will the strategic South Atlantic, with the next target on the Kremlin's list being Brazil." Washington's fury was caused by another Cuban act of "successful defiance." When a U.S.-backed South African invasion was coming close to conquering newly-independent Angola, Cuba sent troops on its own initiative, scarcely even notifying Russia, and beat back the invaders. In what is now the major scholarly study, Piero Gleijeses observes that "Kissinger did his best to smash the one movement that represented any hope for the future of Angola," the MPLA. And though the MPLA "bears a grave responsibility for its country's plight" in later years, it was "the relentless hostility of the United States [that] forced it into an unhealthy dependence on the Soviet bloc and encouraged South Africa to launch devastating military raids in the 1980s."

These further crimes of Cuba could not be forgiven; those years saw some of the worst terrorist attacks against Cuba, with no slight U.S. role. After any pretense of a Soviet threat collapsed in 1989, the U.S. tightened its stranglehold on Cuba on new pretexts, notably the alleged role in terrorism of the prime target of U.S.-based terrorism for 40 years. The level of fanaticism is illustrated by minor incidents. For example, as we meet, a visa is being withheld for a young Cuban woman artist who was offered an art fellowship, apparently because Cuba has been declared a "terrorist state" by Colin Powell's State department.

It should be unnecessary to review how the "terrors of the earth" were unleashed against Cuba since 1962, "no laughing matter," Jorge Dominguez points out with considerable understatement, discussing newly-released documents. Of particular interest, and contemporary import, are the internal perceptions of the planners. Dominguez observes that "Only once in these nearly thousand pages of documentation did a U.S. official raise something that resembled a faint moral objection to U.S.-government sponsored terrorism": a member of the NSC staff suggested that it might lead to some Russian reaction; furthermore, raids that are "haphazard and kill innocents . . . might mean a bad press in some friendly countries." Scholarship on terrorism rarely goes even that far.

Little new ground is broken when one has to turn to House Majority leader Dick Armey to find a voice in the mainstream questioning "an unprovoked attack against Iraq" not on grounds of cost to us, but because it "would violate international law" and "would not be consistent with what we have been or what we should be as a nation."

What we or others "have been" is a separate story.

Much more should be said about continuity and its institutional roots. But let's turn instead to some of the immediate questions posed by the crimes of 9-11:

1. who is responsible?
2. what are the reasons?
3. what is the proper reaction?
4. what are the longer-term consequences?

As for (1), it was assumed, plausibly, that the guilty parties were bin Laden and his al-Qaeda network. No one knows more about them than the CIA, which, together with U.S. allies, recruited radical Islamists from many countries and organized them into a military and terrorist force that Reagan anointed "the moral equivalent of the founding fathers," joining Jonas Savimbi and similar dignitaries in that Pantheon. The goal was not to help Afghans resist Russian aggression, which would have been a legitimate objective, but rather normal reasons of state, with grim consequences for Afghans when the moral equivalents finally took control.

U.S. intelligence has surely been following the exploits of these networks closely ever since they assassinated President Sadat of Egypt 20 years ago, and more intensively since their failed terrorist efforts in New York in 1993. Nevertheless, despite what must be the most intensive international intelligence investigation in history, evidence about the perpetrators of 9-11 has been elusive. Eight months after the bombing, FBI director Robert Mueller could only inform a Senate Committee that U.S. intelligence now "believes" the plot was hatched in Afghanistan, though planned and implemented elsewhere. And well after the source of the anthrax attack was localized to government weapons laboratories, it has still not been identified. These are indications of how hard it may be to counter acts of terror targeting the rich and powerful in the future. Nevertheless, despite the thin evidence, the initial conclusion about 9-11 is presumably correct.

Turning to (2), scholarship is virtually unanimous in taking the terrorists at their word, which matches their deeds for the past 20 years: their goal, in their terms, is to drive the infidels from Muslim lands, to overthrow the corrupt governments they impose and sustain, and to institute an extremist version of Islam. They despise the Russians, but ceased their terrorist attacks against Russia based in Afghanistan—which were quite serious—when Russia withdrew. And "the call to wage war against America was made [when it sent] tens of thousands of its troops to the land of the two Holy Mosques over and above . . . its support of the oppressive, corrupt and tyrannical regime that is in control," so bin Laden announced over U.S. TV four years ago.

More significant, at least for those who hope to reduce the likelihood of further crimes of a similar nature, are the background conditions from which the terrorist organizations arose, and that provide a reservoir of sympathetic understanding for at least parts of their message, even among those who despise and fear them. In George Bush's plaintive phrase, "why do they hate us?"

The question is wrongly put: they do not "hate us," but rather policies of the U.S. government, something quite different. If properly formulated, however, answers to the question are not hard to find. Forty-four years ago President Eisenhower and his staff discussed what he called the "campaign of hatred against us" in the Arab world, "not by the governments but by the people." The basic reason, the NSC advised, is the recognition that the U.S. supports corrupt and brutal governments and is "opposing political or economic progress," in order "to protect its interest in Near East oil." The *Wall Street Journal* and others found much the same when they investigated attitudes of wealthy westernized Muslims after 9-11, feelings now exacerbated by U.S. policies with regard to Israel-Palestine and Iraq.

These are attitudes of people who like Americans and admire much about the United States, including its freedoms. What they hate is official policies that deny them the freedoms to which they too aspire.

Many commentators prefer a more comforting answer: their anger is rooted in resentment of our freedom and democracy, their cultural failings tracing back many centuries, their inability to take part in the form of "globalization" in which they happily participate, and other such deficiencies. More comforting, perhaps, but not too wise.

These issues are very much alive. Just in the past few weeks, Asia correspondent Ahmed Rashid reported that in Pakistan, "there is growing anger that U.S. support is allowing [Musharraf's] military regime to delay the promise of democracy."

And a well-known Egyptian academic told the BBC that Arab and Islamic people were opposed to the U.S. because it has "supported every possible anti-democratic government in the Arab-Islamic world. . . . When we hear American officials speaking of freedom, democracy and such values, they make terms like these sound obscene." An Egyptian writer added that "Living in a country with an atrocious human rights record that also happens to be strategically vital to U.S. interests is an illuminating lesson in moral hypocrisy and political double standards." Terrorism, he said, is "a reaction to the injustice in the region's domestic politics, inflicted in large part by the U.S." The director of the terrorism program at the Council of Foreign Relations agreed that "Backing repressive regimes like Egypt and Saudi Arabia is certainly a leading cause of anti-Americanism in the Arab world," but warned that "in both cases the likely alternatives are even nastier."

There is a long and illuminating history of the problems in supporting democratic forms while ensuring that they will lead to preferred outcomes, not just in this region. And it doesn't win many friends.

What about proper reaction, question (3)? Answers are doubtless contentious, but at least the reaction should meet the most elementary moral standards: specifically, if an action is right for us, it is right for others; and if wrong for others, it is wrong for us. Those who reject that standard can be ignored in any discussion of appropriateness of action, of right or wrong. One might ask what remains of the flood of commentary on proper reaction—thoughts about "just war," for example—if this simple criterion is adopted.

Suppose we adopt the criterion, thus entering the arena of moral discourse. We can then ask, for example, how Cuba has been entitled to react after "the terrors of the earth" were unleashed against it 40 years ago. Or Nicaragua, after Washington rejected the orders of the World Court and Security Council to terminate its "unlawful use of force," choosing instead to escalate its terrorist war and issue the first official orders to its forces to attack undefended civilian "soft targets," leaving tens of thousands dead and the country ruined perhaps beyond recovery. No one believes that Cuba or Nicaragua had the right to set off bombs in Washington or New York or to kill U.S. political leaders or send them to prison camps. And it is all too easy to add far more severe cases in those years, and others to the present.

Accordingly, those who accept elementary moral standards have some work to do to show that the U.S. and Britain were justified in bombing Afghans in order to compel them to turn over people who the U.S. suspected of criminal atrocities, the official war aim announced by the President as the bombing began. Or that the enforcers were justified in informing Afghans that they would be bombed until they brought about "regime change," the war aim announced several weeks later, as the war was approaching its end.

The same moral standard holds of more nuanced proposals about an appropriate response to terrorist atrocities. Military historian Michael Howard advocated "a police operation conducted under the auspices of the United Nations . . . against a criminal conspiracy whose members should be hunted down and brought before an international court, where they would receive a fair trial and, if found guilty, be awarded an appropriate sentence." That seems reasonable, though we may ask what the reaction would be to the suggestion that the proposal should be applied universally. That is unthinkable, and if the suggestion were to be made, it would elicit outrage and horror.

Similar questions arise with regard to the doctrine of "preemptive strike" against suspected threats, not new, though its bold assertion is novel. There is no doubt about the address. The standard of universality, therefore, would appear to justify Iraqi preemptive terror against the United States. Of course, the conclusion is outlandish. The burden of proof again lies on those who advocate or tolerate the selective version that grants the right to those powerful enough to exercise it. And the burden is not light, as is always true when the threat or use of violence is advocated or tolerated.

There is, of course, an easy counter to such elementary observations: WE are good, and THEY are evil. That doctrine trumps virtually any argument. Analysis of commentary and much of scholarship reveals that its roots commonly lie in that crucial principle, which is not argued but asserted. None of this, of course, is an invention of contemporary power centers and the dominant intellectual culture, but it is, nevertheless, instructive to observe the means employed to protect the doctrine from the heretical challenge that seeks to confront it with the factual record, including such intriguing notions as "moral equivalence," "moral relativism," "anti-Americanism," and others.

One useful barrier against heresy, already mentioned, is the principle that questions about the state's resort to violence simply do not arise among sane people. That is a common refrain in the current debate over the modalities of the invasion of Iraq. To select an example at the liberal end of the spectrum, *NYT* columnist Bill Keller remarks that "the last time America dispatched soldiers in the cause of 'regime change,' less than a year ago in Afghanistan, the opposition was mostly limited to the people who are reflexively against the American use of power," either timid supporters or "isolationists, the doctrinaire left and the soft-headed types Christopher Hitchens described as people who, 'discovering a viper in the bed of their child, would place the first call to people for the Ethical Treatment of Animals.'" To borrow the words of a noted predecessor, "We went to war, not because we wanted to, but because humanity demanded it"; President McKinley in this case, as he ordered his armies to "carry the burden, whatever it may be, in the interest of civilization, humanity, and liberty" in the Philippines.

Let's ignore the fact that "regime change" was not "the cause" in Afghanistan—rather, an afterthought late in the game—and look more closely at the lunatic fringe. We have some information about them. In late September, the Gallup organization surveyed international opinion on the announced U.S. bombing. The lead question was whether, "once the identity of the terrorists is known, should the American government launch a military attack on the country or countries where the terrorists are based or should the American government seek to extradite the terrorists to stand trial." As we recently learned, 8 months later the identity of the terrorists is only surmised, and the countries where they were based are presumed to be Germany, the UAE, and elsewhere, but let's ignore that too. The poll revealed that opinion strongly favored judicial over military action, in Europe overwhelmingly. The only exceptions were India and Israel, where Afghanistan was a surrogate for something quite different. Follow-up questions reveal that support for the military attack that was actually carried out was very slight.

Support for military action was least in Latin America, the region that has the most experience with U.S. intervention. It ranged from 2 percent in Mexico to 11 percent in Colombia and Venezuela, where 85 percent preferred extradition and trial; whether that was feasible is known only to ideologues. The sole exception was Panama, where only 80 percent preferred judicial means and 16 percent advocated military attack; and even there, correspondents recalled the death of perhaps thousands of poor people (Western crimes, therefore unexamined) in the course of Operation Just Cause, undertaken to kidnap a disobedient thug who was sentenced to life imprisonment in Florida for crimes mostly committed while he was on the CIA payroll. One remarked "how much alike [the victims of 9-11] are to the boys and girls, to those who are unable to be born that December 20 [1989] that they imposed on us in Chorrillo; how much alike they seem to the mothers, the grandfathers and the little old grandmothers, all of them also innocent and anonymous deaths, whose terror was called Just Cause and the terrorist called liberator."

I suspect that the director of Human Rights Watch Africa (1993–95), now a Professor of Law at Emory University, may have spoken for many others around the world when he addressed the International Council on Human Rights Policy in Geneva in January 2002, saying that "I am unable to appreciate any moral, political or legal difference between this *jihad* by the United States against those it deems to be its enemies and the *jihad* by Islamic groups against those they deem to be their enemies."

What about Afghan opinion? Here information is scanty, but not entirely lacking. In late October, 1000 Afghan leaders gathered in Peshawar, some exiles, some coming from within Afghanistan, all committed to overthrowing the Taliban regime. It was "a rare display of unity among tribal elders, Islamic scholars, fractious politicians, and former guerrilla commanders," the press reported. They unanimously "urged the U.S. to stop the air raids," appealed to the international media to call for an end to the "bombing of innocent people," and "demanded an end to the U.S. bombing of Afghanistan." They urged that other means be adopted to overthrow the hated Taliban regime, a goal they believed could be achieved without death and destruction.

A similar message was conveyed by Afghan opposition leader Abdul Haq, who was highly regarded in Washington, and received special praise as a martyr during the Loya Jirga, his memory bringing tears to the eyes of President Hamid Karzai. Just before he entered Afghanistan, apparently without U.S. support, and was then captured and killed, he condemned the bombing and criticized the United States for refusing to support efforts of his and of others "to create a revolt within the Taliban." The bombing was "a big setback for these efforts," he said, outlining his efforts and calling on the United States to assist them with funding and other support instead of undermining them with bombs. The United States, he said, "is trying to show its muscle, score a victory and scare everyone in the world. They don't care about the suffering of the Afghans or how many people we will lose." The prominent women's organization RAWA, which received some belated recognition in the course of the war, also bitterly condemned the bombing.

In short, the lunatic fringe of "soft-headed types who are reflexively against the American use of power" was not insubstantial as the bombing was undertaken and proceeded. But since vir-

tually no word of any of this was published in the United States, we can continue to comfort ourselves that "humanity demanded" the bombing.

There is, obviously, a great deal more to say about all of these topics, but let us turn briefly to question (4).

In the longer term, I suspect that the crimes of 9-11 will accelerate tendencies that were already underway: the Bush doctrine on preemption is an illustration. As was predicted at once, governments throughout the world seized upon 9-11 as a "window of opportunity" to institute or escalate harsh and repressive programs.

Russia eagerly joined the "coalition against terror," expecting to receive tacit authorization for its shocking atrocities in Chechnya, and was not disappointed. China happily joined for similar reasons. Turkey was the first country to offer troops for the new phase of the United States "war on terror," in gratitude, as the Prime Minister explained, for the U.S. contribution to Turkey's campaign against its miserably-repressed Kurdish population, waged with extreme savagery and relying crucially on a huge flow of U.S. arms, peaking in 1997; in that single year arms transfers exceeded the entire post-war period combined up to the onset of the counterinsurgency campaign. Turkey is highly praised for these achievements and was rewarded by grant of authority to protect Kabul from terror, funded by the same superpower that provided the means for its recent acts of state terror, including some of the major atrocities of the grisly 1990s. Israel recognized that it would be able to crush Palestinians even more brutally, with even firmer U.S. support. And so on throughout much of the world.

Many governments, including the U.S., instituted measures to discipline the domestic population and to carry forward unpopular measures under the guise of "combating terror," exploiting the atmosphere of fear and the demand for "patriotism"—which in practice means: "You shut up and I'll pursue my own agenda relentlessly." The Bush administration used the opportunity to advance its assault against most of the population, and future generations, serving the narrow corporate interests that dominate the administration to an extent even beyond the norm.

One major outcome is that the United States, for the first time, has major military bases in Central Asia. These help to position U.S. corporate interests favorably in the current "great game" to control the resources of the region, but also to complete the encirclement of the world's major energy resources, in the Gulf region. The U.S. base system targeting the Gulf extends from the Pacific to the Azores, but the closest reliable base before the Afghan war was Diego Garcia. Now that situation is much improved, and forceful intervention should be facilitated.

The Bush administration also exploited the new phase of the "war on terror" to expand its overwhelming military advantages over the rest of the world, and to move on to other methods to ensure global dominance. Government thinking was clarified by high officials when Prince Abdullah of Saudi Arabia visited the U.S. in April to urge the administration to pay more attention to the reaction in the Arab world to its strong support for Israeli terror and repression. He was told, in effect, that the U.S. did not care what he or other Arabs think. A high official explained that "if he thought we were strong in Desert Storm, we're ten times as strong today. This was to give him some idea what Afghanistan demonstrated about our capabilities." A senior defense analyst gave a simple gloss: others will "respect us for our toughness and won't mess with us." That stand has many precedents too, but in the post-9-11 world it gains new force.

It is reasonable to speculate that such consequences were one goal of the bombing of Aghanistan: to warn the world of what the "legitimate enforcer" can do if someone steps out of line. The bombing of Serbia was undertaken for similar reasons: to "ensure NATO's credibility," as Blair and Clinton explained—not referring to the credibility of Norway or Italy. That is a common theme of statecraft. And with some reason, as history amply reveals.

Without continuing, the basic issues of international society seem to me to remain much as they were, but 9-11 surely has induced changes, in some cases, with significant and not very attractive implications.

DISCUSSION QUESTIONS

1. Chomsky argues that there are two choices for anyone trying to make sense of the unrest in the world today: one involves applying rational standards and the other involves dismissing the historical and contemporary record. Discuss the two devices he sees being used to dismiss or evade the historical and contemporary record. Then discuss what he means by adopting rational standards in foreign affairs. It would seem obvious that using rational standards is, well, rational. Why would U.S. foreign policy elites not want to use rational, consistent standards?

2. The "war on terror" announced after 9-11 actually amounted to a redeclaration. Why was the original "war" announced, and what is Chomsky's point about the periodic announcement that the United States is at "war" with some nation. Specifically, what does the United States object to when it elevates its displeasure with a nation to a bellicose status? Cite some of Chomsky's many examples.

3. Review the four post-September 11 questions Chomsky raises in the second half of his essay. Throughout his response to these questions he makes a case for applying "elementary moral standards" or "the standard of universality" to international relations. From your reading of these questions and answers, why aren't consistent moral standards applied to all countries? The principal defense of adopting different standards is that the United States is "good" and our enemies are "evil." Evaluate that good/evil dichotomy.

Visions of a New Democracy

Your actions, and inactions, have an impact on the world. The status quo, the political norm, is either challenged, or left unchallenged, by what you do with your life. In this way no one, not even the most ardent hater of things "political," is politically neutral.

Though in different ways, the readings in this final chapter all have at their core a belief that you can and should be politically involved in the United States through careful reflection and sustained action. Citizenship demands that we attempt to "do the right thing," even in the face of a political culture that too often seems mired in lethargy and disengagement. Obviously unanimity does not exist on what constitutes the "right thing." Political and economic elites may say that political participation is a good thing, for example, while actually being suspicious of the impact of citizen involvement on societal stability. And, of course, ordinary citizens themselves disagree on many issues. The point is that there is a place for *you in* debating, and perhaps changing, the priorities of the nation you live in. Discussion and debate over the ends of public life, the give-and-take, is what politics is all about.

LETTER FROM BIRMINGHAM JAIL

"Letter from Birmingham Jail" is a classic statement of the civil rights movement. Written on scraps of paper found in his jail cell, this 1963 essay by the Reverend Dr. Martin Luther King, Jr., crystallizes many of the themes that served as catalysts to the movement for racial equality he helped lead. The letter was written in response to a statement issued by eight white Alabama clergymen who criticized King and other demonstrators for causing violence with their protests against segregation. King's searing moral response in support of nonviolent civil disobedience makes a powerful and impassioned call for democracy and human freedom. Among the many compelling points he makes, King criticizes political moderates—in this case the "white moderate" who, in King's words, "is more devoted to 'order' than to justice." To people who follow the doctrinaire belief that the truth always lies in the middle, his position may be surprising. He suggests that we should question the wisdom of assuming that gradual change and piecemeal reforms are the best way to approach a problem.

April 16, 1963

My Dear Fellow Clergymen:

While confined here in the Birmingham city jail, I came across your recent statement calling my present activities "unwise and untimely." Seldom do I pause to answer criticism of my work and ideas. If I sought to answer all the criticisms that cross my desk, my secretaries would have little time for anything other than such correspondence in the course of the day, and I would have no time for constructive work. But since I feel that you are men of genuine good will and that your criticisms are sincerely set forth, I want to try to answer your statement in what I hope will be patient and reasonable terms.

I think I should indicate why I am here in Birmingham, since you have been influenced by the view which argues against "outsiders coming in." I have the honor of serving as president of the Southern Christian Leadership Conference, an organization operating in every southern state, with headquarters in Atlanta, Georgia. We have some eighty-five affiliated organizations across the South, and one of them is the Alabama Christian Movement for Human Rights. Frequently we share staff, educational and financial resources with our affiliates. Several months ago the affiliate here in Birmingham asked us to be on call to engage in a nonviolent direct-action program if such were deemed necessary. We readily consented, and when the hour came we lived up to our promise. So I, along with several members of my staff, am here because I was invited here. I am here because I have organizational ties here.

But more basically, I am in Birmingham because injustice is here. Just as the prophets of the eighth century B.C. left their villages and carried their "thus saith the Lord" far beyond the boundaries of their home towns, and just as the Apostle Paul left his village of Tarsus and carried the gospel of Jesus Christ to the far corners of the Greco-Roman world, so am I compelled to carry the gospel of freedom beyond my own home town. Like Paul, I must constantly respond to the Macedonian call for aid.

Moreover, I am cognizant of the interrelatedness of all communities and states. I cannot sit idly by in Atlanta and not be concerned about what happens in Birmingham. Injustice anywhere is a threat to justice everywhere. We are caught in an inescapable network of mutuality, tied in a single garment of destiny. Whatever affects one directly, affects all indirectly. Never again can we afford to live with the narrow, provincial "outside agitator" idea. Anyone who lives inside the United States can never be considered an outsider anywhere within its bounds.

You deplore the demonstrations taking place in Birmingham. But your statement, I am sorry to say, fails to express a similar concern for the conditions that brought about the demonstrations. I am sure that none of you would want to rest content with the superficial kind of social analysis that deals merely with effects and does not grapple with underlying causes. It is unfortunate that demonstrations are taking place in Birmingham, but it is even more unfortunate that the city's white power structure left the Negro community with no alternative.

In any nonviolent campaign there are four basic steps: collection of the facts to determine whether injustices exist; negotiation; self-purification; and direct action. We have gone through all these steps in Birmingham. There can be no gain saying the fact that racial injustice engulfs this community. Birmingham is probably the most thoroughly segregated city in the United States. Its ugly record of brutality is widely known. Negroes have experienced grossly unjust treatment in the courts. There have been more unsolved bombings of Negro homes and churches in Birmingham than in any other city in the nation. These are the hard, brutal facts of the case. On the basis of these conditions, Negro leaders sought to negotiate with the city fathers. But the latter consistently refused to engage in good-faith negotiation. . . .

You may well ask: "Why direct action? Why sit-ins, marches and so forth? Isn't negotiation a better path?" You are quite right in calling for negotiation. Indeed, this is the very purpose of direct action. Nonviolent direct action seeks to create such a crisis and foster such a tension that a community which has constantly refused to negotiate is forced to confront the issue. It seeks so to dramatize the issue that it can no longer be ignored. My citing the creation of tension as part of the work of the nonviolent resister may sound rather shocking. But I must confess that I am not afraid of the word "tension." I have earnestly opposed violent tension, but there is a type of constructive, nonviolent tension which is necessary for growth. Just as Socrates felt that it was necessary to create a tension in the mind so that individuals could rise from the bondage of myths and half-truths to the unfettered realm of creative analysis and objective appraisal, so must we see the need for nonviolent gadflies to create the kind of tension in society that will help men rise from the dark depths of prejudice and racism to the majestic heights of understanding and brotherhood.

The purpose of our direct-action program is to create a situation so crisis-packed that it will inevitably open the door to negotiation. I therefore concur with you in your call for negotiation. Too long has our beloved Southland been bogged down in a tragic effort to live in monologue rather than dialogue.

. . . My friends, I must say to you that we have not made a single gain in civil rights without determined legal and nonviolent pressure. Lamentably, it is an historical fact that privileged groups seldom give up their privileges voluntarily. Individuals may see the moral light and voluntarily give up their unjust posture; but, as Reinhold Niebuhr has reminded us, groups tend to be more immoral than individuals.

We know through painful experience that freedom is never voluntarily given by the oppressor; it must be demanded by the oppressed. Frankly, I have yet to engage in a direct-action campaign that was "well timed" in the view of those who have not suffered unduly from the disease of segregation. For years now I have heard the word "Wait!" It rings in the ear of every Negro with piercing familiarity. This "Wait" has almost always meant "Never." We must come to see, with one of our distinguished jurists, that "justice too long delayed is justice denied."

We have waited for more than 340 years for our constitutional and God-given rights. The nations of Asia and Africa are moving with jetlike speed toward gaining political independence, but we still creep at horse-and-buggy pace toward gaining a cup of coffee at a lunch counter. Perhaps it is easy for those who have never felt the stinging darts of segregation to say, "Wait." But when you have seen vicious mobs lynch your mothers and fathers at will and drown your sisters and brothers at whim; when you have seen hate-filled policemen curse, kick and even kill your black brothers and sisters; when you see the vast majority of your twenty million Negro brothers smothering in an airtight cage of poverty in the midst of an affluent society; when you suddenly find your tongue twisted and your speech stammering as you seek to explain to your six-year-old daughter why she can't go to the public amusement park that has just been advertised on television, and see tears welling up in her eyes when she is told that Funtown is closed to colored children, and see ominous clouds of inferiority beginning to form in her little mental sky, and see her beginning to distort her personality by developing an unconscious bitterness toward white people; when you have to concoct an answer for a five-year-old son who is asking: "Daddy, why do white people treat colored people so mean?"; when you take a cross-country drive and find it necessary to sleep night after night in the uncomfortable corners of your automobile because no motel will accept you; when you are humiliated day in and day out by nagging signs reading "white" and "colored"; when your first name becomes "nigger," your middle name becomes "boy" (however old you are) and your last name becomes "John," and your wife and mother are never given the respected title "Mrs."; when you are harried by day and haunted by night by the fact that you are a Negro, living constantly at tiptoe stance, never quite knowing what to expect next, and are plagued with inner fears and outer resentments; when you are forever fighting a degenerating sense of "nobodiness"—then you will understand why we find it difficult to wait. There comes a time when the cup of endurance runs over, and men are no longer willing to be plunged into the abyss of despair. I hope, sirs, you can understand our legitimate and unavoidable impatience.

You express a great deal of anxiety over our willingness to break laws. This is certainly a legitimate concern. Since we so diligently urge people to obey the Supreme Court's decision of 1954 outlawing segregation in the public schools, at first glance it may seem rather paradoxical for us consciously to break laws. One may well ask: "How can you advocate breaking some laws and obeying others?" The answer lies in the fact that there are two types of laws: just and unjust. I would be the first to advocate obeying just laws. One has not only a legal but a moral responsibility to obey just laws. Conversely, one has a moral responsibility to disobey unjust laws. I would agree with St. Augustine that "an unjust law is no law at all."

Now, what is the difference between the two? How does one determine whether a law is just or unjust? A just law is a man-made code that squares with the moral law or the law of God. An unjust law is a code that is out of harmony with the moral law. To put it in the terms of St.

Thomas Aquinas: An unjust law is a human law that is not rooted in eternal law and natural law. Any law that uplifts human personality is just. Any law that degrades human personality is unjust. All segregation statutes are unjust because segregation distorts the soul and damages the personality. It gives the segregator a false sense of superiority and the segregated a false sense of inferiority. Segregation, to use the terminology of the Jewish philosopher Martin Buber, substitutes an "I-it" relationship for an "I-thou" relationship and ends up relegating persons to the status of things. Hence segregation is not only politically, economically and sociologically unsound, it is morally wrong and sinful. Paul Tillich has said that sin is separation. Is not segregation an existential expression of man's tragic separation, his awful estrangement, his terrible sinfulness? Thus it is that I can urge men to obey the 1954 decision of the Supreme Court for it is morally right; and I can urge them to disobey segregation ordinances, for they are morally wrong.

Let us consider a more concrete example of just and unjust laws. An unjust law is a code that a numerical or power majority group compels a minority group to obey but does not make binding on itself. This is *difference* made legal. By the same token, a just law is a code that a majority compels a minority to follow and that it is willing to follow itself. This is *sameness* made legal.

Let me give another explanation. A law is unjust if it is inflicted on a minority that, as a result of being denied the right to vote, had no part in enacting or devising the law. Who can say that the legislature of Alabama which set up that state's segregation laws was democratically elected? Throughout Alabama all sorts of devious methods are used to prevent Negroes from becoming registered voters, and there are some counties in which, even though Negroes constitute a majority of the population, not a single Negro is registered. Can any law enacted under such circumstances be considered democratically structured?

Sometimes a law is just on its face and unjust in its application. For instance, I have been arrested on a charge of parading without a permit. Now, there is nothing wrong in having an ordinance which requires a permit for a parade. But such an ordinance becomes unjust when it is used to maintain segregation and to deny citizens the First Amendment privilege of peaceful assembly and protest.

I hope you are able to see the distinction I am trying to point out. In no sense do I advocate evading or defying the law, as would the rabid segregationist. That would lead to anarchy. One who breaks an unjust law must do so openly, lovingly, and with a willingness to accept the penalty. I submit that an individual who breaks a law that conscience tells him is unjust, and who willingly accepts the penalty of imprisonment in order to arouse the conscience of the community over its injustice, is in reality expressing the highest respect for law.

Of course, there is nothing new about this kind of civil disobedience. It was evidenced sublimely in the refusal of Shadrach, Meshach and Abednego to obey the laws of Nebuchadnezzar, on the ground that a higher moral law was at stake. It was practiced superbly by the early Christians, who were willing to face hungry lions and the excruciating pain of chopping blocks rather than submit to certain unjust laws of the Roman Empire. To a degree, academic freedom is a reality today because Socrates practiced civil disobedience. In our own nation, the Boston Tea Party represented a massive act of civil disobedience.

We should never forget that everything Adolf Hitler did in Germany was "legal" and everything the Hungarian freedom fighters did in Hungary was "illegal." It was "illegal" to aid and comfort a Jew in Hitler's Germany. Even so, I am sure that, had I lived in Germany at the time, I would have aided and comforted my Jewish brothers. If today I lived in a Communist country where certain principles dear to the Christian faith are suppressed, I would openly advocate disobeying that country's antireligious laws.

I must make two honest confessions to you, my Christian and Jewish brothers. First, I must confess that over the past few years I have been gravely disappointed with the white moderate. I have almost reached the regrettable conclusion that the Negro's great stumbling block in his stride toward freedom is not the White Citizen's Counciler or the Ku Klux Klanner, but the white moderate, who is more devoted to "order" than to justice; who prefers a negative peace which is the absence of tension to a positive peace which is the presence of justice; who constantly says: "I agree with you in the goal you seek, but I cannot agree with your methods of direct action"; who paternalistically believes he can set the timetable for another man's freedom; who lives by a mythical concept of time and who constantly advises the Negro to wait for a "more convenient season." Shallow understanding from people of good will is more frustrating than absolute misunderstanding from people of ill will. Lukewarm acceptance is much more bewildering than outright rejection.

I had hoped that the white moderate would understand that law and order exist for the purpose of establishing justice and that when they fail in this purpose they become the dangerously structured dams that block the flow of social progress. I had hoped that the white moderate would understand that the present tension in the South is a necessary phase of the transition from an obnoxious negative peace, in which the Negro passively accepted his unjust plight, to a substantive and positive peace, in which all men will respect the dignity and worth of human personality. Actually, we who engage in nonviolent direct action are not the creators of tension. We merely bring to the surface the hidden tension that is already alive. We bring it out in the open, where it can be seen and dealt with. Like a boil that can never be cured so long as it is covered up but must be opened with all its ugliness to the natural medicines of air and light, injustice must be exposed, with all the tension its exposure creates, to the light of human conscience and the air of national opinion before it can be cured.

In your statement you assert that our actions, even though peaceful, must be condemned because they precipitate violence. But is this a logical assertion? Isn't this like condemning a robbed man because his possession of money precipitated the evil act of robbery? Isn't this like condemning Socrates because his unswerving commitment to truth and his philosophical inquiries precipitated the act by the misguided populace in which they made him drink hemlock? Isn't this like condemning Jesus because his unique God-consciousness and neverceasing devotion to God's will precipitated the evil act of crucifixion? We must come to see that, as the federal courts have consistently affirmed, it is wrong to urge an individual to cease his efforts to gain his basic constitutional rights because the quest may precipitate violence. Society must protect the robbed and punish the robber.

I had also hoped that the white moderate would reject the myth concerning time in relation to the struggle for freedom. I have just received a letter from a white brother in Texas. He writes: "All Christians know that the colored people will receive equal rights eventually, but it is possible that you are in too great a religious hurry. It has taken Christianity almost two thousand years to accomplish what it has. The teachings of Christ take time to come to earth." Such an attitude stems from a tragic misconception of time, from the strangely irrational notion that there is something in the very flow of time that will inevitably cure all ills. Actually, time itself is neutral; it can be used either destructively or constructively. More and more I feel that the people of ill will have used time much more effectively than have the people of good will. We will have to repent in this generation not merely for the hateful words and actions of the bad people but for the appalling silence of the good people. Human progress never rolls in on wheels of inevitability; it comes through the tireless efforts of men willing to be co-workers with God, and without this hard work, time itself becomes an ally of the forces of social stagnation. We must use time creatively, in the knowledge that the time is always ripe to do right. Now is the time to make real the promise of democracy and transform our pending national elegy into a creative psalm of brotherhood. Now is the time to lift our national policy from the quicksand of racial injustice to the solid rock of human dignity.

You speak of our activity in Birmingham as extreme. At first I was rather disappointed that fellow clergymen would see my nonviolent efforts as those of an extremist. I began thinking about the fact that I stand in the middle of two opposing forces in the Negro community. One is a force of complacency, made up in part of Negroes who, as a result of long years of oppression, are so drained of self-respect and a sense of "somebodiness" that they have adjusted to segregation; and in part of a few middle-class Negroes who, because of a degree of academic and economic security and because in some ways they profit by segregation, have become insensitive to the problems of the masses. The other force is one of bitterness and hatred, and it comes perilously close to advocating violence. It is expressed in the various black nationalist groups that are springing up across the nation, the largest and best-known being Elijah Muhammad's Muslim movement. Nourished by the Negro's frustration over the continued existence of racial discrimination, this movement is made up of people who have lost faith in America, who have absolutely repudiated Christianity, and who have concluded that the white man is an incorrigible "devil."

I have tried to stand between these two forces, saying that we need emulate neither the "do-nothingism" of the complacent nor the hatred and despair of the black nationalist. For there is the more excellent way of love and nonviolent protest. I am grateful to God that, through the influence of the Negro church, the way of nonviolence became an integral part of our struggle.

If this philosophy had not emerged, by now many streets of the South would, I am convinced, be flowing with blood. And I am further convinced that if our white brothers dismiss as "rabble-rousers" and "outside agitators" those of us who employ nonviolent direct action, and if they refuse to support our nonviolent efforts, millions of Negroes will, out of frustration and despair, seek solace and security in black-nationalist ideologies—a development that would inevitably lead to a frightening racial nightmare.

Oppressed people cannot remain oppressed forever. The yearning for freedom eventually manifests itself, and that is what has happened to the American Negro. Something within has reminded him of his birthright of freedom, and something without has reminded him that it can be gained. Consciously or unconsciously he has been caught up by the *Zeitgeist,* and with his black brothers of Africa and his brown and yellow brothers of Asia, South America and the Caribbean, the United States Negro is moving with a sense of great urgency toward the promised land of racial justice. If one recognizes this vital urge that has engulfed the Negro community, one should readily understand why public demonstrations are taking place. The Negro has many pent-up resentments and latent frustrations, and he must release them. So let him march; let him make prayer pilgrimages to the city hall; let him go on freedom rides—and try to understand why he must do so. If his repressed emotions are not released in nonviolent ways, they will seek expression through violence; this is not a threat but a fact of history. So I have not said to my people: "Get rid of your discontent." Rather, I have tried to say that this normal and healthy discontent can be channeled into the creative outlet of nonviolent direct action. And now this approach is being termed extremist.

But though I was initially disappointed at being categorized as an extremist, as I continued to think about the matter I gradually gained a measure of satisfaction from the label. Was not Jesus an extremist for love: "Love your enemies, bless them that curse you, do good to them that hate you, and pray for them which despitefully use you, and persecute you." Was not Amos an extremist for justice: "Let justice roll down like waters and righteousness like an ever-flowing stream." Was not Paul an extremist for the Christian gospel: "I bear in my body the marks of the Lord Jesus." Was not Martin Luther an extremist: "Here I stand: I cannot do otherwise, so help me

God." And John Bunyan: "I will stay in jail to the end of my days before I make a butchery of my conscience." And Abraham Lincoln: "This nation cannot survive half slave and half free." And Thomas Jefferson: "We hold these truths to be self-evident, that all men are created equal. . . ." So the question is not whether we will be extremists, but what kind of extremists we will be. Will we be extremists for hate or for love? Will we be extremists for the preservation of injustice or for the extension of justice? In that dramatic scene on Calvary's hill three men were crucified. We must never forget that all three were crucified for the same crime—the crime of extremism. Two were extremists for immorality, and thus fell below their environment. The other, Jesus Christ, was an extremist for love, truth and goodness, and thereby rose above his environment. Perhaps the South, the nation and the world are in dire need of creative extremists.

I had hoped that the white moderate would see this need. . . .

Before closing I feel impelled to mention one other point in your statement that has troubled me profoundly. You warmly commended the Birmingham police force for keeping "order" and "preventing violence." I doubt that you would have so warmly commended the police force if you had seen its dogs sinking their teeth into unarmed, nonviolent Negroes. I doubt that you would so quickly commend the policemen if you were to observe their ugly and inhumane treatment of Negroes here in the city jail; if you were to watch them push and curse old Negro women and young Negro girls; if you were to see them slap and kick old Negro men and young boys; if you were to observe them, as they did on two occasions, refuse to give us food because we wanted to sing our grace together. I cannot join you in your praise of the Birmingham police department.

It is true that the police have exercised a degree of discipline in handling the demonstrators. In this sense they have conducted themselves rather "nonviolently" in public. But for what purpose? To preserve the evil system of segregation. Over the past few years I have consistently preached that nonviolence demands that the means we use must be as pure as the ends we seek. I have tried to make clear that it is wrong to use immoral means to attain moral ends. But now I must affirm that it is just as wrong, or perhaps even more so, to use moral means to preserve immoral ends. Perhaps Mr. Connor and his policemen have been rather nonviolent in public, as was Chief Pritchett in Albany, Georgia, but they have used the moral means of nonviolence to maintain the immoral end of racial injustice. As T. S. Eliot has said: "The last temptation is the greatest treason: To do the right deed for the wrong reason."

I wish you had commended the Negro sitinners and demonstrators of Birmingham for their sublime courage, their willingness to suffer and their amazing discipline in the midst of great provocation. One day the South will recognize its real heroes. They will be the James Merediths, with the noble sense of purpose that enables them to face jeering and hostile mobs, and with the agonizing loneliness that characterizes the life of the pioneer. They will be old, oppressed, battered Negro women, symbolized in a seventy-two-year-old woman in Montgomery, Alabama, who rose up with a sense of dignity and with her people decided not to ride segregated buses, and who responded with ungrammatical profundity to one who inquired about her weariness: "My feets is tired, but my soul is at rest." They will be the young high school and college students, the young ministers of the gospel and a host of their elders, courageously and nonviolently sitting in at lunch counters and willingly going to jail for conscience' sake. One day the South will know that when these disinherited children of God sat down at lunch counters, they were in reality standing up for what is best in the American dream and for the most sacred values in our Judaeo-Christian heritage, thereby bringing our nation back to those great wells of democracy which were dug deep by the founding fathers in their formulation of the Constitution and the Declaration of Independence.

the persecutions of the White Citizen's Counciler or the Ku Klux Klan.

· · ·

Yours for the cause of Peace and Brotherhood, Martin Luther King, Jr.

DISCUSSION QUESTIONS

1. Explain why Martin Luther King may have come to the conclusion that the white moderate's devotion to order has been "the Negro's great stumbling block" rather than

2. In what way does King criticize the white moderate? What does he mean by the statement "justice too long delayed is justice denied"?

3. Why would King object to the pluralist understanding of American politics as explained in the introduction to this reader? How is the kind of action that King calls for viewed in our society today?

NAOMI KLEIN

RECLAIMING THE COMMONS

One of the most striking developments in U.S. and world politics in recent years has been the growth of a diverse and broad-based movement against corporate domination of the global economy. Misleadingly labeled the "antiglobalization" movement, this new wave of activism reached mass awareness with the protests in Seattle at the meeting of the World Trade Organization in 1999. One of the most articulate thinkers of the movement is the Canadian author and activist Naomi Klein, whose book No Logo *(2000) found an international audience. In this article Klein clarifies the nature and goals of the movement, which opposes the privatization and commodification of everyday life rather than globalization as such. She explains that activists have targeted "free-market" trade agreements as a way of resisting "McGovernment"—the "happy meal" of cutting taxes, privatizing services, slashing regulations, busting unions, and removing any obstacles to the unfettered reign of the market which is the hidden agenda of the free trade agenda. Far from seeing democracy and the free-market as synonymous, Klein asserts that the dominant form of corporate globalization amounts to "a crisis in representative democracy." For her the spirit of the oppositional campaigns and movements is one of the "reclaiming the commons"—acting to create a public sphere in which grassroots democracy can flourish and resist the boundless drive of the corporate project.*

What is 'the anti-globalization movement'? I put the phrase in quote-marks because I immediately have two doubts about it. Is it really a movement? If it is a movement, is it anti-globalization? Let me start with the first issue. We can easily convince ourselves it is a movement by talking it into existence at a forum like this—I spend far too much time at them—acting as if we can see it, hold it in our hands. Of course, we have seen it—and we know it's come back in Quebec, and on the U.S.–Mexican border during the Summit of the Americas and the discussion for a hemispheric Free Trade Area. But then we leave rooms like this, go home, watch some TV, do a little shopping and any sense that it exists disappears, and we feel like maybe we're going nuts. Seattle—was that a movement or a collective hallucination? To most of us here, Seattle meant a kind of coming-out party for a global resistance movement, or the 'globalization of hope,' as someone described it during the World Social Forum at Porto Alegre. But to everyone else Seattle still

Source: Naomi Klein, "Reclaiming the Commons." *New Left Review* 9, May–June 2001, pp. 81–89.

means limitless frothy coffee, Asian-fusion cuisine, e-commerce billionaires and sappy Meg Ryan movies. Or perhaps it is both, and one Seattle bred the other Seattle—and now they awkwardly coexist.

This movement we sometimes conjure into being goes by many names: anti-corporate, anti-capitalist, anti-free trade, anti-imperialist. Many say that it started in Seattle. Others maintain it began five hundred years ago—when colonialists first told indigenous peoples that they were going to have to do things differently if they were to 'develop' or be eligible for 'trade.' Others again say it began on 1 January 1994 when the Zapatistas launched their uprising with the words *Ya Basta!* on the night NAFTA became law in Mexico. It all depends on whom you ask. But I think it is more accurate to picture a movement of many movements—coalitions of coalitions. Thousands of groups today are all working against forces whose common thread is what might broadly be described as the privatization of every aspect of life, and the transformation of every activity and value into a commodity. We often speak of the privatization of education, of healthcare, of natural resources. But the process is much vaster. It includes the way powerful ideas are turned into advertising slogans and public streets into shopping malls; new generations being target-marketed at birth; schools being invaded by ads; basic human necessities like water being sold as commodities; basic labour rights being rolled back; genes are patented and designer babies loom; seeds are genetically altered and bought; politicians are bought and altered.

At the same time there are oppositional threads, taking form in many different campaigns and movements. The spirit they share is a radical reclaiming of the commons. As our communal spaces—town squares, streets, schools, farms, plants—are displaced by the ballooning marketplace, a spirit of resistance is taking hold around the world. People are reclaiming bits of nature and of culture, and saying 'this is going to be public space.' American students are kicking ads out of the classrooms. European environmentalists and ravers are throwing parties at busy intersec-

tions. Landless Thai peasants are planting organic vegetables on over-irrigated golf courses. Bolivian workers are reversing the privatization of their water supply. Outfits like Napster have been creating a kind of commons on the internet where kids can swap music with each other, rather than buying it from multinational record companies. Billboards have been liberated and independent media networks set up. Protests are multiplying. In Porto Alegre, during the World Social Forum, José Bové, often caricatured as only a hammer of McDonald's, travelled with local activists from the Movimento Sem Terra to a nearby Monsanto test site, where they destroyed three hectares of genetically modified soya beans. But the protest did not stop there. The MST has occupied the land and members are now planting their own organic crops on it, vowing to turn the farm into a model of sustainable agriculture. In short, activists aren't waiting for the revolution, they are acting right now, where they live, where they study, where they work, where they farm.

But some formal proposals are also emerging whose aim is to turn such radical reclamations of the commons into law. When NAFTA and the like were cooked up, there was much talk of adding on 'side agreements' to the free trade agenda, that were supposed to encompass the environment, labour and human rights. Now the fight-back is about taking them out. José Bové—along with the Via Campesina, a global association of small farmers—has launched a campaign to remove food safety and agricultural products from all trade agreements, under the slogan 'The World is Not for Sale.' They want to draw a line around the commons. Maude Barlow, director of the Council of Canadians, which has more members than most political parties in Canada, has argued that water isn't a private good and shouldn't be in any trade agreement. There is a lot of support for this idea, especially in Europe since the recent food scares. Typically these anti-privatization campaigns get under way on their own. But they also periodically converge—that's what happened in Seattle, Prague, Washington, Davos, Porto Alegre and Quebec.

BEYOND THE BORDERS

What this means is that the discourse has shifted. During the battles against NAFTA, there emerged the first signs of a coalition between organized labour, environmentalists, farmers and consumer groups within the countries concerned. In Canada most of us felt we were fighting to keep something distinctive about our nation from 'Americanization.' In the United States, the talk was very protectionist: workers were worried that Mexicans would 'steal' away 'our' jobs and drive down 'our' environmental standards. All the while, the voices of Mexicans opposed to the deal were virtually off the public radar—yet these were the strongest voices of all. But only a few years later, the debate over trade has been transformed. The fight against globalization has morphed into a struggle against corporatization and, for some, against capitalism itself. It has also become a fight for democracy. Maude Barlow spearheaded the campaign against NAFTA in Canada twelve years ago. Since NAFTA became law, she's been working with organizers and activists from other countries, and anarchists suspicious of the state in her own country. She was once seen as very much the face of a Canadian nationalism. Today she has moved away from that discourse. 'I've changed,' she says, 'I used to see this fight as saving a nation. Now I see it as saving democracy.' This is a cause that transcends nationality and state borders. The real news out of Seattle is that organizers around the world are beginning to see their local and national struggles—for better funded public schools, against union-busting and casualization, for family farms, and against the widening gap between rich and poor—through a global lens. That is the most significant shift we have seen in years.

How did this happen? Who or what convened this new international people's movement? Who sent out the memos? Who built these complex coalitions? It is tempting to pretend that someone did dream up a master plan for mobilization at Seattle. But I think it was much more a matter of large-scale coincidence. A lot of smaller groups organized to get themselves there and then found to their surprise just how broad and diverse a coalition they had become part of. Still, if there is one force we can thank for bringing this front into being, it is the multinational corporations. As one of the organizers of Reclaim the Streets has remarked, we should be grateful to the CEOs for helping us see the problems more quickly. Thanks to the sheer imperialist ambition of the corporate project at this moment in history—the boundless drive for profit, liberated by trade deregulation, and the wave of mergers and buy-outs, liberated by weakened anti-trust laws—multinationals have grown so blindingly rich, so vast in their holdings, so global in their reach, that they have created our coalitions for us.

Around the world, activists are piggy-backing on the ready-made infrastructures supplied by global corporations. This can mean cross-border unionization, but also cross-sector organizing—among workers, environmentalists, consumers, even prisoners, who may all have different relationships to one multinational. So you can build a single campaign or coalition around a single brand like General Electric. Thanks to Monsanto, farmers in India are working with environmentalists and consumers around the world to develop direct-action strategies that cut off genetically modified foods in the fields and in the supermarkets. Thanks to Shell Oil and Chevron, human rights activists in Nigeria, democrats in Europe, environmentalists in North America have united in a fight against the unsustainability of the oil industry. Thanks to the catering giant Sodexho-Marriott's decision to invest in Corrections Corporation of America, university students are able to protest against the exploding U.S. for-profit prison industry simply by boycotting the food in their campus cafeteria. Other targets include pharmaceutical companies who are trying to inhibit the production and distribution of low-cost AIDS drugs, and fast-food chains. Recently, students and farm workers in Florida have joined forces around Taco Bell. In the St. Petersburg area, field hands—many of them immigrants from Mexico—are paid an average $7,500 a year to pick tomatoes and onions. Due to a loophole in the law, they have no bargaining power: the farm bosses refuse even to talk with them about wages. When they started to look into who bought what they pick, they found that Taco Bell was the largest purchaser of the local tomatoes. So they launched the campaign *Yo No Quiero Taco Bell* together with students, to boycott Taco Bell on university campuses.

It is Nike, of course, that has most helped to pioneer this new brand of activist synergy. Students facing a corporate take-over of their campuses by the Nike swoosh have linked up with workers making its branded campus apparel, as well as with parents concerned at the commercialization of youth and church groups campaigning against child labour—all united by their different relationships to a common global enemy. Exposing the underbelly of high-gloss consumer brands has provided the early narratives of this movement, a sort of call-and-response to the very different narratives these companies tell every day about themselves through advertising and public relations. Citigroup offers another prime target, as North America's largest financial institution, with innumerable holdings, which deals with some of the worst corporate malefactors around. The campaign against it handily knits together dozens of issues—from clear-cut logging in California to oil-and-pipeline schemes in Chad and Cameroon. These projects are only a start. But they are creating a new sort of activist: 'Nike is a gateway drug,' in the words of Oregon student activist Sarah Jacobson.

By focusing on corporations, organizers can demonstrate graphically how so many issues of social, ecological and economic justice are interconnected. No activist I've met believes that the world economy can be changed one corporation at a time, but the campaigns have opened a door into the arcane world of international trade and finance. Where they are leading is to the central institutions that write the rules of global commerce: the WTO, the IMF, the FTAA, and for some

the market itself. Here too the unifying threat is privatization—the loss of the commons. The next round of WTO negotiations is designed to extend the reach of commodification still further. Through side agreements like GATS (General Agreement on Trade and Services) and TRIPS (Trade-Related Aspects of Intellectual Property Rights), the aim is to get still tougher protection of property rights on seeds and drug patents, and to marketize services like health care, education and water-supply.

The biggest challenge facing us is to distil all of this into a message that is widely accessible. Many campaigners understand the connexions binding together the various issues almost intuitively—much as Subcomandante Marcos says, 'Zapatismo isn't an ideology, it's an intuition.' But to outsiders, the mere scope of modern protests can be a bit mystifying. If you eavesdrop on the movement from the outside, which is what most people do, you are liable to hear what seems to be a cacophony of disjointed slogans, a jumbled laundry list of disparate grievances without clear goals. At the Democratic National Convention in Los Angeles last year, I remember being outside the Staples Centre during the Rage Against the Machine concert, just before I almost got shot, and thinking there were slogans for everything everywhere, to the point of absurdity.

MAINSTREAM FAILURES

This kind of impression is reinforced by the decentralized, non-hierarchical structure of the movement, which always disconcerts the traditional media. Well-organized press conferences are rare, there is no charismatic leadership, protests tend to pile on top of each other. Rather than forming a pyramid, as most movements do, with leaders up on top and followers down below, it looks more like an elaborate web. In part, this web-like structure is the result of internet-based organizing. But it is also a response to the very political realities that sparked the protests in the first place: the utter failure of traditional party politics. All over the world, citizens have worked to elect social democratic and workers' parties, only to watch them plead impotence in the face of market forces and IMF dictates. In these conditions, modern activists are not so naive as to believe change will come from electoral politics. That's why they are more interested in challenging the structures that make democracy toothless, like the IMF's structural adjustment policies, the WTO's ability to override national sovereignty, corrupt campaign financing, and so on. This is not just making a virtue of necessity. It responds at the ideological level to an understanding that globalization is in essence a crisis in representative democracy. What has caused this crisis? One of the basic reasons for it is the way power and decision-making has been handed along to points ever further away from citizens: from local to provincial, from provincial to national, from national to international institutions, that lack all transparency or accountability. What is the solution? To articulate an alternative, participatory democracy.

If you think about the nature of the complaints raised against the World Trade Organization, it is that governments around the world have embraced an economic model that involves much more than opening borders to goods and services. This is why it is not useful to use the language of anti-globalization. Most people do not really know what globalization is, and the term makes the movement extremely vulnerable to stock dismissals like: 'If you are against trade and globalization why do you drink coffee?' Whereas in reality the movement is a rejection of what is being bundled along with trade and so-called globalization—against the set of transformative political policies that every country in the world has been told they must accept in order to make themselves hospitable to investment. I call this package 'McGovernment.' This happy meal of cutting taxes, privatizing services, liberalizing regulations, busting unions—what is this diet in aid of? To remove anything standing in the way of the market. Let the free market roll, and every other

problem will apparently be solved in the trickle down. This isn't about trade. It's about using trade to enforce the McGovernment recipe.

So the question we are asking today, in the run up to the FTAA, is not: are you for or against trade? The question is: do we have the right to negotiate the terms of our relationship to foreign capital and investment? Can we decide how we want to protect ourselves from the dangers inherent in deregulated markets—or do we have to contract out those decisions? These problems will become much more acute once we are in a recession, because during the economic boom so much has been destroyed of what was left of our social safety net. During a period of low unemployment, people did not worry much about that. They are likely to be much more concerned in the very near future. The most controversial issues facing the WTO are these questions about self-determination. For example, does Canada have the right to ban a harmful gasoline additive without being sued by a foreign chemical company? Not according to the WTO's ruling in favour of the Ethyl Corporation. Does Mexico have the right to deny a permit for a hazardous toxic-waste disposal site? Not according to Metalclad, the U.S. company now suing the Mexican government for $16.7 million damages under NAFTA. Does France have the right to ban hormone-treated beef from entering the country? Not according to the United States, which retaliated by banning French imports like Roquefort cheese—prompting a cheese-maker called Bové to dismantle a McDonald's; Americans thought he just didn't like hamburgers. Does Argentina have to cut its public sector to qualify for foreign loans? Yes, according to the IMF—sparking general strikes against the social consequences. It's the same issue everywhere: trading away democracy in exchange for foreign capital.

On smaller scales, the same struggles for self-determination and sustainability are being waged against World Bank dams, clear-cut logging, cash-crop factory farming, and resource extraction on contested indigenous lands. Most people in these movements are not against trade or industrial development. What they are fighting for is the right of local communities to have a say in how their resources are used, to make sure that the people who live on the land benefit directly from its development. These campaigns are a response not to trade but to a trade-off that is now five hundred years old: the sacrifice of democratic control and self-determination to foreign investment and the panacea of economic growth. The challenge they now face is to shift a discourse around the vague notion of globalization into a specific debate about democracy. In a period of 'unprecedented prosperity,' people were told they had no choice but to slash public spending, revoke labour laws, rescind environmental protections—deemed illegal trade barriers—defund schools, not build affordable housing. All this was necessary to make us trade-ready, investment-friendly, world-competitive. Imagine what joys await us during a recession.

We need to be able to show that globalization—this version of globalization—has been built on the back of local human welfare. Too often, these connexions between global and local are not made. Instead we sometimes seem to have two activist solitudes. On the one hand, there are the international anti-globalization activists who may be enjoying a triumphant mood, but seem to be fighting far-away issues, unconnected to people's day-to-day struggles. They are often seen as elitists: white middle-class kids with dreadlocks. On the other hand, there are community activists fighting daily struggles for survival, or for the preservation of the most elementary public services, who are often feeling burnt-out and demoralized. They are saying: what in the hell are you guys so excited about?

The only clear way forward is for these two forces to merge. What is now the anti-globalization movement must turn into thousands of local movements, fighting the way neoliberal politics are playing out on the ground: homelessness, wage stagnation, rent escalation, police violence, prison explosion, criminalization of migrant workers, and on and on. These are also struggles about all kinds of prosaic issues: the right to decide where the local garbage goes, to have good public schools, to be supplied with clean water. At the same time, the local movements fighting privatization and deregulation on the ground need to link their campaigns into one large global movement, which can show where their particular issues fit into an international economic agenda being enforced around the world. If that connexion isn't made, people will continue to be demoralized. What we need is to formulate a political framework that can both take on corporate power and control, and empower local organizing and self-determination. That has to be a framework that encourages, celebrates and fiercely protects the right to diversity: cultural diversity, ecological diversity, agricultural diversity—and yes, political diversity as well: different ways of doing politics. Communities must have the right to plan and manage their schools, their services, their natural settings, according to their own lights. Of course, this is only possible within a framework of national and international standards—of public education, fossil-fuel emissions, and so on. But the goal should not be better far-away rules and rulers, it should be close-up democracy on the ground.

The Zapatistas have a phrase for this. They call it 'one world with many worlds in it.' Some have criticized this as a New Age non-answer. They want a plan. 'We know what the market wants to do with those spaces, what do *you* want to do? Where's your scheme?' I think we shouldn't be afraid to say: 'That's not up to us.' We need to have some trust in people's ability to rule themselves, to make the decisions that are best for them. We need to show some humility where now there is so much arrogance and paternalism. To believe in human diversity and local democracy is anything but wishy-washy. Everything in McGovernment conspires against them. Neoliberal economics is biased at every level towards centralization, consolidation, homogenization. It is a war waged on diversity. Against it, we need a movement of radical change, committed to a single world with many worlds in it, that stands for 'the one no and the many yesses.'

DISCUSSION QUESTIONS

1. How does Klein characterize the "corporate agenda" in the age of globalization? Why does she think that this agenda is a threat to democracy in any meaningful sense?

2. Contemporary political discourse often speaks of "free market democracy" as an ideal that all countries strive to attain. Why would the movements that Klein discusses take issue with this easy equation of democracy and free markets?

ELAINE BERNARD

WHY UNIONS MATTER

In 1995 John Sweeney won the first-ever contested election for the presidency of the nation's largest labor organization, the AFL-CIO. Compared to all past presidents of this relatively middle-of-the-road labor federation, Sweeney was an aggressive, fairly militant leader who promised to breathe some life into a tired and troubled U.S. labor movement. Against this backdrop of hope for a revived labor movement, Elaine Bernard, executive director of the Harvard Trade Union Program, offered her analysis of why unions are so vital to a healthy democracy. Bernard places the union movement in the context of capitalist worksites that undermine any semblance of democracy for workers. Contrary to the myth of "free labor," workplaces are "factories of authoritarianism" where the power imbalance between employers and employees is stark. Workers essentially give up their rights, such as free speech, once they enter a place of employment. As Bernard puts it: "It's almost as if the worksite is not part of the United States." She views the revival of labor unions, the extension of worker rights, and the pursuit of "workplace democracy" as crucial ingredients in the construction of the broad social vision necessary for the struggle to achieve political and economic justice. In the twenty-first century, according to Bernard, the cause of unions will be linked to the cause of building the kind of strong communities necessary for social values to triumph over crude, antidemocratic market values. Without vibrant unions, democracy languishes as the economic and political power gap widens between the rich and the poor. With strong unions, real democracy has a greater chance of flourishing.

The new leadership in the AFL-CIO is committed to putting the "movement" back into the "labor movement," and there is now an opportunity for reflection on the role and strategy of organized labor in our society. Do unions really matter anymore? And if they do, what should be their mission? Specifically, shall we build a movement simply to represent our own members, or does this movement have a wider role in society as a whole? And does the fate of the labor movement and workers' rights in the workplace concern more than the ranks of organized labor?

Worksites, Organized and Unorganized

For too long, there has been an irrational and self-defeating division of duties among progressives in the U.S. Unions organize workplaces, while other groups—the so-called social movements and identity groups—organize in the community. Even the term "labor movement" has been reduced to mean simply trade unions, which are supposed to focus on narrowly defined bread-and-butter workplace issues—wages and benefits. This topical and organizational division of turf misleadingly implies that there is an easy division between workplace issues and other social struggles. Furthermore, it suggests that wages and benefits are somehow unifying and other social issues are divisive. These separate spheres of influence have resulted in the sad fact that U.S. progressives have often marched in solidarity with labor movements and workers around the world, but often fail to consider the working majority here at home.

For activists striving for social and economic justice, the workplace is a crucial environment for organizing. It is often already organized, and not only when it is unionized; even non-union employees tend to share common hours, lunches and breaks, and most still go every day to a common location. By definition, everyone at the workplace is earning money, so it's a resource-rich community in comparison to many other locations. The production of goods and services occurs there. Decisions of great importance are made and acted upon. It is a place where global capital puts its foot down. And anywhere capital puts its foot down, there is an opportunity for people to act upon it and influence it. For all these reasons, the workplace is an important location for organizing—and not just for immediate bread-and-butter issues, important as they may be.

Democracy and Participation, or Benevolent Dictatorship?

The worksite is also a place where workers learn about the relations of power. They learn that they actually have few rights to participate in decisions about events of great consequence to their lives. As power is presently distributed, workplaces are factories of authoritarianism polluting our democracy. It is no surprise that citizens who spend eight or more hours a day obeying orders with no rights, legal or otherwise, to participate in crucial decisions that affect them, do not then engage in robust, critical dialogue about the structure of our society. Eventually the strain of being deferential servants from nine to five diminishes our after-hours liberty and sense of civic entitlement and responsibility.

Thus, the existing hierarchy of employment relations undermines democracy. Of course, this is not to suggest that all workers are unhappy, or that all workplaces are hellish. Rather, the workplace is a unique location where we have come to accept that we are not entitled to the rights and privileges we normally enjoy as citizens. Consider how employers, even very progressive employers, feel when asked how they would react to an effort by "their" employees to form a union. The normal response is that such an act is a personal rebuke, a signal of failure and a rejection of their management. Why is such a paternalistic attitude, which would be quickly recognized as such in politics, so widely accepted in employment relations?

But is the workplace really so autocratic? Why such an extreme characterization? Some illustrations of the uniqueness of the work environment, in which the normal rules of our legal system simply do not apply, are worth noting. For it is in the workplace that citizens are transformed into employees who learn to leave their rights at the door.

Take, for example, a fundamental assumption in our legal system—the presumption of innocence. In the workplace, this presumption is turned on its head. The rule of the workplace is that management dictates and workers obey. If a worker is accused of a transgression by management, there is no presumption of innocence. Even in organized workplaces the rule remains: work first, grieve later. Organized workers protected by a collective agreement with a contractual grievance procedure can at least grieve an unjust practice (or more specifically, one that violates the rights won through collective bargaining). Unorganized workers, on the other hand, have the option of appealing to their superiors' benevolence or joining the unemployment line. The implied voluntary labor contract—undertaken by workers when they agree to employment—gives management almost total control of the work relationship. "Free labor" entails no rights other than the freedom to quit without penalty. That's one step up from indentured servitude, but still a long distance from democracy.

There is not even protection in our system against arbitrary and capricious actions by management. There is no general right to employment security and no prohibition against unjust dismissal in the private sector such as exists in most other advanced industrial countries. The law of the U.S. workplace is governed by the doctrine of "employment at will." There is some protection to ensure that an employee may not be dismissed for clearly discriminatory reasons of race, gender, disability or age. But that same employee can be Black, female, older, white, male or whatever, and as long as the dismissal is for "no reason," it's legal. Most Americans believe that there is a law that protects them from being fired for "no cause." But they're wrong.

FREE SPEECH FOR WHOM?

A most glaring example of the power imbalance on the job concerns the freedom of speech. Often celebrated as the most cherished right of a free citizen, most Americans are astonished to learn that freedom of speech does not extend to the workplace, or at least not to workers. It is literally true that free speech exists for bosses, but not workers. The First Amendment of the Bill of Rights applies only to the encroachment by government on citizens' speech. It does not protect workers' speech, nor does it forbid the "private" denial of freedom of speech. Moreover, in a ruling that further tilted the balance of power (against workers) in the workplace, the Supreme Court held that corporations are "persons" and there-

fore must be afforded the protection of the Bill of Rights. So, any legislation (e.g. the National Labor Relations Act) or agency (e.g. the National Labor Relations Board) that seek to restrict a corporate "person's" freedom of speech, is unacceptable. Employers' First Amendment rights mean that they are entitled to hold "captive audience meetings"—compulsory sessions in which management lectures employees on the employers' views of unions. Neither employees nor their unions have the right of response.

It's almost as if the worksite is not a part of the United States. Workers "voluntarily" relinquish their rights when they enter into an employment relationship. So, workers can be disciplined by management (with no presumption of innocence) and they can be denied freedom of speech by their employer. The First Amendment only protects persons (including transnational corporations designated as persons) against the infringement of their rights by government—but not the infringement of rights of real persons (workers) by the private concentration of power and wealth, known as corporations.

Such limitations on workers' rights are incompatible with the requirements of a genuine democracy. In comparison to European countries, the legal rights of workers in the U.S. are remarkably limited. For a country that prides itself on individual rights, how can we permit the wholesale denial of those rights for tens of millions of American workers?

INDUSTRIAL DEMOCRACY OR AN END TO WORKPLACE CONFLICT?

History counts. Few people today remember that when the National Labor Relations Act, the cornerstone of U.S. labor law, was adopted by Congress in 1935, its purpose was not simply to provide a procedural mechanism to end strife in the workplace. Rather, this monumental piece of New Deal legislation had a far more ambitious mission: to promote industrial democracy. To achieve this extension of democracy into the workplace, the NLRA instituted "free collective bargaining" between workers and employers. Unions were to be encouraged, as it was understood that workers could not engage in meaningful collective bargaining without collective representation.

Needless to say, it has been a long time since we've heard any President or Administration, much less Congress, talk about promoting industrial democracy. In fact, the very term "industrial democracy" seems like a contradiction in terms. While we might not expect politicians to lead the charge for democracy in the workplace and the right of workers to participate in workplace decisions, what about organized labor? Has labor been on the defensive so long that we have lost sight of this long-term goal?

While the occasional union document makes a passing reference to "workplace democracy," there has been little effort by labor in recent years to draw the connection between worker rights in the workplace and the overall struggle of working people for democracy in the United States. Rather then relegating workplace democracy to an abstract long-term goal, labor today needs to tap into the desire for the extension of democracy into the workplace. The new labor movement must place industrial democracy front and center if we are to create a wider appeal for unions. Fighting for democracy in the workplace, and not simply the right to form unions, is vital to the restoration of labor's social mission. While unions are the pre-eminent instrument in our society to actualize workplace rights, it is important for unions to lead the charge against the entire antidemocratic workplace regime.

It is not only right, but smart too. Viewing labor rights as part of a wider struggle for democracy is essential for the growth of the labor movement today. With organized labor down to only 15 percent of the total workforce and 11 percent in the private sector, the vast majority of today's workers have no direct experience with unions. But as citizens, they have a conception of democracy and the rights of citizens. Unfortunately, American workers are schooled every day at work to believe that democracy stops at the factory or office door. But democracy is not an extracurricular activity that can be relegated to evenings and weekends. And citizens' rights should not be subject to suspension at the whim of one's employer. The labor movement is the natural vehicle to lead the struggle for basic democratic rights inside and outside the workplace.

THE NATURAL STATE OF THE WORKPLACE—UNION FREE?

Organized labor, of course, has long sought to restore some balance to U.S. labor law. The current regime is so stacked against workers that unionization is very difficult everywhere, and almost impossible in some sectors of the economy. Supreme Court decisions rolling back union and worker rights, as well as management-inspired amendments to labor law, have tied the hands of union organizers while freeing management to penalize workers who attempt to exercise their rights.

While the battle to restore "fairness" in labor law is important, even a victory in this campaign would simply bring us back to 1935. Instead, we should question the basic assumption of U.S. labor law that the natural state of the workplace is union-free with workers having no rights. We need to re-establish among a new generation of workers that one of the key purposes of a union is to bring democratic rights of participation, enjoyed in the rest of society, into the workplace.

In a truly democratic society, all workers would have rights, and collective decision-making would be the norm. If workers wish to give up their rights in the workplace, they should be required to demonstrate that they are doing so of their own free will. Yet most of our laws operate in a completely opposite manner. U.S. labor law is largely a series of barriers over which workers must climb to gain elementary rights. And each year these barriers are getting higher and higher. Management can, of course, voluntarily recognize unions or permit workers to participate in decision-making, but this is nothing more than a form of benevolence, the granting of privileges which can be retracted at any time—not to be confused with rights which cannot be arbitrarily taken away. Why do we assume that workers should not meaningfully participate in workplace decisions? In a democracy would it not make more sense to assume such rights and to apply strict scrutiny to those workers who relinquish their rights rather than those who exercise them?

Seen in this light, even the much touted right to collective bargaining is a very limited right. Like a hunting license, it does not guarantee anything but an opportunity which may or may not yield results. It should not be confused with actually conferring rights on workers, though it does help workers create a power than can win them rights. Workers who win bargaining rights through their unions have the right to collectively bargain with the employer, who has a duty to bargain in good faith; however, the employer is under *no obligation* to come to a settlement.

The authoritarianism of the workplace in the United States diminishes our standing as a democracy. Indeed, in the latter part of this century, instead of the democratization of the American workplace, the hierarchical corporate workplace model is coming to dominate the rest of society.

BEYOND "BREAD AND BUTTER" UNIONISM

With the United States reporting the highest levels of inequality in the advanced industrial world, and the majority of U.S. workers experiencing declining real wages for 20 years, we might be tempted to think that the problems of democracy in the workplace should be put on the back burner for more settled times and that the labor movement should focus only on this growing economic inequality. Yet the two are linked. Democracy and workers' rights in the workplace are crucial issues for organizing. And without greater levels of organization, inequality will continue to rise.

If the aims of unions are, as stated by the AFL-CIO, to "achieve decent wages and conditions, democracy in the workplace, a full voice for working people in society, and the more equitable sharing of the wealth of the nation," then unions must be more than service organizations for their members. Yet unions cannot meet these admirable goals if they are simply a type of business—"Contracts 'R Us"—or if they operate merely as a non-profit insurance company seeking to protect its client/members from unexpected trouble.

This is not a new tension. Servicing the membership has often been held as incompatible with fulfilling the wider social mission of labor to serve the needs of all working people, whether they are organized or not. But it is now becoming increasingly clear that unions need to do both. Unions, like any organization, will not survive if they do not serve the needs of their members. Nor will unions survive if they *only* serve the needs of their members.

The experience of organized labor in the U.S. demonstrates that simply delivering for their own members is not sufficient for success in the long run. Measured in this narrowest sense of "delivering" for members, U.S. trade unions have been the most "successful" labor movement in the world. Unions won for their members a social wage (benefits such as pensions, health care, paid vacations) that working people in other advanced industrial countries were able to win only through political as well as industrial action. In addition, U.S. trade unionists enjoy the highest wage premium of unionists in any country—that is, the difference in pay and benefits between organized workers and the unorganized workers in the same sector.

Thus, if serving the membership was the key to building unions, then the U.S. should have the highest rate of unionization in the world, not one of the lowest. The low levels of unionization underline the fact that there is a downside to labor's achievement for its members: *The higher the wage premium, the greater the employer resistance to unionization.* The sad lesson for labor is that by failing to extend the gains made by unions to the rest of working people, these gains have come to be threatened. By comparison, in Canada, where unions have been more successful in spreading the gains first achieved through collective bargaining, rates of organization are double what they are in the U.S. Management resistance to unionization in Canada is less vigorous than in the U.S. If management busts a union in Canada, it cannot take away Canadian workers' health care because this benefit has been socialized and is an entitlement of all Canadian residents. By winning benefits first through collective agreements and then extending them to all working people through political action, labor in Canada has not only assisted all working people, but has made its own victory that much more secure.

A second problem for unions in winning benefits only for their own members is that over time this approach has led to the isolation of unionists from other working people. Unionists are left with little sense of a broad class movement that includes all workers, organized and unorganized. Unions come to see themselves and their members see them as businesses narrowly servicing members needs (McDonald's unionism—"we do it all for you.") These attitudes replace a sense of solidarity among members ("an injury to one is an injury to all") with a sense of entitlement ("What can the union do for me?"). Members see joining the union as purchasing a service, not participating in a movement for social change.

This business or servicing approach weakens unions and reinforces anti-union, individualistic ideology. And unions eventually lose their ability to mobilize members in their own defense. Ultimately, this approach depoliticizes working people, including union members who start to see unions as simply another "special interest" rather than organizations representing the interests of the vast majority of people—workers.

UNIONS AND POLITICS: CONSTRUCTING THE POSSIBLE

For unions to succeed today they need to have a wider social vision. Pure and simple trade unionism is not possible. Most unionists recognize that politics is important to the labor movement and that there is nothing that labor can win at the bargaining table that cannot be taken away by regulation, legislation or political decision-making. It's therefore urgent for organized labor and working people in general to organize on two fronts—politically, in the community through political parties and social movements, and industrially in the workplace through unions. Unionists cannot leave politics alone, because politics will not leave unions alone.

To operate effectively in the contemporary political context, the labor movement must understand the challenge that the New Right presents for unions and the rights of working people. At 14 million members, the labor movement remains the largest multi-racial, multi-issue membership organization in the country. As such, it is a prime target of the New Right's assault on working people's rights, both in and out of the workplace.

Politics has always been fundamentally a contest of ideas. Political scientist Robert Dahl has defined politics as "the art of the possible," but for the working person today, it might be more useful to see politics as the process of *constructing the possible*. In essence, it is the process of deciding which issues warrant a societal response and which are best left to the individual.

The 1994 debate over health care reform—already a fading memory—exemplified this process in politics. The question was whether we should leave this critical service to individuals seeking private solutions through a maze of various insurance plans or whether society as a whole should organize a system of insurance to assure universal, comprehensive, affordable, quality coverage for all. The Canadian single-payer system was held up as an example of how the provision of insurance could be socialized, while leaving the practice of medicine private and assuring freedom of choice of doctors. Although we have already socialized health insurance for the elderly through Medicare, many Americans seemed to balk at the prospect of socialized medicine for all. Yet in U.S. history we have often done precisely this—socialized a service—transforming it from an individual responsibility to a community-provided right of all.

The fire department and fire service throughout the country at the turn of the century were private; fire service was an individual responsibility. Those who could afford it, and those who had the most to lose in case of fire, financed private fire companies. The companies gave their patrons iron plaques which they could post on the outside of their buildings to assure that in case of fire the local fire service would know they were insured and act promptly.

Of course fire does not confine itself to purchasers of fire service. And while the uninsured could engage in expedited negotiations with the fire service over fees when fire struck, fire spreads easily from the uninsured to the insured, and so it gradually dawned on the insured that the only protection for anyone in the community was to insure everyone. So, the insured sought to socialize the service, that is, extend fire service to everyone—through a universal, single payer, high quality, public system. Taxes, rather than private insurance fees, financed the universal system. And the universal system was cheaper, and more efficient. The quality was assured because rich and poor alike were covered by the system. Everyone could access the system as needed and everyone paid into the system through their taxes to the community. No doubt, the cynics of the day argued that the poor would take advantage of this social service, or that people would simply not be able to appreciate what they had unless they paid for it. Through the political process, the problem of fires was moved from the realm of individual concern to collective responsibility. Today, the need for universal fire service seems obvious. Interestingly, the need for health care is still not regarded as a societal right. But that is the essence of the political challenge—to construct what is possible.

WHO DECIDES: MARKET VALUES OR SOCIAL VALUES?

Clearly understanding this point, the New Right has a program to construct a new political consensus. In the U.S. and elsewhere, this program designates virtually all problems as the responsibility of the individual, whose fate is left to the mercy of the market. Former British Prime Minister Margaret Thatcher summarized this approach succinctly: "there is no such thing as society, only individuals and their families." If there is no such thing as society, then there is no role for government, or indeed collective institutions of any sort—including unions. We are thus left only with individuals and their families, working in isolation, making decisions within the narrow context of the market, thinking only of themselves. This program seeks nothing less than the destruction of civil society, without which there can be no democracy.

The market must not be permitted to replace social decision-making. Markets have their uses, but they should not be confused with democratic institutions. Markets, for example, might be useful in determining the price of goods, but they should not be mechanisms for determining our values as a community. Markets are oblivious to morals and promote only the value of profit. To take an example from our own history, a slave market thrived on this continent for over 300 years. Nor did this market collapse on its own. It took political intervention and armed resistance—in a communal assertion of values—to abolish slavery. Markets are no substitute for the democratic process.

In a democracy, it's "one person, one vote." But in the marketplace, it's "one dollar, one vote," which, despite an appearance of neutrality, is an inherently unjust equation that privileges the rich at the expense of the poor. In such statements as "let the market decide," promoted as principle by the New Right, the market disguises human agency, while serving the demands of the wealthy whose dollars shape the rules of the market. According to "free market" ideology, government intervention is futile at best, disruptive of the natural order at worst, and always unwelcome (though in practice the New Right uses government shamelessly for its own purposes, e.g., corporate welfare).

The elevation of markets as the sole arbitrator of values deprives people of a sense of belonging to a community. Instead, people feel isolated, which in turn leads to demoralization. If each of us is on our own, none of us can change very much, so we should just accept things as they are. No single individual can answer the big questions in our society. An individual can't opt for single-payer health care, or rapid transit, or address the problems in our public schools. So by default these problems become "unsolvable."

This frightening world view forces people to seek individual solutions and pits people against one another, reducing social responsibility and cohesion. If there is no such thing as society, then government is a waste, and redistributive programs are robbery. Anything that goes from my pocket to the community is a scam. Worse yet, anything that goes from my pocket makes it that much harder for me and my family to survive. This is a zero-sum view of society in which your gain is my loss, and an injury to one is their problem. And this is the view that will ultimately prevail if the New Right succeeds in its attempt to eviscerate democratic institutions—from government to communities to unions.

UNIONS AND CIVIL SOCIETY

By destroying all collective institutions and making government regulations appear to be illegitimate and infringements of individual rights—the New Right is destroying the last vestiges of social solidarity. They are, in essence, expanding the undemocratic regime in the workplace to all aspects of civil society, thus their determination to end entitlement programs and destroy unions.

The labor movement builds communities—that's what unions do. By bringing together workers, who have few rights, who are isolated as individuals and often competing against each other, unions forge a community in the workplace. They help workers understand that they have rights, and they provide a collective vehicle

for exercising those rights. Beyond the defense and promotion of individual union members' rights, unions also provide a collective voice for workers. They provide a powerful check to the almost total power of management in the workplace. And they fight for the right of workers to participate in decision-making in the workplace.

But labor movements and other communities of common interest don't just happen. They have to be consciously constructed, with a lot of hard work, discussion and engagement. Constructing democratic communities is an ongoing process, rather like democracy. And like democracy, it's a process that can be rolled back or reversed.

The cause of unions in the twenty-first century United States reaches far beyond their own survival. Because we have not yet succeeded in extending democracy to the workplace, democracy and civil society themselves are threatened. The labor movement cannot be seen in isolation from the political environment, and any revitalization of unions will require an effective response to that environment. While the New Right tries to reduce everything to an individual responsibility, we must create democratic communities—in the workplace and beyond. That's the challenge that faces the new leadership of the AFL-CIO, as well as every local official, stop steward, and union member in the U.S. today.

DISCUSSION QUESTIONS

1. Discussions of democracy do not usually address the worksite. Why does Bernard think it is important to include workplace relations of power when we consider the foundations of democracy?

2. Interpret Bernard's statement that "Unionists cannot leave politics alone, because politics will not leave unions alone."

CLOSING THE DEMOCRACY GAP

Ralph Nader has been battling corporate America on behalf of social and economic justice for four decades as a consumer advocate, author, and presidential candidate. Though marginalized or ignored in the mainstream media, and shut out of the presidential debates, his 2000 campaign consistently drew far larger audiences than either Governor Bush or Vice President Gore at rallies from Portland to Minneapolis to Boston and New York City. Analysts, when they paid any attention at all, noted that young, idealistic college-aged people were heavily represented amid the throngs in attendance. The following article is the text of Nader's speech announcing his candidacy for the 2000 presidential nomination as a member of the environmental Green Party. The speech is filled with lots of details. But what frames the specifics of Nader's analysis is a belief in the need to close the "democracy gap" in America—that is, the gap between the control that the "corporate government" exercises over our "political government." As Nader puts it: "Active citizens are left shouting their concerns over a deep chasm between them and their government." While many former Nader supporters were critical of his 2004 presidential campaign, we encourage you to seriously consider Nader's 2000 message, think about how his views differs from those of mainstream Republicans and Democrats that dominate the news each night, and decide whether you too are tired of politics as usual. Perhaps Nader's spirit and program may inspire you and your friends to do some creative and challenging thinking, some political organizing, and perhaps some shouting of your own.

Today I wish to explain why, after working for years as a citizen advocate for consumers, workers, taxpayers and the environment, I am seeking the Green Party's nomination for President. A crisis of democracy in our country convinces me to take this action. Over the past twenty years, big business has increasingly dominated our political economy. This control by the corporate government over our political government is creating a widening "democracy gap." Active citizens are left shouting their concerns over a deep chasm between them and their government. This state of affairs is a world away from the legislative milestones in civil rights, the environment, and health and safety of workers and consumers seen in the sixties and seventies. At that time,

Source: Ralph Nader, "Announcement Speech For the Green Party's Nomination for President." http://www.votenader.com, Washington, D.C., 21 February, 2000.

informed and dedicated citizens powered their concerns through the channels of government to produce laws that bettered the lives of millions of Americans.

Today we face grave and growing societal problems in health care, education, labor, energy and the environment. These are problems for which active citizens have solutions, yet their voices are not carrying across the democracy gap. Citizen groups and individual thinkers have generated a tremendous capital of ideas, information, and solutions to the point of surplus, while our government has been drawn away from us by a corporate government. Our political leadership has been hijacked.

Citizen advocates have no other choice but to close the democracy gap by direct political means. Only effective national political leadership will restore the responsiveness of government to its citizenry. Truly progressive political movements do not just produce more good results; they enable a flowering of progressive citizen movements to effectively advance the quality of our neighborhoods and communities outside of politics.

I have a personal distaste for the trappings of modern politics, in which incumbents and candidates daily extol their own inflated virtues, paint complex issues with trivial brush strokes, and propose plans quickly generated by campaign consultants. But I can no longer stomach the systemic political decay that has weakened our democracy. I can no longer watch people dedicate themselves to improving their country while their government leaders turn their backs, or worse, actively block fair treatment for citizens. It is necessary to launch a sustained effort to wrest control of our democracy from the corporate government and restore it to the political government under the control of citizens.

This campaign will challenge all Americans who are concerned with systemic imbalances of power and the undermining of our democracy, whether they consider themselves progressives, liberals, conservatives, or others. Presidential elections should be a time for deep discussions among the citizenry regarding the down-to-earth problems and injustices that are not addressed because of the gross power mismatch between the narrow vested interests and the public or common good.

The unconstrained behavior of big business is subordinating our democracy to the control of a corporate plutocracy that knows few self-imposed limits to the spread of its power to all sectors of our society. Moving on all fronts to advance narrow profit motives at the expense of civic values, large corporate lobbies and their law firms have produced a commanding, multi-faceted and powerful juggernaut. They flood public elections with cash, and they use their media conglomerates to exclude, divert, or propagandize. They brandish their willingness to close factories here and open them abroad if workers do not bend to their demands. By their control in Congress, they keep the federal cops off the corporate crime, fraud, and abuse beats. They imperiously demand and get a wide array of privileges and immunities: tax escapes, enormous corporate welfare subsidies, federal giveaways, and bailouts. They weaken the common law of torts in order to avoid their responsibility for injurious wrongdoing to innocent children, women and men.

Abuses of economic power are nothing new. Every major religion in the world has warned about societies allowing excessive influences of mercantile or commercial values. The profiteering motive is driven and single-minded. When unconstrained, it can override or erode community, health, safety, parental nurturing, due process, clean politics, and many other basic social values that hold together a society. Abraham Lincoln, Theodore Roosevelt, Franklin Roosevelt, Supreme Court Justices Louis Brandeis and William Douglas, among others, eloquently warned about what Thomas Jefferson called "the excesses of the monied interests" dominating people and their governments. The struggle between the forces of democracy and plutocracy has ebbed and flowed throughout our history. Each time the cycle of power has favored more democracy, our country has prospered ("a rising tide lifts all boats"). Each time the cycle of corporate plutocracy has lengthened, injustices and shortcomings proliferate.

In the sixties and seventies, for example, when the civil rights, consumer, environmental, and women's rights movements were in their ascendancy, there finally was a constructive responsiveness by government. Corporations, such as auto manufacturers, had to share more decision making with affected constituencies, both directly and through their public representatives and civil servants. Overall, our country has come out better, more tolerant, safer, and with greater opportunities. The earlier nineteenth century democratic struggles by abolitionists against slavery, by farmers against large oppressive railroads and banks, and later by new trade unionists against the brutal workplace conditions of the early industrial and mining era helped mightily to make America and its middle class what it is today. They demanded that economic power subside or be shared.

Democracy works, and a stronger democracy works better for reputable, competitive markets, equal opportunity and higher standards of living and justice. Generally, it brings out the best performances from people and from businesses.

A plutocracy—rule by the rich and powerful—on the other hand, obscures our historical quests for justice. Harnessing political power to corporate greed leaves us with a country that has far more problems than it deserves, while blocking ready solutions or improvements from being applied.

It is truly remarkable for almost every widespread need or injustice in our country, there are citizens, civic groups, small and medium-sized businesses and farms that have shown how to meet these needs or end these injustices. However, all the innovative solutions in the world will accomplish little if the injustices they address or the problems they solve have been shoved aside because plutocracy reigns and democracy wanes. For all optimistic Americans, when their issues are thus swept from the table, it becomes civic mobilization time.

Consider the economy, which business commentators say could scarcely be better. If, instead of corporate yardsticks, we use human yardsticks to measure the performance of the economy and go beyond the quantitative indices of annual economic growth, structural deficiencies become readily evident. The complete dominion of traditional yardsticks for measuring economic prosperity masks not only these failures but also the inability of a weakened democracy to address how and why a majority of Americans are not benefiting from this prosperity in their daily lives. Despite record economic growth, corporate profits, and stock market highs year after year, a stunning array of deplorable conditions still prevails year after year. For example

- A majority of workers are making less now, inflation adjusted, than in 1979.
- Over 20 percent of children were growing up in poverty during the past decade, by far the highest among comparable western countries.
- The minimum wage is lower today, inflation-adjusted, than in 1979.
- American workers are working longer and longer hours—on average an additional 163 hours per year, compared to twenty years ago—with less time for family and community.
- Many full-time family farms cannot make a living in a market of giant buyer concentration and industrial agriculture.
- The public works (infrastructure) are crumbling, with decrepit schools and clinics, library closings, antiquated mass transit and more.
- Corporate welfare programs, paid for largely by middle-class taxpayers and amounting to hundreds of billions of dollars per year, continue to rise along with government giveaways of taxpayer assets such as public forests, minerals and new medicines.
- Affordable housing needs are at record levels while secondary mortgage market companies show record profits.
- The number of Americans without health insurance grows every year.
- There have been twenty-five straight years of growing foreign trade deficits ($270 billion in 1999).

Now, these checkpoints face a relentless barrage from rampaging corporate titans assuming more control over elected officials, the workplace, the marketplace, technology, capital pools (including workers' pension trusts) and educational institutions. One clear sign of the reign of corporations over our government is that the key laws passed in the 1960s and 1970s that we use to curb corporate misbehavior would not even pass through Congressional committees today. Planning ahead, multinational corporations shaped the World Trade Organization's autocratic and secretive governing procedures so as to undermine non-trade health, safety, and other living standard laws and proposals in member countries.

Up against the corporate government, voters find themselves asked to choose between look-a-like candidates from two parties vying to see who takes the marching orders from their campaign paymasters and their future employers. The money of vested interests nullifies genuine voter choice and trust. Our elections have been put out for auction to the highest bidder. Public elections must be publicly financed and it can be done with well-promoted voluntary checkoffs and free TV and Radio time for ballot-qualified candidates.

Workers are disenfranchised more than any time since the 1920s. Many unions stagger under stagnant leadership and discouraged rank and file. Furthermore, weak labor laws actually obstruct new trade union organization and leave the economy with the lowest percentage of workers unionized in more than sixty years. Giant multinationals are pitting countries against one another and escaping national jurisdictions more and more. Under these circumstances, workers are entitled to stronger labor organizing laws and rights for their own protection in order to deal with highly organized corporations.

At a very low cost, government can help democratic solution building for a host of problems that citizens face, from consumer abuses, to environmental degradation. Government research and development generated whole new industries and company startups and created the Internet. At the least, our government can facilitate the voluntary banding together of interested citizens into democratic civic institutions. Such civic organizations can create more level playing fields in the banking, insurance, real estate, transportation, energy, health care, cable TV, educational, public services, and other sectors. Let's call this the flowering of a deep-rooted democratic society. A government that funnels your tax dollars to corporate welfare kings in the form of subsidies, bailouts, guarantees, and giveaways of valuable public assets can at least invest in promoting healthy democracy.

Taxpayers have very little legal standing in the federal courts and little indirect voice in the assembling and disposition of taxpayer revenues. Closer scrutiny of these matters between elections is necessary. Facilities can be established to accomplish a closer oversight of taxpayer assets and how tax dollars (apart from social insurance) are allocated. This is an arena which is, at present, shaped heavily by corporations that, despite record profits, pay far less in taxes as a percent of the federal budget than in the 1950s and 1960s.

The "democracy gap" in our politics and elections spells a deep sense of powerlessness by people who drop out, do not vote or listlessly vote for the "least-worst" every four years and then wonder why after another cycle the "least-worst" gets worse. It is time to redress fundamentally these imbalances of power. We need a deep initiatory democracy in the embrace of its citizens, a usable brace of democratic tools that brings the best out of people, highlights the humane ideas and practical ways to raise and meet our expectations and resolve our society's deficiencies and injustices.

A few illustrative questions can begin to raise our expectations and suggest what can be lost when the few and powerful hijack our democracy:

- Why can't the wealthiest nation in the world abolish the chronic poverty of millions of working and non-working Americans, including our children?
- Are we reversing the disinvestment in our distressed inner cities and rural areas and using creatively some of the huge capital

pools in the economy to make these areas more livable, productive and safe?

- Are we able to end homelessness and wretched housing conditions with modern materials, designs, and financing mechanisms, without bank and insurance company redlining, to meet the affordable housing needs of millions of Americans?

- Are we getting the best out of known ways to spread renewable, efficient energy throughout the land to save consumers money and to head off global warming and other land-based environmental damage from fossil fuels and atomic energy?

- Are we getting the best out of the many bright and public-spirited civil servants who know how to improve governments but are rarely asked by their politically-appointed superiors or members of Congress?

- Are we able to provide wide access to justice for all aggrieved people so that we apply rigorously the admonition of Judge Learned Hand, "If we are to keep our democracy, there must be one commandment: Thou Shall Not Ration Justice"?

- Can we extend overseas the best examples of our country's democratic processes and achievements instead of annually using billions in tax dollars to subsidize corporate munitions exports, as Republican Senator Mark Hatfield always used to decry?

- Can we stop the giveaways of our vast commonwealth assets and become better stewards of the public lands, better investors of trillions of dollars in worker pension monies, and allow broader access to the public airwaves and other assets now owned by the people but controlled by corporations?

- Can we counter the coarse and brazen commercial culture, including television which daily highlights depravity and ignores the quiet civic heroisms in its communities, a commercialism that insidiously exploits childhood and plasters its logos everywhere?

- Can we plan ahead as a society so we know our priorities and where we wish to go? Or do we continue to let global corporations remain astride the planet, corporatizing everything, from genes to education to the Internet to public institutions, in short planning our futures in their image? If a robust civic culture does not shape the future, corporatism surely will.

To address these and other compelling challenges, we must build a powerful, self-renewing civil society that focuses on ample justice so we do not have to desperately bestow limited charity. Such a culture strengthens existing civic associations and facilitates the creation of others to watch the complexities and technologies of a new century. Building the future also means providing the youngest of citizens with citizen skills that they can use to improve their communities.

This is the foundation of our campaign, to focus on active citizenship, to create fresh political movements that will displace the control of the Democratic and Republican Parties, two apparently distinct political entities that feed at the same corporate trough. They are in fact simply the two heads of one political duopoly, the DemRep Party. This duopoly does everything it can to obstruct the beginnings of new parties including raising ballot access barriers, entrenching winner-take-all voting systems, and thwarting participation in debates at election times.

As befits its name, the Green Party, whose nomination I seek, stands for the regeneration of American politics. The new populism which the Green Party represents, involves motivated, informed voters who comprehend that "freedom is participation in power," to quote the ancient Roman orator, Cicero. When citizen participation flourishes, as this campaign will encourage it to do, human values can tame runaway commercial imperatives. The myopia of the short-term bottom line so often debases our democratic processes and our public and private domains. Putting human values first helps to make business responsible and to put government on the right track.

It is easy and true to say that this deep democracy campaign will be an uphill one. However, it is also true that widespread reform will not flourish without a fairer distribution of power for the key roles of voter, citizen, worker, taxpayer, and consumer. Comprehensive reform proposals from the corporate suites to the nation's streets, from the schools to the hospitals, from the preservation of small farm economies to the protection of privacies, from livable wages to sustainable environments, from more time for children to less time for commercialism, from waging peace and health to averting war and violence, from foreseeing and forestalling future troubles to journeying toward brighter horizons, will wither while power inequalities loom over us.

Why are campaigns just for candidates? I would like the American people to hear from individuals such as Edgar Cahn (Time Dollars for neighborhoods), Nicholas Johnson (television and telecommunications), Paul Hawken, Amory and Hunter Lovins (energy and resource conservation), Dee Hock (on chaordic organizations), James MacGregor Burns and John Gardner (on leadership), Richard Grossman (on the American history of corporate charters and personhood), Jeff Gates (on capital sharing), Robert Monks (on corporate accountability), Ray Anderson (on his company's pollution and recycling conversions), Johnnetta Cole, Troy Duster and Yolanda Moses (on race relations), Richard Duran (minority education), Lois Gibbs (on community mobilization against toxics), Robert McIntyre (on tax justice), Hazel Henderson (on redefining economic development), Barry Commoner and David Brower (on fundamental environmental regeneration), Wendell Berry (on the quality of living), Tony Mazzocchi (on a new agenda for labor), and Law Professor Richard Parker (on a constitutional popular manifesto). These individuals are a small sampling of many who have so much to say, but seldom get through the evermore entertainment-focused media. (Note: mention of these persons does not imply their support for this campaign.)

Our political campaign will highlight active and productive citizens who practice democracy often in the most difficult of situations. I intend to do this in the District of Columbia whose citizens have no full-voting representation in Congress or other rights accorded to states. The scope of this campaign is also to engage as many volunteers as possible to help overcome ballot barriers and to get the vote out. In addition it is designed to leave a momentum after election day for the various causes that committed people have worked so hard to further. For the Greens know that political parties need also to work between elections to make elections meaningful. The focus on fundamentals of broader distribution of power is the touchstone of this campaign. As Supreme Court Justice Louis Brandeis declared for the ages. "We can have a democratic society or we can have great concentrated wealth in the hands of a few. We cannot have both."

Thank you.

DISCUSSION QUESTIONS

1. Throughout his address Nader speaks of a "democracy gap" in the United States. What does Nader mean by this term? How is the democracy gap related to the political power of corporate business?

2. Nader argues that only "active citizenship" and a "powerful, self-renewing civil society" can overcome the democracy gap. Why does Nader believe that the current two-party system is an obstacle to citizen-based democracy? To what extent do you agree with Nader's critique of the two-party system?

Resources for Further Study

MEDIA

AlterNet
77 Federal St.
San Francisco, CA 94107
Tel: 415–284–1420
http://www.alternet.org

Common Dreams News Center
P.O. Box 443
Portland, ME 04112–0443
Tel: 207–775–0488
http://www.commondreams.org

FAIR Fairness and Accuracy in Reporting
112 West 27th St.
New York, NY 10001
Tel: 212–633–6700

http://www.fair.org

Free Press
100 Main St.
PO Box 28
Northampton, MA 01061
Tel: 413–585–1533
http://www.freepress.net

Independent Media Center (Washington Office)
PO Box 21372
Washington, DC 20009
Tel: 202–452–5936
http://www.indymedia.org

Media Access Project
1625 K St., N.W.

Washington, DC 20006
Tel: 202–232–4300
http://www.mediaaccess.org

Progressive Media Project
409 E. Main St.
Madison, WI 53703
Tel: 608–257–4626
http://www.progressive.org/
    mediaproj.htm

Z Net
18 Millfield St.
Woods Hole, MA 02543
Tel: 508–548–9063
http://www.zmag.org

RESEARCH, POLICY, AND ADVOCACY

Center on Budget and Policy Priorities
820 First St., N.E., Suite 510
Washington, DC 20002
Tel: 202–408–1080
http://www.cbpp.org

Center for Defense Information
1779 Massachusetts Ave., N.W.
Washington, DC 20036
Tel: 202–332–0600
http://www.cdi.org

Center for Responsive Politics
1101 14th St., N.W., Suite 1030
Washington, DC 20005-5635
Tel: 202–857–0044
http://www.opensecrets.org

Center for Voting and Democracy
6930 Carroll Ave., Suite 601
Takoma Park, MD 20912
Tel: 301–270–4616
www.fairvote.org

Children's Defense Fund
25 E St., N.W.
Washington, DC 20001
Tel: 202–628–8787
http://www.
    childrensdefense.org

Citizens for Tax Justice
1311 L St., N.W., Suite 400
Washington, DC 20005
Tel: 202–626–3780
http://www.ctj.org

Economic Policy Institute
1660 L St., N.W., Suite 1200
Washington, DC 20036
Tel: 202–775–8810
http://www.epinet.org

Foreign Policy In Focus
Interhemispheric Resource Center
PO Box 2178
Silver City, NM 88062
Tel: 505–388–0208
http://www.fpif.org

Institute for Policy Studies (IPS)
733 15th St., N.W., Suite 1020
Washington, DC 20005
Tel: 202–234–9382
http://www.ips-dc.org

Physicians for a National Health Program
29 E. Madison St. 602
Chicago, IL 60602
Tel: 312–782–6007
http://www.pnhp.org/

Public Campaign
1320 19th St., N.W., Suite M–1
Washington, DC 20036
Tel: 202–293–0222
http://www.publiccampaign.org

Public Citizen (Includes: Buyers Up, Congress Watch, Critical Mass Energy Project, Global Trade Watch, Health Research Group, Litigation Group)
1600 20th St., N.W.
Washington, DC 20009
Tel: 202–588–1000
http://www.citizen.org

United for a Fair Economy
37 Temple Pl., 2nd Floor
Boston, MA 02111
Tel: 617–423–2148
http://www.faireconomy.org

U.S. PIRG (Public Interest Research Groups)
218 D St., S. E.
Washington, DC 20003
Tel: 202–546–9707
http://www.uspirg.org

PUBLICATIONS

Magazines

Defense Monitor (CDI)
1779 Massachusetts Ave., N.W.
Washington, DC 20036
Tel: 202–862–0700
http://www.cdi.org/dm/

Dollars and Sense
740 Cambridge St.
Cambridge, MA 02141
Tel: 617–876–2434
http://www.dollarsandsense.org

Extra! (FAIR)
112 West 27th St.
New York, NY 10001
Tel: 212–633–6700
http://www.fair.org/extra/

In These Times
2040 N. Milwaukee Ave.
Chicago, IL 60647
Tel: 773–772–0100
http://www.inthesetimes.com

Left Business Observer
38 Green St., Floor 4
New York, NY 10013–2502
Tel: 212–219–0010
http://www.
    leftbusinessobserver.com

Ms.
20 Exchange Place, 22nd floor
New York, NY 10005
Tel: 212–509–2092
http://www.msmagazine.com

Mother Jones
731 Market St., 6th Floor
San Francisco, CA 94103
Tel: 415–665–6637
http://www.motherjones.com

Multinational Monitor
P.O. Box 19405
Washington, DC 20036
Tel: 202–387–8030
http://www.
    multinationalmonitor.org

Nation
33 Irving Place
New York, NY 10003
Tel: 212–209–5400
http://www.thenation.com

The Progressive
409 East Main St.
Madison, WI 53703
Tel: 608–257–4626
http://www.progressive.org

Utne Reader
1624 Harmon Place #330
Minneapolis, MN 55403
Tel: 612–338–5040
http://www.utne.com

Z Magazine
18 Millfield Street
Woods Hole, MA 02543
Tel: 508–548–9063
http://www.zmag.org

Journals

Boston Review
E53–407 MIT
Cambridge, MA 02139
Tel: 617–253–3642
http://bostonreview.net

Dissent
310 Riverside Dr., Suite 1201
New York, NY 10025
Tel: 212–316–3120
http://www.dissentmagazine.org

Monthly Review
122 West 27th St., 10th floor
New York, NY 10001
Tel: 212–691–2555
http://www.monthlyreview.org

New Left Review
6 Meard St.
London W1F 0EG
United Kingdom
Tel: 011 44 (0)20 7734 8830 30
http://www.newleftreview.net/

Tom Paine.com
A Public Interest Journal
http://www.tompaine.com

POLITICAL PARTIES

Green Parties of North America
The Greens/Green Party USA
P.O. Box 1134
Lawrence, MA 01842
Tel: 978–682–4353
http://www.greens.org/na.html

Labor Party (U.S.)
P.O. Box 53177
Washington, DC 20009–3177
Tel: 202–234–5190
http://www.thelaborparty.org

Northeast Action
621 Farmington Ave.
Hartford, CT 06105
Tel: 860–231–2414
http://www.neaction.org

Vermont Progressive Party
P.O. Box 281
Montpelier, VT 05601
Tel: 802–229–0800
http://www.progressiveparty.org

Working Families Party
88 Third Ave.
Brooklyn, NY 11217
Tel: 718–222–3796
http://www.
          workingfamiliesparty.org

RELATED ORGANIZATIONS

AIDS

ACT UP/New York
332 Bleecker St., G5
New York, NY 10014
http://www.actupny.org

**Community HIV/AIDS
Mobilization Project (CHAMP)**
80A 4th Ave.,
Brooklyn , NY 11217
Tel: 212–437–0254
http://www.aidsinfonyc.org/
          champ

**Health Global Access Project
(GAP)**
584 Castro St., #416
San Francisco, CA 94114
Tel: 415–863–4676
http://www.healthgap.org

Civil Rights

Rainbow/PUSH Coalition
930 E. 50th St.
Chicago, IL 60615–2702
Tel: 773–373–3366
http://www.rainbowpush.org

NAACP
4805 Mt. Hope Drive,
Baltimore, MD 21215
Tel: 877–NAACP–98
http://www.naacp.org

Human Rights Campaign
1640 Rhode Island Ave., N.W.
Washington, DC 20036–3278
Tel: 202–628–4160
http://www.hrc.org

Environmental
Organizations

Friends of the Earth
1717 Massachusetts Ave., N.W.
600
Washington, DC 20036–2002
Tel: 877–843–8687
http://www.foe.org

Greenpeace
702 H. Street, Suite 300
Washington, DC 20001
Tel: 202–462–1177
http://www.greenpeaceusa.org

Labor

AFL-CIO
815 16th St. N.W.
Washington, DC 20006
Tel: 202–637–5000
http://www.aflcio.org

Harvard Trade Union Program
Harvard Law School
125 Mt. Auburn St., 3rd Floor
Cambridge, MA 02138
Tel: 617–495–9265
http://www.law.harvard.edu/
          program

**National Labor Committee for
Worker and Human Rights**
540 West 48th St., 3rd Floor
New York, NY 10036
Tel: 212–242–3002
www.nlcnet.org

Women's Organizations

**NOW (National Organization
for Women)**
733 15th St. N.W.–2nd Floor
Washington, DC 20005
Tel: 202–628–8669
http://www.now.org

Appendix

The Declaration of Independence
In Congress, July 4, 1776

The unanimous Declaration of the Thirteen United States of America,

When in the Course of human events, it becomes necessary for one people to dissolve the political bands which have connected them with another, and to assume among the Powers of the earth, the separate and equal station to which the Laws of Nature and of Nature's God entitle them, a decent respect to the opinions of mankind requires that they should declare the causes which impel them to the separation.

We hold these truths to be self-evident, that all men are created equal, that they are endowed by their Creator with certain unalienable Rights, that among these are Life, Liberty and the pursuit of Happiness. That to secure these rights, Governments are instituted among Men, deriving their just powers from the consent of the governed. That whenever any Form of Government becomes destructive of these ends, it is the Right of the People to alter or to abolish it, and to institute new Government, laying its foundation on such principles and organizing its powers in such form, as to them shall seem most likely to effect their Safety and Happiness. Prudence, indeed, will dictate that Governments long established should not be changed for light and transient causes; and accordingly all experience hath shown, that mankind are more disposed to suffer, while evils are sufferable, than to right themselves by abolishing the forms to which they are accustomed. But when a long train of abuses and usurpations, pursuing invariably the same Object evinces a design to reduce them under absolute Despotism, it is their right, it is their duty, to throw off such Government, and to provide new Guards for their future security. Such has been the patient sufferance of these Colonies; and such is now the necessity which constrains them to alter their former Systems of Government. The history of the present King of Great Britain is a history of repeated injuries and usurpations, all having in direct object the establishment of an absolute Tyranny over these States. To prove this, let Facts be submitted to a candid world.

He has refused his Assent to Laws, the most wholesome and necessary for the public good.

He has forbidden his Governors to pass Laws of immediate and pressing importance, unless suspended in their operation till his Assent should be obtained; and when so suspended, he has utterly neglected to attend to them.

He has refused to pass other Laws for the accommodation of large districts of people, unless those people would relinquish the right of Representation in the Legislature, a right inestimable to them and formidable to tyrants only.

He has called together legislative bodies at places unusual, uncomfortable, and distant from the depository of their Public Records, for the sole purpose of fatiguing them into compliance with his measures.

He has dissolved Representative Houses repeatedly, for opposing with manly firmness his invasions on the rights of the people.

He has refused for a long time, after such dissolutions, to cause others to be elected; whereby the Legislative Powers, incapable of Annihilation, have returned to the People at large for their exercise; the State remaining in the meantime exposed to all the dangers of invasion from without, and convulsions within.

He has endeavoured to prevent the population of these States; for that purpose obstructing the Laws for Naturalization of Foreigners; refusing to pass others to encourage their migrations hither, and raising the conditions of new Appropriations of Lands.

He has obstructed the Administration of Justice, by refusing his Assent to Laws for establishing Judiciary Powers.

He has made Judges dependent on his Will alone, for the tenure of their offices, and the amount and payment of their salaries.

He has erected a multitude of New Offices, and sent hither swarms of Officers to harass our people; and eat out their substance.

He has kept among us, in times of peace, Standing Armies without the Consent of our legislatures.

He has affected to render the Military independent of and superior to the Civil Power.

He has combined with others to subject us to a jurisdiction foreign to our constitution, and unacknowledged by our laws; giving his Assent to their acts of pretended Legislation:

For quartering large bodies of armed troops among us:

For protecting them, by a mock Trial, from Punishment for any Murders which they should commit on the inhabitants of these States:

For cutting off our Trade with all parts of the world:

For imposing taxes on us without our Consent:

For depriving us in many cases, of the benefits of Trial of Jury:

For transporting us beyond Seas to be tried for pretended offences:

For abolishing the free System of English Laws in a neighboring Province, establishing therein an Arbitrary government, and enlarging its Boundaries so as to render it at once an example and fit instrument for introducing the same absolute rule into these Colonies:

For taking away our Charters, abolishing our most valuable Laws, and altering fundamentally the Forms of our Governments:

For suspending our own Legislatures, and declaring themselves invested with Power to legislate for us in all cases whatsoever.

He has abdicated Government here, by declaring us out of his Protection and waging War against us.

He has plundered our seas, ravaged our Coasts, burnt our towns, and destroyed the lives of our people.

He is at this time transporting large armies of foreign mercenaries to compleat the works of death, desolation and tyranny, already begun with circumstances of Cruelty & perfidy scarcely paralleled in the most barbarous ages, and totally unworthy the Head of a civilized nation.

He has constrained our fellow Citizens taken Captive on the high Seas to bear Arms against their Country, to become the executioners of their friends and Brethren, or to fall themselves by their Hands.

He has excited domestic insurrections amongst us, and has endeavoured to bring on the inhabitants of our frontiers, the merciless Indian Savages, whose known rule of warfare, is an undistinguished destruction of all ages, sexes and conditions.

In every stage of these Oppressions We have Petitioned for Redress in the most humble terms: Our repeated Petitions have been answered only by repeated injury. A Prince, whose character is thus marked by every act which may define a Tyrant, is unfit to be the ruler of a free people.

Nor have We been wanting in attentions to our British brethren. We have warned them from time to time of attempts by their legislature to extend an unwarrantable jurisdiction over us. We have reminded them of the circumstances of our emigration and settlement here. We have appealed to their native justice and magnanimity, and we have conjured them by the ties of our common kindred to disavow these usurpations which, would inevitably interrupt our connections and correspondence. They too have been deaf to the voice of justice and of consanguinity. We must, therefore, acquiesce in the necessity, which denounces our Separation, and hold them, as we hold the rest of mankind, Enemies in War, in Peace Friends.

We, therefore, the Representatives of the united States of America, in General Congress, Assembled, appealing to the Supreme Judge of the world for the rectitude of our intentions, do, in the Name, and by authority of the good People of these Colonies, solemnly publish and declare, That these United Colonies are, and of Right ought to be Free and Independent States; that they are Absolved from all Allegiance to the British Crown, and that all political connection between them and the State of Great Britain, is and ought to be totally dissolved; and that as Free and Independent States, they have full power to levy War, conclude Peace, contract Alliances, establish Commerce, and to do all other Acts and Things which Independent States may of right do. And for the support of this Declaration, with a firm reliance on the Protection of Divine Providence, we mutually pledge to each other our Lives, our Fortunes and our sacred Honor.

THE CONSTITUTION OF THE UNITED STATES

WE THE PEOPLE OF THE UNITED STATES, IN ORDER TO FORM A MORE PERFECT UNION, ESTABLISH JUSTICE, INSURE DOMESTIC TRANQUILITY, PROVIDE FOR THE COMMON DEFENSE, PROMOTE THE GENERAL WELFARE, AND SECURE THE BLESSINGS OF LIBERTY TO OURSELVES AND OUR POSTERITY, DO ORDAIN AND ESTABLISH THIS CONSTITUTION FOR THE UNITED STATES OF AMERICA.

ARTICLE I

Section 1.   All legislative Powers herein granted shall be vested in a Congress of the United States, which shall consist of a Senate and House of Representatives.

Section 2.   The House of Representatives shall be composed of members chosen every second Year by the People of the several States, and the Electors in each State shall have the Qualifications requisite for Electors of the most numerous Branch of the State Legislature.

No person shall be a representative who shall not have attained to the Age of twenty five Years, and been seven Years a Citizen of the United States, and who shall not, when elected, be an Inhabitant of that State in which he shall be chosen.

Representatives and direct Taxes shall be apportioned among the several States which may be included within this union, according to their respective Numbers, which shall be determined by adding to the whole Number of free Persons, including those bound to Service for a Term of Years, and excluding Indians not taxed, three fifths of all other Persons. The actual Enumeration shall be made within three Years after the first Meeting of the Congress of the United States, and within every subsequent Term of ten Years, in such Manner as they shall by Law direct. The Number of Representatives shall not exceed one for every thirty Thousand, but each State shall have at Least one Representative; and until such enumeration shall be made, the State of New Hampshire shall be entitled to chuse three, Massachusetts eight, Rhode-Island and Providence Plantations one, Connecticut five, New York six, New Jersey four, Pennsylvania eight, Delaware one, Maryland six, Virginia ten, North Carolina five, South Carolina five, and Georgia three.

When vacancies happen in the Representation from any State, the Executive Authority thereof shall issue Writs of Election to fill such Vacancies.

The House of Representatives shall chuse their speaker and other Officers; and shall have the sole Power of Impeachment.

Section 3.   The Senate of the United States shall be composed of two Senators from each State, chosen by the Legislature thereof, for six Years; and each Senator shall have one Vote.

Immediately after they shall be assembled in Consequence of the first Election, they shall be divided as equally as may be into three Classes. The Seats of the Senators of the first Class shall be vacated at the Expiration of the second Year, of the second Class at the Expiration of the fourth Year, and of the third Class at the Expiration of the sixth Year, so that one third may be chosen every second Year; and if Vacancies happen by Resignation, or otherwise, during the Recess of the Legislature of any State, the Executive thereof may take temporary Appointments until the next Meeting of the Legislature, which shall then fill such Vacancies.

No Person shall be a Senator who shall not have attained to the Age of thirty Years, and been nine Years a Citizen of the United States, and who shall not, when elected, be an Inhabitant of that State for which he shall be chosen.

The Vice President of the United States shall be President of the Senate, but shall have no Vote, unless they be equally divided.

The Senate shall chuse their other Officers, and also a President pro tempore, in the Absence of the Vice President, or when he shall exercise the Office of the President of the United States.

- Consumer debt is at an all time high, totaling over $6 trillion.
- Personal bankruptcies are at a record level.
- Personal savings are dropping to record lows and personal assets are so low that Bill Gates' net worth is equal to that of the net assets of the poorest 120 million Americans combined.
- The tiny federal budgets for the public's health and safety continue to be grossly inadequate.
- Motor vehicle fuel efficiency averages are actually declining and, overall, energy conservation efforts have slowed, while renewable energy takes a back seat to fossil fuel and atomic power subsidies.
- Wealth inequality is greater than at any time since WWII. The top one percent of the wealthiest people have more financial wealth than the bottom 90 percent of Americans combined, the worst inequality among large western nations.
- Despite annual declines in total business liability costs, business lobbyists drive for more privileges and immunities for their wrongdoing.

It is permissible to ask, in the light of these astonishing shortcomings during a period of touted prosperity, what the state of our country would be should a recession or depression occur? One import of these contrasts is clear: economic growth has been decoupled from economic progress for many Americans. In the early 1970s, our economy split into two tiers. Whereas once economic growth broadly benefited the majority, now the economy has become one wherein "a rising tide lifts all yachts," in the words of Jeff Gates, author of The Ownership Solution. Returns on capital outpaced returns on labor, and job insecurity increased for millions of seasoned workers. In the seventies, the top 300 CEOs paid themselves forty times the entry-level wage in their companies. Now the average is over 400 times. This is an economy where impoverished assembly line workers suffering from carpal tunnel syndrome frantically process chickens which pass them in a continuous flow, where downsized white and blue collar employees are hired at lesser compensation, if they are lucky, where the focus of top business executives is no longer to provide a service that attracts customers, but rather to acquire customers through mergers and acquisitions. How long can the paper economy of speculation ignore its effects on the real economy of working families?

Pluralistic democracy has enlarged markets and created the middle class. Yet the short-term monetized minds of the corporatists are bent on weakening, defeating, diluting, diminishing, circumventing, coopting, or corrupting all traditional countervailing forces that have saved American corporate capitalism from itself.

Regulation of food, automobiles, banks and securities, for example, strengthened these markets along with protecting consumers and investors. Antitrust enforcement helped protect our country from monopoly capitalism and stimulated competition. Trade unions enfranchised workers and helped mightily to build the middle class for themselves, benefiting also non-union laborers. Producer and consumer cooperatives helped save the family farm, electrified rural areas, and offered another model of economic activity. Civil litigation—the right to have your day in court—helped deter producers of harmful products and brought them to some measure of justice. At the same time, the public learned about these hazards.

Public investment—from naval shipyards to Pentagon drug discoveries against infectious disease to public power authorities—provided yardsticks to measure the unwillingness of big business to change and respond to needs. Even under a rigged system, shareholder pressures on management sometimes have shaken complacency, wrongdoing, and mismanagement. Direct consumer remedies, including class actions, have given pause to crooked businesses and have stopped much of this unfair competition against honest businesses. Big business lobbies opposed all of this progress strenuously, but they lost and America gained. Ultimately, so did a chastened but myopic business community.

The Senate shall have the sole Power to try all Impeachments. When sitting for that Purpose, they shall be on Oath of Affirmation. When the President of the United States is tried, the Chief Justice shall preside: And no Person shall be convicted without the Concurrence of two thirds of the Members present.

Judgment in Cases of Impeachment shall not extend further than to removal from Office, and disqualification to hold and enjoy any Office of honor, Trust or Profit under the United States: but the Party convicted shall nevertheless be liable and subject to Indictment, Trial, Judgment and Punishment, according to law.

Section 4.   The Times, Places and Manner of holding Elections for Senators and Representatives, shall be prescribed in each State by the Legislature thereof; but the Congress may at any time by Law make or alter such regulations, except as to the Places of chusing Senators.

The Congress shall assemble at least once in every Year, and such Meeting shall be on the first Monday in December, unless they shall by Law appoint a different Day.

Section 5.   Each House shall be the Judge of the Elections, Returns and Qualifications of its own Members, and a Majority of each shall constitute a Quorum to do Business; but a smaller Number may adjourn from day to day, and may be authorized to compel the Attendance of absent Members, in such Manner, and under such Penalties as each House may provide.

Each House may determine the Rules for its Proceedings, punish its Members for disorderly Behaviour, and, with the Concurrence of two thirds, expel a Member.

Each House shall keep a Journal of its Proceedings, and from time to time publish the same, excepting such Parts as may in their Judgment require Secrecy; and the Yeas and Nays of the Members of either House on any question shall, at the Desire of one fifth of those Present, be entered on the Journal.

Neither House, during the Session of Congress, shall, without the Consent of the other, adjourn for more than three days, nor to any other Place than that in which the two Houses shall be sitting.

Section 6.   The Senators and Representatives shall receive a Compensation for their Services, to be ascertained by Law, and paid out of the Treasury of the United States. They shall in all Cases, except Treason, Felony and Breach of the Peace, be privileged from Arrest during their Attendance at the Session of their respective Houses, and in going to and returning from the same; and for any Speech or Debate in either House, they shall not be questioned in any other Place.

No Senator or Representative shall, during the Time for which he was elected, be appointed to any civil Office under the Authority of the United States, which shall have been created, or the Emoluments whereof shall have been encreased during such time; and no Person holding any Office under the United States, shall be a Member of either House during his Continuance in Office.

Section 7.   All Bills for raising Revenue shall originate in the House of Representatives; but the Senate may propose or concur with Amendments as on other Bills.

Every Bill which shall have passed the House of Representatives and the Senate, shall, before it become a Law, be presented to the President of the United States; If he approve he shall sign it, but if not he shall return it, with his Objections to that House in which it shall have originated, who shall enter the Objections at large on their Journal, and proceed to reconsider it. If after such Reconsideration two thirds of that House shall agree to pass the Bill, it shall be sent, together with the Objections, to the other House, by which it shall likewise be reconsidered, and if approved by two thirds of that House, it shall become a Law. But in all such Cases the Votes of both Houses shall be determined by Yeas and Nays, and the Names of the Persons voting for and against the Bill shall be entered on the Journal of each House respectively. If any Bill shall not be returned by the president within ten Days (Sundays excepted) after it shall have been presented to him, the Same shall be a Law, in like Manner as if he had signed it, unless the Congress by their Adjournment prevent its Return, in which Case it shall not be a Law.

Every Order, Resolution, or Vote to which the Concurrence of the Senate and House of Representatives may be necessary (except on a question of Adjournment) shall be presented to the President of the United States; and before the Same shall take Effect, shall be approved by him, or being disapproved by him, shall be repassed by two thirds of the Senate and House of Representatives, according to the Rules and Limitations prescribed in the Case of a Bill.

Section 8. The Congress shall have Power To lay and collect Taxes, Duties, Imposts and Excises, to pay the Debts and provide for the common Defence and general Welfare of the United States; but all Duties, Imposts and Excises shall be uniform throughout the United States;

To borrow Money on the credit of the United States;

To regulate Commerce with foreign Nations, and among the several States, and with the Indian Tribes;

To establish an uniform Rule of Naturalization, and uniform Laws on the subject of Bankruptcies throughout the United States;

To coin Money, regulate the Value thereof, and of foreign Coin, and fix the Standard of Weights and Measures;

To provide for the Punishment of counterfeiting the Securities and current Coin of the United States;

To establish Post Offices and post Roads;

To promote the Progress of Science and useful Arts, by securing for limited Times to Authors and Inventors the exclusive Right to their respective Writings and Discoveries;

To constitute Tribunals inferior to the supreme Court;

To define and punish Piracies and Felonies committed on the high Seas, and Offences against the Law of Nations;

To declare War, grant Letters of Marque and Reprisal, and make Rules concerning Captures on Land and Water;

To raise and support Armies, but no Appropriation of Money to that Use shall be for a longer Term than two Years;

To provide and maintain a Navy;

To make Rules for the Government and Regulation of the land and naval Forces;

To provide for calling forth the Militia to execute the Laws of the Union, suppress Insurrections and repel Invasions;

To provide for organizing, arming, and disciplining, the Militia, and for governing such Part of them as may be employed in the Service of the United States, reserving to the States respectively, the Appointment of the Officers, and the Authority of training the Militia according to the discipline prescribed by Congress;

To exercise exclusive Legislation in all Cases whatsoever, over such District (not exceeding ten Miles square) as may, by Cession of particular States, and the Acceptance of Congress, become the Seat of the Government of the United States, and to exercise like Authority over all Places purchased by the Consent of the Legislature of the State in which the Same shall be for the Erection of Forts, Magazines, Arsenals, dock-Yards, and other needful Buildings; And

To make all Laws which shall be necessary and proper for carrying into Execution the foregoing Powers, and all other Powers vested by this Constitution in the Government of the United States, or in any Department or Officer thereof.

Section 9. The Migration or Importation of such Persons as any of the States now existing shall think proper to admit, shall not be prohibited by the Congress prior to the Year one thousand eight hundred and eight, but a Tax or duty may be imposed on such Importation, not exceeding ten dollars for each Person.

The Privilege of the Writ of Habeas Corpus shall not be suspended, unless when in Cases of Rebellion or Invasion the public Safety may require it.

No Bill of Attainder or ex post facto Law shall be passed.

No Capitation, or other direct, Tax shall be laid, unless in Proportion to the Census or Enumeration herein before directed to be taken.

No Tax or Duty shall be laid on Articles exported from any State.

No Preference shall be given by any Regulation of Commerce or Revenue to the Ports of one State over those of another: nor shall Vessels bound to, or from, one State be obliged to enter, clear, or pay Duties in another.

No money shall be drawn from the Treasury, but in Consequence of Appropriations made by Law; and a regular Statement and Account of the Receipts and Expenditures of all public Money shall be published from time to time.

No Title of Nobility shall be granted by the United States: And no Person holding any office of Profit or Trust under them, shall, without the Consent of the Congress, accept of any present, Emolument, Office, or Title, of any kind whatever, from any King, Prince, or foreign States.

Section 10. No State shall enter into any Treaty, Alliance, or Confederation; grant Letters of Marque and Treaty; Alliance, or Confederation; grant Letters of Marque and Reprisal; coin Money; emit Bills of Credit; make any Thing but gold and silver Coin a Tender in Payment of Debts; pass any Bill of Attainder, ex post facto Law, or Law impairing the Obligation of Contracts, or grant any Title of Nobility.

No State shall, without the Consent of the Congress, lay any Imposts or Duties on Imports or Exports, except what may be absolutely necessary for executing its inspection Laws: and the net Produce of all Duties and Imposts, laid by any State on Imports and Exports, shall be for the Use of the Treasury of the United States; and all such Laws shall be subject to Revision and Control of the Congress.

No State shall, without the Consent of Congress, lay any Duty of Tonnage, keep Troops, or Ships of War in time of Peace, enter into any Agreement or Compact with another State, or with a foreign Power, or engage in War, unless actually invaded, or in such imminent Danger as will not admit of delay.

ARTICLE II

Section 1. The executive Power shall be vested in a President of the United States of America. He shall hold his Office during the Term of four Years, and, together with the Vice President, chosen for the same term, be elected, as follows

Each State shall appoint, in such Manner as the Legislature thereof may direct, a Number of Electors, equal to the whole Number of Senators and Representatives to which the State may be entitled in the Congress: but no Senator or Representative, or Person holding an office of Trust or Profit under the United States, shall be appointed an Elector.

The Electors shall meet in their respective States, and vote by Ballot for two Persons, of whom one at least shall not be an Inhabitant of the same State with themselves. And they shall make a List of all the Persons voted for, and of the Number of Votes for each; which List they shall sign and certify, and transmit sealed to the Seat of the Government of the United States, directed to the President of the Senate. The President of the Senate shall, in the Presence of the Senate and House of Representatives, open all the Certificates, and the Votes shall then be counted. The Person having the greatest Number of Votes shall be the President, if such Number be a Majority of the whole Number of Electors appointed; and if there be more than one who have such Majority, and have an equal Number of Votes, then the House of Representatives shall immediately chuse by Ballot one of them for President: and if no Person have a Majority, then from the five highest on the List the said House shall in like Manner chuse the President. But in chusing the President, the Votes shall be taken by States, the Representation from each State having one Vote; A quorum for this Purpose shall consist of a Member or Members from two thirds of the States, and a Majority of all the States shall be necessary to a Choice. In every Case, after the Choice of the President, the Person having the greatest Number of Votes of the Electors shall be the Vice President. But if there should remain two or more who have equal Votes, the Senate shall chuse from them by Ballot the Vice President.

The Congress may determine the Time of chusing the Electors and the Day on which they shall give their Votes; which Day shall be the same throughout the United States.

No Person except a natural born Citizen, or a Citizen of the United States, at the time of the Adoption of this Constitution, shall be eligible to the Office of President; neither shall any person be eligible to that Office who shall not have attained to the Age of thirty five Years, and been fourteen Years a Resident within the United States.

In case of the Removal of the President from Office, or of his Death, Resignation, or Inability to discharge the Powers and Duties of the said Office, the Same shall devolve on the Vice President, and the Congress may by Law provide for the Case of Removal, Death, Resignation or Inability, both of the President and Vice President, declaring what Officer shall then act as President, and such Officer shall act accordingly, until the Disability be removed, or a President shall be elected.

The President shall, at stated Times, receive for his Services a Compensation, which shall neither be encreased nor diminished during the Period for which he shall have been elected, and he shall not receive within that Period any other Emolument from the United States, or any of them.

Before he enter on the Execution of his Office, he shall take the following Oath or Affirmation:- "I do solemnly swear (or affirm) that I will faithfully execute the Office of President of the United States, and will to the best of my Ability, preserve, protect and defend the Constitution of the United States."

Section 2.   The President shall be Commander in Chief of the Army and Navy of the United States, and of the Militia of the several States, when called into the actual Service of the United States; he may require the Opinion, in writing, of the principal Officer in each of the executive Departments, upon any Subject relating to the Duties of their respective Offices, and he shall have power to grant Reprieves and Pardons for Offences against the United States, except in Cases of Impeachment.

He shall have Power, by and with the Advice and Consent of the Senate, to make Treaties, provided two thirds of the Senators present concur; and he shall nominate, and by and with the Advice and Consent of the Senate, shall appoint Ambassadors, other public Ministers and Consuls, Judges of the supreme Court, and all other Officers of the United States, whose Appointments are not herein otherwise provided for, and which shall be established by Law; but the Congress may by Law vest the Appointment of such inferior officers, as they think proper, in the President alone, in the Courts of Law, or in the Heads of Departments.

The President shall have Power to fill up all Vacancies that may happen during the Recess of the Senate, by granting Commissions which shall expire at the end of their next Session.

Section 3.   He shall from time to time give to the Congress Information of the State of the Union, and recommend to their Consideration such Measures as he shall judge necessary and expedient; he may, on extraordinary Occasions, convene both Houses, or either of them, and in Case of Disagreement between them, with Respect to the Time of Adjournment, he may adjourn them to such Time as he shall think proper; he shall receive Ambassadors and other public Ministers; he shall take Care that the Laws be faithfully executed, and shall Commission all of the officers of the United States.

Section 4.   The President, Vice President and all civil Officers of the United States, shall be removed from Office on Impeachment for, and Conviction of, Treason, Bribery, or other High Crimes and Misdemeanors.

ARTICLE III
Section 1.   The judicial Power of the United States, shall be vested in one supreme Court, and in such inferior Courts as the Congress may from time to time ordain and establish. The Judges, both of the supreme and inferior Courts, shall hold their offices during good Behaviour, and shall, at stated Times, receive for their Services, a Compensation, which shall not be diminished during their Continuance in Office.

Section 2.   The judicial Power shall extend to all Cases, in Law and Equity, arising under this Constitution, the Laws of the United States, and Treaties made, or which shall be made, under their

Authority; to all Cases affecting Ambassadors, other public Ministers and Consuls; to all Cases of admiralty and maritime Jurisdiction; to Controversies to which the United States shall be a party; to Controversies between two or more States; between a State and Citizens of another State; between Citizens of different States; between Citizens of the same State claiming Lands under Grants of different States, and between a State, or the Citizens thereof, and foreign States, Citizens or Subjects.

In all Cases affecting Ambassadors, other public Ministers and Consols, and those in which a State shall be Party, the supreme Court shall have original Jurisdiction. In all the other Cases before mentioned, the supreme Court shall have appellate Jurisdiction, both as to Law and Fact, with such Exceptions, and under such Regulations as the Congress shall make.

The Trial of all Crimes, except in Cases of Impeachment, shall be by Jury; and such Trial shall be held in the State where the said Crimes shall have been committed; but when not committed within any State, the Trial shall be at such Place or Places as the Congress may by Law have directed.

Section 3. Treason against the United States, shall consist only in levying War against them, or in adhering to their Enemies, giving them Aid and Comfort. No Person shall be convicted of Treason unless on the Testimony of two Witnesses to the same overt Act, or on Confession in open Court.

The Congress shall have Power to declare the Punishment of Treason, but no Attainder of Treason shall work Corruption of Blood, or Forfeiture except during the Life of the Person attainted.

ARTICLE IV
Section 1. Full Faith and Credit shall be given in each State to the public Acts, Records, and judicial Proceedings of every State. And the Congress may by general Laws prescribe the Manner in which such Acts, Records, and Proceedings shall be proved, and the Effect thereof.

Section 2. The Citizens of each State shall be entitled to all Privileges and Immunities of Citizens in the several States.

A Person charged in any State with Treason, Felony, or other Crime, who shall flee from Justice, and be found in another State, shall on Demand of the executive Authority of the State from which he fled, be delivered up, to be removed to the State having Jurisdiction of the Crime.

No Person held to Service or Labour in one State, under the Laws thereof, escaping into another, shall, in Consequence of any Law or Regulation therein, be discharged from such Service or Labour, but shall be delivered up on Claim of the Party to whom such Service or Labour may be due.

Section 3. New States may be admitted by the Congress into this Union; but no new State shall be formed or erected within the Jurisdiction of any other State; nor any State be formed by the Junction of two or more States, or Parts of States, without the Consent of the Legislatures of the States concerned as well as of the Congress.

The Congress shall have Power to dispose of and make all needful Rules and Regulations respecting the Territory or other Property belonging to the United States; and nothing in this Constitution shall be so construed as to Prejudice any Claims of the United States, or of any particular State.

Section 4. The United States shall guarantee to every State in this Union a Republican Form of Government, and shall protect each of them against Invasion; and on Application of the Legislature, or of the Executive (when the Legislature cannot be convened) against domestic Violence.

ARTICLE V
The Congress, whenever two thirds of both Houses shall deem it necessary, shall propose Amendments to this Constitution, or, on the Application of the Legislatures of two thirds of the several States, shall call a Convention for proposing Amendments, which, in either Case, shall be valid to all Intents and Purposes, as Part of this Constitution, when ratified by the Legislatures of three fourths of the several States, or by Conventions in three fourths thereof, as the one or the other

Mode of Ratification may be proposed by the Congress; Provided that no Amendment which may be made prior to the Year One thousand eight hundred and eight shall in any Manner affect the first and fourth Clauses in the Ninth Section of the first Article; and that no State, without its Consent, shall be deprived of its equal Suffrage in the Senate.

ARTICLE VI

All Debts contracted and Engagements entered into, before the Adoption of this Constitution, shall be as valid against the United States under this Constitution, as under the Confederation.

This Constitution, and the Laws of the United States which shall be made in Pursuance thereof; and all Treaties made, or which shall be made, under the Authority of the United States, shall be the supreme Law of the Land; and the Judges in every State shall be bound thereby, any Thing in the Constitution of Laws of any State to the Contrary notwithstanding.

The Senators and Representatives before mentioned, and the Members of the several State Legislatures, and all executive and judicial Officers, both of the United States and of the several States, shall be bound by Oath or Affirmation, to support this Constitution; but no religious Test shall ever be required as a Qualification to any Office or public Trust under the United States.

ARTICLE VII

The Ratification of the Conventions of nine States shall be sufficient for the Establishment of this Constitution between the States so ratifying the Same.

Done in Convention by the Unanimous Consent of the States present the Seventeenth Day of September in the Year of our Lord one thousand seven hundred and Eighty seven and of the Independence of the United States of America the Twelfth. In witness whereof We have hereunto subscribed our Names.

[The first 10 Amendments were ratified December 5, 1791, and form what is known as the Bill of Rights.]

AMENDMENT 1

Congress shall make no law respecting an establishment of religion, or prohibiting the free exercise thereof; or abridging the freedom of speech, or of the press; or the right of the people peaceably to assemble, and to petition the Government for a redress of grievances.

AMENDMENT 2

A well regulated Militia, being necessary to the security of a free State, the right of the people to keep and bear Arms, shall not be infringed.

AMENDMENT 3

No Soldier shall, in time of peace be quartered in any house, without the consent of the Owner, nor in time of war, but in a manner to be prescribed by Law.

AMENDMENT 4

The right of the people to be secure in their persons, houses, papers, and effects, against unreasonable searches and seizures, shall not be violated, and no Warrants shall issue, but upon probable cause, supported by Oath or affirmation, and particularly describing the place to be searched and the persons or things to be seized.

AMENDMENT 5

No person shall be held to answer for a capital, or otherwise infamous crime, unless on a presentment or indictment of a Grand Jury, except in cases arising in the land or naval forces, or in the

Militia, when in actual service in time of War or public danger; nor shall any person be subject for the same offence to be twice put in jeopardy of life or limb; nor shall be compelled in any criminal case to be a witness against himself, nor be deprived of life, liberty, or property, without due process of law; nor shall private property be taken for public use, without just compensation.

AMENDMENT 6
In all criminal prosecutions, the accused shall enjoy the right to a speedy and public trial, by an impartial jury of the State and district wherein the crime shall have been committed, which district shall have been previously ascertained by law, and to be informed of the nature and cause of the accusation; to be confronted with the witnesses against him; to have compulsory process for obtaining witnesses in his favor, and to have the Assistance of Counsel for his defense.

AMENDMENT 7
In Suits at common law, where the value in controversy shall exceed twenty dollars, the right of trial by jury shall be preserved, and no fact tried by a jury, shall be otherwise reexamined in any Court of the United States, than according to the rules of the common law.

AMENDMENT 8
Excessive bail shall not be required, nor excessive fines imposed, nor cruel and unusual punishments inflicted.

AMENDMENT 9
The enumeration in the Constitution, of certain rights, shall not be construed to deny or disparage others retained by the people.

AMENDMENT 10
The powers not delegated to the United States by the Constitution, nor prohibited by it to the States, are reserved to the States respectively, or to the people.

AMENDMENT 11
[Ratified February 7, 1795]

The Judicial power of the United States shall not be construed to extend to any suit in law or equity, commenced or prosecuted against one of the United States by Citizens of another State, or by Citizens or Subjects of any Foreign State.

AMENDMENT 12
[Ratified July 27, 1804]

The Electors shall meet in their respective states and vote by ballot for President and Vice-President, one of whom, at least, shall not be an inhabitant of the same state with themselves; they shall name in their ballots the person voted for as President, and in distinct ballots the person voted for as Vice-President, and they shall make distinct lists of all persons voted for as President, and of all persons voted for as Vice-President, and of the number of votes for each, which lists they shall sign and certify, and transmit sealed to the seat of the government of the United States, directed to the President of the Senate; The President of the Senate shall, in the presence of the Senate and House of Representatives, open all the certificates and the votes shall then be counted; The person having the greatest number of votes for President, shall be the President, if such number be a majority of the whole number of Electors appointed; and if no person have such majority, then from the persons having the highest numbers not exceeding three in the list of those voted for as President, the House of Representatives shall choose immediately by ballot, the President. But in choosing the President, the votes shall be taken by states, the representation from each state having one vote; a quorum for this purpose shall consist of a member or members from two-thirds of the states, and a majority of all the states shall be necessary to a choice. And if the House of Representatives shall not choose a President whenever the right of choice shall devolve upon them, before the fourth day of March next following, the Vice-President shall act as President, as in the case of the death or other constitutional disability of the President. The person having the greatest number of votes as Vice-President, shall be the Vice-President, if such number be a majority of the whole number of Electors appointed, and if no person have a majority, then from the two highest numbers on the list, the Senate shall choose the Vice-President; a quorum for the purpose shall consist of two-thirds of the whole number of Senators, and a majority of the whole number shall be necessary to a choice. But no person constitutionally ineligible to the office of President shall be eligible to that of Vice-President of the United States.

AMENDMENT 13
[Ratified December 6, 1865]
Section 1.   Neither slavery nor involuntary servitude, except as a punishment for crime whereof the party shall have been duly convicted, shall exist within the United States, or any place subject to their jurisdiction.

Section 2.   Congress shall have the power to enforce this article by appropriate legislation.

AMENDMENT 14
[Ratified July 9, 1868]
Section 1.   All persons born or naturalized in the United States, and subject to the jurisdiction thereof, are citizens of the United States and of the State wherein they reside. No State shall make or enforce any law which shall abridge the privileges or immunities of citizens of the United States; nor shall any State deprive any person of life, liberty, or property, without due process of law; nor deny to any person within its jurisdiction the equal protection of the laws.

Section 2.   Representatives shall be appointed among the several States according to their respective numbers, counting the whole number of persons in each State, excluding Indians not taxed. But when the right to vote at any election for the choice of electors for President and Vice President of the United States, Representatives in Congress, the Executive and Judicial Officers of a State, or the members of the Legislature thereof, is denied to any of the male inhabitants of such State, being twenty-one years of age, and citizens of the United States, or in any way abridged, except for participation in rebellion, or other crime, the basis of representation therein shall be reduced in the proportion which the number of such male citizens shall bear to the whole number of male citizens twenty-one years of age in such State.

Section 3.   No person shall be a Senator or Representative in Congress, or elector of President and Vice President, or hold any office, civil or military, under the United States, or under any State, who, having previously taken an oath, as a member of Congress, or as an officer of the United States, or as a member of any State legislature, or as an executive or judicial officer of any State, to support the Constitution of the United States shall have engaged in insurrection or rebellion against the same, or given aid or comfort to the enemies thereof. But Congress may by a vote of two-thirds of each House, remove such disability.

Section 4.   The validity of the public debt of the United States, authorized by law, including debts incurred for payment of pensions and bounties for services in suppressing insurrection or rebellion, shall not be questioned. But neither the United States nor any State shall assume or pay any debt or obligation incurred in aid of insurrection or rebellion against the United States, or any claim for the loss or emancipation of any slave; but all such debts, obligations and claims shall be held illegal and void.

Section 5. The Congress shall have power to enforce, by appropriate legislation, the provisions of this article.

AMENDMENT 15
[Ratified February 3, 1870]

Section 1. The right of citizens of the United States to vote shall not be denied or abridged by the United States or by any State on account of race, color, or previous condition of servitude.

Section 2. The Congress shall have power to enforce this article by appropriate legislation.

AMENDMENT 16
[Ratified February 3, 1913]

The Congress shall have power to lay and collect taxes on incomes, from whatever source derived, without apportionment among the several States, and without regard to any census or enumeration.

AMENDMENT 17
[Ratified April 8, 1913]

The Senate of the United States shall be composed of two Senators from each State, elected by the people thereof for six years; and each Senator shall have one vote. The electors in each state shall have the qualification requisite for electors of the most numerous branch of the State legislatures.

When vacancies happen in the representation of any State in the Senate, the executive authority of such State shall issue writs of election to fill such vacancies; *Provided,* That the legislature of any State may empower the executive thereof to make temporary appointments until the people fill the vacancies by election as the legislature may direct.

This amendment shall not be so construed as to affect the election or term of any Senator chosen before it becomes valid as part of the Constitution.

AMENDMENT 18
[Ratified January 16, 1919]

Section 1. After one year from the ratification of this article the manufacture, sale, or transportation of intoxicating liquors within, the importation thereof into, or the exportation thereof from the United States and all territory subject to the jurisdiction thereof for beverage purposes is hereby prohibited.

Section 2. The Congress and the several States shall have concurrent power to enforce this article by appropriate legislation.

Section 3. This article shall be inoperative unless it shall have been ratified as an amendment to the Constitution by the legislatures of the several States, as provided in the Constitution, within seven years from the date of the submission hereof to the State by the Congress.

AMENDMENT 19
[Ratified August 18, 1920]

The right of citizens of the United States to vote shall not be denied or abridged by the United States or by any State on account of sex. Congress shall have the power to enforce this article by appropriate legislation.

AMENDMENT 20
[Ratified January 23, 1933]

Section 1.   The terms of the President and Vice President shall end at noon on the 20th day of January, and the terms of Senators and Representatives at noon on the 3rd day of January, of the years in which such terms would have ended if this article had not been ratified; and the terms of their successors shall then begin.

Section 2.   The Congress shall assemble at least once in every year, and such meeting shall begin at noon on the 3d day of January, unless they shall by law appoint a different day.

Section 3.   If, at the time fixed for the beginning of the term of the President, the President elect shall have died, the Vice President elect shall become President. If a President shall not have been chosen before the time fixed for the beginning of his term, or if the President elect shall have failed to qualify, then the Vice President elect shall act as President until a President shall have qualified; and the Congress may by law provide for the case wherein neither a President elect nor a Vice President elect shall have qualified, declaring who shall then act as President, or the manner in which one who is to act shall be selected, and such person shall act accordingly, until a President or Vice President shall have qualified.

Section 4.   The Congress may by law provide for the case of the death of any of the persons from whom the House of Representatives may choose a President whenever the right of choice shall have devolved upon them, and for the case of the death of any of the persons from whom the Senate may choose a Vice President whenever the right of choice shall have devolved upon them.

Section 5.   Sections 1 and 2 shall take effect on the 15th day of October following the ratification of this article.

Section 6.   This article shall be inoperative unless it shall have been ratified as an amendment to the Constitution by the legislatures of three-fourths of the several states within seven years from the date of its submission.

AMENDMENT 21
[Ratified December 5, 1933]

Section 1.   The eighteenth article of amendment to the Constitution of the United States is hereby repealed.

Section 2.   The transportation or importation into any State, Territory, or Possession of the United States for delivery or use herein of intoxicating liquors, in violation of the laws thereof, is hereby prohibited.

Section 3.   This article shall be inoperative unless it shall have been ratified as an amendment to the Constitution by conventions in several States, as provided in the Constitution, within seven years from the date of the submission hereof to the States by the Congress.

AMENDMENT 22
[Ratified February 27, 1951]

Section 1.   No person shall be elected to the office of the President more than twice, and no person who has held the office of President, or acted as President, for more than two years of a term to which some other person was elected President shall be elected to the office of the President more than once. But this Article shall not apply to any person holding the office of President when this Article was proposed by the Congress, and shall not prevent any person who may be holding the office of President, or acting as President, during the term within which this Article becomes operative from holding the office of President or acting as President during the remainder of such term.

Section 2.   This article shall be inoperative unless it shall have been ratified as an amendment to the Constitution by the legislatures of three-fourths of the several States within seven years from the date of its submission to the States by the Congress.

AMENDMENT 23
[Ratified March 29, 1961]

Section 1.   The District constituting the seat of Government of the United States shall appoint in such manner as the Congress may direct:

A number of electors of President and Vice President equal to the whole number of Senators and Representatives in Congress to which the District would be entitled if it were a state, but in no event more than the least populous State; they shall be in addition to those appointed by the States, but they shall be considered, for the purposes of the election of President and Vice President, to be electors appointed by a State; and they shall meet in the District and perform such duties as provided by the twelfth article of amendment.

Section 2.   The Congress shall have power to enforce this article by appropriate legislation.

AMENDMENT 24
[Ratified January 23, 1964]

Section 1.   The right of citizens of the United States to vote in any primary or other election for President or Vice President, for electors for President or Vice President, or for Senator or Representative in Congress, shall not be denied or abridged by the United States or by any State by reason or failure to pay any poll tax or other tax.

Section 2.   The Congress shall have power to enforce this article by appropriate legislation.

AMENDMENT 25
[Ratified February 10, 1967]

Section 1.   In case of the removal of the President from office or of his death or resignation, the Vice President shall become President.

Section 2.   Whenever there is vacancy in the office of the Vice President, the President shall nominate a Vice President who shall take office upon confirmation by a majority vote of both Houses of Congress.

Section 3.   Whenever the President transmits to the President pro tempore of the Senate and the Speaker of the House of Representatives his written declaration that he is unable to discharge the powers and duties of his office, and until he transmits to them a written declaration of the contrary, such powers and duties shall be discharged by the Vice President as Acting President.

Section 4.   Whenever the Vice President and a majority of either the principal officers of the executive department or of such other body as Congress may by law provide, transmit to the President pro tempore of the Senate and the Speaker of the House of Representatives their written declaration that the President is unable to discharge the powers and duties of his office, the Vice President shall immediately assume the powers and duties of the office as Acting President.

Thereafter, when the President transmits to the President pro tempore of the Senate and the Speaker of the House of Representatives his written declaration that no inability exists, he shall resume the powers and duties of his office unless the Vice President and a majority of either the principle officers of the executive department or of such other body as Congress may by law provide, transmit within four days to the President pro tempore of the Senate and the Speaker of the House of Representatives their written declaration that the President is unable to discharge the powers and duties of his office. Thereupon Congress shall decide the issue, assembling within forty-eight hours for that purpose if not in session. If the Congress, within twenty-one days after receipt of the latter written declaration, or, if Congress is not in session, within twenty-one days after Congress is required to assemble, determined by two-thirds vote of both Houses that the President is unable to discharge the powers and duties of his office, the Vice President shall continue to discharge the same as Acting President; otherwise, the President shall resume the powers and duties of his office.

AMENDMENT 26
[Ratified June 30, 1971]

Section 1.   The right of citizens of the United States, who are eighteen years of age or older, to vote shall not be denied or abridged by the United States or by any State on account of age.

Section 2.   The Congress shall have the power to enforce this article by appropriate legislation.

AMENDMENT 27
[Ratified May 18, 1992]

No law, varying the compensation for the services of the Senators and Representatives, shall take effect, until an election of Representatives shall have intervened.

THE FEDERALIST NO. 10

(James Madison)

To the People of the State of New York:

Among the numerous advantages promised by a well-constructed Union, none deserves to be more accurately developed than its tendency to break and control the violence of faction. The friend of popular governments never finds himself so much alarmed for their character and fate, as when he contemplates their propensity to this dangerous vice. He will not fail, therefore, to set a due value on any plan which, without violating the principles to which he is attached, provides a proper cure for it. The instability, injustice, and confusion introduced into the public councils, have, in truth, been the mortal diseases under which popular governments have everywhere perished; as they continue to be the favorite and fruitful topics from which the adversaries to liberty derive their most specious declamations. The valuable improvements made by the American constitutions on the popular models, both ancient and modern, cannot certainly be too much admired; but it would be an unwarrantable partiality, to contend that they have as effectually obviated the danger on this side, as was wished and expected. Complaints are everywhere heard from our most considerate and virtuous citizens, equally the friends of public and private faith, and of public and personal liberty, that our governments are too unstable; that the public good is disregarded in the conflicts of rival parties; and that measures are too often decided, not according to the rules of justice and the rights of the minor party, but by the superior force of an interested and overbearing majority. However anxiously we may wish that these complaints had no foundation, the evidence of known facts will not permit us to deny that they are in some degree true. It will be found, indeed, on a candid review of our situation, that some of the distresses under which we labor have been erroneously charged on the operation of our governments; but it will be found, at the same time, that other causes will not alone account for many of our heaviest misfortunes; and, particularly, for that prevailing and increasing distrust of public engagements, and alarm for private rights, which are echoed from one end of the continent to the other. These must be chiefly, if not wholly, effects of the unsteadiness and injustice with which a factious spirit has tainted our public administrations.

By a faction, I understand a number of citizens, whether amounting to a majority or minority of the whole, who are united and actuated by some common impulse of passion, or of interest, adverse to the rights of other citizens, or to the permanent and aggregate interests of the community.

There are two methods of curing the mischiefs of faction: the one, by removing its causes; the other, by controlling its effects.

There are again two methods of removing the causes of faction: the one, by destroying the liberty which is essential to its existence; the other, by giving to every citizen the same opinions, the same passions, and the same interests.

It could never be more truly said than of the first remedy, that it is worse than the disease. Liberty is to faction what air is to fire, an aliment without which it instantly expires. But it could not be less folly to abolish liberty, which is essential to political life, because it nourishes faction, than it would be to wish the annihilation of air, which is essential to animal life, because it imparts to fire its destructive agency.

The second expedient is as impracticable as the first would be unwise. As long as the reason of man continues fallible, and he is at liberty to exercise it, different opinions will be formed. As long as the connection subsists between his reason and his self-love, his opinions and his passions will have a reciprocal influence on each other; and the former will be objects to which the latter will attach themselves. The diversity in the faculties of men, from which the rights of property originate, is not less an insuperable obstacle to a uniformity of interests. The protection of these faculties is the first object of government. From the protection of different and unequal faculties of acquiring property, the possession of different degrees and kinds of property immediately results; and from the influence of these on the sentiments and views of the respective proprietors, ensues a division of the society into different interests and parties.

The latent causes of faction are thus sown in the nature of man; and we see them everywhere brought into different degrees of activity, according to the different circumstances of civil society. A zeal for different opinions concerning religion, concerning government, and many other points, as well of speculation as of practice; an attachment to different leaders ambitiously contending for preeminence and power; or to persons of other descriptions whose fortunes have been interesting to the human passions, have, in turn, divided mankind into parties, inflamed them with mutual animosity, and rendered them much more disposed to vex and oppress each other than to co-operate for their common good. So strong is this propensity of mankind to fall into mutual animosities, that where no substantial occasion presents itself, the most frivolous and fanciful distinctions have been sufficient to kindle their unfriendly passions and excite their most violent conflicts. But the most common and durable source of factions has been the various and unequal distribution of property. Those who hold and those who are without property have ever formed distinct interests in society. Those who are creditors, and those who are debtors, fall under a like discrimination. A landed interest, a manufacturing interest, a mercantile interest, a moneyed interest, with many lesser interests, grow up of necessity in civilized nations, and divide them into different classes, actuated by different sentiments and views. The regulation of these various and interfering interests forms the principal task of modern legislation, and involves the spirit of party and faction in the necessary and ordinary operations of the government.

No man is allowed to be a judge in his own cause, because his interest would certainly bias his judgment, and not improbably, corrupt his integrity. With equal, nay with greater reason, a body of men are unfit to be both judges and parties at the same time; yet what are many of the most important acts of legislation, but so many judicial determinations, not indeed concerning the rights of single persons, but concerning the rights of large bodies of citizens? and what are the different classes of legislators but advocates and parties to the causes which they determine? Is a law proposed concerning private debts? It is a question to which the creditors are parties on one side and the debtors on the other. Justice ought to hold the balance between them. Yet the parties are, and must be, themselves the judges; and the most numerous party, or, in other words, the most powerful faction must be expected to prevail. Shall domestic manufactures be encouraged, and in what degree, by restrictions on foreign manufactures? are questions which would be differently decided by the landed and the manufacturing classes, and probably by neither with a sole regard to justice and the public good. The apportionment of taxes on the various descriptions of property is an act which seems to require the most exact impartiality; yet there is, perhaps, no legislative act in which greater opportunity and temptation are given to a predominant party to trample on the rules of justice. Every shilling with which they overburden the inferior number is a shilling saved to their own pockets.

It is in vain to say that enlightened statesmen will be able to adjust these clashing interests and render them all subservient to the public good. Enlightened statesmen will not always be at the helm. Nor, in many cases, can such an adjustment be made at all without taking into view indirect and remote considerations, which will rarely prevail over the immediate interest which one party may find in disregarding the rights of another or the good of the whole.

The inference to which we are brought is, that the *causes* of faction cannot be removed, and that relief is only to be sought in the means of controlling its *effects*.

If a faction consists of less than a majority, relief is supplied by the republican principle, which enables the majority to defeat its sinister views by regular vote. It may clog the administration, it may convulse the society; but it will be unable to execute and mask its violence under the forms of the Constitution. When a majority is included in a faction, the form of popular government, on the other hand, enables it to sacrifice to its ruling passion or interest both the public good and the rights of other citizens. To secure the public good and private rights against the danger of such a faction, and at the same time to preserve the spirit and the form of popular government, is then the great object to which our inquiries are directed. Let me add that it is the great desideratum by which this form of government can be rescued from the opprobrium under which it has so long labored, and be recommended to the esteem and adoption of mankind.

By what means is this object attainable? Evidently by one of two only. Either the existence of the same passion or interest in a majority at the same time must be prevented, or the majority, having such coexistent passion or interest, must be rendered by their number and local situation unable to concert and carry into effect schemes of oppression. If the impulse and the opportunity be suffered to coincide, we well know that neither moral nor religious motives can be relied on as an adequate control. They are not found to be such on the injustice and violence of individuals, and lose their efficacy in proportion to the number combined together, that is, in proportion as their efficacy becomes needful.

From this view of the subject it may be concluded that a pure democracy, by which I mean a society consisting of a small number of citizens, who assemble and administer the government in person, can admit of no cure for the mischiefs of faction. A common passion or interest will, in almost every case, be felt by a majority of the whole; a communication and concert result from the form of government itself; and there is nothing to check the inducements to sacrifice the weaker party or an obnoxious individual. Hence it is that such democracies have ever been spectacles of turbulence and contention; have ever been found incompatible with personal security or the rights of property; and have in general been as short in their lives as they have been violent in their deaths. Theoretic politicians, who have patronized this species of government, have erroneously supposed that by reducing mankind to a perfect equality in their political rights, they would, at the same time, be perfectly equalized and assimilated in their possessions, their opinions, and their passions.

A republic, by which I mean a government in which the scheme of representation takes place, opens a different prospect, and promises the cure for which we are seeking. Let us examine the points in which it varies from pure democracy, and we shall comprehend both the nature of the cure and the efficacy which it must derive from the Union.

The two great points of difference between a democracy and a republic are: first, the delegation of the government in the latter to a small number of citizens elected by the rest; secondly, the greater number of citizens and greater sphere of country over which the latter may be extended.

The effect of the first difference is, on the one hand, to refine and enlarge the public views, by passing them through the medium of a chosen body of citizens, whose wisdom may best discern the true interest of their country, and whose patriotism and love of justice will be least likely to sacrifice it to temporary or partial considerations. Under such a regulation, it may well happen that the public voice, pronounced by the representatives of the people, will be more consonant to the public good than if pronounced by the people themselves, convened for the purpose. On the other hand, the effect may be inverted. Men of factious tempers, of local prejudices, or of sinister designs, may by intrigue, by corruption, or by other means, first obtain the suffrages, and then betray the interests of the people. The question resulting is, whether small or extensive republics are more favorable to the election of proper guardians of the public weal; and it is clearly decided in favor of the latter by two obvious considerations.

In the first place, it is to be remarked that, however small the republic may be, the representatives must be raised to a certain number in order to guard against the cabals of a few; and that, however large it may be, they must be limited to a certain number in order to guard against the confusion of a multitude. Hence, the number of representatives in the two cases not being in proportion to that of the two constituents, and being proportionally greater in the small republic, it follows that, if the proportion of fit characters be not less in the large than in the small republic, the former will present a greater option and consequently a greater probability of a fit choice.

In the next place, as each representative will be chosen by a greater number of citizens in the large than in the small republic, it will be more difficult for unworthy candidates to practise with success the vicious arts by which elections are too often carried; and the suffrages of the people being more free, will be more likely to centre in men who possess the most attractive merit and the most diffusive and established characters.

It must be confessed that in this, as in most other cases, there is a mean, on both sides of which inconveniences will be found to lie. By enlarging too much the number of electors, you render the representative too little acquainted with all their local circumstances and lesser interests: as by reducing it too much, you render him unduly attached to these, and too little fit to comprehend and pursue great and national objects. The federal Constitution forms a happy combination in this respect; the great and aggregate interests being referred to the national, the local and particular to the State legislatures.

The other point of difference is, the greater number of citizens and extent of territory which may be brought within the compass of republican than of democratic government; and it is this circumstance principally which renders factious combinations less to be dreaded in the former than in the latter. The smaller the society, the fewer probably will be the distinct parties and interests composing it; the fewer the distinct parties and interests, the more frequently will a majority be found of the same party; and the smaller the number of individuals composing a majority, and the smaller the compass within which they are placed, the more easily will they concert and execute their plans of oppression. Extend the sphere, and you take in a greater variety of parties and interests; you make it less probable that a majority of the whole will have a common motive to invade the rights of other citizens; or if such a common motive exists, it will be more difficult for all who feel it to discover their own strength and to act in unison with each other. Besides other impediments, it may be remarked that, where there is a consciousness of unjust or dishonorable purposes, communication is always checked by distrust in proportion to the number whose concurrence is necessary.

Hence, it clearly appears that the same advantage which a republic has over a democracy in controlling the effects of faction is enjoyed by a large over a small republic,—is enjoyed by the Union over the States composing it. Does the advantage consist in the substitution of representatives whose enlightened views and virtuous sentiments render them superior to local prejudices and to schemes of injustice? It will not be denied that the representation of the Union will be most likely to possess these requisite endowments. Does it consist in the greater security afforded by a greater variety of parties, against the event of any one party being able to outnumber and oppress the rest? In an equal degree does the increased variety of parties comprised within the Union, increase this security. Does it, in fine, consist in the greater obstacles opposed to the concert and accomplishment of the secret wishes of an unjust and interested majority? Here, again, the extent of the Union gives it the most palpable advantage.

The influence of factious leaders may kindle a flame within their particular States, but will be unable to spread a general conflagration through the other States. A religious sect may degenerate into a political faction in a part of the Confederacy; but the variety of sects dispersed over the entire face of it must secure the national councils against any danger from that source. A rage for paper money, for an abolition of debts, for an equal division of property, or for any other improper or wicked project, will be less apt to pervade the whole body of the Union than a particular member of it; in the same proportion as such a malady is more likely to taint a particular county or district, than an entire State.

In the extent and proper structure of the Union, therefore, we behold a republican remedy for the diseases most incident to republican government. And according to the degree of pleasure and pride we feel in being republicans, ought to be our zeal in cherishing the spirit and supporting the character of Federalists.

PUBLIUS

Credits

THE
M·Y·S·T·I·C
fOUNDATION

About the Author

Christopher Penczak is an award-winning author, teacher, healing practitioner, and eclectic Witch. His practice draws upon the foundation of modern Witchcraft blended with the wisdom of mystic traditions from across the globe. He has studied extensively with Witches, mystics, and healers in various traditions to synthesize his own practice of Witchcraft and healing. He is an ordained minister, herbalist, flower essence consultant, and certified Reiki Master (Teacher) in the Usui-Tibetan and Shamballa traditions. He is the author of several books, including *The Inner Temple of Witchcraft, The Temple of Shamanic Witchcraft, Gay Witchcraft, Magick of Reiki,* and *Instant Magick*.

CHRISTOPHER PENCZAK

THE

M·Y·S·T·I·C
FOUNDATION

UNDERSTANDING & EXPLORING

THE MAGICAL UNIVERSE

Llewellyn Publications
Woodbury, Minnesota

First Edition
First Printing, 2006

Book design and layout by Donna Burch
Cover design by Kevin R. Brown
Edited by Andrea Neff
Interior illustrations by Llewellyn art department and © Mary Ann Zapalac on pages 43, 56, 58, 68, 188, and 189
Tarot cards from the *Universal Tarot* by Roberto de Angelis © 2000 by Lo Scarabeo and reprinted with permission from Lo Scarabeo

Llewellyn is a registered trademark of Llewellyn Worldwide, Ltd.

Library of Congress Cataloging-in-Publication Data
Penczak, Christopher.
    The mystic foundation : understanding & exploring the magical universe / Christopher Penczak.
        p. cm.
    Includes bibliographical references.
    ISBN-13: 978-0-7387-0979-6
    ISBN-10: 0-7387-0979-4
    1. Mysticism. 2. Magic. 3. Occultism. I. Title.

    BL625.P45 2006
    204'.22—dc22   2006046528

Llewellyn Publications
A Division of Llewellyn Worldwide, Ltd.
2143 Wooddale Drive, Dept. 0-7387-0979-4
Woodbury, Minnesota 55125-2989, U.S.A.
www.llewellyn.com

Printed in the United States of America

Also by Christopher Penczak

City Magick: Urban Spells, Rituals and Shamanism
(Samuel Weiser, 2001)

Spirit Allies: Meet Your Team from the Other Side
(Samuel Weiser, 2002)

The Inner Temple of Witchcraft: Magick, Meditation and Psychic Development
(Llewellyn Publications, 2002)

The Inner Temple of Witchcraft Meditation CD Companion
(Llewellyn Publications, 2002)

Gay Witchcraft: Empowering the Tribe
(Samuel Weiser, 2003)

The Outer Temple of Witchcraft: Circles, Spells and Rituals
(Llewellyn Publications, 2004)

The Outer Temple of Witchcraft Meditation CD Companion
(Llewellyn Publications, 2004)

The Witch's Shield
(Llewellyn Publications, 2004)

Magick of Reiki
(Llewellyn Publications, 2004)

Sons of the Goddess
(Llewellyn Publications, 2005)

The Temple of Shamanic Witchcraft
(Llewellyn Publications, 2005)

The Temple of Shamanic Witchcraft Meditation CD Companion
(Llewellyn Publications, 2005)

Instant Magick
(Llewellyn Publications, 2005)

Forthcoming by Christopher Penczak

Ascension Magick
(Llewellyn Publications, 2007)

Acknowledgments

Profound thanks go to my husband, Steve Kenson, and my parents,
Ronald and Rosalie, for keeping me grounded.

Thank you to Laurie Cabot, for teaching me the science behind the Craft.

Thank you to Timothy Bedall, Kevin Castelli, and David Boyle for inspiring me to write
this book and showing me that it was needed. As always, students make the best teachers.

For all the thoughts, teachings, and input, a very special thanks to Crystal Bear,
Chris Bashaw, Stephanie Rose Bird, Steve Bir, Gita Bryant, Sandi Liss, Stephanie Rutt,
Danielle Serge Everton-Bouchard, and Beth Washington.

Contents

Exercises

Charts and Figures

Chapter Eleven

INTRODUCTION

A few weeks after teaching a meditation class, I got an e-mail from a student who was concerned about demons. Someone told him that if you meditate and open yourself up spiritually, you will attract dark forces. This person then proceeded to tell my student ugly stories that mixed urban legend with Hollywood horror script. The meditation technique he learned was perfectly safe, but when someone knows only one technique and doesn't have a strong foundation in mystical thinking, a little misinformation can cause a lot of fear. Fear is one of the biggest obstacles to spiritual growth and mystical understanding. I would be more concerned about fear than demons, since such demons and devils are most often reflections of our fears.

Most fears come from misunderstanding. Those of us living in the modern Western world were not raised in a culture of metaphysics. Our mystical knowledge has survived only as superstition. It is easy to either dismiss a superstition as having no wisdom, or become fearful of it, because the idea that has devolved into an ignorant superstition is not understood.

Most of our superstitions come from metaphysical ideas. Meditation, psychic development, healing, spirit communication, and magic all are based on sound philosophies and concepts and can be found in cultures across the world and across time. Our modern Western culture is one of the few that allowed this wisdom to devolve into superstition. In an effort to exert greater control, certain institutions within our society allowed this empowering wisdom to be lost, or imbued it with fear and misunderstanding. Even as we enter a time of increased personal empowerment through these techniques, we lack a basic understanding of the building blocks of mystical and holistic principles. With the new interest in herbalism, holistic healing, crystals, yoga, and other topics considered New Age by the public at large, we need to develop a common metaphysical tongue. The subjects most people consider to be New Age actually come from an older age—they simply have been reestablished in our current time.

One of the reasons so many people describe those involved in metaphysical pursuits as "flaky" is that the foundation behind their beliefs is not understood. Unfortunately, a lot of people who consider themselves part of the New Age community don't understand the foundation either. They have some experience or a little bit of information, but do not understand the whole picture. Some have had such a moving spiritual experience that they discard facts accepted by most of the mainstream without having another foundation firmly in place, which can cause them to become ungrounded, unbalanced, and misinformed. They don't know where the foundation of their experiences and beliefs can be found. They discard the modern mainstream paradigms of life without establishing a new paradigm. In the scope of a lecture, workshop, or book on a particular topic, it is difficult to get a full foundation in the mystic arts. It is up to the student to seek out this information and begin his or her education as a quest into the unknown. The modern mystical paradigm is a synthesis of many diverse cultures, traditions, and philosophies, and, contrary to popular opinion, does not exclude modern science or common sense.

I began my mystical quest not with a spiritual experience but with skepticism. I believed in a divinity of some kind, but my traditional religious background hadn't helped me directly experience it, if it was even possible to do so. I doubted the possibility of direct divine experience. I studied Eastern thought and found wonderful philosophies, but didn't explore them further, because at that time, to me, they were just words, and sounded like carnival-barker double talk. I now know that spirituality contains many paradoxes, because the very thought of putting something spiritual (which is thereby beyond shape and form) into words creates problems with communication. Our modern languages, as beautiful as they are, lack much of the sophistication found in ancient languages, which had words to describe these mystical ideas and experiences. For example, in the English language we have only one word for love, though many different kinds of love are possible. We don't have a sufficient number of words to make the distinctions. This lack of clear communication with metaphysical topics gives the impression that those involved in the mystical are deluding themselves, or worse yet, purposely misleading others.

Then I met a woman who taught metaphysics, magic, and Witchcraft as a science, and she gave me a scientific and philosophical background to understand these metaphysical concepts. She taught quantum physics and ancient philosophy, and compared the two. The similarities were shocking. I wasn't asked to believe in anything on blind faith. Once I had an understanding of the ideas involved, I was given demonstrations and was then asked to participate in exercises, to give me real-world, personal experiences in the topics. They weren't the province of the special or elite, but experiences that could be shared by all.

This scientific, philosophical, and experiential approach gave me the tools to understand other teachings. The more I learned, the more I realized that all the mystic traditions and world religions say very similar things. They each seek to describe universal principles, but their descriptions of these universal concepts are colored by their individual cultures, time periods, locations, and founders. They use different words and symbols to describe similar truths.

To have a strong mystic foundation, you must understand the greater pattern of truths as well as the pieces that make up the pattern. Each tradition calls the pattern and pieces something different, but most recognize the same things. For example, a yogi, rabbi, alchemist, monk, Witch, and shaman all recognize life force, but each may call it something different. Terms also depend on the location and time period. Having a familiarity with a variety of metaphysical terms is helpful when studying new material or speaking with people from different traditions. The concepts behind each term have universal applications. A good text will provide succinct definitions of terms, but you can't always count on New Age texts, or even the ancient classics they draw from, to clearly define terms to a modern, twenty-first-century person.

An understanding of metaphysical terms prevents the jargon of the guru. A guru is simply a teacher who bestows divine grace, and can refer to both an outer spiritual teacher and inner guidance. Ideally, an outer guru will help you connect to your source, and to your inner guru, what many consider the higher self or inner guide. The word guru has received a lot of criticism in recent times, because many gurus have abused their position of power and respect. This abuse is not limited to Eastern gurus, but can be found throughout the human condition, from orthodox religious leaders to politicians and public servants.

Unfortunately, many would-be gurus seek dependence from their students and use a combination of charisma, minor feats, and spiritual jargon that is never clearly defined to dazzle the students into submission rather than truly teach the tools for self-awareness, independence, and self-mastery. As a student, if you don't know a word, ask the teacher to define it clearly. You may already know the concept, but not this particular term for it. Other teachers will use the same word, but with a different meaning. When in doubt, ask. Spiritual teachings are often much simpler than most of us believe.

The Mystic Foundation introduces basic spiritual concepts in easy-to-understand language and teaches a variety of terms and labels associated with these concepts. Some of the words will seem occult. Many people are scared by that word. Occult refers to the word ocular, relating to the eye. It does not mean evil, as many mistakenly believe. When something is occult, it simply is hidden, obscured from view, from the eyes, and refers to material that most people don't see or study, the mystical arts. This book is an effort in the tradition of practical, sane occultism both to explain the spiritual mysteries and to show how this information can be applied in daily life.

I love using the term mystic, because each tradition has a mystical aspect to it. A mystic is one who explores spirituality through a personal relationship with it. Mystics are the truth seekers and visionaries, regardless of the culture. Mystics are found in ancient cultures as well as the traditional monotheistic religions.

The word metaphysics refers to the structure of reality beyond the known physics of science. *Meta* can mean transcending or beyond, so in this case it is beyond the physical sciences, into territory that is not validated by science. Metaphysics is another word that many people find intimidating. Someone once asked me if I had to study at M.I.T. in a lab to learn metaphysics. I explained that it was more of a philosophy and not a physical laboratory science. Strangely enough, such a big word gives more validation to the study to people in certain circles who laugh at the term New Age. New Age seems flaky, but the study of metaphysics sounds serious.

Each mystic tradition is like a paradigm, a systematic point of view. Each one is correct, if you are standing in that position. If you move to another position, you can change your view and see the truth from a different window. None is an absolute truth, but rather an individual truth, when looking at the universe from that point of view. Each is helpful in understanding the whole, but none is complete and all-encompassing in itself.

Each paradigm is a belief system, a tool to organize into a coherent whole the experiences of those who have gone before, adding to the tradition's stories, myths, proverbs, rules, and advice. There is nothing wrong with such paradigms; in fact they are quite helpful to learn. But every student must remember that a paradigm is simply a description of the truth, not an absolute truth. Mystics learn to divide truth into personal truth, or revelation, and absolute truth, which to some is unknowable or, at the very least, indescribable. In Taoism, the Tao is described quite similarly in the first two lines of the Tao Te Ching: "The Tao that can be spoken is not the eternal Tao. The Name that can be named is not the eternal Name."

Many religions were founded on one person's personal truth and divine experience, and these religious movements led to the creation of the more institutional traditions. They can be called prophetic religions, because they are based on the prophecies, the mysticism, of an individual or series of individuals. These prophecies were recorded and interpreted as the foundation of a tradition. The problem is, they have been mistranslated over thousands of years, and the original meaning and cultural context have been lost. Seekers hope to find a guide for a personal experience in recorded text, but usually the text becomes a foundation for dogma.

Though the teachings of Christianity are based on the life experiences and teachings of a man called Jesus, many in the Christian faith have had personal experiences of the divine, seeing visions, hearing voices, and witnessing miracles. To see the most dramatic examples, one only has to look to the lives of the saints, but anyone in the Christian faith can have a personal relationship, a mystical experience, with the divine, if he or she chooses and is encouraged to do so. Sacred texts can act as roadmaps, but you have to walk the path yourself if you are a mystic.

A good mystic can walk between paradigms, moving to see things from a different point of view, without having his or her personal beliefs and experiences challenged. A fundamentalist, of any tradition, believes that his or her point of view is the only point of view, and all others are false. Fundamentalism stems from fear, a fear that one's point of view is not correct. Ideally, everyone has a slightly different point of view, even people in the same tradition, because no two people can stand at the same exact place at the same exact time. Many teachers, masters, and prophets disagree with their peers and their predecessors. If you agree completely and have nothing to change or add from your own experience, you are not having a mystical experience—you are simply accepting another's experience as your own truth.

The Mystic Foundation contains four main sections, four corners of a foundation, to provide stability and knowledge. Each one explores an aspect of the mystical experience, covering a variety of paradigms and models used in modern metaphysics. Their similarities and differences will be demonstrated. The chapters alternate between seemingly outer and inner experiences, though a mystic knows they are one and the same. One classic mystic

teaching is the Principle of Correspondence: "As above, so below; as within, so without."
Inner and outer truths are the same. Subjective and objective experiences are not as different as you might think. The fifth section of this book, like the apex of the pyramid, contains information on a variety of mystic traditions and disciplines. With the four corners
supporting you, the traditions will help you climb to the top.

Eastern mystics say there are many paths that lead up the mountain. The mountaintop,
like the top of our four-cornered pyramid, is spiritual enlightenment. The journey is our
exploration of spirit. The paths on the mountain are the different traditions. Each path has
a different point of view. Some spiritual paths are easier to walk, while others are much
harder. Each path requires different things of us, but in the end, all of these paths lead to
the top of the same mountain. Some just take a more scenic route. A good mystic can
simply step off of one path and spend a little time on another. Ultimately, we each have
a path that is perfect for us and us alone, and it may wander to and from the well-known,
well-worn paths of mainstream religions.

Today, with this renewed interest in mystical lore, we have an opportunity to reclaim
spiritual wisdom from long-ignored traditions and let this knowledge stand side by side
with our scientific and technological paradigms. Only by understanding the foundations
of all these traditions can we find a truly holistic fusion that is practical, spiritual, and
grounded in reality. One tradition need not fight the others. Science, art, and spirituality
not only can coexist, but must coexist and find harmony together as we move into the next
epoch.

With an understanding of the spiritual worlds, we never need fear the demons of the
dark coming to get us when we meditate or at any other time. Knowledge, and the wisdom to use it correctly, dispels all fears. Together, these strands of wisdom can be woven
into a healthy, balanced interpretation for the New Age mystic.

ONE

THE FUNDAMENTAL FORCES OF THE UNIVERSE

1

THE POWERS OF CREATION

Mystics from around the world believe the universe, material and spiritual, is made up of a variety of forces. Their interactions are what create, sustain, and transform the universe. Scientists haven't yet learned to classify all the energies known to the mystic, but we do find their echoes in the forces studied by modern physicists. People of different cultures divide and name these forces in different ways, but essentially they are all working with the same energy. Naming these forces is just a way to communicate about them with others. When you understand these powers and the patterns they make, you can identify how they affect you, the people around you, and the world. With understanding comes a greater sense of empowerment.

The One

All things are connected. All people are connected to each other, as well as to the Earth and everything on it. We are connected to everything beyond what we know, seen and unseen, on all levels of the universe. What one person does affects and influences the whole. On this planet, we are all connected by the water we drink, the air we breathe, and the land we stand upon. From a metaphysical point of view, we also are connected on a subtle level. There is one spirit running through all things, one great creative force, but it has many different expressions. Each expression of spirit sees itself as an individual. On one level of creation, this is true—each person, place, or thing is separate and distinct upon first glance. But on another level, from another viewpoint, each expression is part of a greater whole that created and sustains it.

Shamans might say that we are all branches from the same tree. Though we grow in different directions, we all come from the same roots. Our fates are all tied together. What affects part of the tree will eventually affect the rest.

Witches might say that we are all strands in the web of life. When you move one part of the web, you move the entire thing. The web carries the movement, or vibrations, from one end to the other. The Goddess weaves creation into life, creating the web and all that is in it. She sits in the center of the web.

The Hindus say we live in the Maya. The Maya is the dream. It is an illusion of separation. We think we are separate, but we are part of the whole, which is the truth. When one awakens from the dream, or reaches a level of spiritual awareness or enlightenment, one truly lives from a sense of knowing that we are all connected. We are like waves upon the ocean. Each wave seems like a separate thing, and for most practical purposes it is separate, but it cannot survive without the ocean. The wave will eventually reach the shore and lose its individuality, becoming one again with the ocean.

To demonstrate this oneness, Hermetic mages might quote the Principle of Mentalism: "We are all thoughts in the Divine Mind." The great connecting spirit mentally creates the universe, and all its creations are thoughts within its vast, omnipotent mind. All things, on all levels, are contained within the Divine Mind, yet the Divine Mind is greater still. Just as each person has thoughts, and each thought seems individual, each thought is contained within the greater matrix of that person's mind. Each person mentally creates his or her own inner world, populated with his or her own thoughts. Each thought appears individually, yet is part of a greater whole. In the world, we each appear individually, yet are a part of a greater whole, the Divine Mind. We are part of the divine matrix, the mind of God, Goddess, or Great Spirit. You can call this creative force whatever you'd like. In the modern mythology that is found in the movie *Star Wars*, this energy is called "the Force." It is the energy connected to all things. Modern scientists have explored this concept through the holographic model of the universe, theorizing that the universe works much like a hologram. Each part contains the information of the whole. Each part is connected to every other part. We live in an age where scientists sound like Hindu scholars and age-old mystics.

This concept of connection is the heart of magic and psychic ability. Magic is the ability to create change in the world. You could not create change if you were not connected to everything. The change would not manifest if your will was contained only within your own body. Psychic ability is much like magic, but instead of projecting out a thought, those with developed psychic ability are listening or watching. They can receive information in a variety of ways, because they are connected to the greater whole. If they were not, all they would hear would be their own minds, and they would never be accurate in their perceptions and predictions. Some people have a greater inborn awareness of this connection. Mystics develop their psychic and magical abilities to truly know and understand their connection to all, and strengthen this bond as a part of their mystical development. Legendary mystics are known for their seemingly paranormal abilities, but these abilities are simply a result of being consciously aware of the connection among all things.

The Power of Two

Just as all of creation can be seen as one creative, animating spirit, this spirit can be divided in a number of ways. When you divide the fundamental energy into two, you see polarity. Hermetic wisdom calls this the Principle of Polarity: "Everything has its poles; everything has its pair of opposites." Although often described as opposites, being opposite ends of a pole or range of qualities, mystics see such pairs as dual. They are not necessarily in complete opposition to each other; they are complementary to each other.

The most common polarity with which humans are familiar is male/female. Although male and female seem to be at opposite ends of the spectrum, they are complementary. One cannot survive for long without the other. In fact, when you think about it, no one person or thing is wholly one gender. Sure, each of us may have a distinctively male or female physical anatomy, but in terms of male and female qualities, however a society defines them, we each contain a bit of both. How we balance these gender energies is what makes us unique. Hermetic wisdom expands on this concept, calling it the Principle of Gender, which states that all things contain both genders.

Most people involved in nature religions, such as Neo-Paganism, Wicca, and modern Witchcraft, see the divine with both genders. The divine creation is the interaction of male and female, God and Goddess. They are the Great Mother and Great Father, and we are their children. Their union sustains creation. Their continual love generates the cycles of life within the universe.

In Chinese medicine, polar forces are described in terms of yin and yang. Yin is the feminine, passive, receptive energy, and yang is the masculine, active, projective energy. Part of this healing system is about maintaining the proper balance of these two forces within the patient.

In Hindu traditions, the qualities of male and female energies are somewhat reversed, showing that the assignment of gender qualities can reflect a cultural bias. Goddess energy, called Shakti, after the goddess of the same name, rises upward from the Earth and is usually considered active. God energy, named for the god Shiva, descends downward. Shiva is the great dissolver.

Other polarities exist. Any pair of seemingly opposite or complementary words can be considered a polarity. We have polarity in up and down, demonstrated by sky and Earth or heaven and hell. We have it in the Sun and Moon, which many consider masculine and feminine as well. Most Western cultures think of the Sun as male and the Moon as female, because the Sun is direct, warming, and drying, and the Moon is cooling and stimulates the inner worlds, intuition, and dreams. But other cultures see the Sun as the mother principle, being the source of light, and the Moon as masculine, being a precise and intricate timekeeper. Other polarities include light/dark, good/evil, love/fear, hot/cold, mental/emotional, soft/hard, light/heavy, and positive/negative.

Somewhere along the line, particularly in Western society, in an effort to simplify things, all the different polarities got lumped together. Rather than being distinct pairs, all the sets began to blend together. Qualities such as light, good, love, male, Sun, mental, and positive all were put on one end, while their counterparts of dark, evil, fear, female, Moon, emotional, and negative were categorized together on the other end. This created a great shift in our consciousness, to the detriment of more "feminine" cultures reverent of the mysteries, the arts, and the unknown world. These divisions put us in polar conflict with our own nature and selves. Instead of having complementary pairs that can coexist, we now have absolute opposites in constant conflict.

Unfortunately, our myths of the last couple of thousand years, including those in our modern literature, movies, and television programs, have reinforced this conflict. The myth of absolute evil in the Devil and absolute good in God has emerged, but if all things contain their opposite, as symbolized in the familiar yin/yang symbol, then nothing is absolute. Even our modern myth example of *Star Wars* divides the Force into the light side (good) and the dark side (evil). But if you remember the movies, the film series is about the prophecy of the one who will bring balance to the Force, so in the end, director George Lucas is really emphasizing an age-old wisdom, even if the point is lost on many viewers who see the film as an epic of light versus dark.

I think a healthier way to look at polarity is in the yin/yang symbol. In each side, the seed of the opposite is contained. A balance must be struck between pairs to find the peaceful center.

Figure 1: Yin/Yang Symbol

These days we use the term positive to denote all things "good" and negative to denote all things "bad," but this terminology is imprecise. Many people in the New Age world seek to dispel the negative, but positive and negative are simply electrical charges. What mystics mean when they say "banish all negative" is that they want to banish all energies that would cause harm or imbalance. Too much of anything can cause an imbalance, even if it is something that would be labeled "good." Too much of a healing medicine, which is "good," can lead to an overdose. A small amount of a poison, which is "bad," can be a cure, such as a homeopathic remedy. Labels such as good and bad are relative.

All things are relative, even in polarity. Even the definitions of light and dark depend on what you compare them to. We think of the qualities of light and dark as absolute, but they are not. Take a stormy day, for example. Some would describe it as dark, and others would describe it as light. Compared to a sunny summer day, it is dark. Compared to a windowless room with no illumination, the stormy day is bright.

So the next time you say a prayer, affirmation, or spell to be protected from "all negative forces," perhaps you should ask for protection from "all forces that bring me harm."

The Trinity

Although most people think of the universe solely in terms of polarities, the forces of change for the universe can be seen as a trinity as well. The power of the trinity is the power of change. Mythologies from diverse cultures acknowledge triune deities, but they all represent the same fundamental forces.

Mystics use many names to describe the three universal forces. The first is the power of initiation, the power to begin and create. It is the impetus to move energy in the creative process. The second power is the energy of consolidation and manifestation. It is the power that binds and sustains a creation. It brings the energy that initiated the creation into form. The third power is the energy of dissolution. It breaks a creation into components so something else can be created. It is the power of adaptation. Though it is often considered to be the destructive element, it is not evil. Modern society considers the end of something to be bad, but something new cannot begin until the old ends. We often fear change, but it is a necessary part of life. The third power of the trinity is the power of change.

In the language of astrology, the trinity is divided into cardinal, fixed, and mutable energies. When the Sun enters a cardinal zodiac sign, a season begins. The cardinal signs are Aries, Cancer, Libra, and Capricorn. When the Sun enters a fixed zodiac sign, we enter the middle of a season, and the energy of the season is sustained. The fixed signs are Taurus, Leo, Scorpio, and Aquarius. When the Sun enters a mutable zodiac sign, the season prepares to change to the next. The mutable signs are Gemini, Virgo, Sagittarius, and Pisces. A new cycle then begins in the next cardinal sign.

When you are born, the sign the Sun occupies is considered your "Sun sign" and can tell a lot about the energies you are working with in this lifetime. Although we all work with all three energies in life, we might have a particular focus on the type of energy reflected in our Sun sign.

Aries: March 21–April 19
Taurus: April 20–May 20
Gemini: May 21–June 21
Cancer: June 22–July 22
Leo: July 23–August 22
Virgo: August 23–September 22
Libra: September 23–October 22

Chart 1: Traditional Sun Sign Dates

Scorpio: October 23–November 21
Sagittarius: November 22–December 21
Capricorn: December 22–January 19
Aquarius: January 20–February 18
Pisces: February 19–March 20

Chart 1 *(continued)*

In Hindu mythology, three gods hold this triple power. Brahma is the creator god, much like cardinal energy; Vishnu is the preserver, relating to fixed energy; and Shiva is the dissolver or destroyer, corresponding with mutable energy.

In modern Witchcraft, the Triple Goddess can be seen as the trinity. In Norse myth, she is called the Norns, or Wyrd sisters. These three are the Fates, the weaver goddesses of past, present, and future, or what was, what is, and what may yet be. A similar trinity of Fates, known as the Moirai, is found in Greek mythology. You can also see the Triple Goddess in Hecate, the triune goddess of Witches from the Greco-Roman era, as well as in the Morgan, the Celtic triune goddess who is the patroness of war and battlefields. The popular modern image of the Triple Goddess draws from these legends, manifesting now as the maiden, mother, and crone, seen both in the phases of the Moon and the seasons of the Earth.

In Catholicism, the Trinity is described as three aspects of the one God. The first aspect is the Father, often relating to Yahweh of the Old Testament. He is usually interpreted as the creator god. The second aspect is the Son, Jesus of Nazareth, viewed as the savior. It is said that upon his Second Coming, the faithful will be brought to an everlasting paradise. The third aspect is the Holy Spirit, or Holy Ghost, the formless power of inspiration and miracles. In earlier forms of Christianity, such as certain sects of Gnostic Christianity, the third aspect is represented by the Holy Sophia, a feminine aspect of divinity. This power of inspiration brings revelation and change.

In ceremonial magic, which often blends the mystical aspects of Paganism, Christianity, and Judaism, the threefold formula is written and chanted as IAO, for Isis, the Mother Goddess; Apophis or Apophis-Typhon, the serpent monster of destruction; and Osiris, Isis's husband-brother, who is the risen and resurrected god. For those familiar with Egyptian myth, Apophis-Typhon is often equated with Set, Osiris's brother and murderer. This formula alters the order, with the destructive force in the middle, and the regenerating force (the eternal and solid power of Osiris, the god of fertility and of the eternal underworld) at the end.

In alchemy, a spiritual discipline of transformation as well as laboratory work, the universal forces were originally a polarity, described as sulfur and mercury. They are not literal sulfur and mercury, as in the periodic table of elements, but names symbolizing the forces of nature. Originally, sulfur was the fiery, active, male principle, while mercury was the silvery, cool, receptive, feminine principle. As alchemical philosophies gained greater complexity, later alchemists added the principle of salt—fixed form, rigidity, and solidness. With the addition of salt to alchemical symbolism, the ideas developed along different lines. Sulfur became more like the cardinal energy and mercury like the mutable, while salt claimed the fixed form. Some look to salt as the body, while sulfur is the soul and mercury the spirit, or vice versa, depending on the teaching and the different definitions of soul and spirit used. These words can have different meanings and symbolism, based on the alchemical text, time period, culture, and author used. Each alchemical tradition built on the previous one, but had its own system of codes.

A teacher of mine once told me that the word God is an acronym for the three universal forces: G is for the generating force, O is for the organizing force, and D is for the destructive force. I love that definition of God, because it can apply to any tradition without any dogma, or even gender, attached to it.

Every creation has a beginning, middle, and end. Everything in the universe contains these three energies. Some we can see more easily, because their cycles and patterns are readily observed by humans. We can see the seasons, phases of the Moon, and human lives. Other patterns play out over time periods that are much longer than our life span, and are thereby harder to observe, but still exist. Hermetics call these cycles the Principle of Rhythm: "All things have their tide. All things have their season." By understanding the cycles of creating, sustaining, and destroying, we know the universe and ourselves.

2

THE ELEMENTS

Our creative forces can also be subdivided in terms of qualities and described as classic elements. Mystic traditions across the world describe these powers with similar names and images, though the specific systems are different. We usually look at the elements in divisions of four or five.

The Four Powers

Patterns of universal energy are subdivided most popularly into four categories. Most people know these forces as the classical elements of earth, water, air, and fire. These names are the ones most commonly used in Western traditions. Mystics honor these four forces by honoring the four sacred directions, although practitioners of different traditions, from Witches and hermetic magicians to native shamans and medicine people, associate different elements with each direction.

Everything consists of these four elements, four forces, in various combinations. It is important to recognize that the four elements represent energies, and the physical elements themselves are *symbols* of the energies. This is similar to alchemy, where sulfur, mercury, and salt refer to energies and not literal chemicals. Fire the element is not fire from a burning torch; it is an energy whose nature is similar to that of a burning torch. The burning torch symbolizes the element of fire, and, in ritual, will even embody it. Some texts refer to the mystical elements as the "elements of the wise," so elemental fire is referred to as "fire of the wise," to distinguish it from the torch. Elemental earth is "earth of the wise," to differentiate it from garden soil or stones. Largely because they misunderstand this symbolism, modern scientists have devalued and essentially thrown away the profound wisdom in magic and alchemy. Modern psychologists, particularly those whose work is based upon the alchemical works of Carl Jung, are reclaiming these esoteric symbols.

Each of the elements is not only an energy, an energy found in all things, but also a level of consciousness, a dimension or plane of existence that interpenetrates all things. Each of the elements exists at a different energetic vibration, and each one brings different qualities from the rest. Each person can relate to certain elements because he or she has a natural affinity for those qualities, and may have difficulties with other elements because he or she lacks those qualities. Working with the elements means learning to work with the principles of balance.

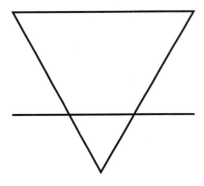

Figure 2: Earth Triangle

Earth

Earth is the element we all know the best. The energy of the earth element represents the physical form and physical world. All that can be seen and measured by the physical senses consists of the earth element. Our homes, food, plants, trees, stones, and all humanmade items, such as cars, toys and jewelry, are composed of earth energy. Our bodies, our bones, and all the minerals and metals within us are representations of the earth element.

Earth energy rules all physical concerns, so it also influences our physical health and financial security. In the tarot, earth energy is represented by discs, sometimes called coins or pentacles. The five-pointed star can indicate manifestation or protection on the physical plane. People with strong earth energy are powerful in the physical and financial worlds, while those who are learning about earth energy are challenged in those areas. The highest form of the earth element is sovereignty, meaning you control your own body, home, and fate. Astrologically, the earth signs are Taurus, Virgo, and Capricorn, since each of these signs deals with the physical world in some way. The north is usually the direction of earth, at least in the Northern Hemisphere, because of the strong, solid magnetic earth energy of the North Pole.

Figure 3: Pentacle

Taurus   Virgo   Capricorn

Figure 4: Earth Signs

The element of earth, of earth of the wise, is usually distinguished from the planet Earth. When mystics talk about the planet Earth, they are usually referring to the consciousness, the soul, of the planet, which is usually personified as a feminine mother figure. The Earth has many names. One of the most popular is the Greek name Gaia, or Gaea, because in our recent history, a scientist named James Lovelock proposed the Gaia Theory, which theorizes that the planet's biosphere is one intelligent organism and we are all smaller parts of that organism. We are like cells within the body of the planet. What affects one of us affects the greater whole.

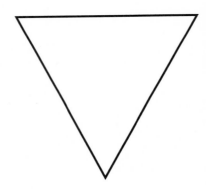

Figure 5: Water Triangle

Water

Water is the energy of the astral plane, the level of symbolic reality where shape and form are fluid. Water is the element of dreams. In our body, water is symbolized by the liquid in our blood and cells, but the elemental energy of water is actually our astral body, which travels when we sleep and dream. The astral body is our self-image influenced by our emotions. Like water, this energy is fluid and changes form easily. Our astral body is like the container for our emotions, just as a glass contains liquid. When our emotions are clear, the liquid is clear. When our emotions are confused, the liquid is murky. The watery level of the universe is known as the astral plane, or emotional plane.

The glass analogy also symbolizes another issue of water energy—boundaries. One challenge of water is to establish boundaries in relationships. Emotion is a building block for any type of relationship, with a family member, friend, lover, or spouse. Developing emotional connections and relationships is one of the spiritual challenges that water presents to us.

Water also involves psychic ability and delving into the mystical depths of consciousness. Western European traditions usually associate water with the west. Though the strongest symbolism is the large ocean to the west, the Atlantic, the direction of the setting sun is also the place of death, mystery, and the unknown. For many, the lands of the dead and water are synonymous, and are found to the west.

The highest and purest form of the water element is unconditional love, which is associated with miraculous healing, cleansing, and compassion. In the tarot, water is associated with the cups, and in a mythic sense, water is associated with the Holy Grail, a magical cup or cauldron with both Christian and Pagan associations. The water signs of the zodiac are Cancer, Scorpio, and Pisces. Each of these signs deals with emotional relationships in some way.

Cancer   Scorpio   Pisces

Figure 6: Water Signs

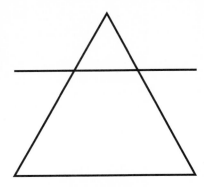

Figure 7: Air Triangle

Air

Air is the element of the mental plane, the realm of ideas, concepts, and thoughts. Like the sky, our minds can be clear and peaceful. At other times, they are turbulent with thought, or clouded by the water vapor of clouds, our emotions. The link between the emotional body and the mental body is like the relationship between the sea and sky. Before something takes shape on the astral plane, a mental idea, a thought, must animate it.

Air is the element of communication. We use the air of our breath to speak our words. The air between us carries sound waves, so our words can be heard. Many who study the element of air think it is only about talking, but it also involves the power to listen. Air is logic and memorization, but also poetry and cleverness. In the tarot, air is symbolized by the swords. We use imagery like "her mind is sharp" to describe a person who is strong with the air element. Being double-edged, swords represent the two-way power of communication, which requires both listening and speaking. They also symbolize the power of words to connect, and the power to hurt. We use sword imagery for betrayal, such as "he stabbed me in the back." The ultimate sword symbol is found in Arthurian myth—Excalibur is the sword of truth. Air's ultimate power is truth, but how that truth is expressed is up to the wielder of the sword.

In most Western traditions, air is associated with the direction of east, but sometimes is associated with the south, to pair the earth and air as opposites in the north and south. The air signs of the zodiac are Gemini, Libra, and Aquarius, as each works in the sphere of communication and connection.

Gemini   Libra   Aquarius

Figure 8: Air Signs

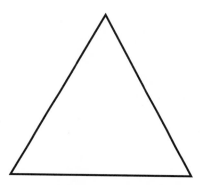

Figure 9: Fire Triangle

Fire

The most intangible element is fire. Earth you can hold, water you can drink, and air you can breathe, but fire cannot be held. The element of fire is symbolized within our bodies as our metabolism. We know it is present, but we cannot extract it like the other three elements. Fire is described by mystics in different ways. Fire is the energetic reality, the power of creation. The energy of fire inspires an idea, a concept, on the mental plane. The energy flows from the mental plane to the emotional plane, giving the idea a shape or image in the astral world. The energy continues to flow from the emotional plane to the physical, earthly plane, where it manifests as a reality

For some people, fire expresses itself as career, while for others, it expresses as sex or artistic endeavors. Fire is the drive to find identity through our passions. Fire in its highest form expresses our will, which comes in many forms. The most basic definition of will is what we want, what we desire. This is considered the ego will, or personal will. Transcending the ego will is higher will, or divine will. It is the will of our highest, most divine identity. Some call it the higher self. You could think of it as the soul, the divine spark of individuality in each of us. When we merge our personal will with our divine will, we find our true spiritual identity, and all doors are open to us.

In the tarot, fire is symbolized by wands, spears, or torches. The wand is the symbol of the Wizard or Witch, who uses it to focus his or her magical will. Mythically, the spear is the Spear of Destiny, the spear that pierced Christ's side, or the spear of Lugh, the leader of the gods in Irish myth. Destiny is another way to think of the higher will. Even with destiny, we must choose to accept it and implement it. Most people associate fire with the south, since the noonday sun is associated with the south in the Northern Hemisphere, and that is the hottest time of day. Also, the further south you go, the closer you get to the equator, and the warmer it is. Others put fire in the east for the rising sun. Obviously, some of the four directional associations would be different in the Southern Hemisphere.

The astrological fire signs are Aries, Leo, and Sagittarius. Each of these signs questions identity, ego, and the will in its own way.

Aries   Leo   Sagittarius

Figure 10: Fire Signs

Some traditions switch the symbolism of fire and air, associating fire with the blades, as they are forged in fire and are sharp weapons of the warrior, considered a fiery discipline, while the wands are air, as the branches are found in the windy treetops. This is simply another symbol system, no better or worse than the first.

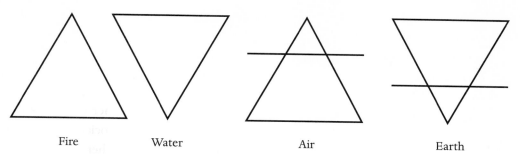

Fire   Water   Air   Earth

Figure 11: Elemental Triangles Together

Fire and air are considered male elements and have upward points, while water and earth are considered female elements and have downward points.

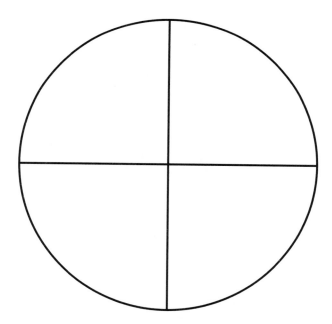

Figure 12: Earth Cross

The equal-armed cross in the circle is a symbol of the four elements and directions in the sacred circle. It is also the astrological symbol of the planet Earth.

The Quintessence

Beyond the four elements is a fifth element, which is even more difficult to describe than fire. All things start with this element, and all things return to it. The fifth element is the sum of all the previous four elements and beyond. The fifth element is known as spirit.

Spirit is not the most descriptive title, since some traditions describe fire as spirit, and also call nonphysical entities spirits, or refer to the divine creative force as Spirit or the Great Spirit. Other traditions call the fifth element ether, akasha, or prana, though prana is also linked to the life energy of the air element, as Hindu traditions call breath work pranayama. Alchemists call the fifth element quintessence, the very essence of the other four. When the energies of the four previous elements are removed from an object, all that remains is the quintessence, the animating force of all things. In its primal state, it is also known as the first matter, though it is not really matter, but the subtle energy that sustains matter.

While the quintessence is the fundamental force behind all things, objects, and, theoretically, people, it can be transformed by manipulating the qualities of the elements. The elements are each described in terms of warm/cold and wet/dry. Earth is cold and dry, fire is warm and dry, air is warm and wet, and water is cold and wet.

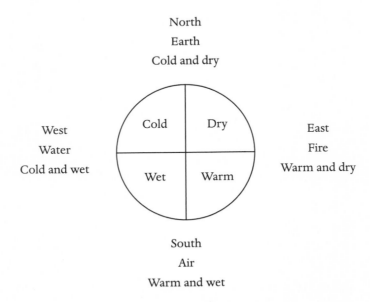

Figure 13: Elemental Quality Wheel

By manipulating these qualities, you can transform one element into a neighboring element. To transform an element into the opposing element requires two steps. Water is cold and wet. In the case of seawater, if you remove some of the moist quality by allowing it to evaporate, you get salt (and any other remaining minerals), which is a symbol of earth, being cool and dry. If you take cold and dry matter (earth), such as dry wood, and apply enough warmth through heating, it will combust and create fire. If you remove the dry quality of fire by adding moisture, you get water vapor, a gas that is warm and wet, like the element of air. If you cool the water vapor, it will condense and become water. Symbolically, for the practitioner these images represent shifts in energy that create a transformation.

Mystically, the five elements represent the balance of five qualities within each of us. We each use the tools of the body, emotions, mind, soul, and spirit. By maintaining a healthy, dynamic balance of these forces, we will have all the resources we need to lead healthy, joyful lives.

Figure 14: Pentagram

The pentagram of the five elements is one of the most misunderstood mystical symbols. It has many different meanings and is considered to be one of the most ancient and perfect symbols. Technically, a pentagram is a five-pointed star drawn in one line, and a pentacle is the same star within a circle. Both are used by mystics across the world.

Within the pentagram's proportions is the phi ratio, a ratio that is found in the proportions of all life, creating the spiral. The phi ratio is also found in the proportions of the human body. Symbolically, it stands for humanity—two arms, two legs, and a head. It also symbolizes the five physical senses of life encircled by the sixth sense. In the Greek mystery schools it was referred to as the pentalpha, or five alphas, the first letter of the alphabet, symbolizing beginnings. These are a few of the reasons that the five-pointed star is associated with Goddess worship, for the Goddess is classically considered the source of life. The sixth sense, or psychic intuition, is also the gift of the Goddess. The planet and the goddess Venus are particularly associated with the five-pointed star, as five-petalled flowers are sacred to Venus.

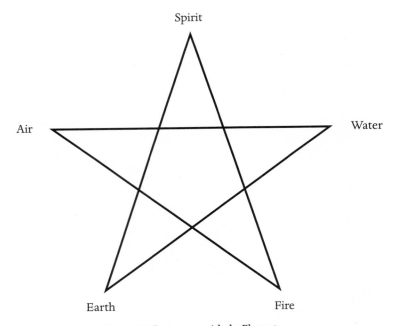

Figure 15: Pentagram with the Elements

Each point of the pentagram is associated with an element, with the fifth element being the top point. Much of the confusion about the pentagram comes from this symbolism. Many people believe the five-pointed star, particularly when drawn upside-down, is a symbol of evil or the Devil. Others believe it symbolizes energy moving downward and into the earth, so they use it for banishment rituals. The reversed pentagram also depicts the four worldly elements ruling over spirit, rather than spiritual principles ruling over the four elements. In essence, you've lost the "point" of the spiritual journey when you have it upside-down. Some traditions have lower-level initiates wear a reversed pentagram to denote that they have not yet mastered the elements, and only those of a higher degree can wear it upright.

In the tarot deck, the traditional image of the Devil card has an upside-down pentagram, and the card can symbolize materialism, being shackled to the world, and being ruled by the senses and desires rather than the spirit, an esoteric interpretation of temptation. The figures "chained" by the Devil image in the card are held only loosely. They are free to go at any time, but choose to remain.

Figure 16: Devil Tarot Card from Lo Scarabeo's Universal Tarot

Many mystics don't believe in an ultimate source of evil such as the Christian Devil, because of its social and political origins. They believe that the true source of evil is temptation and abuse of power by humans. Though there are tales of temptation and harmful spirits in many myths and legends, the concept of an ultimate source of evil and ultimate source of good really came with the advent of turmoil in the Christian church, when many concepts and teachings were fused into the image of the Devil, drawing from principles of Gnostic Christianity and even earlier Zoroastrianism. The familiar horned image of the Devil was borrowed from horned Pagan gods, in an effort to make Pagans convert to Christianity by proclaiming their old gods evil in the eyes of the new faith.

With its upright point, the pentagram is a symbol of spiritual power and command and is used for protection. The pentacles or coins in the tarot are also described as shields, tools of protection. Pentacles and coins are associated with earth, because it takes all five elements to manifest something on the physical plane, and with the symbol of the five-pointed star in the circle, you are protected on all five levels of reality. Though many people assume the symbol on King Solomon's magic ring to be the Star of David, or six-pointed hexagram, the ring's symbol, used to command spirits to do his bidding, might just as likely have been the five-pointed star, also known as the Witch's knot. The hexagram is also a symbol of the elements in integration, for the hexagram is the combination of the four elemental triangles.

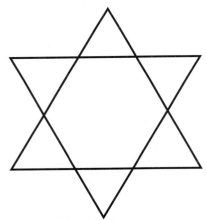

Figure 17: Hexagram

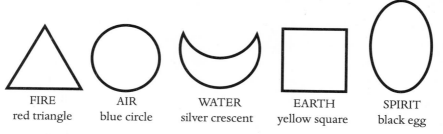

FIRE | AIR | WATER | EARTH | SPIRIT
red triangle | blue circle | silver crescent | yellow square | black egg

Figure 18: Tattwas

You will also find images of the elements in Hinduism and Sufism, in the form of tattwas. These symbols are used in Hinduism to represent the elements, much like Western seekers would use the elemental triangles. Western magicians use a system of scrying, or gazing into these tattwa symbols, to connect with the elemental planes.

EXERCISE
Elemental Journaling

Write the answers to the following questions in your journal. If you don't want to keep a journal, simply record your answers in a notebook or computer file for future reference. If you don't like to write, see if you can find someone else in your life interested in mystical topics who will have a discussion about this elemental exercise with you.

What element resonates with you the most? Why? Do you simply like the physical representation of the element? Do you feel that element's experiences are easy or hard for you personally? Do you identify its qualities with your personality? Does it correlate with the element of your astrological Sun sign? Does it remind you of anyone in your life?

What element resonates with you the least? Why? Describe or qualify your feelings for it. Do you simply dislike it, hate it, feel unmoved by it? Do you dislike its physical representation? Do you feel the element's experiences are easy or hard for you personally? Does it represent something about yourself that you don't like or feel is lacking? Does it correlate with the element of your astrological Sun sign? Does it remind you of anyone in your life?

Chinese Elements

The Chinese have a similar system of five elements, which uses the pentacle to demonstrate its creation and destruction cycles. Like the Western system, the Chinese system contains fire, water, and earth. The energy described as air in the Western tradition is symbolized as metal in this system. The elemental energy is not literally air or metal; these are simply symbols to help people understand the energy. Elemental air is symbolized by the sword, which is metal itself, so the symbolism is not so different.

Instead of the element of spirit or ether, the Chinese call the fifth element wood. Out of the five, it is the only one associated with cellular life. "Elemental" wood in the Eastern system is the same energy as ether or spirit in the Western system, and both hold a unique position in their respective elemental systems.

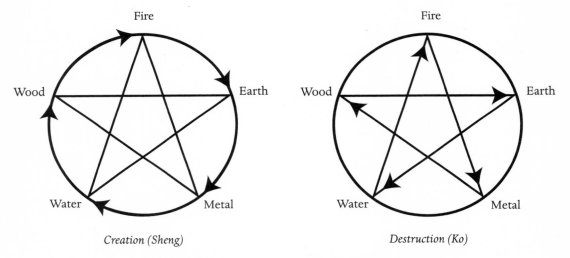

Creation (Sheng)   Destruction (Ko)

Figure 19: Chinese Pentacle with Creation and Destruction Cycles

When laid out on the five-pointed star, somewhat differently in than the Western layout, the order can be used to describe the cycles of creation, known as the Sheng cycle, moving clockwise around the circle. As fire burns, it creates ash, which adds to the earth.

Earth creates metals in its depths. Metal, as a pipe, carries water across great distances. Water feeds the seed that grows into the tree. The wood of the tree fuels the fire, beginning the cycle all over again.

To describe the cycle of destruction of the Chinese elements, called the Ko cycle, the order follows the pattern of star. Fire melts and purifies metal, preventing it from holding solid form. Metal, as a blade, chops down wood. The tree's roots absorb the minerals and power of the earth. Earth absorbs water, preventing it from flowing. Water extinguishes fire.

Comparing the Western and Eastern systems of elements is an excellent way to show that mystics across the world study the same fundamental forces of the universe, but find different ways to describe and explain these forces, based on their cultural conditions and aesthetics.

From the power of one, of unity, to the division of five and elemental theory, you now understand the powers of the universe. The universe is one whole, two polarities, a trinity, four quarters, and five elements, all simultaneously.

EXERCISE
Cleansing Space

The five elements are used in traditional rituals to bring balance and purification to the self and to the space. Many rituals include them, though you might be familiar with the rituals yet never know that they are based on the concept of the elements. Growing up Catholic, I never really understood the use of holy water and the sign of the cross before entering the church, or the use of incense, yet there is elemental symbolism in these practices.

Water, salt, incense, and flame (physical symbols of the four elements) are traditionally used to cleanse a space. Usually, you hold each of these for a few moments, while concentrating on the concepts of cleansing and balance. This act of concentration, directing your energy and intent into the object, is called charging, consecrating, or hallowing an object in magical practices, but is quite similar to the mainstream practice of blessing an object.

Water can be used to anoint and bless a person or object. It can be sprinkled on the ground or traced around the edges of objects and door frames. Salt, known for the purifying qualities inherent in its color and earthy crystalline nature, can also be sprinkled, but many practitioners find it more effective to mix a small amount of salt, usually sea salt or kosher salt, in water, and use them simultaneously. Table salt usually has chemical additives in it that are less than ideal for spiritual purposes, and for your health. Salt is said to absorb the harmful energies near us, and ground them. When salt is spilled, folk custom has us toss it behind us, to symbolically throw away any bad luck.

Incense smoke is symbolic of air, though incense could stand for both fire and air, being burning plant matter. Certain substances burned for incense are considered by occultists to be "high vibrational" incense. Burning these substances releases strong and pure spiritual vibrations that automatically cleanse any lower or harmful vibrations from the environment where they are burned. A mixture of frankincense and myrrh is my favorite, since they are considered masculine and feminine, respectively. Sandalwood, lavender, cinnamon, cloves, dragon's blood, mugwort, and patchouli are also protective and cleansing. Sage, or mixtures of sage with cedar, sweet grass, and pine, are favorites in Native American traditions to banish harmful energy. Copal is the favorite resin in South American traditions. Incense or herb is used to "smudge," meaning the area is filled with the smoke, then the person is exposed to the smoke or the object is passed through the smoke. A ritual feather is often used to help direct the smoke.

For fire alone, the flame of a white candle, blessed for protection and purification, is quite powerful. I have a white candle burning in my meditation space, or in my home after any disturbance has occurred.

In traditional cleansing rituals, the tools are brought to the four directions. Salt and water can be sprinkled in the four directions, or incense smudged, usually starting in the north or east and moving clockwise around the room, home, or yard. Not only is each compass direction associated with an element, but each element is associated with a variety of beings, spiritual entities that act as guardians and guides who aid a practitioner in creating sacred space (see part 3). Different traditions look to different forms of spirits for the four elements. Western magicians often call upon the four archangels, while shamanic traditions will call upon animal spirits.

For now, cleanse the space where you will be performing your mystical exercises and meditations. Keep the process simple. You don't have to use all four elements, but choose the techniques that resonate the most with your personal preferences. Honor the four directions with your cleansing tool, and notice how the space feels afterward. Periodically cleanse the space of unwanted energies and forces. If possible, cleanse the space and yourself before every meditative exercise or ritual.

EXERCISE

Meditation on the One

Since our polarity, trinity, and quintessence develop out of the one energy, the Divine Mind, mystics often begin their quest with the contemplation of the one.

Set up a comfortable space in which to meditate and practice your exercise. Have a seating space either on the floor, where you can comfortably sit cross-legged, or in a straight-backed chair or couch, where you can sit upright, with feet flat on the floor and hands in your lap. These are the two classically accepted meditation positions. Across from you should be a table or flat working space. Cleanse the space as directed in the previous exercise, "Cleansing Space." Have a single white candle burning on the surface. If you want, you can have some incense burning. See the previous exercise for incense recommendations.

Relax your body. Start at the top of your head, and tell yourself to relax all the muscles in your head and neck. Inhale, and when you exhale, release all tension or stress. Continue down your body. Relax all the muscles in your shoulders and your arms, right down through your fingertips. Relax your back and chest. Relax your belly and waist. As you breathe, feel waves of relaxation sweep through you. Relax your hips and lower back. Relax your buttocks. Relax your legs, starting with your thighs. Relax your knees, calves, and shins. Relax your ankles and your feet, down through the tips of your toes. Relax completely and feel yourself sink into your chair or the floor.

Focus all your attention on the candle flame. Stare into the candle flame, and think about how the essence of this fire is the same as that of all fires, from the fire of your metabolism to the fire in the heart of a star. Think about how there is one spirit, one energy, running through everything. Feel the power of the one force that connects all things, everywhere. The light in this room is the same light that is in the stars and that shines from your spirit. Focus all your will and attention on the candle, to the exclusion of everything else, for as long as possible. When you start this practice, you might only be able to hold your attention for a few minutes, but with practice, you will build up your endurance.

Take breaks as needed, but over a period of time, try to build up your powers of concentration and focus. When done, bring your awareness back to your body. Stretch and blink. Feel yourself back in your body, and snuff out the candle. Many traditions of magic discourage the practice of blowing out candles. Some say that blowing out a charged candle will create a curse or create ill will between you and the spirit of the element of fire. In the end, it will simply unbalance any intention you have placed in the candle, so I suggest getting into the habit of snuffing them out.

This meditation is a basic foundation and will help you develop subsequent skills. Meditation simply means to contemplate. It induces an altered state of consciousness. As you relax your body and awareness, your brain waves shift to a lower cycle, opening to the gifts of imagination, insight, intuition, and inner vision. Some people experience a profound sense of awareness in meditation. Many see images or hear messages. Some people simply feel things intensely, or "know" when something is happening in this state. They don't know things in pictures or words, but simply have a sense of knowing information on an intuitive level.

There is no right or wrong way to experience meditation. Use whatever techniques work best for you. Most written or guided meditations work with the visual medium, because it is the most descriptive to the largest number of people, but all the senses work on the psychic level, not just vision. A person who see visions during meditation is not more spiritually advanced than another who does not. Don't be discouraged if you don't envision things suggested in future meditations in this book. Visualization skills can be built over time, but they are not as important as trusting your own intuition and inner wisdom, however it manifests. Go with the senses and experiences that resonate best with you. Meditation helps focus and discipline the mind to other realities and mystical truths, but we all perceive them in our own unique way. Honoring your own path is part of the mystic's journey.

TWO

THE FUNDAMENTAL FORCES WITHIN US

3

VITAL ENERGIES

"As above, so below. As below, so above." This is the Principle of Correspondence, quoted in various forms in mystic traditions. Basically, it means that patterns repeat themselves on all levels. Whatever you see in the larger world, or macrocosm, is reflected in the smaller world, the microcosm.

Patterns of the universe repeat in the body. Look at the shape of the planet—crust, mantle, and core—and then look at the structure of a cell—membrane, liquid, and nucleus. Just as the universe has invisible mystical forces in unity, polarity, and the elements, so we have these same principles within us. The outer world parallels the inner world. By studying one, we gain a greater awareness of the other.

Modern scientists, studying the so-called outer world, often arrive at profound metaphysical concepts that parallel the discoveries of devout mystics devoted to the study of the inner worlds. All that was described in chapter 2, "The Elements," also applies to us as individuals. The elements of fire, air, water, and earth correspond to four energies, four levels of reality found in the universe, but their microcosmic versions within us are the soul, mind, emotions, and body. One pattern is reflected in the other. All the forces of the universe are within each of us.

Life Force

Each person consists of a subtle but vital energy that sustains and animates the body, mind, emotions, and soul. This life force is found in everything, but its shape and form vary when we compare different substances and even different people. It is known all over the world by various names and has different cultural associations attached to it. Mystics who can see this energy can measure a person's health and vitality. By manipulating the energy, mystics can heal and create change.

In India, this life force is called prana and is associated with the breath. Pranic healers manipulate this energy for hands-on and distance healing work. Prana has become a popular name for this force in the modern New Age community. Hawaiian mystics call it mana, in Japan it is called ki, and in China it is chi. Some branches of modern futuristic science call it orgone, od, odyle, or odic force.

Many people relate this vital life force to the fifth element, our akasha or quintessence. But different people, locations, and substances have different types of life force. At their core, the different types of life force energy all may be the same, but mystics can sense them differently. The life force of certain crystals is more powerful than that of others. The life force of each plant is different, and in part, it is the quality of life force in certain herbs and foods that creates medicines. Certain people seem to have a different quality or greater amount of life force. Others have a lesser amount. Forms of exercise, meditation, and diet can change this energy.

Life force energy itself is not good or bad, but the form in which we perceive it carries certain connotations. I tell students that spiritual energy or life force is like electricity—it depends on what it is used for. Electricity can light a room and dispel darkness, or electrocute someone. The general vibe of a lamp is very different from that of an electric chair.

Everything has a perceivable energy to those who are sensitive enough to tune in to it. Some call it resonance, and others harmony. I simply say "vibe" out of a desire to recapture the colorful sixties, which I never experienced firsthand. Many people perceive energy, but don't understand their perceptions. When they meet a new person or enter a room, they have an immediate sense of safety, danger, joy, nausea, or some other unexplained feeling or sensation. The experience did not initiate with them, but it causes a reaction within their body or consciousness.

With experience, a mystic can perceive these feelings without being overwhelmed by them. This is a basic part of psychic health and self-defense. Without this defense, you may often feel like you are taking on the feelings and thoughts of others around you. It is difficult enough at times to process your own energy. You do not necessarily have to take on other people's energy. It can be confusing until you learn to distinguish between the two, which is what you will do in the following exercise.

EXERCISE

Feeling Energy

Still down in a quiet place where you won't be disturbed, and take a few deep breaths. Deep breathing helps clear your mind, relaxes your thoughts, and gives you greater awareness. If you can pay attention to the subtleties of your breath, you can perceive all sorts of things most people miss.

Rub your hands together vigorously, like you are trying to warm them. This sensitizes them to feel energy. Then spread your arms so your hands are as far apart as possible. Slowly, bring your hands together, palms facing each other. With each moment, try to perceive a tactile sense of the space between your hands. You are feeling the energy of your body. Everyone feels it differently, but it has been described to me as heat, vibration, or pins and needles, or like two positive ends of a magnet coming together. I personally think the sensation is much more subtle than any of those descriptions, but this is a good starting place to feel energy.

Move your hands back and forth, playing with the energy between them. You may feel different layers of sensation or resistance. You may not feel a lot at first, but the more you play with this exercise and refine your perceptions, the more you will feel. It will help you feel the energies of different people and locations and gain an awareness of the general vibe, or resonance, of the energies.

Energy Centers

Our bodies process this primal life energy, and it moves through our energetic centers like food, oxygen, and waste move through our cells and organs. Primal energy manifests in our bodies as it does in the universe, creating polarity energy, or yin and yang. We also have the triple energy and the four elemental energies within us, though the different mystic traditions all can't agree on exactly how they work or where they are. I prefer to think of these energies as being in a dynamic balance, ever changing, rather than in a static state that can be definitively measured.

The various traditions do seem to agree that there are spiritual "organs" within the human body that process life energy. In certain primal shamanic traditions, as well as Qabalistic ceremonial magic traditions, the major centers are at the top of the head, chest, belly, and feet, connected by a central column of energy.

Chinese medicine maps out intricate systems of meridians that carry energy through the body. Meridians are like energetic blood vessels. They carry energy, not blood, and since they are not physical entities, they cannot be detected like blood vessels. One cannot remove a meridian during a traditional operation or autopsy, though injuries and illnesses can block and damage them. You could also think of meridians as subtle nerves, as energetic pathways for life energy, with no physical tissue. Acupuncture and acupressure are based on this system of energy flow. Although Chinese medicine and its art of acupuncture meticulously map these pathways, and their systems of healing have been documented to be effective, other traditions have different systems of meridian lines that do not coincide with the more mainstream systems, yet still seem to work.

The system of energy centers that has benefited me the most is the chakra system. The term chakra is very popular in the Western New Age movement and is believed to be universally known by mystics, at least in part, though the most complete system of chakras, including the term chakra itself, comes from the Hindus. The word chakra usually translates to spinning wheel or spinning disc, because many psychics see these centers of energy as spinning vortexes of light embedded in the body.

Although many have added to and adapted this system, the basic form consists of seven chakras running along the spine. Starting at the base of the spine, with red, the chakras ascend the colors of the rainbow. Each center is like a spiritual organ, representing a level of consciousness. As they ascend, they range from basic needs to highest ideals. Energy is exchanged through each center, powering that particular level of consciousness within us. Think of each chakra as a transformer, regulating the energy as it travels from level to level, from the lowest to the highest and back down again.

Unfortunately, this system of high and low has led many teachers to think of the lower chakras as "bad" and the upper chakras as "good." Remember, a building can't survive without its foundation. The basement might not be as aesthetically beautiful as the architecture above, but it is a vital part of the building. It is the same with the lower chakras.

The Principle of Polarity, discussed in chapter 1, teaches us that balance, not absolutes, is the key.

When someone tells me the lower chakras are bad, I like to think of the colors of a rainbow. Purple isn't better than red, though many people assume one color to be more "spiritual" than the other. Both are needed to form a rainbow. I think of them as gifts from the divine natural world. Many myths describe rainbows as bridges between the worlds. We each may have our favorite color, but it takes all colors to make a rainbow. We are each a rainbow in the world. We are each a natural gift of beauty and contain all colors. Without all the colors, we cannot be a bridge between the worlds within us, and the worlds around us.

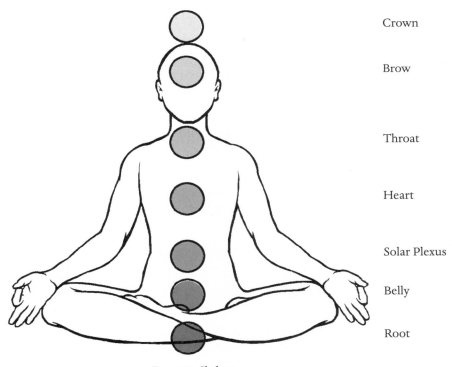

Crown

Brow

Throat

Heart

Solar Plexus

Belly

Root

Figure 20: Chakras

Root Chakra: Muladhara

The root chakra is the root of consciousness, grounded in the physical world. Viewed as a vortex of red energy at the base of the spine or the perineum, it represents the consciousness of survival, focusing on physical survival and the ability to enjoy physical pleasure. Reproduction and elimination, sex and death, are associated with this chakra. Sexuality for reproduction and pleasure, rather than emotional intimacy, is the primary concern. Survival in the physical world also relates to procreation, so the reproductive system has two connections to the root chakra. People who are capable of maintaining their physical needs of food, protection, safety, and pleasure have a well-functioning root chakra. People who are ungrounded or escapist, or who struggle when dealing with worldly concerns, have imbalances in the root chakra. Western magicians often view this chakra as being located between the feet, because much of their work is done standing, while Eastern yogis perceive it at the base of the spine, since their meditation is done on the floor, making contact with the ground and the root chakra. I think of the space between my feet as the extension of the center at the base of my spine. The root chakra is traditionally associated with the earth element, but its red color also gives it fire attributes.

Belly Chakra: Svadhisthana

The second level of consciousness is viewed as a vortex of orange light near the navel (the belly button) and is sometimes referred to as the sacral, navel, or spleen chakra. When we move past the simple need for survival, the next step is to develop trust and intimacy and connect with others. The belly chakra relates to the basic gut instinct we have, which tells us whom to trust and not to trust. Through this consciousness, we learn to build a relationship with ourselves, to trust ourselves, and then to build relationships with others. The spleen and intestines are connected to the belly chakra. These organs discern what is nutrition and what is waste or poison, the ultimate physical form of discernment. Water is the element of the second chakra.

Solar Plexus Chakra: Manipura

The solar plexus is the power plant of the chakra system. Here, we enter the realm of consciousness dealing with power and will. Through exercising our will, we learn a great deal about our relationships with ourselves, others, and the world. As a yellow orb of light just below the diaphragm, this center deals with how we project our will and energy, physical and psychic. When we feel unsafe, we enter the consciousness of fear. The solar plexus is associated with the adrenal glands and the fight or flight response. Power, fear, and self-image are all connected. When we feel our power sapped by others or our environment, we use our natural body language to cover the solar plexus area, to shield it. This is the place where we are most likely to lose energy or even take it from others. Fire is the element of the solar plexus.

Heart Chakra: Anahata

Anahata means unstruck and refers to the unstruck sound of the heart. This level of consciousness goes beyond the survival, connection, and power of the lower three chakras, the foundations, to the level of compassion and emotions, beyond our own personal needs. The heart chakra, located at the sternum, is viewed as green. Some people view it as green with a pink or red center. The fourth chakra acts a bridge between the lower and upper three chakras, grounding the experiences of both extremes through love. When you are in touch with your emotions, your heart chakra is more open and balanced. When you are blocking your emotions, and your ability to love is denied, then your heart chakra is unhealthy. The gland of the heart, the thymus, rules the immune system. When we are in touch with love, we are naturally healthy and balanced. Air, water, and earth have all been linked with the heart chakra.

Throat Chakra: Vishuddi

The throat chakra represents the power of communication, our ability to speak to others and the universe, but also our ability to listen and receive information. Visualized as a blue orb of light, the throat center allows us to bring our thoughts, ideas, and intentions into form and express them to others. The throat chakra is also an expression of our will. If we can't say something, we often can't make it happen. Mystic traditions often talk about the power of magic words. Words make things happen. People with issues involving the throat, respiratory system, or thyroid gland, all of which are parts of the body ruled by this chakra, have imbalances in their throat energy. The ears are also related to the throat chakra, for the ability to listen as well as speak. Air and spirit are the elements of this chakra.

Brow Chakra: Ajna

The brow chakra, also known as the third eye, is traditionally associated with psychic visions and powers. Although it is the center of consciousness of psychic ability, visualized as purple

or indigo between and above the eyes, its primary function is vision. Even people without any apparent psychic ability have a third eye. When you dream, visualize, or imagine,
you are using your third eye. When you envision yourself in the future, or receive divine
visions filled with information that helps you on your path, you are using your psychic eye.
The pineal gland and lower brain are associated with the brow chakra, and water and spirit
are its elements.

Crown Chakra: Sahasrara

The crown chakra is your connection to the divine, and is visualized as white or violet.
While the root chakra represents physical survival, the crown is spiritual survival, giving
you a sense of higher purpose and spiritual guidance. Some people feel the crown is a
chakra of potential, not actual manifestation, since it is located at the top of the head,
mostly outside of the body, but it is associated with the upper brain and pituitary gland.
Any imbalance or illness that causes a person to awaken to higher spiritual awareness is
considered an issue of the crown chakra. Though some traditions ascribe the pituitary
gland to the brow chakra and the pineal gland to the crown chakra, the pituitary is the
master gland, so it is fitting that it is the gland of the crown chakra. Most people consider
the crown chakra to be beyond any element, but the closest corollary is spirit.

Chakra	Colors	Elements	Planets	Body Systems & Organs
Root	Red	Earth, fire	Saturn, Mars	Reproductive system, excretory system, ovaries/gonads
Belly	Orange	Water	Moon, Mercury, Jupiter	Lower digestive system, reproductive system, skeletal system, large intestine, spleen
Solar plexus	Yellow	Fire	Sun, Mars	Upper digestive system, musculature system, liver, stomach, adrenal glands
Heart	Green, green with a pink or red center	Air, water, earth	Venus, Sun	Circulatory system, immune system, heart, blood vessels, thymus gland

Chart 2: Chakra Correspondences

Chakra	Colors	Elements	Planets	Body Systems & Organs
Throat	Blue	Air, spirit	Mercury	Respiratory system, metabolism, lungs, throat, mouth, vocal cords, larynx, ears, thyroid gland
Brow	Purple, indigo	Water, spirit	Moon, Jupiter	Nervous system, lower brain, nerve tissue, eyes, pineal gland
Crown	White, violet	Spirit	Sun, Saturn	Endocrine system, higher brain, spinal cord, pituitary gland

Chart 2 (continued)

Some traditional Hindu teachings assign completely different, nonprismatic colors to the seven chakras, along with slightly different locations. Each chakra is a mandala based on the image of a lotus flower, with specific associations, colors, petals, and symbols. Much of our New Age chakra lore is very Westernized and differs from traditional Hindu lore, but both contain valuable teachings based on experience. Modern lore gives us many more "minor" energy centers in the body, and also includes "higher" chakras outside of and above the body. My understanding of the traditional Eastern lore has in no way diminished my experiences with more modern interpretations. It just shows yet again that there are many ways to view the same thing. Our experiences with chakra energies are subjective.

EXERCISE
Grounding

Grounding is one of the basic skills every mystic should have. Grounding simply means to be fully present in the physical world. When you alter your consciousness, either intentionally or unintentionally, you are not fully present in your body. To be grounded, you must return your consciousness fully to the here and now, anchored in the body. When you wake up in the morning, you feel like part of you is still asleep, still dreaming—you are ungrounded. After meditation, people feel slightly dizzy or dazed when they are not fully grounded. If you are shocked, frightened, or in sudden pain, you can become ungrounded. The most extreme experience of being ungrounded is what is called an OBE, an out-of-body experience. All manner of hallucinations and visions indicate being ungrounded. When you are absent-minded or daydreaming, you are ungrounded. Some people are naturally less grounded than others. Those who are more creative, or embody the archetype of the dreamer or escapist, are less grounded than those who embody more pragmatic concerns.

Being ungrounded is fine under certain circumstances. When doing various meditations, psychic exercises, and rituals, you want to be ungrounded, because you are intentionally expanding your consciousness. When shocked, becoming ungrounded is a self-defense mechanism in response to the trauma.

The trick of a good mystic is to be able to come back fully at will to a state of normal waking consciousness. Many techniques for this exist. Eating grounds you, bringing your energy back to your body for digestion. This is one reason to have breakfast in the morning, or to have a feasting celebration after a ritual. Even drinking water can help. Caffeine is very grounding, although that sounds contrary to conventional wisdom. The caffeine high is centered in energizing the body and boosting the metabolism, much like eating in general raises the metabolism. A small burst of caffeine can do so faster, but it's not good to become dependent on it for your grounding. I use it only in extreme situations, and my favorite source is chocolate. Other substances that give a high, such as alcohol and most recreational drugs, actually unground you, so they cannot be used for this purpose. Certain stones, usually dark stones such as hematite, smoky quartz, and onyx, are also grounding when held. The best grounding techniques are internal and psychic and don't require any tools. The following are just a few that are helpful to me.

You can ground yourself by imagining a beam of light from your root chakra digging deep into the earth, anchoring you like a balloon. Focus on the feeling of gravity pulling you back to center.

Imagine your feet are growing like the roots of a big tree, digging deep into the land and holding you down, yet at the same time nourishing you. Feel yourself become sturdy and solid, like a tree.

Pretend you are sinking your feet deep into beach sand. Feel yourself firmly anchored in the material world. You can even just press down on your feet, and bring all your attention to the soles of your feet, bringing the energy down the body, grounding you.

If you feel too energized after a ceremony, get down on your hands and knees and press into the floor. Imagine grounding the excess energy into the earth, like a lightning rod. You can even bow your head, imagining only the excess energy pouring out and into the earth. You can send an intention of earth healing with it, so as not to waste the energy. If you can't bend over, then hold a ritual object, such as a staff, walking stick, or sword, and use it like a lightning rod to ground the energy into the earth. You can even lean into the altar and use that like a lightning rod to ground the energy. With the release of energy, root yourself with the other techniques just discussed and you will be fully grounded.

Experiment with these grounding techniques, and find the ones that work best for you. Make sure to ground after every exercise that expands your awareness beyond the physical world. Integrate the technique into your daily life when needed.

EXERCISE

Chakra Balancing

Sit down in a quiet place, as you did in the previous meditation. Take a few deep, clearing breaths. Focus your awareness on your feet, if you are sitting with your feet flat on the floor. You can also sit cross-legged, focusing your attention on the base of your spine.

As you inhale, imagine you are sucking up energy from the earth below through the straw of your spine. Imagine a beam of light extending from your spine deep into the earth, into the center of the Earth itself. Inhale and draw the energy up this personal tube. Exhale normally. Continue to breathe, and with each inhalation, feel the energy rise up. The energy will feel much like it did in the previous exercise. As you inhale, concentrate on your root chakra. Feel it fill with energy and glow with a dazzling ruby-red energy. The red light clears the chakra of any unbalanced, unwanted energy. Release any blocks to survival and pleasure. Feel yourself rooted in the world, grounded and centered.

After spending a few moments on the root chakra, draw the energy up to the belly chakra, transforming it into a warm orange color. The light cleanses this chakra of unbalanced energy. Release any blocks to trust and intimacy. Feel your sense of knowing grow and strengthen.

Move on to the solar plexus chakra. As the energy ascends with your breath, it turns a golden yellow. Take several breaths, energizing the solar plexus and cleansing it. Release your fears, your need to control, and anything that contributes to an unhealthy self-image. See yourself as you desire to be—strong, confident, and self-assured. You draw your power from yourself and your divinity, not from other people's perceptions of you.

Draw the energy up to your heart chakra, changing it to green light. Fill yourself with great, loving light. Let the light heal and cleanse you, releasing all that prevents you from giving and receiving love. Feel yourself become love, a universal unconditional love, connecting you to all things.

Move the energy up with your breath to the blue throat chakra. Feel it fill with light, and energize it. Cleanse all blocks to true communication and understanding with the blue light. Feel yourself find your own personal inner truth.

Feel the energy ascend to your third eye, turning a dark purple or indigo. Feel the light cleanse your third eye and awaken your powers of inner vision and psychic ability.

Spend a few moments on your third eye, then let the energy rise to your crown chakra. Feel the crown open in multicolored lights. Feel the energy of the Earth ascend like a geyser, spraying a shower of light all around you, clearing your crown and the space around you. Spend a few moments feeling your divine connection, bridging the Earth and heavens.

When you are done, stop willing Earth energy up through your spine. Let the remaining Earth energy in your spine come out of your crown. Take a few moments to bring your attention back to your root, and the beam of light grounding you to the Earth. Feel yourself centered, grounded, and anchored in the world, energetically clear and free.

Some texts urge you never to focus on the chakras consciously, because such exercises will cause great harm and imbalance in your body and energy. Though misuse of the chakras' energy can cause harm, in my experience I have found no detrimental effects in performing this simple cleansing and balancing exercise. Quite the contrary. It's brought great benefits on all levels in my life, and in the lives of my students, friends, and family who practice it.

If you are worried about causing harm to yourself or any others in your mystical pursuits, begin your exercises with this firm intention: "I ask that all I do here be for the highest good, harming none. So mote it be." So mote it be, which simply means "it is so," is used in the traditions of magic that I practice. You could also use "So be it" or even "Amen," if that is more comfortable for you.

4

SUBTLE ANATOMY

Surrounding and interpenetrating the physical body are the energy bodies, the subtle bodies. As each chakra regulates the energy of a particular level of consciousness within us, each chakra is based in a particular energy body, the field of energy that helps us express that consciousness. Through the four elements we create a model of our physical and nonphysical anatomy that includes four levels: the physical, emotional, mental, and spiritual. The fourfold model is only one way to look at it. Some occultists divide our physical and nonphysical anatomy into seven subtle bodies, based upon the imagery of the seven chakras.

Although we think of our consciousness, our mind and soul, as being contained within the body, and the body is a shell, these energies are simply too expansive to be contained within the mortal form, so they "spill" out and radiate outward. This is your vibe, or resonance, that people pick up on when you enter the room. You could think of your energy field as being generated by your spiritual organs, your chakras, much as heat radiates from your physical body due to the metabolic processes of your physical organs.

Collectively, mystics refer to the subtle bodies as the aura. Some perceive the aura as a sphere or bubble of energy around an individual. On the subtle psychic level, the aura has many layers and colors, and those skilled at interpreting the colors and symbols in the aura can diagnose the health, state of mind, and state of spiritual awakening within an individual.

The energy bodies are actually greater than what most people see as the aura, expanding far and wide, but the most cohesive energy appears to be a field reaching a little further than

53

arm's length all around a person, and slightly above the head and below the feet. The more "energy" a person has, spiritually, the bigger or brighter the person's aura. The less spiritual energy a person has, the less intense or more contracted or diffuse the aura will be.

The aura is also the boundary of personal space. Those with healthy personal boundaries will have a healthy auric boundary. Those who are constrained or tense or who lack personal presence will have contracted auras. Those who lack boundaries, strongly identify with others, or can't separate themselves from other people's problems or successes will have large, diffuse auras that melt and mingle with other people's auras. The aura is not limited to just people. All things contain and radiate a subtle energy. We perceive the strongest energy from living beings, the cellular life of the animal and plant world, but minerals and even crafted objects have detectable auras.

Though many mystic traditions describe the subtle bodies as specific layers with definite names and boundaries, the energy is more like a personal ocean. The ocean has many layers of temperature and pressure, but there is no membrane separating each layer. The layers blend into each other. You experienced one of the denser layers when you felt the energy between your hands in the "Feeling Energy" exercise in chapter 3. The energy around you extends beyond just your hands. If you look at a true rainbow, and not a drawing of one with neatly drawn separate lines, you will realize that a rainbow, too, is a blended spectrum. No lines divide the colors.

Systems of division occur when a tradition draws lines in this ocean of energy to describe its properties. There is nothing wrong with that, as long as you understand that these are no hard lines or absolute truths. Some traditions draw more lines than others, or call the same layer by different names. When you study the subtle bodies, try to keep in mind that they are part of a dynamic whole, and not separate, divisible layers. Some systems have three, four, five, or seven layers. Other systems are even more complex.

A simple way of looking at the body is through the eyes of a shaman. Though most shamanic models are very complicated and subtle, dividing the self into many parts, most shamanic traditions divide the self into three parts. The middle self is the body and linear mind, including the ego. It is the part of the self to which most nonmystics relate. The modern world focuses on the middle self. The lower self is the body of instinct, psychic ability, and primal emotion. The higher self is the spiritual, divine, and enlightened self that most people feel detached from. It is connected to the other selves, but the middle self must use the lower self to consciously connect and commune with the higher self. The lower self acts as a bridge, informing us of the higher self's message through our intuitions, dreams, impressions, and visions. Our higher and lower selves take part in the process of manifesting our life, our reality. When we send out our intentions into the world, through our thoughts, words, and deeds, the lower self collects the energy of our intentions, and brings this energy to the higher self. The higher self uses this energy to metaphorically "pave" the road to our future life. The higher self can only create a life based upon the raw building material we give it. If we give it shoddy intentions, our road is rougher. If we are clear in our intentions, the road of our future comes with fewer bumps. This three-self shamanic road-building model might be symbolic, yet the experience and relationship of the three selves is very real.

Another system of division looks at the subtle bodies in terms of elements. Your physical body, the one the modern world knows the most about, relates to the earth element. What is called the astral or emotional body, the body of shape, form, and feeling, corresponds to the water element. The air element relates to the mental body, and the element of fire corresponds to the soul. Each level extends progressively outward from the physical body, so you can think of the physical body, earth, being inside the soul body, or fire. Most people think of the soul as residing in the body, but many occultists see the soul as much larger than the physical body.

Energy in the physical body is exchanged with energy in the emotional body. The emotional body, too, exchanges energy with the mental body, and the mental body exchanges energy with the spiritual body. You can vividly see this chain of exchange when you focus your thoughts on something that resonates powerfully for you. It doesn't matter if the focus creates harmony or discord. Pick something that makes you really happy or something that upsets you. Your intense thoughts on the subject create feelings. Many people believe their feelings are uncontrollable, because they well out of their initial thoughts. Discipline of the mind can bring greater emotional control. The emotional feelings can create sensations in the body and, if they persist in generating discord, eventually a physical disruption in the body, manifesting as illness or injury.

For example, if a person were to focus on the fact he or she lacked any income, and thought about it intensely, the possible ramifications of having no money—such as bill collectors, debts, loss of home and possessions, and possible starvation—would set in. These are uncomfortable thoughts that can generate feelings of anger, sadness, shame, and worry. The feelings could translate into loss of appetite, anxiety, or tension, which, if they persisted, could create digestive and nervous system ailments, and eventually disease.

On the opposite side of the spectrum, a person who has no money, but is happy about living off the land, or living in a monastery or ashram retreat, and is otherwise satisfied with the status of no income, can generate feelings of happiness, detachment, and relaxation, allowing the energy to flow freely in the physical body and maintain health. Health and balance depend on a person's thoughts about the current situation.

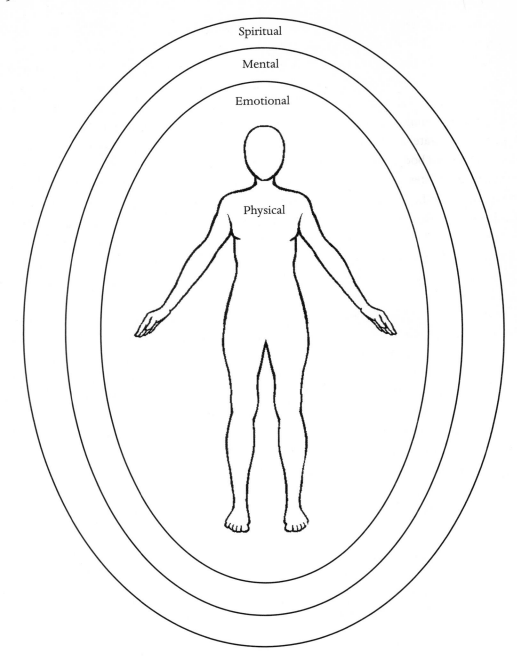

Figure 21: Elemental Bodies

My favorite way of dividing the subtle bodies is based on the chakras, corresponding a different subtle body with each energy center. The root chakra corresponds with the physical body. The belly chakra partners with the etheric body. The etheric body is like an energy template, a pattern of the physical body that radiates out just a few inches from the physical body. The solar plexus chakra connects with the astral body, a more fluid self-image. People think of the astral self as the dream self that journeys when we dream, fantasize, meditate, and do certain forms of psychic work. Some call it the lower astral or lower emotional body, since our emotions change our self-image and intuitive abilities. The heart chakra relates to the emotional body, or upper emotional/upper astral body. This is the body of our higher emotions, compassion, and healing abilities. The throat chakra is the link to our mental body, the realm of thoughts and ideas. Psychics perceive this less as a human body and more as a sphere or egg around the body, being more abstract in nature. The third eye chakra relates to what I call the psychic body, for the psychic eye. Some call it the upper mental body, lower spiritual body, or Buddhic body. The crown chakra relates to the divine body, or soul body. The soul body is another name for the higher self.

Other systems divide the energy bodies in other ways, based on the Tree of Life teachings or other mystical paradigms. Just as there are forces within us, there are also forces beyond us, in the macrocosm. Just as we all have these potential subtle bodies, so does the universe, or universal being, when you think of the universe as alive and conscious.

None of these views are absolutely right or wrong. They simply describe something energetic that cannot be objectively mapped the way physical anatomy can be mapped. The wonderful lesson in exploring multiple views is to know that there are many "truths" in the world, and none are mutually exclusive. Each model seems to work for the practitioners using it.

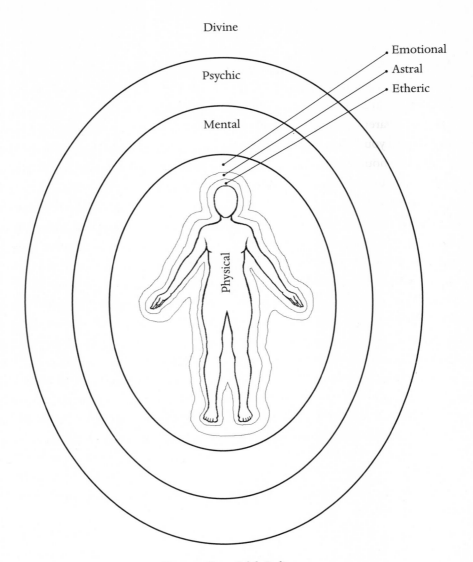

Figure 22: Seven Subtle Bodies

EXERCISE

Aura Cleansing

Periodic cleansing of the aura is a powerful way to maintain spiritual and mental health. It removes unwanted energies from our subtle bodies. For this exercise, sit in a quiet place in a comfortable position. Take a few deep breaths, centering yourself and your awareness. Imagine that you are inside a large bubble or egg. This is the aura around your body. It is like a bubble filled with water, and floating in the water are all your thoughts and feelings. The unhealthy thoughts look and feel dense. The healthier thoughts are fluid and ethereal, without weight or density.

Imagine scanning your aura for dense thoughts and feelings. Even if you are not sure you are feeling or seeing anything, use your imagination. Imagine reaching out with your mind and taking hold of these dense energies. Unwanted thoughts from yourself and from others will appear as dense, heavy, and dark packets floating in the aura, or coating the inside or outside of the "shell." These are often called thoughtforms, but can be composed of emotions as well as thoughts. Fill a dense packet of thought with a dazzling white light, allowing the density to dissolve and break apart. One by one, reach out to your dense, unwanted thoughts and clear them away. Clear your entire aura, to the best of your ability.

Next, imagine filling your aura with light. You can use a dazzling white light, since it is composed of all colors. If you cannot manage to clear the individual dense forms of energy in your aura, fill the entire aura with dazzling white light to clear as many of them as possible at once. You can also use any color you desire. What is your favorite color? Which of the chakra colors represents the level of consciousness you want to fully embody? By using your will to visualize yourself surrounded by that color of light, even for just a few moments, you bring that level of consciousness and its qualities into manifestation.

When you are done, imagine yourself in a clear, clean crystalline field of energy. Charge your protection shield, the edge and boundary of your aura, by putting this intention into its energy: "I charge this shield to protect me from all harm on any level. So mote it be." Repeat this three times. For additional protection, you can visualize four pentagrams, symbols of protection, at the boundary of your aura, one in each of the four directions—before you, behind you, to your left, and to your right. For protection, the pentagram is traditionally drawn starting in the lower left-hand corner and is called the banishing pentagram. Imagine it drawn in a flaming white, blue, or violet light.

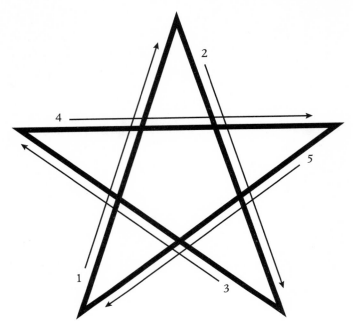

Figure 23: Banishing Pentagram

When done, return yourself to normal waking consciousness with a few breaths. Become aware of your body and the physical world. Feel yourself centered, grounded, and anchored in the world, energetically clear and free.

You might not be able to clear your entire aura in one session. You can do several sessions spread out over time. Be gentle with yourself, since cleansing the aura might force you to confront your unhealthy, unwanted feelings. I have found journaling to be extremely helpful when doing energetic clearing. Journaling allows us to process mentally what we have already processed energetically, to fully purge and release our past experiences yet still draw upon valuable lessons and teachings.

A balance of personal life force, through the chakras and subtle bodies, is what creates health and well-being. Only by knowing the forces inside ourselves can we command greater awareness and clarity and inspire healing, creativity, and enlightenment.

THREE

EXPLORING THE UNIVERSE

5

THE WORLDS BEYOND

"There be dragons" used to be written on old maritime maps, before the world was truly explored. It denoted the edges of the known world, where the mysterious, unknown, exciting, and possibly dangerous forces dwelled. Although the seafaring explorers feared such "dragons," there was also a sense of romantic excitement to be the first to see one.

When I read about mystical philosophy, I often think the books should have "there be dragons" written somewhere on them. Although many authors write about the spiritual universe as if it were a set of perfectly defined facts, mystical texts are much more like medieval maps. They are models, maps of reality that are not absolute. Their edges are less defined the further away you get from the world you know. At the edges, there is the unknown. There are dragons. And I, for one, am quite glad that this is the case, because the world would be a boring place without dragons. Life would be dull without mysteries to be explored and different points of view to consider.

Even though the mystical realms cannot necessarily be measured by the physical senses, and therefore cannot be objectively defined, we humans, by our very nature, define and label our experiences. There's nothing wrong with that, since it gives us the ability to discuss experiences with a common language. In fact, as mystics compare experiences, they realize there is a lot of common ground. They record benchmark experiences in meditation and ritual to create their maps, and find that many others have taken the same sort of path. Explorers' experiences are colored by their own cultures and expectations, but a lot of the fundamental ideas are the same.

The Spiritual Dimensions

Mystics have divided reality into many different levels. Some view these levels as different places, like different locations on a map. By using spiritual models that describe the levels of reality, you can travel to those levels, just like following the lines on a map. These levels are called dimensions or worlds. Others see these realities as different vibrations, realms that exist in the same place as the world we know but at different densities. The different realms overlap, yet they do not conflict with each other, since they are vibrating at different rates. Experienced mystics can "tune in" their consciousness to the right vibration, and shift their awareness.

In a sense, both views are right. Each description is one way of looking at a truth. They each attempt to describe something that is beyond linear description. Like many topics in both science and metaphysics, they are models, not absolute truths.

The first model of spiritual realms, the dualistic model, is the one most ordinary people are familiar with. Reality is divided into two worlds—the physical, known universe and the spiritual, intangible, unknown world. Most think the physical world is completely charted, while the spirit world is filled with strange, unsubstantiated life forms, ghosts, and other things that go bump in the night. The dualistic model is pretty simple, and is the first step toward acknowledgment of a realm beyond the physical. In reality, there are mysteries still to be explored in both worlds, particularly where they overlap. The separation between the physical and spiritual worlds is often called the "veil" or "veil between the worlds," though the term veil can refer to the separation between any two spiritual worlds. Another symbol for the veil is the magic mirror, as the spiritual world is said to be on the other size of the mirror. All reflections are gateways to the other side of the veil. Pools of water act like mirrors, and in mythology are gateways to the spirit worlds. Our experiences in this other world, this reflected spirit world, can appear contradictory or backward, and the customs of the spiritual inhabitants of this world may seem strange. To us, we are watching a reflection of the physical world, and the energies of the spirit world appear backward or reversed because they are reflections of the energies in our familiar physical world.

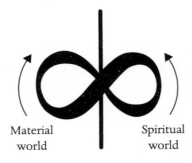

Material   Spiritual
world   world

Figure 24: The Veil and the Infinity Loop

Within the microcosm of humanity, this dualistic view is the body-and-soul theory of mainstream religious thinking. We have both a physical body, residing in the physical world, and a mysterious spiritual aspect, unseen and seemingly unknowable, that belongs to the other side when our physical shell ceases to live.

The Shamanic World Tree

For the shaman, the universe is divided into three basic worlds. The first is the middle world, which consists of the physical world we know, but also includes what science would call the space-time continuum. The middle world is the present time, but also the past and future.

Surrounding the middle world is a lower world and an upper world. The lower world is the place of ancestors, where the spirits of the dead go to rest. It is a place of earthy power, healing, and emotion. Visitors to the underworld can experience love and healing, or find strength through facing their fears. All who enter the lower world are transformed. Many people think of it as the collective unconsciousness. The nature of the lower world is like the mirror, the veil we pass through to enter the realm of spirit. The energy of this realm shows us whatever we are, like gazing at our reflection. Everybody's experience of it is different. Those who come to the lower world with fear can experience fear, and the opportunity to overcome it. Those who visit with joy experience joy. The lower realm takes on the characteristics of the visitor's thoughts and emotions.

The upper world is the realm of spirituality, enlightenment, direct knowledge, and detachment. Psychologists would relate it to the superconsciousness. Here is the realm of the heavens and eternal reward. It is the realm of the enlightened ancestors, saints, gurus, and gods.

Different mythologies further subdivide these realms, but the basic three are found in many shamanic or mystic traditions. Connecting all three worlds is a cosmic axis, referred to by scholars as the *axis mundi*, or main axis, usually viewed as a tree, mound, mountain, or ladder. Just as the planet rotates on its axis, so does the spiritual universe rotate on its axis, but this center of the universe is accessible to any shaman who does the proper meditations, rituals, and visualizations. Many traditions call the cosmic axis the world tree.

You may notice the similarity between the world tree and the shamanic model of the self, having a middle, higher, and lower self. These three essential natures relate to the three worlds of the shaman.

Upper World

Middle World

Lower World

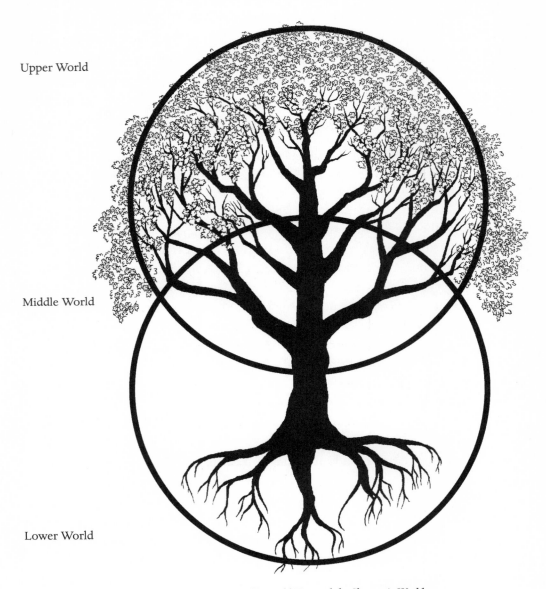

Figure 25: The World Tree and the Shamanic Worlds

The Elemental Worlds

In the elemental model, the world is divided into four realms, based on the four elements. The physical world, which is the densest, is the realm of earth. The astral world, the realm of energetic shape and form as well as emotions, since the two are so strongly connected, is the realm of water. The intellectual world of the mind is the realm of air. Finally, the realm of the pure energy animating all things is the realm of fire. Spirit/quintessence is the energy that encompasses them all. Within these realms exist aspects of ourselves. Our individual bodies reside in the physical realm, our emotions function on the astral level, our minds operate in the mental realm, and our souls dwell in the divine spirit realm.

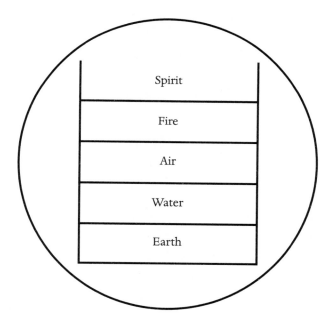

Figure 26: Elemental Ladder

Notice that the elemental planes are ordered from the most ethereal on the top to the densest on the bottom, and are surrounded by the fifth element, quintessence. Just as some systems switch fire and air symbolically, some place the realm of air above that of fire. Another system, drawing from the system of philosophy called the Qabalah, puts the elemental worlds in an even different order, with fire on top, followed by water, air, and earth. Each system works, and shows how energetic reality is symbolic. There is no one way to see it. Different mystics can see things differently, and still have success.

The Seven Layers of Reality

Though the elemental model of reality seems complete, the layers of reality can be further subdivided. In this division, I use the chakras as my guide. As the chakras represent levels of consciousness within us, think of these levels of reality as the levels of consciousness in the divine body of the universe. Each one corresponds to one of the previous seven subtle bodies discussed in relationship to the chakras.

The root chakra corresponds to the physical realm. The belly chakra works with what I call the etheric realm, a level of energy that is very close to the physical, where patterns of everything physical exist—they are the energetic templates to the physical universe. The solar plexus chakra relates to the astral plane, a more fluid pattern and template that is influenced by our will, emotions, and self-esteem. The heart chakra corresponds to the emotional plane, what some call the higher astral plane. At this level we find the energy of relationships and connections. The throat chakra is the realm of the mind, the mental plane. The third eye chakra relates to what I call the psychic level, the level of pure information. Some call it the higher mental plane. The crown chakra is the level of the divine, the spiritual plane. Here, everything is connected in divine bliss. This is where our highest selves exist.

Some mystics even view the seven magical planets of the ancients as the seven chakras of the solar system's "body," each truly functioning on the corresponding subtle plane or energetic "layer." The physical planet we see is only the physical expression of that solar being's "chakras." Each of the planets has key spiritual associations related to its realm of consciousness, associations used in both astrology and ritual magic. Modern mystics dispute which planet is related to which chakra. One of the most common methods is to start with Saturn, the planet used by the ancients that was the furthest out, and correspond it to the root chakra, and then move in, ending with the Moon and Sun. In astrology, the Sun and Moon are considered planets, although technically they are really luminaries, or celestial lights. The physical planets astronomers have charted are the physical representations of these spheres of consciousness.

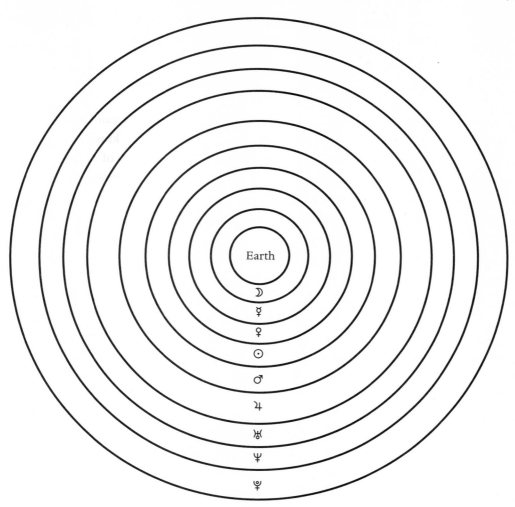

Figure 27: Planetary Spheres

The Tree of Life

In the Qabalah, a form of Hebrew mysticism that exists in both a traditional Jewish form and one blended with Western hermetic ceremonial magic, the universe is divided into ten realms of consciousness, said to be emanations from the divine creator. The Tree of Life is a map of these ten realms. The tree is said to have its roots in the heavens, and the physical world is its fruit. On the tree, the spheres—called sephiroth, though sephiroth technically translates to emanations or numerical emanations—are connected by linear pathways. The sephiroth are all associated with planets, and the paths are associated with the Major Arcana cards of the tarot. Each sphere is a plane of consciousness, a state of being, both within ourselves and in the universe. Each path, and its corresponding tarot card, represents the process to reach that level of consciousness from another level.

Although the Tree of Life is one of the most complicated systems of mapping reality, many others exist. The advantage of the Qabalah map is that it is complete, and most other systems or traditions can be "mapped" upon its branches.

Qabalah is spelled in many different ways, denoting its tradition and use. Qabalah usually denotes Western magical Qabalah. Kabalah or Kaballah usually indicates the more orthodox Hebrew system. Cabala denotes a Christian version of the system. Not all authors and scholars use the *Q*, *K*, and *C* differentiations. All of these systems essentially contain the same information, though they each treat it differently, colored by their particular belief system and culture. The names of the sephiroth also have many variant spellings.

The lowest sphere on the Tree of Life—number ten, called Malkuth, meaning Kingdom—represents the physical realm and the Earth. In this system, the four elemental planes are related to the tenth sphere, since they all are the powers of manifestation in the physical realm, though the various upper spheres, based on planetary or astrological associations, also have further elemental associations. On the tree, this sphere is often divided into four equal parts for that reason. It is the realm of the elements and the seasons.

The ninth sphere, Yesod, meaning Foundation, refers to the astral plane, which is the foundation of the physical realm. All things must occur on the astral plane, and have an astral double, to exist in the physical realm. Yesod relates to the Moon.

The eighth realm is Hod, the realm of the mind, which translates to Glory. It is the glory and splendor of the mind, knowledge, and truth. Mercury is the planet of Hod. Paired with Hod is Netzach, the sphere of Venus and the realm of emotion and attraction. Netzach means Victory, indicating the victory and triumph of emotion.

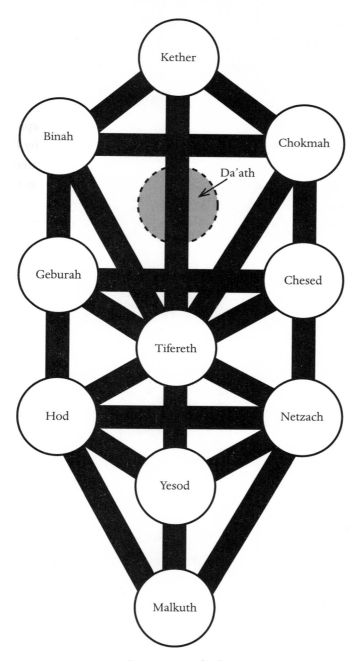

Figure 28: Tree of Life

The center of the tree is Tifereth, the realm of the Sun, meaning Beauty. It is the realm of the higher self, what ceremonial magicians call the Holy Guardian Angel, because it embodies our most noble self. Tifereth is the consciousness of selfless sacrifice for the higher good.

Next on the tree is the sphere of Geburah, or Might. This is the consciousness of Mars, the warrior, and willpower. Paired with it is Chesed, meaning Mercy. It is the realm of Jupiter and the benevolent father consciousness.

Highest on the tree are the last three spheres, Binah, Chokmah, and Kether. They can be viewed as the divine manifestations of the Goddess, God, and Divine Spirit. Binah is Understanding. It is the sphere of Saturn and holds the pattern of creation from the primal mother. It is the cosmic ocean of potential. Chokmah, meaning Wisdom, is the seed of consciousness, the energy of the divine father. Unlike the other spheres, Chokmah does not correspond with one of the seven magical planets of the ancients. Qabalists correspond Chokmah with the zodiac signs, though modern mystics, desiring to fit the "new" outer planets into the Tree of Life, assign Neptune or Uranus to Chokmah. The seed of Chokmah fertilizes the oceans of Binah, bringing about the creation of the sephiroth below.

Kether, although often visualized as male in Judeo-Christian mysticism, is beyond gender and represents the divine light of creation. Modern mystics relate Kether to the planet Pluto. Kether, which means Crown, is the most knowable form of the divine source, emitted from the veils of nothingness to manifest creation. Before the last triad is the unconnected sphere, Da'ath, meaning Knowledge. It sits in the abyss between the levels of Geburah/Chesed and Binah/Chokmah. One must pass through this abyss to reach the highest realms. Those beneath the abyss in consciousness can't truly understand the realms above it.

EXERCISE
Rising on the Planes

"Rising on the planes" is a term given to a meditative experience of the ten spheres of the Qabalah, though in a variety of traditions it could be used to describe psychic travel or shamanic journey. Some practitioners use precise formulas and rituals to open the paths between the spheres, and more detailed meditations also focus on specific pathways, using associations with tarot cards and Hebrew letters, to make the connections between spheres. In this exercise, we will be doing a simple, basic version of rising on the spheres, to give you an experiential understanding of the Tree of Life and its components.

Sit in a quiet place in a comfortable position. Take a few deep breaths, centering yourself and your awareness. As you breathe, be aware of the physical world, the world of Malkuth. You are in Malkuth, the kingdom or garden, the realm of four directions and four seasons. As you breathe in and out, feel your awareness grow lighter and lighter, as you feel your sense of self rise up out of your body. Imagine the Tree of Life above you.

Become aware of a purple moon above you, a purple sphere of light, soft and pulsing. The purple may be flecked with silver. Enter the realm of purple light, the sphere of Yesod. Feel the power of emotions flowing back and forth. Enter a realm that is much like your dreams. This is the sphere of Moon goddesses and gods, sacred timekeepers, and gateways to the higher realms. Feel your intuition, not your reason, guide you in this place, as you float in the sea of purple energy.

Feel yourself rise out of the purple light of Yesod. Above you resides a bright orange sphere. As you enter the sphere of Hod, feel your mind become quick and sharp. Enter the realm of language, the sphere of logic, reason, and communication. The very realm seems to be made of language. This is the realm of messengers and magicians.

Rise from the sphere of Hod into the emerald green light of Netzach. Enter the land of nature, the green, growing faerie realm, abundant in life and light. Feel your senses come alive amid a garden paradise. This is the realm of nature spirits and fertility gods. This is the realm of Venus, also known as the Greek Aphrodite, goddess of love, born of the foamy ocean. This is the realm of attraction and love.

From the clear skies of Netzach, see the golden yellow sun shining above you. Its rays invite you upward. Draw yourself upward. Enter the sphere of Tifereth, the realm of the Sun kings and sacrificed gods. Here is the realm of unconditional, spiritual love, the realm of your higher, noble self. Feel the love of this level radiate and fill you, sustaining you, like a plant soaking up the rays of the sun.

Rise from the golden yellow of Tifereth to the fiery red sphere of Geburah. This is the sphere of the warrior, of judgment. Geburah is the realm of the warrior gods, like the god Mars himself, but it is also of the realm of the spiritual warrior, those on the path who pursue their truth with honor and discipline, dedicated to the will of the divine. Many war goddesses are associated with Geburah. The fires of Geburah burn away all that does not serve your highest good. It stimulates and activates your inner fire, and challenges you to use your power and will.

The purifying fires give way to the cooling blue light of Chesed, the sphere of mercy and compassion. This is the realm of the ascended masters, teachers, and saints. It is the realm of benevolence and grace, and of the loving father gods.

After resting in the gentleness of the blue sphere, imagine yourself crossing over a dark abyss, a chasm, into the sphere of knowledge, the realm of Da'ath. Da'ath is the sphere of ultraviolet, otherworldly light. It's like looking into a peacock's feathers or an oil slick. It mesmerizes. Don't let yourself get stuck in Da'ath, but rise above it.

The abyss gives way to a dark sphere of blackness, the sphere of the dark mother goddess. This realm is known as Binah, a vast primordial ocean of potential. Feel yourself floating in the currents of the starless night sky, like a black, inky sea.

Move from the realm of Binah to the fountains of light in the gray sphere of Chokmah. Chokmah is the seed, the potential, the form that is implanted into the sea of Binah to bring life from the cosmic oceans. Feel the starry light of the star fathers within this realm.

The last stop on the cosmic ladder is Kether, the brilliant light of the crown, the purest state we can conceive of. Feel the dazzling light around you and in you. Become one with the light.

When ready, slowly descend back through the spheres, one by one, in reverse order, returning to Malkuth. Imagine that you are following a string, a path you have left for yourself. Feel yourself move from the absolute pure white light of Kether to the gray light of Chokmah, then to the inky blackness of Binah. Descend through the abyss of Da'ath, through the blue and red spheres of Chesed and Geburah. Pass through the gold of Tifereth, down through green Netzach, orange Hod, and purple Yesod, making your way back to the physical plane of Malkuth and your body.

Ground yourself in your body. Feel the physical world around you. When ready, rise from your position and reorient yourself.

What makes the Qabalistic Tree of Life even more complex is the simultaneous belief in a fourfold system, along with the ten-sphere tree. The four worlds of the Qabalah are modeled very similarly to the four-element system, though the traditional order given, from the most sublime to the densest element, is usually fire, water, air, and earth, differing from other elemental models.

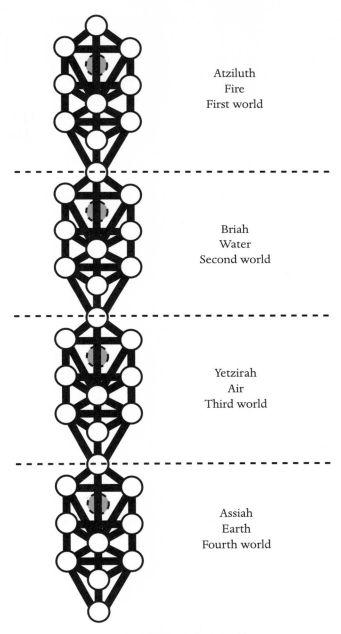

Atziluth
Fire
First world

Briah
Water
Second world

Yetzirah
Air
Third world

Assiah
Earth
Fourth world

Figure 29: Four Qabalistic Worlds

The ten-sphere tree exists in all four realms. A particular sphere's inherent nature can be more attuned to one of the four worlds. Malkuth is more aligned with the fourth world of manifestation, but can also be found in the other three worlds. Therefore, you can discuss the qualities of Malkuth in the first world, which would be slightly different from those in the second, third, or fourth world, but the fourth world would be closest to its traditional nature.

Many would argue about the "Rising on the Planes" meditation just given, stating that you cannot conceive of, or really experience, the upper spheres of the tree. But in this meditation, you are experiencing their lowest, fourth-world aspects, rather than their highest, most exalted states in the first world. Each of the spheres exists in all four worlds.

6

ENTITIES OF SPIRIT

The spiritual realms are not uninhabited. Our myths and mystic texts talk quite extensively about the natives in these realms. Like the models of reality, these spiritual beings vary from one magical model and culture to the next. A general term for these forms of life is spirits. Most mystical cultures recognize that consciousness goes beyond the physical realm, and mystics have learned to communicate with those spirits. Only in our modern scientific age have we doubted the possibility of consciousness without physicality. World religions recognize that consciousness survives after death, though there is much debate about what happens to the soul after death. Mystical lore tells us there are spirits that move beyond the human realm, including some that have never been human.

Nonphysical beings that take an interest in human affairs and aid in the spiritual development of individuals and communities are generally referred to as spirit guides. They have a higher perspective, and can often see things more clearly than we can, but their wisdom is not absolute. Different cultures have a variety of opinions as to what types of spirits become spirit guides, along with their forms, functions, powers, and motivations. The following are some types of entities you might encounter in your spiritual exploration.

Spirits

Ancestors

Ancestors are relatives who have passed from this world and guide us from the other side of the veil. Many cultures believe that ancestor reverence is vital for continued health and prosperity. Ancestors act as guides and intermediaries between the living and the higher powers. They guard us and grant us blessings. Some people consider only blood relatives to be ancestors, while others use a modern definition of ancestors and include those in their spiritual lineage, or those whose lives have greatly inspired them.

Masters

Masters, or ascended masters, refer to humans who have passed on from this world in a state of enlightenment. While on Earth, they are reputed to be advanced spiritual beings, mystics with abilities beyond the average person, yet they demonstrate the potential within us all. They remain connected to the earth plane to act as inner teachers and guides to humanity, and in this spiritual state they are available to help a multitude of people rather than be confined to only one physical location, as was the case when they were in body. The ascended masters are often thought of as saints in the West and bodhisattvas in the East. Many people relate them to the great scholars, religious leaders, and even Pagan demigods and deities. Sometimes they are called inner plane masters or inner plane adepts.

Power Animals

Tribal cultures believe that an animal spirit is associated with each person or tribe. That animal's traits and habits, its "medicine," help bring humans back into balance with nature. The animal spirit guides us, defends us from the spirits of sickness, and teaches us its abilities. Some people think your animal spirit, called your power animal or totem animal, is a part of your soul, while others believe your animal spirit to be a separate entity. You can work with more than one animal spirit at a time, though most traditions believe you have one primary animal that stays with you for a long time, if not a lifetime. Many traditions believe that all animals in a species come from one animal spirit, as if each species has an archetypal group soul. When you work with a crow totem animal, you are working with Crow, the same spirit all people who work with crow call upon. Other traditions believe that each animal totem is separate and distinct, and each practitioner has his or her own individual crow spirit. The animal's basic nature corresponds with your own inner nature, or the functions and lessons you are learning in this lifetime. Each animal holds an animal medicine, a teaching based on its natural character and qualities that helps bring us back into balance. These medicines are discovered by observing the animals, as well as looking at cultural folklore. The most common example would be Dog medicine, which reminds us of the virtue of loyalty. The wisdom of the zodiac, which means "wheel of animals," is found in shamanic animal medicine, even though our image of the zodiac is no longer based entirely upon animals.

Angels

Angels are an order of spiritual beings that has many different subdivisions. They are found in various cultures and sometimes have animal associations, particularly in the ancient traditions of the Middle East. In Tibetan lore, they are sometimes referred to as the Dakini. Various Jewish and Christian texts divide the angels into different choirs, or hierarchies, such as angels, archangels, cherubs, and thrones. Different archangels and angelic orders are associated with the ten spheres of the Tree of Life. Though our popular image of an angel is of an androgynous figure in a gown with feathered wings, Judeo-Christian lore paints fearsome images of angels, with many wings, many eyes, or wheels of fire. Angels are messengers and oversee an aspect of creation for the divine. Guardian angels are protectors of individuals, while other angels may embody a variety of principles, from healing to war. The most popular among the angels are the archangels of the four quarters: Raphael, the healer for the east and the air element; Michael, the warrior for the south and the fire element; Gabriel, the messenger for the west and the water element; and Uriel, the gatekeeper for the north and the earth element. In ceremonial magic, the Holy Guardian Angel, or HGA, is not simply your protective angel, but your highest consciousness, your divine self, known as the Higher Self.

Faeries

There are many different definitions of faeries. Our popular image of faeries as small, winged creatures comes mainly from the Victorian era, but myths of faeries are found all over the world. The spelling "faery" is often used to differentiate them from the stereotypical images of pop culture. In myth, sometimes they are big, and sometimes they are small. Many faeries are beautiful, while others are frightening. They are all connected to the land and the old ways that honor the land. They are sometimes associated with the wild nature spirits of mythology, including satyrs, dryads, elves, brownies, and goblins. In many myths, the faeries have kingdoms beneath the hills, leading shamanic practitioners to believe that they are really underworld spirits. In magical hierarchies, faeries are thought of as earth or underworld angels, the mirror images of the angelic realm. They could be guardians of the land. New Age mythology identifies faeries with the devas of Vedic lore, and considers them the architects or overarching spirits of nature, different from the underworld spirits. Some think they are aspects of old Pagan gods who are no longer actively worshipped. Faeries are not small in stature, but our perception of them has diminished, so they seem small to us. They can be allies to those who honor the old ways, but not all faeries are automatically benign. They demand respect, and when they don't receive it, they can be tricksters, and sometimes even malicious. In Celtic traditions, they are often called the "good folk." Offerings of milk and honey are left for them to ensure healthy crops and a healthy family.

Elementals

Elementals are the spirits who embody the elements of earth, air, fire, and water. Traditional lore tells us the earth elementals appear as gnomes or dwarves, tiny men who dig in the earth. Air elementals appear as sylphs, thin, small beings with gossamer wings, like our Victorian image of faeries. Fire elements are reptilian, called fire salamanders or fire drakes. Water elements are undines, mermaids, and mermen. Elementals don't always appear in these forms. They can simply be balls of colored light, or take on the literal quality of the element—a humanoid shape made of earth, air, fire, or water. Elementals guide the four forces of creation used in magic and healing. Each elemental originates from a spiritual realm that corresponds with its nature. Fire elementals come from the elemental realm of fire, water elementals come from the elemental realm of water, and so on. Each realm has a spiritual hierarchy of life, lead by an elemental ruler, an elemental king or queen, guiding the elementals of that realm. Some people believe that the archangels of the four quarters—Raphael, Michael, Gabriel, and Uriel—guide the corresponding elemental rulers. The elementals answer our calls in ritual because they wish to learn more about using their element in the world for manifestation. As they help us by providing elemental energy for our rituals, we help them by giving them opportunities to learn. As they learn more, they can either ascend their own elemental hierarchy or seek to master all four elements before becoming another type of spirit. Some people think that once an elemental masters all the elements, it moves on and becomes an angel, nature spirit, dragon, faery, or even human soul.

Nature Spirits

Nature spirits is a catch-all phrase for the consciousness and energies of plants, trees, stones, and the land. Some people think that nature spirits and faeries are the same beings, while others feel they are separate and distinct. When I speak to the consciousness of a particular herb, such as yarrow, I know I am talking to Yarrow, and not to a faery. To me, the faery realm is something guiding the natural world, but is not incarnate in plants or trees.

Devas

The word deva comes from the Hindu culture and can be translated to gods or shining ones, often referring to the gods who govern over nature. Some people think of devas as faeries or nature spirits, while others think of them as angels. I learned that devas are like the angels of nature; they are the spirits that oversee creation, while nature spirits are the ones who actually do the constructing. A deva will hold the pattern, the architectural blueprint, of a type of plant, and will give that pattern to the nature spirits to grow into. A friend of mine described it to me using the analogy of a foreman and a construction crew. The deva of the plant yarrow holds the pattern for all yarrow plants, and guides their growth, but individual nature spirits fill the individual yarrow plants.

Gods

The gods are an interesting topic that causes a lot of controversy, depending on your mystic tradition. Originally, most cultures were polytheistic, believing in many gods. They saw that the divine has an abundant nature, with male and female aspects, and named all aspects of the divine. There became a goddess of the Earth, a goddess of the Moon, a god of the Sun, a god of writing, a god of travel, a goddess of love, and so on, until every aspect of nature, every location and every quality, had a divine ruler. Modern psychologists think of these divine aspects as archetypes. Many cultures had an Earth goddess, but each had a different name and story for her. Then polytheistic cultures lost control to monotheism, a belief in one god. Some monotheistic groups were simply cults devoted to one god of many gods, and they wished to wipe out the worship of all others. Other monotheistic groups sought to unify the nature of the divine, so practitioners could see they were all connected to one spirit. Such cultures often converted the Pagan gods to saints, heroes, and villains in the mythologies. Goddess worship was funneled into reverence of Mother Mary. The Irish goddess Brid, or Bridget, became St. Bridget. The horned gods Pan and

Cernunnos were fused with the Christian concept of the Devil. The modern revival of Paganism and other nature-based religions has created a revival of the old, pre-Christian images of the gods. They appear in meditations, dreams, and visions and can act as guides and healers to mystics. My personal philosophy is a combination of monotheism and polytheism. I think of the gods as aspects of the divine creative spirit. I call the creative spirit the Great Spirit, without gender, but personally work with aspects of the Great Spirit I can relate to, the gods and goddesses. Both realities exist for me. Such attitudes are prevalent in the Hindu forms of polytheism, which recognize many aspects of the divine one, as well as in Qabalistic concepts of the divine. One saying is that the gods are all shadows cast from the same flame of the one spirit.

Avatars

Avatars are physical incarnations of divine gods. They are aspects of the divine spirit manifested on the Earth. Usually found in Hindu mythology, a god would incarnate to become a teacher of humanity. The god Vishnu has had nine avatars of various forms, including the well-loved hero god Krishna. This tenth avatar has not yet appeared. Some would say that Jesus was an avatar of Yahweh. Others claim he is an ascended master who reached a level of enlightenment. Aradia, a semi-mythical figure of Italian Witchcraft, could be considered an avatar of the goddess Diana. Though many people may strongly embody a particular archetype in their lives, they are not necessarily avatars of that archetype or divinity. An avatar implies a certain level of spiritual mastery that one did not necessarily attain in this lifetime, like an enlightened master, but rather that one already possessed before coming into this lifetime.

Mythical Creatures

Mythical creatures are beings who show up in fairy tales, folklore, and mythology, though there is no physical evidence of them living on the earth plane. They include unicorns, dragons, griffons, basilisks, giants, elves, sirens, and sea serpents. Some mystics experience these creatures during meditation or shamanic journey, believing them to be living spiritual energies beyond the earth plane. Others feel their value is only symbolic and believe they are not living beings.

Devils and Demons

Devils, demons, and other malevolent entities are always difficult to explain. Most mystics believe that spirits are much like people, and while some mean to help and hold good intentions, there are also those that mean to harm. Such malevolent spirits can be warded away with protection rituals. Ignoring them or laughing at them are also great ways to banish them. They feed off of fear, and the more attention you give them, the stronger they seem. Some traditions believe demons are our own repressed traits, both personally and for the collective human consciousness. They represent our shadow side, and once confronted, they can no longer harm us. In the Tree of Life, the shadow sides of the ten sephiroth are called the Qlippoth, which means shells. The Qlippoth are not the antithesis of good, but rather represent the lack of the ten divine qualities. When you are faced with the lack of a divine quality, it is easy to see the emptiness as evil. For example, the divine principle of the sphere of Chesed is mercy. When you are faced with the Qlippoth and demonic forces of Chesed, they manifest with the qualities of no mercy and no compassion. The way to overcome that evil is to manifest the missing divine quality, compassion. In the end, such forces are really teachers. Many people blame their misfortunes on demons, devils, or other people around them, but if you keep these definitions in mind, you will find yourself more empowered to handle any situation. Acknowledge these malevolent entities, but do not give your power away to them. They simply represent our worst traits, just as angels are said to embody many of our best, while the gods have a balance of both. By acknowledging and owning your shadow side, the demonic world has no power over you.

Ghosts

Ghosts usually refer to the spirits of the deceased who have not passed over into the next world. They are bound to the physical plane through intense emotion, such as fear or anger, or feel they have left something undone. Such spirits are not necessarily evil, but they are no more enlightened now than they were when they were alive. In fact, since they are stuck, they are probably not the best spirits from whom to seek advice. Some ghosts are not conscious souls; they are just echoes of a person, a fragment of that person's energy left behind. Some ghosts are recordings. They are an event that is etched into the ethers of a particular location. Some places have a ghost that can be seen going up the same flight of stairs at the same time every day. Battlefields have "ghost battles" etched into their energy, but the souls of the soldiers are not necessarily trapped there. Intense feelings and energies can record themselves in the energy of a location, just as sound or information is recorded on a magnetic tape. Poltergeists are thought of as violent ghosts who have the ability to physically manipulate reality by throwing objects. According to most lore, poltergeists are not ghosts at all, but are the pent-up energies of a prepubescent or pubescent teen demonstrating unconscious telekinetic ability, or a disturbed nature/faery spirit unhappy with the disruption of its current environment.

As you may have noticed, all these spiritual entities do not have easy descriptions and definitions. Each tradition has its own view of them, its own truth. These traditions disagree or contain paradoxes. There is not one absolute viewpoint but a multitude of perspectives when you explore the inhabitants of the spiritual planes.

The spiritual models of the universe classify spirits by the "locations" where they reside in the spirit world. Each of the three worlds of the shaman has different inhabitants. Sky gods and angelic spirits live in the upper world; underworld gods, faeries, and demons are in the lower world; and nature spirits reside in the middle world. In the Tree of Life, each sphere has its associated archangel, angelic order, deities, and spirits, along with ritual correspondences, such as tarot cards, incense, and mantras to be chanted. These correspondences help you tap into the energy of the sphere, and allow you to connect with its inhabitants. Sometimes connecting to a particular level of consciousness involves journeying to its realm, or communicating with its associated spirits.

Spirit Talk

There are many ways to communicate with spirits, from the use of divination devices, such as pendulums and spirit boards, to the deeper trances of mediums and shamans, who act as bridges, in their own way, to the spirit world. No one way is correct, but practitioners of the various traditions have strong feelings about which is best.

Mediums perform a process called invocation, though few refer to it as such. When a person channels a spiritual entity, from a deceased human to an ascended master or angel, letting it speak through his or her body, he or she is performing an invocation. At the end of the nineteenth century and into the twentieth, séances involving speaking with the dead were quite popular, and they still are in their modern TV show form. Modern New Age invocations have made connecting with hidden masters and aliens a new venue for information.

Channelers differ in style with the type of channeling they perform, usually divided into conscious channeling and full-body, or trance, channeling. Practitioners of conscious channeling simply repeat back the message as they psychically "hear" it from the entity. They never "leave" their body and remain aware of all that transpires. The advantage is that they are in full control of the experience. The disadvantage is that their ego might tamper with the message, letting them hear only what they want to hear or what they fear, and not the true message.

Full-body channelers either submerge or dismiss their consciousness to the entity they are channeling, and the spirit entity controls the voice and movements of the channeler's body. When their consciousness returns, they typically have no recall of the session, and if any message was given for the channeler personally, others in the session must relay that message. The advantage of this type of channeling, according to some, is a purer message, because the ego is bypassed. Others believe that the ego of the channeler is anchored to the physical self, and is simply taken on by the entity. The message is still filtered through it. The disadvantage is that the channeler is not conscious and is giving over his or her body to an entity that doesn't have a body. Some feel that these spiritual entities will care for it greatly, and having such high spiritual vibrations in his or her body will aid the channeler's own enlightenment, while others feel that such energies are not meant to be in a body, and will burn out the channeler's energy system. They also worry that an entity without a pure and loving intent could do harm if allowed the opportunity to channel. In the end, intuition, discernment, clarity, and common sense are the watch words of channeling. The practice goes beyond the scope of this book and will be not listed as an exercise here. If you pursue this path, make sure you read up on the psychic self-defense techniques in part 4. You can also find more information on channeling in my book *Spirit Allies: Meet Your Team from the Other Side*.

Various magicians and Pagan priests and priestesses perform invocations, allowing the energy of a god or goddess to come through them during ritual. Even the ceremonies in the African diaspora religions, such as Voodoo, have spontaneous invocations that often occur as part of the ritual. The spirits involved, called loa or lwa, are said to "ride" the participants, offering messages and blessings and accepting offerings. Unlike most forms of invocation, such "mounts" can involve incredible feats of magic, such as holding burning coals or drinking copious amounts of rum without getting drunk or suffering alcohol poisoning.

Many people fear possession by spirits, but invocation differs from possession. Possession indicates involuntary interface with a spirit and is much rarer than most people think. Invocations involve some form of ritual, with a clear beginning, a purpose, and an ending that dismisses the spirit and grounds the practitioner back in the physical world.

The word evocation is often used synonymously with invocation, but technically they are two different practices. Evocation manifests a spirit outside the body, either in the physical world or on the psychic planes, where those who are sensitive enough to see them will know their presence and possibly communicate with them. The medieval magician's techniques for summoning spirits are forms of evocation. Traditionally medieval magicians would create a magic circle, drawn on the floor, and a magic triangle, also drawn on the floor outside of the circle, to separate themselves from the spirit they were evoking into the triangle. Calling upon elementals and watchtowers from a Pagan ritual circle is another form of evocation. Asking your guardian angel for protection is yet another form.

Evocation and invocation have one thing in common. In both practices, the practitioner asks the spirit to cross the veil and make its presence known in the material world. The last option you have in spirit work is to make the journey yourself to their realm to communicate with them. Or ideally you can meet them in an "in-between" space that will facilitate communication for you both. This is a more common undertaking for the shamanic practitioner. Though practitioners of some forms of shamanism also do invocation and evocation, most focus on the shamanic journey, altering consciousness and entering the realms of the spirits. Modern practitioners refer to this state of mind as Shamanic State of Consciousness, or SSC. Journeying also occurs for those who do dream work and those who favor guided meditations to the inner planes. Rising on the planes is another way of accessing the different realms of spirit. At each level, you can encounter different types of spirits. Magical knowledge of each sphere on the Tree of Life, or any other system used to move between worlds, lets you know where to go to find the appropriate spirits for your intention. Magical systems are like maps, allowing us to navigate the territory and avoid the potential harmful "dragons" at the edges.

EXERCISE
Speaking with Spirit Guides

Since the practice of invocation goes a bit further than the foundation we have built so far, and evocation through ritual magic will be touched upon in chapter 11, this exercise will focus on journeying, specifically a guided meditation to go to one of those in-between places where you can communicate comfortably with your spirit guide. If you have done the aura cleansing exercise in chapter 4, as well as the space cleansing exercise in chapter 2, then you will be fully protected from any unwanted or mischievous entities. When you are clear and centered, you have a better sense of personal boundaries and protection. If you have any apprehension about this exercise, or working with spirits, skip it until you have had a chance to review the specific and extended psychic self-defense material in part 4, which includes the Lesser Banishing Ritual of the Pentagram. In my experience, this ritual should be unnecessary, but if you have any concerns at all, make sure you have all the information you need to be comfortable.

Sit in a quiet place in a comfortable position. Take a few deep breaths, centering yourself and your awareness. Feel yourself relaxing from head to toe, getting into a deeper meditative state. Be aware of the four directions. Be aware of the space in front of you. Bring your attention to the space to your right. Be aware of the space behind you. Bring your attention to the space to your left. Now take a moment to focus on the space above you, then below you. Finally focus on the space you are in, the center. You are in the center of the crossroads, a sacred space where all roads meet.

Imagine that before you is a great staircase, perhaps carved in stone, crystal, metal, or even pure light. Take notice of the steps as you ascend it. At the top is a doorway, and around the edges of the door frame, streams of light and energy pour forth. This staircase leads to a temple of communication and guidance, a place where you can communicate with the spirit guides that are perfect for you, who are already in your life, even if you are not aware of them.

Open the door and enter into the light. You feel almost blinded by its dazzling colors. As you feel your awareness adjust to the light, within it you see one or more shapes, the shapes of your spirit guides. Moment by moment they become clearer in your consciousness. When they come into full clarity, speak with them. Introduce yourself and ask them their names. Ask the spirits to describe their purposes and functions in your life. What types of spirits are they? What work will you be doing together? Have a conversation with them, and listen with an open heart and mind. Allow whatever messages they have to come through. The messages might be auditory, visual, or acquired through simply a sense of knowing. If you can't understand them, ask them to communicate in a way you can understand. If possible, they will accommodate you. Ask them any questions you have. Spirits often give spiritual guidance, answers on the important issues in our lives, but they can be asked anything. Many of my guides have helped me with quite mundane problems related to home or business.

When done with your conversation, thank your guides. Ask them how you may communicate with them in the future. Affirm to yourself that you will remember all the details of your experience when you go back to the physical world.

Return the way you came, closing the doorway and heading back down the staircase. Acknowledge the directions around you again. Start with the space before you, then to your left, behind, right, above, below, and center. Center and ground yourself as you bring your awareness back to the physical world. Write down any messages you got, so you won't forget them. Information received in this state can be wispy and dreamlike, and easily lost in the light of the day.

7

SACRED SPACE, SACRED TIME

Mystical traditions from all over look at both place and time as important on the spiritual path. Each tradition has holy places, often marked by a temple, and holy days and times, when the community of practitioners comes together at these places. Sacred space and time play roles in our own personal development, but those of us in the modern world often neglect these two important factors.

Sacred Sites

As we explore the universe's subtle planes of reality, the intangible locations of the inner planes, we must acknowledge the sacred all around us. The natural world is filled with mystical energy. The physical world is the densest aspect of spirit. It is spiritual energy manifest, but it is still spirit. Mystics across time and space have found their truth by spending time in nature, be it the forests of Celtic seers such as Merlin, or the top of the mountain favored by Eastern yogis.

Though all matter, all land, is sacred, some places are considered more sacred than others. Particular rivers, mountains, and ancient temple sites are in alignment with both Earth energies and stellar energies, making them particularly powerful sites for meditation and ritual. Temples were created to align with the Sun, Moon, and stars at specific times of the year. The most popular ritual times are the summer and winter solstices. Rituals done on sacred sites and at sacred times align the participants with the flow of universal energies through the planet, creating more intense or powerful results.

Though we tend to associate sacred sites with ancient temples, such as the Egyptian pyramids, Stonehenge, or Central American Mayan ruins, sacred sites are all around us. You can find locations of powerful energy in the woods, near rivers, bogs, and mountains, and even in cities.

Such sites, both the well-known ancient temples and lesser-known local natural sites, are said to anchor vortexes of energy. Recently, the vortexes in Sedona, Arizona, have become a popular hotbed of New Age attention. They were always there, but only local mystics knew of them until the news made its way to others. Although travel to sacred sites is wonderful, first try finding the sacred in your own area.

Vortexes are spiraling fields of energy, like chakras of the Earth. Major vortexes are the major chakras of the Earth, and are considered to be the sacred sites of the ancient world. The smaller vortexes are the other minor chakra points. They are still part of the overall system and still powerful. Vortexes are intersections of the subtle planes of reality with the physical world, and feel like gateways to the inner planes. Some legends say the temples built on these sites lead to the other worlds.

Vortexes feel like they are moving. The energy is much subtler than most people think, and can fluctuate with the seasons and astrological alignments. When I felt my first vortex energy in Sedona, I thought, "This is it? What's the big deal?" The energy was subtle but powerful. Other people in my group were extremely sensitive to the vortex energy and became physically hot or cold, or strong emotions welled up in them. Since then, I've visited a number of sacred sites in the United States and England, and have found that other Earth vortexes feel different to me. Each site seems to have its own personality and characteristics.

Just as chakras are connected with lines of energy used in healing work, vortexes also are connected with lines of energy. In the modern world, these lines are often called ley lines. In the East, they are called dragon lines. Some European traditions call them faery lines or Witch lines, which may or may not be the same things as ley lines. I usually call them Earth energy lines. Though many people have attempted to map them and create definitive systems to categorize all the different types of Earth lines, no one system has become the standard. Those familiar with dowsing rods or divining rods can use these tools to find these energy lines.

EXERCISE

Dowsing

For this exercise, a pair of dowsing rods can be made from a metal wire coat hanger. If you can get the kind of coat hanger with the cardboard tube at the bottom, so much the better. Using a wire cutter, cut off the hook of the hanger. Then cut the longest end of the triangle in two, so you are left with two sides of the hanger.

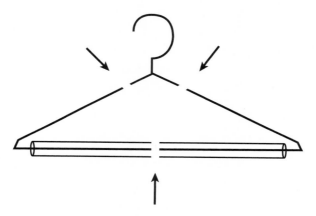

Figure 30: Cutting the Coat Hanger

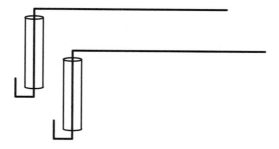

Figure 31: Dowsing Rod

For each piece, bend the remaining wire to form roughly a ninety-degree angle. Cut your cardboard tube in half, and put one half on the shorter end. If you hold the tube, the wire will rest on it, but will be able to move and rotate as it senses energy.

If it is too much trouble to make your own dowsing rods, you can purchase them at a metaphysical shop. Before using them, cleanse your dowsing rods with the space cleansing techniques found in chapter 2, to remove any unwanted energies. It is a good practice to cleanse spiritual tools before using them, to prevent other energies from interfering with your results.

To work with the dowsing rods, hold them by the tubes, roughly shoulder length apart, with the wires parallel to each other. The wires will move when reacting to an energy field. If you hold the dowsing rods and walk toward someone, the rods will swing open as you approach the person's energy field, or aura.

My first experience with dowsing rods was in a class exploring the human energy field. Holding our dowsing rods, we determined that our target person's energy field was a bit further than arm's length. Next, the teacher wanted to demonstrate how quartz amplifies energy. She instructed those of us with dowsing rods to back up, and had our target person hold a large quartz-crystal cluster. As we walked toward the target, our rods swung open at least three times further away than they had done before.

In another workshop, I learned how to dowse for Earth energy lines. By moving slowly from side to side, rather than forward, holding the dowsing rods, the wires will cross whenever they come into contact with an energy line. By walking in a grid pattern over an area of land, you can map out the energy lines. I was surprised to find these lines everywhere, even in my backyard. The lines near sacred sites, such as the site called America's Stonehenge in New Hampshire, produce bigger and more tangible lines, but I have found lines in many different sites, even one going through an old neighborhood church.

The results of this technique are amazingly consistent, though not always foolproof. If you walk under a power line, or get too close to a generator or underground wire, the wires also will cross. Dowsing rods pick up all sorts of energy, and are often used to find underground water, since the water's flow creates an energetic current. I have found that applying other spiritual tools to this technique improves accuracy. After I cleanse the rods, I ask for the help of my spirit guides, and ask to find only what I am looking to find, which are usually Earth energy lines; but I could change my intention when communing with my spirit guides in a quiet moment of meditation, and ask them to work with the dowsing rods to find water, or anything else that I desire. Using intention and spiritual guidance with your dowsing rods seems to filter out unwanted readings, such as those generated by humanmade energy fields and underground water.

Feng Shui

Feng shui is a Chinese art and science concerned with the flow of energy shaping the land. The ancient Chinese saw the sacred in everything, outdoors and indoors, and sought to promote healthy relationships with all things by exploring these principles of balance in all areas of life, from the construction of tombs to the arrangement of towns and cities. Feng shui has erroneously been referred to as geomancy, using the term to refer to working with Earth energies, but technically geomancy is divination, foretelling the future, through interpreting lines and markings made upon the earth.

Feng shui (pronounced "fung shway") is a relatively new term for this long-standing tradition. It literally translates to "wind and water," referring to the energies that subtly and not so subtly flow through the landscape, much like the invisible movement of wind and the ungraspable flow of water, which can only be directed, harnessed, or blocked. This living, vital force is referred to as chi. Feng shui is the tradition of working with these forces to remove obstacles and misfortunes and enhance health, wealth, and happiness. The original Chinese characters for this art were Ham and Yu. Ham basically means to receive the heavens, while Yu is the connective force from the Earth to the heavens; thus feng shui is really the connection of the heavens and the Earth. Overly simplified and diluted by many practitioners, particularly those in the West, feng shui is part of a complex system of esoteric knowledge, including Chinese astrology, numerology, medicine, and mystical philosophy.

Originally, feng shui was concerned with the geographic evaluation of the land, rooted in the Chinese landscape and weather patterns of the time. This type of feng shui is known as the Form School, and since its inception, many other traditions of feng shui have been developed. Once the compass was invented, feng shui became much more personal and developed into systems of home placement, creating the Compass School. The Black Hat sect of feng shui, started in the 1960s, has been one of the most popular forms in the New Age movement.

Feng shui encourages the accumulation of chi, of flowing energy, but is greatly concerned with the quality of the energy. The chi, like blood, must keep flowing to effectively bring blessings into our lives. Slow-moving water or air encourages a "good" chi, while fast-moving water or wind dissipates it. Stagnant water might have chi, but it's not necessarily "good." Disharmonious shapes, harsh corners, sharp angles, and clutter can interrupt the flow of healthy chi. Harmonious shapes encourage its healthy flow. You don't want the chi to flow too fast, which can be the result in corridors and with doors opposite each other. Careful placement of household objects, as well as plants, flutes, mirrors, and crystals, is used to slow the chi and encourage a harmonious flow of energy. The placement of the house in relationship to the land affects how energy, chi, flows in and out of the dwelling. Objects in the household are arranged to facilitate an optimum flow of this energy. The occupant's own energy can also affect the arrangement of objects in the building. Practitioners use information based on the birth date of the owner or occupant to aid them in determining the optimum arrangement. Ideally, a home would be built with these considerations in mind, but now we use feng shui to correct any problems inherent in the home and to promote harmonious chi flow.

Feng shui is concerned not only with pure chi, but also with the balance of yin and yang energies. Yin energy is often equated with feminine and receptive forces, and yang with masculine and projective forces. An appropriate balance of each, for the home or individual, is needed. The balance of the elements, as described in Chinese five-element theory, is also a concern.

Most systems of feng shui work with the eight trigrams of the I Ching, arranged around an octagon called a pa kua, to determine the area of influence for each part of the building (figure 32). The pa kua is laid over the floor plan of the home or office. It can also be placed over a single room, or even used as the method of laying out your desk.

Wealth	Home	Love
Family & Health		Creativity
Knowledge	Career	Friends & Mentors

Figure 32: Pa Kua Modern Nine-Square Image

Figure 33: Pa Kua Traditional Octagon

When working with a building or room, the front door is aligned with the side of the pa kua that has Knowledge, Career, and Friends & Mentors. Many believe the front door is the entrance you use most often. If you have a traditional front door that you never use, then align the pa kua with the door that you do use. That is where the chi is flowing.

Another method, known as the Eight Trigrams method, or Nine Stars method, aligns the pa kua to the compass directions (figure 33). Both systems work. The state of harmony or disarray, and the flow of chi in a particular section, will affect the corresponding area of life. Many in the West encourage the use of "intuitive" feng shui, either using your own intuition to feel the flow of energy that is best for you and your home, or using other mandala systems to help balance and align your environment.

Some critics of feng shui say that its principles are based on China's climate, weather patterns, and culture, and do not meld well with those in the Western world, but the principles of harmony, flow, and health resonate with every culture. If you find sound advice that works for you through feng shui, intuition, or any other system, then by all means use it.

Sacred Timekeeping

Not only are places sacred, but all time is sacred as well. Mystics have been the keepers of the calendars. Sometimes mystics follow cycles of the Earth and Sun, the visible patterns of the seasons that are obvious to all. Other times we follow the paths of the stars and the Moon. Systems of numerology and astrology are applied to calendar dates. There is a true art and science to timekeeping.

Timing is incredibly important in mysticism. Each day contains a variety of energies. Certain days are auspicious for certain actions, and other days provide challenges. We all have sacred cycles, sacred patterns within us that mimic the rhythms of the world around us. The inner world and outer world are synchronized. In ancient days, the priests and priestesses would be consulted before beginning a project, to start with the best possible energy to ensure success. They could predict times of challenge in a person's life and give advice as to how to handle the challenges.

Cycles and seasons are marked by celebrations and rituals led by priestesses or priests. Most of our modern holidays relate to seasonal celebrations, though they have been disguised by many traditions and levels of meaning. By recognizing the rhythms of the world, and synchronizing yourself to them through ritual, you bring yourself greater awareness, balance, and health on all levels.

The Wheel of the Year

One of my favorite sacred calendars is the Wheel of the Year, which is a modern adaptation of the ancient solar and agricultural holidays found in Pagan cultures. The holidays were celebrated differently all over the world, but modern Pagan traditions brought them together in a cohesive form. Although they are usually described in terms of northern European mythology, the individual holidays were celebrated in many different cultures. Through looking at the Wheel, one sees the interaction of the Goddess and God energies, as the land, sun, vegetation, and decay.

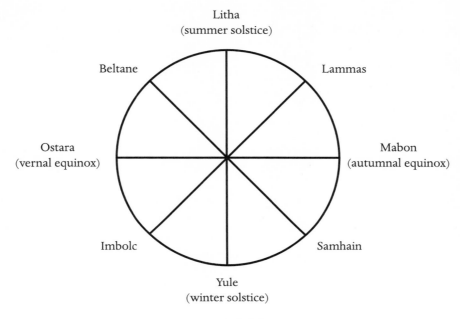

Figure 34: Wheel of the Year

The Wheel of the Year consists of eight holidays that mark the changes of the seasons and humanity's interaction with them. Four holidays are solar in nature, the two equinoxes and two solstices. Though many believe these solar days to be the holy days of the ancient Celts, they probably played a more significant role for the Teutonic tribes. The Celtic high festivals were four agricultural holidays, called fire festivals, held between the solar holidays.

The following is a basic description of the Wheel of the Year. Keep in mind that different cultures and different modern traditions celebrate differently, so many variations exist. The imagery is biased toward those in the Northern Hemisphere, since the traditions of modern Paganism arose in the Northern Hemisphere. Pagans in the Southern Hemisphere have opposite seasons, and often celebrate festivals at opposite times of the year as Pagans in the North. Others feel the astrological correspondences are most important, and the earthly season is less important. For example, Samhain, the feast of the dead, is celebrated in October, when the Sun is in Scorpio, the sign of death and regeneration, regardless of the season being fall or spring.

Samhain: October 31

Samhain, usually pronounced "Sow-wen," is traditionally the Celtic new year and a celebration of the ancestors. Celebrated on October 31 or November 1 of the modern calendar, Samhain is the basis of modern Halloween traditions, with a Christian lens distorting the Pagan traditions. Due to the change of season—as all things wither in the fall, and the life energy withdraws to the underworld—the veil between the land of the living and the land of the dead is said to be thinnest at this time. The God and Goddess of life are said to retire to the underworld for rejuvenation. Many traditions have the lord of the hunt, the horned god or the underworld god, ruling the land until the God of life returns. Samhain is a time to make offerings to our ancestors by leaving out their favorite food and drink and setting up ancestor altars. It is also an excellent time for divination and scrying, to ask questions about the future year, as our psychic abilities are at their peak and the loving ancestors can give us clear guidance.

Yule: Winter Solstice, near December 21

Celebrated on the winter solstice, this holiday is a celebration of the rebirth of the God as the child of the Sun. From this point on, the Sun will grow in power, giving us longer days and shorter nights, until the summer solstice, when the process will be reversed. The custom of celebrating the birth of the God at this time was so prevalent in the ancient world that the early Christian church changed the birthday celebration of Jesus Christ to December 25, to more closely fit the Pagan traditions. The birthday of the god Mithras is also celebrated on December 25 by those in his Roman mystery tradition. Many of our traditional Christmas customs, such as evergreen trees, holly, mistletoe, and Yule logs, are actually Pagan practices.

Imbolc: February 2

Known in the Christian world as the celebration of Candlemas, Imbolc is the Pagan celebration of the lights, held in honor of the fire goddess Brid (pronounced Breed or Bride), who was later transformed to Bridget and then St. Bridget. Her priestesses became the nuns of St. Bridget. Candles are lit to awaken the Goddess in the underworld, so she may rise and bring the spring at the next holiday. Imbolc refers to "ewe's milk" and is marked by the lactation of the herd. It is a time of nourishment for the young child God, who is growing up as the rising Sun.

Ostara: Vernal Equinox, near March 21

At this time, the great Goddess rises from the underworld, bringing the spring. The land is resurrected with the rise of greenery and early flowers. Ostara is named after the Teutonic goddess Ostre, the goddess of eggs and seeds. Seeds are blessed and planted. Eggs are decorated and left as offerings and magical talismans of fertility for the coming year. Many of the symbols of Ostara, most importantly the theme of resurrection at this time of year, were coopted into the Christian celebration of Easter.

Beltane: May 1

Beltane is the Celtic celebration of spring and the growing season. The God is seen as the growing green, a young and virile man, while the Goddess is the flower maiden. They join together at this time to ensure the fertility of the land. Traditionally, bales of hay and sacred woods were lit on fire, and the herds were driven between two of these fires, for purification from the last traces of winter illness. Modern Pagans translate Beltane to mean "the fires of Bel," Bel being the Celtic fire or solar deity. Dancers weave ribbons around the pole, a symbol of union between the God and Goddess, in celebration of fertility. These practices were adopted into the festival of May Day, a vestige of the Pagan Beltane, though many traditional Christians might be surprised at what the Maypole represents.

Litha: Summer Solstice, near June 21

Litha is the modern name for the celebration of Midsummer, the peak of the Sun's power. The divine couple are queen and king of the land, preparing for the royal bounty of the harvest. From this point forward, the energy of the God begins to wane. Some traditions believe he fights his shadow and loses to his dark side. Others associate this day of longest twilight with the faery folk, believing the door to their realm to be open. Solar magic is worked on this day, to store up on the healing energy of the Sun to survive during the darker months of winter.

Lammas: August 1

Lammas, known as Lughnassadh in the Irish Celtic traditions, is the first harvest, the grain harvest. On this day, the first grains are cut and a celebration is had. In modern Wheel celebrations, the cutting of the grain symbolizes the death of the grain and solar God. The world will be ruled by his shadow, the dark underworld God, for half the year. Like an old-world funeral, feasts and games are held to celebrate his life. The theme is also taken from Lughnassadh, which translates to "the funeral feast of Lugh." Lugh is the Irish Celtic god of many skills, equated with the solar and grain figures, and leader of the tribe of gods known as the Tuatha de Danaan, the Children of Danu. The funeral feast in traditional myth, however, refers to his mother and not to Lugh himself. Modern Pagans still celebrate this time with ritual, games of skill, and feasting.

Mabon: Autumnal Equinox, near September 21

Mabon is the second harvest, the fruit harvest, followed by Samhain's third and final "harvest," the meat harvest. At this time, the fruits are collected and made into intoxicating beverages. Intoxication is one of the Pagan methods of opening the gates between the worlds. On Mabon, the gates are said to be swinging open. As the spirit of the light God descends to the underworld, to be reborn, all vegetation soon follows him, bringing the fall season. The Goddess mourns her lover, and begins her descent into the underworld. Mabon is named after the Celtic god Mabon, who as a child was lost in the underworld until later rescued, being reborn in the world. Rituals of trance and journey are common on this day.

Astrology

Astrology is another pattern of sacred timekeeping. It is the study of the skies to understand the patterns of energy in our lives. At the moment of your birth, the sky symbolically contains the patterns—the lessons, abilities, and challenges—that you will face. My astrology teacher, Jan Brink, describes it as the curriculum your soul chooses to learn in this lifetime. When an astrologer creates a chart of this moment, it is called your natal chart, or birth chart. By studying the current patterns in the sky in relationship to your birth chart, a talented astrologer can predict how various energies will affect you and can advise you in handling challenges.

In astrology, particularly magical forms of astrology, various times are "ruled," or influenced, by different planets and signs. The ancients worked with the seven planets that were known at the time, and the seven days of the week were named after them. Some of our modern names are derivatives of the names of Norse gods, the closest archetypal equivalents of their planetary Roman counterparts.

Day	Mythic Name	Planet	Colors	Energies
Sunday	Sun's day	Sun	Yellow	Energy, health, vitality
Monday	Moon's day	Moon	Silver	Emotion, psychic, family
Tuesday	Tyr's day	Mars	Red	Power, force, action, protection
Wednesday	Wotan's day	Mercury	Orange	Communication, mind, travel
Thursday	Thor's day	Jupiter	Blue, violet	Expansion, prosperity, spirituality
Friday	Freya's day	Venus	Green	Love, romance, attraction
Saturday	Saturn's day	Saturn	Black	Contraction, protection, karma

Chart 3: Planetary Days

Each day is influenced by the ruling planet's energy. This sevenfold pattern is found in many ways, from the days of the week and the planets to the chakras and the subtle bodies. Some people relate each day and planet to a "ray" of light, an aspect of the divine shining upon humanity, with various spirits, powers, angels, and even forms of yoga and exercise corresponding to the ray and the day. Friday's ray, for example, is the green ray, dealing with love and matters of the heart. Unfortunately, some systems of rays do not always correspond with the classic color associations of the planets. Very few people in the New Age world talk about working with the "black" ray, yet black is the color of Saturn.

More detailed systems of astrological timing will calculate a planet's influence on each hour of the day. For example, you can be in the day of Venus, the day of love, romance, and relationship, but be in the hour of Mercury, the hour of communication. This would be an auspicious time to speak with your partner about your relationship. Calculation of planetary hours goes beyond the range of this work, but you can find out more about them in any book detailing magical timing, including my book *The Outer Temple of Witchcraft*.

Other aspects of astrology are based on the zodiac signs. We have already discussed the signs in relationship to the four elements (fire, earth, air, water) and the three qualities (cardinal, fixed, mutable). Each sign is also considered masculine or feminine, in alternating order. As a planet passes through the signs, it takes on the qualities of each sign. The planets are like actors, and the signs are the roles they take on and play out. The signs are like colored filters over a light. They change the quality of the light and how it interacts with us. The same light can pass through twelve different filters, and take on twelve different qualities.

Aries ♈

Symbol: The ram
Gender: Male
Triplicity: Cardinal
Element: Fire
Ruling planet: Mars
Color: Red
Part of the body: Face

Aries is the cardinal fire sign, starting the zodiac wheel. The process of Aries is beginning. Aries is the sign of the leader, the one who must charge forward to explore new territory. All fires signs are about identity, exploring your will and desire. Aries is the quest for identity through action, learning to overcome fear through action. Its classic statement is "I am," but it could equally be phrased as the question "Who am I?" The part of the body associated with Aries is the face, because it is the biggest outward sign of identity. The drawbacks to such leadership qualities include being too headstrong, dominant, or aggressive, or acting before you know where you are going or have all the facts.

Taurus ♉

Symbol: The bull
Gender: Female
Triplicity: Fixed
Element: Earth
Ruling planet: Venus
Colors: Green, red-orange
Part of the body: Throat

Taurus is the sign of the bull, fixed earth. Taurus is the fertility of the Earth itself, and its ability to give us the things we need and want. Taurean qualities include a desire for comfort, often in the form of material luxuries, food, music, and art. Pleasing the senses appears to be a hallmark of Taurean energy, but the true spiritual quest is for security. Taurus's key statement is "I have." Some Taureans seek security in material comforts, and others in financial strength. They take refuge in their talents that bring material comfort, including artistic talents such as singing, for the throat is the part of the body associated with Taurus. Other negative qualities of Taurean energy are materialism and stubbornness, as well as difficulty taking risks, breaking routines, or being spontaneous. Ultimately, the quest of Taurus leads to finding security in oneself, not the material world.

Gemini ♊

Symbol: The twins
Gender: Male
Triplicity: Mutable
Element: Air
Ruling planet: Mercury
Colors: Orange, blue, multicolored patterns
Parts of the body: Hands

Gemini is the first sign of communication, and focuses on communication with those closest to us, including self-communication. The talk of the twins, often mistakenly seen as a quality of multipersonality or schizophrenia in the nonastrologically versed student, is really about the internal dialogue in each of us. When we are multitasking by saying one thing but thinking about something else, we are using the power of Gemini. Gemini qualities include skills in speech and writing, but the challenge is to speak deeply, truly, and in a focused manner. The key phrase of Gemini is "I communicate." The hands are associated with the sign of the twins, both because they are mirror images of each other and because they can be used to communicate information, creating an animated or social exchange, another hallmark of the sign. Gemini's virtue of doing many things at once can also be its downfall, scattering its energy until nothing is done.

Cancer ♋

Symbol: The crab
Gender: Female
Triplicity: Cardinal
Element: Water
Ruling planet: Moon
Colors: Silver, yellow, lavender
Parts of the body: Stomach, breasts

Cancer is the sign of the Great Mother, rising from the primordial ocean and protective, like the shell of the crab. The shell is indicative of the emotional boundaries those with strong Cancer energy must learn to develop for self-defense. The key phrase being "I feel,"

Cancer energy is the most empathic, bordering on psychic, as such intuition is the realm of water. The mothering instinct of Cancer naturally makes these people great caregivers and nurturers. The parts of the body associated with this sign are the stomach, the watery container that gives us all nourishment, and in women, the breasts, which provide sustenance to offspring. Although the qualities of love, caring, and support are strong, the downsides of Cancer include being overly sensitive, defensive, or emotionally unavailable when things get overwhelming. One of the great lessons of Cancer is learning how to nurture and mother yourself.

Leo ♌

Symbol: The lion
Gender: Male
Triplicity: Fixed
Element: Fire
Ruling planet: Sun
Colors: Gold, yellow
Part of the body: Heart

The symbol of Leo is the golden lion, a symbol of nobility and pride. The lion leads like the archetypal king of the jungle, recognized for his abilities and gifts. This outward recognition and the search for recognition, or identity, through others are key aspects of the spiritual lessons of Leo. Those with strong Leo energy are stereotypically said to be entertainers and performers, those with "look at me" professions, but anybody who seeks recognition is working with Leo lessons. Many astrologers cite the phrase "I perform" as the key mantra to understanding this sign. Leos play a central role, a vital role, in the lives of those around them, as symbolized by this sign's body part, the heart. The heart is in the center, and without it, the other organs could not function. Leo's strengths are qualities of leadership and charisma, as well as formation of a healthy ego, while the drawbacks include the pitfalls of ego, arrogance, and being overly sensitive to criticism.

Virgo ♍

Symbol: The harvest
Gender: Female
Triplicity: Mutable
Element: Earth
Ruling planet: Mercury
Colors: Brown, green
Parts of the body: Intestines

Virgo's symbol is one of the most misunderstood. Often called the virgin, a more accurate title would be the corn maiden, associating her with an aspect of the fertility and underworld goddess Persephone. Virgo's true symbol is the harvest, the grains and corn produced when the Sun is in this sign. Virgo applies the mental process of Mercury to the physical world, because it is an earth sign. Separating the wheat from the chaff gives us an understanding of the process, analyzing and discerning what is nutritional, or helpful, and what is not. The parts of the body associated with Virgo are the intestines, which separate food from waste. The key statement of Virgo is "I analyze," though the downside of Virgo energy is to make the process too personal, creating perfectionist or anal-retentive tendencies. The virtue of Virgo is the ability to separate and analyze all the components of a situation to make the most informed choices.

Libra ♎

Symbol: The scales
Gender: Male
Triplicity: Cardinal
Element: Air
Ruling planet: Venus
Colors: Pastels, gray, green
Parts of the body: Kidneys

Libra is the sign of the scales, the sign of balance. Being a cardinal air sign, the process of Libra is learning to find a balance in relationships—your own needs versus another person's needs. This symbol shows that it takes both sides to bring balance to a situation. Often one side takes responsibility for both, creating further imbalance. The ruler of Libra, Venus, indicates that such balances fall in the romantic and personal spheres as well. Libra's key phrase is "I balance," and it is represented in the body by the two kidneys. Venus also lends a sense of artistic sensibility to this sign, while the scale symbol naturally implies a link to justice and fairness. Librans have a hard time making decisions, because they can easily see the merits and flaws of both sides, but once they make a choice, they usually hold firm to their decision.

Scorpio ♏

Symbol: The scorpion
Gender: Female
Triplicity: Fixed

Element: Water
Ruling planets: Pluto
Colors: Scarlet, black
Parts of the body: Reproductive and eliminative systems

This fixed water sign is one of the most misunderstood signs of the zodiac, and often gets a bad rap. Scorpio represents a range of qualities involving the mysteries of life—sex, death, and transformation. This sign involves areas of life where we often have no conscious control, and although intense desire is a hallmark of Scorpio, one often must surrender personal desires to a higher will. In its lower form, this sign is expressed as the scorpion. It may seem strange to have a desert creature as the symbol of a water sign, but to me, it's always been the poison in the tail that is Scorpio. Poisons can be deadly or, in small doses, cures. That is the double-edged power of Scorpio. Another lower form is the snake, which sheds its skin to transform. Scorpio's key statement is "I transform," as it transforms from lower forms to higher forms. It is the process of surrendering the ego will to the higher will. The higher images of Scorpio are more spiritual, being the eagle or phoenix. Qualities associated with Scorpio include the desire to penetrate mystery by understanding and investigating, often with an interest in the paranormal or psychic, while remaining intensely private. The parts of the body associated with this sign are the reproductive and eliminative systems—sex and death. Scorpio energy is stereotypically seen as stinging, because the truths it expresses on both the higher and lower levels can be sharp. Scorpios can express a strong sexual current or magnetic charm.

Sagittarius ♐

Symbol: The archer
Gender: Male
Triplicity: Mutable
Element: Fire
Ruling planet: Jupiter
Colors: Blue, purple
Parts of the body: Thighs

The archetype of Sagittarius is the seeker. The sign of the archer, centaur, or horse is the explorer or traveler. Sometimes its energy is expressed in physical exploration and travel, learning directly from other people and other cultures and lands. Other times it is the power of intellectual and philosophical travel, being the sign of higher education. Sagittarius will often take on the role of spiritual understanding and exploration. Its key phrase is "I understand," and its body parts are the thighs, helping these natives travel from place to place. Those with strong Sagittarian energy are athletes in the physical realm, or visionary managers and publishers, facilitating other people's explorations in the mental realms. Qualities associated with this sign include the desire for freedom, expressed on many levels, as well as joy, excitement, and optimism. The search for freedom can give some Sagittarians a reputation for being unable to commit or be dependable. For Sagittarius, what matters most is the quest, the journey, not the goal or outcome.

Capricorn ♑

Symbol: The sea goat
Gender: Female
Triplicity: Cardinal
Element: Earth
Ruling planet: Saturn
Colors: Black, magenta
Parts of the body: Skeletal system

The symbol of Capricorn, the sea goat, is the odd mythical animal with the hindquarters of a fish and the front of a mountain goat. Many modern astrologers use the image of the mountain goat, or even the mountain, exclusively, as Capricorn is a cardinal earth sign, reaching for the heavens. Climbing higher—in power, stature, view, or community standing—is a pattern of Capricorn. The lessons of Capricorn include the use of ever increasing power, and learning that with such power comes responsibility. "I use" is the phrase of this sign. The knees, shins, calves, and in fact the entire skeletal system are ruled by Capricorn, giving the body the structure it needs to stand tall. At times, Capricorn can seem overburdened by responsibility and too set in structure and rules, without the ability to be flexible. The challenge is to temper responsible use of power with an understanding of each situation, and to strive to reach the highest outcome.

Aquarius ♒

Symbol: The water bearer
Gender: Male
Triplicity: Fixed
Element: Air
Ruling planet: Uranus (formerly Saturn)

Colors: Dazzling blue, white
Parts of the body: Ankles

The water bearer, like many of the non-animal signs of the zodiac, is often misrepresented. One would assume that Aquarius, being a water bearer and having the word aqua in its name, would be a water sign. However, Aquarius is an air sign. It is the bearer, not the water itself. The bearer is a human being, and humans are capable of thought and speech, aspects of the mind. The waves it bears are likened to the waves of electricity, of communication systems, connecting us all invisibly. Aquarian ideas are of community, equality, brotherhood/sisterhood, and social service. Aquarius is also about being an individual, your unique self contributing to the whole. The downsides of Aquarius energy include being unique bordering on eccentric, and producing innovations that no one can understand or appreciate. Aquarius's key phrase is "I am aware" or "I know," and its body parts are the ankles.

Pisces ♓

Symbol: The twin fish
Gender: Female
Triplicity: Mutable
Element: Water
Ruling planet: Neptune (formerly Jupiter)
Colors: Sea green, sea blue, violet
Parts of the body: Feet

The twin fish, one swimming toward the heavens and the other toward Earth, are the symbol of Pisces. Seemingly incompatible, the fish represent the struggle between the ideal and the actual. Pisces qualities are idealistic, romantic, and inspirational. When reaching for the highest ideals, Pisces is the mystic, the healer, and the artist, sent to inspire all with visionary qualities. The key phrase of Pisces is "I believe" or even "I merge," to symbolize both the spiritual power of faith and the ultimate goal of merging with the one divine nature. The feet—of the traveler, the ecstatic dancer, the journeying into the mystical realms—are its body parts. Unfortunately, these visions sometimes fall short of the reality, creating a sense of disillusionment and despair. The lower qualities of Pisces include a desire to escape. Forms of escape may include addictions, from the traditional addictions of drugs and alcohol, substances that can give quick glimpses into the visionary world, to excessive television or music, ways of shunning the outside world. Those with strong

Pisces energy are often very sensitive to the feelings of others and must learn to strive for their ideals while still living in the imperfect material world.

Many people resonate with the gemstones associated with their birth Sun sign. Unfortunately, this system has gone through many transitions, as different cultures associated different gems with each sign, often based on what was available to them at the time and place. The system was later adapted to birthstone months, but is truly founded in zodiac signs, not humanmade calendar months. Here is the system that I use for the zodiac gems, based on magical associations, colors, the gem's properties, and a mix of precious and semiprecious stones.

Aries: Ruby, garnet, diamond
Taurus: Emerald, rose quartz
Gemini: Agate, carnelian
Cancer: Moonstone, pearl, beryl
Leo: Citrine, topaz, diamond, amber
Virgo: Agate, sapphire
Libra: Peridot, jade
Scorpio: Diamond, obsidian, jet
Sagittarius: Sapphire, lapis, turquoise
Capricorn: Onyx, garnet, jet
Aquarius: Opal, aquamarine
Pisces: Amethyst, aquamarine

Chart 4: Gemstones of the Zodiac

Most important for day-to-day living, and the most easily noticed, are the changes of the Sun and Moon. The Moon travels through all twelve signs in under a month. Since the Moon is the planet of emotion, you may find particular signs emotionally difficult or emotionally empowering.

The Sun passes through the same twelve signs, but does so in a year's time. The Sun is less volatile and changeable than the Moon, but its energy directly influences us. The Wheel of the Year is influenced by Sun signs. The Sun changes signs on the solar holidays, moving from a mutable sign, which ends a season, to a cardinal sign, which initiates a new season. The Sun is in the middle of a fixed sign on the fire festivals.

By journaling, and using an astrological calendar, we can look for our own personal patterns and discover that the Sun or Moon in particular signs can have a strong effect on us.

Astrology readings are based on the generation of an astrological chart. The most popular reading is an interpretation of the natal chart, the chart of the sky when and where you were born. The art and science of astrology is based on the belief that the moment of your birth contains the lessons and qualities you will be working with in this lifetime. You can also glean valuable information by comparing your natal chart with another person's chart, to show the compatibilities and challenges between you and that person in relationship—including romantic, family, personal, and business areas of life. You can compare your natal chart to the current position of the planets, and see how the current forces are influencing you. Such comparisons are called transit charts. With this knowledge, you can gain a greater understanding of the forces at play and the potential spiritual lessons, challenges, and boons available to you at any time.

Interpretation of an astrology chart focuses on the planets, and what roles they are playing, as well as where they are playing them. The sky is divided into twelve sections, called houses. The houses are the areas in life where the planets play out their roles. Although there are many ways to calculate the houses, called house systems, the houses remain in relatively fixed positions in the sky. Six houses are above the horizon, and the other six are unseen, below the horizon. The first house is always on the eastern horizon. The planets and signs rotate through the houses, making each moment a slightly different alignment of planets and signs. On its daily journey, it takes the Sun roughly two hours to move through each house. Each house has a "natural" ruler, a sign that resonates with the energy of the house. For example, Aries is the sign of personal discovery, having qualities of leadership and drive. The first house is the house of self-identity. It's where you learn about yourself. But if Taurus is ruling the first house of your natal chart, your relationship with yourself will have Taurean qualities. Houses indicate "where" things occur, both in your life and in your psyche. Signs describe how things occur in the houses. They represent the process that guides the house.

The location of a planet in a sign or house can indicate characteristics of an individual, but most importantly it represents places in life where the individual invests a lot of energy, and has learning to do. "Empty" houses represent places where less energy is invested, and thus where less learning occurs.

First House: House of Self-Identity

In the first house you learn to relate to yourself and know the true you. The cusp, or edge, of the first house, the eastern horizon, is called your Ascendant. The sign of your Ascendant is also known as your rising sign, and can be the sign that influences how others view you, the mask you wear in the world. The Ascendant plays an even more significant role in how people perceive you if you were born at night, as your natal Sun is on the dark side of

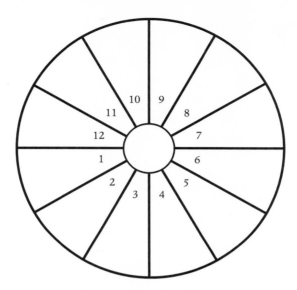

Figure 35: Twelve Houses

the planet. If you were born during the day, your Sun sign energies are more noticeable to people. If you were born at night, your Ascendant energies are more noticeable.

Second House: House of Resources

In the second house you work with material resources, and the skills, talents, and gifts that help you amass resources in the world. The second house influences the body, because your body is the first resource you have in this world, and it is through the skills you develop in your body that you earn your way in the world and gain other resources and valuables.

Third House: House of Communication

The third house involves learning to communicate in your day-today life to the people around you. It indicates how we think and how we learn. Relationships with siblings are also influenced by this house.

Fourth House: House of Family

In this house you develop your relationship with your formative family, as well as the family you create later in life, based on your childhood experiences. The fourth house is usually associated with the mother, but truly is associated with the primary caregiver or nurturer. The cusp of the fourth house is often referred to as the Nadir.

Fifth House: House of Children and Lovers

This is the house of ego, where you are most sensitive to others, especially your children and lovers. Here you learn about your identity in relationship to others and their feedback. Here is the house where you shine, and where you are most easily crushed and have to learn to move past ego reactions.

Sixth House: House of Service

The sixth house is where you serve on a daily basis. It represents your day-to-day work in the community. Since your work, and your relationship with it, affects your health so greatly, it is also the house of health and well-being.

Seventh House: House of Partnership

This is the realm of public relationships, and includes partnerships of all kinds, because they are publicly declared relationships. Most people think of it as the house of marriage. Private romantic relationships fall in the domain of the fifth house. When a public declaration is made, as in a marriage ceremony, it moves the relationship into the seventh house. Found opposite the Ascendant (the cusp of the first house), the cusp of the seventh house is called the Descendant.

Eighth House: House of Transformation

Here is the house where we learn to relinquish control, or at least let go of our ego's need for control, and trust in the spiritual transformation process. Medieval astrologers used to call this the house of sex, death, and taxes, because ultimately these are things we have no control over. The lessons of the eighth house provoke our transformation, and often have an element of mystery or sexuality to them.

Ninth House: House of Higher Learning

The ninth house defines higher learning, not just in an academic sense but also including philosophy, spirituality, and studying other cultures. The ninth-house challenge is to expand our viewpoint and see the potentials of the greater world. We often experience higher learning through spiritual paths or world travel.

Tenth House: House of Career

While the sixth house represents day-to-day work, the tenth represents career or vocation. The tenth house indicates our purpose, what we are here to do in the world and share with others. The cusp of the tenth house, called the Midheaven, is the midpoint of the sky. Here we find what we are learning to be in the world. Some feel that the issues of the father, or the primary earner in the family, manifest in the tenth house, being the opposite of the family/mother associations of the fourth house.

Eleventh House: House of Social Consciousness

The eleventh house is the realm of social communication and service to the greater community. It is sometimes referred to as the house of friends, because here we develop lateral relationships rather than hierarchical relationships. This is the realm of community and cooperative service.

Twelfth House: House of Merging

In this house we find divine inspiration and creativity, but also a tendency to escape from the rigors of the material world. Medieval astrologers called it the house of hidden enemies, because it indicates where we are most likely to be self-defeating. Some think of it as the house of addictions or illusions, because they are self-defeating behaviors. The twelfth house was also called the house of institutions, ruling everything from convents to mental institutions, because in both places we find the solitude for true introspection and potential merging with the divine, as well as escape from reality.

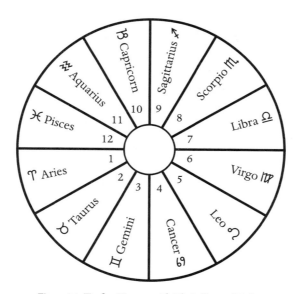

Figure 36: Twelve Houses with Their Natural Rulers

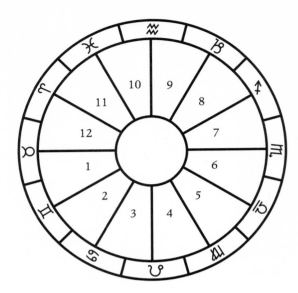

Figure 37: Twelve Houses as the Signs Rotate

A sign other than the natural ruling sign can rule a house in an actual astrological chart.
In this chart, Taurus (2), the natural ruler of the second house, is on the eastern horizon,
so it is ruling the first house. Here, Taurus is considered the Ascendant.

Chart interpretations vary in style, focus, and details, and can include not only the placement of a planet in a sign and house but also the various relationships, symbolized by specific angles called aspects, between the planets. By understanding the basic vocabulary and definitions, you can gain a great appreciation of astrological movements, seasonal shifts, and even astrological readings. Most people find knowledge of their Sun sign, Moon sign, and Ascendant (rising sign) to be of primary significance. Consulting a professional astrologer—particularly one with a mystical and spiritual orientation who can give you insight into your life's purpose rather than just simple predictions—can be a valuable asset on the mystical path.

Astrological Ages

We can observe the sacred cycles not only in the days of the week, lunar month, solar year, and cycle of human life, but we can find the patterns of astrology, the greater seasons of cosmic development, played out in the history of the world. Each culture marks periods of history differently, and calls them by different names. The mythologies of Greece speak of a Golden Age, and relate the time periods by metals corresponding to levels of enlightenment. Practitioners of ceremonial magic in the traditions of Aleister Crowley follow three historic epochs named for Isis, Osiris, and Horus. Our anthropologists, historians, and artists use different measuring sticks to categorize historic periods. Each of these systems measures the periods in different ways, yet all are leading to an important shift, and we are on the cusp of it. For me, the astrological calendar, using the astrological ages, has been a fascinating one to watch, and plays an important role in understanding what we now call the New Age.

Before we can understand the astrological ages, we must know that there are two distinctly different, yet related, zodiacs (figure 38). This is the biggest point of confusion and controversy. Astrology, even mythic astrology, is based on our viewpoint from the Earth, not on the reality of the solar dynamics. From our point of view, it looks like the Sun is orbiting our planet through the zodiac. Viewpoint relates to the Principle of Correspondence. Patterns repeat themselves, and it is our view of the patterns that affects us.

The word zodiac usually translates to "wheel of animals," relating to the ring of constellations through which the Sun, Moon, and other planets seem to pass, from our viewpoint on Earth. This zodiac based on stellar constellations is called the sidereal zodiac, and is used in Vedic, or Hindu, astrology. Most Westerners use the tropical zodiac, based on the ring of space around the Earth divided neatly into thirty-degree segments. The first thirty degrees of space in this wheel, after the point where the Sun is located at the vernal equinox, is Aries. The next thirty degrees is Taurus, continuing the pattern of all twelve signs. The tropical zodiac relates to the seasons on Earth rather than the actual stars.

At one point in time, the sidereal and tropical zodiacs were aligned, but due to a wobble in the Earth's axis, the stellar constellation behind the Sun on the vernal equinox slowly changed. It seemed to lose one degree every seventy-two years. While astrologers debate the exact starting and ending times of each age, it takes 2,166 years to shift from one sign to another.

This transition, called the precession of the equinoxes, has led to a theory that each age of roughly 2,000 years is dominated by the energy of the stellar, or sidereal, sign the Sun occupies during the vernal equinox. Many people believe that we as a culture are transitioning out of the Age of Pisces and into the Age of Aquarius, the New Age, with the potential from past prophecies to be a new golden age of enlightenment and peace. Astrologers argue as to when and how this could possibly manifest, but when we look at history through this astrological lens, patterns of change and development seem to be clearer in a larger context.

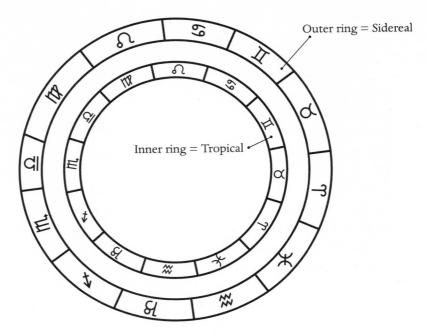

Figure 38: Sidereal and Tropical Zodiacs

The Age of Leo

10,966 to 8830 BCE*

Although it depends on your definition of civilization, the Age of Leo is said to be the start of what we think of as the earliest human culture and civilization. Although the *Homo sapiens* species evolved much earlier, the end of the last great Ice Age marked the dominance of its hunter-gatherer tribal civilization, with earthen fertility goddesses and horned god consorts. Mythologically, the Age of Leo was said to mark the end of the last great civilizations and golden ages, often described as Atlantis in the Western magical traditions. Though great debate continues over the physical evidence of Atlantis, myth says that the people of this advanced culture abused their power, be it scientific or mystical, and, due to this act of ego, destroyed themselves, returning to the stone age, but the survivors planted the seeds of mystical advancement in the ancient cultures. Ego and pride are classic lessons of Leonine energy, where we ultimately learn to find self-esteem through inner identity and spiritual power rather than outer achievements.

* BCE, short for Before Common Era, is often used along with CE, Common Era, instead of BC and AD. Not all mystic traditions look at the birth of Christ as the pivotal shift in time.

The Age of Cancer

8830 to 6664 BCE

The sign of the Great Mother marked the rise of the goddess civilizations and the Neolithic period. The shift to the domestication of animals began, along with aspects of agriculture. The life of the nomad was replaced by the life of settled village, marking territory, land, and ultimately home, the province of Cancer. Fertility and phallic images from this time have also been found. The civilization of Crete, as well as the town of Jericho, were founded during this time period.

The Age of Gemini

6664 to 4498 BCE

During this age, the first truly accepted sense of "civilization" began. The land known as Sumer was settled. More advanced ideas, the hallmark of Gemini, were introduced to improve agriculture and irrigation. Towns and villages swelled to form cities, and the first form of urban life appeared. Language became more standardized, and the first true writing systems were created. From them developed our notions of trade and industry, ways of exchanging ideas, information, and resources. Traditional fertility cults, depicted in the Sumerian myths, still abounded, as the Goddess took more triple images as maiden, mother, and crone, or upper world, middle world, and underworld, but pantheons became more complex and worship more diverse.

The Age of Taurus

4498 to 2332 BCE

The Age of Taurus is known as the age of builders, as various cultures developed into their recognizable civilizations, including the Egyptian, Minoan, Mesopotamian, and Indian regions. The bull became a major icon, the horned God, as the Goddess's sacred consort and sacrificed lover. Mythologies and mysticism became more "solid" and stable in the minds of the people of these cultures, dividing the various gods and goddesses into pantheons that are recognizable today. The signs of the zodiac were fixed into their current system, which is still recognized by modern astrology students.

The Age of Aries

2332 to 166 BCE

Aries, as a fire sign, also has solar attributes, as the Sun is said to be exalted in Aries, meaning the energies are very harmonious and compatible. Solar religions grew to great heights in the lands of Egypt. A royal cult created by the controversial figure Akhenaton focused on the solar disc itself, as the god Aten, to the exclusion of all other gods. This first bout of monotheism did not last long, and after Akhenaton's death the old religions were reestablished. According to some biblical scholars, the rise of Abraham and then Moses occurred during this age. Abraham is known for his sacrifice of the ram to his god. The archetype of Aries is often the warrior, one who charges ahead fearlessly, and the Age of Aries was marked by the migration of warrior cultures across the European continent and the rise of empires. The Trojan War, as well as the rise of the Roman Empire, occurred during this period. Weapons of war were the technological leaps of the time, as the metal of Aries, and its ruling planet, Mars, is iron. Due to the influence of Aries' opposing sign, Libra, there also was a rise of justice and laws, arts, literacy, and language. A zodiac sign's opposing sign, its shadow, acts as its complement and will always influence its partner.

The Age of Pisces

166 BCE to approximately 2000 CE

The age that is currently ending is the age of the Fish, marked by the rise of Christianity as a dominant world power. Though most often viewed as a monotheistic religion, Christianity is also a fertility cult based around a sacrificed god figure, who is both the redeemer and healer. Though Christ is one of the final expressions of the theme, the seeds of the sacrificed-god archetype were planted with Dumuzi, Tammuz, Osiris, Dionysus, and Mithras. On the highest level, Pisces is the mystic, merging with the divine and returning to the world with great healing power, insight, and inspiration for all. Ideally, with this insight comes a sense of spiritual, unconditional love, which really is the highest expression of Christianity. The other side of Pisces is institutions, confinement, seeking escape, romanticism, fanaticism, disillusionment, and addiction. We have also seen expressions of these over the last two thousand years. Great advancements in philosophy, science, and politics have occurred, truly with divine inspiration, but the shadow of Pisces is also present in this age. It is interesting how the sign of the Fish—which is actually the sacred-geometry form of the vesica pisces, two interlocked circles creating an "eye"—became the symbol of Jesus and Christianity, as it is the herald of the Age of Pisces, the sign of the Fish.

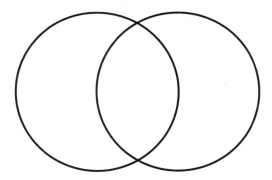

Figure 39: Vesica Pisces

The Age of Aquarius

2000 (approximately) to 4166 CE

This is the coming age surrounded by much prophecy and excitement. Some think it is the end of the world, but in many ways it is the end of *a* world, and the start of another, meaning the start of another world consciousness. No one agrees when the new age really starts, since the time span is so large from a human perspective. Years such as 1905, 1969, 1972, 1987, 2000, 2003, 2005, 2010, 2012, 2020, and 2080 have been given. I think that, like all shifts, the change will be powerful but initially subtle, though Aquarian qualities can shock and surprise everybody, defying expectations. Aquarian qualities at their highest include a universal equality, a sense of kindred sisterhood/brotherhood, the removal of hierarchies in favor of lateral relationships, community service, true friendship, a celebration of diversity and individuality, revolution, and innovation on the technological and spiritual planes leading to a utopian society or another golden age of peace and prosperity on all levels. Though these are the highest ideals, Aquarian energy struggles with individuality versus the needs of the whole, being eccentric and unable to relate to others, and creating sudden changes that are often violent, whether natural earth changes or uprisings and military revolutions. Because of this, there are an equal number of prophecies of violence and destruction surrounding the New Age, though the general mystical belief is that we create our own reality. If we raise our consciousness to a higher state, we will avoid such difficulties. If we do not, they will be the vehicle by which we learn how to realize Aquarian energy. The blessings and challenges of an age often manifest simultaneously, and pragmatic mystics are well advised to keep that in mind, rather than looking to be rescued by other divine or extraterrestrial beings. The Aquarian current is about taking responsibility for ourselves yet being part of a larger community, uniquely contributing to the greater whole. Utopia will come only if we work for it.

Western astrology is not the only model of sacred calendars and sacred ages. Eastern astrology, from the Chinese zodiac to Vedic astrology, plays a prominent part in sacred timekeeping. Vedic astrology divides the great ages a bit differently, calling them yugas. The great ages also appear in a variety of indigenous tribal lore. The Hopi have the story of many worlds. Their myths closely parallel the mythic history of the Aztecs and Mayans, who have intricate timekeeping systems that are growing in modern awareness and popularity. The sacred Mayan calendar is said to be one of the most accurate and complex systems; it can accurately predict the solar sun spot cycles, something that modern scientists only recently discovered.

EXERCISE

Balancing the Day

Tribal people all over the world honor not only the four sacred directions but also the four sacred times—dawn, noon, dusk, and midnight. Classically, they are magical times between the worlds, when faeries and otherwordly Witches can be glimpsed. Each relates to one of the four directions. Dawn is associated with east, and often the element of air, beginning the day, although some traditions put the rising Sun with fire. Noon relates to the south, at least in the Northern Hemisphere. Most think of the hot noon Sun as relating to fire, and the further south you go in the Northern Hemisphere, the warmer it gets. Some think of the south as the direction of air, for the wide open sky. West is the direction of sunset, the land of endings, relating to the realm of water. Magically, water is associated with the west, even for people on an east coast, because water relates to the dead, to the ancestors, and the sunset relates to the land of the ancestors. The Sun "dies" and goes to the underworld. Midnight relates to the north, and most often to the element of earth.

I have honored the four points of the day in my own practice with the following poetry. It continues to evolve and change as I do.

Dawn (Waking)
East

To the powers of the east
I feel the call of the rising Sun
I ask that your breath fill me up
And guide my thoughts.

Midday
South

To the powers of the south
I feel the essence of the midday Sun
I ask that your fire fill me up
And guide my soul.

Sunset
West

To the powers of the west
I feel the call of the twilight Sun
I ask that your waves fill me up
And guide my heart.

Midnight (Bedtime)
North

To the powers of the north
I feel the call of the midnight Sun
I ask that your soil fill me up
And guide my body.

Find your own way to honor the four times of day. If you are not conscious
at dawn and/or midnight, count waking up as your dawn and going to sleep as
your midnight. Face the direction at the appropriate time, and think of its qualities
and powers. Take time to give thanks to the divine. Some traditions have elaborate
poetry, but you can simply say or think whatever is in your heart at the time. The
important thing is to take time out of your day for the sacred times.

The ancient calendar keepers, be they Western, Eastern, old world or new, understood the power of time and its relationship to the flow of mystical energy, and used it to their advantage, for their own evolution and expansion. Time, space, dimension, and vibration are only a few of the markers we have for understanding and exploring the universe around us, on all levels.

FOUR

EXPLORING OURSELVES

8

GOING WITHIN

Through understanding the magical maps of the universe, and the symbol systems used by mystics, we gain the foundational skills to walk the magical path. By understanding traditional views on the universe, we understand ourselves, fulfilling the "as above, so below" teaching. We can put the esoteric concepts into practice. Ultimately, building a closer relationship with the divine means you come into a closer relationship with yourself. By building a closer relationship with yourself, you find your own divine center and can more easily find the divine in everyone and everything else.

Meditation

Regardless of the tradition, meditation is a key to greater spiritual awareness. Each tradition thinks of meditation in different ways. Particular differences arise between Eastern and Western traditions, but ultimately, each definition, and each technique, serves the same purpose: mastering consciousness.

Meditation simply means contemplation. Meditation is a method of altering consciousness through contemplation on a focus. Our brain waves are measured at various states of mind. Beta level is thirteen to sixteen hertz, or brain-wave cycles per second. We call beta level our normal waking consciousness. By consciously shifting our brain waves into states other than our normal waking state, we create opportunities for inner awareness, psychic experience, magic, and spiritual epiphanies. Alpha level, measured at eight to thirteen hertz, is associated with daydreaming but also with creative visualization and psychic experience. Theta, the next lower state, measured at four to eight hertz, is a place of deep journey and meditation. The lowest level, delta, measured at four or less hertz, is a place of deep sleep or coma. Some mystics consciously penetrate these deep areas during meditation.

The various meditation techniques give us a focus. The focus of thought allows a shift in brain waves. Through this contemplation we can learn many things. Each level of consciousness can unlock various mysteries. Each practitioner's experience will be different, and will grow and develop over time, but some of the common basic experiences include the following.

Mind-Body Connection

The relationship between the mind and the body is demonstrated during meditation. By changing the focus of your thoughts, your body and its systems naturally change in accordance with your thoughts. When your thoughts are agitated, excited, nervous, or angry, your body reacts in an equivalent manner. When you focus your thoughts on rhythm and relaxation, your body responds in kind. Improving health through meditation occurs through this connection.

Mind-Emotion Connection

Many people think they are subject to the whims of their emotions, which they believe to be entirely beyond their control or influence. Though some people are more easily influenced than others, we all have the ability to alter our emotions, through control of our thoughts. When learning meditation techniques, you learn to focus your mind, and see how it changes your mood. You can bring the techniques into your daily life by using them to focus through emotional situations. This doesn't mean that you don't feel the emotions, or that you deny them, but that you have a measure of control in responding to them, rather than being subject to seemingly uncontrollable emotional reactions.

Consciousness Control

Through the awareness of the mind's connection to the body and emotions, a practitioner naturally learns how to shift consciousness when appropriate. With meditation techniques, by literally using your mind and will, you can alter your brain waves and move between various levels of consciousness. You can use the techniques to ground yourself when you feel flighty or spacey, to enter the creative or intuitive state of alpha brain waves, or to get into a deeper trance. You can alter your point of view, entering a form of "witness consciousness" where you observe your own behavior and thoughts and can consciously change them to suit your own personal goals. Magical practitioners can enter a state of consciousness where they have a greater awareness of energy and more acute psychic impressions, and can project their will to create change in their lives.

Figure 40: Magician Tarot Card from Lo Scarabeo's Universal Tarot

The True Nature of Consciousness

The greatest gift that comes from practicing both Eastern and Western meditation techniques is understanding the true nature of consciousness. As a practitioner, you will come to the realization that "you" are having the thoughts, but "you" are not the thoughts. So many people identify with their mind, mental body, or ego. We even have the philosophical saying "I think, therefore I am." Untrue. You are having thoughts. Your mental body is a possession of the true you, the spiritual you, the soul, or higher self. The true you owns your mind, and your emotions, as much as your body. They are all temples that house and express "you," but they are extensions. They are not more you than your car or your house. Because we live in a society that closely identifies with acquiring material possessions, it is even harder to embody this concept. Western magic has four sacred tools—the wand, sword, cup, and disc; but the true spiritual self—the will, mind, heart, and body—

owns these four tools. The imagery in the Magician card of the tarot displays this truth. One popular saying that embodies the true nature of consciousness is: "You are a spiritual being having a human experience, not a human being having a spiritual experience." Your true identity includes the human realm, but is much larger and vaster than it.

Unity

Meditation practitioners often come to a state of consciousness, both in and out of the meditative state, pervaded by a sense of unity and connection to all things seen and unseen. It brings a sense of truly knowing that we are all connected, that we always have been and always will be. The Hindus call this seeing through Maya, or illusion, that we are separate, and recognizing the truth of our unity. You can learn this principle intellectually, but until you experience it, it is meaningless.

How you come to these realizations is different with each form of meditation. The forms do not have to be mutually exclusive. I practice both Western and Eastern forms of meditation, and use various techniques, but it's good to stick with one technique for a while and get some benefit from it. Many people give up on meditation too easily. They think that something is "supposed to happen," and when an amazing spiritual experience doesn't occur the first day, week, or even month, they quit. As with all disciplines, the benefits of meditation take time to manifest, and are different for everybody. The purpose of meditation is to focus and clear the mind, which will automatically bring benefits. Some people have transcendental visions or epiphanies, but that is not the goal of meditation. Many feel that meditation has no goal, that it is an experience for the sake of the experience, which is like saying the path is about the journey and not the destination.

Though for simplicity's sake we divide many of the meditation techniques into perceived Eastern and Western styles and divisions, such divisions are not clear-cut. Various traditions use a combination of all these techniques, or even define them very differently. In the end, what's important is to find the spiritual techniques that suit your own mystic path and tradition.

Eastern meditation techniques focus on clearing the mind. Through a sense of quiet stillness, what is described as an emptiness, the gifts of the universe flow. Many say the difference between Eastern and Western meditation techniques is that the East turns the mind inward on the self while the West turns the mind outward, though this is not entirely true. Both have their inner and outer tools. The focus is no thought, just pure consciousness. The mind's chatter is quieted by a focus, such as counting the breaths or repeating a mantra.

The first meditation technique I learned was a simple breath count. While breathing slowly and deeply, you count eight breaths and then begin again. In other styles, you count how many seconds you inhale, hold, then exhale. I learned the eight-four-eight breath, in which you inhale for a silent count of eight, hold for a silent count of four, exhale for a silent count of eight, then repeat. You focus on the breath and count, and nothing else. You exhale all stray, unwanted thoughts until it is just you and the breath.

Mantras are words and phrases, often in a "sacred" language, that are said out loud or internally, with the intention of altering consciousness. The word or phrase is used to direct the consciousness and hold the attention to one focus. Repeating a mantra—either out loud, with or without a specific melody, or internally, using the mind—is a method of directing consciousness. Mantras are used in devotional meditations, healing, and what some might consider magic, to create a change, such as manifesting prosperity or love in the user's life.

While the term mantra is usually associated with Buddhist and Hindu traditions, the concept of sacred words of power is found in many ancient cultures and systems of mysticism. Unlike affirmations, which are simply intentional phrases, many believe the very structure of sacred words and phrases—the sounds they make and the way the mouth forms and the tongue moves to pronounce them—contributes to their mystical power. Studies show that the way the tongue strikes the palette can have a healing response much like reflexology.

Some people feel the mantras themselves are divine powers. Others believe mantras are the names, the vibrational energies, of particular gods and creative forces, and when chanted, they control those entities. There is a long-standing tradition that says if you have the "true name" of something, you have power and control over it. Others see mantras as prayers to the divine forces, and by resonating with those forces, you can create change.

Though most mantras come from a language associated with a mystic tradition, modern mystics use their own names, either their given birth name or their spiritual name, as the focus for their mantra meditations. In some forms of meditation, such as Transcendental Meditation, or TM, the practitioner is given a special mantra that is not to be shared with others. Most mantra systems allow the sharing of mantras, believing that each mantra works effectively for everybody.

Bija, or seed mantras, are used to build larger mantras. Each of the seven chakras is said to have a seed mantra, the sound that is at the core of the chakra when it is healthy and balanced. By reciting a seed mantra, you align with the chakra's power. Some systems disagree on the exact mantras for the upper chakras.

Chakra	Seed Mantra
Root chakra	LAM
Belly chakra	VAM
Solar plexus chakra	RAM
Heart chakra	YAM
Throat chakra	HUM
Brow chakra	KSHAM
Crown chakra	AUM

Figure 41: Om Symbol

AUM, or OM, is probably the most popular mantra. Said to be the sound of creation, everything resonates with AUM. The three distinct sounds of A-U-M are said to stand for the three principles of creation, sustenance, and destruction, which are embodied by the Hindu gods Brahma, Vishnu, and Shiva.

Here are some mantras used for manifestation, focusing on the divine feminine.

OM GUM GANAPATAYEI NAMAHA
(Om Gum Guh-nuh-puh-tuh-yeah Nahm-ah-ha)
Mantra to Ganesha, the elephant-headed god, to remove all obstacles from one's path.

OM SHRIM MAHA LAKSHMIYEI SWAHA
(Om Shreem Mah-ha Laksh-mee-yeah Swah-ha)
Mantra to salute Lakshmi, the great goddess of abundance.

OM SHRIM SIDDHAYE NAMAHA
(Om Shreem Sid-hah-yea Nahm-ah-ha)
Mantra to salute the Goddess who releases the inner magical powers.

OM DUM DURGAYEI NAMAHA
(Om Doom Door-Gah-Yei Nahm-ah-ha)
Mantra to salute the goddess Durga, the divine protectress.

Kundalini yoga uses a series of mantras, usually in the language of Ghurmeki, used by the Sikhs. The translations are not always precise, but are said to convey an energy that is not always bound by earthly languages. Here are a few of my favorites from the kundalini tradition.

SAT NAM
This is the seed mantra most often used in kundalini yoga. It means "true name." You recite "SAT" on the in breath and "NAM" on the out breath, silently, while exercising. This mantra aligns your personal identity with your divine self.

ONG NAMO, GURU DEV NAMO
This is the mantra used at the start of every kundalini yoga session. Its purpose is to help you tune in to your higher self and the great "golden chain" of kundalini yoga teachers of the past. Through it, you are calling upon divine wisdom and your inner teacher.

SA TA NA MA
This mantra is said to embody the primal powers of the universe. The first syllable stands for infinity, the second for life, the third for death, and the fourth for rebirth. This is often done with the hand movement, or *muddra*, of the first finger and thumb when reciting SA, thumb and second finger for TA, thumb and third finger for NA, and thumb and pinky for MA, repeated over and over again.

AD GURAY NAMEH, JUGAD GURAY NAMEH, SAT GURAY NAMEH, SIRI GURU DEVAY NAMEH
This mantra is a chant of reverence, meaning the reciter of it bows to the primal guru, the inner teacher, to the ancient wisdom of the ages, to true wisdom, to the unseen wisdom. For practical purposes, it is a chant of protection, and is said to surround the aura with light.

RA MA DA SA, SA SAY SO HUNG
This mantra is a chant for healing. The syllables embody the primal powers. RA stands for the Sun, MA is for the Moon, DA represents the Earth, and SA is infinity. These four are

known as the Earth mantra. The final four syllables, known as the Ether mantra, mean "Total infinity, I am thou."

WAHE GURU, WAHE GURU, WAHE GURU, WAHE JEEO
This mantra elevates the spirit, putting you in touch with the ecstasy of your inner teacher and pure divine consciousness.

EK ONG KAR, SAT NAM, SIRI WHA HE GURU
This mantra awakens the kundalini and brings the mind to bliss. A combination of many powerful words, it is said to mean "There is one Creator whose name is Truth. Great is the ecstasy of that Supreme Wisdom."

GOBINDE, MUKUNDE, UDARE, APARE, HARING, KARING, NIRNAME, AKAME
This mantra means "Sustainer, liberator, enlightener, infinite, destroyer, creator, nameless, desireless." It balances the right and left sides of the brain, and aligns the brain and heart to unite with the infinite creator.

ADI SHAKTI, ADI SHAKTI, ADI SHAKTI, NAMO NAMO,
SARAB SHAKTI, SARAB SHAKTI, SARAB SHAKTI, NAMO NAMO,
PRITHUM BHAGAWATI, PRITHUM BHAGAWATI, PRITHUM BHAGAWATI,
NAMO NAMO, KUNDALINI, MATA SHAKTI, MATA SHAKTI, NAMO, NAMO
The First Shakti Mantra attunes the user to the power of the Divine Mother. It is protective, but it also generates energy. It is the primal power and is used to create your life and fulfill your desires. This mantra is also said to eliminate fear.

Here are some other popular mantras.

OM MA NI PAD ME HUM
(Om Mah Nee Pahd May Hum)
This mantra is the best-known Tibetan Buddhist chant, originating in India. Though most often translated as "Behold the Jewel in the Lotus," the mantra is really beyond those simple words, and contains a deeper meaning and teaching that cannot be translated into English but only experienced through using the mantra in your spiritual practice.

BA BAK BENNU
A mantra attributed to the Egyptians and used in Egyptian-influenced New Age circles, the term Ba is depicted as part of the soul, according to the Egyptians, and symbolized as

a bird like a dove. Bak is symbolized by a hawk, and stands for the physical body, while the Bennu bird, in this phrase, means the phoenix, symbolizing the transformed or transcendent consciousness.

Traditionally, mantras, particularly Eastern mantras, are recited in multiples of three. Three, nine, thirty-three, and 108 repetitions are not uncommon. Sometimes a set of beads, known as mala beads, are used, consisting of 108 beads, with one head bead known as the "sumeru." Traditionally, you hold the beads in your right hand, index finger extended. You either can hang the mala between the thumb and the ring finger, and use the second finger to rotate one bead at a time, toward yourself, or you can hang the mala on the middle finger, and use the thumb to rotate one bead at a time, toward yourself. One bead is moved for each complete mantra recited. The index finger never touches the beads. You start on the summit, or head bead, and end never crossing over the sumeru. If you choose to do more than one round of 108 mantras, you turn the mala around and proceed in the reverse direction. The mala can be worn as a piece of spiritual jewelry, bringing its vibration to your daily life. Some feel the mala you use in daily meditation should never be displayed to others, and should be kept in a separate bag.

Catholics will mention that the mala bears a striking resemblance to the rosary, but the use of prayer beads in many cultures and traditions is ancient. Witches have a similar practice of using the Witch's ladder to recite incantations. Mantras are not restricted to the unfamiliar syllables of the Eastern world. Greek, Hebrew, Latin, and even English prayers and phrases can have similar effects and benefits.

Other forms of Eastern meditation techniques include physical yogic exercises and martial arts. The focus is brought to the body, and the connection between the body and mind. Often our mind tells us we can't do something physically that in truth we can do, if we move past the mind and into our divine consciousness. Such physical activities give us an opportunity to move past the mind. These discipline traditions provide far more than physical exercise or even mental fortitude, and embody a rich spiritual wisdom.

Western meditation techniques are more directed and conscious. Instead of focusing on clearing the mind and using repetition to get into that pure, empty state, Western techniques use directed and guided visualizations and intentions to occupy the mind and move past stray, unwanted thoughts.

The basic meditation in these traditions, taught in both modern ceremonial magic and modern Paganism, is focusing on the light of a candle. You sit in a darkened room and stare at a candle flame, directing your attention to the flame to the exclusion of all else. Some traditions have you then close your eyes, and re-create the image in your mind's eye, focusing on it clearly and making its inner manifestation more and more real. This prepares you for deeper visualization experiences.

Such guided meditations are often called pathworkings, based on the concept of the Qabalistic Tree of Life, diagramming ten states of consciousness, with twenty-two "paths" linking them. Each path has associated images, letters, and even a pictorial "key" in the form of a tarot card from the deck's Major Arcana. This information is used to connect the two levels of consciousness. Contemplation of the images and symbols of the path gives rise to a meditative experience, leading from one level of consciousness to the next.

The word pathworking has been applied to all manner of guided imagery meditations using sacred or mythic images but not necessarily directly related to the Qabalistic Tree of Life. Basically, a general set of images that are archetypal in nature, drawn from traditional lore, are suggested, either self-suggested to the more experienced practitioner, or guided by a teacher or even a recording. The spontaneous images that occur symbolically reveal clues to the issues at hand that the practitioner needs to work on, and may provide information on how to work with this knowledge.

For example, if the meditation guides you down through a cave tunnel to take you to your sacred temple, and once you get there, it's on fire, think about what fire could mean to you. Is it aflame with your divine will and light? Is it burning with your anger? What does it feel like? You might not even "see" it clearly, but simply know or feel what is happening. If you ask for help and see a large pen that is spraying water like a hose, and it succeeds in putting out some of the flame, you might construe that writing would be a way to resolve your anger issues.

Other times, these psychic archetypal scenes are areas not only to interact with our own consciousness but to act as launch pads for spiritual journeys and common rooms to meet with nonphysical beings.

Eastern techniques may focus on a visual, such as a sacred symbol or yantra, or use guided imagery when relaxing or focusing on the chakras. Some techniques do not fall clearly on either side of East or West. The repetitive drumming and dancing of shamans and ecstatic cults contain elements of both traditions. These techniques seem wilder and less physically and mentally disciplined than those of the East, but lead to "no thought."

They use symbols and imagery of many Western traditions, such as visualizing a great world tree connecting all realms, yet they are not guided in specific steps, but are freeform. Some would argue that such techniques are not contemplative enough to be meditations, and are more magical or mystical rituals.

EXERCISE

Meditation

You have already done some pathworkings, or visualizations, more in harmony with the Western traditions, in chapters 5 and 6. Though such experiences can be quite wonderful and informative, and grant you a firsthand experiential understanding of the paradigm from which the visualization is drawn, they might not lead to the discipline, awareness, and awakening of a consistent meditation practice. You can learn to integrate meditation into your daily regime by practicing it regularly and applying its wisdom to your everyday life.

To help you build this discipline, I suggest you take some time to work with a more contemplative technique. Choose either the simple breath count meditation or the eight-four-eight breath on page 131, or the candle-staring meditation on pages 135 and 136. Set a timer. Start with two minutes. This may not seem like a long time, but it can be. Practice the meditation for two minutes and see how you do. Can you remained focused and clear, or do a lot of stray thoughts manifest? Don't worry if they do, and don't be mad at yourself for not being perfect. Clearing your consciousness is part of the process. The practice is what helps. If you were perfect at it, you wouldn't need a meditation practice. Few people are perfect at anything, but it's the experience that counts.

Perform your timed meditation regularly, and try to lengthen it a little bit each time. You will develop your focus and meditation skills, as well as patience. As you become more and more successful, you will get to a state of "no time," where your perception of time alters with your consciousness. What was once an exceedingly long period of time will seem to be over quickly, because you will truly be in the moment, not thinking about the past or worrying about the future.

You might be tempted to omit this type of contemplative exercise from your mystical routines, because it is not as flashy as some of the others. You might feel it is too basic, particularly if you had vivid experiences in the earlier pathworking exercises in chapters 5 and 6. Those exercises were designed primarily to illustrate the teachings in those chapters, but the foundation of a life-changing meditation practice starts with simple contemplative exercises.

———————————————————

9

DEVELOPING INTUITION

One of the greatest benefits of regular meditation is an increase in the faculty of intuition. Many people notice this effect of meditation almost immediately. Their increased universal awareness has an added practical benefit of helping them make decisions and be in the right place, at the right time, doing the right thing. Doors seem to open that were always closed before. In fact, many people who seek to develop their psychic abilities are told to learn to meditate first.

The connection between meditation and psychic ability is strong, but not obvious to most people. So many think that psychic ability is some kind of super power, reserved for the rare individual, and that most of us mere mortals are not capable of it. In true mystical wisdom, the psyche is the soul, the divine inner wisdom that each of us possesses. In the modern medical context, it has been reduced to the mind, and is the root of our mental disciplines of psychology and psychiatry. But the psyche is not the mind, and its original lore is rooted in much of the mystical and intuitive goddess-born wisdom.

When people say they are psychic, they really mean they can listen to this inner wisdom, they can listen to the voice of their soul. We all have this divine essence. When we slow down long enough to tune in to it and find the unique way that it communicates with us, then we become more intuitive.

Psychic Ability

A lot of fancy names have been used to describe psychic "powers." They are simply ways of describing how the psyche communicates with you. Clairvoyance means seeing psychically. Someone with developed psychic sight might see people's auras as color, see spirits, or have visions of the past, present, and future. Clairaudience means psychic hearing. Many think of it as the still voice within us. Clairaudients can hear the voices of spiritual beings as well as their own inner voice. They might hear vibrations, and the tone, pitch, and quality can be indicative of the situation. Haunted houses might have a high, piercing psychic background noise, while sacred earth sites have a low hum. At times the energetic vibration is perceived as literal sound through the ears, but most times it is an inner sound, much like when you remember a sound, voice, or song with your inner ear. Psychic impressions can be translated as music. Certain kinds of music mean different things. Harmonious music identifies harmonious energy, and discordant music symbolizes discordant energy. Some mediums report hearing high bells when making contact with spirits. Some practitioners have developed both gifts, seeing and hearing things psychically.

All the physical senses can be conduits for psychic information. Although some practitioners have difficulty distinguishing psychic sight and hearing from physical sight and hearing, in general the impressions are usually more subtle and sometimes vague. You are not using your physical eyes and ears, but your psychic equivalents. Others use their sense of smell, touch, or taste to receive psychic impressions. I once knew a healer who would psychically "smell" people, and the scents were symbols for various states of health and illness. Someone who carried the psychic scent of roses was healthy and spiritual, while the person with the scent of gasoline was sick. The people didn't literally smell of those substances. The scents were just a way that this healer's psychic mind communicated with her. Though all five physical senses can be conduits for psychic impressions, sight and hearing are the most common.

Clairsentience means psychic knowing, and doesn't involve sight, hearing, or any other sense. One simply knows the information. Often this sense of knowing is like a gut feeling that needs to be translated into words. Other times the ideas and words are present in the mind, though they were not heard or seen; they simply became present. Some psychics call this ability "the knowing."

In my experience, psychic ability can be developed by anybody. Some people have natural ability, while others struggle. Like any art or skill, those with natural gifts can develop them even further. Developing psychic abilities can help a person develop relationships with spirit guides and develop deeper meditation skills for problem solving and healing.

Those without natural psychic gifts may not become amazingly proficient, but can develop basics skills. I can learn to play basketball and develop the skills necessary to enjoy the game, but I will never play for the NBA. It's not my calling, just as being a professional psychic is not for everybody, yet everybody can learn the basics if they want. Psychic skills can be quite helpful in life, and fun.

I've noticed that many students have a "grass is greener" attitude when it comes to how their psychic abilities manifest. Those who see visions are upset that they don't hear any messages. Those who get messages wonder whom they are coming from, because they can't see anything. Both skills can be developed, but in the end, it doesn't really matter how you receive the information. Is the experience helpful, no matter how the information comes to you? That is the important question. Everybody thinks they are missing out on the experience if it is not exactly like their friend's experience. Everyone is unique, and works with his or her intuition in unique ways. That is a wonderful part of the mystic's gift.

EXERCISE

The Psychic Game

The "psychic game" is not a specific exercise, but something to incorporate into your life. It works best if you have a friend or companion you see often who is also interested in psychic development.

Simply take every opportunity you can to practice quieting yourself and listening to your first intuition regarding any matter. Play the game with inconsequential situations. When the phone rings, psychically ask yourself who it is, and then pick it up. Right or wrong, it doesn't matter, but as you develop your skills, you might find more right "guesses" and know that your intuition is developing. Ask yourself how many phone messages are waiting for you when you get home, or if your bus/train is running on schedule before you get to the station. Ask yourself if there will be a wait at a restaurant where you want to dine.

As you become aware of feelings, quick flashes of vision, or quiet voices within you, notice what happens when you follow them, and when you don't. I used to be really bad about listening to my inner wisdom about driving and taking different roads. I would pick the shortest route, even if my intuition said to go another way. Each time I would end up in a traffic jam and then be late for my appointment.

None of these examples are that important, but paying attention to them will help you develop your skills for more important situations and learn to recognize the feeling of a psychic impression, versus one of your own hopes or fears. These inconsequential games have no great emotional charge to them, so you will learn how to filter out the strong emotions that can cloud your psychic impressions. Regular meditation helps clear the mind and emotions for a clearer "signal" as well. That is one of the main reasons that meditation is so helpful. Play games to see how psychic you are when you are meditating regularly, and when you are not. Think of the game as practice, honing your skills like any athlete, artist, or musician.

Many people think that developing psychic ability is a power trip, for those who desire to be special. Some people seek to develop their psychic ability because they think it will give them an advantage over others.

The best reason to develop your psychic ability is for spiritual advancement. We talk grandly about how all things, people, places, and times are connected, yet if you don't have a personal experience of this connection, then it is just simply an idea. When you are able to get information about someone or something of which you have no linear knowledge, you realize how connected you are. When you can affect something or someone beyond the normal channels that modern science readily accepts, you feel this connection. The more you make such realizations a part of your everyday life and outlook, the more you will live like you are connected to everything else.

Western mystic traditions often encourage the development of psychic abilities in moderation, to demonstrate these truths. We need such proof to help fuel our mystical quest, particularly because most of us, myself included, come from a skeptical background.

In Eastern traditions, particularly of India, such abilities are considered to be the natural byproducts of spiritual evolution. As you develop spiritually, your psychic abilities grow. These psychic talents, called sidhis in the Hindu traditions, are greatly detailed and catalogued. If you focus on the psychic abilities, however, rather than the spiritual quest, they will become a distraction and even a hindrance to your quest for enlightenment. You can become seduced by your growing power, and forget that it was a desire for spiritual awareness that helped you gain that power in the first place.

I suggest striking a balance between the Eastern and Western views on psychic development, knowing they both have lessons to share with us. For me, psychic development was a big part of my awakening to spirituality, beyond the dogma of religion. It has helped me greatly on my mystical path. But I know the focus is not on perfecting or increasing my psychic abilities. I still have a fairly normal life and can relate to people who are more mainstream or conventional. As I develop in knowledge and awareness, I am sure I am receptive enough to the messages and experiences I need without having to be a super psychic. In the end, psychic development is a practical exercise for me.

Divination

Many people, regardless of their psychic ability, use tools as triggers for their ability. These tools are used in divination. Divination simply means "to make divine," and popularly refers to techniques to know the past, present, and future, or divine guidance, when making a decision. Divination is truly a way of getting divine advice, though most people think of it as fortunetelling.

The simplest divination tools are usually yes/no devices. The pendulum, a weight on the end of a string or chain, is used as an interface with your psychic ability, or perhaps even your spiritual allies, to gain answers. The answers usually come in a yes/no format. Tradition says a clockwise motion of the pendulum means yes, while counterclockwise means no, though I have found that different people, and different pendulums, behave differently. If you use a pendulum to connect to a specific spirit or guide, the yes and no responses can be different from your usual ones as well. The best thing to do is to start your session by asking for a yes answer, then a no answer. The pendulum can be developed into a more sophisticated device, often with place cards with a spectrum of answers, and the motion will point to the appropriate answer.

A pendulum with a place card is similar to a Ouija board. The Ouija board is surrounded by much fear and misunderstanding. It is another interface, like the pendulum, but it is used specifically to connect with nonphysical entities. A planchette is moved across a board, pointing to yes or no, or specific letters and numbers to spell out responses to questions. The concept behind it is that the spirit helps guide the planchette to answer your questions.

The technique came into fashion at the turn of the twentieth century, as mediumship and spiritualism gained popularity. Technically, the term Ouija belongs to Parker Brothers, which holds the trademark for the term, but it has been used generically for any spirit talking board. The commercial board and planchette set originated in 1890 with Elijah Bond and Charles Kennard, who patented the first board. William Fuld, an employee of Kennard, later started his own board line under the name "Ouija." Fuld's estate sold it to Parker Brothers. It's important to realize that the techniques behind this method of communication predate the modern spiritualism movement, though the development of a commercial product rose from the interest and experimentation that spiritualism encouraged among the public.

Many people tried to use the Ouija board as a way to speak to the dead. Though it has been demonized by the media, it is just a game, manufactured by game companies. Most serious spirit guides are not attracted to it, or they see it as a game, not a tool of spirituality. It usually attracts lower spirits—spirits that are not necessarily evil, but not necessarily wise or serious either, accounting for the vague and jumbled answers most people receive when using it. I know that in my own experiments, my friends, fellow mystics, and I received vague answers when using it. Then we did a ritual of purification and protection, to banish all unhealthy, unbalanced spirits, and the board went dead. We couldn't get any of our regular spirit guides to communicate through it. I think other, less sensational techniques are best for spiritual work, but don't be afraid of the Ouija board. Just don't take it too seriously.

I've had the best luck using pendulums with the simple yes/no response rather than the more complicated cards, but the pendulum is not my favorite tool. If you explore divination tools, you will find the ones that work best for you.

Another form of divination that can yield similar results is muscle testing, also known as applied kinesiology. Through a series of movements, you test the strength or weakness of the body in a gentle manner, to connect with the body's wisdom. Muscle testing was initially used by practitioners to test medicines and holistic remedies, to see what strengthened the body and what weakened it. When the body is strengthened, the response is taken as a yes, or positive response, and when the body is weakened, it is taken as a no, or negative response. The technique was refined for solo use, to connect with the intuitive gut wisdom of the body, and even as a vehicle to communicate with spirit guides. The yes/no response went beyond just finding out what is good for the body in terms of physical health, and became a medium to interface with higher wisdom and spiritual guides.

The simplest yes/no divination device is a coin toss. When using coins, pendulums, and even Ouija boards, I suggest that you spiritually cleanse these tools and then say a blessing or prayer that they be used for the highest good, and that they answer truly.

More symbolic forms of divination exist, allowing the information received to be much broader than a simple message or yes/no answer. The problem lies in how the broader message is interpreted. Symbolic divination basically comes in two forms: freeform symbolism and a traditional symbol system.

Freeform symbol divination is done by getting into a light altered state and staring at a reflective surface or changing pattern that can suggest a variety of shapes. Such systems were at one time done with animal entrails. An animal was sacrificed, and its innards were spilled out onto the altar and examined. Originally it was an act done when a tribe moved into an area, to see if the land could support and maintain the health of the animal, or if the animal was ill. Later, the shapes suggested in the symbolism of the various organs became a method of divination. Most mystics do not perform animal sacrifice today for divination.

Gazing at floating tea leaves or coffee grounds, clouds, or oil/wax in water can suggest shapes. Also used are reflective surfaces, such as a crystal ball, blacked mirror, bowl of water, or still pool. When divining in reflective surfaces, the act is often called scrying, or skrying, as the surface is believed to be opening a window into the astral world, or providing a space for you to project your mind's eye. Some people even scry in fire, smoke, or tapestry patterns.

If you ask a question about money, and you see a crown, dollar sign, or coin in the shapes, then the answer is probably beneficial to you. If you see an empty bowl or a house collapse, then the answer is probably negative. The answers are symbolic, but the issue becomes one of interpretation. With a trained meditative mind, you can learn to separate your own strong emotions, desires, and fears from your reading, to avoid coloring the information and interpretation. If you can't do this, then you should seek out another practitioner. In general, you can get more psychic impressions and specific information for others when you are not attached to their situation and outcome. That is the reason that many say you should not do divinations for yourself. I don't agree, but I think you have to learn to separate yourself and become detached from your expectations. Seeing other practitioners is very helpful at times, but you can learn to do divination for yourself. The fixed systems are often more helpful for self-divination.

Fixed systems of divination include the tarot, runes, and I Ching. Each is a complex system associated with the mystical powers of the universe, as conceived by a specific time and culture. Each key—card, rune, or hexagram—has a specific cultural meaning, though its meaning in relationship to your question is open to interpretation. The cultural associations and traditional meanings make it harder for you to project your fears or desires into the reading, though it's not impossible. The drawback is that it can give less personal information. Layouts of the symbols can give you the context from which the information can be taken. Layouts often include spaces for the past, present, and future.

Figure 42: I Ching Hexagram

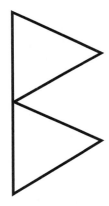

Figure 43: Rune

Many psychics use the symbols as a psychic springboard. They might disregard the traditional meanings of the system and focus on whatever symbol is suggested, and allow a chain of associations to give them a psychic impression.

For example, the Fool in the tarot is traditionally depicted with a small dog at his feet. If, during a reading, you look at the dog and think, "Shepherd—Thigh—Sick," without censoring yourself or breaking the chain, you might then ask your client if he or she has a Shepherd dog with an injured leg. The card really has nothing to do with dogs, legs, or health, but since that image association suggested itself to you through the card, it might be completely accurate, even though it sounds crazy. The card acts as a springboard for psychic intuition through word and image associations.

Figure 44: Fool Tarot Card from Lo Scarabeo's **Universal Tarot**

Augury is a form of divination between the fluid and fixed symbolism, in which meaning is taken from seeing natural occurrences, such as the flight of birds. Each type of bird, and the number of birds counted, has a specific meaning in the tradition, though traditions and meanings vary between cultures and time periods.

Learning a system of divination, and gaining proficiency in its practical use, can be an excellent way of developing your psychic abilities.

EXERCISE
Pendulum

The pendulum is one of the simplest divination tools to use. If you don't have a commercial pendulum, you can use a weight on a string. Silk or cotton string is said to work best, with silver as the metal, so a silver ring hanging from a piece of silk thread or a silver chain is excellent. I've also used silver chains and necklaces, and even a regular washer on cotton thread, with excellent results. Commercial pendulums are usually crystals hung on a length of chain.

Cleanse your pendulum and "consecrate" it by holding it and saying or thinking this, or something similar:

> *I charge this pendulum for the highest good, to answer all my questions truly and accurately.*

I like to repeat this every time I use a pendulum. Then dangle the weight from the cord, and say or think: "I call upon my highest wisdom. Show me a yes answer." Close your eyes, and imagine yourself someplace very peaceful. Don't think about the pendulum. Then open your eyes after a few moments and watch the movement. How is it moving? That is your yes. Repeat this step, asking for a no response. Then you can ask your yes-or-no questions. Start with questions to which you know the answers, to get your bearings with the device, and then ask the rest of your questions.

Close your eyes and think of a peaceful place in which to learn to disconnect your conscious mind from the pendulum. By focusing on a peaceful place, you are not focusing your mind directly on the pendulum, subtle influencing it based on your desires or fears. Once you know your yes and no answers, many people think "yes, yes, yes" when they ask a question and want a yes, or visualize the pendulum moving to indicate a yes. It can be hard to know when your own personal power is moving the pendulum, what is called telekinesis or psychokinesis, and when your higher guidance is responding. This step helps you connect with your higher guidance and disconnect from your ego.

When done, say or think: "I thank my highest wisdom for these answers." Put down the pendulum. Many people keep it in a special bag or other sacred space, so it won't get mixed in with mundane items and energies.

The pendulum, and in fact any method of divination, is not infallible. Our egos can always potentially get in the way. I also believe in free will when it comes to divination. A divinatory reading shows you what is most likely at that moment, but with this information you can change your future. If you get information about something unhealthy or unwanted, you have the opportunity to change it, much like Scrooge in *A Christmas Carol*. Nothing is set in stone. You are empowered to create your own life.

10

PSYCHIC DEVELOPMENT

A natural extension of developing intuition is the expansion of other psychic gifts and abilities. In the Eastern traditions, they are said to be side effects of pursuing a mystical path, though the aspirant is warned not to be seduced by his or her power. In the West, we develop these skills to understand our connection to the universe and experience self-empowerment.

Psychic Defense

One of the key reasons I chose to write this book was to address the issue of psychic defense. Without education in the occult, many people are afraid of what could happen to them if they pursue an unorthodox spiritual path. Our culture is filled with books, movies, and stories that generate a great deal of fright, and without firmly rooted knowledge, it's hard to know what is real and what isn't. People are afraid that if they dabble in the mystical arts, demons and devils will carry them off into the night, but that is simply not true. Such images are truly part of a propaganda campaign that is strongest in the Western world, initially started to discourage people from exploring direct experience of the divine, or from seeking counsel from practitioners who were not authorized by the dominating church or government.

A lot of magical rituals and techniques are about purification and protection. In the traditions I teach, we create a sacred space and state that we are protected from all harm. We light incense to banish all harm. We wear potions and oils for protection. I wear a silver pentacle for protection. A friend once came to a ritual I was conducting and said, "Why do you need all that protection? If this isn't dangerous or evil, then why do you need so much protection?"

What a great question! I taught the rituals as I learned them, and they made sense to me, but until that point, I never really had to explain why protection is such a focus in magic rituals. Mysticism is not evil, and is not inherently harmful; it's a part of life. Like most things in life, there are risks and dangers. When you cross a street, you take the risk of getting hit by a car, so you take actions to make that unlikely. You learn to look both ways before you cross. You know not to cross during rush-hour traffic, or lounge in the middle of the road. These rules make sense, because the potential dangers of an oncoming car are apparent. You know the potential dangers and take the appropriate measures to protect yourself.

In the mystical world, any potential dangers are subtler than in the physical world. Subtle energy, the energy of the nonphysical planes, is potentially a danger when doing mystical work. This energy is very real, but not inherently harmful. Like a car, you can use it to drive from place to place, serving your needs and making things easier, or you can get hit by it without warning. It all depends on your relationship with the car, or with the energy.

Most often, we do protection and purification rituals to protect ourselves from the energy of our thoughts and feelings, which can conflict with our purpose. If you feel doubt, tension, fear, or even simple nervousness, it can work against your mystical pursuit. If you are working in a group, other members of the group can affect you too. Mystical work is usually done in a group, because group energy can be more powerful and can support you. Some people experience much more vivid meditations and energy in a group setting than on their own. Ritual creates a group consciousness, but at times group consciousness can detract from the magical working, particularly if there is someone who is not in harmony with everybody else in the group. Such preventive rituals can clear unwanted energies and prevent them from intruding again, in a solo or group situation.

I would like to be able to say that our own harmful energies are the only things we have to watch out for, but unfortunately that's not the case. Dangers can come in many forms, though they are usually not as colorful as Hollywood movies make them out to be.

If thoughts have energy, and "good" healing thoughts and prayers can help us, then harmful thoughts can hurt us. Most harmful energy comes from the environment around us. Our buildings, homes, and living conditions are not as naturally cleansing of energy as outdoor environments. Exposure to the elements—sun, wind, water, and land—is very purifying. Without this direct contact with nature, the energy of our thoughts and emotions builds up in our dwellings. If you live in a place with tension, arguments, illness, or violence, those energies can become imprinted on the dwelling and can influence its occupants. The flow of subtle life energy can become stagnant and prevent helpful influences from entering the lives of those who work or live there. One of the first exercises you learned in this book was "Cleansing Space," in chapter 2. It is an excellent protective ritual as well, to purify a space of stagnant, harmful energies.

When a person directs harmful thoughts, anger, fear, or hate toward you, the energy is real and can affect your daily health and well-being. That's one of the reasons that many magical practitioners keep their practices secret, so no one else can affect their work. If you are secure and anchored in yourself and your personal power, you usually will not be greatly affected by other people's harmful thoughts. If you are ungrounded, uncentered, and unsure, lack personal boundaries, or are overly sensitive to psychic energy, such thoughts can dramatically affect you.

Most people don't know that their thoughts have true power, so their thoughts usually don't have a lot of "wattage" behind them. Such people are not intentionally wishing you harm. They simply may be frustrated and directing their frustration at you because you are a convenient target. Sometimes people realize the power behind their thoughts, and use it maliciously. This is what some consider to be the "evil eye." Though it is not common, it is possible for practitioners of mystical arts who know their power to intentionally use their psychic or magical abilities to harm others, creating a curse of some sort.

Nonphysical beings are also potential dangers on the subtle planes. "Lower" entities are said to reside on the denser planes. The words "denser" and "lower" are just descriptions of discordant or inharmonious energy. The more subtle and refined the energy, the more spiritual, enlightened, and loving it is said to be. When we work with entities who act as our guides and teachers, we look to such refined beings for aid. Denser beings simply don't have the perspective or insight to help. Most are not inherently malevolent. Some are simply scavenger spirits. They have their place in creation as psychic scavengers, just like we have carrion feeders in the physical world.

When you first become magically, psychically, or spiritually "active," it is as if you are lighting up the spiritual planes, and many spirits, from all levels, will be checking out the new activity. Most people don't notice such things, but those with some sensitivity will feel as if they are being watched, or get a sense of what my students have described as the "creepy crawlies." As you continue your practice, such sensations will go away. You will become a part of the background, since you are no longer "new." For a time, your spiritual work will attract attention, but the more aligned you become with your part in the universe, the more you will become a harmonious part of the spiritual background and will not attract undue attention, unless your role requires you to attract attention. In fact, the greatest protection you can have from all psychic attack—intentional, unintentional, human, or spirit—is to find and fulfill your life purpose. When you live in harmony with the divine pattern, there is little that can deter you. Such purpose is often called true will, divine will, magical will, or dharma, and will be discussed in detail in the next chapter on magic and manifestation.

Some spirits are more harmful, creating the mythic images we have of demons and monsters, though the most serious and dangerous of these creatures are not spirits "outside" of ourselves but representations of the repressed parts of ourselves, our shadows and personal demons. We disarm them by becoming conscious of them and confronting the issues they embody.

Other harmful spirits are like harmful people, in that they can be helpful or harmful, and for the most part don't really care about you individually. The same commonsense rules about trusting people apply to spirits as well. If you intuitively don't trust someone, don't associate with that person. Don't put energy into a relationship. Draw a boundary, and clearly demonstrate that you do not want any contact.

Harmful spirits simply seek energy. Those that thrive on fear and anger want to feed off of fear and anger. If you want to stop them, stop taking them seriously. Harmful spirits get very upset when you stop taking them seriously and you laugh at them. By doing so, you transform your energy into something that will no longer feed them. You break the energetic circuit, the connection a spirit has. If you are not satisfying a spirit's needs, it will stop bothering you.

You have already learned some powerful protection techniques, such as cleansing, grounding, and creating protection shields and banishing pentagrams. Cleansing a space is very helpful, even when there is not a specific problem or danger present. It lightens the energy, making all mystical pursuits easier and more peaceful. Cleansing is a great preventive measure.

Charging your aura to create a protection shield around you is another great protection technique. I recharge mine frequently. You will find, as you become better versed in the technique, that everything has energy and you can charge that energy to create a protection shield. I also put up protection shields around my home, office, and car.

The banishing pentagram is a powerful and trusted technique. Drawn in the four directions around you, it not only can help heal and protect the aura, but can banish any unwanted spirits or clear an entire room. If you feel harmful energy being sent toward you from a particular direction, you can draw a banishing pentagram in that direction to break the connection. If you feel you are under psychic attack, you can draw banishing pentagrams all around you. I also like to draw them on all the doors, windows, and other entry points to a building.

When drawn in the four directions, the banishing pentagram is a simple version of a more complex ritual known as the Lesser Banishing Ritual of the Pentagram, or LBRP. This is one of the first rituals taught to those in a ceremonial magic tradition. It is a preliminary process that prepares you for deeper work, continually healing and clearing your energetic field. Strangely enough, I have found that the ritual has made its way into many different nonceremonial traditions and settings. I was surprised to find a yogi using it to clear his studio before classes. He felt it cleared any influences from the last class and gave a fresh, new start. Many involved in Wicca learn about ceremonial magic in their training, and use the LBRP to prepare the space prior to a ritual.

EXERCISE

Lesser Banishing Ritual of the Pentagram

The Lesser Banishing Ritual of the Pentagram involves several parts. It is drawn from the modern ceremonial tradition of the order most commonly known as the Hermetic Order of the Golden Dawn. In the ritual, symbolism from Jewish, Christian, and Pagan sources are fused into a harmonious whole.

This type of ritual involves coordinating movements, sounds, and visualizations. Combined, they move and transform energy to fulfill the purpose of the ritual. Intention is the key to bring together the individual parts. The first part, called the Qabalistic Cross, is similar to the traditional Lord's Prayer and Sign of the Cross. The practitioner imagines himself or herself as the Qabalistic Tree of Life, with the top sphere at the crown and the bottom sphere at the feet. The words of power are intoned or vibrated, meaning that they are not simply recited, but are spoken with power and intention. The practitioner draws out the power of the sound by holding the note, much like a chant. The words are not sung with melody, but simply intoned. Many books create great confusion over the correct way to vibrate such words, making the process more complicated than it needs to be. Simply try intoning the words, and see how it feels. You will find your own style and method of doing it. I've never found two magicians, or two traditions, that do it exactly the same way.

Qabalistic Cross

Stand firm and tall. Face east and take a few deep breaths. Feel the world below you and a sphere of heavenly white light above you.

Point to your forehead with your right hand or with a ritual blade. Visualize a beam of white light entering your crown chakra. Imagine your crown is the top of the Tree of Life.
Intone: **Ata**

Point to the root chakra or ground with your right hand. Visualize the beam of light descending from your crown, down to your root, then down to the Earth between your feet. Imagine the bottom sphere of the Tree of Life between your feet. Feel a connection between your crown and the Earth.
Chant: **Malkuth**

Point to your right shoulder with your right hand. Visualize a beam of light from the space to your right that comes into your right shoulder.
Chant: **Veh Gebura**

Point to your left shoulder with your right hand. Visualize the beam of light moving across from your right shoulder to your left shoulder, crossing the first, vertical beam at the heart/throat area. Feel the beam of light move out of your left shoulder and into the space to your left.
Chant: **Veh Gadula**

Bring your hands to your heart center in prayer position, palms pressed together.
Chant: **Le Oh Lam**

Focus on the cross of light running through the middle of your body. Feel yourself grounded and balanced. Focus on your connection to all.
Chant: **Amen**

The purpose of this part of the ritual is to root the image of the Tree of Life within your aura. You are connecting to the highest sphere in the vertical line, Kether, and the lowest sphere, Malkuth. Divine light for protection and wisdom will flow through you. You are also connecting to spheres on each side pillar, Geburah and Chesed (which is also known as Gadula). Through the Qabalistic Cross, you become one with the Tree of Life and the forces of creation.

Next, you can commence with the true banishing ritual. If you are in a small room, or simply banishing harm from your aura, turn in one-quarter steps as directed. If you are clearing a larger room or temple, move one quarter of the way around the room as you perform the banishing.

Banishing Ritual
Face east and draw a banishing pentagram in blue light.
Chant: **Yud Heh Vahv Heh**
With your finger, point to the center of the pentagram and slowly turn clockwise ninety degrees, visualizing one quarter of the circle being drawn in white light, connecting east to south.

Facing south, draw a banishing pentagram in blue light.
Chant: **Adonai**
With your finger, point to the center of the pentagram and slowly turn clockwise ninety degrees, visualizing one quarter of the circle being drawn in white light, connecting south to west.

Facing west, draw a banishing pentagram in blue light.
Chant: **Eh Heh Eh**
With your finger, point to the center of the pentagram and slowly turn clockwise ninety degrees, visualizing one quarter of the circle being drawn in white light, connecting west to north.

Facing north, draw a banishing pentagram in blue light.
Chant: **Agla**

Complete the circle and face east again. Visualize one quarter of a circle in light, connecting north to east.

Feel yourself surrounded in a ring of light, with a blazing blue pentagram in each of the four cardinal directions. Each pentagram is energized by chanting one of the four names of God found in ceremonial magic, associated with the four directions.

Call upon the archangelic guardians of the four directions with the following chant. Since this is a banishing ritual, many perceive them to be facing outward, guarding and protecting.

Chant:
Before me, Raphael.
Behind me, Gabriel.
On my right hand, Michael.
On my left hand, Uriel.
Before me shines the pentagram.

Stretch out your arms and legs, and visualize yourself as a banishing pentagram. Visualize a hexagram, a six-pointed star, in your heart chakra.
Chant: **Within me shines the six-rayed star.**

Repeat the Qabalistic Cross. Then the ritual is complete. Notice the changes in the feel and energy of the room.

The LBRP is a foundation exercise in psychic self-defense. Many people are afraid to use it because of the seemingly complicated gestures, visualizations, and words involved. I know I was intimidated when I first learned it. From my experience, I've found that even though each part of the ritual is important, the intention is the most important of all. The LBRP is a great exercise to have to maintain basic psychic self-defense, balance, and health. I know many advanced practitioners who still practice this ritual regularly. I do recommend that you try it, and if it doesn't suit your tastes, you can find a way to adapt it that is more comfortable for you.

Psychic Travel

Psychic travel, also known as astral travel, mental travel, or remote viewing, depending on the technique, is one of the most sought-after psychic talents. I have students who take long-term classes just to learn this technique. It can be a powerful and useful tool, but always keep in mind that it is one tool of many.

Psychic travel refers to projecting your awareness beyond your body. Many people have the ability to retrieve and retain information from whatever location they visit. Technically, psychic travel can refer to any activity that projects your consciousness away from your body. All our pathworking meditations are a form of psychic travel. Dreams are a form of psychic travel. Any type of guided meditation or shamanic journey is a form of travel. Near-death experiences, or NDEs, which are becoming more prevalent in our culture, are a form of psychic travel. Most people, when they refer to psychic travel, are referring to traveling psychically along the physical plane, finding accurate details about locations they have never physically visited.

Most people think of psychic travel as astral travel, which involves projecting the astral body out of the physical body. Expectations run high, and many believe, due to other reports and descriptions, that psychic travel and out-of-body experiences are always identical. They expect all psychic travel to be a dramatic, detailed experience, with full sensations of being out of body. Technically, the astral body is just one component of your energy, and projecting it outward doesn't leave your body "empty." Sometimes it can feel that way, and many people believe that elusive empty feeling is what makes the experience real. Most psychic travel experiences are not as dramatic and, at least initially, can simply be vague impressions. But with experience you will find that those vague impressions are often right, and with time and practice you can refine your skills.

Some traditions divide psychic travel into astral travel, mental travel, and soul travel, referring to the part of your psyche that you are projecting forward. Though I personally don't think such distinctions are important in the overall effect of the exercise, they can be helpful in understanding the various sensations and perceived experiences. Though many of my students don't have vivid out-of-body experiences with these psychic development exercises, most are able to become fairly proficient at a form of mental travel, where their awareness is viewing things remotely, yet they are still vaguely aware of their body and the physical surroundings of their body.

Some think of this as bilocation, where your consciousness is located in two places at once. Those with keen psychic senses might be able to perceive their "double" at their target location. Other traditions refer to bilocation as full physical manifestation at two places at the same time, visible to all regardless of psychic ability. I don't know of too many people who can credibly claim that skill, though I believe anything is possible.

Why do people focus so much on psychic travel? Well, there are a lot of reasons, though most seekers are unaware of them. Generally, people want to do it because it seems cool. They think of psychic ability as a superpower, and psychic travel seems very super indeed. They want to have a real and vivid experience to prove that mystical experiences are real, and psychic travel seems so far out of the range of "normal" skills that it qualifies as something truly mystical. People chalk up many other mystical experiences to coincidence or luck. Being able to visit a location you have never physically been to, and then verify that your impressions are correct, is a very powerful experience, opening you up to a new worldview that is not only possible in theory but possible personally.

As for practical, earthly purposes, there are not a lot of reasons to do this work unless you are involved in espionage or otherwise need to gather information and bypass conventional routes. If you learn other magical arts, such as healing, you can use psychic travel to send healing energy to others distantly and check in on their condition. Psychic travel can be mixed with many other disciplines. For example, you can send messages via dreams.

Psychic travel along the physical plane helps validate psychic travel on the subtle planes. Many people think of their earthly remote-viewing experiences as "real" because they can be objectively verified, but they consider their experiences beyond the physical, where shape and form are more symbolic and subjective, as less than real. Both are realities, but different kinds of realities. With success in the objective experiences, and the realization that you are using the same faculties in the more subjective experiences, your subtle-plane journeys—from guided meditations to dreams—carry more weight, meaning, and importance. They become more real and not idle fantasies or daydreams.

Before doing the following psychic travel exercise, reaffirm any of your protection disciplines and make sure you will not be disturbed. Many seekers and teachings talk about how you will not be able to find your body if it is moved during psychic travel, or that if someone tries to wake you, you will die. Some talk of a silver or gold cord that attaches your astral body to your physical body, and if the cord is cut, you will be lost or dead. From my own personal experience, as well as my students' experiences, I have found that the worst thing that happens if you are disturbed during psychic travel is you get a really bad headache. I believe the perception of the cord, usually from the solar plexus, is a projection of your energy from that point. It is as if your awareness is projected and stretched out from that chakra, giving the appearance psychically of a cord. What seems to happen is your energy "snaps" back, creating a sense of psychic whiplash, and while that can be rather unpleasant, it is not life-threatening. Still, I try to avoid it.

Pick a target location that you have never been to, but you can easily visit. I suggest a store where you know the location, but have not been inside. Independent stores, rather than large chains, are often a bit more of a challenge, keeping us from using our associations with other stores of the same name.

You can also "visit" a particular person you know, someone who is willing to be your partner for this exercise. You can write down whatever you see or hear the person doing at a particular time, and the individual can report his or her activities at that moment, to see if you are accurate. Since the astral plane is technically beyond time, make sure you hold the intention that you wish to visit the person "at this moment, on the physical plane," and note the times at the start and end of your exercise, so no confusion will result.

EXERCISE
Psychic Travel

Sit in a quiet place in a comfortable position. Take a few deep breaths, centering yourself and your awareness. Feel yourself relaxing from head to toe, getting into a deeper meditative state. Be aware of your surroundings, but focus on your own breath and body, allowing yourself to relax deeply and become more centered.

Think about your target. Focus all your attention and will on the target. Imagine yourself projecting out toward your target. Feel your energy, aspects of your psyche, going toward the target. Don't worry if you don't know the way physically via streets and roads. You will be guided by your magical will. I often imagine I am traveling through a tunnel of pure light. One end is at my body, and the other end at the target.

When you arrive at your destination, take a look around. Be aware of all your impressions, using all your senses. Traditionally, this is a more visually oriented exercise, but those who feel they lack visualization abilities might be surprised at the strong feelings and impressions they get. Your information may not be visual, but instead you simply know the shape, color, and layout of the target. Don't worry if your impressions are not crystal clear. Go with your first impression and trust it. Things will become clearer if you relax and simply go with the process.

With practice, you will discover your own style and methods of psychic travel. If you work well with spirit guides, you can call upon a spirit guide to help you in the process, and may take the journey together. If the location is dark at the time you are visiting, psychically create light, or ask your guides for light, to see things more clearly.

When you are done, return the way you came. Ground yourself in your body. Feel the physical world around you. When ready, rise from your position and reorient yourself. Quickly write down all your impressions, so you don't forget them.

When you are ready, check out the location or speak to your partner. Don't worry about being 100 percent accurate, at least at first. As with all things, it takes time and patience to develop this skill. Every "hit" you have is a major accomplishment, even if the impression was vague, such as "I feel the color blue to the left of the entrance." You might not have known it was a rack of blue jackets, but that is still very impressive. Take enjoyment in all your successes. With acceptance of these blessings, your abilities will improve.

Dreams

Dreams are another way we explore our psychic abilities and ability to travel to other realms. Though mystics seek to consciously control these abilities, some have far more success when their conscious mind is asleep, and out of the way, allowing for a greater intuitive or mystical experience to occur. Many traditions, and in particular Tibetan mysticism, highly encourage seekers to develop an active dream life as a part of the spiritual development process.

So what are dreams, and where do they come from? There are no easy answers. Modern science looks at dreams as the product of involuntary biological processes occurring when we sleep. Dreams are associated with rapid eye movement (REM) sleep, and occur with elevated breath, heart rate, and body paralysis. Our minds interpret the random brain impulses occurring while we sleep as sensory information. Dreams are a series of images, sounds, and sensations that we experience in this sleep state, ranging from pleasant dreams to nightmares, as well as sexual dreams. On one level, this scientific viewpoint of dreams is correct, yet it doesn't really explain them.

From a psychologist's point of view, dreams are contact from our subconscious or unconscious mind. Through them we gain insights about ourselves, our motivations, behaviors, and issues that need to be addressed. Often, people who are disturbed by unresolved feelings of guilt, anger, or shame will find these themes in their dreams. Issues and information we don't want to consciously recognize or verbalize can become the themes of some dreams, though most dreams stem from day-to-day occurrences, as the mind unwinds from the stresses of waking life during sleep. Other dreams are stray thoughts, fantasy fulfillment, or a whole range of themes that might not have any deep significance or point the way toward any issue. Though dream interpretation, made famous by Sigmund Freud, is a popular aid in some forms of psychotherapy, most academics don't necessarily believe that dreams have clear meanings or messages.

From the mystic's point of view, dreams are an opportunity for your consciousness to enter a different state of being. Through sleep, you open a gateway to other worlds, where thoughts, emotions, and reality are not as keenly separated as they are in the physical world. Your thoughts and feelings manifest in symbolic form in the dream world. In the model of our cosmos, the dream world is associated with the astral and emotional planes of existence. Every night, everybody, regardless of their mystical interest in the conscious world, has an opportunity to interface with other dimensions as well as deepen their relationship with their own psyche. Mystics, however, learn to retrieve this dream-time information, and bring it back to the conscious world.

Yes, some dreams are simply the chatter of your mind taking on shape and form, but there are dreams that are significant, that seem different or important. The memory of them often fades, but with training you can learn to remember your dreams, and program them to aid you in your waking life. You can even "wake up" in the dream itself, realize that you are dreaming, and take charge of the dream. This type of clear dreaming is known as lucid dreaming. Some people do it naturally, but the rest of us can learn techniques for it. We can learn to do lucid dreaming for our own enjoyment, but also to practice the powers of manifestation, to know that our thoughts create our reality, but to do this practice in a safe environment. Lucid dreaming is a great preparation and enhancement for magical work. Lucid dreaming can also be seen as a form of psychic projection, projecting your consciousness to the dream world of the astral plane rather than to a physical location on Earth.

Prophecy and psychic prediction are a large part of dream workings. You can dream something, and then sometime later it literally comes true. Many people receive information through a dream about whatever is about to happen in their lives. According to Ward Hill Lamon, a friend of Abraham Lincoln, the president, had a dream that predicted his assassination. Dream prophecy, also known as oneiromancy, was a popular art in ancient cultures, including biblical times, as Joseph interpreted the dreams of the Egyptian court.

Oftentimes, prophetic dreams are not direct messages, but are related in symbolism. You don't see exactly what is going to happen, but through the dream's story you can relate it to your life in a way that speaks to you. The symbols have to be decoded. We use psychology, mythology, and modern symbolism to understand what dreams are telling us. Some dream symbols are universal, part of our collective human databanks, while others are more localized. The culture you live in can affect the dream symbolism. Someone living in an urban section of the United States will have some associations different from someone living in a tribal culture in the Brazilian rain forest.

Although oneiromancy technically refers to the prophetic aspect of dreams, it has developed into more mainstream dream interpretation that delivers messages and insights, if not direct prophecies and psychic predictions. Dream interpretation is an artistic skill as well as a psychological one, requiring both intuition and knowledge of stories, myths, and archetypes, as well as a sense of how they would relate to that individual. Often, the meaning of a dream is not completely clear until much later, if ever.

Greek literature and myth state that dreams come to us from one of two gates. Dreams that come to use through the Gate of Horn are true, while those that come through the Gate of Ivory are deceitful and empty. Sometimes it's hard to tell which type of dream is which. Trusting our intuition is a key to determining which dreams feel right and which ones don't. Other spiritual practices, such as meditation, and treatments, such as psychotherapy, help us distinguish between our hopes and fears and our intuitive impressions.

If they are not random brain impulses, then where do these dream messages come from, according to our spiritual model? Some would say they are communications from your own self, your higher consciousness, as filtered through the unconscious mind. In modern Huna, the controversial system of spirituality drawn from Hawaiian traditions, dreams are said to be messages from the higher divine self, as couriered by the lower, psychic self. When we are not conscious of our higher self, the messages come through garbled and are hard to understand. When we are more spiritually tuned in, we hear the higher self's message more clearly and know which dreams to pay attention to and which are unimportant. Other teachings would say they are communications not from the higher self but from other nonphysical entities—spirits guides, angels, deities—using the gateway of dreams to send a message to you, since in your waking life you pay little attention to the unseen world. Communication with spirits is easier in the world of dreams, yet difficult to remember.

Here are some tips to help you activate your dream life:

- Keep a notebook or recorder by your bedside. When you wake up, record the first thing you remember, even if it's "I don't remember." This practice will get you in the habit of retrieving dream memories when you first wake up.

- Set a snooze alarm a half hour before you have to get up. Wake up a few times to the snooze alarm, and each time you do, try to remember your dreams and record them. When REM sleep is interrupted, the dream memory is much more present in the conscious waking mind.

- Look at your dreams over the course of a month, or Moon cycle, and see if you notice any themes or patterns. The dreams might not make a lot of sense individually, but over a cycle you may see similar themes. Or you might notice that when the Moon is full, or dark, you have clearer, more meaningful dreams. It is well worth it to get an astrological calendar and take note of the Moon signs. Certain signs and phases of Moon activity can facilitate dream work. The Moon is the astrological body that rules over dreams and the unconscious, as well as psychic ability.

- The following herbs are helpful in dream working: chamomile, catnip, lavender, lemon, lemon balm, mugwort, rose, sandalwood, valerian, vanilla, and wormwood. Put a combination of these herbs that is pleasing to you in a small pouch, and place it under your pillow to enhance your dreams.

- The following stones enhance dreams: aquamarine, beryl, clear quartz, Herkimer diamond, moonstone, mother of pearl, opal, pearl, selenite, and the metal silver. Cleanse the stone in incense smoke, water (except selenite, since it's a water-soluble salt), or pure intention, and place it under your pillow or in a bag with the herbs mentioned above.

- If you have a question, problem, or issue in life that you need insight and understanding to solve, write it out as clearly as possible and put it under your pillow. When you wake up the next day, see if your dream contains some clue to the answer.

11

MAGIC

Magic is a powerful, evocative word. All cultures and traditions recognize magic, but not all use the same word for it. Magic is the process of creation. All creation stories are really magic stories, regardless of the mythology. They often start with a word, sound, or song. In the New Testament, John 1:1 says: "In the beginning was the Word, and the Word was with God, and the Word was God." The Word is a magic word. Sound and word are vibrations. Vibration is energy. Harnessing and directing energy is magic. Your own words have the same creative power and energy.

Energy comes in many forms. Not only are our words energy, but our thoughts and actions are too. Herbs, metals, stones, symbols, and colors are all forms of energy. Traditional forms of magic involve all sorts of exotic paraphernalia and recipes. Though they have powerful symbolic value as well, each resonates with a particular type of energy. Magic rituals harness this energy, along with the magician's will, to create a change in reality.

Magic is described as a science. Though many people would disagree with that description, magic conforms to basic principles and parameters that are consistent. If you look across many cultures, the paradigms describing magic are different, but each contains some basic similarities that can be boiled down to what metaphysical students call magic theory.

A popular thought stated in science fiction literature is that any science or technology not understood by an observer appears to be magic. When we think of all the technological marvels at hand in the current era, people in the past would probably be awestruck by our technology, and assume it has a magical origin. The same process works in reverse. Technologies from the past, relying on principles not generally understood in the modern era, seem fantastic or unbelievable, but at one time they were a part of the ordinary view of reality.

Nonmagical practitioners often think of magic as a science as well, but do not understand how the practitioner is intrinsically tied to the process. Magic is a science, but it is also an art, a skill to be learned. Modern stories propagate the idea that if you simply say the right magic word, at the right time, and in the right place, or mix together the right combination of exotic ingredients, poof, something amazing will happen. As in modern science, they expect all experiments to be repeatable by anyone. Under the right laboratory conditions, two parts hydrogen to one part oxygen always makes H_2O, or water. This chemical reaction is predictable and repeatable. Sugar dissolves in water, a process that's also repeatable. It doesn't matter who does it. The results are always consistent if the conditions and the procedure are the same.

With art, it's an entirely different matter. Imagine a room full of people with a wide variety of skills, tastes, and backgrounds. We can all start with the same box of paints, have all the same resources available, and all be shown a model whose portrait we are to paint. Each rendition will be different, unique to that artist and to that moment in time. The principles of painting, design, and color are consistent, but what you do with them is unique. Magic is much the same.

Unlike traditional science, magic doesn't recognize truly consistent and controlled laboratory conditions. The principles are universal, but each moment in time is unique, adding to the many variables. Different times of day, year, and astrological cycles have an influence in magic. Each person is unique, and brings the greatest variable. Magical formulas fuse with the practitioner's will, focus, concentration, and intent. We each have those qualities in different measures, and the variations between practitioners doing the same spell will affect the intended outcome.

Because of the mythical qualities surrounding magic, many people are surprised to discover how magical their lives are. We are all doing magic all the time. The difference between a true magician and everybody else is that a magician is consciously aware of the magical reality, and uses this awareness as a part of his or her personal and spiritual path. To the practitioner of magic, every thought, word, and action is part of our magical reality.

Those on the spiritual paths of ceremonial magic, Witchcraft and Wicca, and Pagan-ism are traditional practitioners of magic, reclaiming old ways and adapting them to the modern world. They often spell magick with a *k*, to distinguish esoteric, spiritual forms of magick from sleight-of-hand stage tricks. Other people use the power of magic, but call it prayer, positive thinking, creative visualization, or manifestation. A shamanic practitioner might call it medicine. All have a different worldview, a different paradigm in which they believe their system works. Many follow the mystical techniques outlined in this book, though they would use different words.

Most other practitioners would be aghast to think their techniques have anything to do with magic. A good Catholic praying for healing would not think of it as magic, but there is not much difference between that and forms of folk magic. Some like to say that meditation is listening to the divine, while prayer or magic is speaking to the divine. Both are needed for a balanced mystical practice. More conventional people, not on a path of magical spirituality, sometimes seek out magic as a quick fix to their problems. They will seek out a money spell, love charm, healing, or even curse in times of desperation. Some-times magic can be the solution to a problem, but ultimately magic works best when it is part of a spiritual practice, done in the context of a spiritual tradition. Those who are trained in magic will also be trained to think about the ethics and consequences of their actions. Those who dabble in emergencies, or seek out less-than-reputable practitioners for aid, often cross moral and spiritual lines that have far-reaching consequences they did not contemplate at the start of the magic.

The manifestation of magic can disappoint those looking for Hollywood movie excite-ment. If you expect lightning bolts from your fingers, it may be theoretically possible, but I've never seen it, and quite frankly the amount of effort it would take to attempt such a thing would not be worth it. Many people ask me, as a practitioner of magical arts, ques-tions like, "Can you telekinetically levitate a book across a room?" Why would I do so, when I can just as easily pick it up and move it across the room? Magic is a practical, earthy art in many respects, and follows the path of least resistance. Practitioners are not con-cerned with exactly how the result manifests, just that it does manifest. If it's easier to get up and do something, we do it. Much of our magic relies on real-world follow-up.

Magic will more likely manifest through a series of coincidences. Sometimes the results are immediate, but other times they take days, weeks, and even months to manifest. Though some amazing things can happen, usually the results are mundane. They are synchronicities, but not out of the realm of possibility. The practitioner casts a spell, a specific act of magic, with a specific intent, a desired result that changes reality. The change is first created on the subtle planes of reality, and eventually the energy trickles down, or precipitates, into the physical world. Like flowing water, magical energy will take the path of least resistance to manifest something, unless you "program" it to do otherwise.

Energy is programmed through a spell, given a specific set of instructions. This programmed energy is called a thoughtform. Unwanted thoughtforms, or unhelpful programs, can get stuck in your energetic field, and are removed when you clear your aura. Helpful thoughtforms can be very beneficial. Usually they last until the spell is completed, but some are semipermanent. In fact, many people believe that certain spirits are thoughtforms created by a tradition, sustained by the knowledge and belief of the practitioners.

If you do a spell to get a new job, you should specify the type of job, pay range, or any other requirements you have. If you don't, you might get the new job at a fast food restaurant, being fired from your quiet office job, and feel like it was a step down for you. Neither job is inherently good or bad. You asked for a new job, and the universe gave it to you. You should have asked more wisely. Keep in mind the old saying "Be careful what you wish for, because you just might get it." Make sure you really want what you have done a spell for, not what you think you have done a spell for. Intention is powerful, but intention must be coupled with clarity.

On the other hand, you might be so specific in your spell craft that you make the fulfillment of the spell impossible. If you ask to immediately become the head of a department at a specific company, make double your current salary, and have the corner office and the best parking spot, the universe might not be able to fulfill that request. If you left your intention open to a specific type of job and a specific type of company, with an acceptable pay range and benefits, then more possible openings could fit your desire.

Lastly, you have to follow up with real-world action. If you do a job spell, get your resumé together. Network. Answer help wanted ads. Practice interviewing skills. Prepare. Magic can knock on the door, but if you are not prepared to answer it and let a new blessing in, then a spell will be of no help. Sometimes a spell manifests so quickly that you don't have time to follow it up with extensive real-world action, and that's wonderful when it happens, but it's not always the case. You might do a job spell and immediately get a phone call with a job tip or offer. Still, you must be prepared to follow up.

One of the most important stipulations that I put into all my spells is that the result be "for the highest good." I want to make sure that my desires do not hurt anybody else. Some people say "for the good of all involved, harming none" or "for higher divine will." Another favorite is that the result be "completely acceptable to me on all levels." Many people fear, particularly if they are not comfortable with the idea of magic in terms of religion, that if they do a spell, something horrible will happen to fulfill it, making it a curse. Sometimes that does happen. You do a money spell, and get into an accident and win an insurance settlement. Yes, you got money, but are you enjoying it with your injuries? I'd rather have less money and be pain-free. If you do such a spell with the intention "for the highest good, harming none," you can usually avoid such problems, though not always. Magic is a blessing, but it's not always safe. It doesn't always give you what you think you asked to get.

Though many people think practicing magic is selfish and immoral, most practitioners have the highest morals and ethics. There are very few rules to magic, though different traditions of magic have their own spiritual codes. The reason magicians are ethical is because they know firsthand about something called the Law of Return. Basically stated, what you do comes back to you, usually amplified. It's the fundamental reason that magic works. Through words, rituals, and visualization, you take what appear to be your insubstantial thoughts and make them reality. The thoughts return to you amplified as a reality. The thoughts and emotions that fuel your magic return to you. If you do a spell with anger and malice, then more anger and malice will return to you. In the end, all magicians have to be responsible for their creations, because they know they are creating their own reality, through their spells, and through all thoughts, words, and deeds. Spells are just the most focused and powerful of their thoughts, words, and deeds.

So if magic can backfire if you are not careful, and carries all this weight of responsibility with it, why would anyone do it? Each practitioner has his or her own reasons for walking the path.

Many of these reasons are practical in nature. You are already doing magic, so why not really understand what you are doing? It's not selfish. Most people are already trying to manifest their will on Earth, but most don't take the time to think about their motivations and actions, and take responsibility for them. Although magic is described as supernatural, it's really just natural, and we all tap into the powers of the universe in different ways.

The other main reason to practice magic is spiritual in nature. Through knowledge and study of the various correspondences associated with magic, we learn about the universe. Humanity is a reflection of the cosmos, and the cosmos is a reflection of humanity. We learn to see, hear, and feel the life in all worlds, human and nonhuman, physical and nonphysical. Spell work helps us focus our will with the use of herbs and stones that resonate with our intention, and helps us partner with these energies to create a harmonious world for us all.

By communing with the plant, animal, and mineral kingdoms, as well as studying the seasons and stars, we learn more about ourselves. We begin to see patterns and make connections that most people do not. Magic is truly a path of introspection. Magical practitioners were the first psychologists, healers, and ministers in the ancient world. Esoteric systems have profound systems of soul psychology that many people find more helpful than modern psychological models.

Magic is any change that conforms with a person's will. Magicians recognize many realities, not just the physical. Sometimes the most profound magic is a shift in your own consciousness. By changing your awareness, you change the way you interact with the physical world and thus change your reality. As practitioners become more proficient, they often start focusing less on making changes in the physical world, knowing how to do so if needed, and turn their attention to changing their own thoughts, feelings, and body, to create the change they desire.

Magic is associated with will. Some distinguish between different types of will. Most people are familiar with personal will, which is your desire. What do you want? That is your will. Another way to look at will is higher will, also known as divine will, true will, or magical will. What is it that your soul, your highest consciousness, wants? What is your true purpose in life?

Exploring spiritual magic is exploring your divine purpose. Sometimes your personal will is in conflict with your divine will. If you do magic consistently for a specific purpose, and it doesn't succeed, then you must take time to reflect. Were the technique and execution of the spell flawed, or is the universe not supporting you because the spell's intent is not for your highest good? If the universe is supporting your will, then you will have a clearer understanding of your purpose and true will. The more you understand and execute your true will, the more you live in communion with the divine. Eventually, every thought, word, and action becomes an act of devotion and partnership with the divine, to manifest your true will in the world.

You can study and execute magic in many different ways. Many people assume that magic is divided into white magic and black magic. Most practitioners don't use those terms, and even those who do don't use the Hollywood stereotypes attached to them. The average person on the street would say that white magic is good and black magic is evil. Magicians don't see it that way. Yes, black magic is technically any magic that is used to harm another, or impose one's will on another. White magic is not just good magic, but any magic with the intent of spiritual alignment with the divine. Continually conscious spiritual alignment with the divine is called Enlightenment in the East. Ceremonial magicians and alchemists in the West call it the Great Work.

So in what category is a healing spell? Most people assume a healing spell is white magic, because it is good. Not necessarily. Technically, it is gray magic, effecting a change in the physical world but not necessarily causing harm to another. If you do a healing spell against someone else's wishes, you are doing black magic. Perhaps on some level the person wants to be ill, and you are subverting his or her personal or divine will. The same goes for those who "pray" for others without their consent, if they are praying for a specific outcome not in alignment with the wishes of the recipients of the prayer. Many "pray" for Pagans to find Jesus or for homosexuals to become straight, and technically those prayers are a form of black magic. Some pray with the intent of "the highest good" or for "grace," leaving it up to the divine as to whether and how the prayer should manifest. That is much less potentially harmful and potentially quite helpful. The best thing to do is ask permission of the intended recipient, and only do magic or pray if you have permission. We often think we know best, but we don't always see past what we want for others.

Black, white, and even gray magic have fallen out of favor as magical terms, particularly among Pagan practitioners who embrace both the dark and light as descriptions of the divine, and do not associate either with purely good or purely evil. They look at the aspects of polarity as nature, expressed as female and male, Goddess and God. Some practitioners use the color terms until their students understand magic well enough to discard them. Other practitioners attribute certain colors to magic for specific purposes, such as green magic for money magic or purple magic for spirit magic.

Magic and Western mysticism have been called the "black arts" throughout the ages, conjuring images of "black" magic and curses, though there is a very good reason that all magic can be considered the black arts. In Western alchemy, there is the step of spiritual putrefication, or darkening, associated with the black depths of darkness and despair. Spiritually, we can think of this as the profoundly moving "dark night of the soul." The light is temporarily expunged, and the mystic is faced with what is dark and dense before coming to a greater sense of spiritual awareness and fortitude. All mystics must face the shadow. It is like the darkness before the dawn.

Other practitioners divide magic based on technique, referring to high and low magic. High magic is intricate ceremonial magic, with elaborate ritual tools, specific gestures, rituals often in foreign languages, and usually a more lofty spiritual pursuit. Historically, high magic was shrouded in secrecy and practiced only by those with the luxuries of time, education, and financial resources, but now it is available to anyone through popular books and the Internet.

Low magic is the magic of the peasant folks, using simple household tools, herbs, and stones with an intuitive style. The goals of low magic are more practical, day-to-day concerns, such as prosperity, love, fertility, and protection. Many think of high magic as spiritual and low magic as practical, but in the end they encompass both realms.

Spells

How do you cast a spell? Some basic techniques exist. Just as with artistic techniques, start with the ones that capture your imagination first. They will work best for you, but don't be afraid to expand your repertoire beyond your normal boundaries and explore something new.

For me, the key component of magic is ritual. Though the word conjures quite a vivid image for the magical practitioner, a ritual is simply any repeated action done with meaning. Rituals are different from habits, because they are repeated actions that serve your will, that you are fully conscious of; habits, on the other hand, are usually unconscious and sometimes harmful. Rituals can involve complicated ceremonies and exotic tools, but many of our magic rituals are simple actions. They are symbolic actions of what we want to create. Symbolic actions are one of the best ways of speaking to the universe, and having the universe respond and create what we want. If all that we do returns to us magnified, a ritual clearly communicates what we want to create and efficiently allows it to manifest in our world. Rituals allow us to gather, focus, and release energy. The stronger and clearer the energy, the more likely that it will manifest our desire.

Traditional magic rituals use time-honored techniques, though that doesn't mean new techniques cannot be discovered. Most "new" techniques follow the same patterns and theories, but simply express these ideas in a new way. Some traditional rituals are done repeatedly, the same way, for the same purpose. The Lesser Banishing Ritual of the Pentagram is one such ritual. Others are more open-ended, for more specific acts of manifestation, such as the Witch's magic circle.

Simple folk rituals, which can be used by anybody, frequently mimic the actions they seek to accomplish. To the magician, you are creating an action on a smaller scale, or microcosm, and it will be reflected on the larger scale, or macrocosm. If you want to create rain, pouring a little water during a ritual is a way to communicate that desire to the universe. If you want to cleanse your home of harmful energy, try physically cleansing the space. You can use soap and water, but add a few ingredients that are known for protection and cleansing, such as salt or lavender oil. As you cleanse physically, use your intent and imagine the space psychically cleansed. Such actions are also called sympathetic magic. You literally perform an action that symbolizes what you want to occur. In this case, physical cleaning corresponds to psychic cleaning. Other examples of sympathetic magic include cutting a string to break ties with someone harmful to you; planting a seed for some quality you want to grow in your life, such as prosperity; or sticking pins in a poppet or Voodoo doll to heal or harm the one for whom the doll was made and named.

Here are some popular magical techniques found in the modern era.

Affirmations

To traditionalists, affirmations don't seem like magic, but they are a powerful tool in manifestation, using word magic. Some people think of it as positive thinking or reprogramming the consciousness. An affirmation is usually a positive statement of what you want to create. Instead of focusing on your desire, saying "I want," you focus your energy as if you already have what you want, with such positive statements as "I have" or even more popularly "I am." The energy you send out is of abundance, of having, not wanting, so having is what manifests. Many people use the affirmation "I am prosperous," repeating it daily. That affirmation does create prosperity, but if you were to say "I want prosperity," all you would do is magnify your own want of it, rather than create actual prosperity. I have found that using affirmations repeated in sets of a sacred number—such as three, four, five, seven, nine, and, in general, multiples of three, such as thirty-three and one hundred eight—has a powerful effect. In the study of numerology, three is the number of manifestation.

Visualization

Visualization is another popular skill that most people don't associate with magic. Many call it creative visualization and think of it as a modern psychological technique, but it is the basis for much of our more esoteric magical work. The technique consists of getting into a focused yet relaxed state, a light meditative state often known as the alpha state in scientific terms. While in this state, visualize what you want to create in your life. As when doing affirmations, don't focus on the "want" of it; imagine yourself already having it. How does it feel to have it? Though we call this technique visualization, it is not totally visual, and many people who feel they are not "good" at visualization can still do it. Magical visualization is really imagination, imagination with intent. Some students say that they feel they are making it up. That it's not real. It's not magical. They are just using their imagination. I say, yes! Then you are doing it perfectly. Use your imagination. That is magic. Bells and whistles will not go off because it is magic. The state of mind you are in is very similar to a daydream, except you are focused and willing it, rather than letting it take you aimlessly. That is the only difference. The quality of creative visualization still feels like imagination. The best practitioners use all their senses. See yourself successful with your desired outcome, but also feel it. When you reach your goal, what do you see, hear, feel, smell, and taste? What does the excitement in your body feel like? Use all your feelings and senses as the foundation for your visual magic. Hold the image for a few moments to a few minutes. You can repeat the visualization several times, and then when you are done, bring your awareness back to the waking world and let go of the image. Let go of the energy. Let it go and manifest.

Words and Letters of Power

Certain traditions use specific languages and words to create changes. They are the archetypal magical words. The belief is that either the sonic quality of the words, or the language itself, interacts with the energy of reality and the energy of your own consciousness to produce change. In the ceremonial magic tradition, the Hebrew names of God found in the Lesser Banishing Ritual of the Pentagram are used to empower, clear, and protect. Many feel the very letters of the Hebrew alphabet encode magical power and meaning. The same is true of Sanskrit, where specific mantras and chants are repeated to create a change in conscious-ness. Such names and mantras are like sonic formulas created and used for specific purposes, although unlike affirmations, the meaning might not always be clear to the practitioner.

Petition Spells

Petition spells are simple, direct, and powerful. Basically, you write down what you want as a petition to the divine. The papers are usually destroyed, through burning or burying, to release the intention. For myself, I might write a petition spell like this:

> I, Christopher, ask in the name of the Great Spirit, Goddess, and God to grant me [and then list whatever I want, with whatever stipulations or conditions I feel are appropriate]. I thank the Great Spirit, Goddess, and God, and ask that this be correct and for the good of all involved, harming none. So mote it be.

As mentioned earlier, in Wicca and forms of ceremonial magic, "so mote it be" means "it is so," and is like ending a prayer with "amen." It's a phrase that turns the petition into a positive affirmation-like statement. It's like saying, this is already real and manifest in my future, so I no longer have to worry abut it. I like petitions because they are so direct. The "harming none" part is usually thought about and intended in all other magic, but in the petition spell it is directly stated and very clear. Petition for the final result you want, not for how it will manifest. If you want to go on a vacation, ask for the vacation, with everything you want for it, rather than for the money to go on vacation. That way, someone might give you a trip, or you could win a contest, but no one would directly give you the money.

Symbols and Sigils

Spells involving geometric elements come in two basic forms. One uses traditional symbols for a traditional purpose. Spell books, from ancient to medieval sources, have lists of symbols and their meanings. Modern practitioners have even cobbled together a basic form of symbols used in many traditions of magic. Other symbols are unique to the practitioner and are created using a geometric system. Such symbols, known as sigils, have gained quite a bit of popularity in the modern era. Your magical intention is reduced to a simple statement. Any repeated letters are crossed out, and you are left with a few letters to represent the essence of your intent. Traditionalists, particularly ceremonial magicians, will plot the letters on a grid of letters and/or numbers that would work well with the spell, such as a planetary square of the Witch's wheel. Then the new sigil is lifted off the grid and used in magic. It is empowered in a ritual and then either drawn in the air, burned on paper, or carried as a charm. More modern magicians will artistically arrange the letters into a pleasing geometric form.

PEACEFUL SLEEP

P̶E̶A̶C̶E̶F̶U̶L̶ S̶L̶E̶E̶P̶

ACFUS

Intention Reduced to Nonrepeating Letters

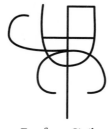

Freeform Sigil

Figure 45: Sigil Creation Examples

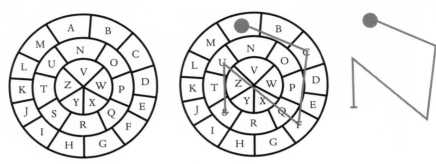

Sigil Plotted on the Witch's Wheel

Figure 45: Sigil Creation Examples (continued)

Charms

Charms are a catchall form of magical device. In some traditions, a charm that attracts forces to you is called a talisman, while a charm that banishes unwanted forces and protects you is called an amulet. Other traditions think of a talisman as a three-dimensional container of magical substances for your spell, such as a vial of herbal powder, while a charm is more two-dimensional, involving a flat surface and a symbol of your magical intention. Charms work through the system of correspondences, relating natural substances or geometric symbols to your magic. By carrying them around, you automatically attract or banish forces in alignment with your spell. Many charms are simple bags of cloth, with the color matched to the intention, and filled with herbs, stones, metals, or other tools that are connected to the intention. A charm to attract romantic love might have rose petals, yarrow, hot pepper flakes, a rose quartz, and a copper penny.

Candle Magic

Candle magic is a powerful form of magic. Though many think of it as an ancient art, it is most likely a bit more modern, since candles are relatively modern and only now affordable and readily available. The practice of candle magic probably originated in lamp and fire magic. The candle is so powerful because it inherently represents the four elements in magic. The wax is earthy. The flame is obviously the fire element and consumes air to burn. The wax melts, becoming like water. To do candle magic, use a candle with a color that matches your intention. Cleanse it. You can "dress" the candle by carving any appropriate magical symbols or letters into it, or carving the name of the person whom the spell will affect, the person's astrological sign, or anything else. You can combine candle magic with affirmations and carve the affirmation on the candle. Carving can be done with any small implement, such as a small knife, pen knife, or letter opener. You can even use your fingernail. You can also dress the candle by anointing it with oils that correspond with the intention. Other practitioners will take it a step further and roll the oiled candle in dry herbs that match the intention. Some even carve out the bottom of the candle and pack the end with herbs, so they will burn at the end of the spell. Once the candle is cleansed and dressed, hold it and think about your intention. Get clear and focused. Visualize your intent. Speak it as an affirmation. Focus your will however you can. Imagine filling the candle with your energy. When you are done, light the candle. Ideally, you should let it burn out, but if you can't, snuff it and then relight it later. Never blow it out or dip it in water. You want to keep its unique balance of the elements, and not add air or water to it. Once the candle burns completely, your energy has been released, and your spell will manifest.

Color	Elements	Chakras	Planets	Zodiac Signs	Intentions
Red	Fire	Root	Mars	Aries, Scorpio	Strength, power, success, victory, aggression, will
Orange	Fire, air,	Belly	Mercury, Sun	Gemini	Creativity, insight, intuition, healing, expression, clarity
Yellow	Fire	Solar plexus	Sun	Leo	Energy, success, inspiration, wealth, illumination, optimism
Green	Earth, water air	Heart	Venus	Taurus, Libra, Virgo	Healing, money, prosperity, love, growth, nature, empathy, new life, compassion, emotion

Chart 5: Magical Color Correspondences

Color	Elements	Chakras	Planets	Zodiac Signs	Intentions
Blue	Air, water, spirit	Throat	Mercury, Jupiter	Gemini, Sagittarius	Communication, peace, clarity, dreams
Indigo	Water, air	Brow	Moon, Jupiter	Sagittarius	Psychic ability, intuition, revealing the unseen
Purple	Water, air, spirit	Brow	Jupiter, Moon, Neptune	Sagittarius, Pisces	Royalty, influence, power, rulership, good fortune, expansion, peace, spiritual balance, optimism
Violet	Spirit	Crown	Jupiter, Neptune	Pisces	Transmutation, cleansing, divinity, spirituality, all magic
White	Spirit	Crown	Uranus	Aquarius	All-purpose, healing, cleansing, protection
Black	Earth	Root	Earth, Saturn, Pluto	Capricorn, Scorpio	Relaxation, grounding, solidness, protection, transformation, facing fear, shadow work

Chart 5: Magical Color Correspondences (continued)

Color	Elements	Chakras	Planets	Zodiac Signs	Intentions
Gold	Fire	Solar plexus	Sun	Leo	Masculine power, solar energy, health, wealth, overcoming fear, inspiration, intelligence, divinity
Silver	Water	Belly, brow	Moon	Cancer	Feminine power, lunar energy, psychic ability, intuition, dreams, motherhood, wisdom, goddesses
Pink	Water	Heart	Venus	Taurus, Libra	Love, self-esteem, happiness, uplifting
Brown	Earth	Root	Earth, Saturn	Taurus, Capricorn	Physical healing, animal magic, nature magic
Gray	Water, air		Neptune, Mercury	Pisces, Gemini, Virgo	Invisibility, spirit communication

Chart 5 (continued)

Cord Magic

Cord magic is another simple folk magic technique. Start by taking a length of string or cord. Natural material is preferable to synthetic but not absolutely mandatory, as the power is manifested through the knotting. The medium simply aids the flow of energy. Match the color with your intention. Some people choose three colors and braid them together. Then, as you think of your intent, tie a knot. Some spells do one knot. Others do three. Traditional spells often have nine or thirteen knots. I've known some people to do as many as thirty-three or forty-two knots, with a really long cord. With each knotting, focus on your intent. Put all your energy into the knot as you tie it. Multiple knots are good for spells with multiple components to them. Some spells will have similar themes, but have a few parts. Each knot can be for a different part. This is a simple yet powerful technique. This method of cord magick is for specific spell work, while another type of cord magic uses a longer cord to make a more elaborate charm that holds a general intention, such as protection or health, rather than a specific goal.

These spell techniques are some of the more popular forms of magic, but they are not the only kinds. There are many traditions of magic, using footprints, alchemical processes, the flow of the rivers, playing music, and gardening. Everything can be turned into a magical act.

The Magic Circle

One of my favorite magic rituals, the cornerstone of my personal magical and spiritual practice, is known as the magic circle. Other names and variations of it are the Moon circle, Witch's circle, or magician's circle. Basically, in this ritual, the practitioner creates sacred space by acknowledging and evoking divinity, the four directions, and the four elements as the powers of creation. Traditions across the world have ceremonies that similarly honor the four directions and sacred powers, though each culture and tradition has different associations with it. Those who have experienced Native American medicine wheel rituals remark how similar the magic circle is to these tribal teachings. Some ceremonies are used for celebration, and others for healing. More still are used for magic.

In this sacred space of the magic circle, your thoughts, words, and deeds are in a more direct communication with the divine. Witches say you are "between the worlds." Your intentions are catalyzed and become even more powerful. I like to do both meditation and formal spell work inside the confines of a magic circle. I do visualizations and petitions and consecrate charms, candles, and symbols in the magic circle, and I find it much more effective and spiritual for me than performing these actions in other ways.

Most circle work involves building an altar before creating the sacred space. An altar is simply a magical workspace. Upon it are tools used to help create the sacred space of your circle. In the Magician card of the tarot, you can see the four most popular tools in Western magic: the wand, cup, blade, and pentacle. They are the tools related to the four elements—fire, water, air, and earth, respectively. The tools on the altar represent the powers called upon in the ritual. Items that represent the God and Goddess, the male and female life forces, are often placed on the altar. In my tradition, the practitioner places a black candle on the left for the Goddess and a white candle on the right for the God. The altar faces north in the traditions I teach, for the magnetic power of the Earth, though in many traditions it faces east, in honor of the power of the rising Sun. Other altar items are both symbolic and practical, to set the tone of the ritual, such as matches, incense, oils, flowers, stones, crystals, and bells.

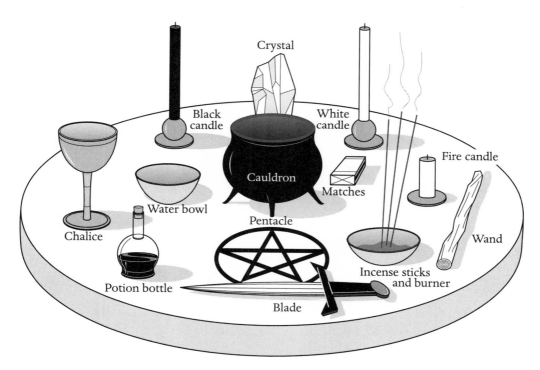

Figure 46: Altar

In the following exercise, you will be guided through a general form of the magic circle ritual, based on many of the most popular and traditional correspondences.

EXERCISE
The Magic Circle Ritual

The first step in most forms of ritual magic, including the magic circle, is purification. Both the practitioner and the environment are cleansed. Cleanse the space as taught in the Cleansing Space exercise in chapter 2. You can also use the same principle to cleanse yourself. The Aura Cleansing exercise in chapter 4 can also be used for personal cleansing. The Lesser Banishing Ritual of the Pentagram from chapter 10 is useful for cleansing yourself and the space.

Many ritualists use the technique of ritual bathing. Some take a bath of sea salt and purifying herbs, such as lavender, rosemary, or frankincense and myrrh. Here is one of my favorite versions, based on a recipe by Scott Cunningham, found in the chapter on herb baths in *The Complete Book of Incense, Oils & Brews*.

4 parts lavender
4 parts rosemary
3 parts thyme
3 parts basil
2 parts fennel
2 parts hyssop
1 part mint
1 part vervain
1 pinch valerian root
4 parts sea salt

Other ritualists take a shower, and visualize the water as a shower of light, cleansing both the physical body and all the spiritual bodies. The tools on your altar should be periodically cleansed of energy and charged with intent, just like your pendulum and other divination tools. I thoroughly cleanse my ritual tools and altar once a year and periodically cleanse and consecrate them as needed.

Once your self, space, and tools are set, prepare for your ritual to create your sacred space. Get into a light meditative state. Hold your magical wand in your dominant hand. Your dominant hand is usually considered to be projective and allows your energy to be sent out, while your nondominant hand is considered receptive. Some traditions rigidly follow the right hand as projective and left hand as receptive model, but I believe you should follow your intuition in these situations and use what you feel is best.

With your wand in hand, face north and feel with each breath that you are drawing energy up from the ground into your feet and down from the sky and stars into your crown. Feel the pure magical energy mix within you, then with your imagination and will, feel it flow down through your arm. Project it out through your wand as a beam of light. Starting in the north, use this beam of light and move clockwise around yourself to create a ring of light, much like the ring created in the Lesser Banishing Ritual of the Pentagram, but in one continuous movement, without stopping to draw the four pentacles. Create the ring three times to make the boundary of your sacred space. As I do this, I usually say the following words or something similar:

I cast this circle to protect me from all harm on all levels.
I charge this circle to draw the most perfect energies to this space for my working.
I charge this circle to stand as a sacred temple, a space beyond space, a time beyond time, a temple of perfect love and perfect trust, where the highest will is sovereign.

Take a moment to feel the shift in the energy around you. I feel a stillness that indicates I have erected a boundary. Unlike with the LBRP, once you have created the boundary, do not cross it until the ritual is over and you have released the circle. To make something real on the psychic level, you must treat it as real. The more your will and intent reinforce the reality, the more all entities on the subtle planes will treat the circle as a reality. The LBRP cleanses you and your space, but doesn't erect a stationary energetic container, a sacred space, the way the magic circle does. In various ceremonial magic traditions, practitioners create sacred space using more elaborate rituals that are similar to the magic circle, such as the Greater Rituals of the Pentagram, Supreme Invoking Ritual of the Pentagram, and Opening by Watchtower.

The circle is then anchored by calling upon the four powers, the four elements associated with the four directions. Different traditions use different associations for them, so I will be sticking to some of the most traditional correspondences. Many traditions, from Wicca to ceremonial magic, call upon the four archangels. Since you are already familiar with these four powers from the LBRP, I will use them in the quarter calls for the magic circle.

Stand before the altar, face the north, and hold out your receptive, nondominant arm, hand outstretched. Traditionally it is the left hand. If you have a ritual pentacle, you can hold it. If you don't, spread out your fingers like the five points of a star. Say:

To the north, I call to the powers of the element of earth. I call upon the archangel Uriel to aid me in my magic. Hail and welcome.

Feel the power of the earth, the solid, cool, and dry power of the land beneath your feet. Feel the stability and power of the earth.

Face the east, with your arm similarly outstretched. Say:

To the east, I call to the powers of the element of air. I call upon the archangel Raphael to aid me in my magic. Hail and welcome.

Feel the power of air, the warm and moist power of the wind and breath. Feel the clarity and quickness of the air.

Face the south, with your arm similarly outstretched. Say:

To the south, I call to the powers of the element of fire. I call upon the archangel Michael to aid me in my magic. Hail and welcome.

Feel the power of fire, the warm and dry power of light and combustion. Feel the dynamic force and illumination of the fire.

Face the west, with arm outstretched. Say:

To the west, I call to the powers of the element of water. I call upon the archangel Gabriel to aid me in my magic. Hail and welcome.

Feel the power of water, the warm and moist power of the seas and rivers. Feel the love and healing of the water.

Stand in the center, before the altar, and hold up the pentacle with both hands, or raise your outstretched arms. Say:

I call upon the Goddess, God, and Great Spirit to join me in this sacred space. I call upon my spirit guides and guardians that are perfect for this working. Hail and welcome.

Feel the presence of the divine and the element of spirit in the circle. Feel yourself between the worlds, where everything is possible. This space protects you, gathers your energy, and amplifies your magical intent.

In the traditions of Wicca and other forms of Paganism, we honor the divine as both Goddess and God. If this is not comfortable for you, adapt it. You can call upon the archangel Metatron for the center and the element of spirit/ether/akasha instead.

In a bowl on the altar, keep a solution of sea salt and water. Anoint yourself on your wrist with a banishing pentagram. In other traditions, an oil or potion of protection is used, but the salt solution is perfectly fine.

In Wicca, the anointing is usually followed by the Great Rite, but since this is an all-purpose ritual, even though it has a strong Wiccan flavor to it, it will not be included.

Once you have created the sacred space, you can do your magical spell work. Some traditions "raise" energy to be contained by the circle and charged by the spell craft. Raising energy can take the form of intense will, singing, chanting, dancing, trance work, sex, burning herbs and woods, and a variety of other techniques developed by practitioners. I do my spell craft at this point, anything from candle magic to a petition spell.

When releasing the energy of a spell, I raise my arms in what is known as the Goddess position (figure 47). Imagine a burst of energy going out of the circle, sending out your intention in what is known as the Cone of Power. Then take a moment to reflect on your spells in the God position (figure 48), arms crossed over your heart, much like an Egyptian pharaoh figure. When you have completed all your spell work, ground the energy. To do this, you can get down on your hands and knees and feel the remaining unneeded energy leave your body and enter the land. You can also visualize the energy going through the roots of your legs and feet and extending into the earth, or project it through your altar, wand, blade, or a staff into the land. If you are indoors, visualize the energy going through the building structure into the land. In some Wiccan traditions, cakes are eaten as well, since digesting food helps one ground into the physical world. Traditionally, each practitioner can do no more than three spells per circle.

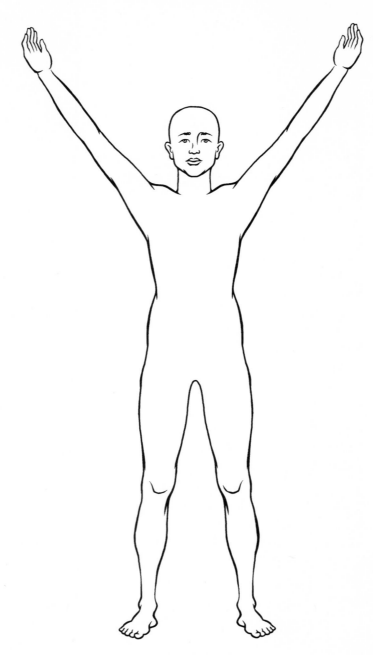

Figure 47: Goddess Position

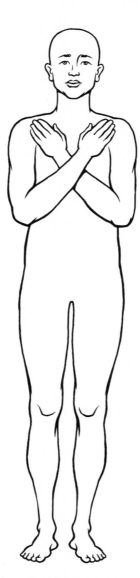

Figure 48: God Position

When the spell work is completed and the grounding is done, it is time to release the quarters, thank divinity, and release the circle. Start by facing the north again, and stand before the altar. Raise your dominant, projective hand, traditionally the right hand, and hold up your ritual pentacle or outstretched fingers. Say:

To the north, I thank and release the element of earth and the archangel Uriel. I thank you for your aid. Hail and farewell.

Feel the connection to the element of earth recede from the circle and its guardian take leave. Turn counterclockwise and face the west. Say:

To the west, I thank and release the element of water and the archangel Gabriel. I thank you for your aid. Hail and farewell.

Feel the connection to the element of water recede from the circle and its guardian take leave. Turn counterclockwise and face the south. Say:

To the south, I thank and release the element of fire and the archangel Michael. I thank you for your aid. Hail and farewell.

Feel the connection to the element of fire recede from the circle and its guardian take leave. Turn counterclockwise and face the east. Say:

To the north, I thank and release the element of air and the archangel Raphael. I thank you for your aid. Hail and farewell.

Feel the connection to the element of air recede from the circle and its guardian take leave. Turn counterclockwise and face the center. Hold up the pentacle in both hands, or raise your outstretched arms. Say:

I thank the Goddess, God, and Great Spirit, the powers of creation. I thank you for all your aid. I thank all spirits who come in perfect love and perfect trust, stay if you will, go if you must. Hail and farewell.

Point your wand to the north, and trace the circle of light, moving counterclockwise. Some practitioners imagine the light getting sucked back into the wand, while others imagine the light expanding out infinitely. Either is fine. Follow your intuition. As you do this, say:

I cast this circle out into the cosmos as a sign of my work here. The circle is undone, but never broken. So mote it be.

Take time after the ritual to ground yourself and return fully to the regular world. Eating is very helpful, as is any other real-world, mundane action that brings your attention back fully to the physical realm.

12

HEALING

Out of all the forms of magic and mysticism, the one that is most often sought out is the art and science of healing. Healing traditions have arisen and made themselves known, moving through the modern world in the form of alternative healing or holistic health. Interest has risen in traditional forms of healing, particularly herbalism, aromatherapy, energy healing, crystals, and even shamanism. Since many of these practices are brought to use through alternative healing, many people have no knowledge of their mystical and magical associations. These modern applications are based on the more ancient mystical practices. Here are a few variations on the healing traditions.

Energy Healing

Many forms of energy healing exist. Most consist of a system where the practitioner draws on a source of vital energy, of life force, often known as chi, ki, or prana, and transfers the energy to the recipient. The recipient's body uses this life force to effect the healing. Techniques exist for transferring energy both in person through touch and via distance. Energy healing can be combined with other techniques, and is often used in conjunction with methods to clear and balance the chakras and the aura. Reiki, a form of energy healing from Japan, is a very popular, safe, easy, and effective form of energy healing.

Psychic Healing

Psychic healing is the process of using your will and intention to effect a change in healing. Practitioners often visualize the healing taking place. They imagine broken bones being knit together or malignancies shrinking. Some visualize colored lights, yet with this technique, if they are using energy healing, they are not filtering the energy through their body, but psychically directing the energy to the recipient. Colored light is a symbol of their healing intention.

Psychic Surgery

Psychic surgery is a hotly debated topic among those in the mystical world, and opinions on it vary, depending on how it is defined. When it reached the more mainstream society, some charlatans were proponents of it and, with their deceptions, polluted the possibility of the most dramatic form of healing for most people. The more dramatic definition of psychic surgery is using psychic ability to literally and physically reach into the body and perform surgery, removing or changing physical tissue, without scalpel, anesthesia, or any other modern surgical device. Though I believe in the psychic possibility of this healing, I have never seen it performed, though I have reliable friends who state they have witnessed it. Unfortunately, charlatans have "removed" from people what in reality is chicken guts, claiming to remove tumors. Through sleight-of-hand gestures, they appear to pull out the tumors, tricking patients into believing they were cured. In a more psychic arena, what is also known as shamanic surgery is the process of energetically removing the illness or injury with surgerylike techniques. This does not involve a literal manipulation of tissue. The theory is that if you remove the energy of a sickness, such as a tumor, the physical substance will more easily collapse and will be healed by the immune system naturally. Shamanic surgery is not the immediate miracle cure many people expect when they hear the term psychic surgery, but it's able to be performed by more people involved in healing arts, and has a great track record when used in conjunction with other forms of holistic healing.

Spirit Healing

Spirit healing is a shamanic technique using the healing powers of various nonphysical spirits. Such spirits are embodiments of the natural realm, from animal spirits to plant and mineral spirits. Such spirit healing is often called spirit medicine, because the spirit embodies a healing lesson that helps bring the person back into balance. Much of what a Witch or magician considers to be healing magic is called "medicine" in shamanic traditions, because it heals and brings the recipient's consciousness and life force back into harmony with the universe and the person's own divine nature.

Faith Healing

Faith healing is found in a number of metaphysical traditions, including some expressions of the dominant monotheistic faiths. It involves very few of the metaphysical principles or models. The concept relies on the faith of the practitioner and/or the client in a higher power that will bring complete health. This form of healing might include a prayer or reading, but not what a magical practitioner would consider an evocation or ritual. Illnesses are not visualized as being healed or banished. It's a very simple technique based solely on the power of faith.

Crystals

Crystal healing is the process of altering energy and consciousness by laying stones upon the body or carrying them with you. Each stone, based on its structure, color, composition, and spiritual qualities, is used to heal a particular area of life. Most crystals have properties to heal on the physical, mental, emotional, and spiritual levels. Crystals, like all things, have unique vibrations. Their colors correspond to the chakras. Their structure not only vibrates healing qualities of energy, but many crystals, particularly those of the quartz family, can amplify any intentions placed in them, much as a magnifying glass amplifies the heat of sunlight. This quality makes crystals very powerful in healing and magic.

Vibrational Remedies

Vibrational remedies are dilute solutions made from flowers, stones, and other substances. Originally known as flower remedies, from the pioneering work of a homeopath named Dr. Edward Bach, vibrational remedies encode in a water and preservative mix the healing vibrations, the subtle spiritual qualities, of a substance. The most popular vibrational remedies are made from flowers and are often called flower essences or flower remedies. Working according to principles that are similar to those in homeopathy—such as the concepts of like cures like, and small, frequent doses can be more effective than larger high-chemical doses—vibrational remedies work to heal on the emotional, mental, and spiritual levels. When the consciousness of the essence recipient is changed by taking the remedy, then the process that supports the disease also changes and is no longer supported by the individual thoughts and feelings, and the body can more easily and gently correct itself. Each flower, or any other natural substance, has a healing property based on its signature—its physical shape, color, medicinal qualities, and folklore. For example, a rose is universally associated with love, and the opening of a rose is symbolic of opening the heart. Rose flower essence is used to open the heart to love and to heal relationships. The powers of vibrational remedies are subtle, but they can have powerful effects, particularly with long-term use. Practitioners act as consultants, helping those in need choose essences and create harmonious combinations of essences, but individuals can also intuitively or deductively choose and self-administer essences quite successfully.

Healing Rituals

Healing rituals are magical formulas that are used in many traditions, combining and adapting many of the techniques presented in this chapter. Witches, magicians, and shamans use ritual techniques to direct their will toward healing both themselves and others. They also use the rituals to alter the consciousness of their healing recipient, to help induce self-healing. Healing changes are effected by petitioning deities, spirits, and elements, and using the power of color, visualization, candles, herbs, and stones.

EXERCISE
General Healing Spell

This healing spell can be used by anyone, for any healing purpose. It is not dependent on faith or any specific metaphysical system, other than the belief in energy and magic. You can do it in a magic circle, if you'd like, but this is not absolutely necessary. Do what feels most comfortable for you. For this working, you will need the following:

1 white candle

1 quartz crystal

A photo or personal item of the healing recipient, if it is not you

Take this time to get into a meditative state. Center yourself. Feel yourself at peace with your world and the universe. Call upon the divine, in whatever form you feel comfortable. In my own practice, I call upon "the Goddess, God, and Great Spirit." Call upon the divine to let the healing powers of the universe flow through you, for "the highest good, harming none."

Feel a beam of light descend from the heavens. Intuitively choose the color of light, or intellectually choose an appropriate color based on your knowledge of the chakras and magical correspondences. If you are uncertain with either technique, focus on white light.

Hold the personal object or photo, and think about the person in need of healing. With the following words or something similar, call upon the person's higher consciousness and spirits:

I call upon the higher self and highest guides of [name of healing recipient]. I ask for your permission and help in guiding this healing energy, for the highest good, harming none. If this healing is not for the highest good, please direct the energy to where it is needed and will be accepted. So mote it be.

Set the personal object down, then hold the candle. Think about the light of energy descending from the heavens into you. Feel the healing energy flow through your body. Fill the candle with it. You are not using your personal energy, but this universal energy flowing through you. Think about the recipient, and imagine the person bathed in healing light. It might change color in your mind's eye. I imagine it as "crystal white" light, an opalescent or prismatic light filled with a rainbow of colors. You can imagine the recipient healthy and vital. You can imagine illness declining and disappearing and health being bolstered. Place the candle in a holder next to the personal object and light it.

Repeat the process with the crystal. First fill the crystal with light, and imagine the light cleansing the crystal of all unwanted energies and programs. Then put your magical healing intention into the crystal. Imagine the crystal taking the light of the candle and amplifying it, directing it out to the recipient. Place the crystal next to the candle. Let the candle burn out. If you cannot leave it, snuff it out and relight it later. Repeat the process as often as necessary. This will send a vital healing light to the recipient, to be used for the person's highest healing good.

FIVE

EXPLORING THE PATHS

13

MYSTIC TRADITIONS

All cultures have their mystic traditions. In our modern terminology, it's hard to distinguish between various spiritual titles and vocations. For the purpose of this book, I am using the word mystic to describe an individual seeking a direct experience with the divine. Some people would distinguish a mystic from a magician, Witch, or sorcerer, but I think of mystic as a larger category, and magicians, Witches, shamans, martial artists, yogis, ecstatics, seers, healers, and members of various spiritual orders as part of this broader category. Anybody who seeks a direct spiritual experience can be a mystic, regardless of the tradition, culture, or time period. In more secular places and times, philosophers, scientists, artists, dancers, and musicians have walked the path of the mystic, seeking transcendental experiences to know themselves, the worlds, and the divine.

Spiritual traditions use the metaphor of climbing a mountain to describe the path of enlightenment. As you ascend the mountain, you gain a wider, more encompassing viewpoint, and better appreciate the beauty around you. The spiritual climb gives you many of the same benefits. You see the whole and learn to appreciate many of the paths leading to the top.

There are many paths to get to the top of the spiritual mountain. We each start at a different place. We might find our own paths, or walk well-worn paths cut by those who came before us. We might use a path as a guide, but walk slightly off the path, finding our own way, but looking for similar landmarks.

Mystic traditions are the paths up the mountain. We can walk them, or use them as guides. We might cross from one path to the next, trying several ways of life. Eventually, all routes lead us to the top of the mountain, though some might be more difficult or easier for us. Many people take time to appreciate parts of the mountain, while others race quickly to the top. Each path suits a different climber, but all are good. Even people who seem to be lost, wandering aimlessly at the base of the mountain, appearing to have no mystical interest at all, eventually find their way to the top.

East and West

The previous chapters contain basic information that has become fairly standard in the modern New Age mystic traditions, with a broad cultural view yet with a general bias toward what most people would call the Western traditions. Various spiritual paths, in the West and East, have their own take on the information, with specific terminology, cultural biases, and insights. The previous descriptions offer generalizations and common denominators, but do not encompass a complete and whole tradition. Each tradition is unique, with its own traits and personality.

Some people divide mystic traditions into Western patterns and Eastern patterns, though this is a great oversimplification, and many traditions do not fit neatly into either division. People in the West often describe Eastern traditions as passive, introspective, and aesthetic. The practitioner withdraws from the world to understand the true nature of consciousness. But Eastern traditions such as yoga or the various martial arts are quite active and vigorous. The practitioner has to perform the exercises to get the spiritual benefit. While the stereotype of Eastern traditions is of "non-doing" and detachment, the Western traditions are seen as actively pursuing, studying, and affecting the material world. Through building a relationship with the physical world, and the energy that sustains it, the practitioner comes to understand the powers of the universe. Creating change in the world is known as magic, though magic encompasses both internal and external changes. The arts of Witchcraft, hermetic magic, and alchemy follow this path. Though the image is one of active participation, the Western traditions contain a fair amount of introspection and quiet contemplation. Traditions on both sides require discipline and introspection, but simply pursue them in different ways. In truth, they are like two sides of the same coin. Both are needed. The yogis of the East are often viewed as magicians. The Western Qabalah, as a system of mystical union, is often called the yoga of the West. Many shamanic practices have both Western and Eastern traits, and appear to be a universal fount of wisdom for people on both sides of the globe.

Institutions

Those on the spiritual path invariably codify their experiences into traditions. The first seers and shamans came back with their tales of otherworld adventures and divine beings, creating tribal mythology, songs, and customs. They passed on their techniques, experiences, and interpretations of those experiences to their students. They shared information and influenced the spiritual views of the tribe.

When humankind became agrarian, settled down, built cities, and developed writing, the oral traditions became solidified into various teachings. Some of the teachings became mystery traditions, rituals and techniques to induce personal contact with the divine. Others became institutional religions. Civilization created a divide between the esoteric, or inner mysteries, and the exoteric, or outer religions. The average person in the ancient world was Pagan, but not necessarily a mystic. In many societies there has always been a caste of people who are focused on the mystical and esoteric.

Religion and mysticism are not mutually exclusive. Both are often very entwined, depending on how you define religion. Many mystical systems have grown into formal institutions, and many exist side by side. The most famous of the institutional religions—Judaism, Christianity, and Islam—all have their own inner mystic traditions that are not as widely known. At various points in history, such institutions have discouraged the personal mystical experience, but mysticism and institutional religion are not incompatible. The difference between the two is that mystics learn techniques for direct experience of the divine. That is the focus of their traditions. Institutional religions are more prophetic, based on the revelation of an honored mystic in that tradition. Rather than encourage personal revelation and interpretation, institutions base their theology on the experiences of accepted and approved prophets. The wisdom and experiences of these prophets are recorded as sacred scripture and become the basis of the religion's teachings.

The teachings of institutional religions can become dogmatic, not evolving with the changing consciousness of people over time. What was appropriate for one era might not be universally appropriate for another. Difficulties also arise when scriptures are translated into many different languages, as the original meanings often become muddled, colored by cultural and personal prejudices.

No matter your personal belief system, you cannot look at figures such as Moses, Abraham, Jesus, the Apostles, and Mohammed and not see that they are all mystics, with direct experience of the divine. But instead of using their lives as models for our own mystical experiences, their experiences and the words attributed to them became the foundations of the religions. These mystics are held in high esteem as having the divine truth revealed to them, for the good of all. In many ways, the mystic's experience is the foundation of metaphysics, magic, and religion.

Initiation

Initiation is an important experience for practitioners of mystic traditions. The word initiate literally means "to begin." Although many people think of an initiation ritual as a graduation ceremony, because it occurs at the end of a length of training or testing, just like a graduation from school, the ending is also a new beginning. A ceremonial initiation occurs when a mystic is accepted into a tradition or order as a full member, after completing a period of training or series of tests. Traditions with more than one rank or level can have an initiation ceremony for each level. Initiation rituals occur in mystical as well as mundane groups. The best-known and most notorious are the initiation rituals of fraternities and sororities at institutions of higher education. The trials and hardships are said to build character, and connect the person to all of those in the group who have experienced the same initiation. Initiation can be a bonding experience, as only those who have gone through it can truly understand what it means to be a part of a particular group. We find initiations in Freemasonry, blending elements of a social group with past mystic traditions.

Initiation is more than a ceremonial acknowledgment. It is a spiritual connection to the energy of a tradition, as those who carry the energy of the tradition pass on that connection to the newest members. It links the initiates to all the sisters and brothers in the tradition who have come before them, and all those who will come after them. Many people believe that certain abilities or talents are passed on during initiations. In traditions that encourage psychic or magical development, those abilities often expand after the initiation. In the healing tradition of Reiki, one becomes a practitioner of the art through an initiation into the energy of Reiki. Though most call the process an "attunement," it is quite literally an initiation, and after this ceremony, the practitioner naturally channels the healing energy of Reiki. Other initiation ceremonies can grant different gifts, but the greatest gift is the sense of accomplishment and belonging to a spiritual tradition. The initiates become part of a spiritual lineage, linking them to the founder of that tradition. This is a key teaching in the Christian concept of Apostolic succession, sharing a link to the founding of the church.

Initiations are often awakening experiences. Teachers of the mystery traditions design their initiation rituals to awaken the initiate's inner powers. Up until that point, much of the esoteric lore the person studies may be objective and intellectual, but the initiation rituals awaken the divine within, and alter the initiate's worldview. Initiations involve surprises, challenges, and oaths.

The most primal initiations occur spontaneously, and were the foundation of the ritual initiations of mystical orders. The first mystics would alter their consciousness and open themselves to the paths of a new reality and understanding through a trial or traumatic experience. Many times this would occur during an extended period of illness, particularly with a fever. The person's spirit would leave the body during this time of sickness and commune with the spirit world. These near-death experiences would forever alter the worldview of the new mystic. Other initiates have an awakening of psychic ability or insight that alters them. Though I've undergone ritual initiations, I think my most important initiation experience involved my first attempt at psychic diagnosis and healing. Using the techniques I had learned in a Witchcraft class, I put the esoteric knowledge into action, and it became real for me. I was able to connect with a person I had never met, intuitively diagnose her illnesses and pain, and send healing energy to her. Going into the exercise, I didn't quite believe it was possible, but had an open mind. As with many initiation rituals, I was afraid of failure, yet pressed onward. When we were done, my mind was completely blown. All the theories of magic and meditation became a reality for me, and after that I believed that anything was possible. I was forever changed in a night, though it took me quite a while to integrate the experience. Like many initiation experiences, it was a rebirth process for me. Life initiations, or personal ordeals, can be the most powerful initiations of all.

Formal rituals sometimes imitate and reenact the mythic resurrection stories, such as those of Osiris and Isis, Persephone, Dionysus, or even Jesus. The death symbolizes the loss of the old self, and the initiation is the rebirth of the new, more mystically realized self. Initiation does not necessarily mean enlightenment. Many people misunderstand and think they will become fully enlightened, saved, or perfected automatically through the ritual. The ritual gives us the opportunity to expand our consciousness, but it's up to us as to how we integrate the experience. I don't know anybody who has become instantly enlightened and perfected from an initiation experience, but I know people who have totally transformed their lives for the better after a successful initiation.

Some initiations are not as successful. Many people simply go through the steps, but do no inner preparation to expand their consciousness through the ritual. Many take time to really contemplate the meaning of the initiation, and the results are not immediate. It takes time for them to fully manifest. For others, the sudden realization of a larger world-view and expanded consciousness is frightening or overwhelming. With an increased sense of power comes an increased sense of responsibility—for yourself and your world. Many people, especially those who are blame-oriented for their life situations, cannot handle the newfound responsibility.

Initiation, like any spiritual experience, comes with many blessings, but is a great responsibility. Before deciding upon an initiatory path of training, give it plenty of thought. Understand the roles and responsibilities expected of you when you join a tradition. Make sure it is compatible with your spiritual path and calling. Many people feel the need to be formally initiated into a tradition in order to feel like a legitimate mystic. A true mystic is one who has done the work and had the experiences, regardless of lineage. Most great innovators founded their own tradition by finding their own way. Names, titles, certificates, and initiations are less important than the experiences themselves. The most important initiations are the natural, spontaneous awakenings that happen on the mystic's path.

Spiritual Names

A common theme in many initiations is renaming. After a pivotal experience that becomes a rebirth, such traditions feel a renaming is appropriate. Most of us don't get to consciously pick our birth names. Our parents or guardians do so for us. When we turn to the mystic's life, we often get the opportunity to rename ourselves.

Specific traditions have various guides in the naming process. Some have a teacher rename the student. Others use astrology and numerology as guides. Many allow the initiate to choose his or her own name. Sometimes the name of a mythic figure that the initiate aspires to emulate is chosen. Some initiates create unique names using a combination of sacred sounds and phrases from the tradition. Still others make combinations of words from nature—including animals, plants, and astrology—to symbolize their new journey. Lastly, many initiates meditate and receive their name directly from their own guidance.

In traditions with several initiation steps, the seeker may be encouraged to take a new name at each step, either adding to previous names or discarding the older ones as the path unfolds.

Many people feel their mystical experiences reveal their true name or soul name. Some traditions of magic use names in both healing and cursing. Practitioners of such traditions take care never to reveal their true spiritual names, because to know someone or something's true name is to have power over it. Many traditions of spirit evocation and control are based on knowing the name and symbol of the spirit. Cautious practitioners might have a public name or even a public spiritual name that is much like a guise. The name is true to themselves and their character, but not something intimately used. It could be a spiritual name from an early initiation. Another name may be used in magical circles that are intimate, such as a coven, order, or lodge, but kept secret. Still another name may be used privately, between the spirits and the mystic.

On the other end of the spectrum, certain people feel it is vitally important for practitioners to use their true spiritual names whenever and wherever possible, to own them and to radiate their inner magical power in all aspects of their lives. Many spiritual seekers use their spiritual names in public, but in spiritual circles only. Others use them in public all the time, and some even change their legal names to match their spiritual names.

You don't have to be an initiate of a specific tradition to take a spiritual name. If you feel called to do so, particularly after a transformative experience on your mystical path, then follow your inner wisdom and intuition and use the name that is appropriate for you.

Secrecy

Secrecy is one aspect of the mystic traditions that can cause great difficulty for seekers. By its very nature, the mystical is esoteric, not exoteric. The teachings are not for everybody. They are only appropriate for a certain group of people. Mystical study requires a certain discipline and desire to experience the divine directly. Most people who are involved in religion are involved in the institutional forms of religion, with guidelines on life, morality, and belief systems set by scriptures and prophets. For most people, that is enough. Not everybody is looking for a direct experience. Many are called to do other work and service in the world, fulfilling their own unique role. They are still spiritual beings with a unique, wonderful part to play in creation. Some may dabble in the esoteric, but not devote themselves to the path of the mystic.

The consciousness-expanding techniques of the mystic traditions are intense. They can bring awareness of the unconscious aspects of the self into full awareness. Without the support system of a responsible teacher, order, or class, the realizations the mystical techniques bring can be shattering rather than healing.

Mystic traditions are based upon a set formula. Archetypal themes are followed that speak to the deep inner wisdom and active consciousness. Teachings are followed in a specific order, with the student expected to understand and master a set of basic experiences before going on to learn more advanced techniques. Traditions that teach magic and psychic abilities fear the potential of the teachings being abused to the detriment of others. Orders often ask initiates to take oaths of secrecy to protect the teachings, or take vows to use the information in the most reputable and honorable ways.

With the expansion of the printed media, and the bustling New Age metaphysical market, mystical material is available to those without a teacher in a way that has never before occurred in our history. Many traditionalists see this as a problem, because many of the structures and safeguards have been taken away. There is a possibility of the information from one tradition being mingled with another and diluting the teaching.

More modern practitioners and teachers look at this openness as a potential blessing. As we enter the New Age, the similarities between wisdom traditions all across the world will be revealed. In this age, certain teachers and orders will hold the job of keeping traditions pure, while others will be spiritually responsible for showing the common threads and making the information accessible to all. In books such as this one, the views of many traditions are distilled into common ground and made accessible to a greater number of people.

Many mystics have had transformative experiences from books, CDs, videos, and weekend workshops, following their own unique path and using ancient wisdom as an aid and signpost on the path. Though there is a danger in any kind of experimentation, mystical or otherwise, there can be great rewards as well. I, among many other modern authors, feel that the accessibility of the ancient wisdom for greater numbers of people far outweighs the potential risks. As we enter a new time, there are simply not enough orders, temples, ashrams, and teachers to personally oversee all the mystical seekers. Modern media allow access to information for those who truly dare to take the next step. Many people buy books and take classes related to spirituality, but don't actually put any of the teachings or techniques into practice. They are armchair mystics, collecting information but not experience. Those who move beyond the intellectual exercise of collecting data and put the teachings and techniques into practice are rewarded with a rich spiritual life. A mystic realizes that even seeming difficulties on the path can be great teachers and, in the end, wonderful blessings.

Though most people are not necessarily seeking the mystic's path as their own, those viewing the New Age through a lens of equality feel that the consciousness-expanding experiences of the past will be made available to all on some level. One of the more positive prophecies of the next age is that it will be a golden age of enlightenment. Each human being will be more developed and self-realized. The mystics of the next age will do their part by taking consciousness to the next level of human development. In the age of light, much of our secret traditions will come out of the shadows and be available to all.

14

THE PATHS UP THE MOUNTAIN

The teachings of this book have simplified and distilled the common points of many different mystic traditions, Eastern and Western. This represents a foundation of metaphysical thought found in the modern New Age community. A thorough understanding of it gives an aspiring mystic sure footing, no matter what tradition he or she follows.

Each path, however, is unique, with its own terminology, beliefs, and history. The unseen worlds are difficult to describe, even when we experience them firsthand, and each mystic's description is colored by his or her own tradition, culture, and time.

The following is a list of mystic traditions and systems. It is by no means complete, but includes some of those that I have drawn upon for this book, and those that have affected my life in a direct way. The purpose is to give you an understanding of the many paths up the mountain of spirituality, so you can determine for yourself which, if any, you seek to study.

Alchemy

Alchemy is a tradition that focuses on the act of transmutation. Though it eventually transformed into modern-day chemistry, losing its spiritual value except with the most isolated of seekers, alchemy is a worldwide tradition, with roots in Egypt, Greece, Asia, and the Middle East. The classic alchemical text, the Emerald Tablet, is ascribed to the Greek

figure Hermes Trismegistus, known to the Egyptians as the god Thoth. Hermetic manu-
scripts attributed to Hermes or his followers continue to influence alchemy and Western
magic. We are most familiar with the image of the European alchemist. This tradition
is an amalgam of many different cultures, mixing Qabalah, Hermeticism, astrology, and
some Christian symbolism. The secrets of European alchemy are encoded in a variety of
images and esoteric symbols involving nature and the stars. The most popular image is
that of transforming lead into gold. Most people misunderstood this teaching, assuming
it was about greed, where one looked to take something worthless and transform it into
something financially valued. Such alchemists seeking only fortune were labeled "puffers"
by those who sought the spiritual value of alchemy.

Spiritual alchemists sought to change their darkness, or what might be known as karma,
their personal lead, into refined spiritual energy, enlightenment, or gold. Some looked at
the lead-to-gold imagery as just symbolism, while others thought of it as literal fact—if a
person could literally transform the qualities of lead into gold, then he was a spiritual master, like Jesus turning water into wine. It was a sign that the person had reached that state
of enlightenment and understanding of the universe. This transmutation was often called
the Philosopher's Stone or the Perfected Stone, and was said to change lead into gold,
grant immortality, and cure all illnesses. Many thought it was an outer rock, a synthesized
mineral, but in reality the Philosopher's Stone was an inner tool, the perfected alchemist's
soul. The various chemical processes the alchemist performed to distill and refine matter—such as calcination, distillation, separation, fermentation, and coagulation—were also
occurring on the alchemist's energy, to refine his or her consciousness. Prayer, ritual, and
meditation played as big a role in the success of an experiment as actual chemistry, for the
alchemist sought change in the inner and outer worlds.

Ascension

The ascension paradigm is not one specific religious path, but an amalgam of the mystic traditions around the world. Most people would consider it a subset of the overall
New Age movement, with some of its own specific theology and terminology. Rooted in
the modern spiritualist movement and the inspired works of Theosophy and its offshoots,
including the works of H. P. Blavatsky, Alice Bailey, and Guy Ballard, ascension lore has incorporated aspects of Hinduism, Buddhism, Gnostic Christianity, Qabalah, Taoism, alchemy,
ceremonial magic, Paganism, and shamanism into a synthesis that is dependent upon the

practitioner. No one consistent doctrine or set of core beliefs defines all the participants in the movement, other than the belief that humanity is "ascending" to another level of consciousness, what is often referred to as a higher dimension or higher vibrational level. Otherwise, the beliefs and practices vary widely from practitioner to practitioner. Many believe a variety of other beings, including angels, spirit guides, deities, faeries, enlightened aliens, and ascended masters, are aiding our evolution to the next level. In fact, these ascended masters, enlightened beings from every culture and time period, are the model for our own ascension process.

Some ascension practitioners also believe that another set of forces—both physical and nonphysical beings, characterized as "dark brothers"—is seeking to stop or slow the ascension process by creating a battle with the forces of light. They see Earth's history as being riddled with mysterious societies, conspiracies, and secret agendas, battles that have been hidden from mainstream society, and include in their history a belief in locations such as Atlantis, Lemuria, and Shamballa. Ascensionists sometimes refer to themselves instead as "light workers," meaning they work with the principles of esoteric light, psychic energy, to create healing and harmony. The focus is on world peace, healing, unconditional love, and the belief that we all come from the same source and will return to it, and the essence of this source is love. Complementary practices, including healing arts such as Reiki and crystal healing, as well as channeling, psychic development, and holistic health, are a part of the overall paradigm.

Astrology

Astrology is not a religious or even a spiritual tradition, but a tool found in many cultures that aids the mystic in understanding his or her spiritual development. Though some may follow it like a religion, it is a practice found in both Western and Eastern occultism, based on the observation of the patterns of the sky and how these patterns correspond to what is occurring on Earth and in our lives. We find its influence in modern Hinduism, alchemy, ceremonial magic, Witchcraft, and popular psychology. Though there are several forms of astrology—from Western astrology, based on the tropical zodiac, to Vedic, or Hindu, astrology, based on the sidereal zodiac—each is based on the patterns of the sky, from the zodiac signs to the movement of the planets, to understand the energies present at any given moment. The systems teach that the alignment of the sky at a person's birth determines the potentials and challenges in that person's life, and the current movements of the sky in comparison to the birth chart can provide insight into the forces at hand in the person's life. Each of the signs is an archetypal energy, and each planet corresponds to a part of the person's psyche that acts out that archetype. Where the signs and planets fall in the sky determines "where" in the person's life they influence him or her.

As a tool, astrology acts as a lens to understand the past and present and to work with the future, for the best possible outcomes. Some focus on the spiritual pursuits of astrology, understanding the development of consciousness through life's lessons. Others use it simply to observe personality traits and personal strengths and weaknesses, or to find fortunate moments of opportunity in business or love. Astrology is even used to plan appropriate times for ritual, ceremony, and meditation. Working through the Principle of Correspondence, "As above, so below; as below, so above," this science and art operates on many levels, and its benefit is determined only by the scope of the user.

Bahá'í

Bahá'í is a religion that grew out of the Islamic tradition in the 1800s, but is distinct from Islam. It is a monotheistic tradition based on the teaching of the prophet Bahá'u'lláh from Persia. His name means "the Glory of God" in Arabic, and his teachings include the belief in one supreme god who is unknowable to man. There is one humanity, and all people are equal in the eyes of God. In our oneness, Bahá'í encourages cultural diversity. Men and women are equal, and the tradition seeks to eliminate prejudice and create world peace. Bahá'í recognizes that all religions were brought by prophets of God, including the teachings of Judaism, Christianity, Islam, Hinduism, and Buddhism. Followers see Bahá'í as the next stage of religion, in which God will reveal his will in the modern world. The Bahá'í stance on traditions such as Paganism is not clear. Practitioners of the Bahá'í faith believe in a covenant between God and humanity to send prophets to bring God's teachings, as well as the succession of prophetic authority.

Bahá'í teaches moderation as a key principle and lacks a rigid structure, though there are fasts once a year, restrictions against alcohol and recreational drug use, and mandatory financial contributions. In addition, chastity before marriage is required, and homosexual relationships are prohibited. There are few specific rituals in the Bahá'í faith, though the rituals that are a part of the tradition include specific marriage and funerary practices, daily prayer facing the "Point of Adoration," and reading the sacred writings of the faith each morning and evening.

Buddhism

Buddhism is an Eastern religion and philosophy based on the teachings of the Buddha, named Siddhartha Gautama, who was born approximately 550 years before Jesus Christ. Starting in India, Buddhism spread throughout Asia, including Tibet, China, Korea, Mongolia, and Japan. Though the basic core of the teachings is the same, different cultures have manifested different strains of Buddhism. One of the most popular branches is Tibetan Buddhism, which bonded Buddhism with the Tibetan native religion of Bon. In the modern era, Buddhism has spread all over the world.

The aim of Buddhism, through its moral and philosophical code and meditative practices, is to awaken the practitioner to true reality and to be liberated from the cycle of death and rebirth. In essence, anyone can become enlightened, and thereby become a Buddha. The title is not restricted to any one person or spiritual leader. Siddhartha Gautama, who is called Shakyamuni Buddha by Buddhists, does not claim any special status, and simply shows the way for those who want to follow the path of awakening and realization of nirvana. On Siddhartha's journey, he discovered the Four Noble Truths, teaching that suffering and dissatisfaction in life come from craving. This condition of humanity is curable, and the cure is to follow the Noble Eightfold Path of Buddhism, emphasizing "right" action. Five precepts to aid the practitioner are given, including refraining from harming other living creatures, stealing, sexual misconduct, incorrect speech, and intoxication. Traditions of Buddhism use ritual, prayer, mantra, and meditation as a part of their practice in achieving Buddhahood.

Christianity

Christianity is the religion based on the life, teachings, and death of Jesus of Nazareth, known as Jesus Christ. The word Christ is derived from the Greek *Christos*, and means "anointed one." Followers of Christianity believe that Jesus of Nazareth is the messiah prophesied in the Old Testament. Christians base their teachings on both the Old Testament and the New Testament, a record of Jesus's life and teachings recorded by his followers, as well as the actions of the early Church. Like Judaism, Christianity is a monotheistic religion, yet many Christian sects believe in the Creator as a trinity as well as a sole being. God manifests as the Father, the god of the Old Testament; the Son, Jesus Christ; and the Holy Spirit, also known as the Holy Ghost or Holy Sophia. A main precept is that Jesus, as the messiah, was literally the son of God, a manifestation of the divine, who became flesh to redeem all those believers from their sins as he suffered, died by crucifixion, and literally resurrected himself from the dead to return to heaven. Followers are promised resurrection and everlasting life in heaven on Judgment Day. The essence of Christianity is to be "Christlike," meaning to follow the actions of Jesus in the Gospels, emphasizing love, forgiveness, and healing. Although Christians follow the Ten Commandments of the Old Testament, the Golden Rule takes precedence: "All things whatsoever ye would that men should do to you, do ye so to them; for this is the law and the prophets," or more simply, "Do unto others as you would have done unto you" (Matthew 7:1).

Christianity has broken into a variety of sects. The most dominant and largest groupings include Roman Catholicism, Eastern Orthodoxy, and Protestantism. The early branches of Christianity included various sects of Gnostic Christianity, a more mystical, personal take on the tradition, marked by the theology that only personal knowledge of the true reality grants salvation from this world. As the Roman Catholic Church was formed, various Gnostic texts and practitioners, demonstrating alternate views on Christ's teachings, were suppressed. The early church in the British Isles was known as the Celtic Christian Church, and for a time incorporated Pagan beliefs and teachings into its structure. Some people believe the Druids of the Celtic people eventually became part of the orders of priests, monks, and brothers of the church, and preserved some of their teachings in the Celtic Church. Eventually the more traditional forms of Christianity became dominant in the isles.

Discordianism

Discordianism is a religion that is not taken seriously, even by its practitioners. It is based on a book called Principia Discordia by Greg Hill, and the tradition began in 1958 or 1959. Its principal deity is the Greek goddess of discord, named Eris, and her Roman counterpart, Discordia. Though such godforms might evoke an image of serious ancient ritual magic, Discordianism is anything but serious. It is based on the concept that while other religions focus on harmony and order in the universe, Discordians feel that the forces of chaos and disharmony are just as valid. While most religions are serious, with poetic texts, Discordianism is silly and doesn't make much sense from a logical perspective, and its texts read like jokes. There are several principles about the apparent order or apparent disorder of the universe, but the true reality is pure chaos. There are various sects of Discordianism, though their organization, structure, and hierarchy are not readily apparent.

One of the symbols of Discordianism is the Sacred Chao, a spinoff of the yin/yang symbol, where one of the "dots" of the symbol is a pentagon, while the other is apple-shaped. The pentagon is associated with the Aneristic Principle, or perception of order, as well as a teaching known as the Law of Five. The apple is a nod to the goddess Eris, in her story with the golden apple of discord, and related to the Eristic Principle. The Apple of Discord story involving Eris is known to Discordians as the "Original Snub." Discordian teachings are called catma rather than dogma, and the pineal gland is seen as the source of answers to life's questions, with the popular saying "Consult your pineal gland." Becoming a Discordian is described on page 00032 of the Principia Discordia: "If you want in on the Discordian Society then declare yourself what you wish do what you like and tell us about it or if you prefer don't. There are no rules anywhere. The Goddess Prevails."

Druidism

The word Druid refers to a member of the priestly caste of the ancient Celtic people. There is great debate about the nature of the Druids, their culture, and their practices, because the Druids held an oral tradition, with little being written down. Much of what we do know about the Druids comes from scholars and historians outside of their culture and traditions, with various biases. The Romans, when expanding into the Celtic territories, wrote about the Celtic tribes, yet many believe their reports, though containing facts, reveal an obvious bias against the people the empire was seeking to conquer.

The name Druid is most commonly associated with the word duir, meaning oak, and having associations with wisdom. The romantic view of these priests is of age-old wizards, wise men who were capable of great feats of magic, and who held within their minds a veritable storehouse of wisdom and occult knowledge. They acted as religious priests, judges, and the keepers of cultural knowledge. They were the guardians of history, myth, and genealogy, as well as medicine, astrology, law, divination, and ritual. Though we have an image of men wearing white robes and acting like courtly magicians, due to some modern reconstructions of Druidic practices in the eighteenth century, historically the Druids were most likely animal-skin wearers (fitting in with the times of their people), both men and women, and much more like tribal shamans, with a more codified oral tradition and a role that expanded beyond one tribe to be recognized among many of the tribes. Because of this great political and social influence, the Romans feared the power of the Druids to unite the separate and feuding Celtic tribes.

Ancient Druids were said to train for at least nineteen years, going through several training periods. First they were trained as bards, the keepers of the music, myths, and lineages; then as ovates, the soothsayers and judges of disputes; and then as priests, or Archdruids themselves, who were in charge of religious rites of passage and seasonal celebrations. Druids acted as intermediaries between the Celtic Pagan gods and the Celtic people, overseeing many offerings, sacrifices, and rituals. Though many people associate the solstices with the Druids, the Celtic people considered the fire festivals (known today as Samhain, Imbolc, Beltane, and Lammas) more sacred than the solar festivals. The solar association comes with the image of Stonehenge, being aligned with these solar holidays. Though the Druids most likely knew of these times and days, and possibly celebrated them in ritual, they were not as pivotal to the Celtic people. Many people believe the Druids built Stonehenge, but ancient Stone Age people, predating the Druids' arrival in the British Isles, were the true engineers of Stonehenge, though some speculate the Druids used the site as a place of worship. The Druids more likely worshiped in nature, in groves of sacred trees (particularly oak trees), in caves, or near sacred bodies of water. Human sacrifice is attributed to the Druids, primarily by the Romans, and we are still unclear if this is true or a part of Roman propaganda. Even if it is true, as many suspect, both animal and human sacrifice have been a part of ancient cultures, often with either a willing victim, who gives his life for the rejuvenation of the land, or the execution of criminals, since there was no penal system in the Celtic culture.

As Christianity soon replaced the Roman Empire as the dominant force against Pagan Celtic culture, many believe the Druids, realizing the future, embedded themselves in the Christian Church as monks, brothers, priests, and scribes, to preserve many of the old ways, myths, and holidays of the early Celtic Christian Church, or used their bardic skills to become wandering storytellers and musicians, keeping the old ways alive. From the revival in the eighteenth century, modern Druidism, or Neo-Druidism, has evolved along several lines. Some look to the cultural context of Druidism, the poetry, myths, and storytelling, and those of a religious bent, more akin to modern Neo-Paganism and Wicca. Such Druids usually work with an Earth Mother and a variety of Pagan deities from the Celtic culture, may use Celtic words and phrases in ritual, and celebrate the seasons. Many modern Pagans and Witches see the Druids as their Celtic ancestors and feel a kinship with their traditions. There is a lot of overlap between both the cultural and the religious expressions of modern Druidism, because many religious groups do not require a conversion to Paganism, and many cultural groups do not inquire as to your religion. This has resulted in both monotheistic and polytheistic Druids. Some see Druidism simply as a philosophy and apply it to their lives in any manner they see fit, incorporating aspects of Christianity, Paganism, or a variety of other traditions. Though the eighteenth-century revival was often not historically accurate in the light of modern research, many are still influenced by it, while others in the Druidic movement are strict Celtic Reconstructionists, and hold to an exacting standard of scholarship in their personal spiritual practices. If there is no historical evidence that the Druids performed a ritual in a particular way, then they will not adopt the ritual. No even partially complete Druidic ritual has survived in writing into the modern era, so such reconstructions are based on the classical writers who had contact with the Druids, as well as the mentions of Druids in the Celtic tales. Such practitioners often reject modern creations, such as many Wiccan and ceremonial magic practices, even if they fit into the belief systems of the Druids. In the modern era, two organizations responsible for promoting the Druidic tradition are the Order of Bards, Ovates and Druids (OBOD), the oldest and largest order of Druids based in England, and Ár nDraíocht Féin, the largest American order of Druids.

Faery Faith

The faery faith is not a specific faith or formalized religion, but a collection of folk traditions, customs, mores, and lore passed on in certain parts of the world, particularly in Celtic territories and places where their descendents have settled. The faery faith involves a partnership with spiritual beings defined as faeries, who come from another world but are intimately tied to the land and seasonal cycles. Though much of our modern faery lore depicts these beings as tiny and winged, traditionalists in the faery faith know that they come in all shapes and sizes, often as tall and shining warriors, and, like humans, they come in all temperaments, not just docile or playful.

The faith involves a healthy exchange with the "good folk" through offerings of milk, honey, and bread in return for blessings of health and good harvest. It also includes following other customs and prohibitions, such as the avoidance of all iron or steel when working with these shining ones. Those who are particularly attuned to the faery world are often labeled seers, being able to see into the faery realm and deepen the pact. Some do specific acts of magic, learned from, or in cooperation with, the fair folk, including blessing and cursing, faery healing, divination, prophecy, and artistic inspiration. For quite a while, faery traditions had lived side by side with Christian traditions in the British Isles and parts of the United States. Some have influenced, and been influenced by, forms of mystical and Gnostic Christianity.

Hermetic Ceremonial Magic

Hermetic ceremonial magic is a long European tradition considered "high" magic, using specialized tools, foreign languages, and elaborate ceremonies with an emphasis on spiritual enlightenment over mundane life changes through spell craft, differentiating it from the folk magic of the peasantry, which uses common tools and simple objects available to everyone. Hermetic magic draws upon the mystical teachings of Hermes, teaching that are also heavily entwined with the practice of alchemy. Many involved in Hermetic magic draw upon whatever mystical resources are available, from astrology to Eastern yogic and tantric practices, as well as Gnostic Christianity, Hebrew Kabalah, and angelic/demonic lore, eventually creating a form of magical Qabalah, often spelled with a *Q* to differentiate it from the Hebrew and Christian versions. Modern practitioners, most notably the founders of the Order of the Golden Dawn, drew upon these older sources and synthesized a new practice of ceremonial magic. The modern public lodge of the Golden Dawn was founded in 1888. The Golden Dawn rituals were eventually made public, over the protests of many practitioners, and have become the default foundations for subsequent study.

Though not a religion in the strictest sense—for ceremonial magicians often also identify as Christian, Jewish, or Pagan—ceremonial magic is a spiritual tradition that guides the seeker into deeper levels of mystery and understanding, providing a framework of initiation based on the Tree of Life Qabalistic glyph. Initial training is focused on mastery of the elements within the practitioner, as symbolized by the magician's tools of the pentacle, blade, wand, and cup, also found in the tarot. Though the Golden Dawn was a lodge of magicians, with group practices, many practitioners successfully use the techniques and follow the path solitarily. Though ceremonial magic shares much in common with, and has influenced and been influenced by, traditions of Witchcraft, it is not a celebratory or community service-oriented path, but one of self-enlightenment, seeking completion of the "Great Work," much like an alchemist. Modern ceremonial magic was highly influenced by a text known as *The Sacred Magic of Abra-Melin the Mage*, and the ritual contained within became known as the Abra-Melin Operation. The purpose was to make contact with your higher self, also known as knowledge and conversation with your Holy Guardian Angel, or HGA for short. Variations of this ritual have been created by modern practitioners. Though the Golden Dawn's initial curriculum has provided a modern foundation, many seek their own way into the Hermetic mysteries, looking at the original source material starting with the works of Eliphas Lévi, Cornelius Agrippa, Francis Barrett, and John Dee and working backward to older Hermetic texts. Many traditions and practices have emphasized a specific culture, such as Egyptian, Greek, or Sumerian. Like other mystical paths, those of ceremonial magic are quite diverse.

Hinduism

Hinduism is a religion based upon the sacred texts known as the Vedas, as well as the traditions and belief system of the people of India. Depending on how you define religion, it is considered by many to be the world's oldest formal religion still in practice. Though it is often perceived as a single religion, within Hinduism is a wide range of traditions, rituals, and sects. The term Hindu comes from Sindhu, which is the Indus River specifically and also a term for any river. Hindu became the name for those people living beyond the Sindhu. In the religious text of the Rig Veda, these Indo-Aryans mentioned come from the land of the seven rivers, to the northwest of the Indian subcontinent. One of those rivers is the Indus.

Hinduism involves the belief in dharma, traditionally defined as individual ethics, duties, and obligations; samsara, or reincarnation of the soul; karma, one's actions and the consequences of those actions; and moksha, or salvation for every soul. Salvation is not seen in the Christian sense as salvation from sin, but release from the cycle of death and rebirth to become one with the divine cosmic spirit. The soul is known as the atman, and continues the cycle of birth, death, and rebirth. There are many paths of action that lead to this salvation, including devotional service to the divine, selfless actions for the work, enlightenment through knowledge and study, and simply belief in the divine.

The divine can be viewed as one vast cosmic being, both immanent and transcendent, known as Brahman, but the divine can also manifest through a variety of deities, which are expressions of Brahman. These deities are seen as both male and female, gods and goddesses. There is also a belief in a variety of entities, including those known as devas, or celestial spirits, and demons. Though Hinduism may appear to be polytheistic, particularly when compared to Judaism, Christianity, and Islam, technically this is not correct, as the tradition espouses one supreme creator that manifests in many ways, creating a sort of paradox. It is one of the few traditions that openly states that the divine is both immanent and transcendent. Practitioners of Hinduism can develop an impersonal relationship with the divine, or form a very personal relationship with a specific manifestation of the divine. Many temples, rituals, and traditions have been developed around the devotion to one manifestation of the divine.

Islam

Islam is the prophetic religion following in the traditions of Judaism and Christianity, referring to the followers of the lineage of prophets that runs through Judaism, Christianity, and Islam as the People of the Book, in reference to the Old Testament, New Testament, and Qur'an. The name Islam means submission or surrender, and implies a surrender to the one God of Islam. Followers of Islam, known as Muslims, make up the second largest religion of the world at this time. The prophet of Islam is Muhammad, and God revealed to him his divine word through the Qur'an, or Koran. Though following a prophetic succession that could conceivably be started with Adam from the Garden of Eden, Muslims believe that the Qur'an is God's final word and Muhammad is the final prophet, and this perfect word supersedes all others, as the Bible and Torah can be flawed. The Qur'an is only perfect in Arabic, and any translations of it are simply commentaries and potentially fallible.

Muslims are monotheistic, believing in one supreme god worthy of worship, and this god is known as Allah. Though monotheistic, Islam finds messengers, both in the form of prophets and in the form of angelic beings, acceptable. The basic belief required to become Muslim is that there is no god but Allah, and that Muhammad is his messenger. There are no visual images or depictions of Allah, though there are ninety-nine "names" or "qualities" attributed to him, such as The All Beneficent, The Most Merciful, and The Most Holy. Along with angels, there is also a belief in djinn, or beings of fire that are not entirely material or spiritual. A belief in magic or sorcery of any kind is forbidden. There are a number of branches of Islam, including Sunni, Shi'ite, and Kharijite, which have some differences in theology, but all Muslims believe in one god, Allah, and that he is the only one worthy of worship. They also believe in the prophets, including Muhammad, in the sacred books sent by God, in angels, in a judgment day and resurrection, and in destiny. Islamic practitioners believe in the immortality of the human soul and the fulfillment of a divine plan, where the faithful will be rewarded in a divine paradise and the unfaithful and unjust will be punished. Some branches of Islam are more progressive, while others are more conservative, and views, actions, and customs can vary widely.

Jainism

The religion known as Jainism, or Jain Dharma, finds its roots as an ancient faith and philosophy in India, attributed to the Hindu prince Mahavira (599–527 BC) but possibly predating him by several thousand years in the early Indus Valley culture. Having similarities to other aspects of Hinduism, and greatly influencing Indian society, Jainists believe in karma, reincarnation, nonviolence, asceticism, and the time cycles known as Yugas. Jainists do not believe in a creator god, and feel the universe is eternal, with no beginning or end. It simply moves through these yugic cycles of ascension and descension. Jainists believe their tradition preserves the eternal truths that are periodically lost by humanity over the cycles of time and rediscovered as various people reach a level of enlightenment when these truths become evident.

Jainism is dualistic, as an emphasis is placed on the spiritual world and material world, with the material world trapping the spiritual essence and causing suffering. Jainist society is divided into monks and religious persons, who seek to devote all their efforts to escaping the wheel of rebirth, and the laypeople of the society, who work in traditional jobs. All Jainists believe in non-injury, non-lying, non-stealing, chastity (monks are celibate, and laypeople can have sexual relations only within the confines of marriage), and non-possession. Jainists believe in tolerance for other beliefs, and that nothing is absolute, as we have a flawed perspective of reality and the divine, and no one tradition has a hold on the only truth. It is not a religion of absolutes, even though its requirements seem strict. Jainists believe that absolutism results in fanaticism and does not facilitate the liberation from suffering. Jainist rituals often include rice, which is used to trace the holy symbol of the right-facing swastika. Another symbol is the hand with the wheel in the palm, written with the Jainist vow of Ahimsa, the vow of non-injury and non-violence. It represents the search for the truth through the cycles of reincarnation. Jainists take the vow of non-injury and non-violence beyond strict vegetarianism and will not eat certain root vegetables, because their harvest is seen as unnecessarily harsh.

Judaism

Judaism was one of the first recorded monotheistic religions and is still practiced in a variety of forms today. The history and customs of Judaism have become the basis of the Abrahamic religions, named after the Jewish prophet Abraham, and have gone on to influence Christianity and Islam. Though viewed as a religion in the context of this book, it is difficult to separate the concepts of Judaism from ethnicity, culture, and history. The traditions of Judaism have been influenced by those in ancient Egypt, Babylon, Persia, and Greece. Central to Judaism as it is known today is the concept of monotheism, or of a single creator. Some people would argue that Judaism was not originally monotheistic, and their central concept of God began as a tribal god among many gods, who then forbade his people from worshipping and even acknowledging other gods. Today most involved in Judaism believe it to have always been a monotheistic tradition. Judaism is a prophetic religion, with many messengers sent by God to deliver his word and law. These sacred scriptures come from divine revelation and are considered the true word of God. The Hebrew Bible, known to Christians as the Old Testament, guides the tradition, and includes the famous Ten Commandments. According to legend, Abraham was the first Jew, in covenant with the God of Israel, and he rejected idolatry and Paganism and preached monotheism. The most famous of the Prophetic line was Moses, known for freeing his people from servitude in Egypt.

Jews believe in a divine covenant with God, that they are the chosen people. They believe in and await a messianic figure, but do not believe Jesus Christ to be the messiah. The practice of Judaism includes prayer, temple services, and observance of holy days, including the Sabbath. Sin, as wrong or unacceptable actions, is believed in, though atonement of sin can be undertaken directly with God. Though there is a belief in beings such as angels, they are not to be prayed to. Only God receives prayer. There is a priestly caste known as rabbis, acting as ritualists, counselors, and community leaders. Traditionally, one was considered Jewish if born of a Jewish mother, though most forms of modern Judaism accept converts. People who are born Jews but who leave the traditions for another, or to be agnostic, are still considered Jews, but lose their status in the Jewish spiritual community.

Currently, there are many forms and branches of Judaism, each with its own interpretation of the sacred teachings and its own way of putting them into action in the world. The Kabalah is the mystical teachings of Judaism, traditionally reserved for married men over the age of forty. The Kabalah details creation through ten sephiroth, and the twenty paths connecting these emanations of creation. The theories of Kabalah were later codified into a map of reality known as the Tree of Life. Kabalah became a major portion of the Western mystery traditions, as some speculate its principles were a part of the magical systems of Egypt and Sumeria. Kabalistic lore has been adopted by those outside of the Jewish faith, tradition, and culture. It was absorbed into medieval forms of ceremonial magic and alchemy and has played a major role in the revitalization of the Western mystery traditions, such as the Order of the Golden Dawn. As a system, the Tree of Life schematic can organize and explain vast amounts of esoteric ideas and occult terminology, from numerology and astrology to various non-Jewish mythologies. Ceremonial magic traditions often use the spelling Qabalah, while Christian mystics might use Cabala. Though each is interpreting the wisdom in a different way, they are all essentially describing the same view of reality.

Martial Arts

Though not a religious tradition, the Eastern martial arts play a significant role in the development of many people's spirituality, much like the disciplines of yoga or the practice of Reiki healing. Like yoga and Reiki, each martial art has its roots in a spiritual tradition, though being a member of such a tradition is not a requirement to explore the art itself. Though martial arts technically means a military art of combat, it now usually refers to the traditions of self-defense and fighting from the Eastern world. Martial arts in the Western world exist, though our popular cultural mind has linked most martial arts to Eastern traditions and spirituality. Primarily known as fighting systems of unarmed combat, or when involving weapons, not using conventional modern weapons such as handguns, the underlying systems promote physical fitness, health, self-development, self-defense, meditation, and an understanding of energy and the flow of the universe. Martial arts traditions include Aikido, Jiu Jitsu, Judo, Karate, Kendo, Kung Fu, Ninjutsu, Tai Chi Ch'uan, Chi Kung, and Taekwondo, among others. Each has its own style, traditions, and philosophy. Many see the martial artist as the spiritual warrior.

Mithraism

Mithraism is a mystery tradition passed on through initiation, much like those of the Eleusinian Mysteries. Based upon the god Mithras, or Mehr, found in the traditions of Zoroastrianism, Mithraism originated in the Eastern territories of the Mediterranean around the first or second century BC. Though it would be easy to equate the Persian Mithras with the Mediterranean one, their myths are not always the same, and Zoroastrianism, although it has a dualistic slant, is a monotheistic religion, and its one god is Ahura Mazda. It was later practiced in the Roman Empire, finding its popularity among the soldiers until Pagan rites were banned and the tradition became extinct. We have very little on which to base our knowledge of Mithraism, since few texts survive. It was an experiential, and not scripture-based, tradition. Seen as a male-dominant warrior tradition, women were not allowed to join. The image of Mithras springing forth from an egg, as well as the sacrifice of a bull, seem central to the tradition. Some see in this a motif of life, death, and rebirth, while others view Mithras as being a mediator between humanity and the divine source. There appears to be a connection between the solar cults and Mithraic worship, and some believe that the Cult of Mithras influenced the early Christians' view of Jesus Christ. Even though Mithraism was outlawed, it continued briefly until it was completely supplanted by Christianity.

Paganism

Paganism, or more accurately Neo-Paganism, is the revival of the pre-Christian Pagan traditions of Europe. The word Pagan comes from the Latin *Paganus*, meaning "country dweller" or "of the land." Now it is used to refer to practitioners of the old religions that were intimately tied to the land. When Christianity first began to grow, it took root in the urban environments, and those in the outskirts who were considered Pagan eventually were associated with the older religions. Pagan does not mean someone who has no religious beliefs, or someone who is solely a hedonist. Although Pagans enjoy the physical pleasures of the world, this is but one aspect of life, and not the sole focus.

Modern Pagans seek to recapture the Earth-reverent, nature-oriented traditions of ages past, where nature was seen as an expression of divinity. Pagan traditions are considered polytheistic, meaning a belief in many gods. In ancient mythology, each culture had diverse pantheons of beings, each embodying one or more natural or societal concepts. In Greek myth, we have Gaia, the Earth Mother; Zeus, the storm king and ruler of the gods;

Hades, the god of death and the underworld; Aphrodite, the goddess of love; and Ares, the god of war; among many others. Some modern Pagans work with an amalgam of polytheistic gods and philosophies, while others focus on a specific culture, such as Celtic Paganism. Paganism has many traditions within it. Modern Witchcraft and Wicca are subsets of Paganism. When teaching new students, I use the simile "Paganism is to Witchcraft as Christianity is to Catholicism." One is a larger grouping, and the other is a subset. Some in the Northern European traditions, particularly the Norse, seek to separate their traditions and beliefs from the overall Neo-Pagan movement. They prefer the term heathen, rather than Pagan, reclaiming the word used to refer to people of the heath, the wild, uncultivated lands often covered with various evergreen trees and shrubs. Within heathenism there are specific traditions and movements, such as Asatru, followers of the Norse gods known as the Aesir.

Reiki

Reiki is a form of energy healing that originated in Japan in the late 1800s with a man named Dr. Mikao Usui. Reiki translates to "universal life force." Many mystical cultures have recognized life force. Known in Japan as ki, this is the second syllable of the name Reiki. As a system, Reiki is a tradition in which the practitioner is "attuned," or connected, to this pure universal life force through a ritual given by the teacher. From that attunement, Reiki energy flows through the practitioner and is usually applied through contact with the hands. It is characterized by a warm or tingling sensation, for both the practitioner and the recipient, that emanates from the hands of the practitioner. Later training teaches methods of distance healing and modern techniques of "beaming" this energy to a recipient.

The philosophy of Reiki as a system is that the practitioner offers the Reiki energy to the one in need of healing. The recipient controls the flow of energy on an intuitive, or higher consciousness, level. The practitioner acts like a straw, a channel letting the energy come through. The energy has its own intelligence, working with the recipient, and knows where to go for the highest good. The practitioner and the client cannot consciously control how the healing will manifest. The Reiki practitioner cannot overload or harm the recipient with too much energy. When the recipient is "full" of energy, the flow naturally stops, just as one would stop drinking from a straw.

Though Reiki is not a religion, it has many spiritual benefits. It can be practiced by any-body, of any religion. The precepts are rooted in Japanese Buddhism, even though some stories claim a Christian origin, or genesis in a mythic ancient culture. The concepts of nonattachment and surrender are key to Reiki. The Reiki attunements themselves awaken the student spiritually to more divine energy, and facilitate the student's own healing pro-cess. Each level of training has one of these rituals. When one offers Reiki to another, the practitioner is also nourished by this energy. The Reiki principles, given by Dr. Usui, have continued to be a guiding part of this spiritual discipline. Many people use Reiki as a spiri-tual structure for life, as others use yoga, martial arts, or meditation.

Satanism

Though most people would not include Satanism in a list of spiritual traditions, it most certainly is a valid spiritual choice. Many mystics are fond of saying that all paths lead to the top of the mountain. Satanism is no exception, though many Satanists might dis-agree. There are several manifestations of Satanism, and in general, the public is ignorant of most of them. Satan translates to "adversary," and in the Old Testament was the name of an agent of God, sent to test the faith of believers. In that context, many people believe Satan, or Satanael, to be an angelic figure, one doing God's will, and not a fallen angel. Satan has been liked with many figures in Judeo-Christian-Islamic and Pagan mytholo-gies, including the fallen angel Lucifer, the snake in the Garden of Eden, the Beast of the Apocalypse, the Islamic Iblis, the Roman god Saturn, the Greek Pan, the Celtic Cernunnos, and the Devil. They are not all considered the same archetype and entity. The Greek term diablos meant to throw something in your way, to make an obstacle, and the later term Devil first meant a force trying to slow your spiritual development by giving you obstacles. Eventually this term was equated with an ultimate entity of evil and a social, political, and spiritual scapegoat.

On one level, most see Satanism as an inversion of Jewish or Christian traditions. Images of Satanic masses parodying Catholic rituals are popular, though they do not constitute the full Satanic tradition. Some people have practiced this brand of Satanism, choosing to identify and worship the figure of evil in Christian myth as an act of rebellion against the church's morals and values. Fundamental interpretations of Judeo-Christianity would look at any religion not of the Abrahamic line as Satanic, including Hinduism, sha-manism, Buddhism, and Paganism. Others think of Satanists as illegal groups of murderers, animal sacrificers, and child pornographers as portrayed in the popular media in the United States, even though there is no evidence of a great brotherhood of evil conspirators actively pursuing occult crime and the downfall of Western civilization. At best, such a view is an unsubstantiated conspiracy theory fueled by isolated incidences.

The esoteric philosophy of Satanism is best described as a left-hand path, though the definitions of a left-hand path and a right-hand path differ depending on the organization you are in. Some erroneously think that the left-hand path equates with evil and the right-hand path with good. Some look to the social customs and taboos regarding eating and washing in terms of left- and right-hand connotations. Perhaps these taboos and negative connotations are reflections of the cultural bias against left-handed people. Others see the left-hand path as feminine, or sexual in nature, and the right-hand path as aesthetic and based more in discipline or hardship than pleasure. In a modern Satanic context, the left-hand path is about self-realization, becoming like a god, a creator, rather than submission or union with the creative force. Individuality and individual consciousness are emphasized, rather than union. Some would see it as an ego-based tradition, and at some levels it is, though for many it is a tradition of self-realization and self-actualization, honest enough to look at the desires of the practitioner in a clear light. Some see the left-hand path as the tradition of dissent and rebellion against the status quo, only for those daring enough to go against societal expectations and follow their own callings and impulses. Strangely enough, many traditions that deify individuals, such as the ascended masters of Theosophy and the New Age ascension movement, would be considered, at least in part, left-hand paths by modern practitioners of left-hand paths, though the practitioners of these traditions would assume they were right-hand paths; while traditions such as Wicca, which have a more sinister reputation with the public, are considered far more right-hand paths by true left-hand practitioners. Some would even say, contrary to public opinion, that Jesus Christ's life was an example of a left-hand path, as he fought the status quo, was rejected by the mainstream, followed his own callings and teachings, and eventually was deified as an individual entity by his followers.

Personally, I think most mystic traditions are not exclusively left- or right-hand, as these two concepts do not have to be at odds with each other. Individualization and simultaneous union are spiritual mysteries. The most popularly known branch of Satanism is based on Anton LaVey's Church of Satan and his book *The Satanic Bible*. This might be the least spiritually oriented modern branch, influenced by more modern intellectual philosophers than mystical philosophers, though Aleister Crowley was also an influence on LaVey, and this has erroneously caused Crowley to be labeled a Satanist. In this branch, Satan is seen as a symbol of both nature and human nature, and not a literal entity. These Satanists don't actually believe in Satan. Each practitioner is viewed as his or her own god, and ritual magic is done to further the practitioner's own desires. Followers of the Temple of Set broke off from LaVey's organization and see Set as an actual entity, as a prince of darkness, one of the first divine spiritual rebels or dissenters to the orthodox order. Set is not to be worshipped or served, but used as role model in the practitioner's own process of becoming more godlike.

Other groups of a similar tradition have splintered from the Church of Satan and Temple of Set. Another misunderstood branch, which is technically not a form of Satanism, is Luciferianism, or Gnostic Luciferianism. The varying traditions related to this concept see Lucifer as the light bringer, and the redeemer and lord of the world, as a positive figure rather than the antithesis of God or a destructive force. Like the Greek Prometheus, Lucifer brings individual light, consciousness, awareness in the dark. He sacrificed himself to redeem the world, and many look at him as the precursor of Jesus Christ, as both are redeemers. Some faery traditions and forms of Witchcraft are considered Luciferian in nature. Some look at Lucifer as the equivalent of the Gnostic Demiurge, or God of the World, and the Demiurge is equated with the God of the Christians and Jews, Jehovah or Yahweh. They then use this to either elevate the image of Lucifer or paint Jews and Christians as devil worshippers. In the Middle East, there is a small sect of ethnic Kurds known as the Yezidi, who are labeled Satanists and devil worshippers but actually worship Malak Ta'us, a pre-Islamic fallen angel or fallen god associated with the peacock. Their religion has some strong links to Zoroastrianism, Mithraism, and Gnosticism, as well as elements of Christianity, Judaism, Islam, and pre-Islamic Kurdish beliefs. As all these traditions have valid mystical concepts to share with the world, the Satanic traditions should also be looked at in our mystical survey. Some of the most self-aware, insightful, and responsible mystics I know identify with one of these branches of Satanism.

Shamanism

Shamanism popularly refers to the spiritual medicine traditions of indigenous people across the world. Technically, the word shaman, or saman, comes from Siberian tribes, and is properly used to refer to the healers of the tribes who share a similar genetic origin to the indigenous cultures of Siberia. It has come into common usage to describe a set of a techniques and ideas, now known as "core shamanism," that can be applied to a variety of cultures and time periods. This has led to the creation of terms such as Celtic shamanism or Norse shamanism, even if those cultures did not use the term shaman. The practices of core shamanism for healing, insight, and problem solving date back to the Stone Age, yet each culture experienced and created its own rituals, myths, and symbols around the basic core framework, making it personal and consistent with the values and customs of its tradition. Many consider shamanism to be the impetus for the creation of human civilization and the foundation for other forms of magic, mysticism, and religion. Core shamanism is set apart from other indigenous tribal spiritual and healing practices, as its focus is on entering an altered state to travel to the nonphysical worlds and commune with the spirits. Through a relationship with these spirits, a shaman brings change, healing, and wisdom back to the material world.

Shamanic cosmology usually looks to a cosmic axis known as the *axis mundi* and often thought of as a great tree at the center of the world. This axis holds together at least three worlds: a middle world of space, time, and general humanity; a lower world of the ancestors and earthly spirits; and an upper world of sky, solar, and stellar spirits. Common themes in many shamanic traditions include connecting to a primary spirit ally who guides, protects, and teaches, often in an animal form, as well as eventually forming a "team" of spirits who aid in the shaman's work. As the core techniques are brought to people in the West—most notably by Michael Harner, through his book *The Way of the Shaman* and his organization, the Foundation for Shamanic Studies—terms such as shamanic practitioner and shamanist have been created to distinguish a traditional tribal shaman from those simply using the techniques.

Shinto

Shinto, which means "way of the gods," combines two characters: Shin, or the gods, referring to the Kami, the gods, spirits, and presences of nature; and To, or Tao, the way or path, in a spiritual sense. Often described by Westerners as Japanese Pagans, Shinto practitioners honor the spirits of nature. Some of these are local spirits, while others are grand natural phenomena, such as the Sun and Moon. Shinto was the official state religion of Japan until the end of World War II, though it is still a part of Japanese life and culture and continues to influence the community, even in subtle and often unrecognized ways. Shinto has influenced the "new" religions established in Japan, particularly Japanese Buddhism.

The tradition itself has no set dogma, scripture, or hierarchy, other than a past recognition of the Japanese royal family, whose influence has dwindled since World War II. There is little emphasis on the afterlife, but instead a collection of rituals, prayers, and methods to develop a relationship with the Kami. Shrine worship is part of the practice, along with folk customs such as divination, spirit possession, and healing. An emphasis on family and tradition, nature, physical cleanliness, purification, and honoring the Kami and the many festivals dedicated to them are all part of the tradition.

Sikhism

Born in the environment of the conflict between Hinduism and Islam, the Sikh religion sought to bridge the gap between the two traditions and welcome all people equally to its doors. Sikhism is based on the unity of one God, neither male nor female (though often the male pronoun is used but understood to encompass both genders), as well as the teachings of ten great gurus. Sikhism was founded by Guru Nanak near the end of the fifteenth century. After taking four epic journeys, he began to preach to both Hindus and Muslims. Desiring to go beyond both religions, he incorporated elements of each, from reformed Hinduism to Islamic Sufism.

The term Sikh means a strong and able disciple. Guru Nanak attracted these disciples for which the tradition is named. Sikhism fuses this monotheism with some esoteric ideas from Hinduism, such as the concepts of karma, reincarnation, and the maya, or the illusion of the material world veiling the true nature of God. The caste system is rejected in favor of a view of equality for all before God, and seeing God as divine Father/Mother. Women do not hold a lower status, nor do they have to wear veils. Practitioners meditate, usually early in the morning, recite prayers and mantras, and have a holy text known as the Guru Granth Sahib. Traditionally, Sikhs are required to wear turbans to cover the head, as well as to wear or carry the five K's, words that translate to uncut hair, comb, circular bracelet, shorts, and a small curved sword. Each of the five K's is a symbol of spiritual activities and attitudes that should be integrated into the daily life of a Sikh—a balance between work, devotion to god, and charity, or good works.

In Sikhism, practitioners are judged according to their actions rather than a strict moral code. Salvation is breaking from the wheel of rebirth to be absorbed back into God. As an esoteric tradition without a priestly caste, practitioners are encouraged to live a family life and be a part of the world. Asceticism is not allowed, though practitioners are discouraged from collecting too many worldly goods and getting attached to them. The tradition encourages an optimistic view of life as well as learning to not be attached to both the joys and tragedies of everyday reality. Sikhs have a strong sense of morality and ethics, believing we should stand up for our own rights and the rights of others, as we are all inherently part of the divinity of God. Alcohol, tobacco, drugs, and other intoxicants are prohibited. There are also prohibitions against behavior that is considered nonlogical, such as religious "superstitions," and rituals that have no meaning for them as a tradition, including fasting, women wearing veils, religious pilgrimages, sacrifices, and idols. As spiritual warriors, Sikhs fight the five "thieves" known as ego, anger, greed, attachment, and lust. Their weapons in this battle include contentment, charity, kindness, a positive attitude, and humility.

Sufism

Sufism is considered the esoteric, or mystical, branch of the Islamic religion. Where Sufis fit into the Islamic map of beliefs is not always clear. While some of the Sufi organizations, brotherhoods or sisterhoods, are sometimes considered Shiah or Sunni, many of them are not associated with any of the main branches of Islam, so Sufism can be considered a force unto its own in the Islamic world. It has even made inroads into non-Islamic communities, particularly in the West, though it is rooted Islam. According to most Sufis, the name Sufi means "one who purifies the heart." The core teaching of Sufism is love, that love is the projection of God to the universe. Sufis seek to be touched by God, and to see this love in themselves and all others, creating a system of tolerance and personal experience.

Sufism is often taught in small groups, by a master, as many practitioners believe such a spiritual teacher is necessary to aid their spiritual growth. Parables, metaphors, stories, and poetry are used as teaching tools. Sufis also have a spiritual cosmology comparable to such esoteric teachings as the Qabalistic Tree of Life, and a belief in six personal energy centers in the body that develop over time and with spiritual practices, similar to the chakra system. Disciples of Sufism are known as dervishes and often take a vow of poverty. Their spinning dance, which is a method to induce a trance state and have a personal experience of God, has given rise to the popular image of the whirling dervish, yet not all Sufis practice this style of dance. The rituals and prayers of Sufi groups can be quite varied.

Thelema

Thelema is a mystic tradition founded in 1904 by Aleister Crowley through the transmission of a book known as *The Book of the Law*, or *Liber Al vel Legis*, from a divine source while in Cairo, Egypt. As most Thelemites consider themselves ritual magicians, Thelema is rooted in Crowley's practice of ceremonial magic, being a former member of the Golden Dawn, yet has its own variations of its rituals. Some of the symbolism of these rituals, such as the Star Ruby, one of Crowley's variations of the Golden Dawn's Lesser Banishing Ritual of the Pentagram, is erroneously thought of as being Satanic in nature. Though Crowley's works influenced some branches of modern Satanism, Thelema would not be considered a Satanic path. In his tradition, Crowley draws upon the systems of ceremonial magic, alchemy, yoga, tantra, tarot, and astrology. Because of its birthplace, Thelema is ripe with Egyptian and pseudo-Egyptian symbolism and mythology mixed with its own powerful philosophies. Crowley was considered the prophet of the next Aeon, or Age, with the Aeon of Horus replacing that of Horus's father, Osiris.

The basic tenet of Thelema is to find and perform your True Will, what might be known to others as your Magical Will, Higher Self's Will, or, in some contexts, your dharma. Your purpose is to fulfill your True Will in this world, and your True Will doesn't conflict with anyone else's. Thelemites must respect other people's True Will, even if it conflicts with their personal, or ego, will. Prime keys to Thelema include a recognition of humanity's inherent divinity and a natural inclination toward freedom, as well as finding a balance between personal responsibility and discipline, though critics would argue that Crowley did not live up to them in his personal life. Key phrases from *The Book of the Law* are cited as the basis for these philosophies, such as "Do what thou wilt shall be the whole of the Law" (*AL*, I:40) and "Love is the law, love under will" (*AL*, I:57).

Various organizations have adopted Thelemic tenants in whole or in part, in particular the Ordo Templi Orientis, or O.T.O., an organization of which Crowley was the head. Others see Crowley's law as the basis for the modern-day Wiccan Rede, and believe that either Crowley influenced Gerald Gardner, of the Gardnerian Wicca tradition, since they knew each other, or the two had access to similar traditional material. One of the most popular and moving rituals of Thelema, practiced by branches of the O.T.O., is the Gnostic Mass, which includes this powerful communal statement made by each participant: "There is no part of me that is not of the gods."

Theosophy

Theosophy comes from the words Theo, meaning god, and Sophia, meaning wisdom, and is said to be the search for or study of God found in all religions. As a formal tradition, it was brought to light by one of the founders of the Theosophical Society, a controversial figure known as Madame Helena Blavatsky. Blavatsky wrote some seminal books that highly influenced the New Age movement, including *The Secret Doctrine* and *Isis Unveiled*. She claimed to be in touch with "ascended masters," beings who were once human but have completed their experiences in the physical world and reached a level of enlightenment where they can reside between human consciousness and complete union with the divine, where they are available to many seekers simultaneously. Though many believed Blavatsky's ascended masters were physical beings, or could choose to be and appear to others, most in the modern Theosophical movement look at ascended masters as discarnate beings contacted during meditation and trance work. Theosophy and subsequent modern "channels" were influenced by the work of the Spiritualist Movement. Though not directly endorsed by the Theosophical Society, the author Alice Bailey followed in Blavatsky's steps, acting as the "secretary" to the masters with whom she was in psychic contact. Bailey wrote a large number of texts on spiritual topics, including *A Treatise on White Magic* and *Esoteric Psychology*.

Theosophy as a philosophy itself seeks to find the underlying truths, the search for God, in all religions. Though it definitely has an Eastern flavor, as many of the masters claimed Tibetan Buddhism as their path in the last lifetime before they ascended, it incorporates the wisdom of the ancient Greeks, Egyptians, Hindus, and mystical Christians. Many people feel the early teachers in this paradigm were anti-Semitic, though those who have continued on, particularly those in the ascension movement that Theosophy inspired, have made efforts to incorporate mystical Judaism, including Kabalah, into Theosophical teachings. Though one of the biggest criticisms of Theosophy is that its inclusiveness leaves it with little clear theology or structure of its own, it is because of this inclusiveness that we can see the common points between so many mystic traditions.

Wicca and Witchcraft

Wicca is considered to be the modern revival of the religion of Witchcraft. Witchcraft is an art, science, and spiritual tradition based on the Pagan traditions of the ancient world.

The word Wicca is often translated as to bend or to shape, referring to the Witch's ability to bend and shape the forces of nature, but also to flow with them, not break them, to make changes in life known as magic. Others believe there is a connection between the word Witch and the word wise, referring to the Witch as one with knowledge. Modern Witchcraft, or technically Neo-Witchcraft, is rooted mostly in European traditions such as those of the Celts, Teutons, Greeks, and Romans, with some influence from Egyptian and Middle Eastern mythologies such as Sumerian. Witches look at the priestesses and priests of the ancient world, the cunning men/women of Europe, the hedge Witches and traditional herbalists, the Druids, and the Pagan seers and magicians as spiritual ancestors and inspirations. Witchcraft comes in many forms and traditions and is considered a subset of the larger Neo-Pagan movement.

All Witches are Pagans, but not all Pagans identify as Witches. As a tradition with no central authority or fundamental spiritual text, Witchcraft is defined in many different ways, depending on the practitioner. Key concepts to most of the traditions include a reverence for or veneration of nature, as the material world and the divine are seen as being inexorably linked. Divinity manifests primarily through a Goddess and a God, though each can have many expressions. The Goddess is seen in the Earth, Moon, and stars, while the God is often viewed as a horned animal lord, or deity of the grain, Sun, and sky. Modern Witches often look at a cosmology of a triple goddess—maiden, mother, and crone—with a dual god, a god of light and a god of darkness. Though many Wiccan traditions seek to balance female and male energies, if any gender is favored, it is traditionally the feminine. The high priestess and the Goddess are favored, as the Goddess is seen as the source from which all things flow and to which all things return. Witches celebrate eight yearly main holidays, or sabbats, known collectively as the Wheel of the Year, including two equinoxes, two solstices, and four fire festivals in between, drawing on both Celtic and Teutonic symbolism. They also celebrate Moon rituals, known as esbats, on the full and/or dark Moon. Witches seek to develop psychic and magical abilities as part of their spiritual path and communion with the divine. The Witch's main tools are much like those of the magician, with the wand, pentacle, chalice, and athame (double-edged blade) being primary. The pentacle is the most popular symbol of Witchcraft for modern Witches. In their work they also use the cauldron, broom, scourge, tarot cards, and a variety of natural substances such as herbs and stones.

The words Witchcraft and Wicca are equated by some practitioners and firmly separated by others, yet the definitions are not consistent globally. One school of thought views

Wicca as the religion, and Witchcraft as the collection of techniques. Others see Witchcraft as the more traditional practices, and Wicca as the modern eclectic form of the Craft. Yet another group sees Wicca as solely the initiatory forms of the tradition, and Witchcraft as available to anybody, regardless of initiation or training. Wicca was first brought to public light by the controversial figure Gerald Gardner, who was the founder of the initiatory tradition of Witchcraft known as Gardnerian Wicca. Formal traditions often emphasize initiation from teacher to student, while modern traditions allow and even encourage self-dedication, self-initiation, and direct experience between the Witch and the gods.

Voodoo

Voodoo is the spiritual tradition that grew from the synthesis of the West African tribal traditions, such as the Fon (Dahomey) and the Yoruba (West Africa), with Catholicism and the natives in the Caribbean, when the slave trade brought many Africans into Haiti and eventually the United States. Voodoo is the popular spelling and often refers to the practice in New Orleans, while the spellings Vodou or Voodou refer to the Haitian practice, though all are related. The religion is monotheistic, with one creator and a variety of intermediary spirits originally known in West Africa as the vodu but now known as the loa or lwa. These spirits are not gods, angels, or ancestors in the strictest sense, as they are unique to the Voodoo tradition, but they share archetypal qualities with all three of these classifications of spirits. The loa are not worshiped, but served and honored. Each loa has an archetypal resonance that matches it well with a variety of Pagan godforms. There is a trickster who opens the gates, known as Legba. There is a loa of love and relationship, known as Erzulie, and a loa of the dead, known as Baron Samadi. From a Western magic view, these loa would be comparable to Mercury, Venus, and Pluto, respectively. Voodoo practitioners also revere the ancestors, and the line between the loa and the ancestors often seems to blur.

When the African slaves were forced to convert to Christianity, they noticed common themes with Catholicism, with one creator god and a variety of more personal intermediaries in the saints. The parallels were so close that the practitioners of the African religion were able to disguise their spirits under the mantle of various saints with similar attributes. In Voodoo, altars are built to honor each of the loa with whom the practitioner works, with candles, colors, specific foods, and offerings made on that loa's favorite day of the week. The loa are not commanded, bound, or bribed, but asked like wise old friends for favors and guidance, while the practitioner makes offerings in thanks to the spirit. Priestesses of the tradition, known as mambos, and priests, known as houngans, will work with people to make offerings to the loa, and craft charms of herbs, roots, stones, and bones. The African American version of root work and magic, which has fewer of the religious and spiritual connotations, is often known as Hoodoo, though it is not the same as Voodoo or Vodou. This spiritual clergy of Voodoo lead rituals with dancing and food. Vevers, or symbols of the loa, are drawn on the floor to invoke the loa, and during the ritual participants are often "ridden," or possessed, in a voluntary manner as a part of the celebration. Certain Voodoo priestesses or priests are dedicated to the work of one or more loa in particular.

Practitioners of Voodoo are most often practicing Catholics as well. A popular saying about the tradition in Haiti is that 90 percent of the country is Catholic, 10 percent is Protestant, and 100 percent is Vodou. Practitioners see no incongruities with this, as the African traditions are quite compatible with other traditions, and absorb them to survive. Though Voodoo has a dark reputation, it has been maligned in popular culture. Some of the misconceptions came about because this spiritual tradition grew from a culture that was disempowered through slavery and racism. Voodoo was a means to combat this disempowerment, which is why so much of the tradition is focused on healing, cursing, and breaking curses. The common religion, as an amalgam of traditions of several African and native tribes, along with Catholicism gave the mixed slave population a bond and an ability to rise up for freedom.

In essence, this spiritual tradition is about aligning with various parts of the soul, referred to with the symbol of angels, which New Age practitioners would find surprising. The gwo bon anj, or great good angel, gives a person his or her unique personality, thoughts, emotions, ideas, creativity, and knowledge. The ti bon anj, or little good angel, is the cosmic life force. This force keeps the body alive and guides a person's morals and conscience. Working with the loa helps practitioners understand themselves better. Voodoo is about service to the spirits who serve the Creator, and service to the community. Along with Voodoo, there are several other similar traditions, with different cultural contexts, such as Lukumi or Santería, based in Yoruban traditions with a Spanish Catholic merging, rather than a French Catholic one. By no means are they the same traditions, but they have much in common with Voodoo in terms of philosophy and execution.

Yoga

Yoga is a system of mysticism, philosophy, and practice designed to bring the individual closer to self-realization, to the cosmos or ultimate source of reality. The word yoga literally translates as "to yoke," meaning one yokes, or joins with, the divine. Most people translate yoga as "union." Yoga predates our recorded history, but finds its roots in the Hindu culture of India and relies heavily on Sanskrit. Many words in Sanskrit cannot be easily translated into other languages, so some confusion can arise around the terms and philosophies when yoga reaches other cultures. The Bhagavad-Gita, a sacred Hindu text from the Sanskrit epic Mahabharata, is a tale of Lord Krishna giving advice to Prince Arjuna on the field of battle, and is often considered a cornerstone in yogic thought and philosophy. Though it comes out of the Hindu culture, yoga is a series of techniques and philosophies, not a religion. While many people erroneously assume that all yoga practitioners are Hindu, many in the West have applied yoga to their lives without necessarily changing religions. It is perfectly valid to be a Christian yogi.

Though most people tend to see yoga primarily as a form of exercise, body posture, movement, and breath, that is only one form. Hatha yoga is the best-known type of yoga in this category, and many other modern forms have been based upon it. Hatha yoga is often a preparation for raja yoga, the meditative branch of yoga. Kundalini yoga is a more callisthenic form of yoga, with exercises designed to clear the energy field and encourage the energy of awareness, the kundalini, to rise up and expand one's consciousness. Other forms of yoga include bhakti yoga, the path of devotion; jnana yoga, the path of intellectual discernment; and karma yoga, the path of selfless service to others.

Zen

Zen is a Japanese form of Buddhism influenced by Taoism that emphasizes meditation. It is a practice of transforming your whole life into a meditation and can be viewed as a religion, philosophy, art, or simply a way of living life. In modern times, some have divorced Zen from the Buddhist religion, considering it a philosophy that anyone of any religious persuasion, such as Christian, can practice.

The goal of Zen is the spiritual awakening, or *satori*, and eventual enlightenment, which is certainly not restricted to practitioners of any one tradition or religion. The role of the teacher, and of direct communication over scripture, are emphasized. Some schools of Zen emphasize sitting in still meditation, or *zazen*, to clear the mind. Other schools of Zen use anecdotes, called *koans*, between teacher and student, to shock or puzzle the student to cut through the mind and ego and reveal his or her true nature. Koans appear to be paradoxes, but it is the solving of the paradox that brings transformation. Zen philosophy influences Japanese culture and activities, including martial arts, writing, painting, gardening, calligraphy, flower arranging, and cultural ceremonies, such as the tea ceremony. Through these rituals, Zen teaches us, with effortless action, that we cannot separate who we are and what we are doing. We enter a zone of awareness of the true nature of reality. We learn to make every action effortless and a part of our divine meditation.

Zoroastrianism

Zoroastrianism is based on the teachings of Zoroaster, or Zarathustra, the legendary prince of the magi, who reportedly lived in ancient Persia around 1000 BC. Scholars speculate that the legend of Zarathustra is based on a composite of magicians from that era. Originally coming out of a more polytheistic faith in Persia and eventually developing into what is considered Iranian dualism, the principles of Zoroastrianism are based on the conflict between two forces. The first force, Ahura Mazda, or Ohrmazd, the "wise lord" and supreme creator, is battling Anghra Mainyu, or Ahriman, the "destructive spirit" and master of the material world. The material world is said to be their battlefield. Ahura Mazda lends his name to another title of this religion, Mazdaism, and is symbolized by fire and light, two important aspects of Zoroastrianism. Most rituals and prayers are centered around a source of light as the focus for the divine creator. Asha, the Zoroastrian way of righteousness, is symbolized by fire. Asha brings happiness and drives away evil.

Due to the lack of written records, we know very little about the rituals of ancient Zoroastrianism. Basic tenets include an equality of gender, keeping the environment clean, charity, hard work, and respect. Most Zoroastrians do not proselytize. Within its theology are the concepts of heaven and hell, final judgment and resurrection of the body, and reuniting with the soul. The tradition spread from the Middle East over a wide area, influencing aspects of many dualistic and monotheistic religions such as Judaism, Mithraism, Christianity, and Gnosticism. Sects of Zoroastrians exist in the modern age, surviving in India, Pakistan, and Iran, although in Iran they are looked at as a persecuted minority. Many Zoroastrians, of both Iranian and South East Asian descent, survive as a diasporic community, in such places as the United States, England, Canada, and Australia.

15

PICKING A PATH

All mystic paths have something wonderful to offer. All of them have their advantages, and they each have disadvantages if they are not suited to your spiritual calling. None of them are perfect, but each is a piece of our global spiritual mosaic, each illuminating the divine in a different way.

One of the strongest suggestions I offer to a seeker on the path is to determine which path is your foundation, the solid stone upon which you will build your own spiritual paradigms. Though I'm a big believer in eclecticism, following intuition and weaving together a path from many faiths, as we are children of the global community in the New Age, I am also a strong believer in picking a path and having it be your center. Many people in the New Age move from one topic and tradition to another, without delving deeply. They don't gain the true benefits of any path because they don't stick with it long enough to explore its mysteries. All mystic paths, in essence, are mystery traditions. You must practice and experience them to have the mystery revealed to you through your work. The image many teachers use is digging many shallow wells, never striking water, rather than digging one deep well that will serve your needs.

I think it is best to dig one well in the place that calls to your soul. What, on an emotional, mental, and spiritual level, "feels" right to you? Right is not necessarily the easiest or the most aesthetically pleasing path, but the one that suits your soul's needs. Then as you grow, you take the digging tools of other traditions and add them to your own central well, learning how to use them to enhance your own practice.

I left my traditional upbringing to follow the earth traditions of modern Witchcraft. That became my umbrella, my toolbox and cultural view through which I saw other mystic traditions. My friends joke that it is my cauldron, or big pointed hat, that contains the other techniques and traditions I've learned. Once I established a solid foundation in the teachings of the Craft, and put them into daily practice, integrating them into my life, I then explored outside of my tradition. At times I thought I would leave Witchcraft, but each exploration only strengthened my connection to the Goddess and God in my core tradition. I studied yoga and Eastern mysteries. I worked with North and South American shamans, and saw the parallels to European core shamanism, and how it related to my Craft. I studied traditional Western herbalism, magical and medicinal, which led to an exploration of alchemy and Hermetic magic. I went into the New Age world, studying Reiki, crystals, Theosophy, and ascension lore. I found parallels to my Witchcraft and new ways to explore similar ideas. I learned to integrate all these healing techniques into my tradition, and for me, they were all under the umbrella of Witchcraft. My "cauldron" helped me synthesize the parts of each of these paths that worked for me, but gave me a solid foundation, a structure and paradigm, from which to use them. Rather than digging several shallow wells, with no central path and calling, I was able to dig deeply into my own witchy well, and receive the water of life that welled up from it.

I know many who have done the same thing on their explorations. Some stick with whatever tradition they were raised in. For many, it is a form of Christianity. They seek out the mystical teachings beneath the orthodox traditions, and integrate more metaphysical concepts from other traditions as they go. But at their core, they have a structure that allows them to explore other paths to enhance their own, rather than play shallowly, with no true understanding. When you fully understand the mysteries of one teaching, you can see how they parallel the mysteries of other teachings. Each further understanding takes you deeper, expanding your consciousness.

Soul-search, using all the techniques at your disposal, to find which mystical path is for you. Make a commitment, and then add to it to make the practice truly yours.

SACRED TEACHINGS

Use these excerpts from sacred texts to find the teachings and images that stir your own soul, and aid you in finding the paths that are right for you at this time. They illustrate the similarities and the differences between the mystic paths.

Allah Is Light . . .
Now We have sent down to you signs
Making all clear, and an example
Of those who passed away before you,
And an admonition for the godfearing.

God is the Light of the heavens and the earth
The likeness of His Light is as a niche
Wherein is a lamp
(The lamp is a glass,
The glass as it were a glittering star)
Kindled from a Blessed Tree,
An olive that is neither of the East nor of the West
Whose oil wellnigh would shine, even if no fire touched it
Light upon light
(God guides to His light whom He will.)
(And God strikes down similitudes for me,

And God has knowledge of everything.)

In temples God has allowed to be raised up,

And His name to be commemorated therein;

Therein glorifying Him, in the mornings and the evenings,

Are men who neither commerce nor trafficking

Diverts from the remembrances of God

And to perform the prayer, and to pay the alms,

Fearing a day when hearts and eyes shall be turned about,

That God may recompense them for their fairest works

And give them increase of His bounty;

And God provides whomsoever He will, without reckoning,

And as for the unbelievers,

Their works are as a mirage in the spacious plain

Which the man athirst supposes to be water

Till, when he comes to it, he finds it is nothing;

There indeed he finds God,

And He pays him his account in full; (and God is swift at the reckoning).

Or the yare as shadows upon a sea obscure

Covered by a billow

Above which is a billow

Above which are clouds,

Shadows piled upon another

When he puts forth his hand, well nigh he cannot see it

And to whomsoever God assigns no light,

No light has he.

Hast thou not seen how that whatsoever is in the heavens and in the Earth extols God

And the birds spreading their wings

Each—He knows its prayer and its extolling; and God knows the things they do.

To God belongs the Kingdoms of the heavens and the earth,

And to Him is the homecoming.

Hast thou not seen how God drives the clouds, then composes them,

Then coverts them into a mass,

Then thou seest the rain issuing out of the midst of them?

And He sends down out of the heaven mountains, wherein is hail

So that He smites whom He will with it, and turns it aside
From whom He will;
Wellnigh the gleam of His lightning snatches away at the sight,
God turns about the day and the night;
Surely in that is a lesson for those who have eyes.
God has created every beast of water,
And some of them go upon their bellies,
And some of them go upon two feet,
And some of them go upon four;
God creates whatever He will; God is powerful over everything.

—Koran XXIV, 33–44. A. J. Arberry, trans.

Atharva Veda (Hindu)

High Truth, unyielding Order, Consecration,
Ardor and Prayer and Holy Ritual
uphold the Earth, may she, the ruling Mistress
of what has been and what will come to be,
for us spread wide a limitless domain.

Untrammeled in the midst of men, the Earth,
adorned with heights and gentle slopes and plains,
bears plants and herbs of various healing powers.
May she spread wide for us, afford us joy!

On whom are ocean, river, and all waters,
on whom have sprung up food and plowman's crops,
on whom moves all that breathes and stirs abroad—
Earth, may she grant to us the long first draught!

To Earth belong the four directions of space.
On her grows food; on her the plowman toils.
She carries likewise all that breathes and stirs.
Earth, may she grant us cattle and food in plenty!

On whom the men of olden days roamed far,

on whom the conquering Gods smote the demons,
the home of cattle, horses, and of birds,
may Earth vouchsafe to us good fortune and glory!

Bearer of all things, hoard of treasures rare,
sustaining mother, Earth the golden-breasted
who bears the Sacred Universal Fire,
whose spouse is Indra—may she grant us wealth!

Limitless Earth, whom the Gods, never sleeping,
protect forever with unflagging care,
may she exude for us the well-loved honey,
shed upon us her splendor copiously!

Earth, who of yore was Water in the oceans,
discerned by the Sages' secret powers,
whose immortal heart, enwrapped in Truth,
abides aloft in the highest firmament,
may she procure for us splendor and power,
according to her highest royal state!

On whom the flowing Waters, ever the same,
course without cease or failure night and day,
may she yield milk, this Earth of many streams,
and shed on us her splendor copiously!

May Earth, whose measurements the Asvins marked,
over whose breadth the foot of Vishnu strode,
whom Indra, Lord of power, freed from foes,
stream milk for me, as a mother for her son!

Your hills, O Earth, your snow-clad mountain peaks,
your forests, may they show us kindliness!
Brown, black, red, multifarious in hue
and solid is this vast Earth, guarded by Indra.
Invincible, unconquered, and unharmed,
I have on her established my abode.

Impart to us those vitalizing forces
that come, O Earth, from deep within your body,
your central point, your navel, purify us wholly.
The Earth is mother; I am son of Earth.
The Rain-giver is my father; may he shower on us blessings!

The Earth on which they circumscribe the altar,
on which a band of workmen prepare the oblation,
on which the tall bright sacrificial posts
are fixed before the start of the oblation—
may Earth, herself increasing, grant us increase!

That man, O Earth, who wills us harm, who fights us,
who by his thoughts or deadly arms opposes,
deliver him to us, forestalling action.

All creatures, born from you, move round upon you.
You carry all that has two legs, three, or four.
To you, O Earth, belong the five human races,
those mortals upon whom the rising sun
sheds the immortal splendor of his rays.

May the creatures of earth, united together,
let flow for me the honey of speech!
Grant to me this boon, O Earth.

Mother of plants and begetter of all things,
firm far-flung Earth, sustained by Heavenly Law,
kindly and pleasant is she. May we ever
dwell on her bosom, passing to and fro! . . .

Do not thrust us aside from in front or behind,
from above or below! Be gracious, O Earth.
Let us not encounter robbers on our path.
Restrain the deadly weapons!

As wide a vista of you as my eye

may scan, O Earth, with the kindly help of Sun,
so widely may my sight be never dimmed
in all the long parade of years to come!

Whether, when I repose on you, O Earth,
I turn upon my right side or my left,
or whether, extended flat upon my back,
I meet your pressure from head to foot,
be gentle, Earth! You are the couch of all!

Whatever I dig up of you, O Earth,
may you of that have quick replenishment!
O purifying One, may my thrust never
reach right into your vital points, your heart!

Your circling seasons, nights succeeding days,
your summer, O Earth, your splashing rains, your autumn,
your winter and frosty season yielding to spring—
may each and all produce for us their milk! . . .

From your numberless tracks by which mankind may travel,
your roads on which move both chariots and wagons
your paths which are used by the good and the bad,
may we choose a way free from foes and robbers!
May you grant us the blessing of all that is wholesome!

She carries in her lap the foolish and also the wise.
She bears the death of the wicked as well as the good.
She lives in friendly collaboration with the boar,
offering herself as sanctuary to the wild pig. . . .

Peaceful and fragrant, gracious to the touch,
may Earth, swollen with milk, her breasts overflowing,
grant me her blessing together with her milk!

The Maker of the world sought her with oblations

when she was shrouded in the depth of the ocean.
A vessel of gladness, long cherished in secret,
the earth was revealed to mankind for their joy.

Primeval Mother, disperser of men,
you, far-flung Earth, fulfill all our desires.
Whatever you lack, may the Lord of creatures,
the First-born of Right, supply to you fully!

May your dwellings, O Earth, free from sickness and wasting,
flourish for us! Through a long life, watchful,
may we always offer to you our tribute!

O Earth, O Mother, dispose my lot
in gracious fashion that I be at ease.
In harmony with all the powers of Heaven
set me, O Poet, in grace and good fortune!

—12:1:1–17, 32–36, 47–48, 59–63. Selections from its "Hymn to the Earth," Raimundo Panikkar, trans., *The Vedic Experience: Mantramanjari*, pp. 123–129.

Bhagavad-Gita (Hindu)

I am the taste in the water, the light of the sun and the moon, the sound in the ether, the ability in the man, the fragrance of the earth, the life of all that lives, the strength of the strong, the intelligence of the intelligent, and the original seed of all existences.

—Sloka XX

Deep in the hearts of all, there is the light of all lights, forever beyond darkness. This is wisdom, the goal of all knowledge and what is to be known. Know this to be the absolute Brahman.

—Sloka 13:17

The Charge of the Goddess (Wiccan)

Listen to the words of the Great Mother, Who of old was called Artemis, Astarte, Dione, Melusine, Aphrodite, Ceridwen, Diana, Arianrhod, Brigid and by many other names:

"Whenever you have need of anything, once in the month and better it be when the moon is full, you shall assemble in some secret place and adore the spirit of Me Who is Queen of all the Wise.

"You shall be free from slavery, and as a sign that you be free you shall be naked in your rites. Sing, feast, dance, make music and love, all in My presence, for Mine is the ecstasy of the spirit and Mine also is joy on earth. For my law is love unto all beings. Mine is the secret that opens upon the door of youth and Mine is the cup of wine of life that is the cauldron of Ceridwen that is the holy grail of immortality.

"I give the knowledge of the spirit eternal and beyond death I give peace and freedom and reunion with those that have gone on before. Nor do I demand aught of sacrifice, for behold, I am the mother of all things and My love is poured out upon the Earth."

Hear also the words of the Star Goddess, the dust of Whose feet are the hosts of heaven, Whose body encircles the universe:

"I Who am the beauty of the green earth and the white moon among the stars and the mysteries of the waters, I call upon your soul to arise and come unto Me. For I am the soul of nature that gives life to the universe. From Me all things proceed and unto Me they must return.

"Let My worship be in the heart that rejoices, for behold—all acts of love and pleasure are My rituals. Let there be beauty and strength, power and compassion, honor and humility, mirth and reverence within you.

"And you who seek to know Me, know that your seeking and yearning will avail you not, unless you know the Mystery: for if that which you seek, you find not within yourself, you will never find it without. For behold, I have been with you from the beginning, and I am that which is attained at the end of desire."

Cleanthes' Hymn to Zeus (Greek—Stoic)

Most glorious of immortals, Zeus
The many named, almighty evermore,
Nature's great Sovereign, ruling all by law—
Hail to thee! On thee 'tis meet and right
That mortals everywhere should call.

From thee was our begetting; ours alone
Of all that live and move upon the earth
The lot to bear God's likeness.
Thee will I ever chant, thy power praise!
For thee this whole vast cosmos, wheeling round
The earth, obeys, and where thou leadest
It follows, ruled willingly by thee.
In thy unconquerable hands thou holdest fast,
Ready prepared, that two-time flaming blast,
The ever-living thunderbolt;
Nature's own stroke brings all things to their end.
By it thou guidest aright the sense instinct
Which spreads through all things, mingled even,
With stars in heaven, the great and small—
Thou who art King supreme for evermore!
Naught upon earth is wrong in thy despite, O God
Nor in the ethereal sphere aloft which ever winds
About its pole, nor in the sea—save only what
Their wicked works, in their strange madness,
Yet even so, though knowest to make the crooked straight.
Prune all excess, give order to the orderless;
For unto thee the unloved still is lovely—
And thus in one all things are harmonized,
The evil with the good, that so one Word
Should be in all things everlastingly.
One Word—which evermore the wicked flee!
Ill-fated, hungering to possess the good,
They have no vision of God's universal law,
Nor will they hear; though if obedient in mind
They might obtain a noble life, true wealth.
Instead they rush unthinking after ill:
Some with a shameless zeal for fame,
Others pursuing gain, disorderly;
Still others folly, or pleasure of the flesh.

[But evils are their lot] and other times
Bring other harvests, all unsought—
For all their great desire, its opposite!
But Zeus, thou giver of every gift,
Who dwellest within the dark clouds, wielding still
The flashing stroke of lighting, save, we pray,
Thy children from his boundless misery.
Scatter, O Father, the darkness from their souls,
Grant them to find true understands—
On which relying though justly rules all—
While we, thus honored, in turn will honor thee,
Hymning thy works forever, as it meet
For mortals, while no greater right,
Belongs even to the gods that evermore
Justly to praise the universal law!

—Stobaeus, "Eclogae," I, 1, 12. Cleanthes of Assos (331–233 BC) is considered to be the real founder of the Stoic school of theology. Translation by Frederick C. Grant, in his *Hellenistic Religions* (New York: 1953), pp. 152–154.

Commandments of the Qur'an

Say, come, I will recite what God has made a sacred duty for you: Ascribe nothing as equal with God;

Be good to your parents;

You shall not kill your children on a plea of want; we provide sustenance for you and for them;

You shall not approach lewd behavior whether open or in secret,

You shall not take life, which God has made sacred, except by way of justice and law. Thus does God command you, that you may learn wisdom.

And you shall not approach the property of the orphan, except to improve it, until he attains the age of maturity.

Give full measure and weight, in justice; no burden should be placed on any soul but that which it can bear.

And if you give your word, do it justice, even if a near relative is concerned; and fulfill your obligations before God. Thus does God command you, that you may remember.

Verily, this is my straight path: follow it, and do not follow other paths which will separate you from God's path. Thus does God command you, that you may be righteous."

—Qur'an, 6:151–153

The Earth, Mother of All

I will sing of well founded Earth, mother of all, eldest of all beings. She feeds all creatures that are in the world, all that go upon the goodly land, and all that are in the depths of the seas, and all that fly: all these are fed of her store. Through you, O queen, men are blessed in their children blessed in their harvests, and to you it belongs to give means of life to mortal men and to take it away. Happy is the man whom you delight to honour! He has all things abundantly: his fruitful land is laden with corn, his pastures are covered with cattle and his house is filled with goods things. Such men rule orderly in their cities of fair women: Great riches and wealth follow them: their sons exult with ever fresh delight, and their daughter with flower laden hands play and skip merrily over the soft flowers of the field. Thus it is with those whom you honour O holy goddess, bountiful spirit.

Hail, Mother of the gods, wife of starry Heaven; freely bestow upon me for this my song substance that cheers the heart! And now I will remember you and another son also.

—The Homeric Hymns. Hugh G. Evelyn-White, trans., *The Loeb Classical Library* (New York: 1914), p. 456.

Emerald Tablet (Alchemy/Hermetic)

In truth, without deceit, certain, and most veritable.

That which is Below corresponds to that which is Above. And that which is Above corresponds to that which is Below, to accomplish the miracles of the One Thing. And as all things have come from this One Thing, through the meditation of One Mind, so do all created things originate from this One Thing through Transformation.

Its father is the Sun; its mother the Moon. The Wind carries it in its belly; its nurse is the Earth.

It is the origin of All, the consecration of the Universe. Its inherent strength is perfected, if it is turned into Earth.

Separate the Earth from Fire, the Subtle from the Gross, gently and with great Ingenuity. It rises from Earth to Heaven, and descends again to Earth, thereby combining within Itself the powers of both the Above and the Below.

Thus will you obtain the Glory of the Whole Universe. All Obscurity will be clear to you. This is the greatest Force of all powers, because it overcomes every Subtle thing and penetrates every Solid thing.

In this way was the Universe created. From this comes many wondrous Applications, because this is the Pattern.

Therefore am I called the Thrice Greatest Hermes, having all three parts of the wisdom of the Whole Universe. Herein have I completely explained the Operation of the Sun.

Four Agreements (Toltec)
Be Impeccable With Your Word
Don't Take Things Personally
Don't Make Assumptions
Always Do Your Best

The Five Precepts of Buddhism
I undertake the precept to refrain from harming living creatures.
I undertake the precept to refrain from taking that which is not freely given.
I undertake the precept to refrain from sexual misconduct.
I undertake the precept to refrain from incorrect speech.
I undertake the precept to refrain from intoxicants which lead to loss of mindfulness.

The Four Noble Truths of Buddhism
Dukkha: All worldly life is unsatisfactory, disjointed, containing suffering.

Samudaya: There is a cause of suffering, which is attachment or desire (tanha) rooted in ignorance.

Nirodha: There is an end of suffering, which is Nirvana.

Marga: There is a path that leads out of suffering, known as the Noble Eightfold Path.

Gatha of the Choice:
Zarathustra Reveals the Exemplary Choice
Which Took Place at the Beginning of the World (Zoroastrian)

1. Now will I speak to those who will hear
Of the things which the initiate should remember
The praises and prayer of the Good Mind to the Lord
And the joy which he shall see in the light who has remembered them well.

2. Hear with your ears that which is the sovereign good
With a clear mind look upon the two sides
Between which each man must choose for himself,
Watchful beforehand that the great test may be accomplished in our favour.

3. Now at the beginning the twin spirits have declared their nature
The better and the evil,
In thought and world and deed. And between the two
The wise ones choose well, not so the foolish.

4. And when these two spirits came together,
In the beginning they established life and non-life,
And that at the last the worst experience should be for the wicked,
But for the righteous one the Best Mind.

5. Of these two spirits, the evil one chose to do the worst things
But the most Holy spirit, clothed in the most steadfast heavens
Joined himself unto Righteousness;
And thus did all those who delight to please the Wise Lord by honest deeds.

6. Between the two, the false gods also did not choose rightly
For while they pondered they were beset by error
So that they chose the Worst Mind.
Then did they hasten to join themselves until Fury,
That they might by it deprave the existence of man.

7. And to him came Devotion, together with Dominion, Good Mind and Righteousness;
She gave perpetuity of body and the breath of life,
That he may be thine apart from them,
As the first by the retributions through the metal.

8. And when their punishment shall come to these sinners,
Then, O Wise One, shall thy Dominion, with the Good Mind,
Be granted to those who have delivered Evil into the hands of the Righteousness, O Lord!

9. And may we be those that renew this existence!
O Wise One, and you other Lords, and Righteousness, bring your alliance.
That thoughts may gather where wisdom is faint.

10. Then shall Evil cease to flourish,
While those who have acquired good fame
Shall reap the promised reward
In the blessed dwelling of the Good Mind, of the Wise One, and of Righteousness.

11. If you, O Men, understand the commandments which the Wise One has given,
Well-being and suffering—long torment for the wicked and salvation for the righteous—
All shall hereafter be for the best.

—Gatha: Yasna 30. Translation by Jacques Duchesne-Guillemin, in his *The Hymns of Zara-thustra* (London: 1952), pp. 102–107.

Give Thanks to Mother Earth (Pawnee Tribe, Oklahoma)

Behold! Our Mother Earth is lying here.
Behold! She giveth her fruitfulness.
Truly, her power gives she us.
Give thanks to Mother Earth who lieth here.

Behold on Mother Earth the growing fields!
Behold the promise of her fruitfulness!
Truly her power gives she us.
Give thanks to Mother Earth who lieth here.

Behold on Mother Earth the spreading trees!
Behold the promise of her fruitfulness!
Truly, her power gives she us.
Give thanks to Mother Earth who lieth here.
We see on Mother Earth the running streams;

We see the promise of her fruitfulness.

Truly, her power gives she us.

Our thanks to Mother Earth who lieth here!

—Alice C. Fletcher, "The Hako: A Pawnee Ceremony," in Twenty-Second Annual Report, part 2, Bureau of American Ethnology (Washington, DC: 1904), p. 334.

The Golden Rule (Multi-Faith)

Buddhism—Hurt not others in ways that you yourself would find hurtful. —Udana-Varga 5,1

Christianity—All things whatsoever ye would that men should do to you, do ye so to them; for this is the law and the prophets. —Matthew 7:1

Confucianism—Do not do to others what you would not like yourself. Then there will be no resentment against you, either in the family or in the state. —Analects 12:2

Hinduism—This is the sum of duty; do naught onto others what you would not have them do unto you. —Mahabharata 5,1517

Islam—No one of you is a believer until he desires for his brother that which he desires for himself. —Sunnah

Judaism—What is hateful to you, do not do to your fellowman. This is the entire Law; all the rest is commentary. —Talmud, Shabbat 3id

Taoism—Regard your neighbor's gain as your gain, and your neighbor's loss as your own loss. —Tai Shang Kan Yin P'ien

Wicca—An' ye harm none, do what ye will. —The Wiccan Rede, Book of Shadows

Zoroastrianism—That nature alone is good which refrains from doing another whatsoever is not good for itself. —Dadisten-I-dinik, 94,5

The Hermetic Principles (Hermetic-Ceremonial Magic)

The Principle of Mentalism—Everything in existence is "creations of THE ALL" or thoughts in the divine mind. We are all one in the divine.

The Principle of Correspondence—"As above, so below." Patterns repeat themselves on all scales imaginable. Microcosms and macrocosms are maps of each other. The inner and outer worlds are intimately connected.

The Principle of Polarity—"Everything is dual; everything has poles; everything has its pair of opposites." One of the active forces of the universe is the attraction and repulsion between the sets of poles.

The Principle of Vibration—"Nothing rests; everything moves; everything vibrates." With the discovery of the atom, science has proved this principle beyond a shadow of a doubt.

The Principle of Gender—"Gender is in everything; everything has its Masculine and Feminine principles." Everything and everyone contains a mixture of feminine attributes and masculine attributes.

The Principle of Rhythm—"Everything flows in and out; everything has its tides." The universe works in cycles and patterns that repeat themselves, like the cycles of nature and the stars.

The Principle of Cause and Effect—"Every cause has its effect; every effect has its cause." This law is similar to our modern belief that "every action has an equal and opposite reaction." Everything occurring has an effect on everything else. Events occurring now are the effects of previous causes.

Hymn to Isis

In the beginning there was Isis:
Oldest of the Old.
She was the Goddess from whom all Becoming Arose.
She was the Great Lady,
Mistress of the two Lands of Egypt,
Mistress of Shelter,
Mistress of Heaven,
Mistress of the House of Life,
Mistress of the word of God.
She was the Unique.

In all Her great and wonderful works She was a wiser magician and more excellent than any other God.

—Thebes, Egypt, fourteenth century BC. From Merlin Stone's *When God Was a Woman*.

The Initiates in the Orphic-Pythagorean Brotherhood Are Taught the Road to the Lower World

(From the Funerary Gold Plates from Petelia, South Italy, fourth-third century BC):
Thou shalt find to the left of the House of Hades a spring,
And by the side thereof standing a white cypress.
To this spring approach not near.
But thou shalt find another, from the Lake of Memory
Cold water flowing forth, and there are guardians before it.
Say, "I am a child of Earth and starry heaven;
But my race is of Heaven (alone). This ye know yourselves.
But I am parched with thirst and I perish. Give me quickly
The cold water flowing forth from the Lake of Memory."
And of themselves they will give thee to drink of the holy spring.
And there after among the other heroes thou shalt have lordship.

(Plate from Eleuthernai in Crete, second century BC):
I am parched with thirst and I perish—Nay, drink of me (or, but give me to drink of)
The ever-flowering spring on the right, where the cypress is.
Who art thou? . . .
Whence art though? I am the son of Earth and starry Heaven.

(Plate from Thurii, South Italy, fourth-third century BC):
But so soon as the spirit hath left the light of the sun,
Go to the right as far as one should go, being right wary in all things
Hail, thou who has suffered the suffering. This thou hadst never suffered before.
Thou art become god from man.
A kid thou art fallen into milk.
Hail, hail to thee journeying in the right hand road.
By holy meadows and groves of Persephone.

(Three more tablets from Thurii, roughly fourth-third century BC):
I come from the pure, pure Queen of those below
And Eukles and Eubuleus, and other Gods and Daemons:
For I also avow that I am of your blessed race.
And I have paid the penalty for deeds unrighteous,
Whether it be that Fate laid me low or the gods immortal
Or . . . with star-flung thunderbolt.
I have flow out of the sorrowful, weary circle
I have passed with swift feet to the diadem desired
I have sunk beneath the bosom of the Mistress, The Queen of the underworld.
And now I come suppliant to holy Peresphoneia
That her grace she send men to the seats of the Hallowed.
Happy and blessed one, though shalt be god instead of mortal.
A kid I have fallen into milk.

—Translation by W. K. C. Gurthrie, in his *Orpheus and Greek Religion* (London: 1935), pp. 172–173.

Kalama Sutra (Buddhist)

Do not believe in anything simply because you have heard it. Do not believe in traditions simply because they have been handed down for generations. Do not believe in anything simply because it is spoken and rumored by many. Do not believe in anything merely on authority of your teachers and elders. But when, after observation and analysis, you find anything that agrees with reason, and is conducive to the good and benefit of one and all, then accept it and live up to it.

The Laws of the Magus (The Powers of the Sphinx or the Witch's Pyramid)

To Know
To Will
To Dare
To Keep Silent

Lord's Prayer/Our Father (Christian)

Our Father, who art in heaven: hallowed be thy name.
Thy kingdom come. Thy will be done on earth as it is in heaven.

Give us this day our daily bread.

And forgive us our trespasses, as we forgive those who trespass against us.

And lead us not into temptation, but deliver us from evil.

For thine is the kingdom and the power and the glory for ever and ever.

Amen.

Man's Soul Identified Both with Osiris and with Nature (Egyptian)

Whether I live or die I am Osiris,

I enter in and reappear through you,

I decay in you, I grow in you,

I fall down in you, I fall upon my side

The gods are living in me for I live and grow in the corn that sustains the Honoured Ones.

I cover the earth, whether I live or die I am Barley.

I am not destroyed.

I have entered the Order,

I rely upon the Order,

I become Master of the Order,

I emerge in the Order,

I make my form distinct,

I am the Lore of the Chennet (granary of Memphis?)

I have entered into the Order,

I have reached its limits . . .

—Coffin Texts 330. Translation by R. T. Rundle Clark, in his *Myth and Symbol in Ancient Egypt* (London: 1959), p. 142.

Namokar Mantra (Jainist)

Namo Arihantanam: I bow to the Arahantas, the perfected human beings, Godmen.

Namo Siddhanam: I bow to the Siddhas, liberated bodiless souls, God.

Namo Aariyanam: I bow to the Acharyas, the masters and heads of congregations.

Namo Uvajjhayanam: I bow to the Upadhyayas, the spiritual teachers.

Namo Loe Savva Sahunam: I bow to all the spiritual practitioners in the universe, Sadhus.

Eso Panch Namoyaro: This fivefold obeisance mantra,

Savva Pavappanasano: Destroys all sins and obstacles,

Mangalanam cha Savvesin: And of all auspicious repetitions,

Padhamam Havai Mangalam: Is the first and foremost.

Navajo Prayer (Native American)

I will be happy forever.
Nothing will hinder me.
I walk with beauty before me.
I walk with beauty behind me.
I walk with beauty above me.
I walk with beauty around me.
My words will be beautiful.

Nicene Creed (Catholic)

We believe in one God, the Father, the Almighty, maker of heaven and earth, of all that is, seen and unseen.

We believe in one Lord, Jesus Christ, the only son of God, eternally begotten of the Father, God from God, Light from Light, true God from true God, begotten, not made, of one being with the Father. Through him all things were made. For us and for our salvation he came down from heaven: by the power of the Holy Spirit he became incarnate from the Virgin Mary, and was made man. For our sake he was crucified under Pontius Pilate; he suffered death and was buried. On the third day he rose again in accordance with the Scriptures; he ascended into heaven and is seated at the right hand of the Father. He will come again in glory to judge the living and the dead, and his kingdom will have no end.

We believe in the Holy Spirit, the Lord, the giver of life, who proceeds from the Father [and the Son]. With the Father and the Son he is worshipped and glorified. He has spoken through the Prophets. We believe in one holy catholic and apostolic Church. We acknowledge one baptism for the forgiveness of sins. We look for the resurrection of the dead, and the life of the world to come. Amen.

The Noble Eightfold Path of Buddhism

Right Understanding
Right Thought
Right Speech
Right Action
Right Livelihood
Right Effort

Right Mindfulness

Right Concentration

Prayers of the Dervishes (Sufi)

I have naught but my destitution

To plead for me with Thee.

And in my poverty I put forward that destitution as my plea.

I have no power save to knock at Thy door,

And if I be turned away, at what door shall I knock?

Of on whom shall I call, crying his name,

If Thy generosity is refused to Thy destitute one?

Far be it from Thy generosity to drive the disobedient one to despair.

Generosity is more freehanded than that.

In lowly wretchedness I have come to Thy door,

Knowing that degradation there find help.

In full abandon I put my trust in Thee,

Stretching out my hands to Thee, a pleading beggar.

—Attributed to Abd al-Qadir al-Jilani or Abuyad al-Tijani

The Prayer of St. Francis (Christian)

Lord, make me an instrument of Your peace.

Where there is hatred, let me sow love;

Where there is injury, pardon;

Where there is doubt, faith;

Where there is despair, hope;

Where there is darkness, light;

And where there is sadness, joy.

O, Divine Master,

Grant that I may not so much seek

To be consoled as to console;

To be understood as to understand;

To be loved as to love;

For it is in giving that we receive;

It is in pardoning that we are pardoned;

And it is in dying that we are born to eternal life.

Psalm 23 (Judeo-Christian)

The Lord is my shepherd; I shall not want.

He maketh me to lie down in green pastures: he leadeth me beside the still waters.

He restoreth my soul: he leadeth me in the paths of righteousness for his name's sake.

Yea, though I walk through the valley of the shadow of death, I will fear no evil: for thou art with me; thy rod and thy staff they comfort me.

Thou preparest a table before me in the presence of mine enemies: thou anointest my head with oil; my cup runneth over.

Surely goodness and mercy shall follow me all the days of my life: and I will dwell in the house of the Lord for ever.

Reiki Principles (Reiki)

Just for today, I will be grateful.

Just for today, I will not anger.

Just for today, I will not worry.

Just for today, I will do my work honestly.

Just for today, I will respect all life.

The Revival of Osiris (Egyptian)

Hail to you, O Knowing One!

Geb has created you anew,

The Divine Company has brought you forth anew!

Horus is satisfied for his father,

Atum is satisfied for his offspring.

The gods of East and West are satisfied with this great event which has come to pass through the action of the Divine Progeny.

Ah Osiris! See! Behold!

Osiris! Hear! Attend!

Ah! Osiris! Lift yourself upon your side! Carry out what I ordain!

O Hater of Sleep! O Torpid One!

Rise up, you that were cast down in Nedit!

Take your breath with Happiness in Pê!

Receive your scepter in Heliopolis!

This is Horus (speaking), he has ordained action for his father,

He had shown himself master of the storm,

He has countered the blustering of Seth,

So that he (Seth) must bare you—

For it is he that must carry him who is (again) complete!

—From the Pyramid of Wenis; this is one of the earliest texts from Osirian rituals. Translation by R. T. Rundle Clark, in his *Myth and Symbol in Ancient Egypt* (London: 1959), p. 111.

Shin Paishi

Humbly, I approach the kami in prayer.

I pray to the kami of Tsubaki Grand Shrine; speaking with reverent heart, I present offerings and prayers.

I come in humility and with great respect.

–Kakema kumo kahikoki

–Tsubaki O Kami yashiro No omae o orogami matsurite

–Kashikomi kashikomi mo maosaku

I beseech all the kami to accept these offerings that are brought with

Gratitude for the blessings and the noble teachings

That have been bestowed upon me

–O kamitachi no hiroki atsuki mi megumi o katajikenami matsuri

–Takaki totoki misohie no mani mani

To the divine, exalted kami, I humbly offer my prayers.

Teach me to live with a pure and sincere heart.

Grant me perseverance and that my heart be genuine, childlike, and true.

Grant that I stay on the path of sincerity and truth.

Grant that I be strong and diligent at my deeds.

–Sumera mikoto o aogi matsuri naoki tadashiki magokoro mochite

–Makoto no michi ni tago koto naku

–Oimotsu waza ni nage mashime tamai

Grant good health to my family; give them strength in spirit, mind, and body.

Grant that I may benefit and serve all mankind.

With awe and reverence, I humbly speak these words.

–Ie kado takaku mi sukoyaka ni

–Yo no tame hito no tame ni tsuku sashime to

–Kashikomi kashikomi mo maosu

—Shinto sacred prayer from *Shinto Norito: A Book of Prayers*

Sufi Verse

Come, come, whoever you are.

Worshiper, Wanderer, Lover of Leaving;

Ours is not a caravan of despair.

Though you have broken your vows a thousand times . . .

Come, come again, come.

—Often attributed to Mevlana Rumi, Sufi philosopher and poet

The Song of Amergin (Irish Celtic)

I am the wind that blows across the sea;

I am a wave of the deep;

I am the roar of the ocean;

I am the stag of seven battles;

I am a hawk on the cliff;

I am a ray of sunlight;

I am the greenest of plants;

I am the wild boar;

I am a salmon in the river;

I am a lake on the plain;

I am the word of knowledge;

I am the point of a spear;

I am the lure beyond the ends of the earth;

I can shift my shape like a god.

—From the Book of Invasions

Song of Solomon (Jewish)

Chapter 1

The song of songs, which is Solomon's.

Let him kiss me with the kisses of his mouth: for thy love is better than wine.

Because of the savour of thy good ointments thy name is as ointment poured forth, therefore do the virgins love thee.

Draw me, we will run after thee: the king hath brought me into his chambers; we will be glad and rejoice in thee; we will remember thy love more than wine: the upright love thee.

I am black, but comely, O ye daughters of Jerusalem, as the tents of Kedar, as the curtains of Solomon.

Look not upon me, because I am black, because the sun hath looked upon me: my mother's children were angry with me; they made me the keeper of the vineyards; but mine own vineyard have I not kept.

Tell me, O thou whom my soul loveth, where thou feedest, where thou makest thy flock to rest at noon: for why should I be as one that turneth aside by the flocks of thy companions?

If thou know not, O thou fairest among women, go thy way forth by the footsteps of the flock, and feed thy kids beside the shepherds' tents.

I have compared thee, O my love, to a company of horses in Pharaoh's chariots.

Thy cheeks are comely with rows of jewels, thy neck with chains of gold.

We will make thee borders of gold with studs of silver.

While the king sitteth at his table, my spikenard sendeth forth the smell thereof.

A bundle of myrrh is my well-beloved unto me; he shall lie all night betwixt my breasts.

My beloved is unto me as a cluster of camphire in the vineyards of Engedi.

Behold, thou art fair, my love; behold, thou art fair; thou hast doves' eyes.

Behold, thou art fair, my beloved, yea, pleasant: also our bed is green.

The beams of our house are cedar, and our rafters of fir.

Chapter 2

I am the rose of Sharon, and the lily of the valleys.

As the lily among thorns, so is my love among the daughters.

As the apple tree among the trees of the wood, so is my beloved among the sons. I sat down under his shadow with great delight, and his fruit was sweet to my taste.

He brought me to the banqueting house, and his banner over me was love.

Stay me with flagons, comfort me with apples: for I am sick of love.

His left hand is under my head, and his right hand doth embrace me.

I charge you, O ye daughters of Jerusalem, by the roes, and by the hinds of the field, that ye stir not up, nor awake my love, till he please.

The voice of my beloved! behold, he cometh leaping upon the mountains, skipping upon the hills.

My beloved is like a roe or a young hart: behold, he standeth behind our wall, he looketh forth at the windows, shewing himself through the lattice.

My beloved spake, and said unto me, Rise up, my love, my fair one, and come away.

For, lo, the winter is past, the rain is over and gone;

The flowers appear on the earth; the time of the singing of birds is come, and the voice of the turtle is heard in our land;

The fig tree putteth forth her green figs, and the vines with the tender grape give a good smell. Arise, my love, my fair one, and come away.

O my dove, that art in the clefts of the rock, in the secret places of the stairs, let me see thy countenance, let me hear thy voice; for sweet is thy voice, and thy countenance is comely.

Take us the foxes, the little foxes, that spoil the vines: for our vines have tender grapes.

My beloved is mine, and I am his: he feedeth among the lilies.

Until the day break, and the shadows flee away, turn, my beloved, and be thou like a roe or a young hart upon the mountains of Bether.

Chapter 3

By night on my bed I sought him whom my soul loveth: I sought him, but I found him not.

I will rise now, and go about the city in the streets, and in the broad ways I will seek him whom my soul loveth: I sought him, but I found him not.

The watchmen that go about the city found me: to whom I said, Saw ye him whom my soul loveth?

It was but a little that I passed from them, but I found him whom my soul loveth: I held him, and would not let him go, until I had brought him into my mother's house, and into the chamber of her that conceived me.

I charge you, O ye daughters of Jerusalem, by the roes, and by the hinds of the field, that ye stir not up, nor awake my love, till he please.

Who is this that cometh out of the wilderness like pillars of smoke, perfumed with myrrh and frankincense, with all powders of the merchant?

Behold his bed, which is Solomon's; threescore valiant men are about it, of the valiant of Israel.

They all hold swords, being expert in war: every man hath his sword upon his thigh because of fear in the night.

King Solomon made himself a chariot of the wood of Lebanon.

He made the pillars thereof of silver, the bottom thereof of gold, the covering of it of purple, the midst thereof being paved with love, for the daughters of Jerusalem.

Go forth, O ye daughters of Zion, and behold king Solomon with the crown wherewith his mother crowned him in the day of his espousals, and in the day of the gladness of his heart.

Chapter 4

Behold, thou art fair, my love; behold, thou art fair; thou hast doves' eyes within thy locks: thy hair is as a flock of goats, that appear from mount Gilead.

Thy teeth are like a flock of sheep that are even shorn, which came up from the washing; whereof every one bear twins, and none is barren among them.

Thy lips are like a thread of scarlet, and thy speech is comely: thy temples are like a piece of a pomegranate within thy locks.

Thy neck is like the tower of David builded for an armoury, whereon there hang a thousand bucklers, all shields of mighty men.

Thy two breasts are like two young roes that are twins, which feed among the lilies.

Until the day break, and the shadows flee away, I will get me to the mountain of myrrh, and to the hill of frankincense.

Thou art all fair, my love; there is no spot in thee.

Come with me from Lebanon, my spouse, with me from Lebanon: look from the top of Amana, from the top of Shenir and Hermon, from the lions' dens, from the mountains of the leopards.

Thou hast ravished my heart, my sister, my spouse; thou hast ravished my heart with one of thine eyes, with one chain of thy neck.

How fair is thy love, my sister, my spouse! how much better is thy love than wine! and the smell of thine ointments than all spices!

Thy lips, O my spouse, drop as the honeycomb: honey and milk are under thy tongue; and the smell of thy garments is like the smell of Lebanon.

A garden inclosed is my sister, my spouse; a spring shut up, a fountain sealed.

Thy plants are an orchard of pomegranates, with pleasant fruits; camphire, with spikenard,

Spikenard and saffron; calamus and cinnamon, with all trees of frankincense; myrrh and aloes, with all the chief spices:

A fountain of gardens, a well of living waters, and streams from Lebanon.

Awake, O north wind; and come, thou south; blow upon my garden, that the spices thereof may flow out. Let my beloved come into his garden, and eat his pleasant fruits.

Chapter 5

I am come into my garden, my sister, my spouse: I have gathered my myrrh with my spice; I have eaten my honeycomb with my honey; I have drunk my wine with my milk: eat, O friends; drink, yea, drink abundantly, O beloved.

I sleep, but my heart waketh: it is the voice of my beloved that knocketh, saying, Open to me, my sister, my love, my dove, my undefiled: for my head is filled with dew, and my locks with the drops of the night.

I have put off my coat; how shall I put it on? I have washed my feet; how shall I defile them?

My beloved put in his hand by the hole of the door, and my bowels were moved for him.

I rose up to open to my beloved; and my hands dropped with myrrh, and my fingers with sweet smelling myrrh, upon the handles of the lock.

I opened to my beloved; but my beloved had withdrawn himself, and was gone: my soul failed when he spake: I sought him, but I could not find him; I called him, but he gave me no answer.

The watchmen that went about the city found me, they smote me, they wounded me; the keepers of the walls took away my veil from me.

I charge you, O daughters of Jerusalem, if ye find my beloved, that ye tell him, that I am sick of love.

What is thy beloved more than another beloved, O thou fairest among women? What is thy beloved more than another beloved, that thou dost so charge us?

My beloved is white and ruddy, the chiefest among ten thousand.

His head is as the most fine gold, his locks are bushy, and black as a raven.

His eyes are as the eyes of doves by the rivers of waters, washed with milk, and fitly set.

His cheeks are as a bed of spices, as sweet flowers: his lips like lilies, dropping sweet smelling myrrh.

His hands are as gold rings set with the beryl: his belly is as bright ivory overlaid with sapphires.

His legs are as pillars of marble, set upon sockets of fine gold: his countenance is as Lebanon, excellent as the cedars.

His mouth is most sweet: yea, he is altogether lovely. This is my beloved, and this is my friend, O daughters of Jerusalem.

Chapter 6

Whither is thy beloved gone, O thou fairest among women? Whither is thy beloved turned aside? that we may seek him with thee.

My beloved is gone down into his garden, to the beds of spices, to feed in the gardens, and to gather lilies.

I am my beloved's, and my beloved is mine: he feedeth among the lilies.

Thou art beautiful, O my love, as Tirzah, comely as Jerusalem, terrible as an army with banners.

Turn away thine eyes from me, for they have overcome me: thy hair is as a flock of goats that appear from Gilead.

Thy teeth are as a flock of sheep which go up from the washing, whereof every one beareth twins, and there is not one barren among them.

As a piece of a pomegranate are thy temples within thy locks.

There are threescore queens, and fourscore concubines, and virgins without number.

My dove, my undefiled is but one; she is the only one of her mother, she is the choice one of her that bare her. The daughters saw her, and blessed her; yea, the queens and the concubines, and they praised her.

Who is she that looketh forth as the morning, fair as the moon, clear as the sun, and terrible as an army with banners?

I went down into the garden of nuts to see the fruits of the valley, and to see whether the vine flourished and the pomegranates budded.

Or ever I was aware, my soul made me like the chariots of Amminadib.

Return, return, O Shulamite; return, return, that we may look upon thee. What will ye see in the Shulamite? As it were the company of two armies.

Chapter 7

How beautiful are thy feet with shoes, O prince's daughter! the joints of thy thighs are like jewels, the work of the hands of a cunning workman.

Thy navel is like a round goblet, which wanteth not liquor: thy belly is like an heap of wheat set about with lilies.

Thy two breasts are like two young roes that are twins.

Thy neck is as a tower of ivory; thine eyes like the fishpools in Heshbon, by the gate of Bathrabbim: thy nose is as the tower of Lebanon which looketh toward Damascus.

Thine head upon thee is like Carmel, and the hair of thine head like purple; the king is held in the galleries.

How fair and how pleasant art thou, O love, for delights!

This thy stature is like to a palm tree, and thy breasts to clusters of grapes.

I said, I will go up to the palm tree, I will take hold of the boughs thereof: now also thy breasts shall be as clusters of the vine, and the smell of thy nose like apples;

And the roof of thy mouth like the best wine for my beloved, that goeth down sweetly, causing the lips of those that are asleep to speak.

I am my beloved's, and his desire is toward me.

Come, my beloved, let us go forth into the field; let us lodge in the villages.

Let us get up early to the vineyards; let us see if the vine flourish, whether the tender grape appear, and the pomegranates bud forth: there will I give thee my loves.

The mandrakes give a smell, and at our gates are all manner of pleasant fruits, new and old, which I have laid up for thee, O my beloved.

Chapter 8

O that thou wert as my brother, that sucked the breasts of my mother! when I should find thee without, I would kiss thee; yea, I should not be despised.

I would lead thee, and bring thee into my mother's house, who would instruct me: I would cause thee to drink of spiced wine of the juice of my pomegranate.

His left hand should be under my head, and his right hand should embrace me.

I charge you, O daughters of Jerusalem, that ye stir not up, nor awake my love, until he please.

Who is this that cometh up from the wilderness, leaning upon her beloved? I raised thee up under the apple tree: there thy mother brought thee forth: there she brought thee forth that bare thee.

Set me as a seal upon thine heart, as a seal upon thine arm: for love is strong as death; jealousy is cruel as the grave: the coals thereof are coals of fire, which hath a most vehement flame.

Many waters cannot quench love, neither can the floods drown it: if a man would give all the substance of his house for love, it would utterly be contemned.

We have a little sister, and she hath no breasts: what shall we do for our sister in the day when she shall be spoken for?

If she be a wall, we will build upon her a palace of silver: and if she be a door, we will inclose her with boards of cedar.

I am a wall, and my breasts like towers: then was I in his eyes as one that found favour.

Solomon had a vineyard at Baalhamon; he let out the vineyard unto keepers; every one for the fruit thereof was to bring a thousand pieces of silver.

My vineyard, which is mine, is before me: thou, O Solomon, must have a thousand, and those that keep the fruit thereof two hundred.

Thou that dwellest in the gardens, the companions hearken to thy voice: cause me to hear it.

Make haste, my beloved, and be thou like to a roe or to a young hart upon the mountains of spices.

The Ten Commandments (Judeo-Christian)

1. I am the Lord thy God. Thou shalt have no other gods before me.
2. Thou shalt not make unto thee any graven image, or any likeness of any thing that is in heaven above, or that is in the earth beneath, or that is in the water under the earth.
3. Thou shalt not take the name of the Lord thy God in vain.
4. Remember the sabbath day, to keep it holy.
5. Honor thy father and thy mother.
6. Thou shalt not kill.
7. Thou shalt not commit adultery.
8. Thou shalt not steal.
9. Thou shalt not bear false witness against thy neighbor.
10. Thou shalt not covet thy neighbor's house, thou shalt not covet thy neighbor's wife, nor his manservant, nor his maidservant, nor his ox, nor his ass, nor any thing that is thy neighbor's.

—From Exodus 20: 1–17

Thelemic Principles

Do what thou wilt shall be the whole of the Law. (*AL*, I:40)

Love is the law, love under will. (*AL*, I:57)

The word of the law is Thelema. (*AL*, I:39)

There is no law beyond Do what thou wilt. (*AL*, III:60)

Every man and every woman is a star. (*AL*, I:3)

—*The Book of the Law (Liber Al vel Legis)*

To Walk the Red Road (Native American)

The Red Road is a circle of people
standing hand in hand,
people in this world, people between
people in the Spirit world.
star people, animal people, stone people,
river people, tree people . . .
The Sacred Hoop.
To walk the Red Road
is to know sacrifice, suffering.
It is to understand humility.
It is the ability to stand naked before God
in all things for your wrong doings,
for your lack of strength,
for your dis-compassionate way,
for your arrogance—because to walk
the Red Road, you always know
you can do better. And you know,
when you do good things,
it is through the Creator, and you are grateful.
To walk the Red Road
is to know you stand on equal ground
with all living things. It is to know that
because you were born human,
it gives you superiority over nothing.
It is to know that every creation carries a Spirit,
and the river knows more than you do,
the mountains know more than you do,
the stone people know more than you do,
the trees know more than you do,

the wind is wiser than you are,
and animal people carry wisdom.
You can learn from every one of them,
because they have something you don't:
They are void of evil thoughts.
They wish vengeance on no one, they seek Justice.
To walk the Red Road
is to know your Ancestors,
to call to them for assistance . . .
It is to know that there is good medicine,
and there is bad medicine . . .
It is to know that Evil exists,
but is cowardly as it is often in disguise.
It is to know there are evil spirits
who are in constant watch
for a way to gain strength for themselves
at the expense of you.
To walk the Red Road,
you have less fear of being wrong,
because you know that life is a journey,
a continuous circle, a sacred hoop.
Mistakes will be made,
and mistakes can be corrected
if you will be humble,
for if you cannot be humble,
you will never know
when you have made a mistake.
If you walk the Red Road,
you know that every sorrow
leads to a better understanding,
every horror cannot be explained,
but can offer growth.
To walk the Red Road
is to look for beauty in all things.
To walk the Red Road

is to know you will one day
cross to the Spirit World,
and you will not be afraid . . .

—Author unknown

Vishnu, The Cosmic God

You are everything, earth, water, fire, air and space,
The subtle world, the Nature-of-All (pradhana),
And the Person who stands forever aloof.

O Self of all beings!
From the Creator (Brahma) to the blade of grass
All is your body, visible and invisible,
Divided by space and time.

We worship you as Brahma, the Immense Being, the first shape,
Who sprang from the lotus of your navel to create the worlds.

We, the gods, worship you in our selves,
We, the King of Heaven, the Sun, the Lord of Tears,
The Indweller, the wing gods of agriculture,
The Lord of Wind, the offering, who are all your shapes
While you are our Selves.

We worship you in your demonic shapes, deceitful and stupid,
Wild in their passions, suspicious of wisdom.

We worship you in the genni, the yakshas,
With their narrow minds obdurate to knowledge,
Their blunt faculties covetous of the objects of worlds.

O Supreme Man! We bow to your fearful evil shapes
Which wander at night, cruel and deceitful.

O Giver-of-Rewards (Junardana)!
We worship you as the Eternal Law
Whence virtuous men, who dwell in the heaven,

Obtain the blissful fruit of their just deeds.
We bow to the Realized (Siddhas) who are your shapes of joy;
Free from contacts, they enter and move within all things.

O Remover-of-Sorrow (Hari)! We bow to you the serpent shapes,
Lustful and cruel, whose forked tongues know no mercy.

O Pervader! We worship you as knowledge
In the peaceful form of the seers,
Faultless, free from sin.

O Dweller in the lotus of the Heart! We bow to you
As the self of Time which at the end of the ages,
Infallibly devours all beings.

We worship you as the Lord of Tears,
Who dances at the time of destruction,
Having devoured gods and men alike.

O Giver of Rewards! We worship your human shape
Bound by the twenty-eight incapacities (badha),
Ruled by the powers of darkness.

We bow to you as vegetable life (mukhya rupa),
By which the world subsists and which—six in kind,
Trees, [creepers, bushes, plants, herbs, and bamboo]—
Supports the sacrificial rites.

O Universal Self! We bow to you under that elemental shape
Gods and living beings, ether and the elements,
Sound and all the qualities.
O Transcendent Self! We bow to you as the Cause of causes,
Beyond Nature (pradhana) and Intellect.
O All-powerful (Bhagavan)! We bow to your shape
Which the seers alone perceive and in which is found
No white nor other color, no length nor other dimension
No density no other quality.

Purer than purity it stands
Beyond the sphere of quality
We bow to you, the birthless, the indestructible,
Outside who there is but nothingness.

You are the ever-present within all things,
As the intrinsic principles of all.
We bow to you, resplendent Indweller (Vasudeva)! The seed of all that is!
You stand changeless, unsullied.
The Supreme stage is your core, the Universe your shape.
You are the unborn, Eternal.

—Vishnu Purana, 3, 17, 14–34. Translation by Alain Daniélou, in his *Hindu Polytheism* (New York: Bollingen Series LXXIII, 1964), pp. 367–368.

The Wiccan Rede (Wiccan)

Bide the Wiccan Laws we must
In perfect Love and perfect Trust
Live and let live,
Fairly take and fairly give.
Cast the Circle thrice about
To keep the evil spirits out.
To bind the spell every time
Let the spell be spake in rhyme
Soft of eye and light of touch,
Speak little, listen much.
Deosil go by the waxing moon,
Changing out the Witches' rune.
Widdershins go by the waning moon,
Chanting out the baneful rune.
When the lady's moon is new,
Kiss thy hand to her, times two.
When the moon rides at Her peak,
Then your heart's desire seek.

Heed the North wind's mighty gale,
Lock the door and drop the sail.
When the wind comes from the South,
Love will kiss thee on the mouth.
When the wind blows from the East,
Expect the new and set the feast.
When the wind blows from the West,
Departed souls will have no rest.
When the West wind blows o'er thee
Departed spirits restless be.
Nine woods into the cauldron go,
Burn them fast and burn them slow.
Elder be your Lady's tree,
Burn it not or cursed ye'll be.
When the Wheel begins to turn,
Let the Beltane fires burn.
When the Wheel has turned to Yule,
Light the log and the Horned One rules
Heed ye Flower, Bush and Tree,
By the Lady, Blessed Be.
Where the rippling waters go,
Cast a stone and truth ye'll know.
When ye have a need,
Hearken not to other's greed.
With a fool no season spend,
Nor be counted as his friend.
Merry meet, Merry part,
Bright the cheeks and warm the heart.
Mind the Threefold Law ye should,
Three times bad and three times good.
When misfortune is enow,
Wear the Blue Star on the brow.
True in love ever be,

Unless thy Lover's false to thee.
Eight words to the Wiccan Rede fulfill
And ye harm none, do what ye will.

GLOSSARY

acupressure: Similar to acupuncture, but instead of using needles it uses slight pressure on special points on the body, to alter the energy system of the person and create health and provide relief from pain.

acupuncture: A form of traditional Chinese medicine that uses needles placed at various points on the body, along energy lines known as meridians, to realign the energy flow, or "chi" flow, and remove energy blockages from the system. Acupuncture can be used to treat physical and emotional illnesses, relieve pain, and even as a preventive measure.

aeromancy: A style of divination based on the atmospheric conditions, cloud patterns, and the weather.

affirmations: Repeated statements designed to form new patterns within the mind and change the consciousness and reality of the user of the affirmations. Such statements are usually present tense, not future tense, and formed in a "positive" manner, rather than negating that which you don't want. For example, you would use the affirmation "I am prosperous" rather than "I will be prosperous" or "I am not poor."

air: The mental principle, associated with thought, communication, memory, language, and writing, as well as the principles of life and truth. Air is warm and moist.

Ajna chakra: The third eye or brow chakra, usually colored indigo or purple, related to the principles of psychic vision and inner sight. The name translates to "command" or "authority."

akashic records: Refers to the sum total information of the past, present, and future, said to be recorded in the "akasha," or spirit energy, around the planet and/or universe. Some psychics are said to be able to "read" the akashic records through their visions, to tell people information about their past, past lives, and potential futures.

aliens: E.T.'s, or Extra-Terrestrials, are common images in New Age metaphysics. Some people believe in the physical existence of beings from other planets and star systems in flying ships, while others feel they are a mask or metaphor for celestial spirits and nonphysical beings. The E.T.'s are presenting themselves in a way in which our modern scientific and fantasy-oriented society can relate to them, as many of the traditional mythologies they could use to interface with humans, such as those involving faeries or angels, are not as popular in our culture. The lore of alien abductions and of past faery abductions are strikingly similar.

alpha: The first letter in the Greek alphabet, symbol of the beginning. Also a state of consciousness below the normal waking state, where intuition, magic, and psychic experiences can occur, usually measured at eight to thirteen cycles per second in brain-wave activity.

amulet: A magical charm that is traditionally used to ward off unwanted influences. An amulet can also refer to a magical charm that is of a geometric or symbolic design, set as jewelry.

Anahata chakra: The heart chakra, related to the principles of love, empathy, harmony, and healing. Its name refers to the "unstruck" sound of the heart, the vibration of love, and is associated with the hexagram.

angels: Divine intermediaries between humankind and the creator source. The word angel is often translated as "messenger." The best-known classical depictions of angels are found in the Abrahamic religions of Judaism, Christianity, and Islam, but the concept of angels does not belong to any one tradition. Practitioners of many traditions, including ceremonial magic and Wicca, call upon angels.

animism: Animism generally refers to the belief that everything is alive, everything has a consciousness, or spirit/soul. Many consider modern Neo-Paganism to be an animist tradition.

Aquarius: The eleventh sign of the zodiac. A fixed air sign known as the water bearer.

Aries: The first sign of the zodiac. A cardinal fire sign depicted as a ram.

aromatherapy: The art and science of working with essential oils of plants to heal others physically, mentally, and emotionally. Through a distillation process, the volatile oils of a plant, which contain a strong scent, are extracted. The body responds to these scents, alone and in combination, to create healing on all levels. Some oils have benefit when applied to the skin, though most essential oils, being concentrated chemicals, need to be diluted in a carrier oil, or nonvolatile oil. Such treatments can be used in conjunction with massage.

ascended master: An enlightened being who has freed him- or herself from the wheel of rebirth, yet forgoes union with the source of all creation to remain behind in an ethereal state beyond the physical to act as a healer, guide, and teacher to those still in the wheel of rebirth. Often equated with a saint in the Christian traditions, or bodhisattva in the Eastern traditions.

ashram: In the physical world, an ashram usually refers to the dwelling of a Hindu sage or teacher, often remote and secluded. Students often reside at the ashram as well, to receive instruction and cloister themselves from the outside world in a religious retreat. Sometimes the term refers to the population of the retreat. In modern times, many believe the ascended masters have "astral" ashrams on the nonphysical planes, where disciples come to learn in dreams and meditations.

asteroids: A number of smaller solid bodies within the solar system existing in a band between Mars and Jupiter. Modern astrologers figure many of the asteroids into astrological chart interpretation. The best-known ones are Ceres, Pallas, Juno, and Vesta.

astral travel: The process of projecting your consciousness away from your physical body, often described as sending out your astral body, or double, to a location in either the physical world or a spiritual world. Astral travel to a physical destination is often known as remote viewing, or mental projection, while it is called journeying or pathworking when the destination is on the spiritual plane.

astrological ages: A period of Earth's cycle roughly 2,166 years long, marked by the sidereal zodiac sign the Sun occupies at the vernal equinox. Each sign confers its lessons, qualities, and challenges upon the Earth for that 2,000-year period.

Atlantis: A fabled island nation in the Atlantic Ocean that sunk beneath the waves. Reported in Plato's writing, and a common theme in many mythologies, it was revived in the works of Edgar Cayce and Madame Blavatsky. Some feel Atlantis is a literal place lost beneath the ocean to someday be rediscovered, while others feel it is a metaphor for the fabled perfect kingdom all cultures aspire to create.

augury: Divination usually based on the behavior and movement of animals.

aura: The energy field that surrounds and interpenetrates the human body. Those skilled psychically to perceive the aura can use the information in the aura to reveal the person's health, mood, and even past lives.

avatar: A deity who is said to incarnate as a human being.

Ayurveda: The indigenous medical system found in India, based on the philosophies of Hinduism. Ayurveda is a holistic treatment that does not discount surgery and medicines, but advocates changes in diet, exercise such as yoga, and herbs. The key principle of Ayurveda is living a life that promotes balance on all levels. Bodies are described in combinations of three doshas, three archetypal forces consisting of combinations of the five elements. By eating right for your dosha mixture, as well as engaging in the proper activities, you create health.

belly chakra: Also known as the navel chakra, sacral chakra, or spleen chakra. The orange energy center in the lower abdomen related to a person's sense of trust, intimacy, and intuition.

Beltane: One of the four Celtic fire festivals, and one of the eight Wheel of the Year holidays. Celebrated in May, usually on May 1, when the Sun is in Taurus, Beltane is a festival of fire, light, dancing, purification, and sexuality.

beta: The level of normal waking consciousness in brain-wave activity, measured at thirteen to sixteen cycles per second.

birth chart: The astrological chart cast for the moment of a person's birth. In astrological terms, it is a "picture" of the sky when and where the person was born. The birth chart, also know as the natal chart, is the seed of the lessons, challenges, and skills a person brings into this life that will unfold as his or her life develops.

black magic: Traditionally a term used for magic that intentionally harms others.

bodywork: Holistic therapies that work on manipulation of the body and its tissues, but also affect the mind, emotions, and spirit. Massage, in its various forms, is considered the primary form of bodywork.

brow chakra: The third eye or Ajna chakra, responsible for psychic vision. Usually depicted as indigo or purple.

Cabala: Usually refers to a Christian version of the Hebrew Kabalah.

Cancer: The fifth sign of the zodiac. A cardinal water sign symbolized by the crab.

candle magic: A spell where you place your intention into a candle through will, visualization, speaking, and/or formal ritual, and then light the candle to release the energy of your intention to manifest as a reality.

Capricorn: The ninth sign of the zodiac. A cardinal earth sign symbolized by the goat or the goat-fish.

cardinal: The initiating or generating principle. The force of beginnings.

centering: The act of aligning yourself with your core, to help you focus on a mystical task at hand, or to orient yourself back to the physical world after ritual and meditation. Often used in conjunction with grounding.

ceremony: Another term for ritual. Some use ceremony to denote a group ritual. Others use the term ceremony for rituals of high magic, as in the term ceremonial magician.

chakra: An energy center aligned with a level of consciousness and a place within the physical body. Chakras can be thought of as spiritual organs that process energy like our physical organs process food and waste. Seven main energy centers exist, running up the spine from the base to the crown.

channeling: The act of connecting to a nonphysical entity and mediating between that entity and either your own human consciousness or that of another person. Channeling is often called mediumship. One who performs channeling is called a channel or channeler. A channel can experience channeling consciously, psychically interpreting and repeating back messages, or through trance, where the entity in question "takes over" the physical body. Each form has its benefits and drawbacks.

charm: A magical tool created for a specific purpose, to manifest a specific intention or spell. Charms usually come in the form of an amulet or talisman.

chela: A term for a spiritual disciple.

chi: The Chinese term for vital life energy.

Chiron: A "planetoid" orbiting between Saturn and Uranus. Astrologers have worked with the archetype of the "wounded healer" and the myth of Chiron the centaur to understand how this body works in the art and science of astrology.

clairaudience: A term for psychic "hearing" or interpreting psychic information through the sense of hearing. A clairaudient "hears" messages, guides, spirits, or an inner guiding voice. Though this voice is usually internal, some feel it is so real they swear they actually hear it with their physical ears, even though no one else can hear it.

clairsentience: A term for psychic "knowing" or interpreting psychic information as a gut-level feeling, or simply knowing information without a visual or auditory experience.

clairvoyance: A term for psychic "seeing" or interpreting psychic information through the sense of sight. A clairvoyant usually receives information as internal pictures through the mind's eye, though some see visions while their eyes are wide open. Those who can "see" auras, energy, and spirits are clairvoyant.

cleansing: The process of removing any unwanted energies or vibrations, from yourself, an object, or an environment. Incense, herbs, sounds, prayers, chants, intentions, and visualizations can be used in a cleansing.

color magic: Using the unique properties of each color in ritual and magic. Each color corresponds to a different range of experiences and effects. Colors can be visualized, or used with tools that are colored to match the desired effect. Color correspondence systems can vary from tradition to tradition.

cord magic: The use of cords and strings, braided and knotted, as a focus for magical intention.

creative visualization: The process of visualizing whatever you desire to manifest in your reality to make it manifest in the physical world. While in a meditative state, "see" in your mind's eye exactly what you want. Use all your senses—see it, hear it, feel it, smell it, taste it, and touch it. Make the image as real as possible, and imagine it in the present tense. Don't think of it coming in the future; imagine it being fully present now. This process is a foundation of many magical traditions that has been brought to mainstream attention.

crown chakra: The seventh chakra, located at the top of the head or, some say, slightly above it. Usually depicted as violet or dazzling white, the crown relates to our spiritual nature and connection with the creative source.

crystal: Any mineral used for metaphysical purposes, usually as a meditation aid, charm, or healing instrument. Technically, a crystal refers to a mineral that has a crystalline structure, such as quartz, but many in the metaphysical world use the term crystal for any mineral associated with metaphysical properties.

crystallomancy: Divination by crystals. Scrying is a form of crystallomancy.

deities: Divine beings of the Pagan mythologies. Each deity embodies one or more aspects of creation, usually paralleling what modern psychology would call an archetype.

delta: The deepest level of brain-wave activity, measuring at four or less cycles per second. Delta is the place of deep sleep, coma, and the deepest trance work.

demon: In classical Christian mythology, a demon is a fallen angel consigned to Hell. In other systems, it is a being that corresponds to the lowest of emotions and desires. Others view demons simply as nonhuman entities, not predisposed with good will toward the human realm.

deva: A deva is a Hindu term originally relating to the "little gods," but in modern times it has come to denote a spirit related to the nature realm, acting as the architect and holding the patterns of some aspect of nature, such as a species of flower or tree. A deva also can be related to an area, such as a mountain, park, or valley. The smaller devas in the larger area make up the "body" of the larger deva.

dharma: In Western terms, your dharma basically refers to fulfilling your life purpose. It is your proper actions and your duty, and can be equated with your magical will, true will, or the creator's "plan" for your life. Dharma is not destiny; it doesn't simply happen. You must be open to it, and choose to make it happen. In various Eastern traditions, dharma has other, specific cultural meanings and connotations.

divination: To divine literally means to align with divinity, and in this case it means to align with divinity to get guidance, usually about the future. Divination can be done without tools, though traditionally it uses some form of oracle system. Tarot, runes, crystal scrying, and horary astrology are all forms of divination.

Divine Mind: Another term from the Hermetic tradition for the great creator or divine spirit.

djinn: In Western magic, a djinn is usually a manifestation of a fire elemental. In Middle Eastern lore, it is a being that is neither wholly spiritual nor physical, and considered a lower spirit when compared to angelic beings.

dogma: The official teachings and doctrines of a religious institution usually set out authoritatively as fact for those belonging to that tradition.

dowsing: Divination using a pendulum or divining rods.

dowsing rod: Another term for divining rods. Usually dowsing rods are made of metal, and in the shape of an *L*. The shorter end is placed in a tube, often cardboard, and the tube is held, so the wire can move freely. A pair of rods is used and the practitioner interprets the movement of the rods, as they cross or separate, to determine the energy present. Dowsing rods are used to find Earth energy lines, water, and the human aura.

dragon: Some equate dragons with spiritual entities associated with the land, as Earth energy lines in the East are referred to as dragon lines. In the West, they seem to be an amalgam of the four traditional elements: earth, with their body, and their affinity for treasure; water, for their serpentine nature; air, for their wings; and fire, with their breath. Some believe elemental spirits that master all four elements go on to become dragon spirits, and act as guardians and keepers of the Earth mysteries.

earth: The physical principle, associated with the physical world, security, finances, and health, as well as the principles of law and sovereignty. Earth is cold and dry.

elemental: A being that embodies one of the four elements: earth, air, fire, and water.

elemental guardians: Elemental beings of greater power who can be called upon to guard and guide the four elemental gateways of a ritual. Often referred to as the watchtowers. Some think of the elemental guardians as the four archangels of the elements, while others call upon the traditional "kings" of the elements. Other traditions call upon animal guides or deities as the guardians and guides of the elements.

energy healing: The use of vital life force, directed by the practitioner to any areas of afflicted health within another person. The energy is used to increase vitality, balance energy, and remove stagnant energy. Reiki, magnified healing, and pranic healing are all forms of energy healing.

enneagram: A system of understanding human nature and personality, based upon the graphic images of a nine-pointed star, each point corresponding to a different set of traits. The tradition comes out of Sufi philosophy and was developed by George Gurdjieff and others in the twentieth century.

Enochian: A system of angelic magic introduced to the modern world through the working of the Elizabethan magicians John Dee and Edward Kelly. Enochian magic consists of various symbols in a new alphabet, and grids spelling out the names of various

Enochian angels. The system was adopted by the Golden Dawn and integrated into its material as well as the works of Aleister Crowley.

equinoxes: The two solar holidays in the spring and fall, indicating equal times of day and night.

ESP: Extra-Sensory Perception. A term covering all psychic abilities, including clairaudience, clairvoyance, and clairsentience, as well remote viewing, telepathy, and divination.

evocation: The process of summoning a spirit. Differs from invocation because you are summoning a spirit to manifest, not summoning it into your body. In some magical traditions, spirits are evoked into a triangle drawn on the floor.

faeries: Otherworldly beings strongly associated with the natural realm. Though some use the term faery for a nature spirit or deva, traditional myths associate faeries with the underworld legends, and the ancestors, depicting them in human stature or even larger, as well as diminutive Tinkerbell-style faeries.

faith healing: A form of spiritual healing that works not through ritual, visualization, spiritual guides, or energy work, but through sheer faith and belief in the divine, and the healer who is acting as the conduit for the divine.

familiar: A term of Witchcraft applied to a helping spirit for a Witch. Many modern Witches use the term familiar to refer to an animal totem spirit, or a physical animal, a pet, with whom they have a spiritual bond.

fire: The energetic principle, associated with identity, intensity, passion, and drive, as well as the principles of light and will. Fire is warm and dry.

fire festival: The four Celtic festivals of the Wheel of the Year, primarily based in agricultural, rather than solar, symbolism. Samhain, Imbolc, Beltane, and Lammas are the four fire festivals. Each takes place when the Sun is in one of the fixed astrological signs.

First Matter: The fifth element before manifesting through the other four elements. The primal creative energy.

fixed: The structuring or organizing principle. The force of sustaining.

flower essences: Vibrational remedies consisting of a dilute solution of a flower soaked in water and preserved with a small amount of alcohol, vinegar, or glycerin. Regular small doses of the liquid create energetic changes in the mind, body, and spirit of the recipient. Each flower has its own remedy, or pattern of consciousness that it heals and balances.

Gabriel: Archangel associated with the direction of west and the element of water, as well as the Moon and the sephira Yesod. Gabriel has been translated as "man of God," "hero of God," or "might of God." He is often seen as the messenger of God, announcing news to those on Earth.

Gaia Hypothesis: Modern scientific hypothesis proposed by James Lovelock, stating that the Earth, in its entirety with its various species and systems, is a living organism.

gematria: A system of Qabalistic numerology. The meanings of words and scripture are studied based on the numeric value of each word. Each Hebrew letter is associated with a number. The numbers are added together, and that word or phrase is compared with other words or phrases of a similar numeric value. Sometimes these equations are remarkably insightful, while others tend to upset the orthodox understanding of scripture. For example, the Hebrew numeric value for "serpent," as in the serpent in the Garden of Eden, is the same as the numeric value for "messiah." Even more controversially, it links the term "Holy of Holies" with the Woman of Whoredom, the archdemon of prostitution.

Gemini: The third sign of the zodiac. A mutable air sign symbolized by the twins.

geomancy: Using shapes on the earth, or an earthlike substance, as a focus for divination.

ghost: The spirit or soul of a being who has physically died but whose soul has not transitioned to the next realm and remains bound to the physical world. Some ghosts appear conscious and aware. Others appear to be echoes, shells, or recordings of the people they formerly were, suggesting that perhaps their souls passed on, but some aspect of their remaining energy bodies remains in the world in an unquiet state.

God: A term of the great creator or divine spirit in patriarchal, monotheistic traditions. In many dualistic traditions that recognize both genders as divinity, it refers to the masculine aspect of the divine.

God Position: A ritual position found in forms Wicca, Witchcraft, and ceremonial magic where the feet are held close together and the arms are crossed over the chest, forming a position reminiscent of an Egyptian sarcophagus. It is also symbolic of the god Osiris and suggests the image of the skull and crossbones. This position is often assumed as a reflection on the work of the ritual.

Goddess: The feminine component of the creative spirit. Some feminist traditions use Goddess to refer to all aspects of the creator, as patriarchal traditions use God. Popularly embodied in modern traditions as a triple goddess—maiden, mother, and crone.

Goddess Position: A ritual position found in forms of Wicca, Witchcraft, and ceremonial magic where the feet are placed shoulder-width apart and the arms are held stretched up, much like a crescent moon or horns. Some forms have the arms straight out, holding the body in the five-pointed star, or pentagram, position. This position is often assumed to release and send out energy for the ritual.

gods: In polytheistic traditions, refers to a multitude of beings that are aspects of the divine spirit. Each of these gods rules over one or more attributes of creation, life, and consciousness.

gray magic: In systems that delineate between white and black magic, gray magic is a blend between the two. It is magic that creates change in the physical world, but is not purposely done to create harm. According to this tradition, most forms of magic, healing, and prayer would be considered gray magic. Many traditions of magic do not use the terms black, white, and gray.

Great Spirit: Another term from the Native American traditions for the great creator or divine spirit.

grounding: The process of being fully present in the physical body. Grounding also refers to releasing excess energy, similar to when a lighting rod grounds electricity harmlessly into the Earth. After ritual or spiritual work, one often needs to ground the excess energy to be fully present in the physical plane.

healing: The process of bringing a person, animal, plant, location, community, or planet into a harmonious balance. Healing can occur on both the physical and energetic levels. In forms of spiritual or energetic healing, the healing must occur first on the energetic level, and the body can later follow suit and return to balance. To the spiritual healing practitioner, Western medicine, which addresses the physical first, is not wrong, but on a holistic level the rest of the being's needs must also be addressed. If the injury or physical symptoms are suppressed without addressing the mental, emotional, or spiritual components of the illness, then it will reoccur or another illness will manifest.

heart chakra: The central chakra found at the sternum. Linking the upper and lower chakras, the heart chakra governs our ability to feel love and empathy. It is usually pictured as green, green with pink, or, in some traditions, red.

herb: Any plant that is used for medicine, magic, or cooking. Each plant has many different properties, and the leaves, flowers, seeds, stems, roots, bark, and oils can be harvested and used. Many herbs are considered weeds by more traditional gardeners.

Hermetic: Refers to traditions associated with the Greek god Hermes, or Hermes Trismegistus, as well as the Egyptian Thoth. Typically refers to modern Western ceremonial magic and alchemy.

hologram: A three-dimensional construct of life created through the interference pattern of two lasers. Each piece of holographic film contains the entire image. If you rip the film in half and shine the laser through it, you get two smaller, complete images, rather than two halves of a whole. A hologram is a symbol for the nature of the universe, where everything contains information on everything else, like the holographic film, demonstrating the idea "As above, so below."

homeopathy: A modern system of alternative medicine based upon the ancient principle of "like cures like." Minimal, diluted doses of substances, often containing no active ingredients, are used to create healing, often in pellet or solution form. For example, in regular doses, onion creates symptoms of watery eyes. A homeopathic dose of onion is said to cure watery eyes. Though associated with modern medicine, homeopathy is a very controversial practice from the medical community's point of view, though users of the system often swear by it and the improved health they gain from it. There is a lack of clinical evidence of homeopathy, and many skeptics believe it to be a remnant of alchemy, and not a science, yet proponents say that the effects work on many different levels, including mental and emotional health, which are not easily measured in terms of clinical lab results. Homeopathy has led to the modern use of flower essences, also drawing upon older, alchemical principles.

house: In astrology, one of the twelve divisions of the sky. Each house represents an area of your life. Six houses are above the horizon, and six houses are below the horizon. Astrological signs and planets occupy the houses, and the signs and planets in a house affect that "area" of your life.

hydromancy: Hydromancy is also called water scrying. You can use the reflective surface of still water as a scrying mirror. In fact, this is often the Witch's favorite medium of all.

The still water can be in the ritual chalice, under the full Moon, or in any still body of water. When done in sacred springs, ponds, or wells, it is called pegomancy.

I Ching: A Chinese form of divination based on sixty-four hexagram shapes, each with a different symbolic meaning. Based on the ancient Chinese text known as the Book of Changes.

Imbolc: A Celtic fire festival usually celebrated on February 2, sacred to the goddess Brid, or Bridget. It is a holiday of awakening the Earth, marked by candlelight. Another name for this celebration in a more Christian context is Candlemas.

initiation: Initiation means "to begin" and in a metaphysical context usually indicates a ceremony that inducts you into a particular path or tradition. Like a graduation ceremony, it indicates a completion of a level of learning, and the beginning of using that knowledge. In terms of spiritual initiation, it is an event, either a visionary experience or a trial of life, that tests you and results in a spiritual awakening or transformation.

institutions: In a spiritual context, institutions are organizations, structures, and groups that hold spiritual information and usually have a system of training for spiritual dedicants and often the general populace. Within each institution is usually a rich mystical tradition that is not often seen by the outside world. The traditional churches, brotherhoods, and other organizations of power can be seen as institutions.

invocation: The process of bringing a spirit, god, or entity into yourself. Some define invocation as the process of calling entities within the ritual magic circle, and evocation as the process of summoning spirits outside of the circle into manifestation. Others define invocation as literally bringing a spirit into your body. Trance channelers, certain mediums, and magical priests and priestesses who Draw Down the God/dess (Wiccan) or Assume the Godform (ceremonial magic) are performing invocation.

Jupiter: A large planet that orbits between Mars and Saturn. It a considered a lucky planet, the "greater benefic." Spiritually Jupiter represents the forces of expansion and has been used for the expansion of good fortune as well as consciousness. Jupiter corresponds to Chesed on the Tree of Life, the sephira of mercy and higher love, depicted as a benevolent king on a throne.

Kabalah: Usually refers to the Jewish system of mysticism. Sometimes spelled Kaballah. Kabalah is also spelled Cabala and Qabalah, referring to Christian and Hermetic branches of mysticism that have adopted and adapted traditional Jewish material.

karma: Karma usually translates to act, action, or deed, and refers to a cosmic principle of cause and effect. Karma is the sum of one's deeds, from this life and past lives, and the repercussions of those actions. The concept comes from Hinduism, and the term has been adopted in both Eastern and Western traditions, ranging from Buddhism to Wicca. Though many Western traditions equate it with reward and punishment from the divine, that is not true in the strictest interpretation. It is more of a universal law rather than a moral law. It is similar to the physical laws of the universe, but operates first in the spiritual dimensions. Some think of it as destiny, but karma can be changed by your actions in the present. The concept is found in many traditions, and is often summed up with the statement "You shall reap what you have sown." Though many seek "good" karma, the most profound teachings on karma urge us to balance all karma, good or bad, and act from our dharma.

ki: Life force energy. Ki, the term used in Japan, lends its name to the energy healing system of Japanese origin known as Reiki. The same energy is known as chi in China.

kundalini: In Hindu lore, an energy usually described as a coiled serpent residing at the base of the spine. The kundalini can become active and rise up the spine, moving through the chakras. Much fear-based lore exists regarding the accidental or improper awakening of the kundalini energy causing madness or physical illness, though most people in a mystic tradition experience the awakening of this energy with no serious problems. It is the energy of awareness, and brings up issues that need to be healed and resolved, but this process is part of the mystic's path.

Lammas: One of the four Celtic fire festivals, usually celebrated on August 1. Lammas, also known as Lughnassadh, is a celebration of the first harvest and the cutting of the grain, as well as the sacrifice of the solar or agricultural god embodied by the grain. Irish traditions hold this day sacred to the god Lugh, and his mother, Tailtiu.

left-hand path: The left-hand path often refers to a path of evil by practitioners who identify with a right-hand path. Originally, it likely referred to a tradition of feminine mysteries, tantra, or rituals that circle in a counterclockwise direction. Some associate this term with modern traditions of Satanism. Ideologically, left-hand paths differentiate themselves from right-hand paths as paths that do not seek undifferentiated union with the divine or seek to escape the material world, but seek to be "like" the divine and emulate divinity by remaining distinct and individual.

Lemuria: According to myth and channeled material, Lemuria was a fabled motherland continent found in the Pacific or Indian Ocean. It was a culture contemporary with Atlantis, yet it preceded Atlantis and sank beneath the waves before the eventual demise of Atlantis. Many believe the Lemurian culture, also known as the land of Mu, was more feminine, intuitive, and spiritual than the cultures that followed it. Some believe the inhabitants were not altogether human as we know humanity today, or were not entirely physical, but consisted of dense etheric bodies of energy, not matter. The modern origin of the name Lemuria is the lemur, a primate that comes in a variety of forms. Lemurs live in Madagascar, but also have been found in parts of Africa, India, and Malaya. Esotericists believe the lemur to be a remnant from the Lemurian civilization, as its wide migration would have been assisted by a large continent.

Leo: The fifth sign of the zodiac. A fixed fire sign symbolized by a lion.

Lesser Banishing Ritual of the Pentagram: Also known as the LBRP, it is a ritual of the Golden Dawn and its various offshoots that clears a space of all lower and unwanted energies by calling forth beams of light to emulate the structure of the Tree of Life within the human body, drawing a circle of blue light, with four banishing pentagrams, and invoking the four archangels for protection.

letters of power: Any letters, words, or names used by a mystic for a specific purpose. Certain languages, such as Hebrew and Sanskrit, are said to have magical power inherent in their structure. You can use these words and phrases to create change in yourself and the environment. Some believe that the words and letters themselves have inherent power, while others believe it is the proper execution of drawing the letters and/or speaking with words, with the proper, focused intent of the practitioner, that actually empowers the letters.

ley lines: Modern mystics define ley lines as the lines of Earth energy running all around the planet and seemingly converging at many ancient sacred sites. These lines are compared to the acupuncture meridians of the human body. The original meaning of ley line didn't refer to an energy path, but to a walking path used by ancient people. Neither definition is widely accepted by the scientific community.

Libra: The seventh zodiac sign. A cardinal air sign symbolized by the scales.

Litha: A Neo-Pagan term for Midsummer or the summer solstice. A celebration of the Sun's peak in power, and often honoring the faery folk. At this time, the Sun is moving from the sign Gemini to Cancer.

lithomancy: A system of divination using stones—precious, semiprecious, or mundane—each with a symbolic meaning.

lodge: A group of magicians, usually in the Western mystery traditions, who practice together regularly and may have a permanent meeting space for their works. Similar in idea, if not in structure, to a Witch's coven. Masonic structure also uses the lodge system, and many speculate about its influence on magicians and Witches in their own hierarchies.

Logos: A Greek term meaning "word," used originally to refer to the logical guiding force of the universe, comparable to the concept of the Tao in Asia or AUM in India. In later Greek periods it referred to an individual's own logic, reason, and soul self, in a form of spiritual anatomy. Today we might think of it as the higher self. The Logos referred to the Word of God from the Old Testament, capable of creation, and was later associated with Jesus Christ. Theosophists use the term Logos more in alignment with the original use, referring to various "octaves" of this guiding force, such as the Planetary Logos, Solar Logos, and Galactic Logos.

lower world: In a shamanic cosmology, the interior world that is a place for the ancestors, faeries, healing, chthonic deities, and trials and tests. The lower world is not a place of evil, but a place of power that reflects your own emotions to you.

Lughnassadh: The Irish name for the celebration of Lammas.

Mabon: The modern Neo-Pagan term for the autumnal equinox. Also the name of the Welsh child god, son of the mother goddess Modron.

mage: One who practices magic. Derived from the Old Persian term magus, and the plural form, magi.

magic: Defined as the "art and science of causing change in conformity with your Will," drawing upon the work of magician Aleister Crowley, who highly influenced the modern magician's concept of magic. It is the process of projecting an intention to the universe, usually through ritual, and having the universe respond and manifest that intention. Magic creates change, in both the inner and outer worlds. Most consider magic the study of the science of nature, and our relationship with it, rather than supernatural forces.

magician: One who practices the spiritual discipline of magic. Sometimes spelled magickian in the modern era.

magic circle: A basic ritual performed with many variations by both Witches and magicians. The circle is a type of boundary to create sacred space, contain energy, and block out unwanted forces during a ritual, celebration, or spell casting.

magus: A term often used synonymously with mage or magician. The plural form is magi. Sometimes used to denote a specific higher rank in a traditional school of magic.

Major Arcana: Twenty-two cards found in the tarot, denoting the major life experiences and spiritual initiations. They correspond with the twenty-two letters of the Hebrew alphabet, the connecting paths on the Tree of Life, and the signs and planets of astrology.

mana: A term for vital life force from the Hawaiian traditions.

mandala: In Hindu and Buddhist traditions, it refers to a circle used for ritual and meditation. Usually the circle is designed in an artistic pattern, symbolizing the universe and filled with patterns of various deities and sacred symbols.

Manipura: The traditional name for the solar plexus chakra, associated with a "city of gems." The solar plexus rules the sense of power and self-image, and is traditionally colored yellow, though some older systems use the color gray.

mantra: A word that is repeated over and over again, silently in the mind or chanted out loud, to act as a focus for meditation. Many believe that mantras from certain spiritual languages, such as Sanskrit, have inherent power in their vibration when spoken aloud or thought about, and the use of such a mantra will confer its power or blessing upon the user.

Mars: The planet associated with will, drive, and force in astrology and magic. Mars is named after the Roman war god.

medicine: Modern terminology defines medicine as a pharmaceutical designed to aid healing or suppress symptoms. From a spiritual context, medicine is anything that aids the recipient on the path of wholeness and healing. Working with the spirits of animals, plants, and stones is often referred to as animal medicine, plant medicine, and stone medicine, respectively, because the spirit is offering its healing qualities to the recipient.

meditation: The process of contemplation through quieting and focusing the mind. Many traditions of meditation exist, and there is no one right way. Eastern forms of meditation focus on mantras, yantras, and breathing techniques. Western forms focus on guided imagery and directing thought toward a specific goal or symbol.

mediumship: The ability to mediate between the spirit world and the human world. A medium, often used synonymously with the term channel, acts as a conduit for a spirit or nonphysical entity seeking to communicate with those in the physical world. Some define a channel as one who interfaces with nonphysical entities, ascended masters, and angels, while a medium speaks with humans who have departed from the physical plane.

mental travel: The psychic skill of sending out your mental awareness to another physical location, also known as remote viewing, or to a nonphysical location, referred to as journeying or pathworking. A traveler can then recall details and experiences of the mental travel destination upon awakening from the meditative state used to induce the journey. Many make the distinction between mental travel, astral travel, spirit travel, and soul travel, believing each term refers to a different portion of your consciousness being projected outward and traveling. In practical application, each has the same end result, though the idea of one type of travel might appeal to the practitioner and make the internal process of projection and traveling easier.

Mercury: The planet associated with communication, memory, and mental processes. Named after the Roman god Mercury and often equated with the Greek Hermes. In alchemy, the mutable, adaptable, receptive principle, associated with quicksilver, the Moon, and water, is named Mercury.

metal: In the Chinese elemental system, metal is the symbol for the element known as air in the West.

metaphysics: A general term used for the philosophical study of the universe and humankind's role in it that is concerned with realities beyond the scope of the physical sciences. Both ancient and New Age philosophies can be considered forms of metaphysics. Metaphysics technically differs from religion, for there is no requirement of belief or any strict dogma, but a system of related ideas and concepts the metaphysician is encouraged to explore. Many mystic traditions could be considered both a metaphysical path and a religion.

Metatron: A very popular angel from the Western mystery tradition. Usually called an archangel in modern lore, depending on the system, though Metatron has also been considered a seraph, cherub, or one of the Chaioth Ha Qadesh, the Holy Living Creatures. He is said to be the highest of all the angels, sitting at the throne right next to God and responsible for the functioning of creation. He is said to be the tallest of all beings, with thirty-six wings and countless eyes. Metatron is sometimes credited with giving the Kabalah to humanity. Some think the prophet Enoch ascended and became Metatron, or merged with Metatron.

Michael: One of the most popular archangels of the Western traditions. Associated with the direction of south and the element of fire, Michael is said to be the keeper of the flaming sword or flaming spear, which he uses to protect and heal humankind. He is the archetype of the divine warrior. His name is usually translated to mean "who is like God." Astrologically he has been associated with the planets Mercury and the Sun. Some see Michael as one of the most powerful, if not the most powerful, of the angelic beings.

middle world: In shamanic practice, the middle world is the world of humanity and nature. It is the world of physical shape and form, as well as time and cycles. It stands between the upper world of heavenly spirits and enlightenment and the lower world of transformation and healing. Most people consciously exist only in the middle world. The middle world is identified with the human mind and persona, while the lower world is associated with instinct and intuition and the higher world with the divine self.

Minor Arcana: The four suites of the tarot deck, including the ace through ten of the pentacles, wands, swords, and cups, as well as the four court cards of each suite. The Minor Arcana is said to represent the more day-to-day process of the individual with the ordinary challenges and blessings of life, while the Major Arcana represents the more profound challenges and transformations.

monotheism: The belief in one divinity, as opposed to polytheism, which is the belief in multiple divinities. Some religions claim monotheism but have polytheistic aspects. Catholicism is monotheistic, but sees divinity manifest in a trinity, Father, Son, and Holy Spirit. It also includes a range of intermediary spirits, in the form of saints and angels.

Moon: In astrology, the planet associated with the emotional self and intuition. Technically not a planet, but a luminary, astrologers and magical practitioners often refer to the Moon as a planet. In forms of Witchcraft and Goddess worship, the Moon is seen as a manifestation of the divine feminine, and often embodies the Triple Goddess, with the maiden as the waxing crescent Moon, the mother as the full Moon, and the crone as the waning to dark Moon. The tides of the Moon, its waxing and waning light, as well as the astrological sign the Moon currently occupies, have a profound effect upon humankind and human magic, as the Moon is the celestial body closest to the Earth. Though smaller than the Sun, from our perspective the sphere of the Moon is as big as the Sun, and carries similar weight in our consciousness.

Mu: Another name for Lemuria. Some believe Mu is the older version of Lemuria, or represents the first age of Lemuria.

Muladhara: Also known as the root or base chakra. Found at the base of the spine and typically colored red. Muladhara also means foundation.

muscle testing: Also known as applied kinesiology, muscle testing finds wisdom in the strength or weakness of the physical body. Typically a substance's suitability for an individual is tested against the individual's physical strength, often by pushing down on the arm extended out horizontally from the body. Those substances, including vitamins, herbs, and crystals, that make the individual stronger test positive and are good for the person's health. Those that make the individual weaker test negative and are not conducive to health. Muscle testing has been adapted in a variety of ways, including self-muscle testing done with the fingers, or muscle testing to communicate with your body's wisdom, or spirit guides, to receive a yes or no answer to questions you have on a variety of healing and spiritual topics.

mutable: The adaptable or dissolving principle in astrology. The force to change or destroy in order to create something new.

mythical creatures: A variety of animals not found in the physical world, including unicorns, dragons, and griffons. Though they don't exist in a biological sense, they are very real in the spiritual worlds, appearing over and over again in popular mythologies and practitioners' experiences. These creatures can act as both guides and antagonists to the mystical practitioner.

natal chart: An astrology chart detailing the location of the planets and signs on the day and at the time you were born, as viewed from the location where you were born. Also known as a birth chart. The natal chart is said to contain the potential life patterns and traits of a person.

nature spirit: A nonphysical entity closely related to an aspect of nature, from plants and trees to rocks, mountains, and bodies of water.

Neptune: The Roman sea god. The planet that rules inspiration, escapism, and unconditional love in Western astrology.

New Age: A term used to describe the next astrological age, the Age of Aquarius, starting roughly near the year 2000 and lasting approximately 2,000 years.

Northern tradition: Any pagan tradition based on the Germanic tribes, including the Norse and Saxons. A term used to differentiate these traditions from many other modern Neo-Pagan practices, particularly Wicca. The term heathen is often preferred to the term Pagan as a general category for the Northern traditions.

numen: A term for life force, often used synonymously with prana.

numerology: Using a system of numbers, primarily for birth dates, names, and addresses, to see the archetypal influence of the number on a person, place, or situation.

od: Another term for life force, or vital energy.

ogham: A Celtic system based on tree symbolism. Though many modern writers cite it as an ancient calendar and zodiac, it was most likely a symbol system for memorization, divination, and magic.

OM: A Hindu chant that has become popular in many New Age circles and rituals. OM, or more appropriately AUM, is said to be the sound of creation. The three distinct sounds A–U–M stand for the trinity of powers responsible for the generation, sustenance, and dissolution of the universe.

omega: The last letter of the Greek alphabet, and symbol of the end.

oneiromancy: A form of divination in which answers come through dreams and dream interpretation.

orgone: A name for subtle life force energy, according to the teachings of Wilhelm Reich.

ornithomancy: Receiving psychic information from the flight, sound, and appearance of birds. A form of augury.

Ostara: One of the four solar holidays and one of the eight Wheel of the Year holidays in the modern Pagan calendar. At this time, the Sun is moving from Pisces to Aries, signaling the beginning of spring and the resurrection of the land.

Ouija board: A divination board used with a planchette, to speak with spirits. The board contains sections for yes, no, and the letters and numbers of the modern alphabet. The spirit is said to direct the planchette to spell out answers to questions posed. Usually sold as a children's game.

Paganism: From the Latin, referring to country dwellers. Reclaimed in the modern era to refer to practitioners of nature-based spirituality.

palmistry: A method of divination using the lines and shapes on the palm of the hand.

pathworking: A visual meditative journey using archetypal symbols and images. Drawn from the Tree of Life, as the various paths connect the ten states of consciousness. Technically a pathworking refers to a meditation based on the imagery of these paths, but in modern use it can refer to any guided imagery meditation.

petition spell: A written intention of what you seek to manifest through magic, usually read during the course of a ritual and burned, to release the intention.

pendulum: A weight on the end of a length of string or chain. The pendulum is used to divine answers, usually yes or no, by watching the motion of the weight as it is suspended from the string.

pentacle: A five-pointed star in a circle. Also refers to the five-pointed star in a circle in a three-dimensional form, such as a ritual tool or piece of jewelry.

pentagram: A five-pointed star. Each point is representative of one of the five elements. Also refers to a flat or drawn version of the five-pointed star, whereas a pentacle is the three-dimensional ritual-tool version of the five-pointed star.

Pisces: The twelfth sign of the zodiac. A mutable water sign depicted by two fish.

planets: The moving bodies of the solar system. In astrology and astrological magic, both the Sun and the Moon, from the perspective of the Earth, are considered magical planets, though technically they are luminaries and not planets in the astronomical sense. Each planet is said to "rule" a different area of life and correspond to a different facet of magic and spirituality.

Pluto: The outermost planet recognized by modern astrologers. Pluto is named after the god of death and the underworld in Roman myth, and the planet rules changes, transformations, and the higher will.

poltergeist: A psychic manifestation of an apparent entity with the ability to move small objects, quite often many at the same time, in a violent or chaotic manner. Some think of a poltergeist as a haunting of a deceased person. Others see it as the manifestation of the unconscious psychic ability of a prepubescent or pubescent teen.

polytheism: The belief in many divinities, usually associated with Paganism and tribal religions. Many traditions claim to be polytheistic, but have monotheistic associations.

Many tribal and Pagan traditions believe in the divine expression of many gods, yet also acknowledge the one force connecting all things.

power animal: Also known as a totem animal. An animal spirit that acts as the spiritual, and sometimes physical, guardian, teacher, and guide to one in a shamanic tradition. Many believe the concepts of the Witch's familiar rose out of the shamanic animal practices of Europe. In some traditions, any one person is guided by numerous animal spirits, but one or two are of primary importance. The key concepts of an animal, known as its teachings, or "medicine," are either embodied by the individual or are experiences the individual is asked to learn and master in this lifetime.

positive thinking: The use of directed thought to change your life for the better. Positive thinking is related to the use of affirmations.

prana: A term for life force energy in the Hindu traditions.

priest/priestess: One who spiritually ministers to others. In Wicca, Witches are considered priestesses and priests of the Old Religion, serving the gods. Many modern mystics identify with the priests and priestesses of the ancient Pagan world. In a modern magical context, a priest/ess is anyone who moves energy through intention and ritual.

psyche: A Greek term often used in reference to the soul, though modern use associates it with the mind.

psychic: The ability to communicate with your "soul" through visual, verbal, and nonsensory means, to receive information not normally received through the physical and linear senses.

psychic healing: The use of techniques involving subtle energy, visualization, will, affirmation, and ritual to create a beneficial change in the physical, emotional, mental, or spiritual health of an individual or community.

psychic surgery: A technique used to remove psychic or subtle energy "blockages" from the energy body—to remove unwanted forces, including physical illness and disease, from the body. This technique does not involve actually cutting the physical body.

psychic travel: Projection of your conscious awareness beyond the physical body, giving you the ability to perceive distant places in the physical world, but also travel to various nonphysical dimensions of reality.

psychometry: A technique to receive information by reading the "vibrations" of an object. The reader holds an object and tunes in to it to receive psychic impressions. This information can come visually (literally or symbolically), or it can be a simple sense of knowing.

pyromancy: The act of divination through fire. Gazing deeply into a fire for images, many practitioners of pyromancy see nothing, but say the fire speaks to them of the future. The flame can be from a candle, or a larger flame. Most Witches prefer a fire of sacred woods and herbs, often burning in a cauldron. Woods often include oak, pine, ash, willow, and hawthorn, to name a few, but I prefer to use whatever is available and then throw some vervain or other psychic herbs into the pyre. You can also divine from the smoke of a sacred fire, or from incense. Certain forms of divination also use as their medium various objects melted in the fire, or the ash and embers from the end of the fire.

Qabala: Usually refers to the Hermetic or magical tradition drawing from the Jewish Kabalah.

Qabalistic Cross: An exercise in ceremonial magic based upon the Qabala that draws a beam of divine light from the heavens through the body into the Earth, and through the right shoulder and the chest, and out the left shoulder, creating a cross of light through the body. The imagery and words that go along with this ritual are akin to the Sign of the Cross. The Qabalistic Cross is the first part of the Lesser Banishing Ritual of the Pentagram.

Qlipoth: The sephiroth of the reverse of the Tree of Life, sometimes known as the Tree of Death. Qlipoth is often translated as "shells."

quarters: The four directions of the compass, associated with the four traditional elements of earth, fire, air, and water in many cultures.

quartz: Crystallized silicon dioxide. One of the most common minerals used for spiritual purposes in both ancient and modern times. Quartz crystals form six-sided points, which are double-terminated or single-terminated, depending on the growing conditions of the crystal when it formed. Depending on other minerals present, or other factors in its formation, quartz can become rose quartz, smoky quartz, rutilated quartz, tourmilated quartz, amethyst, and citrine. Quartz is known for its ability to amplify psychic and magical energy, and is used extensively in healing.

quintessence: The fifth element, the sum of earth, air, fire, and water, yet greater than the sum of its parts.

rabbi: A minister in the Jewish tradition.

Raphael: One of the better known archangels of the Western traditions. Associated with the direction of east and the element of air, Raphael is said to be the divine physician and healer, often pictured carrying the Greek caduceus. His name is usually translated as "God is healing." Astrologically, he is associated with both the Sun and Mercury in Qabalistic magic.

rays: A system of esoteric study based in the tradition of Theosophy and the writings of Alice Bailey. The divine energy is seen reflected through a spectrum of seven rays. The primary rays are red, blue, and yellow, like the primary colors. The remaining four rays are said to emanate from the yellow ray, and are green, orange, indigo, and violet. Each ray has a variety of correspondences and functions in mysticism and spiritual development. Each is said to be ruled by a Cohen, or special ascended master, who oversees its function, as well as by an archangel associated with its power. Positive and negative attributes have been given to each ray, and a system of esoteric psychology is built around working with those attributes. The ray system has highly influenced the modern New Age movement, but traces of it can also be found in certain forms of ceremonial magic. Some believe it to be the true secret science of Tibet, though the majority of material on it is based on modern channeled works.

Reiki: Reiki translates to "universal life force." The Japanese term for vital life energy is ki, the second syllable of the word Reiki. Reiki is a system of energy healing including both distant and hands-on techniques and originating in Japan. Training is passed on in a lineage-based attunement, or initiation, system.

remote viewing: Another term for what many call astral travel or psychic travel, but when specifically applied to viewing physical locations, usually in the present, though the technique can be adapted to see into the past, and potentially into the future.

right-hand path: The right-hand path, in the most simplistic definition, refers to the practice of "good" or spiritual magic. It can also refer to the male mysteries, traditions of asceticism and renunciation of the world, and rituals done in alignment with the Sun and clockwise motion. Ideologically, a practitioner of a right-hand path seeks union with the divine, rather than individual immortality, though the lines between left- and right-hand paths are not always clearly defined.

ritual: Any series of repeated actions designed to help the practitioner alter consciousness and communicate with the inner self or powers of the universe. Ritual actions are done with intention, and the repetition often helps the action build in power.

root chakra: The first chakra found at the base of the spine and sometimes referred to as the base chakra. The root chakra rules our ability to be rooted in the world, to survive and thrive in the material plane, feeling pleasure and taking care of our most basic needs. Usually depicted as red.

runes: A magical symbol system found in Teutonic magic, primarily associated with the Norse god Odin. Runes are not only symbols, but each character stands for a letter, a song or sound when spoken, and a mystery of life, an archetypal force as understood by the Northern tradition. Runes can be used in magic to manifest change, worn as an amulet or talisman, or used for divination. Several different rune systems exist, most notably the Elder Futhark and Younger Futhark.

Sagittarius: The ninth sign of the zodiac. A mutable fire sign depicted as a centaur, archer, or horse.

Sahasrara: The crown chakra, found at the top of the head, usually depicted as dazzling white or violet. The name means "thousand-petalled," referring to the infinite lotus shape of the crown chakra.

salt: In alchemy, the fixed principle giving rise to form and structure. Physical salt is also a ritual item used to cleanse, purify, and protect.

Samhain: One of the four Celtic fire festivals, and one of the eight Wheel of the Year holidays. Celebrated in October or November, usually on October 31, when the Sun is in Scorpio, Samhain is a festival of the ancestors, death, and regeneration. Considered to be the New Year of the Witch's calendar.

Saturn: The last of the traditional ancient planets, associated with endings, limitations, bindings, karma, lessons, and death. Saturn is named after the Roman god whose Greek correspondent is Chronos, the god of the harvest and time, carrying a sickle.

Scorpio: The eighth sign of the zodiac. A fixed water sign that is depicted as the scorpion, but also has associations with the snake, the eagle, and the phoenix. A sign of transformation.

scrying: The use of clairvoyance projected into a medium or tool of some sort. By focusing on a surface such as a crystal, crystal ball, black mirror, or pool of water, the user facilitates the ability to use clairvoyant abilities, "seeing" images in the surface that will answer the user's questions about a given topic. The answers are often symbolic in nature, and not direct or clear.

Shakti: In Hindu cosmology, both a goddess and the symbol of the feminine creative principle. Paired with the god Shiva.

shamanic surgery: Sometimes referred to as psychic surgery, a ritualized process of removing the energy, or "spirit," of an illness, to promote rapid healing.

Shiva: In Hindu cosmology, both a god and the symbol for the male creative principle. Paired with the goddess Shakti.

sigil: A magical symbol that acts as a vehicle for a specific intention. Traditional and modern sigils exist. Often they are generated through the use of planetary squares, or numbered squares whose numerology resonates with a specific planet. Others are created by fusing together several different symbols and letters.

smudging: The spreading of a sacred smoke, often sage, over a ritual tool or person, or throughout an area, to cleanse that area of unwanted and unhealthy energies.

solar plexus chakra: The third chakra located above the navel and below the heart, usually depicted as yellow in color. The solar plexus is the center of will, power, self-esteem, and control.

solstice: Solar alignment when the Sun reaches its peak in power (summer solstice), creating the longest day of the year, or when the Sun reaches its lowest point (winter solstice), creating the shortest day of the year.

sortilege: Methods of divination performed by drawing lots, or set symbols, such as tarot cards or runes.

soul travel: Another term for psychic projection, but denoting that one feels the astral body or mind is not the aspect that is traveling, but the soul is the energetic component that is traveling to other locations.

spell: A specific act of magic. A ritual with a specific intention.

spirit: The fifth element, known as quintessence, akasha, or ether. The sum of all the four elements (earth, water, fire, air), from which they originate and to which they return. The sustaining and animating force behind the four elements.

spirit guides: Nonphysical beings that act as guides, teachers, and friends to those who are physically incarnated.

spirit healing: The process of healing through the relationship the healer has with non-physical entities; healing using the energy of these beings.

spirits: Nonphysical entities.

stone: Solid minerals that are often used in ritual and healing. The stone signifies the element of earth, and various stones, particularly quartz, are used in crystal healing sessions.

subtle bodies: The energetic bodies that form the templates for the physical body.

sulfur: In alchemy, the cardinal or volatile principle necessary in creation. Associated with the Sun and fire.

Sun: The center of our solar system. In astrology, the Sun is considered a planet, and rules the personality, ego, sense of self, and the person an individual is learning to be in this lifetime. In many Pagan traditions, the Sun is seen as the masculine force and the God, paired with the feminine Moon.

Svadhisthana: The second chakra, or belly/navel chakra, usually depicted as orange, though some traditions say vermillion. This energy center rules our instinct, our base emotion and sense of trust and intimacy. Svadhisthana is the dwelling place of the self.

symbol: Any object or glyph that stands for something else. In magic and ritual, most objects and tools symbolize universal forces and powers. Various written images are used in magic to symbolize forces. It is important to note that not only do such tools symbolize forces, but when properly consecrated, they act as gateways to the very forces they symbolize.

sympathetic magic: A technique in magic in which a small symbolic ritual action mimics the larger real-world event you desire to manifest. The smaller ritual is said to be in "sympathy," or resonating, with the forces necessary to manifest the larger event. A ritual in which water is poured onto the ground to produce rain could be an act of sympathetic magic.

talisman: A magical charm carried, worn as jewelry, or hung in a specific place to fulfill an intention. Certain schools of magic identify a talisman as a charm that draws forces to you, such as a money talisman or good luck talisman. Charms that send forces away are known as amulets. Other schools of thought differentiate the two terms, with talismans being charms that are more three-dimensional and contain various items (such as a bag with herbs, stones, and hair; a metal capsule filled with resin; or a glass bottle with a liquid), and amulets being flatter, with geometric symbols etched into them.

tantra: Technically, the tantras refer to sacred texts of the Hindu traditions, with teachings covering a wide range of topics, but to many, the term tantra has become equated with the sexual teachings of the East. Such practices use sexuality as a form of worship and devotion to the divine and as a path to enlightenment by controlling the flow of sexual energy in awakening the various chakra energy centers. In the West, such sexual tantric practices are known as sex magic.

tarot: A deck of seventy-eight cards used for divination, meditation, and personal spiritual development. The deck is divided into the Major Arcana and Minor Arcana, describing major life experiences and minor, day-to-day experiences, respectively. The Minor Arcana is divided into four suites—pentacles, cups, swords, and wands, representing the elements of earth, water, air, and fire. Each suite has ten numbered cards and four court cards. Modern lore relates the tarot cards to the Qabalistic Tree of Life.

tattwas: Symbols of the five elements in the Eastern traditions. Used in ceremonial magic as "portals" to the elemental realms during psychic journeys and meditations. Though compatible with Western elemental traditions, the tattwas use different shapes and colors for each of the elements than what is commonly accepted in most forms of Western magic.

Taurus: The second sign of the zodiac. A fixed earth sign depicted as a bull or a cow. A sign of stability.

tea leaf reading: A form of divination in which the reader looks into a cup, bowl, or saucer of tea leaves soaked in tea to see images and symbols formed by the tea leaves themselves or on the tea's surface. The person for whom the diviner is reading usually sips the tea, to connect the two. This form of divination is also known as tasseography.

Tetragrammaton: The four letters of the unpronounceable name of God from the various Qabalistic traditions. YHVH is often how it is spelled in the Latin alphabet. The letters stand for fire, water, air, and earth, and the first and third are masculine and the second and fourth are feminine. They are related to the kings, queens, knights, and pages in the tarot. From a Qabalistic point of view, God the creator is both male and female, and works through all four elements, dispelling the notion in Hebrew mysticism that God is solely God the Father. The simpler father image is used for those who do not study Qabalistic mysticism.

theology: The study and teachings of a religion; its faith, practice, and particularly its experience of the divine.

theta: The measure of brain waves from four to nine cycles per second, experienced as a place of deep journey and meditation when consciously induced, or sleep when unconscious.

third eye: Another term for the brow chakra, the center of psychic vision.

throat chakra: The energy center found at the base of the throat, ruling the ability to communicate, which includes both speaking and listening. It is usually depicted as blue.

totem: A term used for an animal spirit that guides and protects you. Also known as a power animal.

Tree of Life: The main glyph of the various Qabalistic teachings. Though found in many variations over the centuries, modern traditions have greatly standardized its shape and correspondences. It consists of ten circles, representing the ten sephiroth of consciousness, linked with twenty-two lines, representing the twenty-two paths or processes to reach those levels of consciousness.

tutelary spirit: A spiritual entity that acts as a teacher. Such spirits can be totem animals, spirit guides, angels, or other beings with the knowledge and ability to transfer that knowledge to a mystic.

upper world: In shamanic cosmology, the realm above, also known as the overworld or sky realm, is the home to enlightened beings, sky spirits, and stellar spirits. Symbolically, it is the place of the superconsciousness and the divine self.

Uranus: The first of the "new" planets in astrology outside the orbit of Saturn. Uranus represents the breaking away from constraints, new and unorthodox ideas, divine inspiration, revolution in thought and action, and swift and sudden change. Though named after the Greek sky god, some feel the archetype of Prometheus fits this planet better. Uranus now rules the sign of Aquarius, alone, or some say jointly with Saturn.

Uriel: One of the four main archangels of the Western traditions. Associated with the direction of north and the element of earth. Uriel is associated both with the Earth in fertility and the earth as the receiver of the body. Some images have Uriel, also spelled Ariel, associated with the angel of death. Though angels are considered androgynous, out of the four, Uriel has the most feminine associations. Her name is usually translated as "Fire of God" and much of her more orthodox imagery from scripture is not always in alignment with the images of ceremonial magic. Some associate Uriel with the planet Uranus, electricity, inspiration, and the hidden sphere of Da'ath on the Tree of Life.

veil: A term for the barrier separating the physical world from the spiritual world. The veil is said to be lifted, parted, or passed when doing spiritual work.

Venus: The planet between Mercury and Earth that is associated with attraction, social interaction, and romance in astrology and magic. The planet is named after the Roman goddess of love, Venus. As the morning star and evening star, shining brightest in the sky, Venus has had associations with many love and fertility goddesses, including Aphrodite, Astarte, Ishtar, and Inanna, as well as the fallen angel figure of Lucifer.

vibrational remedies: An umbrella term for all liquid remedies based not on chemical principles but energetic principles. They include flower essences and gem elixirs, as well as new remedies made through experiments with the vibration of a location, colored gels and colored glass, music, and toning. Some would consider homeopathic remedies vibrational in nature as well.

Virgo: The sixth sign of the zodiac. A mutable earth sign represented by the maiden, virgin, or corn maiden. The harvest is the true symbol of Virgo. A sign of discernment and service.

Vishuddi: The traditional name of the throat chakra, ruling the powers of communication and traditionally colored blue. Vishuddi means pure.

vision quest: A Native American ritual to aid one in seeking a "vision," a divine message to direct one's life. Some vision quests reveal power animals as allies, while others provide a vision to guide your life. Traditional techniques include isolation in nature, within a preordained boundary where nothing from the outside world is taken in, as well as fasting and prayer, while undergoing the quest. Quests can last from one to four days. Some use natural substances to help induce a vision. Often the seeker will experience a feeling of insanity or a strong desire to leave before the quest is done. This is not a ritual to do alone, or without an experienced guide or teacher. In the Lakota culture, it is known as Crying for a Vision, or Hanblecheyapi.

visualization: The process of using your imagination, your inner sight, to perceive a mental image of anything you desire. The skills of visualization are developed through guided meditation and the use of magic.

vortex: An energetic center, usually perceived as a swirling motion, like a whirlpool. The chakras within the body are described as vortexes. Sacred sites in nature are also said to be vortexes of energy, comparable to chakra points on the planet itself. Places such as Sedona, Arizona, are known for their sacred vortex sites.

watchtowers: The powers of the four directions, related to the four elements. Many cultures have imagery of the four directions holding up the sky or holding together the Earth. The beings of the watchtowers are sometimes described as archangels (particularly Uriel, Raphael, Michael, and Gabriel), elemental kings, or animal totems.

watcher: A term used for the beings of the watchtowers. Often refers to a race of fallen angels said to teach humanity the arts of magic, astrology, and civilization.

water: The emotional principle, associated with feeling, empathy, healing, spirits, and the ancestors, as well as the principles of love and compassion. Water is cold and moist.

wax divination: Known as carromancy or ceromancy, wax divination is a technique used to find shapes and meaning in melting wax. Usually the wax of a candle is melted and dripped into water, and the shapes it forms are interpreted by the reader.

Wheel of the Year: A cycle of eight holidays based on a variety of ancient Pagan sources, including the four Celtic fire festivals, based on agricultural images and the four solar holidays, two solstices, and two equinoxes. The Wheel of the Year tells the story of the Goddess and God expressed in the seasons and cycles of the Sun and Earth.

white magic: Most refer to white magic as "good" magic aiding others, and in alignment with the divine. For ceremonial magicians, white magic usually refers to any magical operation to help the practitioner connect with the higher self and then the divine source. In this system, any magic that creates a physical change, even healing or protection, is considered gray magic, not white.

Wiccan: A modern term for a practitioner of Wicca. Some use Wiccan and Witch interchangeably, while others do not.

Witch: A practitioner of the art, science, and religion of Witchcraft. Some make a distinction between the word Witch and Wiccan, and some do not. In the United States, many people use the term Wiccan to denote a practitioner of the religion, while a Witch is considered one who practices the art and craft. In the United Kingdom, a Wiccan often refers to one initiated into a formal tradition, such as Gardnerian Wicca, while an uninitiated practitioner of the art is known as a Witch.

Witch's mark: During the persecutions of Witches and those suspected of Witchcraft, an unusual birthmark was said to be evidence of a Witch making a compact with the devil. Some believe that many of those involved in actual esoteric practices and orders (as most people persecuted as Witches were not truly Witches) would receive a ritual initiation mark, burn, or tattoo to mark the new Witch apart from others.

wood: In the Chinese elemental system, wood is the symbol for the element known in the West as spirit.

words of power: Words in various languages, ranging from Sanskrit to Hebrew, Gaelic, and Enochian, that are associated with various mystical effects. By thinking, saying, or chanting the words of power, one can create an inner change, or outer change. Mantras are often considered words of power.

yang: In Chinese mysticism, the projective, masculine energy.

yantra: A mandala or visual focus used in meditation. One directs the gaze at the yantra during meditation to bring the mind to stillness.

yin: In Chinese mysticism, the receptive, feminine energy.

yogi: A practitioner of one of the various forms of yoga.

Yule: Also known as the winter solstice, one of the four solar holidays and one of the eight Wheel of the Year holidays in the modern Pagan calendar. Yule is the celebration of the birth of the young sun God, who grows to maturity as the light increases until the summer solstice.

zodiac: Usually translated to mean the "wheel of animals" and referring to the twelve signs used in astrology. The sidereal zodiac refers to the actual constellations of stars, while the tropical zodiac refers to the space around the Earth, aligned with the seasonal shifts.

BIBLIOGRAPHY

Andrews, Ted. *Animal-Speak: The Spiritual & Magical Powers of Creatures Great & Small.* Saint Paul, MN: Llewellyn Publications, 1993.

Belhayes, Iris, with Enid. *Spirit Guides.* San Diego, CA: ACS Publishing, 1986.

Bonewits, Isaac. *Real Magic.* York Beach, ME: Samuel Weiser, 1989.

Bruyere, Rosalyn L. *Wheels of Light.* New York: Fireside Publishing, 1989.

Cabot, Laurie, and Tom Cowan. *Love Magic: The Way to Love through Rituals, Spells and the Magical Life.* New York: Delta, 1992.

Cabot, Laurie, with Jean Mills. *Celebrate the Earth: A Year of Holidays in the Pagan Tradition.* New York: Delta, 1994.

Cabot, Laurie, with Tom Cowan. *Power of the Witch: The Earth, the Moon and the Magical Path to Enlightenment.* New York: Delacorte Press, 1989.

Chopra, Deepak. *Magical Mind, Magical Body.* Audio cassette series. Chicago, IL: Nightingale Conant, 1990.

Choquette, Sonia, and Patrick Tully. *Your Psychic Pathway.* Audio cassette. Chicago, IL: Nightingale Conant, 1999.

Conway, D. J. *The Ancient & Shining Ones.* Saint Paul, MN: Llewellyn Publications, 1993.

Cowan, Tom. *Fire in the Head.* San Francisco, CA: HarperSanFrancisco, 1993.

Cunningham, Scott. *Incense, Oils and Brews*. Saint Paul, MN: Llewellyn Publications, 1989.

———. *Wicca: A Guide for the Solitary Practitioner*. Saint Paul, MN: Llewellyn Publications, 1988.

Davidson, Gustav. *A Dictionary of Angels, Including the Fallen Angels*. New York: The Free Press, 1967.

DuQuette, Lon Milo. *The Chicken Qabalah of Rabbi Lamed Ben Clifford*. York Beach, ME: Weiser Books, 2001.

Dyer, Dr. Wayne W. *Real Magic: Creating Miracles in Everyday Life*. Audio cassette. New York: Harper Audio/Harper Collins, 1992.

Eliade, Mircea. *Essential Sacred Writings from Around the World*. Formerly titled *From Primitives to Zen*. San Francisco, CA: HarperSanFrancisco, 1967.

———. *Shamanism: Archaic Techniques of Ecstasy*. Princeton, NJ: Princeton University Press, 1972.

Foxwood, Orion. *The Faery Teachings*. Coral Springs, FL: Muse Press, 2003.

Freke, Timothy. *Spiritual Traditions*. New York: Sterling Publishing, 2001.

Greer, John Michael. *The New Encyclopedia of the Occult*. Saint Paul, MN: Llewellyn Publications, 2003.

Grimassi, Raven. *Encyclopedia of Wicca & Witchcraft*. Saint Paul, MN: Llewellyn Publications, 2000.

Guiley, Rosemary Ellen. *The Encyclopedia of Witches and Witchcraft*. New York: Checkmark Books, 1999.

———. *Harper's Encyclopedia of Mystical & Paranormal Experience*. San Francisco, CA: HarperSanFrancisco, 1991.

Gurunam [Joseph Michael Levry]. *Lifting the Veil: Practical Kabbalas with Kundalini Yoga*. New York: Rootlight, 1999.

Harner, Michael. *The Way of the Shaman*. New York: Harper Collins, 1990.

Hay, Louise H. *Heal Your Body A–Z*. Carlsbad, CA: Hay House, 1988.

Homer. *The Odyssey*. New York: Penguin Classics, 2003.

Kraig, Donald Michael. *Modern Magick: Eleven Lessons in the High Magickal Arts*. Saint Paul, MN: Llewellyn Publications, 1988.

Medici, Marina. *Good Magic*. New York: Fireside Publishing, 1988.

Melody. *Love Is in the Earth*. Wheat Ridge, CO: Earth-Love Publishing, 1995.

Myss, Caroline. *Anatomy of the Spirit: The Seven Stages of Power and Healing*. New York: Three Rivers Press, 1996.

Penczak, Christopher. *City Magick: Urban Rituals, Spells and Shamanism*. York Beach, ME: Samuel Weiser, 2000.

———. *The Inner Temple of Witchcraft: Magick, Meditation and Psychic Development*. Saint Paul, MN: Llewellyn Publications, 2002.

———. *Spirit Allies: Meet Your Team from the Other Side*. Boston, MA: Samuel Weiser, 2001.

Sadleir, Steven S. *The Spiritual Seeker's Guide*. Costa Mesa, CA: Allwon Publishing, 1992.

Sams, Jamie, and David Carson. *Medicine Cards: The Discovery of Power Through the Ways of Animals*. Santa Fe, NM: Bear & Co., 1998.

Satchidananda, Sri Swami. *The Living Gita: The Complete Bhagavad Gita*. Yogaville, VA: Integral Yoga Publications, 1988.

Silva, José, and Philip Miele. *The Silva Mind Control Method*. New York: Simon and Schuster, 1977.

Starhawk. *The Spiral Dance: A Rebirth of the Ancient Religion of the Great Goddess*. San Francisco, CA: Harper & Row, 1989.

Stewart, R. J. *The Living World of Faery*. Somerset, UK: Gothic Images, 1995.

Stone, Joshua David. *The Complete Ascension Manual for the Aquarian Age*. Sedona, AZ: Light Technology Publishing, 1994.

Talbot, Michael. *The Holographic Universe*. New York: HarperCollins Publishers, 1991.

Thompson, Gerry Maguire. *The Atlas of the New Age*. London: Quatro Publishing, 1999.

Three Initiates. *The Kybalion: A Study of the Hermetic Philosophy of Ancient Egypt and Greece*. Chicago, IL: The Yogi Publication Society, 1912.

Turlington, Shannon R. *The Complete Idiot's Guide to Voodoo*. Indianapolis, IN: Alpha Books, 2002.

Valiente, Doreen. *An ABC of Witchcraft Past & Present*. New York: St. Martin's Press, 1973.

Walker, Barbara G. *The Woman's Dictionary of Symbols and Sacred Objects*. San Francisco, CA: HarperSanFrancisco, 1988.

Webster, Richard. *101 Feng Shui Tips for the Home.* Saint Paul, MN: Llewellyn Publications, 2004.

Whitcomb, Bill. *The Magician's Companion.* Saint Paul, MN: Llewellyn Publications, 1993.

Whitworth, Belinda. *New Age Encyclopedia: A Mind, Body, Spirit Reference Guide.* Franklin Lakes, NJ: New Page Books, 2005.

Yin, Amorah Quan. *The Pleiadian Workbook: Awakening Your Divine Ka.* Santa Fe, NM: Bear & Co., 1996.

Online Resources

http://en.wikipedia.org/wiki/Bahai
http://en.wikipedia.org/wiki/Buddhism
http://en.wikipedia.org/wiki/Discordianism
http://en.wikipedia.org/wiki/Dream
http://en.wikipedia.org/wiki/Druid
http://en.wikipedia.org/wiki/Feng_Shui
http://en.wikipedia.org/wiki/Islam
http://en.wikipedia.org/wiki/Jainism
http://en.wikipedia.org/wiki/Judaism
http://en.wikipedia.org/wiki/Martial_Arts
http://en.wikipedia.org/wiki/Ouija_board
http://en.wikipedia.org/wiki/Satanism
http://en.wikipedia.org/wiki/Shinto
http://en.wikipedia.org/wiki/Sikhism
http://en.wikipedia.org/wiki/Sufism
http://en.wikipedia.org/wiki/Thelema
http://en.wikipedia.org/wiki/Voodoo
http://en.wikipedia.org/wiki/Yoga
http://en.wikipedia.org/wiki/Zen
http://en.wikipedia.org/wiki/Zoroastrian
http://museumoftalkingboards.com/new.html
http://www.museumoftalkingboards.com/history.html
http://www.aolsvc.worldbook.aol.com/wb/Article?id=ar550580

http://www.healthandyoga.com/html/product/malabeads.html

http://www.kundaliniyoga.org/mantra.html

http://www.mysteries.pwp.blueyonder.co.uk/2,6.htm

http://www.teachingvalues.com/goldenrule.html

To Write to the Author

If you wish to contact the author or would like more information about this book, please write to the author in care of Llewellyn Worldwide and we will forward your request. Both the author and publisher appreciate hearing from you and learning of your enjoyment of this book and how it has helped you. Llewellyn Worldwide cannot guarantee that every letter written to the author can be answered, but all will be forwarded. Please write to:

Christopher Penczak
℅ Llewellyn Worldwide
2143 Wooddale Drive, Dept. 0-7387-0979-4
Woodbury, Minnesota 55125-2989, U.S.A.

Please enclose a self-addressed stamped envelope for reply,
or $1.00 to cover costs. If outside U.S.A., enclose
international postal reply coupon.

Many of Llewellyn's authors have websites with additional information and resources. For more information, please visit our website at http://www.llewellyn.com.